DAVID HUME

David Hume

REASON IN HISTORY

Claudia M. Schmidt

THE PENNSYLVANIA STATE UNIVERSITY PRESS

UNIVERSITY PARK, PENNSYLVANIA

Library of Congress Cataloguing-in-Publication Data

Schmidt, Claudia M.
David Hume : reason in history / Claudia M. Schmidt.
p.   cm.
Includes bibliographical references and index.
ISBN 0-271-02263-9 (cloth : alk. paper)
1. Hume, David, 1711–1776. I. Title.

B1498 .S32 2003

192—dc21   2003005468

It is the policy of The Pennsylvania State University Press
to use acid-free paper. Publications on uncoated stock
satisfy the minimum requirements of American National
Standard for Information Sciences—Permanence of Paper
for Printed Library Material, ANSI Z39.48-1992.

Contents

To Hartland and Ada Schmidt

PARENTS EXTRAORDINAIRE

Preface and Acknowledgments

In preparing this study, I have benefited from the insights, suggestions, and encouragement of a number of individuals. It is a great pleasure to acknowledge them here.

This book had its origins in a dissertation at the Graduate Theological Union in Berkeley, California, under the careful and enthusiastic direction of Claude Welch, who first inspired my interest in Hume. I also received valuable comments on the original dissertation from Vincent Guagliardo at the Graduate Theological Union, Martin Jay at the University of California at Berkeley, and Donald Livingston at Emory University. My study of Hume was greatly enriched by their perspectives from the fields of theology, intellectual history, and philosophy.

The manuscript of this book was expanded and improved at the University of Iowa. My work there on this project was enhanced by conversations with my colleagues among the faculty and graduate students, including Panayot Butchvarov, Evan Fales, Brian Hutchinson, Todd Ryan, and Kathleen Schmidt. I received valuable comments on the content of various chapters from Phillip Cummins, David Stern, and Richard Fumerton. I would also like to thank Günter Zöller, now at the University of Munich, for encouraging me to explore Hume's relation to subsequent developments in German philosophy.

I presented papers based on the material in Chapter 3 at the Pacific Division meeting of the American Philosophical Association in 1993, the Twentieth International Hume Conference in Ottawa in 1993, the History and Philosophy of Science Reading Group at the University of California at Davis in 1994, and the Iowa Philosophical Society in 1994. The central argument of the project was presented in papers at the annual meeting of the American Academy of Religion in 1991, and at the Midwest Seminar in Early Modern Philosophy in 1996. I would like to thank the participants at these meetings, and colleagues with whom I have discussed Hume at other scholarly events, for their comments and conversation; especially Dorothy Coleman, Lorne Falkenstein, Roger Gallie, Daniel Garber, Alan Charles Kors, Rhoda Kotzin, Manfred

Kuehn, William Edward Morris, David Owen, Terry Pinkard, Wade Robison, John Stewart, Paul Teller, Spencer Wertz, and R. Neil Wood.

I have been very fortunate to work with Sanford Thatcher at Pennsylvania State University Press, who has overseen many excellent works in philosophy and intellectual history. I would also like to thank James Noxon, Frederick Whelan, and David Fate Norton, the readers for Penn State Press, for their many stimulating and encouraging comments. This book has been much improved as a result of their suggestions and criticisms. Special thanks are due Andrew Lewis, my copyeditor, and Jennifer Smith, at Penn State Press, for their careful and discerning work with the manuscript.

The final draft of this book was written in the wonderfully congenial and collegial setting of the philosophy department at Marquette University. I would like to thank my colleagues, especially Howard Kainz, Juliana Laumakis, Ginger Lee, Matthew Pierlott, Tom Prendergast, Gregory Schulz, William Starr, and Tim Yoder, for giving me welcome opportunities to develop material included in the introduction, the final two chapters, and the conclusion. I am especially grateful to Marquette University for a Faculty Development Award, to the philosophy department for research support, and to Paul Shinkle and Carrie Peffley, my research assistants, for their help in reviewing the citations system and bibliography. I would also like to thank Michael Wreen and James South for their advice on the final preparation of the manuscript.

This book is dedicated to my parents, Hartland and Ada Schmidt, who, as members of the faculty in chemistry and creative writing at the University of California at Riverside, filled our family life with an enthusiastic commitment to the liberal arts, and prepared me for the rewards and challenges of pursuing an exciting project across interdisciplinary boundaries. They provided invaluable support for my work on Hume through their constant interest and encouragement, and I am happy to thank them at last for waiting so patiently for its fruition.

Abbreviations

A critical edition of Hume's philosophical, political, and literary works, *The Clarendon Edition of the Works of David Hume,* is being published by Oxford University Press under the supervision of Tom L. Beauchamp, David Fate Norton, and M. A. Stewart. The texts in this edition are also provided in the student editions in the Oxford Philosophical Texts series. I have cited the OPT editions of Hume's *Treatise* and *Abstract,* and the Clarendon editions of the *Enquiries,* according to the reference system for both editions as indicated below. In each case, I have also cited the page number in the Selby-Bigge/Nidditch editions of these works as indicated.

Other texts by Hume are cited in standard editions, according to the reference system indicated below. I have listed any additional editions of Hume's works that are referred to in this study in the bibliography under his name.

A   *An Abstract of A Treatise of Human Nature.* In *A Treatise of Human Nature,* edited by David Fate Norton and Mary J. Norton, 403–17. Oxford: Oxford University Press, 2000.

      A 1   Paragraph
      A P.2   Preface, paragraph

A [SBN]   *An Abstract of A Treatise of Human Nature.* In *A Treatise of Human Nature,* edited by L. A. Selby-Bigge, second edition with text revised and notes by P. H. Nidditch, 641–62. Oxford: Clarendon Press, 1978.

CMH   "David Hume's 'An Historical Essay on Chivalry and Modern Honour.'" Edited by Ernest Campbell Mossner. *Modern Philology* 45 (1947): 54–60.

      CMH 1   Page number

DNR   *Dialogues Concerning Natural Religion.* Edited by Norman Kemp Smith. Indianapolis: Bobbs-Merrill, 1947.

      DNR 1.2   Part, page number
      DNR PH.1   Pamphilus to Hermippus, page number

E   *Essays, Moral, Political, and Literary.* Edited by Eugene F. Miller. Indianapolis: Liberty Fund, 1985; revised edition 1987.

             E ET.1   Essay title, page number

             E Var.1   Variant, page number

E Av   Of Avarice

E BG   Whether the British Government inclines more to Absolute Monarchy, or to a Republic

E BP   Of the Balance of Power

E BT   Of the Balance of Trade

E CL   Of Civil Liberty

E Co   Of Commerce

E CP   Of the Coalition of Parties

E DM   Of the Dignity or Meanness of Human Nature

E DT   Of the Delicacy of Taste and Passion

E El   Of Eloquence

E Ep   The Epicurean

E EW   Of Essay Writing

E FP   Of the First Principles of Government

E IC   Idea of a Perfect Commonwealth

E IM   Of Impudence and Modesty

E In   Of Interest

E IP   Of the Independency of Parliament

E IS   Of the Immortality of the Soul

E JT   Of the Jealousy of Trade

E LM   Of Love and Marriage

E LP   Of the Liberty of the Press

E Mo   Of Money

E MP   Of Moral Prejudices

E MS   Of the Middle Station of Life

E NC   Of National Characters

E OC   Of the Original Contract

E OG   Of the Origin of Government

E PA   Of the Populousness of Ancient Nations

E PC   Of Public Credit

E PD   Of Polygamy and Divorces

E PG   Of Parties in General

E PGB   Of the Parties of Great Britain

E Pl   The Platonist

E PO   Of Passive Obedience

E PR   That Politics may be reduced to a Science

E PS   Of the Protestant Succession
E RA   Of Refinement in the Arts
E RC   Of Some Remarkable Customs
E RP   Of the Rise and Progress of the Arts and Sciences
E RW   A Character of Sir Robert Walpole
E Sc   The Sceptic
E SE   Of Superstition and Enthusiasm
E SH   Of the Study of History
E SR   Of Simplicity and Refinement in Writing
E ST   Of the Standard of Taste
E St   The Stoic
E Su   Of Suicide
E Ta   Of Taxes
E Tr   Of Tragedy

EHU   *An Enquiry Concerning Human Understanding: A Critical Edition.* Edited by Thomas L. Beauchamp. Oxford: Clarendon Press, 2000.
    EHU 1.2   Section, paragraph
    EHU Ind.1   Index, page number
    EHU Int.1   Introduction, paragraph

EHU [SBN]   *An Enquiry Concerning Human Understanding.* In *Enquiries Concerning Human Understanding and Concerning the Principles of Morals.* Edited by L. A. Selby-Bigge. Third edition with text revised and notes by P. H. Nidditch. Oxford: Clarendon Press, 1975.

EM   "Hume's Early Memoranda, 1729–1740: The Complete Text." Edited by Ernest Campbell Mossner. *Journal of the History of Ideas* 9 (1948): 492–518.
    EM 2   Page number

EPM   *An Enquiry Concerning the Principles of Morals: A Critical Edition.* Edited by Thomas L. Beauchamp. Oxford: Clarendon Press, 1998.
    EPM 1.2   Section, paragraph
    EPM A.1.2   Appendix, appendix number, paragraph
    EPM D.1   "Dialogue," paragraph
    EPM Ind.1   Index, page number
    EPM Int.1   Introduction, paragraph

EPM [SBN]   *An Enquiry Concerning the Principles of Morals.* In *Enquiries Concerning Human Understanding and Concerning the Principles of Morals.* Edited by L. A. Selby-Bigge. Third edition with text revised and notes by P. H. Nidditch. Oxford: Clarendon Press, 1975.

FE   "An Early Fragment on Evil." Edited by M. A. Stewart. In *Hume and Hume's Connexions,* edited by M. A. Stewart and John P. Wright, 165–68. University Park: Pennsylvania State University Press, 1995.

H   *The History of England, from the Invasion of Julius Caesar to The Revolution in 1688.* 6 vols. Edited by William B. Todd. Indianapolis: Liberty Fund, 1983.

        H 1.2.3   Volume, chapter, page number

        H 1.App.2.3   Volume, appendix, appendix number, page number

        H 1.NoteA.2 Volume, note, page number

        H 1.Var.2   Volume, variant, page number

L   *The Letters of David Hume.* 2 vols. Edited by J. Y. T. Greig. Oxford: Clarendon Press, 1932.

        L 1.2   Volume, page number

LG   *A Letter from a Gentleman to His Friend in Edinburgh.* Edited by Ernest Campbell Mossner and John Valdimir Price. Edinburgh: Edinburgh University Press, 1967.

        LG 2   Page number

LW   "Letter to the Authors of the *Critical Review* Concerning the *Epigoniad* of Wilkie." In *The Philosophical Works of David Hume,* edited by T. H. Green and T. H. Grose, vol. 4, 425–37. London: Longmans, 1874.

        LW 2   Page number

ML   "My Own Life." In *Essays, Moral, Political, and Literary.* Edited by Eugene F. Miller, xxxi–xli. Indianapolis: Liberty Fund, 1985; revised edition 1987.

        ML i   Page number

NHR   *Natural History of Religion.* Edited by H. E. Root. Stanford: Stanford University Press, 1956.

        NHR 1.2   Section, page number

        NHR Int.1   Introduction, page number

NL   *New Letters of David Hume.* Edited by Raymond Klibansky and Ernest Campbell Mossner. Oxford: Clarendon Press, 1954.

        NL 1   Page number

OP   "A Dissertation on the Passions" ["Of the Passions"]. In *The Philosophical Works of David Hume,* edited by T. H. Green and T. H. Grose, 4:139–66. London: Longmans, 1874.

        OP 1.1.1   Section, paragraph, page number

PO   "Of the Poems of Ossian." In *David Hume: Philosophical Historian,* edited by David Fate Norton and Richard H. Popkin, 390–400. Indianapolis: Bobbs-Merrill, 1965.

          PO 1   Page number

RH   "Review of Robert Henry's *History of Great Britain.*" In *David Hume: Philosophical Historian,* edited by David Fate Norton and Richard H. Popkin, 377–88. Indianapolis: Bobbs-Merrill, 1965.

          RH 2   Page number

T   *A Treatise of Human Nature.* Edited by David Fate Norton and Mary J. Norton. Oxford Philosophical Texts. Oxford: Oxford University Press, 2000.

          T 1.2.3.4   Book, part, section, paragraph

          T Adv. 1   Advertisement to Books 1 and 2

          T Adv.3   Advertisement to Book 3

          T App. 1   Appendix, paragraph

          T Int. 1   Introduction, paragraph

T [SBN]   *A Treatise of Human Nature.* Edited by L. A. Selby-Bigge. Second edition with text revised and notes by P. H. Nidditch. Oxford: Clarendon Press, 1978.

Introduction

David Hume has long been recognized as one of the most profound, creative, and widely influential thinkers in the history of modern philosophy. His writings range from epistemology and metaphysics, through discussions of the principles of explanation in the human sciences, to moral theory, political theory, economics, aesthetics, and history. Indeed, during his life and for much of the following century, Hume was more widely known for his writings in economics and history than as a philosopher. However, beginning with his contemporaries such as Reid and Kant, philosophers throughout Europe gradually came to regard Hume's philosophical system as a compelling challenge to the preceding tradition. Over the next two centuries, his works would become a point of reference and a resource for such diverse developments as the idealist tradition in nineteenth-century Germany, the empiricist tradition in nineteenth-century Britain, and both the phenomenological and analytic movements in twentieth-century philosophy. Indeed, Hume has been perpetually rediscovered, either as a source of unappreciated insights or as a target of criticism, by almost every subsequent movement in the Western philosophical tradition.

In light of Hume's influence and importance, it is surprising to find that there have been very few attempts to develop a systematic examination and interpretation of his thought as a whole, including his contributions to the various humanistic and social scientific disciplines, as well as to philosophy. The only direct examples are two studies by Laing and Laird, both from the 1930s, and an introductory study by J. V. Price, originally published in 1968 and updated in 1991.[1] Several more recent works, such as those by Livingston, Baier, Danford, and Herdt, have sought to present a unified account of a number of themes in his thought, although without the explicit order of a systematic survey. On the other hand, the *Cambridge Companion to Hume* provides an overview of his contributions to different fields of inquiry, in essays by different authors which reflect recent developments in the study of Hume, but without attempting to provide a unified interpretation of his thought.[2]

This study is intended to address this lacuna in the literature. It is intended for several types of readers. First, it is offered to beginning students of Hume, as an introduction to the depth and range of his thought, and to the main debates over his thought in the secondary literature. Next, it is directed to those scholars in various disciplines outside philosophy who are interested in Hume's influence in the history and methodology of their own fields. Third, it is offered to specialists in other areas of philosophy, as an overview and synthesis of recent developments in Hume scholarship. Finally, I hope that this study will also be of interest to specialists in the study of Hume, as an attempt to combine a systematic survey of his thought with a distinctive interpretation of his project.

In contrast to many approaches to the interpretation of his philosophy, I argue that Hume presents a constructive account of human reason or, in other words, an account of the elements and principles of human cognition, by which he intends not only to explain but also to justify and improve our reasonings in both the natural and human sciences. At the same time, he also seeks to establish the limits of human reason and the principles governing its subordination to the passions in the activities of human life. Finally, I also argue that he seeks to trace what we today call the social and historical dimensions of human consciousness. This appears in his consideration of how our concepts, beliefs, emotions, and even standards of judgment in different areas of inquiry are shaped by our experience, both in our individual histories and through our participation in the life of a community. In undertaking this project I am accepting the challenge proposed in 1941 by Norman Kemp Smith in his *Philosophy of David Hume,* and reaffirmed by Mossner in the final edition of his biography of Hume and Baier in her study of Hume's *Treatise of Human Nature.* This is Kemp Smith's call for a study of Hume "in all his manifold activities: as philosopher, as political theorist, as economist, as historian, and as man of letters," with the hope that "Hume's philosophy, as the attitude of mind which found for itself

1. Laing, *David Hume;* Laird, *Hume's Philosophy of Human Nature;* and Price, *David Hume.*
2. Norton, *Cambridge Companion to Hume.*

these various forms of expression, will then have been presented, adequately and in due perspective, for the first time."[3]

The history of the interpretation of Hume is an important part of the history of modern philosophy, since many subsequent philosophers have used his writings, often rather loosely, as a point of reference for their own creative inquiries and achievements.[4] Alongside this reception, which would merit a study in its own right, the scholarly interpretation of Hume has developed in a series of overlapping stages, through which he has been regarded variously as a skeptic, as a positivist or a narrow empiricist, and as a more broadly constructive philosopher.

The skeptical interpretation of Hume first appeared in several of the earliest reviews of his philosophical writings and has persisted from the eighteenth century to the present.[5] The earliest of his major critics, Thomas Reid, the leading figure among the Scottish Common Sense philosophers, charged Hume with presenting "a system of scepticism, which leaves no ground to believe any one thing rather than its contrary."[6] Kant rejected the supposed refutation of Hume by his Scottish contemporaries, but also regarded Hume's thought as skeptical and destructive in its tendency, since Hume overlooked the "positive harm" that would arise from depriving human reason of its "most important vistas."[7] In his 1874 edition of Hume's writings, Thomas Green argued that Hume, by pursuing the Lockean theory of ideas to its ultimate conclusion, ended by declaring knowledge to be impossible.[8] This skeptical interpretation was reaffirmed through much of the twentieth century, for example by Bertrand Russell, Karl Popper, and D. C. Stove.

During the first part of the twentieth century, Hume was also regarded as a forerunner of the version of empiricism known as logical positivism. Indeed, the leading figures among the logical positivists, both on the Continent and in England, identified Hume as one of the main predecessors of their movement.[9] Other commentators on Hume, such as G. E. Moore and John Laird in

---

3. Kemp Smith, *Philosophy of David Hume,* vii–viii; Mossner, *Life of David Hume,* vii; Baier, *Progress of Sentiments,* viii–ix.

4. James Fieser has assembled a valuable collection of eighteenth- and nineteenth-century reactions to Hume in his multivolume *Early Responses to Hume.* On the reception of Hume's work by his British contemporaries, and on Hume's response to their criticisms, see Somerville's *Enigmatic Parting Shot.* On Hume's influence in German philosophy, see especially Kuehn, *Scottish Common Sense Philosophy in Germany;* Gawlick and Kreimendahl, *Hume in der Deutschen Aufklärung;* Waszek, *Scottish Enlightenment;* and Murphy, *Hume and Husserl.*

5. Mossner, *Life of David Hume,* 117–33 and 286–300.

6. Reid, *Works,* 1: 95.

7. Kant, *Prolegomena,* 8n, in *Kants gesammelte Schriften,* 4:258n.

8. Green, *Hume and Locke,* 2.

9. See especially Hahn, Neurath, and Carnap, "The Scientific Conception of the World," 304; and Ayer, *Language, Truth and Logic,* 31 and 54–55.

the early twentieth century, along with more recent figures such as Farhang
Zabeeh, Antony Flew, Robert Anderson, David Pears, and Georges Dickers,
have regarded Hume as a leading representative of a more general empiricism
in philosophy.

A third approach to the interpretation of Hume is the allegation that he
does not present any consistent philosophical position. This view again appears
among his earliest critics, such as James Beattie, another Scottish Common
Sense philosopher, who denounced the "paradoxes" in Hume's philosophy.[10]
This view is also echoed by Selby-Bigge in his 1894 introduction to the
Enquiries: "Hume's philosophic writings are to be read with great caution. His
pages, especially those of the Treatise, are so full of matter, he says so many different things in so many different ways and different connexions, and with so
much indifference to what he has said before, that it is very hard to say posi-
tively that he taught, or did not teach, this or that particular doctrine. . . . This
makes it easy to find all philosophies in Hume, or, by setting up one statement
against another, none at all."[11] This criticism has also been directed against
Hume by John Laird, Jonathan Bennett, and Antony Flew. The most elaborate
version of this approach is presented by John Passmore, who rejects the whole-
sale application of the prevailing traditional labels to Hume's thought, but then
applies them to its allegedly conflicting aspects. Hume thus becomes in different respects a positivist, a phenomenalist, a skeptic, and so on.[12] This approach
to Hume, or indeed to any author, is, however, open to the objection that the
critic is simply giving up any sustained effort to trace the underlying unity in
the thought of his author, or to view his entire body of writings as a coherent
project.

The single most influential challenge to these interpretations of Hume as
a skeptic, as a positivist, or as fundamentally incoherent, was developed by
Norman Kemp Smith, especially in his *Philosophy of David Hume.* According to
Kemp Smith, Hume criticized the prevailing conceptions of reason in order to
emphasize the role of feeling and "natural belief" in both cognition and morality. On this view, Hume sought to establish "the thorough subordination—*by
right,* if not always in actual fact, of reason to the feelings and instincts," by
showing that we must rely on feeling and belief, rather than reason, in "all the
really ultimate issues" of life. Kemp Smith also interprets Hume's account of
our ideas of causality, the existence of external objects, and personal identity as
a doctrine of "natural beliefs," or beliefs that arise from "the ultimate instincts
or propensities which constitute our human nature." Indeed, he identifies this

10. Beattie, *Essay on the Nature and Immutability of Truth,* 18.
11. Selby-Bigge, "Editor's Introduction," vii.
12. Passmore, *Hume's Intentions.* For a postmodern defense of this approach, see Parusnikova, "Against
the Spirit of Foundations," 1–17.

as "the most essential, and perhaps the most characteristic doctrine in Hume's philosophy."[13] Kemp Smith's "naturalistic" interpretation of Hume has been further developed by Hendel, Stroud, Wright, and Mounce, while others such as MacNabb, Penelhum, Fogelin, Pears, and Waxman have sought to distinguish the elements of skepticism and naturalism in Hume's thought.

The continuing value of Kemp Smith's approach lies in his attempt to develop a broadly constructive interpretation of Hume's philosophy, and his emphasis on the continuity between Hume's epistemology and his moral philosophy. However, there are several difficulties in Kemp Smith's approach and in his "naturalistic" interpretation of Hume's philosophy. The first of these is his emphasis upon the words "nature," "natural," and "natural belief." Hume himself does not use the phrase "natural belief," and while he often uses the word "nature" in contexts that might seem to support Kemp Smith's interpretation (cf. T 1.4.1.7, 1.4.1.12, 1.4.7.9 [SBN 183, 187, 269]), he gives the term "nature" no emphasis comparable to his typographical emphasis on such words as "CUSTOM" and "HABIT" (T 1.3.8.10 [SBN 102]; cf. EHU 5.5 [SBN 43]). Indeed, Hume frequently calls attention to the ambiguity of the word "natural," in order to indicate that it has little or no explanatory value without further specification or qualification (T 3.1.2.7–10 [SBN 473–75]; EPM App.3.9 [SBN 307]).[14] Kemp Smith also overlooks Hume's account of the principles of probable or scientific reasoning, as we will see in Chapter 3, and therefore gives an inadequate view of the role of critical reflection in Hume's account of human cognition. His "subordination thesis" has also been challenged as a misrepresentation of the relation between "reason" and "feeling" in Hume's thought.[15] Finally, although he explores the relation between Hume's epistemology and his moral theory, Kemp Smith does not extend the scope of his discussion to Hume's writings in other areas of philosophy and intellectual inquiry.

Since the early twentieth century, a number of studies have challenged these prevailing approaches to the interpretation of Hume, and have indicated some of the directions in which an alternative approach to the constructive interpretation of his philosophy might be developed.[16] These challenges have become increasingly prominent in the last forty years, especially since the middle of

13. Kemp Smith, *Philosophy of David Hume,* 84–86 and 545.

14. For these and other criticisms of Kemp Smith, see Lenz, "Hume's Defense of Causal Inference," 169–70; Hearn, "Norman Kemp Smith," 3–7; Beauchamp and Rosenberg, *Hume and the Problem of Causation,* 57–67; Norton, *David Hume,* 3–20; Agassi, "Smith's Term 'Naturalism,'" 92–96; and Gaskin, *Hume's Philosophy of Religion,* 108–19. Mounce provides a discussion of several different uses of the term "naturalism" in *Hume's Naturalism,* 1–14, though I am not convinced that either Mounce's "Scottish naturalism" or his "scientific naturalism" correspond to Kemp Smith's conception of Hume's naturalism.

15. See especially Norton, *David Hume,* 17–20 and 208–38.

16. Some of these valuable earlier studies of Hume include those by Mary Shaw Kuypers, Ralph Church, Constance Maund, William Gordon Ross, and Rachael M. Kydd.

the 1970s. The contributors to this trend, such as John Stewart, Páll Árdal, Nicholas Capaldi, Duncan Forbes, Annette Baier, Fred Wilson, David Fate Norton, Peter Jones, Donald Livingston, John Danford, Jennifer Herdt, Don Garrett, David Owen, and Dale Jacquette, have pursued new investigations into almost every aspect of Hume's philosophy, and also into the relation between his philosophy and the other areas of his thought.[17] I will refer frequently to these and other studies throughout this book. Finally, several recent studies have even regarded Hume's philosophy and his larger intellectual project as anticipations of the so-called postmodern movement in contemporary thought. Hume's affinity to postmodernism has been traced especially in his account of the tension between skepticism and naturalism; in his move from philosophy to the study of history, literature, and politics; in his criticism of earlier approaches to establishing normative principles for cognition and action; and in his use of irony, multiple perspectives, and other playful devices in his writings.[18]

In this book I argue, drawing upon many of these recent studies, that Hume's philosophy can be understood more accurately and completely as an examination of "reason in history," or as an account of the historical dimension of rationality. This unifying theme will become apparent through a systematic study of his account of the elements of human cognition and the standards of justification in the different areas of human life and thought. In the first five chapters I examine Hume's account of cognition, with particular attention to the formation of abstract ideas and their relation to language; the principles of philosophical probable reasoning; the role of imagination in our ideas of space, time, causation, external existence, and personal identity; and his defense of "moderate," "mitigated," or "academic" skepticism. In the remaining eight chapters I consider his application of these principles to the study of human nature, and to our reasonings in what we now call the various humanistic and social-scientific disciplines. Throughout this study I call attention to Hume's consideration of the influence of social context and historical tradition on the various aspects of human thought and consciousness, such as the formation of abstract ideas, the use of language, the acquisition of beliefs, the formulation

17. Waxman criticizes the naturalizing tendency in recent Hume scholarship and seeks to reaffirm the skeptical implications of Hume's philosophy; see *Hume's Theory of Consciousness*, 1–23 and 266–79. However, he then calls attention to Hume's constructive view of the contribution of the human mind to the constitution of its objects and also acknowledges Hume's transition from an examination of the individual mind in Book 1 of the *Treatise* to the social context of the passions and morality in Books 2 and 3.

18. See Deleuze, *Empiricism and Subjectivity*, and Parusnikova, "Against the Spirit of Foundations," 1–17. For an interpretation of Hume's literary career in a postmodern style, see Christensen, *Practicing Enlightenment*. Hume's philosophy has also been regarded as an alternative to both modernism and postmodernism; see Livingston, *Philosophical Melancholy and Delirium*, 383–407; Danford, *Problem of Reason*, 14–25; and Williams, *Cultivated Reason*.

of the standards of scientific judgment, the directing of the passions toward various objects, and the development of moral, political, aesthetic, and religious traditions. I also consider his account of the principles by which various aspects of human life are to be explained as products of human nature in general, of a particular cultural and historical tradition, or of critical reflection.

Hume frequently affirms his intention to establish the principles of the "sciences," or the various intellectual disciplines. In the introduction to the *Treatise* he expresses dismay over the "present imperfect condition of the sciences," where "there is nothing which is not the subject of debate." He then proposes to reassess all of the other areas of human inquiry by beginning with the "science of MAN," since by explaining the principles of human nature "we in effect propose a compleat system of the sciences, built on a foundation almost entirely new, and the only one upon which they can stand with any security." He even suggests that "Mathematics, Natural Philosophy, and Natural Religion" must ultimately be established on the foundations provided by the "science of man," although the *Treatise* is more particularly directed toward the subjects belonging to "moral philosophy," including "Logic, Morals, Criticism, and Politics" (T Int.2–6 [SBN xiii–xvi]; cf. A P.3 [SBN 643–44]).[19] In the first "Advertisement," which was published with the first two volumes of the *Treatise,* he describes the general plan of this work: beginning with a study of the understanding and the passions, and then proceeding to morals, politics, and criticism (T Adv.1 [SBN xii]). He echoes this plan in the concluding sections of both Books 1 and 2 of the *Treatise,* in which he considers our motives for intellectual inquiry as a transition to his topics in the rest of the *Treatise* (T 1.4.7.12–15, 2.3.10.1–12 [SBN 270–74, 448–54]). Similarly, he concludes the *Enquiry Concerning Human Understanding* with a summary of the principles of reasoning that belong to the different natural and human sciences (EHU 12.26–34; cf. 8.18 [SBN 163–65; cf. 90]). He further examines the principles of explanation in the human sciences in his essays, in his writings on religion, and in the *History of England.* Hume's contributions to what we would now identify as the various academic disciplines are important, not only for the development of these disciplines, but also as a sustained effort to explore the implications of philosophical inquiry for understanding the methodological foundations of the sciences. In this respect, he calls attention to the significance and value of philosophy for understanding the methodological principles of the individual academic disciplines.

---

19. In eighteenth-century English usage, "natural philosophy" refers to what we now call the natural sciences, while "moral philosophy" refers to the "human sciences," or what we now call the humanities and social sciences. Indeed, the subsequent German distinction between the *Naturwissenschaften* and *Geisteswissenschaften* is itself derived from Mill's related distinction between the "natural" and "moral" sciences. See Dilthey, *Introduction to the Human Sciences,* 57.

The arrangement of this study will reflect the general order in which Hume's philosophical arguments are developed, and in which his major works were written and published.[20] At least in Hume's case, the sequence of his writings also provides a convenient structure for the systematic organization of his thought.[21] I will accordingly advance from his initial analysis of ideas at the beginning of the *Treatise* (Chapter 1) to his works in religion and history (Chapters 12 and 13).

In Chapters 1 through 5, I consider Hume's epistemology and metaphysics, as these include in his account of ideas, demonstrative reasoning, causal reasoning, the traditional topics of metaphysics, and the various types of skepticism. These topics are addressed in Book 1 of the *Treatise of Human Nature,* in his anonymously published *Abstract* to the *Treatise of Human Nature,* and in the *Enquiry Concerning Human Understanding.* In Chapters 6 and 7, I examine his account of the passions in Book 2 of the *Treatise* and the dissertation "Of the Passions," and his analysis of human action in Book 2 of the *Treatise* and in the first *Enquiry.* In Chapters 8 and 9, I turn to his moral and political theories, as these are developed in Book 3 of the *Treatise,* in the *Enquiry Concerning the Principles of Morals,* and in his essays.[22] In Chapters 10 through 12, I consider Hume's economic theory, as presented in the *Political Discourses* and other essays; his aesthetic theory, especially in the essays "Of Tragedy" and "Of the Standard of Taste"; and his various discussions of religion in the first *Enquiry,* the *Natural History of Religion,* the *Dialogues Concerning Natural Religion,* and in his political and historical writings. Finally, in Chapter 13, I examine his various discussions of historical method, and his approach to the writing of history, especially in his six-volume *History of England.* In the conclusion I provide a summary of the relation between history and reason in Hume's thought by considering his view of the historical dimension of human consciousness. I then

---

20. For a bibliography of Hume's works and their publication history from the original editions through 1937, and of translations and responses, see Jessop, *Bibliography,* 5–43. A more recent and complete catalog of Hume's works, mainly of the editions which appeared during his own lifetime, is included in Ikeda, *David Hume,* 1–181. On the chronology of Hume's manuscripts, see Stewart, "Hume's Manuscripts," 267–314.

21. For valuable biographies of Hume, see Greig, *David Hume;* Mossner, *Life of David Hume;* and Streminger, *David Hume: Sein Leben und sein Werk.*

22. Hume published a collection (his first) of fifteen essays, *Essays, Moral and Political,* in 1741; a second collection of twelve essays in 1742; and a collection of three essays in 1748. Additional essays were published in the *Political Discourses* in 1752 and the *Four Dissertations* of 1757. Most of these essays were included, with the two *Enquiries,* in his collected *Essays and Treatises on Several Subjects.* This collection, in one, two, or four volumes, was first published starting in 1753, and then reissued in a series of revised editions until the posthumous edition of 1777. The essay section in this collection was given the subtitle "Essays, Moral, Political, and Literary" after 1758. Hume retitled several of his essays, withdrew some from publication, and added others over the course of these editions. He also wrote two essays, "Of Suicide" and "Of the Immortality of the Soul," which were circulated but not published under his name during his lifetime because of their controversial treatment of religious topics. See Jessop, *Bibliography,* 5–42; Eugene Miller, "Foreword," xi–xviii; and Ikeda, *David Hume,* xvi–xvii.

consider some of the implications of my interpretation of Hume for under-standing his relation to a variety of later discussions, including subsequent developments in German philosophy, recent discussions within analytic philos-ophy concerning the social and historical dimensions of human cognition, and current discussions of the Enlightenment and modernity across the academic disciplines.

Readers of Hume are often bewitched, or bedeviled, by a variety of inter-pretive problems arising from the literary artistry and subtlety of his writings, including not only the complexity of his prose but also his frequent uses of irony and the dialogue form.[23] Indeed, several recent studies have called atten-tion to the dialectical character of many passages in his writings. These include not only the *Dialogues Concerning Natural Religion,* the coda entitled "A Dia-logue" at the end of the *Enquiry Concerning the Principles of Morals,* and the Epi-curean dialogue in Section 11 of the first *Enquiry,* but also his juxtaposition of voices and opinions in many of his political and philosophical essays, and even his dramatic progression in the *Treatise of Human Nature* from an examination of the principles of the human mind, through the darkness of total skepticism, to a renewed enthusiasm for his further inquiries into the passions, morals, and political theory.[24] I address many of the resulting issues of interpretation as they arise. Most notably, I argue in Chapters 3 and 12 that Philo should be regarded as the main spokesman in the *Dialogues* for Hume's general philo-sophical view; and, in Chapter 5, that Hume intends to provide a constructive account of human cognition in the concluding section of Book 1 of the *Treatise.* I also emphasize the consistency of his thought over the course of his literary career, although I consider some of the changes in presentation between his writings, especially from the *Treatise* to the two *Enquiries.*

Since Hume's intellectual interests are reflected in his correspondence with his friends and fellow *literati,* I also occasionally cite his letters. However, it is important to note that Hume tended to adjust the tone and content of each let-ter according to its intended reader, and that he generally valued goodwill and courtesy over argument and persuasion in written exchanges with his friends, and even with his critics.[25] I will accordingly indicate if he seems to be treat-ing a given topic either more circumspectly or more candidly in a letter than in his published writings, by considering the style of the letter, and the nature of his relationship with the recipient.

23. On Hume's literary style and its relation to his philosophical concerns, see Price, *The Ironic Hume;* Christensen, *Practicing Enlightenment;* and Box, *Suasive Art of David Hume.*

24. Livingston, *Hume's Philosophy of Common Life,* 34–59, and *Philosophical Melancholy and Delirium,* 97–100, 137–40, and 168–71; Baier, *Progress of Sentiments;* Rorty, "From Passions to Sentiments," 165–79; Immerwahr, "Hume's Essays on Happiness," 307–24; Malherbe, "Hume and the Art of Dialogue," 201–23.

25. For examples, see his letters to his friend Hugh Blair in 1761 (L 1.348–51), and also to his critic George Campbell in 1762 (L 1.360–61).

This study is intended to provide a unified and constructive interpretation of Hume's thought in his various writings. Since this is in itself a demanding project, I have not attempted to criticize or evaluate Hume's arguments, at least to the extent that is usual among contemporary philosophers in studies of their predecessors. On the other hand, I would argue that attempts to understand historical texts in philosophy can and should be directed, not only toward evaluating arguments and tracing the history of issues which are currently popular in philosophy, but also toward discovering new perspectives and new problems that might have been overlooked by previous commentators. Accordingly, in the present study I show that many misleading interpretations of Hume's project, both in its details and in its overall character, have become entrenched in the subsequent philosophical tradition. I hope that a renewed consideration of the unity and constructive character of Hume's thought, and of the history of its interpretation, will in itself be a useful and valuable contribution to discussions in contemporary philosophy.

I have not attempted to provide a systematic account of the background and sources of Hume's thought in the works of his predecessors, or a systematic overview of Hume's influence in the history of philosophy.[26] I also have not discussed extensively his own social, intellectual, and cultural context, beyond what is required for considering the theoretical significance of his remarks concerning contemporary life and various current events in Europe, Great Britain, and Scotland.[27] In other words, although I explore Hume's approach to history, including the study of human cognition, emotion, and volition within their historical context, I am approaching these topics by examining the principles formulated by Hume for pursuing these inquiries. While these principles were indeed developed in the context of his own time, place, and intellectual tradition, Hume intended them to be applicable to the study of human nature in any culture, by anyone who is willing to share the intellectual commitments he defends. I will approach the explanation and interpretation of his philosophy in this spirit.

I have been perpetually encouraged, delighted, and challenged in preparing this book by the flourishing community of Hume scholars. It is regrettably no longer possible, if indeed it ever was, to consult every publication that would be relevant to a general study of this nature. I have therefore referred mainly to

26. The editors of the Clarendon and Oxford Philosophical Text editions of Hume's writings have provided valuable references to many of Hume's sources and predecessors. See the notes and editorial apparatus by David Fate Norton and Mary Norton in the OPT edition of the *Treatise,* and by Tom Beauchamp in the Clarendon and OPT editions of the two *Enquiries.*

27. For recent studies of Hume's immediate intellectual context in eighteenth-century Scotland, see Sher, *Church and University;* Allan, *Virtue, Learning, and the Scottish Enlightenment;* and Wood, *Scottish Enlightenment.* For an eminently readable history of Scotland during this period, including economic, political, cultural, and intellectual developments, see Herman, *How the Scots Invented the Modern World.*

those works (and they are many) that I have found to be especially important in the development of my own thinking about Hume, without attempting to provide a comprehensive survey of the secondary literature on every topic included here. I hope that these references will provide a valuable point of departure for readers who wish to pursue any of the topics in my study, or to contest some aspect of my interpretation of Hume.

Finally, a word on the title of this study. The phrase "reason in history" was introduced by Hegel in the *Encyclopedia of the Philosophical Sciences,* and was adopted either by Hegel or by his editor, Johannes Hoffmeister, as the subtitle for Hegel's introduction to his lectures on the philosophy of history, apparently to summarize their underlying theme.[28] Hume and Hegel are often regarded as representing the extreme poles of empiricism and idealism, although Hegel was actually influenced by Hume's historical writings in at least one important respect, as we will see in Chapter 13. However, many recent studies have observed that Hume and Hegel are among the relatively few philosophers who were deeply interested in the study of history, and in pursuing the connections between history and philosophy.[29] In this study I hope to show that Hume, like Hegel, seeks to develop a constructive account of human reason, and that Hume, like Hegel, also locates the activity of human reason in history, although his style in approaching these topics is clearly different from that of his successor. I have, therefore, freely borrowed my subtitle from the realm of Hegelian discourse, since the phrase "reason in history" also expresses what I regard as the unifying theme in Hume's thought.

28. See the selection from Hegel's *Encyclopedia* in Hegel, *Hegel's Philosophy of Mind,* 277 (§549), and Hegel, *Lectures on the Philosophy of World History,* 1.
29. See Livingston, *Hume's Philosophy of Common Life,* 2 and 36; Rorty, "From Passions to Sentiments," 169; and Williams, *Cultivated Reason,* 26.

1

Ideas

Hume introduces his examination of the "nature and principles of the human mind" in the *Treatise* with an account in Book 1, Part 1 of the "origin, composition, connexion, abstraction, &c" of our ideas, which he identifies as "the elements of this philosophy" (T 1.1.2.1, 1.1.1.1, 1.1.4.7 [SBN 8, 1, 13]). Hume's analysis of ideas has often been taken to reflect an atomistic, passive, and individualistic account of the human mind.[1] In this chapter I show that Hume attempts not only to identify the contents of our mental states but also to characterize the different intentional states in which we apprehend this content. I also examine his account of the various activities of the mind, as these appear in our abilities to recall, compare, distinguish, rearrange, connect, and combine the ideas we derive from sensations, in order to formulate fanciful images, abstract ideas, and judgments. In addition, I argue that Hume recognizes the influence of social and historical existence on our formation and application of abstract ideas, by indicating that these operations are facilitated in the individual, and coordinated among individuals, as they learn the language of a particular community. Finally, I show that Hume presents both of the "first principles" in his "science of human nature"—that ideas are copies of impressions, and that

1. See Dilthey, *Introduction to the Human Sciences,* 210–11; Husserl, *Formal and Transcendental Logic,* 255–66; Flew, *Hume's Philosophy of Belief,* 18–52; and Pears, *Hume's System,* 16–30 and 114–15.

the imagination is able to rearrange our ideas—as principles of analysis which we should apply conjointly in order to trace the genealogy of our complex ideas, including ideas which are signified by various philosophical terms.

PERCEPTIONS

Hume introduces the term "perception" in the *Treatise* to designate the contents, or constituent elements, of human consciousness. He initially states that "nothing is ever really present with the mind but its perceptions," and later adds that "the only existences, of which we are certain, are perceptions," since these alone are "immediately present to us by consciousness" (T 1.1.1.1, 1.2.6.7, 1.4.2.47 [SBN 1, 67, 212]). Hume also describes a perception as an "object of our thought," or an "object" in the primary sense of the term. He distinguishes an object in this sense, as the content of any conscious state, from "external objects," which are supposed to have a continued existence apart from the mind, but are known to us only "by those perceptions they occasion" (T 1.2.6.2–7 [SBN 66–67]). Among our perceptions he includes all of the sensory, affective, and cognitive modifications of the human mind, such as "the actions of seeing, hearing, judging, loving, hating, and thinking" (T 3.1.1.2; cf. 1.3.7.5n20, 1.4.2.7 [SBN 456; cf. 96–97n1, 190]). Finally, he argues that individual perceptions may be regarded as "substances," at least according to the definition of a "substance" as whatever may be "consider'd as separately existent, and may exist separately," and has "no need of any thing else" to support its existence (T 1.4.5.5 [SBN 233]). As we will see in Chapter 4, Hume eventually seeks to show that our ideas of external objects and of the self are produced by the mind through its various activities in combining our perceptions, and that we have no foundation or justification for these ideas apart from the constructive activity of the imagination.

Next, Hume divides our perceptions into "impressions" and "ideas," which he initially states are distinguished from each other by the different "degrees of force and liveliness, with which they strike upon the mind." Of these, impressions are generally more forceful and lively, and include "all our sensations, passions and emotions, as they make their first appearance in the soul," while ideas are the "faint images" of these in our "thinking and reasoning." However, Hume also concedes that our impressions and ideas may in some cases "very nearly approach to each other" in vividness. Thus, for example, "in sleep, in a fever, in madness, or in any very violent emotions of soul" our ideas may resemble impressions in their vivacity, while on the other hand our impressions may at times become "so faint and low" that we cannot distinguish them from ideas. Here, in addition to his quantitative distinction between impressions and ideas in terms of their degrees of vivacity, Hume appears to endorse a qualitative distinction between the types of conscious states in which we respectively apprehend impressions and ideas, which we recognize as "the difference betwixt feeling and thinking" (T 1.1.1.1 [SBN 1–2]). This qualitative distinction is more explicitly indicated in the *Abstract,* where he states that "when we feel a passion or emotion," or the influence of external objects on our senses, our perception is called an "impression," while "when we reflect on a passion or an object which is not present, this perception is an *idea*" (A 5 [SBN 647]). Here he suggests that we can recognize a difference in the subjective quality of our conscious states between our immediate apprehension of a sensation or emotion and our reflective apprehension of the same sensation or emotion when it is represented by an idea. This reference to the two types of intentional states involved in our apprehending of perceptions, either as impressions or as ideas, anticipates his account of belief, in contrast to the imagination, as a distinctive "manner" of conceiving ideas, as we will see later in this chapter (cf. T 1.3.7.7 [SBN 629]).[2]

Hume further divides our impressions, or feelings, into "impressions of sensation" and "impressions of reflection." An "impression of sensation" is one that "strikes upon the senses, and makes us perceive heat or cold, thirst or hunger, pleasure or pain of some kind or other" (T 1.1.2.1 [SBN 7–8]). He later divides our impressions of sensation into three apparent types: impressions of shape, motion, and solidity, which we generally regard as qualities of external objects; impressions of color, taste, smell, heat, and cold, which we commonly attribute to objects but which modern philosophers regard as modifications of the mind arising from the influence of external objects; and impressions of pleasure and pain, which everyone regards as mental states rather than qualities of external objects (T 1.4.2.12 [SBN 192]). By contrast, "impressions of reflection" include the "passions, desires, and emotions," which arise in the mind in response to our ideas of pleasurable or painful sensations (T 1.1.2.1 [SBN 7–8]). In the first *Enquiry* Hume characterizes this division of our impressions as a distinction between "outward" and "inward" sensations: a view echoed by Philo's observation in the *Dialogues* that the "materials" of human thought include the ideas derived from "internal sentiment, added to those of the external senses," which together comprise "the whole furniture of human understanding" (EHU 2.9 [SBN 22]; DNR 3.156).

2. This account of Hume's description of the different "manners" in which we conceive our ideas, as an attempt to describe the distinct "phenomenological" qualities of different intentional states, is developed especially by Waxman; see *Hume's Theory of Consciousness,* 18. See also Butler, "Hume's Impressions," 122–36. Stevenson argues that in Hume's view self-consciousness is a product of the phenomenological feelings of vivacity and of an easy transition in our perceptions; see "Humean Self-Consciousness Explained," 95–129.

Finally, Hume introduces a distinction between "simple" and "complex" perceptions, which he applies to both impressions and ideas. Of these, simple perceptions "admit of no distinction nor separation," while complex perceptions may be "distinguish'd into parts" (T 1.1.1.2 [SBN 2]). Unfortunately, Hume's characterization of simple perceptions is almost immediately obscured by his rather haphazard presentation of his own examples, and by an ambiguity in his account of two apparent ways in which ideas may be "distinguished" or "separated" by the mind.

In his initial example, Hume identifies the "colour, taste, and smell" of an apple as simple impressions of sensation, since these qualities are "not the same, but are at least distinguishable from each other" (T 1.1.1.2 [SBN 2]). Here and elsewhere he apparently identifies the idea of a quality, such as a particular color, as a "simple idea" (cf. T 1.1.7.7n5 [SBN 637]). Next, referring to our idea of a winged horse, he indicates that the imagination can separate and rearrange our ideas of the spatially extended parts of complex impressions. In this context he argues that "there are not any two impressions which are perfectly inseparable," so that "wherever the imagination perceives a difference among ideas, it can easily produce a separation," in this case by imagining part of one type of animal body as separated from that type of animal and attached to another (T 1.1.3.4 [SBN 10]). Finally, he describes the union of color and shape in a visual impression, for example in our view of a globe of white marble, as a "simplicity" (T 1.1.7.18 [SBN 25]). In these cases he apparently characterizes first the qualities of a complex perception, then the parts of a complex perception, and finally a given combination of qualities in our perception of an external object, as simple perceptions.

While the parts of an animal body can clearly be imagined as existing separately from that body, and as attached to another object, Hume's analysis becomes less straightforward when he considers the senses in which the qualities of complex perceptions can be "distinguished" from each other. In the discussion of abstract ideas with which he concludes the presentation of his theory of ideas, he reaffirms the principle "that all ideas, which are different, are separable," and further identifies what is "separable" with what is "distinguishable." He then argues that although we cannot separate certain types of qualities, such as color and shape, from each other in a literal sense as separate impressions or images, we can recognize and consider these as separate qualities by comparing one perception to another and attending to their resembling or contrasting qualities: an activity he calls a "distinction of reason." In his example, we cannot distinguish the color of a marble globe from its shape by forming separate images of its color or shape. However, we can distinguish color and shape from each other, and from the object as a whole, in a figurative sense through a distinction of reason, by directing our attention toward various resemblances and differences between our perception of the globe and our perceptions of other objects (T 1.1.7.17–18 [SBN 24–25]). A *"distinction* of ideas" is thus distinguished from the "real *difference"* which subsists between those perceptions we can imagine as existing separately (T 1.2.6.6 [SBN 67]).

Interestingly enough, while he denies in Part 1 that we can imagine the qualities of color and shape as existing separately, in Part 4 he affirms that even though "the colour, taste, figure, solidity, and other qualities, combin'd in a peach or melon, are conceiv'd to form *one thing,"* the mind recognizes these qualities as "different, and distinguishable, and separable from each other." In this context he even maintains that since each quality is "a distinct thing from another," every quality "may be conceiv'd to exist apart, and may exist apart," not only from a supposed substance, but also from every other quality (T 1.4.3.5–7 [SBN 221–22]).

In order to provide a clearer reconstruction of Hume's account of simple perceptions, or those perceptions which are really separable, we may turn to his discussion of our ideas of space and time in Part 2. Here he identifies the minimal points of color and texture which appear in our sensory field as simple perceptions, by describing our minimum possible impressions of color and texture as "simple and uncompounded," and our ideas of these points as "perfectly simple and indivisible" (T 1.2.1.4–5 [SBN 28]).[3] These points have one quality, a color or texture, but no shape; and our perception of a colored or textured shape is actually a complex perception made up of these indivisible points (cf. T 1.2.2.9 [SBN 32]). Hume subsequently characterizes various other uniform but nonspatial impressions, such as pure sounds, tastes, and smells, as simple (T 1.1.7.7n5; cf. 1.2.3.10, 1.4.2.12–16, 1.4.5.10–14 [SBN 637; cf. 36, 191–94, 235–39]), along with various passions (T 2.1.2.1, 2.2.1.1 [SBN 277, 329]). However, it would seem, according to his analysis, that if we attribute simplicity to minimum visible and tangible points in space, we should also attribute simplicity to nonspatial perceptions only as they appear in minimal temporal points of awareness, since one moment in the continuing awareness of a sound or a passion can presumably be separated from another by the imagination.[4]

As we have seen, Hume initially argues that color and shape cannot be separated from each other by "thought and imagination," but only through a "distinction of reason" (T 1.1.7.3, 1.1.7.17–18 [SBN 18, 24–25]). However, in Part 2 he maintains that minimal visible points can only be seen or imagined as points of color, although he does not offer any specific evidence that we can recognize the color of a minimum visible point (cf. T 1.2.3.4–5 [SBN 34]).

---

3. See Hawkins, "Simplicity, Resemblance and Contrariety," 25; Garrett, *Cognition and Commitment,* 60–64; Frasca-Spada, *Space and the Self,* 11–55 and 181–83; and Jacquette, *David Hume's Critique of Infinity,* 43–128.

4. See Hawkins, "Simplicity, Resemblance and Contrariety," 25.

According to this analysis, minimal points of color seem to be simple perceptions that can be perceived and imagined separately, although they can also be combined in the complex perception of a colored shape. By contrast, our idea of a particular shape is a complex idea, which we can only formulate, as a distinction of reason, by comparing the distribution of colored or textured points in a variety of complex perceptions.

On this reconstruction of Hume's view, simple perceptions would thus consist in those minimal points of color and texture, and those momentary appearances of uniform nonspatial qualities such as sounds, smells, and passions, which we can perceive separately, and imagine as existing separately, from other spatially or temporally minimal perceptions.[5]

Finally, Hume also maintains that we can recognize various resemblances and differences even between our simple perceptions, thereby indicating that we may identify different aspects of these uniform perceptions through distinctions of reason, even though these aspects cannot be perceived or imagined as existing separately from a perception. These recognizable aspects of our simple perceptions include the hue or saturation of colors, the pitch or volume of sounds, and the painful or pleasurable character of our passions (T 1.1.7.7n5; cf. 2.1.4.3 [SBN 637; cf. 283]). This ambiguity in Hume's use of the terms "distinguishable," for either a "real" distinction or a "distinction of reason," introduces a surreptitious difficulty into the two maxims of analysis he claims to derive from his "second principle" concerning the activity of the imagination. These are, that "whatever objects are different are distinguishable, and that whatever objects are distinguishable are separable by the thought and imagination," and conversely that "whatever objects are separable are also distinguishable, and that whatever objects are distinguishable are also different" (T 1.1.3.4, 1.1.7.3 [SBN 10, 18]). In light of the present discussion, we should be prepared to distinguish between those perceptions, such as minimum visible points, which are "really" distinguishable and separable, or can be perceived or imagined as existing separately, and those qualities of our perceptions, such as the shape of a spatially extended object or the pitch of a sound, which can we can attend to and identify by a distinction of reason, but which cannot be perceived or imagined as existing separately (cf. T 1.2.6.6 [SBN 67]). We should accordingly always consider whether he intends to identify a real distinction or a distinction of reason in order to understand his application of these maxims in any particular case.[6]

5. For other discussions of Hume's conception of simplicity, see Hawkins, "Simplicity, Resemblance and Contrariety," 24–38; Russow, "Simple Ideas and Resemblance," 342–50; Hausman, "Simple/Complex Distinction," 424–28; Waxman, *Hume's Theory of Consciousness,* 42–46; Cummins, "Hume on Qualities," 49–88; Garrett, *Cognition and Commitment,* 60–64; Frasca-Spada, *Space and the Self,* 11–55 and 181–83; and Jacquette, *David Hume's Critique of Infinity,* 57–65.
6. For a general discussion of Hume's separability principle, see Garrett, *Cognition and Commitment,* 58–75.

Next, Hume calls attention to the "great resemblance betwixt our impressions and ideas," which "appear always to correspond to each other." Here he finds that all of our ideas resemble our impressions of sensation or reflection, and that all of our impressions may be represented by ideas. However, since we may formulate complex ideas that do not exactly resemble any of our complex impressions, he traces this correspondence to resemblances between simple ideas and the simple impressions that make up our complex impressions. We may thus form a complex idea of "the *New Jerusalem,* whose pavement is gold and walls are rubies," by imaginatively rearranging the simple ideas of color and texture in the complex ideas derived from our complex impressions of golden objects, rubies, pavements, and walls (T 1.1.1.3–4 [SBN 2–3]; cf. EHU 2.2–9 [SBN 17–22]).

Hume also maintains that we cannot formulate a simple idea unless it has been preceded by a resembling simple impression. In other words, simple ideas are "images of our impressions" (T 1.1.1.11 [SBN 6]). Here he appeals to the "constant experience" of his readers, in our own memories of the impressions from which we have derived our simple ideas of various qualities, and our observations of how others appear to acquire these ideas from impressions. For example, we find that none of us can form a "just idea" of the flavor of a pineapple until we have tasted one, and we agree that a person who has been blind from birth cannot formulate the idea of a color (T 1.1.1.8–9 [SBN 4–5]).[7] As the "first principle" in his "science of human nature," Hume thus asserts "that all our simple ideas in their first appearance are deriv'd from simple impressions, which are correspondent to them, and which they exactly represent" (T 1.1.1.12, 1.1.1.7 [SBN 7, 4]; cf. EHU 2.5 [SBN 19]).

We may therefore summarize Hume's account of the derivation of our perceptions in the following terms. The initial contents of human consciousness are impressions of sensation, which may then give rise to ideas, or remembered images of these sensations. These ideas may, in turn, give rise to another set of impressions: the passions, or impressions of reflection. Finally, we may also formulate ideas of the passions, as well as "secondary ideas" of our preceding ideas, ideas of these ideas, and so on (T 1.1.1.11 [SBN 6–7]).

After this preliminary analysis, Hume assigns the task of studying human sensations, considered as physiological processes, to the natural philosopher or scientist, while including the study of ideas and the passions in his own project

---

7. Hume considers one possible exception to this principle: the alleged fact that we would be able to imagine a particular shade of color, such as a "missing shade of blue," when confronted by a gap in a sequence of shades of that color in our visual field, even if we had never seen that shade before (T 1.1.1.10 [SBN 6]; SBN 2.8 [SBN 20–21]). However, he evidently regards this as a unique case that does not subvert his copy principle. For several of many attempts to explain and assess this counterexample, see Russow, "Simple Ideas and Resemblance," 342–50; Williams, "Is Hume's Shade of Blue a Red Herring?" 83–99; Garrett, *Cognition and Commitment,* 50–52; and Frasca-Spada, *Space and the Self,* 61–62.

as a moral philosopher (T 1.1.2.1, 2.1.1.2 [SBN 7–8, 275–76]). With the study of sensation set aside, he concludes that in order to examine the "nature and principles of the human mind" we should reverse the method that might at first seem to be the most natural and obvious, by presenting "a particular account of ideas, before we proceed to impressions" (T 1.1.2.1 [SBN 8]). He accordingly devotes Book 1 to an examination of our ideas, before turning in Books 2 and 3 to our impressions of reflection, or the passions and the moral sentiments.

Hume's first principle, which is often referred to as his "copy principle," has been widely described and criticized as an "imagist" theory of meaning, according to which the meaning of a word is determined by its conjunction with a mental image. For example, Flew has denounced Hume's "uncritical assumption that ideas, conceived as mental images, must play an essential part in the significant employment of words," and that "no word can be employed meaningfully unless the user either has, or is disposed to have, appropriate imagery."[8] Other critics of Hume have argued that this theory of linguistic meaning cannot be applied to many of the terms in his own philosophical system, and have suggested that Hume departs almost immediately from his "official theory."[9] In later sections of this chapter I will show that, although he indeed maintains that the use of a general term is always accompanied by imagery, Hume does not simply reduce the meaning of a word to the ability to frame an individual image, and that he does not identify the meaningful use of a word with the production of a complete, distinct, and positive image of the designated object. This discussion will require us to consider his account of abstract ideas and general terms, which he presents in the concluding section of Book 1, Part 1 of the *Treatise,* and his remarks concerning language in Books 2 and 3 of the *Treatise* and in the second *Enquiry.* I will return to these subjects after considering his account of the creative activity of the mind, as this is reflected in the formation of complex ideas and in the associating of our ideas.

MEMORY AND IMAGINATION

After his initial survey of our perceptions, Hume identifies memory and imagination as the two mental operations by which an impression that has been "present with the mind" can appear again as an idea (T 1.1.3.1 [SBN 8–9]).

8. Flew, *David Hume,* 20. See also Flew, *Hume's Philosophy of Belief,* 22–23; Bennett, *Locke, Berkeley, Hume,* 222–34; Hunter, "Concepts and Meaning," 148–49; Pears, *Hume's System,* 16–30; and Dicker, *Hume's Epistemology and Metaphysics,* 5–34. A further discussion of this interpretation is provided by Jacquette in *David Hume's Critique of Infinity,* 206–21.

9. See Kemp Smith, *Philosophy of David Hume,* 205–9 and 279–84; Stroud, *Hume,* 8–10 and 17–41; and Ayer, *Hume,* 32–33.

Hume presents "the liberty of the imagination to transpose and change its ideas" as the "second principle" in his science of human nature (T 1.1.3.4 [SBN 10]). In the *Enquiry* he adds that nothing might seem "more unbounded than the thought of man," which is able to combine "incongruous shapes and appearances" beyond the limits of reality, although it cannot create images without preceding impressions, or in violation of the principle of contradiction (EHU 2.4 [SBN 18]). The imagination when deliberately used to produce novel images is called "fancy," and this activity is especially apparent in "the fables we meet with in poems and romances," where nature is "totally confounded, and nothing mention'd but winged horses, fiery dragons, and monstrous giants" (T 1.1.3.4 [SBN 10]; cf. CMH 56–60). However, in the course of the *Treatise* Hume also presents the imagination as the faculty by which we are able to separate, connect, and combine our ideas in the formulation of concepts and judgments (T 1.1.4.1–2, 1.1.6.2, 1.1.7.3–15; cf. 1.3.7.5n20 [SBN 10–11, 16, 18–24; cf. 96–97n1]), and to extend our ideas of space and time beyond the arrangement of our immediate impressions of sensation (T 1.2.5.14–19, 1.2.5.29 [SBN 58–60, 65]). Indeed, he identifies a further activity of the imagination by observing that "the imagination, when set into any train of thinking, is apt to continue, even when its object fails it," so that once the mind has embarked "in the train of observing an uniformity among objects, it naturally continues, till it renders the uniformity as compleat as possible" (T 1.4.2.22; cf. 1.2.4.24 [SBN 198; cf. 48]). Hume had already described this activity of the imagination in his early manuscript, "An Historical Essay on Chivalry and Modern Honour," in which he observes "of the human Mind" that whenever it is "smit with any Idea of Merit or Perfection beyond what its Faculties can attain," it immediately runs "quite wide of Nature" and generates new passions, objects, desires, laws of nature, and even principles of conduct (CMH 57).[10] As we will see, in his philosophical writings Hume argues that this propensity of the imagination produces our ideas of geometric equality, empty space, empty time, causal connections, the continued existence of external objects, and a continuing personal identity. Indeed, he eventually describes the various activities commonly attributed to human understanding as arising from the "general and more establish'd properties of the imagination," in contrast to the "trivial suggestions of the fancy" (T 1.4.7.7; cf. 1.4.4.1, 2.3.9.10 [SBN 267; cf. 225, 440]).

Hume accordingly maintains that the mind, by the power of the imagination,

---

10. M. A. Stewart has argued, based on the paper, handwriting, and content, that Hume wrote this essay between 1730 and 1734, and most probably in 1731, when he was around twenty; see "Hume's Manuscripts," 267–76. In this account Stewart is challenging Mossner's speculation that this essay was written around 1725 when Hume was a fourteen-year-old student; see Mossner's introduction to "David Hume's 'An Historical Essay,'" 54–60, and *Life of David Hume*, 46–47. Stewart also indicates that there are a number of errors in Mossner's transcription of this essay.

"has the command over all its ideas, and can separate, unite, mix, and vary them, as it pleases" (T App.2 [SBN 623–24]). In the *Enquiry* he describes the imagination as the "creative power of the mind," by which it engages in "compounding, transposing, augmenting, or diminishing the materials" that are afforded us by our impressions (EHU 2.5 [SBN 19]).[11] In his view, the imagination includes, not only the derivative power of fanciful invention, but also the constitutive activity of the mind in its production of a variety of complex ideas that appear to be fundamental to our ordinary cognition.[12]

While Hume frequently asserts that "nothing is more free" than the imagination (T 1.1.4.1 [SBN 10]; cf. App.2 [SBN 623–24]; EHU 5.10 [SBN 47]), this freedom of the imagination is problematic in the larger context of his system in several respects. First, many of the activities of the imagination, such as the extrapolation of extension in space and time, or the attribution of a causal relation to two events, occur without any deliberate intention on the part of the subject. Second, even the creative fancy is influenced by principles of association, although Hume maintains that these principles do not necessarily determine the course of our thoughts, but only act as "a gentle force, which commonly prevails" (T 1.1.4.1 [SBN 10]). On the other hand, he later argues that we must regard the activities of the mind as subject to necessity in the same way as are the voluntary actions of the human body (T 2.3.1.3, 2.3.2.2 [SBN 399–400, 408–9]). I will return to this topic in Chapter 7, where I show that, on Hume's view, our belief in the necessity of human action depends upon our recognition of a regular conjunction between the actions and character of an individual from the perspective of an external observer. However, this point of view is not available to us in any attempt to trace the sequence of ideas in the mind. Accordingly, the question whether human mental activity is to be regarded as free or determined remains unresolved within Hume's system. For now, however, we may merely take note of his preliminary assertion that the imagination is limited only by the principle of contradiction and by the materials provided by our impressions, and that we have a subjective feeling of freedom in our imaginative activities of separating, connecting, and combining our ideas.

Although Hume gives equal status in the *Treatise* to the copy theory of ideas and to the freedom of the imagination, as the basic principles in his science of human nature, the activity of the imagination has received considerably less attention in the secondary literature. This general emphasis on the copy theory has led many of his commentators to regard Hume's view of the mind as

11. For various discussions of Hume on the imagination, see Price, *Hume's Theory of the External World;* Wilbanks, *Hume's Theory of Imagination;* Brand, *Hume's Theory of Moral Judgment,* 9–37; Waxman, *Hume's Theory of Consciousness,* 58–84; Garrett, *Cognition and Commitment,* 11–40; and Owen, *Hume's Reason.*

12. In this respect Hume anticipates Kant's distinction between the reproductive and the productive activities of the imagination; see the *Critique of Pure Reason,* 257 (B 152) and 273–74 (A 141–42 / B 181).

essentially passive. This view has been challenged especially by Robert Paul Wolff, who argues that Hume began by assuming "that empirical knowledge could be explained by reference to the contents of the mind alone," but arrived at the "profound discovery that it was the activity of the mind, rather than the nature of its contents," which must be examined in order to account for the "puzzling features of empirical knowledge." However, on Wolff's view, Hume's "theory of mental activity" is found mainly in his references to "dispositions" or "propensities" of the mind, and must be extracted from "the associationism and copy theory of ideas in which it is embedded." By contrast, Fred Wilson finds a more direct theory of mental activity in Hume's discussion of the process of causal inference.[13] As I have indicated here, Hume offers an even more explicit theory of mental activity in his account of the imagination, which he presents as a counterpart to his account of the receptivity of the mind, as this is articulated in his copy theory of the relation between impressions and ideas.[14]

Hume's attempt to characterize the distinction between memory and imagination proceeds through several stages of development in the *Treatise*. He initially describes the ideas of memory as more "lively and strong" than ideas arising from the imagination; but then adds that memory, unlike imagination, is strictly tied to the "order and position" of a preceding set of perceptions (T 1.1.3.1–3 [SBN 9]). He later reaffirms the superior force and vivacity of memory, and identifies this as the distinguishing characteristic of belief, while also observing that a faint memory may be mistaken for a product of the imagination, and a vivid fictitious image for a memory (T 1.3.5.5; cf. 1.3.10.5–9 [SBN 85–86; cf. 120–23]). However, he then describes the contrast between belief and the imagination as a difference in the "manner" in which we conceive our ideas, although he again presents this as a difference of force and vivacity (T 1.3.7.5 [SBN 96–97]).[15] Finally, he concedes that there may be "a little ambiguity in those words *strong and lively,*" and suggests that memory may be characterized by a distinctive "action of the mind in the meditation" or "a

13. See Wolff, "Hume's Theory of Mental Activity," 99–100, and Wilson, *Hume's Defence of Causal Inference,* 8–110.

14. See also Biro, "Hume's New Science of the Mind," 33–63, and Wood, "Hume, Reid and the Science of the Mind," 119–39.

15. Hume uses the word "belief" for a variety of our intentional states (cf. T 1.3.13.19 [SBN 153–54]). These include our conception of an idea as a product of memory rather than imagination (T 1.3.5.6–7 [SBN 86]); our conception of one object as the cause or effect of another (T 1.3.2.15, 1.3.8.8–11 [SBN 78, 101–3]); our assent to propositions concerning matters of fact which we regard as justified by probable reasoning, including historical as opposed to fictional narratives (T 1.3.7.3, 1.3.10.10 [SBN 95–97, 631]); our acceptance of the causal maxim (T 1.3.3.9, 1.3.8.14–15 [SBN 82, 104–7]); and our conception of the distinct and continued existence of external objects (T 1.4.2.1–2, 1.4.2.43–57 [SBN 187–88, 209–18]). However, he offers his direct discussion of belief mainly with reference to memory, particular causal connections, and probable judgments; and I have drawn upon his reflections in all three contexts in order to trace the development of his view, since they seem intended to apply to all of these cases.

certain *je-ne-sçai-quoi,* of which 'tis impossible to give any definition or description, but which every one sufficiently understands" (T 1.3.8.15–16 [SBN 105–6]).

Hume develops this formulation in several additions made to Book 1 in its Appendix, in which he describes belief variously as a "peculiar *feeling* or *sentiment,*" and also as a distinctive "manner" in which an idea is conceived. However, he now confesses that "when I wou'd explain this *manner,* I scarce find any word that fully answers the case, but am oblig'd to have recourse to every one's feeling." While he had initially sought to describe this feeling as "a superior *force,* or *vivacity,*" he is now dissatisfied with that account, and traces the distinction between belief and imagination instead to a difference in the "feeling or manner of conception" of the idea (T App.2–9, 1.3.7.7 [SBN 623–27, 629]). This allows us to distinguish more effectively between genuine belief and the vivacity produced by "poetical enthusiasm," since the ideas aroused by a "poetical description" may be more vivid, but are "different to the *feeling* from those, which arise from the memory and the judgment" (T 1.3.10.10 [SBN 630–32]). Indeed, in the corresponding passage in the original text of the *Treatise* he refers to the vivacity conferred upon an idea by the poetic imagination as a "counterfeit belief" (T SBN 123).[16] In the Appendix he even describes his initial claim in the *Treatise* that "two ideas of the same object can only be different by their different degrees of force and vivacity" as an "error." Instead, he now states that "there are other differences among ideas, which cannot properly be comprehended under these terms," but are more accurately described as "their different *feeling*" (T App.22 [SBN 636]). In the *Abstract* he argues that belief is "nothing but a peculiar sentiment, or lively conception produced by habit" (A 27 [SBN 657]). In the *Enquiry* he describes the "sentiment" of belief as a "feeling or manner of conception," or an "act of the mind," which he cannot explain or define. However, he has attempted to indicate this, through what he now calls an analogy, by describing belief as "a more vivid, lively, forcible, firm, steady conception of an object" than an idea provided by the imagination alone (EHU 5.12 [SBN 49]).

In these passages Hume gradually replaces his contrast between memory and imagination as a quantitative difference in their degrees of force and vivacity, with a qualitative difference in the "feeling" or "manner of conception" of our ideas in cases of belief as opposed to imagination, although he finds that he is unable to describe this any further, and can only invite his readers to recognize this feeling from their own understanding of the term "belief."[17]

16. This phrase occurs in a paragraph which is marked by Hume in the appendix for replacement with a longer discussion of poetry, in which he refers more moderately to the effect of poetry as "the mere phantom of belief" (T 1.3.10.10–12 [SBN 630–32]). See Norton and Norton, "Substantive Differences," 252–53.

17. See Waxman, *Hume's Theory of Consciousness,* 18–19, 27–42, and 62–63, as well as Butler, "Hume's Impressions," 122–36; Livingston, *Hume's Philosophy of Common Life,* 57–58; Brand, *Hume's Theory of Moral*

Hume also considers the apparent role of judgment, or the understanding, in distinguishing memory from imagination. This is seen, for example, in his initial statement that the ideas of the memory correspond to the original "order and form" of our impressions (T 1.1.3.2 [SBN 9]), and also in his remarks that we may distinguish between history and the "fictions of poetry" by means of probable reasoning (T 1.3.10.12 [SBN 630–32]). In these passages he suggests that the difference between an idea arising from memory and an idea arising from the imagination is to be found, not in any qualities of our subjective conceptions of these ideas, but in our judgment of their relation to an external and public reality. However, he maintains that the distinction between memory and imagination cannot ultimately rest on such judgments, since we cannot compare the ideas arising from our memory to the actual succession of our perceptions in the past in order to determine whether their arrangement is "exactly similar" (T 1.3.5.3 [SBN 85]).

Noxon and Johnson have both argued that Hume is defending a strictly introspective or phenomenological account of the difference between memory and imagination, as opposed to an epistemic account, in his appeals either to "force and vivacity," or to the "manner" in which we conceive our ideas, as the criterion for recognizing an idea as a memory.[18] Flage, on the other hand, proposes that Hume is describing two separate criteria that we recognize as individually necessary, but only conjointly sufficient conditions for determining whether any particular idea arises from memory rather than imagination. These two criteria are the subjective quality of the idea and a judgment regarding its probable correspondence to an external reality. This judgment arises, however, not from a comparison of our present ideas to the original impressions, but from a comparison of our purported memories with our other present perceptions, with the reported memories of others, and with written documents.[19] On Flage's interpretation, Hume's account of memory would correspond, in its implicit structure, to his "two definitions of a cause," in which he distinguishes between the subjective determination of the human mind that initially gives rise to our causal beliefs and the principles of judgment through which we evaluate these beliefs (T 1.3.14.31 [SBN 169–70]; EHU 7.29 [SBN 76–77]), as we will see in Chapter 4.[20]

Judgment, 49–53; Frasca-Spada, *Space and the Self*, 57, 76–83, and 142–52; and Owen, *Hume's Reason*, 147–74. On the role of Hume's account of belief in his mitigated skepticism, see Norton, "How a Sceptic May Live Scepticism," 119–39.

18. Noxon, "Remembering and Imagining the Past," 270–95; Johnson, "'Lively' Memory and 'Past' Memory," 343–59.

19. Flage, "Remembering the Past," 236–44.

20. See also Falkenstein, "Naturalism, Normativity, and Scepticism," 29–72.

THE ASSOCIATION OF IDEAS

Although he repeatedly affirms the freedom of the imagination, Hume also finds that the imagination is generally "guided by some universal principles," or associating qualities, "by which one idea naturally introduces another." As he indicates in the *Enquiry*, we discover through introspection and conversation that ideas usually present themselves "with a certain degree of method and regularity," not only in our "serious thinking or discourse," but also in our "wildest and most wandering reveries." Hume identifies three qualities of our perceptions that appear to facilitate the "connexion or association of ideas," which he also calls the "principles of union or cohesion" among our simple ideas: "RESEMBLANCE, CONTIGUITY in time or place, and CAUSE and EFFECT" (T 1.1.4.1–6 [SBN 10–12]; EHU 3.1–3 [SBN 23–24]).

Hume characterizes the association of ideas as "a kind of ATTRACTION, which in the mental world will be found to have as extraordinary effects as in the natural" (T 1.1.4.6 [SBN 12–13]), and several of his critics have accordingly regarded his theory as a "mechanistic" account of mental operations.[21] However, Hume maintains that we should not regard the association of ideas as "an inseparable connexion; for that has been already excluded from the imagination," nor conclude "that without it the mind cannot join two ideas," since "nothing is more free than that faculty." Instead, we should regard the three principles of association merely as "as a gentle force, which commonly prevails" (T 1.1.4.1 [SBN 10]). He later states that these principles are "neither the *infallible* nor the *sole* causes of an union among ideas," since the mind has "a very irregular motion in running along its objects, and may leap from the heavens to the earth, from one end of the creation to the other, without any certain method or order" (T 1.3.6.13 [SBN 92]).

In comparing the association of ideas to mechanical forces in the physical world, Hume may have been less concerned with any detailed analogy than with calling attention to his use of the theory of association as a fundamental principle for explaining the operations of the human mind. In the introduction to the *Treatise* Hume calls attention to recent advances in the natural and moral sciences, and proposes to contribute to an emerging "science of man" by discovering the principles of the human mind (T Int.4–10 [SBN xv–xix]). He later asserts in the *Abstract* that "if any thing can entitle the author to so glorious a name as that of an *inventor*," it is "the use he makes of the principle of the association of ideas, which enters into most of his philosophy" (A 35 [SBN 661–62]). In the course of the *Treatise* Hume accordingly appeals to the association of

---

21. The mechanistic interpretation of Hume's theory of ideas was established especially by Thomas Reid: see his *Works*, 1: 386–88; and Kallich, *Association of Ideas*, 235–36. See also Kemp Smith, *Philosophy of David Hume*, 71–76 and 223–26; and Wolff, "Hume's Theory of Mental Activity," 104–5.

ideas to explain such mental operations as the formation of abstract ideas, our judgments of causation and identity, the generation of the passions, and the development of rules in social and political life.

Hume gives less explicit attention to the theory of association in his later works. He refers to this theory only sparingly in the two *Enquiries*. Indeed, in his final edition of the first *Enquiry* he shortened Section 3, "Of the Association of Ideas," by more than three quarters of its original length, leaving a mere three paragraphs (EHU 3.1–3 [SBN 23–24]). The deleted part, which Hume apparently came to regard as an unnecessary digression, examines the principles of association in literary composition, and includes a valuable discussion of narratives in epic poetry and history, as we will see in Chapters 11 and 13 (EHU 3.4–18).[22]

Several of Hume's commentators have regarded his lack of later attention to his theory of association as an indication that Hume eventually rejected it, and have even used this claim as the basis for speculations concerning the development of his thought. For example, according to Kemp Smith, Hume developed his theory of association in order to explain the passions and moral sentiments, and then attempted to extend it into his discussion of ideas, only to become dissatisfied with its results in this domain, which led him to abandon the theory of association as a unifying principle for his "science of man." By contrast, Noxon argues that Hume developed his copy theory and his theory of association as principles of philosophical and psychological analysis respectively, and that he combined these projects in the *Treatise* but attempted to separate them in his later works. Among these, the first *Enquiry* is concerned with philosophy rather than psychology, and hence does not require any extensive reference to the theory of association.[23]

However, while Hume does not explicitly present the theory of association in his later writings as a unifying theme of his philosophy, he continues to appeal to this theory as a basic explanatory principle throughout his works. This is especially evident in the first *Enquiry*, where he reaffirms his account of association, and again identifies causation, resemblance, and contiguity as principles of association among our ideas (EHU 3.1–3, 5.14–20 [SBN 23–24, 50–54]). He also returns to this theory in the second *Enquiry*, where he argues that our ideas of utility in particular actions and objects, and accordingly our ideas of their moral and aesthetic qualities, arise through the association of ideas (EPM 5.14, 5.38 [SBN 218, 225]). We also encounter implicit references to the principles of association in his later writings. For example, in the *Natural History of Religion* Hume traces the origins of polytheism to the "universal tendency among mankind to conceive all beings like themselves" and to ascribe

22. Livingston, *Hume's Philosophy of Common Life*, 131–36.

23. Kemp Smith, *Philosophy of David Hume*, 239–55 and 530–40; Noxon, *Hume's Philosophical Development*, 19–25.

"malice or good-will to every thing, that hurts or pleases us." In other words, we have a tendency to attribute emotions and intentions to any being, force, or event in nature which has caused us pleasure or displeasure, on the basis of their resemblance in this regard to human actions (NHR 3.29). The principle of resemblance also gives rise the central concern of the *Dialogues Concerning Natural Religion:* the argument presented by Cleanthes that the "Author of nature is somewhat similar to the mind of man," based on the resemblance of the universe as a whole to the products of human design (DNR 2.143). We may also trace the principles of contiguity and causation in Hume's composition of the main narrative in the *History of England,* and the principle of resemblance in his appendices concerning social, economic, and cultural history, as these reflect his discussion of the principles of literary and historical composition in the first *Enquiry* (cf. EHU 3.4–18).

RELATIONS, SUBSTANCES, AND MODES

After considering the natural or spontaneous principles of association, Hume turns to "those complex ideas, which are the common subjects of our thoughts and reasoning," which he divides into "RELATIONS, MODES and SUBSTANCES" (T 1.1.4.7 [SBN 13]). In his survey of these complex ideas in sections 5 and 6, and his examination of our ideas of both species and qualities in section 7, Hume in effect develops his own version of the list of categories, or the forms of predication, which serve to structure our judgments. However, this continuity with the traditional Aristotelian discussion of the categories is obscured by Hume's characterization of judgments as "complex ideas," and even as "perceptions" (T 1.1.4.7, 3.1.1.2 [SBN 13, 456]). Indeed, in a later footnote Hume rejects any absolute distinction between the cognitive activities of "conception," "judgment," and "reasoning," and maintains that all of these may be regarded as "particular ways of conceiving our objects." On the other hand, he indicates here and elsewhere in the *Treatise* that a judgment may be more specifically characterized as a proposition that affirms or denies a state of affairs (T 1.3.7.5n20 [SBN 96–97n1]; cf. 1.3.9.3–4, 2.3.3.6, 2.3.10.2, 3.1.1.9 [SBN 108, 415–16, 448–49, 458]).

Hume begins by distinguishing two senses of the word "relation." The first of these is apparent in the ordinary sense of the word, and refers to the natural principles of association, or to those qualities "by which two ideas are connected together in the imagination, and the one naturally introduces the other." By contrast, relations in the second sense are discovered through philosophical reflection, and include those qualities according to which "even upon the arbitrary union of two ideas in the fancy, we may think proper to compare them." In other words, "philosophical" relations are those principles by which we compare ideas through understanding and judgment, although these principles are themselves ultimately derived from the spontaneous principles of association. Hume further develops this distinction in his two definitions of a cause, as we will see in Chapter 3 (T 1.1.5.1–2; cf. 1.3.14.31 [SBN 13–14; cf. 170]).[24]

While we discover the natural relations of resemblance, contiguity, and causation by tracing the spontaneous activities of the imagination in the association of our ideas, Hume argues that we may identify the different philosophical relations by considering the different ways in which we may compare particular ideas or objects. Through this principle he identifies seven philosophical relations: these are resemblance, identity, location in time or space, quantity, the degrees of any quality, contrariety, and causation (T 1.1.5.3–9 [SBN 14–15]).

Later in the *Treatise* Hume argues that, "strictly speaking," a relation is not a property in the objects or ideas themselves, but arises "merely from the comparison, which the mind makes betwixt them" (T 1.2.4.21 [SBN 46]). However, he maintains that objects themselves stand in relations of contiguity and succession to each other "independent of, and antecedent to the operations of the understanding" (T 1.3.14.28 [SBN 168]), and that relations between complex perceptions are founded "on some common quality" among those perceptions (T 1.4.5.11; cf. 1.1.7.7n5 [SBN 236; cf. 637]). In Hume's view, a relation appears to be a distinctive type of complex idea that is conceived by the imagination by comparing resembling sets of perceptions, as discovered through the principle of resemblance, which is a natural principle of association among our ideas. We attend to the quality in which these sets of perceptions resemble each other, and identify this quality, or relation, through a "distinction of reason." Finally, by this distinction of reason we formulate a complex idea of this relation as an independent principle of comparison, which we may then apply to sets of perceptions that are not immediately associated together by the spontaneous principles of our imagination.

Several of Hume's critics have cited his discussion of relations as an example of his alleged tendency to confuse logical with psychological explanation.[25] However, Hume is attempting to articulate this very distinction by presenting "natural" relations as the psychological principles that appear to direct the association of our ideas, and "philosophical" relations as the principles of comparison and judgment that may be applied to ideas even where there is no spontaneous connection between them in the imagination.[26] He develops this

---

24. On Hume's theory of relations, see Hausman, "Hume's Theory of Relations," 255–82; Van Steenburgh, "Hume's Ontology," 164–72; Waxman, *Hume's Theory of Consciousness*, 10–13, 46–51, and 78–84; and Owen, *Hume's Reason*, 79–81.

25. See Passmore, *Hume's Intentions*, 23–28, and Bennett, *Locke, Berkeley, Hume*, 250–51.

26. See Hausman, "Hume's Theory of Relations," 255–82.

initial distinction between the psychological principles of association and the logical principles of judgment further in his account of probable reasoning and his two definitions of a cause, as we will see in Chapter 3. Several of Hume's critics have also argued that he cannot account for the idea of a relation in the context of his theory of ideas.[27] However, Hume specifically identifies our idea of a relation as a type of "complex idea," apparently the idea of a set of qualities belonging to a set of perceptions, which we formulate through a distinction of reason by comparing several resembling sets of perceptions (T 1.1.4.7 [SBN 13]).[28]

In Book 1, Part 3, Hume returns to his discussion of philosophical relations in order to develop a further classification of the various types of judgment. Here he indicates that four of these philosophical relations—resemblance, contrariety, degrees of quality, and proportions in quantity—depend solely upon the ideas that we are comparing to each other, and may not be altered while these ideas remain the same. The first three—resemblance, contrariety, and degrees of quality—are "discoverable at first sight," or are directly recognized as they "strike the eye, or rather the mind" in the immediate appearance of our ideas: a recognition which Hume, following Locke, calls "intuition."[29] The fourth, "proportions in quantity or number," may in some cases also recognized by intuition, but in other cases may require the type of reasoning which we call "demonstration" (T 1.3.1.1–2 [SBN 69–70]). By contrast, the other three relations between our ideas—identity, location in time and space, and causation— may be changed without changing the ideas themselves. Two of these, identity and location, are discovered directly through the activity of the senses in "perception." Accordingly, it is only the final relation, causation, which can lead us beyond whatever is immediately present to our senses (T 1.3.2.2 [SBN 73–74]). From his seven philosophical relations, Hume therefore identifies only two, numerical proportions and causation, as possible subjects of "reasoning." Later in the *Treatise* he divides the "operations of human understanding" into two, "the comparing of ideas, and the inferring of matters of fact." In the *Enquiry* he identifies "all the objects of human reason or enquiry" more simply as "*Relations of Ideas* and *Matters of Fact*" (T 3.1.1.18 [SBN 463]; EHU 4.1 [SBN 25]). I will consider these two types of reasoning in Chapters 2 and 3.

27. See Annand, "Hume's Theory of Relations," 581–97, and Gotterbarn, "How Can Hume Know Philosophical Relations?" 133–41.

28. For a similar account of Hume's derivation of the concept of a relation, see Garrett, *Cognition and Commitment*, 104, and Costa, "Hume on the Very Idea of a Relation," 71–94. Bertrand Russell presented an influential argument that a resemblance theory of concepts, such as that offered by Hume, cannot account for relations, and thus cannot justify its own appeal to the relation of resemblance: see *Problems of Philosophy*, 95–97. For a defense of the resemblance theory against this criticism, see Aaron, *Theory of Universals*, 153, and Price, *Thinking and Experience*, 23–26.

29. Locke, *Essay Concerning Human Understanding*, 530–39 (4.2.1–4.3.4).

Hume also includes our ideas of substances and modes, along with our ideas of relations, among "the common subjects of our thoughts and reasoning." Here he argues that our ideas of modes or substances are in every case really "a collection of simple ideas, that are united by the imagination, and have a particular name assigned to them." The idea of a substance is the idea of a "principle of union" among a collection of contiguous or causally related qualities: an idea which is extended by the imagination to produce the "fiction" of an "unknown *something* in which they are supposed to inhere," as we will see in Chapters 4 and 5. Similarly, the idea of a mode is the complex idea of an activity or condition made up of a combination of qualities, either in a set of objects, as in Hume's example of a dance, or within a single object, as in the example of beauty (T 1.1.4.7, 1.1.6.2–3 [SBN 13, 15–17]).[30]

In this discussion of our ideas of natural relations, philosophical relations, modes, and substances, Hume anticipates his themes in the rest of the *Treatise*. In Part 2 he considers the development of our philosophical conceptions of time and space from the natural relation of contiguity. In Part 3 he compares the natural relation of causation to the philosophical idea of causation. In Part 4 he examines the idea of identity and its relation to the idea of a substance, and then applies his analysis to two types of objects that are often regarded as substances: the mind and external objects. Finally, although he does not appeal to his analysis of modes in this context, he considers our ideas of various modes in Books 2 and 3: including the passions in Book 2—insofar as these are expressed in the observable states and behavior of human beings and animals—and also our idea of virtue, with comparisons to our idea of beauty, in Book 3.

ABSTRACT IDEAS

As we have seen, Hume's preliminary discussion of impressions and ideas has frequently been criticized for identifying linguistic meaning with the purely subjective production of mental images. However, in this section I show that this objection emerges from a misreading of his "first principle" or copy theory of ideas, combined with a tendency to overlook the rest of his theory of ideas in Book 1, Part 1 of the *Treatise,* especially his account of abstract ideas in section 7.[31]

Hume presents his discussion of "*abstract* or *general* ideas" as a further contribution to the discussion in modern philosophy of whether abstract ideas are

---

30. Hume's discussion of substances and modes is derived from Locke's analysis: see *Essay Concerning Human Understanding,* 163–66 and 288–318 (2.12 and 2.22–23). For a critical discussion of Hume's brief remarks concerning modes, see Glouberman, "Hume on Modes," 32–50.

31. For a further criticism of the imagist interpretation of Hume's theory of ideas, see Jacquette, *David Hume's Critique of Infinity,* 206–21.

"general or particular in the mind's conception of them." Abstract ideas, or what we might call concepts, are ideas that represent a number of objects as belonging to a particular type.[32] According to the "receiv'd opinion," as attributed especially to Locke, these ideas are "general" in their very conception, which, on Hume's view, entails that they must either include "all possible sizes and all possible qualities" of the various individual objects which they represent, or else "no particular one at all." Hume agrees with the general rejection of the first view as requiring us to affirm, implausibly, "an infinite capacity in the mind." However, he also rejects the second view, since he maintains that "the mind cannot form any notion of quantity or quality without forming a precise notion of the degree of each" (T 1.1.7.1–3 [SBN 17]).[33]

As an alternative to both of these theories, Hume endorses Berkeley's argument that "general ideas are nothing but particular ones, annex'd to a certain term, which gives them a more extensive signification." Indeed, he describes this as one of the "greatest and most valuable" recent discoveries in the "Republic of Letters" (T 1.1.7.1 [SBN 17]). He then offers a further defense of this "new system," by describing the process through which ideas, which are "in themselves individual," are abstracted by the mind "from every particular degree of quantity and quality" and applied "beyond their nature" to become "general in their representation" (T 1.1.7.16, 1.1.7.6–7, 1.1.7.2 [SBN 24, 20, 17]).[34]

According to Hume, the formation of an abstract idea, or more specifically, in the first instance, the idea of a species or a type of object, begins when we observe a "resemblance among several objects" as they appear to us.[35] This discovery of a resemblance leads us to apply the same "name" or "general term" to all of these individual objects, in spite of the differences we may notice among their other attributes, and to develop a "custom" of associating this term with any other objects in which we notice this resemblance. Once this association is established, any consideration of this word "raises up an individual idea," along with the custom of applying the name to various other resembling objects, through which we "keep ourselves in a readiness" to produce further images and recall "any other individual one, for which we may have occasion," as we might

32. I am using the word "concept" here, both as a convenient term to cover what Hume calls separately "abstract ideas" and "distinctions of reason," and to highlight the continuity between Hume's treatment of abstract ideas and subsequent discussions of the logical function and psychological content of concepts, without however attempting to consider any of these later theories in any detail. I am especially indebted in this regard to Price, *Thinking and Experience*, and Heath, "Concept," 177–80.

33. See Locke, *Essay Concerning Human Understanding*, 409–20 (3.3).

34. See Berkeley's introduction to his *Principles of Human Knowledge*, in his *Works*, 2:25–40. See also Ushenko, "Hume's Theory of General Ideas," 236–51, and Bradshaw, "Berkeley and Hume," 11–22.

35. On the issues involved in Hume's account of resemblance, see Hawkins, "Simplicity, Resemblance and Contrariety," 24–38; Russow, "Simple Ideas and Resemblance," 342–50; Brand, *Hume's Theory of Moral Judgment*, 9–17; Waxman, *Hume's Theory of Consciousness*, 46–50 and 81–82; Cummins, "Hume on Qualities," 49–88; Garrett, *Cognition and Commitment*, 62–64; and Frasca-Spada, *Space and the Self*, 18–19 and 146.

be prompted "by a present design or necessity." In other words, after we have formulated a particular image, as an instance of the species which is indicated by the term, this customary association "readily suggests any other individual" if we pursue "any reasoning, that agrees not with it." Thus, even though only one image may be immediately present to the mind "in fact" at a given moment, many others are present "in power," and may be recalled through the "custom" of "surveying them" on the basis of their relevant resemblance. In Hume's example, the general term "triangle" might initially bring to our mind the image of an equilateral triangle, but if we proceed to consider the proposition that all of the angles in a given triangle are equal, we are likely to form the image of an isosceles or a scalene triangle as counter-evidence. A particular image may even be associated with different general terms, and may thus be regarded as a particular instance of different concepts, according to the different resemblances that we may discover among various images. Hume concludes that "a particular idea becomes general by being annex'd to a general term," or a term "which from a customary conjunction has a relation to many other particular ideas, and readily recals them in the imagination" (T 1.1.7.7–10 [SBN 20–22]; cf. 1.2.3.5 [SBN 34]; EHU 12.15, 12.20n34 [SBN 154–55, 158n1]).

According to Hume, abstract ideas are thus a function of the imagination, in its activities of associating the various ideas arising from our impressions according to the natural principle of resemblance "in such an imperfect manner as may serve the purposes of life," collecting images of resembling objects "with a view to that resemblance," and associating these images with a general term.[36] These general terms and their associated concepts may then be used in "reflection and conversation." Hume indeed describes the propensity of the human imagination to associate our ideas with each other according to the various resemblances we discover between them, and to exhibit these whenever they are "necessary or useful" for our thinking and reasoning, as "a kind of magical faculty in the soul," which may be "most perfect in the greatest geniuses" but is also an inexplicable power in every individual (T 1.1.7.7, 1.1.7.15 [SBN 20, 23–24]).

Hume therefore identifies an abstract idea, or a concept, not merely with the ability to frame a particular image, but with the "custom," or disposition, to recall a set of resembling images, not only with a view toward their resembling qualities, but also with a recognition of the range of variation among their other

36. Sedivy has criticized Hume for regarding both the relation of similarity between the images in a resemblance class and the representational function of any single image in a resemblance class as immediately or "objectively" given to the mind prior to any interpretation: see "Hume, Images, and Abstraction," 117–33. However, Hume accounts for this activity of interpretation by considering the selective attention we direct toward the resembling qualities, which he calls a "view to that resemblance" as it serves the "purposes of life," characterizing our intentional state when we use a single image to represent a concept or a set of resembling images (T 1.1.7.15, 1.1.7.7 [SBN 23, 20]).

qualities. This custom is expressed subjectively in the ability to apply the term to appropriate objects, to compare images of these objects to each other, and to use these terms and images in our silent reasoning. This disposition can also be expressed outwardly, in actions that exhibit the ability to recognize a resemblance among objects and to use the term that has been conventionally established within a linguistic community to designate those objects. Hume thus appears to indicate that the meaning of a general term is not a particular image, but the use of this term to designate a set of resembling qualities among a set of objects; although this usage of the term is always accompanied by the subjective production of a particular image in the mind of the person who is using or considering the term.[37] Hume's theory of abstract ideas therefore anticipates Kant's account of the "schema" of an empirical concept, as a "rule" according to which the imagination supplies images of empirical objects, and Price's characterization of a concept as a "recognitional capacity," which may be expressed in various types of private mental activity and public behavior.[38]

We have already encountered Flew's criticism of Hume's alleged assumption in the first section of the *Treatise* that "ideas, conceived as mental images, must play an essential part in the significant employment of words." A similar criticism has been presented by Ayer, who observes that although we might expect to find a theory of reference in Hume's account of abstract ideas, we find instead that "here, more than anywhere else, he is handicapped by the false assumption that the use of a concept consists in the framing of an image."[39] In the present discussion I have indicated that this interpretation is at least subject to qualification, since Hume does not identify abstract ideas simply with the framing of any particular image, but rather with the capacity to recall any one of a number of resembling images. A further examination of his argument, and his examples of various types of ideas, will show that Hume does not always require us to frame a complete and direct image in order to use a concept or a general term meaningfully, although he maintains that the use of a concept or a general term will always involve the framing of some relevant image.

As we have seen, Hume initially characterizes ideas as the "faint images" of impressions (T 1.1.1.1 [SBN 1]). He uses the further phrases "clear idea" (T 1.1.6.1 [SBN 15]), "distinct idea" (T 1.2.1.5 [SBN 28]), and "just idea" (T 1.1.1.9 [SBN 5]) in order to designate an idea which is the complete and direct image of a preceding impression. However, he also observes that we can

37. See Zartman, "Hume and the 'Meaning of a Word,'" 255–60; Tienson, "Hume on Universals and General Terms," 311–30; and Livingston, *Hume's Philosophy of Common Life*, 72–84.
38. Kant, *Critique of Pure Reason*, 273–74 (A 141 / B 180); Price, *Thinking and Experience*, 34–36, 260. For a related discussion of Hume's abstract ideas as "habitudes of comparison," see Waxman, *Hume's Theory of Consciousness*, 85–105.
39. Ayer, *Hume*, 31–32.

use many concepts and general terms without any distinct and complete images of any particular example of the type of object in question. Indeed, Hume maintains that many of our ideas are "so obscure, that 'tis almost impossible even for the mind, which forms them, to tell exactly their nature and composition" (T 1.2.3.1 [SBN 33]; A 7 [SBN 648]). As we will see, this obscurity is in his view the source of much of the confusion in our reasoning, especially in philosophy; and he therefore indicates that the analysis of concepts is among the first tasks of philosophical inquiry.

I have shown that Hume distinguishes between "ideas" or particular images and "abstract ideas" or concepts, in which the latter are understood as dispositions to associate a set of resembling images with each other and with a general term, and to consider any of these images as they might be required in our thinking. Hume develops this distinction further in several passages in which he rejects the requirement that we must frame a clear image in order to understand and use a given word correctly. In his initial account of complex ideas, he observes that even a person who has visited Paris cannot expect to formulate "such an idea of that city, as will perfectly represent all its streets and houses in their real and just proportions" (T 1.1.1.4 [SBN 3]). He later indicates that "every one, who examines the situation of his mind in reasoning" will agree that "we do not annex distinct and compleat ideas to every term we make use of," since for example "in talking of *government, church, negotiation, conquest,* we seldom spread out in our minds all the simple ideas, of which these complex ones are compos'd." In spite of this, however, we are able to "avoid talking nonsense," and to distinguish between true and false statements concerning these concepts, through the "custom" of attributing "certain relations" to these abstract ideas: a custom which "still follows the words" in our reasoning (T 1.1.7.14 [SBN 23]). In both of these cases, including the idea of a named individual, such as the city of Paris, and the abstract idea of a mode such as "negotiation" or "government," we presumably produce particular images, but images which are only partial and incomplete illustrations of the concept, while holding ourselves in readiness to produce other images which might be required by the progress of our reasoning. Hume therefore indicates, with Price, that we often use "scrappy" images in our thinking, rather than a complete and distinct image of the object in question.[40]

Hume considers another type of general term that we may use and understand, without forming a distinct and complete image corresponding to the term, in his account of "distinctions of reason."[41] Here he argues that, in

---

40. See Price, *Thinking and Experience,* 306.

41. Hume's account of "distinctions of reason" arises from preceding discussions in early modern philosophy; see Descartes, *Principles of Philosophy* (1.62), in *Philosophical Writings of Descartes,* 1:214–15, and Arnauld and Nicole, *Logic,* 38 (1.5).

addition to the concept of a species, we can also formulate the concept of a quality, by attending to the particular respects in which individual objects may resemble or differ from each other. Thus, in his example, we develop the concepts of colors and shapes by comparing a globe of white marble to "a globe of black marble and a cube of white," where we find "two separate resemblances, in what formerly seem'd, and really is, perfectly inseparable." Eventually, "after a little more practice of this kind," we are able to "distinguish the figure from the colour," and to identify these and other qualities or aspects of objects "according to the resemblances, of which they are susceptible" (T 1.1.7.18; cf. 1.2.3.5 [SBN 25; cf. 34]). In other words, we can attend to a resembling quality, such as shape, when we notice this among several objects, even if we cannot form the complete and distinct image of that quality apart from an object in which it subsists; or, more accurately, from certain other qualities with which it is conjoined.[42] As we have seen, Hume even indicates that we can attend to the different aspects of simple ideas by comparing them to other simple ideas, even though we cannot form separate images of the different aspects of simple ideas (T 1.1.7.7n5 [SBN 637]).

As a further type of idea which is designated by a word that can be used meaningfully even without a distinct image corresponding to the idea, Flage has called attention to Hume's occasional references to the distinction, originally found in Locke, between a "just" or "positive" idea and a "relative" idea.[43] While "just" ideas are direct images of preceding impressions, Hume indicates that "relative" ideas may be formed without a preceding impression by an inference or an imaginative extrapolation from other previously given impressions.[44] For example, he argues that the closest we can reach "towards a conception of external objects, when suppos'd *specifically* different from our perceptions, is to form a relative idea of them, without pretending to comprehend the related objects" (T 1.2.6.9 [SBN 68]). Hume also describes our ideas of "power" and "cause" as relative ideas (EHU 7.29n17 [SBN 77n1]). Flage suggests that Hume might have used the notion of a "relative idea" in order to account for our idea of the missing shade of blue (T 1.1.1.10 [SBN 5–6]) and the thousandth part of a grain of sand (T 1.2.1.3 [SBN 27]). We might even apply this distinction to Hume's observation that "we cannot form to ourselves a just idea of the taste of a pine-apple, without having actually tasted it" (T 1.1.1.9 [SBN 5]). In

---

42. See Salmon, "Central Problem," 299–499; Butts, "Husserl's Critique of Hume's Notion of *Distinctions of Reason*," 213–21; Butler, *"Distinctiones Rationis,"* 165–76; Tweyman, "Hume on Separating the Inseparable," 30–42; Livingston, *Hume's Philosophy of Common Life,* 49–58; Waxman, *Hume's Theory of Consciousness,* 94–105; Garrett, *Cognition and Commitment,* 58–75; and Jacquette, *David Hume's Critique of Infinity,* 58–61.

43. Locke, *Essay Concerning Human Understanding,* 296 (2.23).

44. Flage, "Hume's Relative Ideas," 55–73; *David Hume's Theory of Mind,* 42–51; and "Relative Ideas Re-Viewed," 138–55. See also Livingston, *Hume's Philosophy of Common Life,* 81–84 and 155–56, and Frasca-Spada, *Space and the Self,* 14.

discussing this example, it would seem that Hume is implicitly conceding that we may form a "relative idea" of the distinctive flavor of a pineapple from the testimony of others and from our previous discovery that different types of fruit have different flavors, although we can only derive a "just idea" of the flavor of a pineapple from the impression of its taste.

In his discussion of complex ideas, abstract ideas, distinctions of reason, and relative ideas, Hume therefore indicates that, although all of our ideas are ultimately derived from our impressions, we are also able to develop various types of abstract ideas or concepts that are not distinct and complete images of particular impressions. Instead, these are dispositions to generate particular images, to attend to certain characteristics of these images, and to produce other images as illustrations of a concept, under the guidance of a general term that is applied to that type of object, mode, or quality. This term therefore becomes useful in our reasoning by allowing us to draw inferences from the resemblances we have observed among various objects. Finally, as I show in the next section, Hume suggests that a general term usually acquires its meaning through its conventional assignment to a concept, or in other words to a set of objects on the basis of a set of resembling qualities, in a given linguistic community.

Many critics of Hume's "imagist" theory of meaning have overlooked these additional dimensions of the theory of ideas, including his discussion of abstract ideas and language. For example, Flew refers to Section 7 of Book 1, Part 1 of the *Treatise* only to suggest that Hume has failed, even here, to develop an account of meaning, while claiming to have discovered in Berkeley's late work, the *Alciphron,* a more satisfactory view of meaning as determined, not by private images, but by the public use of language. Here Flew has overlooked Hume's references in section 7 and elsewhere to the public character of language and its implications for the meaning of a word.[45] Similarly, Bennett and Dicker have both criticized Hume's "meaning-empiricism" without referring to his account of general terms and abstract ideas.[46]

Hume appeals to his analysis of abstract ideas in order to account for the origin of the various ideas that are generated by the imagination to provide the structure for our ordinary experience, and which are among the central concerns of philosophers. As we have seen, he introduces relations, modes, and substances as complex ideas; and he explains our ideas of modes and substances as "nothing but a collection of simple ideas, that are united by the imagination, and have a particular name assign'd them," by which we are enabled to recall the collection. We thus find that the abstract idea of a substance is the idea of "an unknown *something*" in which a set of qualities "are supposed to inhere,"

---

45. See Flew, "Was Berkeley a Precursor of Wittgenstein?" 153–63, and *David Hume,* 20.
46. Bennett, *Locke, Berkeley, Hume,* 222–353, and Dicker, *Hume's Epistemology and Metaphysics,* 5–34.

while the idea of a mode is the idea of a complex quality which is dispersed either among a number of objects or within a single object (T 1.1.6.2–3 [SBN 16–17]). Hume also presents our ideas of spatial extension and temporal duration as abstract ideas, as we will see in Chapters 2 and 4 (T 1.2.3.4–7 [SBN 34–35]). Finally, in a footnote in the Appendix to the *Treatise* and in a 1740 letter to Francis Hutcheson, he indicates that the very concept of a "simple idea" is itself formulated through a distinction of reason, or an activity of comparison through which we recognize and identify "simplicity" as a resembling aspect of certain images (T 1.1.7.7n5 [SBN 637]; L 1.39).

LANGUAGE

Hume's account of the "general terms" we use to designate our concepts is among the very few brief and widely dispersed passages in his writings in which he is directly concerned with language. In these, however, he sets forth a view of language that is interesting in itself, and also provides the background for his further treatment of terms belonging to different domains of human discourse and activity.[47]

As we have seen, Hume indicates that we use general terms in our "reflection," or silent reasoning, where they not only revive the "custom" of considering a number of individual images, but also allow us to pursue a series of inferences concerning their qualities. In a letter to Joseph Spence in 1754 concerning the blind poet Thomas Blacklock, Hume observes that "we always think in some language, viz. in that which is most familiar to us" (L 1.201).[48] In this reference to the role of language in human thought, Hume rejects the view that Hacking attributes to the early modern philosophers, at least from Hobbes and Descartes to Berkeley, that human thinking or "mental discourse" consists in the production of images, in contrast to our public discourse, which is dependent upon language.[49]

In his discussion of abstract ideas Hume indicates that general terms are useful for conversation as well as reflection (T 1.1.7.2 [SBN 18]). Hume's earliest

---

47. For further studies of Hume's view of language, see Árdal, "Convention and Value," 51–68, and "Language and Significance," 779–83; Jones, *Hume's Sentiments,* 136–48; Livingston, *Hume's Philosophy of Common Life,* 91–111; Wilson, "Hume and Derrida on Language and Meaning," 99–121; Baier, *Progress of Sentiments,* 31–32; and Frasca-Spada, *Space and the Self,* 183–93.

48. Hume continues in this letter that it is "but too frequent to substitute words instead of ideas," or to use words in our thinking and discourse without the appropriate positive image, as Blacklock does in referring to different colors, which he associates with different emotions on the basis of the works of other authors. In the terms of my analysis above, Blacklock would appear to have a relative idea of colors, as concepts which represent the usual emotional effect of an object on human beings.

49. Hacking, *Why Does Language Matter to Philosophy?,* 15–25. See also Price, *Thinking and Experience,* 306.

reference to language in the *Treatise* is concerned with what appears to be universal among different languages. Here he suggests that his theory of association might help explain why languages "so nearly correspond to each other," since, in considering the often similar concepts which are indicated by different terms in different languages, we find "nature," or the natural principles of association, "in a manner pointing out to every one those simple ideas, which are most proper to be united into a complex one" (T 1.1.4.1 [SBN 10–11]; cf. EHU 3.1 [SBN 23]). However, in Book 3 and again in the second *Enquiry* Hume calls attention to the social and historical dimension of language by observing that languages are "gradually establish'd by human conventions," and that "speech and words and language are fixed, by human convention and agreement" (T 3.2.2.9 [SBN 490]; EPM App.3.9 [SBN 306]). This suggests that we may account for the use of different terms in different languages, even for a concept that is pointed out to us through the natural principles of association, by considering the development of each term within its particular linguistic community.

Hume's account of the conventional character of words, combined with his account of the role of language in abstract ideas or concept formation, seems to indicate that general terms receive their customary association with a set of resembling objects through a process of mutual accommodation among a number of speakers, and that a conventionally established term may then be adopted as a sign for the corresponding concept by anyone who learns the language.[50] Indeed, he observes much later, in a letter to Baron Mure of Caldwell in 1767, that in learning a living language "the continual Application of the Words and Phrazes teaches at the same time the Sense of the Words and their Reference to each other" (L 2.157).

These indications of the social and historical development of language are further reflected in Hume's account of the development of moral and aesthetic terms, which we use to establish a common point of view transcending the perspective of any individual speaker, as I will show in Chapters 8 and 11. This view of language also provides the context for his occasional references to terms that reflect, not the resemblances among natural objects which might be apparent to all human beings, but the intellectual, institutional, and cultural history of a specific community, as in the cases of political, legal, and religious terminology (cf. EPM 3.40–41 [SBN 201–2]). Hume's interest in the history of a specific word, in the context of a particular cultural tradition, appears especially in his reflections concerning the use of the word "liberty" in English political discourse, which we will consider in Chapter 9.

Finally, with this discussion of Hume's reflections concerning language, we may return to his first principle, in order to consider its general significance for

50. See Livingston, *Hume's Philosophy of Common Life*, 73.

his philosophical system. As we have seen, many commentators have regarded Hume's first principle, or his copy theory of ideas, as a criterion for the significance of a word, which is taken to identify the meaning of a word with an idea that is the direct image of an impression, and to assert that any word which cannot be shown to be associated with such an idea is meaningless. This view is based especially upon his own proposed application of the copy principle to the evaluation of philosophical terminology in Section 2 of the first *Enquiry:* "When we entertain, therefore, any suspicion, that a philosophical term is employed without any meaning or idea (as is but too frequent), we need but enquire, *from what impression is that supposed idea derived?* And if it be impossible to assign any, this will serve to confirm our suspicion" (EHU 2.9 [SBN 22]). This stark assertion appears to express the expectation that many, if not most, traditional terms in philosophy will fail the test of derivability from our impressions, if this test requires that any meaningful term must designate a complete and distinct idea, or image, which is a direct copy of some particular impression (cf. A 7 [SBN 648–49]).

However, when we consider Hume's own application of this test to various philosophical terms, in both the *Treatise* and the first *Enquiry,* we find that in most cases Hume actually does not reject a term as meaningless if it does not designate a set of positive ideas or distinct images. Instead, he generally traces the process by which the imagination produces the concept designated by the term, while conceding that the term may be used meaningfully, even though its meaning must be specified as including the activity of the imagination as well as certain types of preceding impressions. For example, in his first application of the derivability test within the *Treatise* he specifically challenges "those philosophers, who found so much of their reasonings on the distinction of substance and accident, and imagine we have clear ideas of each," to identify an impression of either sensation or reflection from which this idea is derived. Since no one can identify such an impression, he rejects any characterization of the concept of a substance as a "clear idea," or the direct image of a distinct impression. Instead, he asserts that we have "no idea of substance, distinct from that of a collection of particular qualities, nor have we any other meaning when we either talk or reason concerning it." He thus maintains that our idea of any particular substance is really the complex idea of a particular bundle of qualities, and that the abstract idea of a substance is the concept of this type of bundle-relation among a series of contiguous and causally related qualities. However, even in this passage he concedes that a term referring to a bundle of qualities may still be useful in reasoning and conversation, as long as we understand this as a reference to a bundle of qualities united by the imagination and do not pursue any speculations regarding an "unknown *something*" apart from the sensible qualities of an object (T 1.1.6.1–2 [SBN 15–16]).

In the rest of Book 1 of the *Treatise* Hume frequently appeals to the test of derivability in order to explain our ideas of space, time, external existence, causation, necessary connection, and the self, usually to demonstrate that these are complex rather than simple ideas, which can only be derived from simple impressions through the activity of the imagination (T 1.2.3.8–10, 1.2.6.8, 1.3.2.12–16, 1.4.6.1–3 [SBN 32–37, 68, 77–78, 251–52]). He appeals to this principle again in the first *Enquiry,* especially in restating his account of the idea of a necessary connection between a cause and its effect (EHU 7.30 [SBN 78–79]). However, in all of these cases, we will see that he rarely rejects any of our every-day or philosophical terms if these cannot be shown to designate "clear ideas," or the distinct images of particular impressions. Instead, Hume applies his first principle to traditional philosophical terms in order to explain the derivation of the concepts they signify from our impressions and from the activity of the imagination; and to develop a critique of the metaphysical speculations that may arise when these concepts are mistakenly regarded as the direct images of distinct impressions. In a more considered and accurate statement of this proj-ect, he declares it to be more likely that terms such as "power," "force," and "necessary connexion" may in many cases "lose their true meaning by being *wrong apply'd,* than that they never have any meaning," and he invites us to see "if possibly we can discover the nature and origin of those ideas, we annex to them" (T 1.3.14.14 [SBN 162]).

Hume's intention, in applying the test of derivability to philosophical terms, is thus to discover the sources of their associated concepts, whenever pos-sible, in our inward and outward sensations and in the activity of our imagina-tion, in order to specify the content and limitations of these concepts for the purposes of reasoning. In other words, Hume's application of his first principle is intended to promote a more accurate understanding of our concepts, espe-cially our philosophical concepts, by attempting to trace their genealogy (cf. T 1.2.3.1–3 [SBN 33]).[51]

This project of clarifying the meaning of philosophical terms by tracing their derivation from sensation and the imagination is reflected in Hume's con-cern for the proper definition of the terms that are used in philosophical dis-course. In the *Treatise* he describes the process of definition as the activity by which we "fix the meaning of the word" in order to establish "the compass of that collection" which we intend to designate by that general term (T 1.1.7.10 [SBN 22]). He later observes that since the main obstacle to advances in the "moral or metaphysical sciences is the obscurity of the ideas, and ambiguity of the terms," we should attempt, wherever possible, to "fix" their "precise

51. For a similar account of Hume's method and intentions in applying the copy principle to philo-sophical concepts, see Wilson, "Association, Ideas, and Images in Hume," 255–74, and Garrett, *Cognition and Commitment,* 55–57 and 74–75. See also Hoy, "Genealogical Method," 20–38.

meaning" (EHU 7.2–3 [SBN 61–62]). This advice is especially valuable for discouraging philosophers from their tendency to "encroach upon the province
of grammarians; and to engage in disputes of words, while they imagine, that
they are handling controversies of the deepest importance and concern" (EPM
App.4.1 [SBN 312]; cf. DNR 12.217–19). He indeed calls attention to a number of "verbal disputes" in philosophy concerning words such as "identity,"
"liberty," "natural," and "virtue," and attempts to set these aside by articulating the definitions implicit on either side of these controversies (T 1.4.6.7–21,
2.3.2.1–8, 3.1.2.7–10, 3.3.4.1–5 [SBN 255–62, 407–12, 473–75, 606–10]).[52]
He also criticizes the common tendency of philosophers to offer a circular definition of a term by using a synonym for that term in the definition, rather than
providing an account of the derivation of the concept that is designated by the
term (T 1.3.14.4 [SBN 157]). Thus, while it is common for us in ordinary discourse "after the frequent use of terms, which are really significant and intelligible, to omit the idea, which we wou'd express by them" and preserve only
"the custom, by which we recal the idea at pleasure," we must distinguish this
relatively innocuous tendency from the "frequent use" by philosophers "of
terms, which are wholly insignificant and unintelligible," but are imagined "to
be on the same footing with the precedent, and to have a secret meaning, which
we might discover by reflection." This appears in the use of such terms as
"*faculty* and *occult quality*," by which the "antient" or Scholastic philosophers
attempted to explain the sources of the various qualities in objects, and only
succeeded in restating the problem (T 1.4.3.10 [SBN 224]).

In Hume's view, a definition is therefore the analysis of the concept, or an
account of the distinguishing set of resembling qualities among the collection
of objects which is signified by a given general term. This should ultimately be
"an enumeration of those parts or simple ideas, that compose them" (EHU 7.4
[SBN 62]), although it seems that, in his view, a definition may also include an
account of the mental activities through which these ideas are related to each
other, as we indeed see in his second definition of a cause (T 1.3.14.35 [SBN
172]). He thus uses the copy principle and the principle of the activity of the
imagination in order to trace the derivation of our concepts, and to establish the
precise definition of our terms, rather than using the copy principle as the criterion for simply accepting or rejecting them.

---

52. See also Henze, "Linguistic Aspect of Hume's Method," 116–26; Morrisroe, "Linguistic Analysis,"
72–82; and Jones, *Hume's Sentiments*, 142–48.

2

Demonstration

In Book 1, Part 3 of the *Treatise*, Hume opens his discussion of the different types of reasoning, which give rise to judgments of "knowledge and probability," by considering the four philosophical relations, identified as "objects of knowledge and certainty." In the first *Enquiry*, he calls these "Relations of Ideas." Of these relations, he gives particular attention to mathematical relations, as the only type of relations among our ideas that can be determined through a process of reasoning, which he calls in this case "demonstration" (T 1.3.1.2 [SBN 70]; EHU 4.1 [SBN 25]).

Hume's distinction between "relations of ideas" and "matters of fact" has exerted an important and pervasive influence in the subsequent history of philosophy (EHU 4.1 [SBN 25]). In the first place, this distinction is often regarded as a predecessor of Kant's distinction between analytic and synthetic judgments. In it's turn, Kant's distinction was reformulated in the twentieth century as a principle for the demarcation and classification of meaningful statements by the logical positivists, who also appealed to Hume's distinction as an earlier formulation of this principle.

In this chapter I show that Hume's "relations of ideas" do not include analytic judgments in the Kantian sense, or formal relations among propositions as these are considered in deductive logic. While Hume does discuss conceptual and logical relations, he does not include these among what he calls "philosophical relations." Instead, he generally identifies mathematics as the only type of demonstrative reasoning.

RELATIONS OF IDEAS

Hume identifies four of his philosophical relations—resemblance, contrariety, degrees of quality, and proportions in quantity or number—as relations that depend "entirely on the ideas, which we compare together." Among these, the first three are discovered through "intuition," or the immediate comparison of our ideas, since we recognize resemblance, contrariety, and different degrees of a quality "at first sight," as they appear to "the eye, or rather the mind," without any activity of reasoning. The fourth philosophical relation, proportions in quantity or number, is also judged in some cases immediately through intuition, as when we are considering only a small number of objects or merely approximate proportions. However, we may also discover numerical relations, often more exactly, through the "artificial" methods of mathematical reasoning, which Hume refers to as "demonstration." For example, we may apply demonstrative reasoning to our idea of a triangle to find that its internal angles are equivalent to two right angles (T 1.3.1.1–3 [SBN 69–70]).[1]

According to Hume's classification, these four relations are the only sources of "knowledge and certainty" in the strict sense. In his subsequent distinction between the two types of "reasoning," in mathematical reasoning and causal inferences, he applies the term "certainty" only to the assurance arising from mathematical reasoning, and introduces the terms "proof" and "probability" for the different levels of assurance that may attend our causal inferences, as we will see in Chapter 3 (T 1.3.1.2, 1.3.11.2 [SBN 69–70, 124]).[2] In the *Enquiry* he identifies judgments concerning relations of ideas as "intuitively or demonstratively certain." However, the only examples of judgment concerning the relations of ideas he offers in this context are propositions belonging to "the sciences of Geometry, Algebra, and Arithmetic" (EHU 4.1 [SBN 25]).

In the *Critique of Pure Reason* Kant distinguishes between "analytic" and "synthetic" statements, and identifies the problem of accounting for the possibility of synthetic *a priori* statements as the central problem in metaphysics. Kant is often held to have formulated this distinction, at least in part, as a restatement of Hume's distinction in the *Enquiry* between "relations of ideas"

---

1. For a further examination of Hume's account of intuition and demonstration, and its historical antecedents, see Norton, "Editor's Introduction," 124–126, and Owen, *Hume's Reason*, 83–112.

2. For the history of the distinction between knowledge and opinion, or between certainty and probability, see Hacking, *Emergence of Probability;* Shapiro, *Probability and Certainty;* and Franklin, *Science of Conjecture.*

and "matters of fact."[3] This view is supported by Kant's characterization in the *Prolegomena* of the issue of explaining and justifying our synthetic *a priori* judgments as a general formulation of the problem that Hume had raised in his analysis of causation.[4] Kant argues that Hume overlooked the general formulation and the significance of his own question because he mistakenly considered mathematical judgments to be analytic rather than synthetic.[5] As a result of Kant's analysis, Hume's distinction between "relations of ideas" and "matters of fact" has often been identified with Kant's own distinction between analytic and synthetic judgments. Finally, as a result of this identification, Hume's classification has also been regarded as an antecedent of the twentieth-century formulation of this distinction. For example, A. J. Ayer refers to Hume's account of "relations of ideas" as including "the *a priori* propositions of logic and pure mathematics," which according to Ayer are "necessary and certain only because they are analytic."[6]

More recently, however, a number of studies have challenged both the identification of Kantian "analytic judgments" with Humean "relations of ideas" and Kant's own claim that Hume considered mathematical propositions to be analytic statements.[7] In this section I will show that Hume actually regards his examples of mathematical statements as synthetic rather than analytic, according to the Kantian use of these terms. I will also show that his relations of ideas do not include relations either among concepts, as disclosed through analysis, or between propositions, as exhibited through deductive logic.

Kant initially characterizes an analytic judgment as a proposition in which the predicate concept "belongs to" or is "(covertly) contained" in the concept of the subject. Accordingly, this type of judgment explicates the subject by breaking it "by means of analysis into its component concepts, which were already thought in it." By contrast, a synthetic judgment serves to amplify the concept

---

3. For a valuable account of other historical antecedents for Kant's distinction between analytic and synthetic judgments, see Beck, *Essays on Kant and Hume,* 80–100.

4. Kant could not read English, and could thus have been only indirectly acquainted, if at all, with the contents of the *Treatise.* The two *Enquiries,* as well as many of Hume's essays and the *History of England,* were readily available in German and French translations: see Jessop, *Bibliography,* 5–43, and Ikeda, *David Hume,* 1–181. On the question of Kant's direct and indirect acquaintance with Hume's writings, see Wolff, "Kant's Debt," 117–23; Kuehn, "Kant's Conception of 'Hume's Problem,'" 175–93; and Gawlick and Kreimendahl, *Hume in der Deutschen Aufklärung,* 174–98.

5. Kant, *Critique of Pure Reason,* 225–26 (B 127–28), 654–58 (B 760–69 / B 788–97), and *Prolegomena,* 10–12 and 15–23, in *Kants gesammelte Schriften,* 4: 260–62, 266–70.

6. Ayer, *Language, Truth and Logic,* 31. For two versions of this interpretation of Hume, see Zabeeh, *Hume,* 1–5 and 67–94, and Dicker, *Hume's Epistemology and Metaphysics,* 35–60.

7. See Reinach, "Kant's Interpretation of Hume's Problem," 161–88; Atkinson, "Hume on Mathematics," 127–37; Beck, *Essays on Kant and Hume,* 80–100; Gotterbarn, "Kant, Hume and Analyticity," 274–83; Coleman, "Is Mathematics for Hume Synthetic *a Priori*?," 113–26; Steiner, "Kant's Misrepresentations of Hume's Philosophy of Mathematics in the *Prolegomena,*" 400–410; and Frasca-Spada, *Space and the Self,* 125–28.

of the subject by adding to it "a predicate that was not thought in it at all, and which no analysis could possibly extract from it."[8] For example, Kant identifies the statement that "all bodies are extended" as an analytic proposition, since extension is already included in the concept of "body." On the other hand, the proposition that "some bodies are heavy" attributes to "some bodies" a predicate that does not already belong to the concept of body, and is thus synthetic.[9] Kant then argues that mathematical statements are synthetic, and presents this conclusion as a discovery that had hitherto eluded all the "analysts of human reason," including Hume, who indeed recognized the problem of accounting for our synthetic *a priori* judgments in the case of causation, but who mistakenly believed that mathematical judgments were analytic, and thereby failed to recognize the larger significance of the problem of synthetic *a priori* judgments.[10]

In order to evaluate Kant's interpretation of Hume, we may begin by comparing Hume's references to conceptual analysis with Kant's account of analytic judgments, and then turn to Hume's references to the ampliative character of mathematical propositions.

Hume states that it is impossible to "define," or to analyze, a simple idea, and maintains that we can only render these "precise and determinate to our intellectual view" by attending to "the impressions or original sentiments" from which they are copied. On the other hand, we may give a more determinate account of our complex ideas, including concepts, "by definition, which is nothing but an enumeration of those parts or simple ideas, that compose them" (EHU 7.4 [SBN 62]).[11] For example, he offers an analysis of the concept of a cause in his definition of causation as a natural relation: "A CAUSE is an object precedent and contiguous to another, and so united with it, that the idea of the one determines the mind to form the idea of the other, and the impression of the one to form a more lively idea of the other" (T 1.3.14.31 [SBN 170]).

However, Hume then distinguishes between those propositions in which we state the analysis of a concept and those in which we amplify a given concept, and also gives several mathematical propositions as examples of ampliative statements. For example, in the *Treatise* he argues that while mathematicians

8. Kant, *Critique of Pure Reason*, 141 (A 6–7 / B 10–11). Many, though not all, of Kant's commentators regard this as the decisive characterization of this distinction among his several formulations, which thus has priority over the condition that analytic statements are statements of identity or justified by the principle of contradiction. See, for example, Allison, *Kant's Transcendental Idealism*, 73–78.

9. Kant, *Prolegomena*, 16, in *Kants gesammelte Schriften*, 4:266–67.

10. Kant, *Prolegomena*, 18, 20, in *Kants gesammelte Schriften*, 4:268, 272–73; see also the *Critique of Pure Reason*, 143–44 (B 14) and 146–47 (B 19–20).

11. In Hume's usage, the "definition" of a term or an idea is often what we would call the analysis of a concept, although he refers in other contexts to the process of stipulative definition in which we establish or "fix" the meaning of a term (SBN 7.4 [SBN 62]; cf. T 1.1.7.10 [SBN 22]). For a further discussion of Hume's conception of a definition, see Garrett, *Cognition and Commitment*, 102–4.

"pretend they give an exact definition" of a straight line "when they say, *it is the shortest way betwixt two points,*" this proposition expresses "the discovery of one of the properties of a right line," rather than "a just definition of it." Instead he argues that our idea of a straight line is the idea of a "particular appearance," or more accurately the imagined appearance of a fictional standard, which we may consider without recognizing that a line which has this appearance is also the shortest distance between two points. He also notes that we can imagine the appearance of straightness in a line which is considered merely in itself, while the concept of the shortest distance between two points requires us to compare our image of one line with our images of other lines (T 1.2.4.26 [SBN 49–50]). Kant later uses the same proposition, "that the straight line between two points is the shortest," as an example of a synthetic judgment, since "my concept of *the straight* contains nothing of quantity, but only a quality."[12]

At the end of the *Enquiry* Hume explicitly distinguishes a mathematical proposition from the analysis of a concept. In this example, he argues that the relation between the hypotenuse and the other two sides of a right triangle cannot be known merely by analyzing these concepts; that is, even if these terms are "ever so exactly defined, without a train of reasoning and enquiry." By contrast, the relation between property and injustice, at least according to his use of these terms, may be determined simply by analysis, since "to convince us of this proposition, *that where there is no property, there can be no injustice,* it is only necessary to define the terms, and explain injustice to be a violation of property." Accordingly, this proposition is "nothing but a more imperfect definition" (EHU 12.27 [SBN 163]). Hume refers to several other examples of supposedly informative propositions, which are really tautologies, as statements that "mean nothing," since they do not contain both a subject and a predicate, and as "identical" propositions which give us "no insight" (T 1.4.2.26, 1.4.5.31 [SBN 200, 249]; cf. EHU 4.21 [SBN 37]).

In these examples, Hume distinguishes the analysis of a concept from the discovery of any additional properties of the objects included under the extension of the concept, including properties that are discovered through mathematical demonstration. He offers several examples of mathematical propositions as informative statements that do not arise simply from the definition of the initial terms, including an example that would later be presented by Kant as an example of a synthetic judgment.

Turning to a more recent interpretation of the distinction between analytic and synthetic statements, we may consider Ayer's claim that Hume's "relations of ideas" include the relations among propositions that can be exhibited through the deductive methods of formal logic. Here, in opposition to Ayer's

12. Kant, *Critique of Pure Reason*, 145 (B 16); cf. *Prolegomena*, 19, in *Kants gesammelte Schriften*, 4:269.

view, we find that Hume presents only one of his four relations of ideas, the relation of quantity, as a relation that is susceptible to reasoning, while the other
three are recognized immediately through intuition, without any process of
reasoning. In other words, Hume does not present any of his three nonmathe-
matical philosophical relations as relations discovered through deductive reasoning.[13] This is clearly evident in the cases of resemblance and difference in
degree, which are immediately recognized in comparing two ideas. However,
Hume also describes "contrariety" as a relation apprehended immediately
through intuition, apart from any activity of reasoning: and this description
might call for a more detailed examination, since contrariety might seem to pertain more properly to propositions and to the principles of deductive reasoning.

Hume's account of contrariety is often regarded as one of the most obscure
passages in his account of relations.[14] In his brief discussion in the *Treatise* he
states only that "no two ideas are in themselves contrary, except those of existence and non-existence." He later adds that "no real objects are contrary" in
the strict sense of the term (T 1.1.5.8, 1.4.5.30; cf. 1.3.15.1 [SBN 15, 247; cf.
173]). In the *Enquiry* he describes what might appear to be the separate relation of "contrast or contrariety" as a relation that combines the relations of
causation and resemblance, and in which when "two objects are contrary, the
one destroys the other" (EHU 3.16n6 [SBN 24n4]). Elsewhere he uses the word
"contrariety" to describe a relation between two principles, conditions, or objects
when the first tends to supplant or destroy the second. He then describes the
two members of such a pair as "contrary" to each other (T 1.4.2.52, 2.1.2.3,
2.3.9.16–17 [SBN 215–16, 278, 442–43]). Hume also indicates that the recognition of a contrariety between two objects is an empirical discovery, arising
from the observation of causal relations. For example, "fire and water, heat and
cold, are only found to be contrary from experience, and from the contrariety
of their *causes* or *effects*" (T 1.1.5.9 [SBN 15]). However, he also uses the phrases
"contradiction," or "contradiction in terms," to describe a proposition or a conjunction of two propositions that entails a formal contradiction (T 1.1.7.4,
1.4.2.3 [SBN 19, 188]). Finally, a false mathematical statement is "inconceivable"
in that it implies a contradiction, in contrast to a false statement concerning
a matter of fact or an empirical relation, which can be conceived as distinctly
as a true statement and does not imply a contradiction (T 1.2.4.11, 1.3.6.1,
1.3.7.3 [SBN 43, 86–87, 95]; EHU 4.1–2, 12.28 [SBN 25–26, 164]). It is thus

13. On the contrast between Hume's account of demonstrative reasoning and recent accounts of deductive reasoning, see also Owen, *Hume's Reason,* 1–6, 85–112.

14. On Hume's account of contrariety, see Atkinson, "Hume on Mathematics," 127–37; Gotterbarn,
"Kant, Hume and Analyticity," 274–83; Coleman, "Is Mathematics for Hume Synthetic *a Priori?,*" 113–26;
Hawkins, "Simplicity, Resemblance and Contrariety," 24–38; Imlay, "Hume on Intuitive and Demonstrative
Inference," 31–47; Cohen, "Contrariety and Causality in Hume," 129–39; and Frasca-Spada, *Space and the
Self,* 140–52.

"an establish'd maxim in metaphysics, *that whatever the mind clearly conceives includes the idea of possible existence,* or in other words, *that nothing we imagine is absolutely impossible.*" For example, since we can formulate "the idea of a golden mountain," we may conclude "that such a mountain may actually exist." On the other hand, the concepts of certain empirical objects or states of affairs may entail each other necessarily, since "we can form no idea of a mountain without a valley, and therefore regard it as impossible," or as implying a contradiction (T 1.2.2.8 [SBN 32]; cf. A 11 [SBN 650]; EHU 4.2 [SBN 25–26]). Similarly, the figures "round" and "square," when attributed to the same object at the same time, are "contrary and incompatible" (T 1.4.5.25 [SBN 244]).[15] Hume thus maintains that there is nothing beyond the power of our thought and imagination "except what implies an absolute contradiction." Accordingly, he argues that any attempt to demonstrate the necessity of a cause must show that the opposite of the supposed effect in any given case is "a formal contradiction" and hence cannot be imagined (EHU 2.4 [SBN 18]; T 1.3.9.10 [SBN 111]).

Benjamin Cohen argues that many of the apparent inconsistencies in this discussion can be dissolved if we recognize that Hume is working with two separate conceptions of contrariety. According to Cohen's interpretation, the contrariety that Hume presents as a "relation of ideas" is what we might call the "logical contrariety" of a formal contradiction. On the other hand, Hume's descriptions of objects or states as "contrary" to each other are cases of "empirical contrariety," based on our experience that one of them tends to cause the nonexistence of the other.[16]

However, in considering both types of contrariety, either as a relation of ideas or as an empirical relation, we should also recall Hume's classification of contrariety, not only among the four philosophical relations which are objects of "knowledge and certainty," but also among the three of these which are "discoverable at first sight," and fall more properly "under the province of intuition than demonstration" (T 1.3.1.2 [SBN 70]). In other words, the contrariety that Hume describes as a relation of ideas is a relation that we recognize immediately in comparing our ideas, and not one that is discovered through a process of demonstration.

I would suggest that in his discussion of the relation of contrariety Hume is identifying the principle of contradiction as a principle that is known immediately through intuition, in our very consideration of the ideas of existence and nonexistence, or the affirmation and negation of a proposition. However, he does

15. For a discussion of Hume's use of the term "inconceivable," and his view of the relation between psychological impossibility, or unimaginability, and the logical impossibility of a formal contradiction, see Pap, *Semantics and Necessary Truth*, 69–86; Stroud, *Hume*, 46–50; and Dicker, *Hume's Epistemology and Metaphysics*, 140–43.

16. Cohen, "Contrariety and Causality in Hume," 129–39.

not regard the use of the principle of contradiction in the context of a deductive as contributing, per se, to the discovery of any relation among these propositions, or among their constituent concepts, which can be called a "relation of ideas" in his terms, since these are recognized immediately through intuition.

It is also interesting to note that in his survey of the seven philosophical relations Hume includes identity, not among his relations of ideas, but among the relations we discover through experience. However, he is not using the word "identity" for the logical principle $a=a$, which he describes elsewhere as the principle that "an object is the same with itself," but rather for the relation that may subsist between an impression at one moment and an impression at another, which is the basis for our idea of the continuous existence of an external object through time. A judgment of identity is, in this sense, an empirical discovery, or a judgment of fact, whose origin we will consider in Chapter 4 (T 1.4.2.26–28; cf. 1.1.5.4, 1.3.2.2 [SBN 200–201; cf. 14, 73–74]).

Finally, we may consider Hume's own references to formal logic, or the science of deriving propositions by necessary inferences from other propositions. As we have seen, Hume identifies the "artificial" procedures of mathematical reasoning as "demonstration," and appears to characterize mathematical inferences as the only type of demonstrative reasoning (T 1.3.1.2–7, 2.3.3.2 [SBN 70–72, 413–14]; EHU 2.27–28 [SBN 163–65]). Indeed, while he often refers to instances of other deductive reasoning apart from mathematics, Hume never provides any direct treatment of the principles of formal logic, and does not include deductive relations among his "relations of ideas."

Hume's references to deductive reasoning appear in a variety of contexts. At the end of the first *Enquiry* he denounces all of the "pretended syllogistical reasonings, which may be found in every other branch of learning, except the sciences of quantity and number," as nothing but "sophistry and illusion" (EHU 2.27 [SBN 163]). However, Hume appeals to syllogistic reasoning himself on at least two occasions. One example appears in a letter of 1751 to his friend Gilbert Elliot, a theist who was sympathetic to the design argument. Here, in the course of explaining his approach to moral philosophy, Hume considers the various types of reasoning that are appropriate to different subjects, and observes of metaphysics and theology that "nothing there can correct bad Reasoning but good Reasoning: and Sophistry must be oppos'd by Syllogism" (L 1.151). The other appears in the *Dialogues Concerning Natural Religion,* where Philo argues by means of a syllogism that we do not have any satisfactory idea of the divine attributes and operations, and offers this as an example of "just reasoning" which agrees with "sound piety" (DNR 2.142–43).[17]

---

17. For an attempt to develop a Humean theory of syllogistic reasoning, see Echelbarger, "Hume on Deduction," 351–65.

Apart from these passages, which may be partly conciliatory or ironic in their application of syllogistic reasoning to theology, Hume appeals more directly to the principles and operations of formal logic, both in developing his own arguments and in evaluating those of others. We have seen that he occasionally appeals to the principle of contradiction, or rejects a statement or an argument as a "contradiction in terms," for example if it leads to the "flattest of all contradictions, *viz.* that 'tis possible for the same thing both to be and not to be" (T 1.1.7.4; cf. 1.3.9.10, 1.4.2.3 [SBN 19; cf. 111, 188]; EHU 2.4 [SBN 18]). He also distinguishes a genuinely informative proposition from one that states the analysis of a concept: the latter is a disguised tautology, or an "identical" proposition which gives "no insight" (T 1.4.5.31 [SBN 249]; EHU 4.21 [SBN 37]).

Hume occasionally extends his use of the phrase "demonstration" beyond the process of mathematical reasoning to deductive inferences from propositions according to the principles of formal logic. He thus observes that, unlike the various degrees of probability which we attribute to inductive inferences, demonstrative reasoning must be either "just" and "irresistible," or else "a mere sophism" which can have "no manner of force" (T 1.2.2.6 [SBN 31]). He also rejects any attempt to offer a "demonstration" of the necessity of a cause as "fallacious and sophistical" (T 1.3.3.4 [SBN 80]; cf. EHU 4.18 [SBN 35]). Finally, in presenting his own account of probable reasoning as a new departure in "logic," he notes that the word "logic" had previously been used for the study of the principles of deductive reasoning, or "the operations of the understanding in the forming of demonstrations" (A 4 [SBN 646–47]; cf. T Int.5, 1.3.15.11 [SBN xv–xvi, 175]).

Of course, Hume is famous for arguing against any of the prevailing attempts among his predecessors and contemporaries to show that either causal judgments or normative judgments may ultimately be established through demonstration, as we will see in Chapters 3 and 8. On the other hand, Hume does not entirely exclude deductive reasoning from either domain, and several of his commentators have indeed argued that he requires, and even seeks to establish, a place for deductive reasoning in both our causal and our moral judgments.[18] This claim is supported by a footnote in the first *Enquiry,* where he appears to acknowledge that deductive reasoning plays an important role in many areas of human thought, if it is applied to premises that are ultimately derived from "observation and experience" (EHU 5.5n8 [SBN 43–45n1]).[19]

Several commentators have suggested that in excluding "demonstrative reasoning" from judgments of fact and value, Hume is in fact restricting the term

---

18. See Passmore, *Hume's Intentions,* 30–34; Flew, *Hume's Philosophy of Belief,* 270–71; and Cottle, "Justice as Artificial Virtue," 457–66.

19. This discussion challenges the view that Hume is a thoroughgoing "critic of formal logic," which has been set forth in Passmore, *Hume's Intentions,* 12–13 and 18–41, and echoed in Zabeeh, *Hume,* 81–94.

"demonstration" to one specific type of deductive argument: a valid argument from premises which are recognized as necessarily true. On this view, a "demonstration" would be a deductive argument from premises that are established through intuition.[20] Hume is accordingly denying that the causal powers of objects, or the moral qualities of actions, can be established through a deductive argument from intuitively established premises; in other words, from relations of resemblance, contrariety, degrees of quality, or proportions in quantity. We will return to the question of the possibility of demonstrative reasoning concerning facts or morals in Chapters 3 and 8.

In summary, Hume does not regard either those judgments in which we state the analysis of a concept, or judgments that we derive from other propositions through deductive reasoning, as stating per se a "relation of ideas." Instead, his relations of ideas are those relations—including resemblance, contrariety, degrees of quality, and numerical proportions—which we recognize by intuition in the immediate comparison of our ideas; although in the fourth case our intuition may also be assisted by the methods of demonstrative reasoning belonging to mathematics. In other words, he restricts any "reasoning" concerning relations of ideas to the domain of mathematics. Next, we have seen that although he includes mathematical relations among his relations of ideas, Hume presents his own examples of mathematical propositions as synthetic rather than analytic, or as stating an informative discovery rather than an analysis of the initial concept, even though a mathematical discovery is established *a priori* by a demonstration from intuitively recognized relations.[21] Finally, although he appeals to the principles of deductive reasoning, and offers some reflections concerning the nature of concepts, Hume does not develop an explicit account either of the analysis of concepts or of deductive reasoning as it applies to relations among propositions.[22]

MATHEMATICS

In the introduction to the *Treatise* Hume observes that even mathematics, natural science, and natural religion "are in some measure dependent on the science

20. See Stove, *Probability and Hume's Inductive Scepticism*, 35–36; Belshaw, "Hume and Demonstrative Knowledge," 141–62; and Owen's discussion of this interpretation in *Hume's Reason*, 87–112. Stove also claims that Hume regards deductive arguments as the only "reasonable" arguments, overlooking Hume's own account of the different degrees of probability and reasonable belief attending our causal judgments, as we will see in Chapter 3.

21. For further views of Hume on intuition and demonstrative reasoning, see Frasca-Spada, *Space and the Self,* 140–56, and Owen, *Hume's Reason*, 1–6 and 85–112.

22. Hume's only direct discussion of propositions appears in his footnote concerning the traditional division of "acts of the understanding" into "*conception, judgment* and *reasoning,*" in which he argues that judgments

of MAN; since they lie under the cognizance of men, and are judg'd of by their powers and faculties" (T Int.4 [SBN xv]). He examines several aspects of the mathematical or "demonstrative sciences" (T 1.4.1.1 [SBN 180]) from this perspective, including the concept of number, the necessity of mathematical reasoning, the foundations of geometry, the principles of statistical probability, and the role of mathematical reasoning in the activities and concerns of human life. In fact, Hume's interest in mathematics, and also his diffidence in pursing this subject, are reflected in the greatest known loss among his writings. This lost manuscript was an essay on "some Considerations previous to Geometry & Natural Philosophy," or "the metaphisical Principles of Geometry," which he described in a 1755 letter to his London publisher, Andrew Millar, and intended to publish with the *Four Dissertations* in 1757. However, as he informed Millar's junior associate and successor William Strahan in a letter of 1772, he withdrew it from the projected volume after Philip Stanhope, a respected but unpublished amateur mathematician, persuaded him "that either there was some Defect in the Argument or in its perspicuity; I forget which" (L 1.223, 2.253). Unfortunately, Hume did not preserve this manuscript, although his papers include two anonymous essays on geometry that are not in his handwriting, and whose relation to the lost essay can only be conjectured by comparison to his known writings and other contemporary texts.[23]

In the *Treatise* Hume argues that the concept of numerical equality is derived from our discovery that we can establish one-to-one correspondences between sets of objects, so that "when two numbers are so combin'd, as that the one has always an unite answering to every unite of the other, we pronounce them equal." This activity of directing our attention toward the correlation of the units in different sets of objects enables us to develop our concepts of specific numbers, apparently through a distinction of reason, to serve as "a precise standard" by which we can judge relations of equality and proportion (T 1.3.1.5 [SBN 71]).[24] In the strict sense, Hume maintains that "existence in itself belongs only to unity," or to individual objects, "and is never applicable to number, but on account of the unites, of which the number is compos'd." However, unity may also serve as "a fictitious denomination, which the mind may apply to any quantity of objects it collects together," so that "twenty men," or the whole earth,

---

do not always require two distinct ideas, and that all of these may actually be regarded as ways of conceiving an object (T 1.3.7.5 n20 [SBN 96–97n]). See Echelbarger, "Hume on Deduction," 351–65, and Owen, *Hume's Reason*, 75, 91n16, 99, 103, 156, and 167–68.

23. See Mossner, *Life of David Hume*, 321–22 and 665, and Gossman, "Two Unpublished Essays," 442–49.

24. Hume's derivation of the concept of number is cited by Frege as an anticipation of his own theory: see Frege, *Foundations of Arithmetic*, 73 (§63); and Boolos, "Saving Frege from Contradiction," 137–51. For an intriguing account of the implications of Hume's critique of infinite divisibility for recent developments in mathematical logic, see Jacquette, *David Hume's Critique of Infinity*, 284–303.

or even the entire universe "may be consider'd as an unite" (T 1.2.2.3 [SBN 30–33]). In the *Enquiry* he argues that "the component parts of quantity and number are entirely similar," and he identifies this resemblance as the source of the precision and intricacy of mathematical reasoning (EHU 12.27 [SBN 163]). Finally, he argues that we recognize numerical equality immediately through intuition in the case of "very short numbers," while in other cases we must compare numbers "in a more *artificial* manner" by using the techniques of mathematical reasoning (T 1.3.1.3 [SBN 70]).

Hume indicates that mathematical reasoning enables us to form concepts of very large numbers. Indeed, he describes this process in terms which suggest that our idea of a large number is a relative idea, by stating that whenever we consider "any great number, such as a thousand, the mind has generally no adequate idea of it, but only a power of producing such an idea, by its adequate idea of the decimals, under which the number is comprehended," although this limitation is "never felt in our reasonings" (T 1.1.7.12 [SBN 22–23]). Similarly, he maintains that the human mind cannot produce "a full and adequate conception of infinity," although he seems to allow that we can formulate a relative idea of infinity, which is indicated in his own use of the word with the expectation that it will be understood by others (T 1.2.1.2; cf. 1.2.2.2 [SBN 26; cf. 29–30]).

As we have seen, the concept of number gives us a "precise standard" of equality that we may apply in our mathematical reasonings beyond our intuitive recognition of the most obvious relations of equality between small quantities. Since algebra and arithmetic are directly concerned with relations between numbers, Hume describes these in the *Treatise* as "the only sciences, in which we can carry on a chain of reasoning to any degree of intricacy, and yet preserve a perfect exactness and certainty" (T 1.3.1.5 [SBN 71]). In the *Enquiry* he concludes in similar terms that "the only objects of the abstract sciences or of demonstration are quantity and number," which are thus "the only proper objects of knowledge and demonstration" (EHU 12.27 [SBN 163]).

Hume offers several apparently competing accounts of the necessity that we attribute to mathematical demonstrations. In the *Treatise* he argues that all the apparent types of necessity arise from a "determination of the mind." Accordingly, "the necessity, which makes two times two equal to four, or three angles of a triangle equal to two right ones," like the necessity which we attribute to causation, lies "only in the act of the understanding, by which we consider and compare these ideas" (T 1.3.14.23 [SBN 166]). However, in assenting to a conclusion which is reached through intuition or demonstration, the mind "not only conceives the ideas according to the proposition, but is necessarily determin'd to conceive them in that particular manner, either immediately or by the interposition of other ideas." By contrast, in our causal judgments "this absolute necessity cannot take place, and the imagination is free to conceive both sides of the question." In other words, it is impossible "to conceive any thing contrary to a demonstration," since a demonstration, unlike a causal judgment, implies "the absolute contradiction and impossibility of conceiving any thing different" (T 1.3.7.3, 1.3.6.1 [SBN 95, 87]). As an example, he argues in the *Enquiry* that a false conclusion in mathematics, such as "the cube root of 64 is equal to the half of 10," cannot even be "distinctly conceived" (EHU 12.28 [SBN 164]). Finally, Philo observes in the *Dialogues* that although a naive observer might regard a numerical regularity as the product of chance or human contrivance, any "skilful algebraist" recognizes it as "the work of necessity, and demonstrates, that it must for ever result from the nature of these numbers" (DNR 9.191).

In several of the preceding passages, Hume appears to be arguing that the necessity of a mathematical demonstration arises from the apparent psychological impossibility of imagining any other conclusion. However, this interpretation also requires several important qualifications. First, he describes the determination of the mind in assenting to mathematical propositions as an intentional state in which the mind is "necessarily determin'd to conceive them in that particular manner" (T 1.3.7.3 [SBN 95]). He thus describes our assent to a mathematical proposition as a distinctive intentional state that is comparable to, but different from, our manner of conceiving causal relations, since it carries with it the impossibility of assenting to the opposite. Also, Philo states in the *Dialogues* that the mind is determined to assent to a mathematical proposition, or any other intuitively recognized relation, by the nature of the mathematical ideas and relations themselves (DNR 9.191). By contrast, in the case of causation, as we will see in Chapter 3, Hume argues that the necessity we attribute to our judgments arises through custom, or the repeated observation of similar instances, a process that does not operate in the case of demonstrative reasoning.

The necessity of mathematical reasoning is therefore one instance of the determination of the mind through its activity of intuition. In our mathematical judgments, intuition operates either through immediate recognition or through the methods of demonstrative reasoning, by which we recognize and compare the numerical correspondences that we discover in sets of objects, and the numerical concepts that we form by attending to these correspondences (cf. T 1.1.5.6, 1.3.1.3–5 [SBN 14–15, 70–71]). He maintains, however, that relations, including mathematical relations, are not perceived directly as qualities of objects or sets of objects, but are instead formulated by the mind as complex ideas by comparing sets of objects, and then extended as principles for further judgments in which we compare or connect objects. Accordingly, the necessity of a mathematical demonstration lies only in the distinctive "act of the understanding" in which we compare our ideas of numbers (T 1.3.14.23

[SBN 166]), even though the "truth" of a mathematical judgment, or indeed of any proposition concerning a relation of ideas, consists in "the discovery of the proportions of ideas, consider'd as such," or in the conformity of our judgment "to the *real* relations of ideas" (T 2.3.10.1–2, 3.1.1.9 [SBN 448, 458]).

Among the mathematical disciplines, Hume devotes the most attention to geometry, or "the *art*, by which we fix the proportions of figures" (T 1.3.1.4 [SBN 70]).[25] These reflections begin in the *Treatise* with his criticism of the "doctrine of infinite divisibility" and his defense of minimum sensible points, which he presents, not only as the background for his discussion of our ideas of time and space, but also as a contribution to the "foundation of mathematics" (T 1.2.1.1, 1.4.2.22 [SBN 26, 198]). In contrast to the prevailing opinion that space and time are infinitely divisible, and building again upon Berkeley's argument, Hume argues that space and time are composed of indivisible parts, which he calls "atoms" or "points" in the case of space, and "moments" in the case of time (T 1.2.1.1–2, 1.2.2.4, 1.2.3.15, 1.2.4.8–33, 1.4.5.9 [SBN 26–28, 31, 38–39, 42–53, 235]).[26] This analysis is often regarded as one of the most obscure and implausible in Hume's writings. However, I hope to show, here and in Chapter 4, that Hume presents a coherent and intriguing view of the impressions and cognitive dispositions that give us our ideas of space and time (cf. EHU 12.18–20 [SBN 156–58]).[27]

Hume first attempts to prove that the imagination must eventually reach "a *minimum*, and may raise up to itself an idea, of which it cannot conceive any sub-division." He then argues that since these ideas are derived from impressions of sensation, our impressions of visible and tangible shapes must also be composed of minimum visible and tangible points (T 1.2.1.2–5 [SBN 26–28]).

First, Hume attempts to show that our ideas, or images, of extended objects cannot be infinitely divisible. Here he maintains that since the mind can never attain a "full and adequate conception of infinity," it cannot accommodate the individual ideas of the "infinite number of parts" which, according to the prevailing doctrine, make up a finite extension.[28] Accordingly, if we reject an

25. For discussions of Hume's account of geometry, see Laird, *Hume's Philosophy of Human Nature*, 64–83; Zabeeh, *Hume*, 137–43; Van Steenburgh, "Hume's Geometric 'Objects,'" 61–68; Newman, "Hume on Space and Geometry," 1–31; Wright, *Sceptical Realism*, 85–122; Waxman, *Hume's Theory of Consciousness*, 115–24; Johnson, *Mind of David Hume*, 79–107; Frasca-Spada, *Space and the Self*, 123–56; and Jacquette, *David Hume's Critique of Infinity*, 131–303.

26. Berkeley's version of this argument appears in his *New Theory of Vision*, §54 and §§80–88; see Berkeley, *Works*, 1:191 and 204–6. See also Bayle, "Zeno of Elea," note G, in Bayle, *Historical and Critical Dictionary*, 359–72. For a further account of the historical context of this discussion, see Jacquette, *David Hume's Critique of Infinity*, 3–39.

27. For two recent and valuable reassessments of Hume's analysis of the foundations of geometry, see Frasca-Spada, *Space and the Self*, and Jacquette, *David Hume's Critique of Infinity*.

28. For a discussion of the structure and implications of Hume's criticism of the concept of infinity, see Jacquette, *David Hume's Critique of Infinity*, 284–303.

"infinite capacity of the mind," we must recognize that any division of our ideas ultimately ends in images that are "perfectly simple and indivisible." In a thought-experiment to illustrate this argument, Hume invites us to agree that we cannot divide our image of a very small object, such as a grain of sand, into even as few as twenty smaller parts before we reach the limit of what we can distinguish by the imagination. To help us imagine a minimum visible point, he argues that if we were to look at "a spot of ink upon paper" and then move backward, its "image or impression" would become perfectly indivisible at the moment before it vanishes from our visual field (T 1.2.1.2–4; cf. 1.2.4.7 [SBN 26–27; cf. 42]).[29]

Next, after showing that our ideas of extended objects in space are not infinitely divisible, Hume maintains that our impressions of objects as extended in space cannot be infinitely divisible either. Hume's first argument for this conclusion, beyond an appeal to evidence of the receding ink-spot, is formulated as a deduction from his copy theory of the relation between impressions and ideas. This inference moves from the premise, which has already been established, that the imagination must stop at the idea of a minimum point in dividing the image of a visible or tangible object, to the conclusion that the impressions from which they are copied also cannot be divided beyond a minimum. Accordingly, he asserts that "wherever ideas are adequate representations of objects," all of the "relations, contradictions and agreements" that apply to our ideas must also apply to their objects; in other words, to the impressions from which we derive our ideas. He then argues that since (1) "our ideas are adequate representations of the most minute parts of extension," since (2) "whatever *appears* impossible and contradictory upon the comparison of these ideas, must be *really* impossible and contradictory" if it is attributed to our impressions, and since (3) our ideas of extension cannot be divided infinitely, we must conclude (4) that our impressions of extension, and thus (5) extension itself, cannot be infinitely divisible. In a similar move from what is impossible in conceiving our ideas, to what is impossible for our impressions, he argues that any finite extension that is infinitely divisible would contain an "infinite number of parts." However, this assertion is evidently contradictory, since an infinite series of parts when joined together would produce an infinite extension. He concludes that our impressions, and our ideas, of finite extensions must be composites of the impressions or ideas of minimum visible or tangible points (T 1.2.2.1–3 [SBN 29–31]).

In developing his positive account of our idea of space, Hume observes that the minimum points of our perception of extension in space are given to

29. For a detailed analysis and defense of Hume's spot-of-ink thought-experiment, see Jacquette, *David Hume's Critique of Infinity*, 43–128.

us through vision and touch. We may thus describe these points as minimum visible and tangible points, or minimal points of "colour and solidity" (T 1.2.3.15; cf. 1.2.4.3 [SBN 38; cf. 40]).[30] He identifies these minimum points of spatial perception with mathematical points, or the fundamental units in the composition of a geometrical figure. Accordingly, in describing these as sensible points, he challenges the general conception of a mathematical point as a "nonentity," which he argues would be useless in the imaginative construction of a geometrical figure (T 1.2.2.9–10, 1.2.3.14, 1.2.4.3 [SBN 32–33, 38, 40]). Indeed, Hume appeals to the definitions of Euclidean geometry to defend his doctrine of minimum points against the doctrine of infinite divisibility. According to the Euclidean system, "a surface is *defin'd* to be length and breadth without depth: A line to be length without breadth or depth: A point to be what has neither length, breadth nor depth." However, Hume maintains that these definitions are "perfectly unintelligible upon any other supposition than that of the composition of extension by indivisible points or atoms," since we cannot imagine the "terminations" of a solid in a surface, a surface in a line, or a line in a point, unless these terminations are composed of indivisible points (T 1.2.4.8–14 [SBN 42–44]).

In order to understand Hume's rejection of infinite divisibility in time and space, and his defense of minimum sensible points, it will be helpful to consider what he evidently does *not* mean by these arguments. First, as we have seen, he repeatedly affirms that we may engage in demonstrative reasonings involving very large numbers, and very small fractions, even beyond the range of our immediate intuition of numerical relations (T 1.1.7.12, 1.2.1.3, 2.3.10.2–4 [SBN 22–23, 27, 449–50]). However, although we may perform any of an infinite variety of arithmetical calculations, and may further claim to apply these to an extension in space beyond the reach of our senses, such a calculation is neither a literal division of an object in space, nor a precise division of the object in the imagination. If this calculation is accompanied by images of the division of this object, as it apparently must be on Hume's view, the imagination can exhibit this process only as the division of a sensible object, composed of indivisible points, in an imaginary spatial field, corresponding to the spatial field of perception. Any supposed division of an object in space beyond the reach of our faculties of vision and touch is therefore actually an exercise of arithmetical reasoning, which may also be associated with the division of an image by the imagination. However, such a division can never be carried out

---

30. Many recent studies have argued that for Hume these points of color and solidity are the ultimate simple impressions of vision and touch; see, for example, Cummins, "Hume on Qualities," 49–88; Waxman, *Hume's Theory of Consciousness*, 42–46; Garrett, *Cognition and Commitment*, 60–64; and Frasca-Spada, *Space and the Self*, 11–55.

by the imagination in an exact correspondence with the divisions that are performed in the mathematical calculation.[31]

Hume also accepts the contemporary scientific evidence indicating "that there are bodies *vastly* more minute than those, which appear to the senses," although he maintains that any such imperceptible bodies cannot be properly described as "*infinitely* more minute" (T 1.2.4.24 [SBN 48]). He thus argues, for example, that the view through a microscope gives "parts to impressions, which to the naked eye appear simple and uncompounded, and advances to a *minimum*, what was formerly imperceptible." He also rejects the view that our images of minute bodies are vastly "inferior" to the images of everyday objects, maintaining instead that when we form the image of a very tiny body, such as "the smallest atom of the animal spirits of an insect a thousand times less than a mite," we are in effect "enlarging our conceptions," rather than imagining something smaller than a sensible image. In other words, even our idea of an entity that is too small to be perceived by our senses is depicted by the imagination as a complex visible or tangible impression in the imagined counterpart of our sensory field. Thus, in considering the "thousandth and ten thousandth part of a grain of sand," we may indeed formulate "a distinct idea of these numbers and of their different proportions," but cannot form images of these parts that are different in the same proportions from the image representing the original grain (T 1.2.1.3–5 [SBN 27–28]).[32] In a later elucidation of this argument, Hume maintains that "the eye at all times sees an equal number of physical points," and that, for an object to be visible, it must coincide with a certain number of visible points in this field. Accordingly, a very small object must be magnified, and a very large object must be reduced, in order to appear in its entirety within this field of vision (T 1.3.9.11 [SBN 112]).

Finally, Hume does not regard the indivisible points of space and time as distinguishable and measurable in themselves, or useful as a basis for exact measurements. Indeed, he rejects the definition of geometric equality as the correspondence of mathematical points, since the minimum points which compose any lines or surfaces are "so minute and so confounded with each other, that 'tis utterly impossible for the mind to compute their number" (T 1.2.4.19; cf. 1.2.4.24, 1.2.4.31 [SBN 45; cf. 48, 638]). He also initially rejects the interpretation of his theory as a "system of *physical* points," since "a real extension, such as a physical point is suppos'd to be, can never exist without parts" which

---

31. For a similar interpretation of Hume's argument as an account of perceptual space and its relation to geometry, see Waxman, *Hume's Theory of Consciousness*, 116–23, and Jacquette, *David Hume's Critique of Infinity*, 43–303.

32. Hume's distinction between the images and concepts of very small objects is developed in Newman, "Hume on Space and Geometry," 1–31, and in Frasca-Spada, *Space and the Self*, 11–55. For a contrasting view of Hume's discussion, see Franklin, "Achievements and Fallacies," 85–101.

are "different from each other," and would accordingly be "distinguishable and separable by the imagination" (T 1.2.4.3 [SBN 40]). He apparently reverses his terminology in the course of his writings by observing, even later in the *Treatise*, that the eye always sees "an equal number of physical points" (T 1.3.9.11 [SBN 112]). Similarly, in the *Enquiry* he maintains that "whatever disputes there may be about mathematical points, we must allow that there are physical points," which he now identifies as those "parts of extension, which cannot be divided or lessened, either by the eye or imagination." These "physical points" would appear, by this definition, to be what he called "mathematical points" in Book 1 of the *Treatise* (EHU 12.18n33 [SBN 156n1]).[33]

The most promising approach to understanding Hume's account of indivisible visible and tangible mathematical points is to regard this as a discussion of the composition, first of extended objects in space, then of space itself, and finally of our ideas of geometrical figures.

First, Hume argues that our image of any extension in space is composed of the images of a number of minimum visible and tangible points. However, we do not ordinarily imagine these separately, although the idea of a minimum visible point can indeed be isolated through a thought-experiment by imagining the receding ink-spot. Next, on the basis of the copy principle, he argues that these minimal ideas must be regarded as copies, or images, of those minimum visible and tangible points that are given to us as impressions. He concludes that our impression of an extended object must be composed of a number of minimum visible and tangible points, although we cannot distinguish these from each other by vision or touch, apart from any artificial exercises which are designed to isolate a minimum impression.

Next, Hume argues that our apparent idea of space in general, including empty space, is actually derived from our minimal impressions of visible and tangible points, by an imaginative projection of the arrangement that we discover among these points. Thus, even our idea of empty space is composed of ideas of minimum points of extension (cf. T 1.2.4.1–2, 1.2.5.1–29 [SBN 39–40, 53–65]). I will return to this argument in Chapter 4, where I will examine Hume's account of our ideas of space and time in greater detail.

Finally, Hume maintains that our fundamental concepts in geometry, including our ideas of a point, line, and surface, are all composed of ideas of minimum points, corresponding to the minimal points of sensation. As we have

<hr/>

33. Frasca-Spada suggests that Hume is distinguishing his minimal points in the *Treatise* from both physical and mathematical points: see *Space and the Self*, 30–32 and 42. However, it seems likely, in light of his appeal to the definitions of Euclidean geometry, that Hume is presenting his account of minimum visible and tangible points as an alternative account of mathematical points (cf. T 1.2.2.7, 1.2.4.3–4, 1.2.4.14 [SBN 32, 38, 40]). For a similar reading of Hume, see Jacquette, *David Hume's Critique of Infinity*, 158–68; cf. 109–10 and 116–20.

seen, he further argues that our concepts of geometrical figures are derived, through distinctions of reason, by our comparing of the composite objects of perception (T 1.1.7.17–18 [SBN 24–25]). He then suggests that the imagination extends the ideas which we derive from attending to various aspects of the objects of sensory experience in order to develop our images of ideal geometrical figures and ideal standards for their relations. However, he still maintains that our ideas of these relations, such as equality or congruity between figures, and the straightness of a line, are "far from being exact and determinate, according to our common method of conceiving them," since "the ultimate standard of these figures is deriv'd from nothing but the senses and imagination" (T 1.2.4.29 [SBN 50–51]). This analysis appears especially in his account of our ideas of equality and of a straight line.

Hume begins with the concept of equality in geometry, or of equal extension, in contrast to numerical equality. He dismisses several possible sources for our judgments of congruity, such as those appealing to an equal number of points, or to an exact correspondence of parts, since he maintains that the senses cannot discern the individual points from which any given extension is composed (T 1.2.4.18; cf. 1.2.4.24, 1.2.4.31 [SBN 45; cf. 48, 638]). Instead, "the only useful notion of equality, or inequality" between geometrical figures "is deriv'd from the whole united appearance and the comparison of particular objects" (T 1.2.4.22 [SBN 637]). In forming this concept, we begin with a rough idea of equality that is derived from the "general appearance" of approximately congruent dimensions between objects. This preliminary judgment may then be corrected through "review and reflection," either by a direct "juxtaposition of the objects," or, if this is not convenient, through the artificial use of "some common and invariable measure, which being successively apply'd to each, informs us of their different proportions." Every comparison is, in its turn, "susceptible of a new correction, and of different degrees of exactness, according to the nature of the instrument, by which we measure the bodies, and the care which we employ in the comparison." In judging the dimensions of ordinary objects we generally adopt "a mix'd notion of equality," which combines "the looser and stricter methods of comparison." However, the imagination refines our concept of equal measurement by its propensity "to proceed . . . with any action, even after the reason has ceas'd, which first determin'd it to begin."[34] The imagination is thus impelled by its own momentum to continue past the "mix'd notion" of equality which is given through the senses and intuition, and to posit a supposed continuation of the process of correction, extending even to the supposed comparison of bodies that are "*vastly* more minute than those,

---

34. Price has characterized this propensity very effectively as the "inertia" of the imagination; see *Hume's Theory of the External World*, 54–59.

which appear to the senses." Through this impetus we arrive at the concept of "some imaginary standard of equality," which we assume can be applied beyond the limits of our visual and tactile sensations, even though this imaginary correction of our judgments beyond the reach of any observation "is a mere fiction of the mind; and useless as well as incomprehensible." Hume therefore concludes that we can only achieve "an obscure and implicit notion of a perfect and entire equality" between two figures in space, although he also regards this fictional notion as a very natural product of the human imagination (T 1.2.4.23–24, 1.2.4.22; cf. 1.2.4.31, 1.4.2.22 [SBN 47–48; 637; cf. 38, 198]; A 29 [SBN 658–59]).[35]

Hume offers a similar account of our concept of a "right" or a straight line. Here he argues that while the difference between a curved and a straight line might seem immediately evident to the senses and imagination, it is "impossible to produce any definition of them, which will fix the precise boundaries between them," or to provide an "exact method" for distinguishing between them. In other words, it is impossible for us to either describe or recognize a perfectly straight line. However, in spite of this we may form "a distant notion of some unknown standard to these objects" through the imaginative activity of "correcting the first appearance by a more accurate consideration, and by a comparison with some rule, of whose rectitude from repeated trials we have a greater assurance." In this way we develop "the loose idea of a perfect standard to these figures, without being able to explain or comprehend it" (T 1.2.4.25 [SBN 49]). However, he maintains that the "the original standard of a right line is in reality nothing but a certain general appearance," which we observe in certain lines, even though we cannot determine whether any particular visible line is really or only approximately straight (T 1.2.4.30 [SBN 52]). While Hume does not consider any other geometric concepts, he could presumably provide a similar account of our ideas of regular polygons and other geometrical figures, as fictional constructions arising from the tendency of the imagination to develop a perfected image of the figures we perceive in nature. Finally, we may subject the relations between these constructions to exact calculation in the context of a numerical system of measurement, even though we can never exactly measure the objects of sensation (cf. T 1.1.7.8–10, 1.1.7.17–18, 1.3.1.1 [SBN 21–22, 24–25, 69]).

Hume accordingly rejects the view held by many philosophers that the ideas belonging to mathematics and geometry "are of so refin'd and spiritual a nature" that they must arise, not from the imagination, but from some "pure and intellectual view, of which the superior faculties of the soul are alone

---

35. See Traiger, "Impressions, Ideas, and Fictions," 381–99; Brand, *Hume's Theory of Moral Judgment*, 22–27; and Waxman, *Hume's Theory of Consciousness*, 119–23.

capable." He then criticizes the tendency of such philosophers to use "this notion of some spiritual and refin'd perceptions" given to the pure intellect as a justification for many of our other abstract ideas, instead of recognizing that all of our ideas arise from our impressions of sensation and reflection (T 1.3.1.7 [SBN 72]).

Finally, with this discovery that our fundamental concepts in geometry are "so loose and uncertain," since they arise from sensation and imagination, Hume challenges the claim that we can attain any "infallible assurance," not only for the most "intricate and obscure propositions" of geometry, but even for its "most vulgar and obvious principles." For example, he criticizes the attempt to prove that two straight lines cannot share a common segment, or that there is only one straight line between two points, since, while we may regard the opposite opinions as "obviously absurd, and repugnant to our clear ideas," we might indeed find it easier to imagine that two lines approaching each other "at the rate of an inch in twenty leagues" share a common segment rather than a single point where they contact each other. Indeed, Hume traces our belief in the Euclidean parallel postulate, neither to intuition nor to demonstration, but to the supposed difficulty of imagining any other configuration of geometrical figures in perceptual space (T 1.2.4.30, 1.3.1.5–6 [SBN 51–52, 71–72]). Hume's discussion of the parallel postulate might thus be regarded as an indirect contribution to the emerging contemporary discussion over the problem of proving the parallel postulate, which would eventually lead to the development of non-Euclidean geometry: since he distinguishes any conclusions which might be reached through demonstrative reasoning from the question of whether any alternative view is, or could be, achieved by the imagination in its configuration of the material provided by the senses.[36]

Hume concludes in the *Treatise* that since its first principles are derived "merely from appearances," geometry can never reach "greater exactness in the comparison of objects or ideas, than what our eye or imagination alone is able to attain," and thereby "falls short of that perfect precision and certainty, which are peculiar to arithmetic and algebra." In this respect, geometry is an "art" rather than a science, although it still improves upon "the imperfect judgments of our senses and imagination" (T 1.3.1.4–6 [SBN 70–72]). On the other hand, in the *Enquiry* he offers the calculation of the relation between the sides of a right triangle as an example of the exactness and perfection we may attain in our mathematical demonstrations (EHU 4.1, 12.27 [SBN 25, 163]). Flew has accordingly suggested that in writing the *Enquiry* Hume is renouncing his earlier view of geometry as an inexact and imperfect science, and is instead

---

36. A German contemporary of Hume, G. S. Klügel, appears to have been the first mathematician to assert, in 1763, that Euclid's parallel postulate cannot be proved and is only supported by the judgment of our senses. See Trudeau, *Non-Euclidean Revolution,* 154.

"restoring pure geometry to its place" alongside arithmetic and algebra. Flew also claims that in the *Treatise* Hume is entirely concerned with pure mathematics, and that he only considers applied mathematics in the *Enquiry*.[37]

In response to Flew's reading, I would suggest that in the *Treatise* Hume is tracing the inexact character of geometry to its character as an applied discipline, or its function in measuring and comparing the objects of perception. In this regard he contrasts geometry to the cognitive process, which he also considers in the *Treatise*, of exact calculations concerning imaginatively constructed or idealized geometrical figures (T 1.3.1.1–4, 1.3.14.23 [SBN 69–70, 166]). On this view, Hume's references to exact calculations in geometry, in both the *Treatise* and the *Enquiry*, refer to the arithmetical calculation of relations between the parts of imaginatively postulated geometrical figures, which belongs to pure geometry (cf. EHU 12.27 [SBN 163]).[38] However, elsewhere in the *Enquiry* Hume attributes the precision of geometry, surprisingly, not merely to the demonstrations arising from its concepts and definitions, but also to the clarity of its objects as these may be presented to the senses. Even here, however, he maintains that it is the "ideas" of geometrical figures that are "clear and determinate," and between which the smallest differences are "immediately perceptible" (EHU 7.1–2 [SBN 60–61]). He also states in the *Enquiry* that the propositions of geometry would still maintain their "certainty and evidence," even if there were no perfect circles or triangles in nature (EHU 4.1 [SBN 25]). Here again he thus appears to be presenting our ideas of geometrical figures as imaginative constructions, which we use as images to accompany the process of demonstrative reasoning, rather than as direct copies of the figures that we have attended to in natural objects.

Hume also considers the distinction and relation between pure and "mixed" or applied mathematics more directly in the *Enquiry*. More specifically, he argues that the incorporation of geometry into natural philosophy cannot give us any knowledge of "ultimate causes" in nature, since any use of "mixed mathematics" in the natural sciences already requires us to assume "that certain laws are established by nature in her operations." Once we have accepted this premise, the "abstract reasonings" of mathematics may then be used "either to assist experience in the discovery of these laws, or to determine their influence in particular instances" by enabling us to calculate "any precise degree of distance and quantity." Thus, while geometry may assist us in applying a law of motion, by giving us the dimensions "of all the parts and figures, which can enter into any species of machine," the discovery of this law "is owing merely to experience, and all the abstract reasonings in the world could never lead us one step

---

37. Flew, *Hume's Philosophy of Belief*, 61–62.

38. For a related account of the two types of geometry in the *Treatise*, see Frasca-Spada, *Space and the Self*, 136.

towards the knowledge of it" (EHU 4.13 [SBN 31]).[39] Indeed, in the *History of England* Hume especially praises Galileo as the first to apply geometry, "together with experiment," to the natural sciences (H 5.App.4.153).

In addition to the basic principles of arithmetic and geometry, Hume also considers the concepts and principles involved in the calculation of statistical frequencies, or what he calls the "probability of chances," as background for his discussion of causality and probable reasoning. Hume describes "chance" as "the negation of a cause," or a "perfect and total indifference" of the mind in its expectation of any particular event. However, he then argues that in considering a procedure for generating a random series of events within a given range of possibilities, such as multiple tosses of numbered dice, the mind can be influenced, by its recognition of any factors that might indicate a "superior combination of chances," to predict the relative frequencies of various outcomes, even apart from any judgments regarding the causal forces impinging upon the particular events in the series. For example, if we consider "a dye, that has four sides mark'd with a certain number of spots, and only two with another," we expect that a series of tosses will turn up the first figure with greater frequency than the second figure. He explains this expectation by arguing that "the impulses belonging to all these sides must re-unite in that one figure, and become stronger and more forcible by the union," so that the combined ideas of the first are "superior to those of the latter" (T 1.3.11.1–6, 1.3.11.13 [SBN 124–26, 130]; cf. EHU 6.2–3 [SBN 56–57]). In considering a series of random casts, we therefore expect the figure depicted on four sides to appear more frequently than the figure on the other two sides, because the combined ideas of four instances gives greater force and vivacity to our idea of this figure than to our idea of the other.

Hume's account of our assessment of statistical frequencies might seem to be another example of his supposed tendency to reduce the criteria of belief and judgment to the force and vivacity of our ideas. However, here again he appears to distinguish between a phenomenological and an epistemic account of justification in his references to "calculations concerning chances," in which he suggests that we may also give an objective formulation to these subjective degrees of expectation by a demonstrative calculation of statistical probabilities (T 1.3.4.5, 1.3.11.10 [SBN 125, 128]). While he does not offer any more detailed account of the methods of statistical calculation, Hume might have presented this as another "artificial" procedure belonging to mathematics, arising through another imaginative projection from our ordinary observation, and

39. Flew, *Hume's Philosophy of Belief,* 62–64, and "Did Hume Distinguish Pure from Applied Geometry?" 96–100; Newman, "Hume on Space and Geometry," 1–31; Flew, "Hume on Space and Geometry," 62–65; and Newman, "A Rejoinder," 66–69.

formulated as a set of arithmetical principles for calculating the appearance of specific patterns in various sequences of random events.[40]

Hume therefore suggests that the mathematical sciences ultimately arise from our intuitive recognition of proportions in quantity and number, which initially applies to the objects that are given to us through sensation and reproduced as images, and is then extended beyond the range of our immediate intuition through our formulation and application of the "artificial" procedures of demonstrative reasoning, and the "fictional" or imaginatively projected ideas of perfect figures and exact relations in geometry. Finally, once they are defined, these concepts and procedures allow us to generate a system of propositions that we recognize as demonstratively necessary.

We may conclude by considering Hume's account of the place of mathematics in human life. In considering the motives for various types of intellectual inquiry, he notes that the pleasure associated with mathematical demonstrations cannot proceed from the demonstration itself, since in difficult cases of mathematical reasoning "the pleasure is very inconsiderable, if rather it does not degenerate into pain." Instead, our interest in a mathematical demonstration arises from our delight in exercising, or recognizing, the "genius and capacity" involved in the demonstration, and from anticipating the usefulness of the result. We thus find that "nothing can be more curious, as well as useful" than tracing numerical relations (T 2.3.10.2–3 [SBN 449]; EHU 12.27 [SBN 163]). Hume also argues that mathematical reasoning is "useful in all mechanical operations," and indeed "in almost every art and profession," although its usefulness only becomes apparent when it "directs our judgment concerning causes and effects," either in the operations of nature or in different types of human activity (T 2.3.3.2 [SBN 413–14]).

Finally, in the *Treatise,* Hume also considers the social context, as well as the historical dimension, of mathematical inquiry. Here he notes that no "algebraist nor mathematician" can ever become "so expert in his science, as to place entire confidence in any truth immediately upon his discovery of it," or to regard it as more than "a mere probability." However, his confidence in his discovery increases "every time he runs over his proofs," and is further reinforced "by the approbation of his friends," until it is finally "rais'd to its utmost perfection by the universal assent and applauses of the learned world" (T 1.4.1.1 [SBN 180]). Thus, even though we may indeed regard numerical relations as necessary in themselves, Hume suggests that, in practice, our confidence in any particular instance of demonstrative reasoning rests upon probable reasoning,

40. Hacking overlooks Hume's references to the possibility of objective methods of statistical calculation: see *Emergence of Probability,* 176–85, and "Hume's Species of Probability," 21–37. For a more thorough analysis of Hume's discussion, see Gower, "Hume on Probability," 1–19. See also Daston, *Classical Probability,* 198–203.

since we can only reach a high level of probable assurance that we have carried out a particular demonstration accurately: a probable assurance that is strengthened by the evidence provided by repeated calculations and by intersubjective confirmation. In other words, he calls attention here to the objective character of mathematical relations as indicated by their repeatability, to the historical development of human mathematical knowledge, and to the role of a community of researchers in confirming new developments in the world of learning.

3

Probable Reasoning

The most prominent and influential of Hume's philosophical arguments is his analysis of causation, which he develops both in the longest division of the *Treatise* and as the central argument in the *Abstract* and the first *Enquiry*. However, Hume initially presents this analysis in the *Treatise* within a discussion of "knowledge and probability," whose further dimensions have received considerably less attention in the secondary literature. Hume's circuitous treatment of probable reasoning in both the *Treatise* and the *Enquiry* may indeed have encouraged incomplete readings of his argument. In Book 1, Part 3 of the *Treatise* he begins with a preliminary analysis of our idea of causation, including our idea of the necessary connection between a cause and its effect, in Sections 2–10; then turns to the role of probability in our judgments of causation in Sections 11–13; returns to the idea of a necessary connection in Section 14; and then completes his discussion of philosophical probable reasoning in Section 15. In the first *Enquiry* he presents his analysis of causation in Sections 4–7, including a brief discussion of probable reasoning in Section 6; and then considers philosophical probable reasoning, almost incidentally, in his reflections concerning the reasoning ability of animals (Section 9), and concerning the evaluation of testimony (Section 10). In this chapter I restore Hume's analysis of the causal relation to its original context in his account of probable reasoning.

CAUSATION

Hume describes three of his seven philosophical relations in the *Treatise* as depending on "information from experience," or in the *Enquiry* as concerned with "matters of fact." In the *Treatise* he identifies two of these, identity and location, as immediately apparent to the senses through "perception rather than reasoning." By contrast, causation is the only relation concerning matters of fact and existence in which "the mind can go beyond what is immediately present to the senses" to discover "existences and objects, which we do not see or feel" (T 1.3.1.1, 1.3.2.2–3 [SBN 69, 73–74]; EHU 4.1 [SBN 25]). He therefore identifies two types of "reasoning" in human cognition: demonstrative reasonings about numerical relations; and "probable reasoning," or what he also calls "moral reasoning," concerning causes and effects (T 1.3.6.5–6, 1.3.8.12, 1.3.14.17 [SBN 89, 103, 163]; EHU 4.18, 7.1–3 [SBN 35, 60–62]).[1]

Causal inferences play a central role in human thought and activity, since all of our reasonings in the "conduct of life" arise from this source, along with "all our belief in history," and indeed "all philosophy, excepting only geometry and arithmetic" (A 10 [SBN 650]; cf. T 1.3.9.4 [SBN 108]; EHU 5.6–8, 7.29 [SBN 44–46, 76]). However, Hume indicates that the study of our causal inferences had been "little cultivated" thus far in philosophy (EHU 4.3 [SBN 26]). He accordingly presents his analysis of causation, both as a contribution to contemporary discussions in philosophy and as a foundation for his own further inquiries into the moral or human sciences.

Hume has already introduced causation as both a natural and a philosophical relation in Book 1, Part 1 of the *Treatise* (T 1.1.4.1, 1.1.5.9 [SBN 11, 15]). His project in Part 3 of Book 1, and in the corresponding Sections 4–7 of the first *Enquiry,* is to provide an account of the origin of our idea of causation, beginning with causation as a natural relation, and then proceeding to causation as a philosophical relation.

In accordance with his copy principle, Hume approaches the problem of accounting for the origin of our idea of causation by seeking to discover the "primary impression, from which it arises" (T 1.3.2.4 [SBN 74–75]). He then argues that the idea of causation does not arise directly through either perception or intuition, since we do not perceive causality through our senses as a distinctive quality of any object, nor can we discover any causal relations merely by considering or comparing our ideas of any objects. On the contrary, the imagination can always separate the idea of any cause from the idea of its effect, and there is "no object, which implies the existence of any other if we consider

---

1. For a discussion of these two types of "reasoning," or inference, and their importance in Hume's thought, see Owen, *Hume's Reason.*

these objects in themselves" (T 1.3.2.5, 1.3.6.1 [SBN 75, 86–87]; EHU 4.6–13 [SBN 27–32]).[2]

Next, Hume presents his analysis of the causal relation, initially as it appears in cases of direct mechanical causation between physical objects, although he also eventually applies his analysis to "moral" causes, or to the passions and human action (T 1.3.2.16, 1.3.14.33, 1.3.15.11 [SBN 78, 171, 175]). In a case of physical causation, such as one billiard ball striking another and causing it to move, the causal relation essentially includes two natural relations which are directly given to us through perception: conjunction in space and conjunction in time, or *"contiguity* and *succession"* (T 1.3.2.6–9, 1.3.14.19 [SBN 75–76, 164]; cf. A 9–10 [SBN 649–50]; EHU 4.7–10, 7.6 [SBN 28–30, 63]).[3] However, since we often regard objects as contiguous and successive without regarding one as the cause of the other, as in an accidental conjunction, Hume then finds that we attribute a further quality, which we call "necessity," to the causal relation between two objects. Accordingly, he identifies the "NECESSARY CONNEXION" between a cause and its effect as the distinctive characteristic of the causal relation. Finally, he presents the task of tracing our idea of a necessary connection, and its derivation from our impressions, as the central problem in attempting to account for the idea of causation (T 1.3.2.11–13 [SBN 77–78]; cf. 1.3.14.1–36 [SBN 155–72]; EHU 7.1–30 [SBN 60–79]).

With this statement of his problem in the *Treatise,* Hume then postpones his attempt to find the impression that is the source for our idea of necessity until after he has considered two separate but related sets of questions: first, why we believe that any object which begins to exist must always have a cause; and second, why we infer the connection between a particular cause and its effect, and why we believe in it and consider it to be necessary (T 1.3.2.13–15 [SBN 77–78]). In the *Enquiry* he again defers his discussion of our idea of a necessary connection, this time until he has considered our general expectation that the future will resemble the past (EHU 4.14–23 [SBN 32–39]; cf. T 1.3.6.4–11 [SBN 88–92]), and the nature and sources of our particular causal inferences (EHU 5.3–22 [SBN 42–55]).

In the *Treatise* Hume turns next to the assertion that is often called the Causal Principle, which is our belief that every event must have a cause.

---

2. Although Hume usually refers to the *relata* of a causal relation as "objects," many of his examples can also be described as involving two events, such as the movements of two billiard balls. He indeed refers to both objects (T 1.3.2.5–16 [SBN 75–94]; A 8 [SBN 649]; SBN 4.6–13 [SBN 27–32]) and events (T 1.3.12.4–25 [SBN 131–42]; A 11 [SBN 650]; SBN 7.26–28 [SBN 73–75]) in the course of his investigation, and his examples often indicate that he may be using the terms interchangeably (cf. A 9 [SBN 649–50]). See Garrett, *Cognition and Commitment,* 118, and Dicker, *Hume's Epistemology and Metaphysics,* 69 and 111–12.

3. In the *Enquiry* Hume drops any explicit reference to spatial contiguity, although he may be implicitly conflating spatial contiguity and temporal succession by describing an effect as one object that "follows" another (SBN 7.6, 7.29 [SBN 63, 76–77]). See Dicker, *Hume's Epistemology and Metaphysics,* 112–13.

However, he argues that this principle is "neither intuitively nor demonstrably certain," since in contrast to the universality and necessity that we ascribe to the relations discovered through intuition and demonstration, we can always, in our imagination, separate our idea of a particular cause from our idea of its effect. For this reason, we may conclude that "every demonstration, which has been produc'd for the necessity of a cause, is fallacious and sophistical." Hume argues instead that our belief in the universality and necessity of causation arises from the accumulated force of many individual causal inferences. This accordingly brings us to the second question, concerning the nature and sources of our particular causal inferences (T 1.3.3.1–9; cf. 1.3.14.13, 1.3.14.35 [SBN 78–82; cf. 161–62, 172]).

In both the *Treatise* and the *Enquiry* Hume considers another apparent presupposition of our causal judgments. This principle, which is now generally called the Uniformity Principle or Principle of Induction, is our general expectation that the future will resemble the past, or in other words "that instances, of which we have had no experience, must resemble those, of which we have had experience, and that the course of nature continues always uniformly the same" (T 1.3.6.4 [SBN 89]). Like the Causal Principle, the Uniformity Principle cannot be derived from either intuition or demonstration, since there is "no contradiction" implied by stating "that the course of nature may change, and that an object, seemingly like those which we have experienced, may be attended with different or contrary effects." Indeed, a different course of events can always be "distinctly" conceived by the imagination, since we can imagine a future in which all of the causal relations of the past and present have been replaced by an entirely new set of causal relations. We also find that the Uniformity Principle cannot be derived from experience, since the argument that the uniformity of past experience can be used to predict the uniformity of future experience itself rests upon the expectation that the future will resemble the past, and thus cannot be used to establish this principle. Instead, Hume argues that our expectation of a continuing uniformity in nature is a "supposition," which is produced by the cumulative influence of our individual causal inferences on our imagination (EHU 4.18 [SBN 35]; A 14 [SBN 652]; cf. 4.14–20 [SBN 32–36]; T 1.3.6.4–11, 1.3.8.13 [SBN 88–92, 104]).[4]

After considering the Causal Principle in the *Treatise*, and the Uniformity Principle in both texts, Hume turns in both the *Treatise* and the *Enquiry* to consider the origin and nature of our individual causal judgments. In contrast to any supposed arguments from either intuition or perception, he now argues

---

4. For recent discussions of Hume on the Causal Principle and the Uniformity Principle, see especially Waxman, *Hume's Theory of Consciousness*, 141–50, 173–91; Garrett, *Cognition and Commitment*, 82, 86–91, and 126–29; Wilson, *Hume's Defence of Causal Inference*, especially 70–84 and 140–93; and Dicker, *Hume's Epistemology and Metaphysics*, 73–89 and 133–53.

that we can only infer a causal relation between two objects through "EXPERI-
ENCE." This consists in our observation and memory, not merely of a single
instance of contiguity and succession between a pair of objects, but also of the
"CONSTANT CONJUNCTION" between many pairs of similar objects. Experience
in this sense, or repeated observation, leads us to expect objects of the second
type to follow objects of the first type in the future (T 1.3.6.2–3, 1.3.14.16–21
[SBN 87–88, 163–65]; cf. EHU 5.4, 11.30 [SBN 42, 148]; DNR 2.149). We thus
have "no other notion of cause and effect, but that of certain objects, which have
been *always conjoin'd* together," and this "constant conjunction" gives these and
similar objects "an union in the imagination," even though we cannot find any
reason for this regular connection beyond observation (T 1.3.6.15 [SBN 93];
cf. EHU 5.8–9 [SBN 46–47]).

Hume further argues that the experience of a constant conjunction between
similar sets of objects tends to give us, not only an idea of their conjunction,
but also a "belief," or expectation, that we will perceive conjunctions between
similar types of objects in the future. Our immediate impression of an object of
the first type therefore evokes, both an idea of an object of the second type, and
the expectation that an impression of an object of the second type will either
precede or follow our impression of the object of the first type, in the same order
as in our experience of similar pairs of objects in the past.

As we have seen in Chapter 1, Hume moves from characterizing "belief" as
a superior "force and vivacity" in our conception of particular ideas, to describing belief as a "peculiar *feeling* or *sentiment,*" and finally as a distinctive "manner" in which we conceive our ideas (T 1.3.7.1–8, T App.2 [SBN 93–98,
628–29, 623–24]; EHU 5.10–13 [SBN 47–50]). Whatever may be the best
description, he maintains that our belief in a causal relation between two
objects arises from the influence of a series of "past impressions and conjunctions" on the imagination. Since "we call every thing CUSTOM, which proceeds
from a past repetition, without any new reasoning or conclusion," Hume concludes "that all the belief, which follows upon any present impression, is deriv'd
solely from that origin" (T 1.3.8.10 [SBN 102]). In the *Enquiry* he maintains in
similar terms that all inferences from experience are derived from "CUSTOM or
HABIT," which produces "a propensity to renew the same act or operation,
without being impelled by any reasoning or process of the understanding" (EHU
5.5 [SBN 43]).

Next, Hume argues that custom, or the frequent observation of a conjunction between sets of resembling objects, acts upon the imagination to produce
a new impression of reflection, which he calls a "determination" of the mind.
Once we have repeatedly observed a similar conjunction between similar pairs of
objects, we discover that "upon the appearance of one of the objects, the mind is
determin'd by custom to consider its usual attendant," and to form the idea of this

usual attendant in the "stronger light" of our belief or expectation that an object of this type will follow the first object. Hume identifies this internal impression, or determination of the mind, as the impression which is the source of our idea of a necessary connection between a cause and its effect (T 1.3.14.1 [SBN 156]).

Finally, Hume observes that since the human mind has a tendency to "spread itself on external objects," or to project "any internal impressions, which they occasion" onto them, we generally suppose this necessity to lie "in the objects we consider, not in our mind" (T 1.3.14.25 [SBN 167]). In concluding his analysis, he maintains that "necessity is something, that exists in the mind, not in objects," and even that it is impossible for us "to form the most distant idea of it, consider'd as a quality in bodies" (T 1.3.14.22 [SBN 165–66]; cf. EHU 7.26–30 [SBN 73–79]).

Hume presents his analysis of causation especially in response to the attempts among both "antient and modern philosophers," including the Scholastics, the Cartesians, and Locke, to trace the "efficacy of causes" to a distinctive "power" or causal force, which is either found in matter itself, or imparted to matter by a divine being. These philosophers have referred to this type of force by a variety of synonymous terms, such as "*efficacy, agency, power, force, energy, necessity, connexion,* and *productive quality.*" In response, Hume argues that any "just idea" of such a force must arise from an impression of sensation, which would be distinctly given to us in the perception of objects. Since we do not directly perceive such powers when we observe causal conjunctions between objects, he concludes that these terms have been introduced "without any clear and determinate ideas," and then used to formulate circular definitions of each other (T 1.3.14.3–6, 1.3.14.14 [SBN 156–58, 162]; cf. A 26 [SBN 656–57]; EHU 7.29n17 [SBN 77–78n1]). On the other hand, he appears to distinguish this empty idea of a general power that operates in all instances of causation from the idea of a particular but unknown causal power in a natural object. This is seen in his further observation that "there may be several qualities both in material and immaterial objects, with which we are utterly unacquainted; and if we please to call these *power* or *efficacy,*" this choice of words will be "of little consequence to the world." However, if we attempt to use these terms to "signify something, of which we have a clear idea," we are "led astray by a false philosophy," as when we transfer "the determination of the thought to external objects, and suppose any real intelligible connexion betwixt them; that being a quality, which can only belong to the mind that considers them" (T 1.3.14.27 [SBN 168]).

Hume also anticipates an objection to his analysis of causation: the assertion that causal relations are "operations of nature" which must be "independent of our thought and reasoning." However, in response to this criticism he maintains that, according to his account, we repeatedly observe similar objects in similar relations of contiguity and succession to each other: objects and relations which are "independent of, and antecedent to the operations of the understanding." On the other hand, "if we go any farther, and ascribe a power or necessary connexion to these objects," we attribute a quality to them which we cannot derive from external observation, but only "from what we feel internally in contemplating them" (T 1.3.14.28 [SBN 168–69]).

Hume was obliged to answer several further misinterpretations of his account of causation through the course of his career. In 1745, during his unsuccessful candidacy for the chair of moral philosophy at the University of Edinburgh, he found himself charged with "opinions leading to *downright Atheism,* chiefly by denying this Principle, *That whatever begins to exist must have a Cause of Existence.*" He responded in his anonymously circulated *Letter from a Gentleman to his Friend in Edinburgh* by describing this charge, not only as an "extravagant" interpretation of his writings, but also as theologically misguided (LG 21–26). Similarly, in a letter of 1754 to John Stewart, he states that "I never asserted so absurd a Proposition as *that any thing might arise without a Cause:* I only maintain'd, that our Certainty of the Falshood of that Proposition proceeded neither from Intuition nor Demonstration; but from another Source" (L 1.187).

These debates with Hume over the objectivity and necessity of the causal relation have been echoed by more recent controversies over the interpretation of his argument. On the one hand, many commentators have held that Hume presents a regularity theory, in which he analyzes the causal relation as a constant conjunction between resembling objects while denying any objective causal powers to objects in nature, and then supplements this theory with a separate psychological theory of the origin of our concept of causation.[5] On the other hand, Hume's theory of causation has also been regarded as a subjective version of the necessity theory, in which causal relations are distinguished from accidental regularities by a distinctive type of necessity, which, however, is found only in the mind, as an impression arising from the repeated observation of a conjunction between similar objects.[6] In contrast to this disjunction, Beauchamp and Rosenberg have argued that Hume combines a regularity theory with a modified necessity theory in what he intends to be a single and unified theory of causation.[7] This debate turns especially upon various possible interpretations

5. See especially Robinson, "Hume's Two Definitions of 'Cause,'" 129–47, and Mackie, *Cement of the Universe,* 3–28. For discussions of this interpretation, see Beauchamp and Rosenberg, *Hume and the Problem of Causation,* 13–24; Wilson, *Hume's Defence of Causal Inference,* 12–13; and Dicker, *Hume's Epistemology and Metaphysics,* 110–32.

6. See Church, *Hume's Theory of the Understanding,* 81–85; Kemp Smith, *Philosophy of David Hume,* 91–92; and Stroud, *Hume,* 88–92. See also Beauchamp and Rosenberg, *Hume and the Problem of Causation,* 10, 13, and 25–28.

7. Beauchamp and Rosenberg, *Hume and the Problem of Causation,* 3–32. See also Garrett, *Cognition and Commitment,* 76–117; Wilson, *Hume's Defence of Causal Inference,* 11–22 and 33–41; and Falkenstein, "Hume's Answer to Kant," 331–60.

of Hume's concluding two definitions of a cause, and thus of the causal relation, which I will consider below. Finally, several recent studies have sought to argue that Hume is a causal realist, who attributes objective causal powers to objects even while conceding that we might not be able to formulate any adequate idea of these powers.[8] We will consider Hume's apparent attribution of "secret powers" to natural objects in a later section of this chapter.

At the end of Section 14 Hume returns to his original problem in Book 1, Part 3 of the *Treatise*, which is to provide "an exact definition of the relation of cause and effect." However, since we may consider causation "either as a *philosophical* or as a *natural* relation," he argues that we may formulate two definitions of a cause, which differ only by "presenting a different view of the same object" (T 1.3.14.30–31 [SBN 169–70]). He then presents his two definitions, which we may refer to respectively as the "philosophical" and the "natural" definition of a cause. The first to be stated by Hume is the philosophical definition, which he formulates in the following terms: "We may define a CAUSE to be 'An object precedent and contiguous to another, and where all the objects resembling the former are plac'd in like relations of precedency and contiguity to those objects, that resemble the latter.'" He then presents the natural definition of a cause: "A CAUSE is an object precedent and contiguous to another, and so united with it, that the idea of the one determines the mind to form the idea of the other, and the impression of the one to form a more lively idea of the other" (T 1.3.14.31; cf. 1.3.14.35 [SBN 170; cf. 172]).

In the *Enquiry* Hume presents a modified restatement of these definitions without any explicit reference to the distinction between natural and philosophical relations, and adding to his first definition the otherwise unexplained counterfactual condition that "where, if the first object had not been, the second never had existed" (EHU 7.29 [SBN 76–77]).[9]

Hume's philosophical definition thus apparently reduces causation to a set of relations between objects, while his natural definition apparently reduces causation to an impression in the mind, which is produced by the imagination as a result of certain types of observations. In other words, Hume appears to distinguish between an objective conception of causation, as a relation between pairs of objects which are regularly conjoined with each other in space and time; and a subjective conception of causation, in which the impression of one object determines the mind to expect the other (T 2.3.2.4 [SBN 409]).

8. See Wright, *Sceptical Realism,* 2–3 and 123–86; Strawson, *Secret Connexion,* 1–5 and 10–15; and Costa, "Hume and Causal Inference," 141–59, and "Hume and Causal Realism," 172–90. See also Livingston, *Hume's Philosophy of Common Life,* 155–67. For a critical response to this interpretation, see Winkler, "The New Hume," 52–87, and Waxman, *Hume's Theory of Consciousness,* 191–99. See also the essays in Read and Richman, *The New Hume Debate.*

9. For a discussion of Hume's view of the counterfactual implications of causal statements, and various approaches to this in the literature, see Wilson, *Hume's Defence of Causal Inference,* 17–18.

Many commentators have sought to assess these two proposed definitions of causation, and to determine their relation to each other.[10] For example, J. A. Robinson observes that these definitions are neither equivalent in meaning nor coextensive in their domain, and then argues that Hume intended only the first of these to be his genuine definition of a cause: a view which seems to support the interpretation of Hume's analysis as a regularity theory of causation.[11] However, others such as Church and Waxman have argued that Hume intended the second formulation to be his actual definition of a cause, which would seem to support the modified necessity theory.[12]

We may evaluate these proposals by returning to Hume's characterization of the two types of relations. As we have seen, in Part 1 he characterizes a natural relation as a principle of association among our ideas, and a philosophical relation as a principle of comparison which may be applied to our ideas even without the preliminary mediation of a spontaneous association (T 1.1.5.1 [SBN 13]).[13] In applying this distinction to his analysis of causation, Hume states that although causation is indeed "a *philosophical* relation, as implying contiguity, succession, and constant conjunction," it is only "so far as it is a *natural* relation, and produces an union among our ideas, that we are able to reason upon it, or draw any inference from it" (T 1.3.6.16; cf. 1.1.5.9 [SBN 94; cf. 15]). Hume therefore maintains that the very possibility of formulating any particular causal inferences, according to the definition of causation as a philosophical relation, depends on our disposition to regard certain sets of objects as joined by a necessary connection, and to believe that these objects will continue to appear together in that order. This disposition is derived from a habit produced by the repeated observation of such conjunctions between similar pairs of objects, as indicated in the definition of causation as a natural relation.

I conclude that Hume's two definitions should be regarded as descriptions of two aspects of any genuine and recognized causal relation: a subjective disposition to conceive of objects which are given under certain conditions as related in a certain manner, and an objective set of relations among objects that tends to give rise to this disposition when it is observed. Hume's two definitions must

10. See Robinson, "Hume's Two Definitions of 'Cause,'" 129–47; Richards, "Hume's Two Definitions," 148–61; Hausman, "Hume's Theory of Relations," 255–82; Robison, "Hume's Causal Scepticism," 156–66; Stroud, *Hume*, 88–92; Beauchamp and Rosenberg, *Hume and the Problem of Causation*, 3–32; Waxman, *Hume's Theory of Consciousness*, 83–84 and 185–86; Wilson, *Hume's Defence of Causal Inference*, 12–17; Garrett, *Cognition and Commitment*, 96–117 and 250 n. 5; and Dicker, *Hume's Epistemology and Metaphysics*, 110–16.

11. Robinson, "Hume's Two Definitions of 'Cause,'" 129–47; Mackie, *Cement of the Universe*, 3–4; Dicker, *Hume's Epistemology and Metaphysics*, 114–15.

12. See Church, *Hume's Theory of the Understanding*, 81–86, and Waxman, *Hume's Theory of Consciousness*, 185–86. See also Beauchamp and Rosenberg, *Hume and the Problem of Causation*, 16.

13. A valuable account of the Hume's two definitions of a cause and of the various possible interpretations of his argument is provided by Garrett in his *Cognition and Commitment*, 96–101.

therefore be combined in order to produce his complete analysis of the concept of a cause.[14]

There are a number of grounds in Hume's writings, both explicit and implicit, for regarding his two definitions of a cause as two parts of a complete definition. In the *Treatise* he introduces his two definitions by stating his intention to present an "exact" or a "precise definition of cause and effect," and also maintains that his two definitions differ only by providing "a different view of the same object" (T 1.3.14.30–31 [SBN 169–70]). In the *Enquiry* he offers his two definitions as the products of two types of "experience," one looking outward and the other inward (EHU 7.29; cf. 8.27 [SBN 76–77; cf. 97]). The most compelling implicit reason for regarding these two formulations as parts of a complete definition is that, while the separate definitions are neither equivalent nor coextensive, the definition that is produced by combining them designates the set of genuine causes that are also recognized by a human observer. This combined definition then provides the standard by which any other supposed causes are to be judged. Taken in itself, the first definition of a cause reflects our ability to form the concept of causation as a relation that subsists between two objects apart from the human mind, but does not account for our ability to recognize any particular causal relation. On the other hand, the second definition of a cause, when considered in isolation, also applies to any objects which we mistakenly regard as causes, in what Hume himself calls our "unphilosophical" judgments of causation (cf. T 1.3.13.1–20 [SBN 143–55]).

When considered separately, Hume's two definitions may be applied respectively to any supposed unobserved causes on the one hand, and to spurious causes on the other. Neither of these, according to Hume's view, can be described as a cause in the most accurate and complete sense. However, these two definitions may be combined to produce a definition of a genuine and humanly recognized cause: An object of a given type whose instances are constantly conjoined in space and followed in time by an object of another type; in a series of conjunctions which, through repeated observations, determine the mind of a human observer to expect that any object of the first type will be similarly conjoined with an object of the second type. I would suggest that this definition, which designates the intersection of the domains that are circumscribed by Hume's two definitions, represents the "exact definition of a cause" which is never explicitly stated in his discussion, but appears to be its implicit conclusion.[15]

14. Two further and more extensive attempts to reconstruct Hume's theory of causation from these two definitions are presented by Beauchamp and Rosenberg in *Hume and the Problem of Causation*, and by Wilson in *Hume's Defence of Causal Inference*.

15. For related arguments, see also Garrett, *Cognition and Commitment*, 98–99, and Stroud, *Hume*, 88–94. However, Garrett also argues that Hume's two definitions may both be interpreted objectively or subjectively, and are thus coextensive as long as they are considered according to the same interpretation: see *Cognition and Commitment*, 109.

Hume's two definitions, understood as parts of a complete definition of a cause, may also be regarded as indicating the several stages in the development of this concept in the human mind. First, the regular observation of a conjunction between objects produces a determination of the mind to expect instances of one to follow instances of the other. Next, the mind notices the relations of resemblance, contiguity, and succession between these objects by reflecting upon the sources of this determination in its remembered observations. Finally, the mind comes to regard these objective relations as the standard for its judgments of causation, and as the guiding principle of empirical explanation. Thus, our ability to identify the set of relations that constitute a cause, according to the philosophical definition, is derived from an associative tendency of the mind as indicated by natural definition, although the mind can reverse this order by recognizing that our disposition to regard various objects as causally related arises from our observation of certain relations between them, which it then regards as existing prior to and apart from its own activity. The philosophical definition of causation is therefore a statement of the observable set of relations between objects whose repeated appearances are the source of our natural causal associations, and also states the standard by which we may evaluate our judgments concerning causal relations once we have observed or supposed a conjunction between any two objects.[16] I will examine Hume's further account of the relative assessment and justification of our causal judgments in the next section of this chapter.

Although the word "custom" occupies a central place in Hume's account of the causal relation and of our causal judgments, it has received little direct attention in the secondary literature. I will therefore conclude this section by considering several of his further references to custom, before proceeding to his account of probable reasoning.

In Book 1 of the *Treatise* and in the first *Enquiry* Hume uses the word "custom," often interchangeably with "habit," for an acquired disposition of thought in the individual mind. He thus observes that contiguity influences the imagination "by long custom" (T 1.1.4.2 [SBN 11]), and that we may develop the "custom" of applying the same word to a number of resembling images (T 1.1.7.7–11 [SBN 20–22]). In his analysis of causation he argues that our inferences from an object to its cause or effect are "not determin'd by reason, but by custom or a principle of association," since we may call "every thing CUSTOM, which proceeds from a past repetition, without any new reasoning or

---

16. I agree here with Waxman that Hume's philosophical relation of causation is parasitic upon the natural relation, although I would also argue that once the philosophical conception of causation is derived from reflection upon the natural relation of causation, it may then be used to guide us in reconstructing the sources of our particular causal inferences, and even in discovering other causal relations. See Waxman, *Hume's Theory of Consciousness*, 83–84 and 185–86.

conclusion" (T 1.3.7.6, 1.3.8.10 [SBN 97, 102]). In the *Abstract* he adds that "we are determined by CUSTOM alone to suppose the future conformable to the past" (A 15 [SBN 652]). Similarly, in the *Enquiry* he argues that causal inferences are derived from "CUSTOM or HABIT," and that inferences from experience "are effects of custom, not of reasoning" (EHU 5.5 [SBN 43]). He thus maintains that our idea of any particular causal relation, our belief in the Causal Principle or the necessity of causation in general, and our belief in the Uniformity Principle or that the future will resemble the past, are ultimately all derived from a custom or disposition of the mind which is instilled by repeated experience.

Many of Hume's critics have found his assertions concerning the role of custom in our causal inferences to be skeptical, dismissive, and even despairing. For example, G. E. Moore attributes to Hume the view that we have "no better foundation than custom for any conclusion whatever as to facts which we have not observed" and asks if we can be said "really to *know* any fact, for which we have no better foundation than this?" Similarly, Kemp Smith denounces the "excessive emphasis upon custom" in the first book of the *Treatise,* and asks how Hume can justify his apparent distinction between the vulgar and the wise if "custom is king" in all matters of fact, although he later attributes to Hume the view that experience and reflection rather than custom are the ultimate arbiters in our causal judgments. Finally, Karl Popper argues that Hume's reduction of discoveries in the natural sciences to "custom" or "habit" is an unacceptable view, since on the contrary "We do not act upon repetition or 'habit,' but upon the best tested of our theories," which we accept for "good rational reasons."[17]

As we will see in the next section of the present chapter, these criticisms have overlooked Hume's account of philosophical probable reasoning, in which he considers the constructive role of custom in forming the rules for probable reasoning. Before turning to this discussion, however, we may consider several of his additional references to the operation of "custom" in our causal judgments, to see that these are neither uniformly dismissive nor even very pessimistic in their assessment of our ability to pursue causal inferences.

In the *Treatise* Hume observes that the human mind initially develops "a kind of system" from "impressions or ideas of the memory," such that "every particular of that system," when "join'd to the present impressions, we are pleas'd to call a *reality.*" However, once the mind is able to connect its ideas "by custom, or if you will, by the relation of cause or effect," it develops "a new system, which it likewise dignifies with the title of *realities.*" While the first system is "the object of the memory and senses," the second system is the object of judgment, in which the range of our cognition is extended "beyond the reach

17. Moore, "Hume's Philosophy," 356; Kemp Smith, *Philosophy of David Hume,* 387 and 95; cf. 382–88 and 539–40; and Popper, *Objective Knowledge,* 91 and 95.

of the senses and memory" to the historical past and to distant parts of the universe (T 1.3.9.3–4 [SBN 108]). In the first *Enquiry* he praises custom as "the great guide of human life," which alone "renders our experience useful to us," since without its influence "we should be entirely ignorant of every matter of fact, beyond what is immediately present to the memory and senses," and would never learn "how to adjust means to ends," or how to use our natural abilities in order to produce any effects. Without custom we would thus reach "an end at once of all action, as well as of the chief part of speculation" (EHU 5.6 [SBN 44–45]; cf. A 16 [SBN 652]). Finally, in his index to the *Enquiry* he characterizes "Custom or Habit" both as "the Source of experimental Reasoning" and as "the great Guide of Life" (EHU Ind.308).[18]

These passages indicate Hume's own assessment of the constructive role of custom in our experimental or scientific reasoning. We will explore his justification for this positive assessment of custom in the next section by considering his account of philosophical probable reasoning.

PHILOSOPHICAL PROBABLE REASONING

Hume's analysis of causation is initially presented within his discussion of "probability," which he develops especially in Sections 11–13 and 15 of Book 1, Part 3 of the *Treatise* (cf. T 1.3.1.1, 1.3.2.1 [SBN 69, 73]), and reaffirms, though perhaps less directly, in his later writings. In this discussion Hume considers the principles of experimental or scientific reasoning, not only as a part of his theoretical philosophy, but also as the basis for his account of the methodological principles of the various empirical disciplines he considers elsewhere in his writings.

Hume embarks upon this topic in the *Treatise* by noting that other philosophers have divided the activities of human cognition into the "comparison of ideas" and "arguments from causes or effects," and have identified this distinction as the difference between "knowledge and probability" (T 1.3.11.2; cf. 1.3.1.1 [SBN 124; cf. 69]). However, he then proposes to add a further distinction between various levels of assurance in our judgments concerning matters of fact, since "in common discourse we readily affirm, that many arguments from causation exceed probability, and may be receiv'd as a superior kind of evidence." For example, it would appear ridiculous to say "that 'tis only probable the sun will rise to-morrow, or that all men must dye," although we indeed have "no farther assurance of these facts, than what experience affords us." As

---

18. In this index entry and the other passages cited here, Hume echoes Butler's description of probability as "the very guide of life," in Butler's introduction to his *Analogy of Religion*, xlix. See also Connon, "Naturalism of Hume Revisited," 142.

we have seen, Hume has already reserved the words "knowledge" and "certainty" for "the assurance arising from the comparison of ideas." He now suggests that we distinguish between "proofs" and "probabilities," in order to indicate the "several degrees of evidence" in our causal judgments. First, he applies the word "proof" to any judgments concerning causes and effects which are "entirely free from doubt and uncertainty," even though these judgments arise in the same way as causal judgments which we regard with less assurance.[19] Next, he recommends that we should apply the word "probability" to any causal judgments which are "still attended with uncertainty." Finally, he recommends a further distinction between the "probability of chances," or the relative likelihood of any given outcome in a random series of events from a specified range of possibilities, and the "probability of causes," or causal reasonings which have not yet attained the level of a proof (T 1.3.11.1–2, 1.3.12.1 [SBN 124–25, 130]). Hume occasionally refers to our judgments concerning the probability of causes as "probable reasonings" (T 1.3.6.6, 1.3.8.12, 1.3.14.17; cf. 1.3.9.19n22 [SBN 89, 103, 163; cf. 117n1 and 371n1]).[20] I will accordingly adopt this phrase to characterize his account of causal reasoning, since we are now more likely to use the term "probability" for what he calls the "probability of chances."[21]

After a brief discussion of the probability of chances, which we have already considered in Chapter 2, Hume turns in the *Treatise* to his more sustained discussion of the different degrees of assurance which attend our causal judgments. First, drawing upon his preceding account of causation, he argues that since the "habit" which produces our idea of a particular causal relation arises from the "frequent conjunction of objects," the idea of a particular causal relation acquires an increased force "from each instance, that falls under our observation." In other words, while a single observed conjunction between two objects may have "little or no force," each observation of a conjunction between similar objects strengthens our idea of the causal relation between them, leading our judgment through "several inferior degrees" of "presumption or probability," until it may eventually arrive at the "full assurance" of a proof (T 1.3.12.2 [SBN 130–31]).

19. For the use of the word "proof" in seventeen- and eighteenth-century English in a variety of contexts, including law and historical scholarship, see Gower, "Hume on Probability," 4n6, and Shapiro, *Probability and Certainty*, 173–75.

20. Hume moved and expanded the footnote cited here in a page added to the *Treatise* after printing and before binding. See Norton and Norton's notes to the relevant passages in the Oxford Philosophical Texts edition of the *Treatise* (T 1.3.9.19n22, 2.2.7.6), and Norton and Norton, "Substantive Differences," 252.

21. Hacking suggests that Hume's contribution to the history of probability is limited to his statement of the "sceptical problem of induction." In this study I have indicated that Hume also distinguishes between statistical calculation and inductive reasoning; and that he considers what Hacking calls the "analytical problem of induction" concerning the evaluation of evidence. See Hacking, *Emergence of Probability*, 176–85, and "Hume's Species of Probability," 21–37.

A perfectly uniform experience would lead us directly, through a series of resembling observations, to this complete assurance. However, Hume finds that we are frequently confronted by an "imperfect experience," or an experience in which "one observation is contrary to another" and "causes and effects follow not in the same order," or in which the resemblance is weak and amounts only to an "ANALOGY" (T 1.3.12.3–4, 1.3.12.25 [SBN 130–31, 142]). In the case of contrary causes, we find that while indeed "fire has always burned, and water suffocated every human creature" according to universal laws which have never admitted any exceptions, other causes appear "more irregular and uncertain." We thus find that rhubarb has neither "always proved a purge, or opium a soporific to every one, who has taken these medicines" (EHU 6.4 [SBN 57–58]). The unreflective or "vulgar" observer might attribute such a contrariety to some irregular or eccentric behavior in the cause. However, since philosophers recognize that there might still be a "vast variety of springs and principles, which are hid, by reason of their minuteness or remoteness," they are prepared to attribute such inconsistencies to the "secret operation of contrary causes" (T 1.3.12.5 [SBN 132]). Whatever its source, however, this inconsistency in our experience undermines the assurance of our judgment, and diminishes our belief in a causal relation between the two objects. A series of observations often presents us with cases of both similarity and "contrariety," and belief is a "compounded effect" arising from the superior strength and vivacity of the accumulated consistent evidence as opposed to the contrary evidence, arising from "all the different events, in the same proportion as they have appeared in the past" (T 1.3.12.3, 1.3.12.14–18 [SBN 131, 135–37]; EHU 6.4 [SBN 58–59]). Similarly, the experience of only a few examples of resembling conjunctions, or a series of conjunctions with only a weak resemblance to each other, confers less vivacity upon our idea of a causal connection between the objects (T 1.3.12.2, 1.3.12.24 [SBN 130–31, 142]). On the other hand, we attain a "proof" when the conjunction between events "is found by experience to be perfectly constant," and when the object "exactly resembles those, of which we have had experience" (T 1.3.13.19 [SBN 153]). These three imperfections of limitation, contrariety, and dissimilarity in our experience produce the various levels of belief, and the corresponding gradations between proofs and probabilities, in our judgments concerning matters of fact.

After this account of the conditions that determine the different degrees of assurance in our probable reasoning, Hume considers the justification of our causal judgments, or the process by which we distinguish between "philosophical" and "unphilosophical" forms of probable reasoning. This appears especially in his account of general rules, and their role in our causal judgments.[22]

---

22. The importance of "general rules" in Hume's philosophy has been especially emphasized by Hearn in "General Rules in Hume's *Treatise*," 405–22, and "General Rules and the Moral Sentiments," 57–72. See

In this crucial discussion, Hume observes that certain types of probable reasoning are considered by philosophers to be "reasonable foundations of belief and opinion," and suggests that we may accordingly distinguish between "philosophical" and "unphilosophical" forms of probable reasoning (T 1.3.13.1–20 [SBN 143–54]; cf. EHU 10.4 [SBN 110]; DNR 2.147). We are engaged in "unphilosophical" probable reasoning whenever we are influenced by circumstances that tend to diminish the force and vivacity of our idea of the cause, as this would be indicated by the philosophical definition of a cause; or whenever the idea of another object is allowed to exercise a relatively greater influence on our imagination (T 1.3.13.1–20; cf. 1.2.5.21 [SBN 143–54; cf. 60–62]). For example, we may find ourselves making unphilosophical probable judgments "when we have not observ'd a sufficient number of instances, to produce a strong habit; or when these instances are contrary to each other; or when the resemblance is not exact, or the present impression is faint and obscure; or the experience in some measure obliterated from the memory; or the connexion dependent on a long chain of objects" (T 1.3.13.19 [SBN 154]).

Among the "unphilosophical species" of probable reasoning, Hume includes reasoning from "*general rules,* which we rashly form to ourselves, and which are the source of what we properly call PREJUDICE." For example, the opinion among his British contemporaries that "an *Irishman* cannot have wit, and a *Frenchman* cannot have solidity" had attained such force that, "tho' the conversation of the former in any instance be visibly very agreeable, and of the latter very judicious, we have entertain'd such a prejudice against them, that they must be dunces or fops in spite of sense and reason" (T 1.3.13.7 [SBN 146–47]).

On the other hand, Hume also argues that general rules play a central role in our causal judgments, and that even these hasty generalizations proceed "from those very principles, on which all judgments concerning causes and effects depend." As we have seen, all of our causal judgments arise from a custom in the mind, produced by repeated observations of a conjunction between similar sets of objects. This custom then receives cognitive expression in our implicit or explicit formulation of a general rule affirming the regular conjunction between objects or events of these types. However, in observing a series of conjunctions we often find "a complication of circumstances, of which some are essential, and others superfluous," and the latter often exercise a greater influence than the former over the imagination (T 1.3.13.8–9 [SBN 147–48]).

Hume argues that we may correct our propensity to regard a more immediate and vivid object as the cause of an event, in place of the cause that would be indicated by his philosophical definition, through "a reflection on the nature

---

also Vanterpool, "Hume's Account of General Rules," 481–92, and Brand, *Hume's Theory of Moral Judgment,* 38–65.

of those circumstances." Indeed, these reflections lead us to formulate a set of general rules "by which we ought to regulate our judgment concerning causes and effects," based upon what we discover about "the nature of our understanding, and on our experience of its operations in the judgments we form concerning objects." These rules allow us to distinguish "accidental circumstances from the efficacious causes," so that, for example, if we find that an effect "can be produc'd without the concurrence of any particular circumstance," we conclude that this circumstance is not part of the cause, "however frequently conjoin'd with it." In other words, we may evaluate the rash impulses of our imagination by appealing to "the more general and authentic operations of the understanding," which we recognize and codify as the "establish'd principles of reasoning." Hume concludes that while general rules may often lead us into "a very unphilosophical species of probability," it is only by following other general rules "that we can correct this, and all other unphilosophical probabilities" and instead engage in the philosophical or scientific form of probable reasoning (T 1.3.13.9–12 [SBN 147–50]).

Hume therefore argues that the human mind tends to codify the customary associations arising from its repeated experience of similar conjunctions by forming general rules concerning these conjunctions, and tends to be guided by these rules in its expectation of future conjunctions. In this view, the difference between unphilosophical and philosophical probable reasoning arises neither from the influence of general rules in the former but not in the latter case, since general rules are required for all of our causal reasonings, nor from the influence of custom in the former but not in the latter case, since "all reasonings are nothing but the effects of custom" (T 1.3.13.11 [SBN 149]). Instead, philosophical probable reasoning itself arises from custom, although in an "*oblique* and *artificial* manner," through our formulation of the rules, or methodological principles, which enable us to "reason with knowledge and reflection" from our past experience in our own causal judgments (T 1.3.8.14, 1.3.12.13 [SBN 104–5, 135]). Accordingly, the philosophical standards of causal judgment are themselves generalizations from experience, or rules that we formulate and prescribe to ourselves in order to guide our reasonings and counteract the effects of prejudice and other unphilosophical forms of causal judgment.

Finally, Hume completes his account of philosophical probable reasoning in Section 15, by suggesting that since it is possible for all objects to be causes or effects of each other, "it may be proper to fix some general rules, by which we may know when they really are so," and then offering his own list of "Rules by which to judge of causes and effects" (T 1.3.15.1–2; cf. 1.3.13.11 [SBN 173; cf. 149]).

Hume presents eight principles for judging causes and effects. Four of these are already indicated by his philosophical definition of a cause, arising from our reflection upon causation as a natural principle of association. Of these, the first two state the conditions of each individual conjunction: (1) "The cause and effect must be contiguous in space and time," and (2) "The cause must be prior to the effect." The third and fourth rules specify the conditions of a repeated conjunction and a resemblance between the pairs of objects: (3) "There must be a constant union betwixt the cause and effect," followed by (4) "The same cause always produces the same effect, and the same effect never arises but from the same cause." The fifth and sixth rules guide us in applying the first four to those cases in which we discover an inexact resemblance between the objects, by directing us to trace any similarities or differences between their effects to specific properties in these objects. Accordingly, (5) "where several different objects produce the same effect, it must be by means of some quality, which we discover to be common amongst them," while (6) "The difference in the effects of two resembling objects must proceed from that particular, in which they differ." Finally, in the seventh and eighth rules Hume directs us to trace any change in an object, or in its effects, to a concurrence between several causes. Thus (7) "When any object encreases or diminishes with the encrease or diminution of its cause," we should regard this as a "compounded effect" produced by a combination of effects arising from different parts of the cause; while (8) "an object, which exists for any time in its full perfection without any effect" should not be regarded as the "sole cause of that effect," but must be assisted by "some other principle, which may forward its influence and operation" (T 1.3.15.3–10 [SBN 173–74]).[23]

Accordingly, in Rules 1 through 3 Hume prescribes the conditions of temporal succession and spatial contiguity as principles for judging causal relations; while in 4 to 7 he prescribes the principle of resemblance, and also analyzes partial resemblances between objects as resemblances between their qualities, further directing us to consider these resembling qualities and their regular conjunctions in order to improve the accuracy of our causal judgments.

As we have seen, Hume identifies resemblance both as a natural principle of association among our ideas, and as a philosophical relation by which we may compare ideas (T 1.1.4.1–2, 1.1.5.2–3 [SBN 11, 14]). He also regards the natural disposition to recognize resemblances as the source of our ability to form abstract ideas, including distinctions of reason (T 1.1.7.7–18 [SBN 20–25]). In his account of our idea of causation, he presents the natural disposition to recognize resemblances as the basis for our further ability to develop the custom of expecting one object to follow another object (T 1.3.6.1–7 [SBN 86–90]; EHU 4.14–23 [SBN 32–39]). However, he also notes that superficial resemblances are

---

23. For a further discussion of Hume's rules for judging causes and effects, see Wilson, *Hume's Defence of Causal Inference*, especially 33–75, and Falkenstein, "Naturalism, Normativity, and Scepticism," 29–72.

an obvious source of unphilosophical probable reasoning; and therefore describes resemblance as the most fertile source of errors and mistaken reasonings among the three principles of association (T 1.2.5.21; cf. 1.3.13.9–11 [SBN 61; cf. 147–49]).

In his rules for judging causes and effects Hume accordingly prescribes several principles intended to facilitate the evaluation of resemblances in our causal judgments. In Rule 4 he directs us to extend our judgments concerning causal relations from objects we have observed to other objects "of the same kind." However, in Rules 5 and 6 he considers the many cases in which the resemblance between objects is not exact, and directs us to trace any similarities or differences among their effects to those particular qualities in which they resemble or differ from each other (T 1.3.15.7–8 [SBN 173–74]). He therefore indicates that scientific inquiry may attempt to discover the causal capacities in objects, if these are regarded as observable qualities which are correlated with observable effects, rather than as the hidden and unknown sources of this correlation (cf. EHU 4.20–21 [SBN 36–38]).

Hume's account of resemblance and its role in philosophical probable reasoning is also reflected in the many references to analogical reasoning in his writings. In the *Treatise* he argues that although an exact resemblance between objects is the most effective basis for judging causal relations, we may also accept the "probability deriv'd from analogy" if we recognize that "the reasoning becomes proportionably more or less firm and certain" according to the degrees of resemblance (T 1.3.12.25; cf. 1.3.13.8 [SBN 142; cf. 147]). In the *Enquiry* he includes analogy, along with observation and experience, among the principles of reasoning used in the natural sciences. Indeed, he notes in this text that all causal reasonings "are founded on a species of ANALOGY," and are improved in their evidential force "in proportion to the degree of similarity and resemblance" (EHU 4.12, 9.1 [SBN 30, 104]). Finally, in the *Dialogues Concerning Natural Religion* Hume develops a sustained examination of analogical reasoning, especially through the discussion between Cleanthes and Philo. In Part 2 Philo argues that we cannot suppose that the divine perfections have "any analogy or likeness to the perfections of a human creature," while Cleanthes claims to argue "by all the rules of analogy . . . that the Author of nature is somewhat similar to the mind of man." Philo then states, as a general principle, that whenever we depart from an exact resemblance between the objects, we also "diminish proportionably the evidence; and may at last bring it to a very weak *analogy*, which is confessedly liable to error and uncertainty" (DNR 2.142–44). Through the rest of the *Dialogues* Philo then attempts to show that the defense of philosophical theism by Cleanthes rests upon an imperfect analogy, which does not convey a very high degree of probability to his conclusion (DNR 2.150–53, 6.170–72, 7.180, 12.216–19; cf. EHU 11.1–30 [SBN 132–48]).

In presenting his eight rules for judging causes and effects, Hume therefore indicates that the philosophical form of probable reasoning is characterized by extensive observations, accurate judgments of contiguity and succession, acuity in recognizing resemblances and in distinguishing between the qualities of resembling objects, and the ability to develop consistent generalizations concerning the effects arising from these qualities (cf. T 1.3.13.8–12 [SBN 147–50]; EHU 4.11–12, 9.5n20 [SBN 30, 107n1]).

Hume concludes his examination of the rules for causal reasoning with a declaration that "here is all the LOGIC I think proper to employ in my reasoning," adding however that this list might not be necessary for his readers, "but might have been supply'd by the natural principles of our understanding." He recommends these rules for both natural and moral philosophy, although he also notes that while these rules are "very easy in their invention," they may also be "extremely difficult in their application," especially in the moral or human sciences, "where there is a much greater complication of circumstances," and the "views and sentiments, which are essential to any action of the mind" are especially difficult to discover (T 13.15.11 [SBN 175]).

In the introduction to the *Treatise* Hume observes that "the sole end of logic is to explain the principles and operations of our reasoning faculty, and the nature of our ideas," and identifies "*Logic, Morals, Criticism,* and *Politics*" as the main projected topics of the *Treatise* (T Int.5; cf. Adv.1 [SBN xv–xvi; cf. xii]). In this context, "logic" appears to include the general study of human cognition, as well as the study of the principles of cognitive justification. In the *Abstract* Hume presents a clearer view of his project in Book 1 of the *Treatise*, as contributing to the discussion of "logic" among contemporary European philosophers, including an account of the principles of empirical justification:

> The celebrated *Monsieur Leibnitz* has observed it to be a defect in the common systems of logic, that they are very copious when they explain the operations of the understanding in the forming of demonstrations, but are too concise when they treat of probabilities, and those other measures of evidence on which life and action entirely depend, and which are our guides even in most of our philosophical speculations. In this censure, he comprehends *The Essay concerning Human Understanding, Le Recherche de la verité,* and *L'Art de penser.* The author of the *Treatise of Human Nature* seems to have been sensible of this defect in these philosophers, and has endeavoured, as much as he can, to supply it. (A 4; cf. 28 [SBN 646–47; cf. 657])

Hume is therefore deliberately following a new contemporary usage by applying the word "logic" to the principles of experimental or scientific reasoning.

He also indicates in this passage from the *Abstract* that he is presenting his account of the principles of probable reasoning in order to fill a recognized need in contemporary philosophy, a need that had not yet been satisfied by Locke, Malebranche, the Port Royal *Logic,* by Leibniz himself, or by any eighteenth-century author.[24] Hume's account of philosophical probable reasoning may thus be regarded as a contribution to the ongoing discussion of probability and scientific reasoning among his predecessors and contemporaries.[25]

Hume's account of the rules for judging causes and effects also belongs to the history of British reflection concerning the principles of scientific method. Their most direct antecedents are Newton's four "Rules of Reasoning in Philosophy," stating the principles of simplicity, analogy, generalization, and observation.[26] Hume indeed paraphrases the second of these rules, formulated by Newton as "to the same natural effects we must, as far as possible, assign the same causes," not only as his fourth rule for judging causes and effects in the *Treatise,* but also in the second *Enquiry* as "where any principle has been found to have a great force and energy in one instance, to ascribe to it a like energy in all similar instances," which he identifies here as "NEWTON'S chief rule of philosophizing" (EPM 3.48 [SBN 204]).[27] In its turn, Hume's list anticipates Herschel's account of the principles of scientific reasoning and Mill's canons of induction, although Hume's list was not as well known or as influential as theirs.[28]

Hume's account of philosophical probable reasoning in the *Treatise* is also reflected and developed elsewhere in his philosophical writings, and indeed provides the basis for his "system of the sciences," by setting forth the principles of investigation which apply to all of the natural and human sciences (T Int.6 [SBN xvi]).

In the *Treatise* itself, Hume initially announces his intention to apply the method of "experimental philosophy," which had been developed in natural philosophy or the natural sciences, to "moral subjects." In both the natural and the moral sciences, this method involves observing the variety of effects arising from objects in "different circumstances and situations," using "careful and exact experiments," and then endeavoring "to render all our principles as

24. Hume is referring here to the "Preliminary Dissertation" in the *Theodicy:* see Leibniz, *Philosophischen Schriften,* 6: 67–68 (§28 and §31), and *Theodicy,* 90 and 92. In England, Joseph Butler described probability in 1736 as a part of "the subject of Logic" that "has not yet been thoroughly considered." See Butler, *Analogy of Religion,* 1.

25. For histories of this discussion, see Van Leeuwen, *Problem of Certainty;* Hacking, *Emergence of Probability;* Shapiro, *Probability and Certainty;* Ferreira, *Scepticism and Reasonable Doubt;* Daston, *Classical Probability;* and Franklin, *Science of Conjecture.*

26. Newton, *Mathematical Principles of Natural Philosophy,* 2: 398–400.

27. See Force, "Hume's Interest in Newton and Science," 166–216.

28. Laird, *Hume's Philosophy of Human Nature,* 143. See also Blake, Ducasse, and Madden, *Theories of Scientific Method,* 144–52, and Buchdahl, *Metaphysics and the Philosophy of Science,* 325–87.

universal as possible, by tracing up our experiments to the utmost, and explaining all effects from the simplest and fewest causes" (T Int.7–8 [SBN xvi–xvii]). Hume's account of philosophical probable reasoning is also reflected in the set of "corollaries" to his two definitions of a cause, in which he states, for example, that all causes are of the same kind, and that there is no distinction between moral and physical necessity (T 1.3.14.32–36 [SBN 170–72]). He also implicitly affirms this analysis in the concluding sections of both Books 1 and 2 of the *Treatise*, where he defends the principles of critical reflection against both skepticism and dogmatism (T 1.4.7.12–15, 2.3.10.1–12 [SBN 270–73, 448–54]).

In the first *Enquiry* Hume offers a shortened account of probability in Section 6, without any direct consideration of the rules for judging causes and effects (EHU 6.1–4 [SBN 56–59]). However, in a footnote to Section 9 he affirms his earlier distinction between philosophical and unphilosophical probable reasoning by considering the characteristics of human reasoning which help explain why human beings "so much surpass animals in reasoning," and also why "one man so much surpasses another." These include the ability to draw upon an extensive experience, to consider the context of an event, to pursue a long chain of reasoning, to recognize analogies and form accurate rules, to distinguish relevant from irrelevant circumstances, and to consult the experience of others through "books and conversation" (EHU 9.5n20 [SBN 107n1]). Immediately after this, in Section 10, "Of Miracles," he observes that a "wise man . . . proportions his belief to the evidence." We should accordingly follow this principle by accepting uniform experience as a "proof," while balancing the "opposition of experiments and observations" in cases of conflicting evidence, to reach a probable judgment concerning the cause of any event (EHU 10.4 [SBN 110–11]). Again, as the narrator of the dialogue in Section 11, he endorses the principle that experience should be "the only standard of our judgement" in all questions of fact, and commends his friend for applying this principle to the design argument (EHU 11.24, 11.12–15; cf. 11.26n31, 11.30 [SBN 142–43, 136–38; cf. 145n1, 148]). Finally, in Section 12 he defends "*mitigated* scepticism or ACADEMICAL philosophy" as the outlook of the "just reasoner," who recognizes that "philosophical decisions are nothing but the reflections of common life, methodized and corrected" (EHU 12.24–25 [SBN 161–62]).

Hume offers a further defense of philosophical probable reasoning in the *Dialogues Concerning Natural Religion*, through the character of Philo. At the beginning of the *Dialogues*, Philo defends a moderate skepticism that acknowledges the "uncertainty and narrow limits of reason." He then observes that the moderate skeptic who "philosophises" on natural or moral subjects will recognize that even in ordinary life we continually advance "in forming more general principles of conduct and reasoning," and that any expansion of our experience will enable us to render our principles more "general and comprehensive" (DNR 1.134). In his subsequent debate with Cleanthes he examines the principles of experimental reasoning, especially the use of analogy (DNR 2.144; cf. 2.147). This application of the principles of probable or scientific reasoning distinguishes Philo not only from Demea, who is not especially interested in the methods of the empirical sciences, but also from Cleanthes, whose arguments concerning the existence and nature of God, according to Philo, rest upon weak analogies.

Hume appeals to several of his individual rules for judging causes and effects elsewhere in his writings, although without explicitly referring to his list of rules in the *Treatise*. As we have seen, he rephrases Rule 4, not only in the second *Enquiry* as Newton's chief rule, but also in the *Treatise* as the principle "that like objects, plac'd in like circumstances, will always produce like effects" and in the *Dialogues* as "like effects prove like causes," which Philo simply calls "the experimental argument" (T 1.3.8.14 [SBN 105]; DNR 5.165). Hume also appeals to Rule 5 in several contexts, for example in his attempt to reduce the causes of pride and humility "to a lesser number," and to find "something common, on which their influence depends" (T 2.1.4.1 [SBN 282]; cf. EHU 1.2, 4.12 [SBN 6, 30–31]). He also appeals to Rule 6 by noting that "when the absence of an object or quality removes any usual or natural effect, we may certainly conclude that its presence contributes to the production of the effect" (T 2.2.8.20 [SBN 380]). In addition, earlier in the *Treatise* he describes Rule 8, or the principle that a completely static object requires the assistance of another principle to produce any effect, as "an establish'd maxim both in natural and moral philosophy" (T 1.3.2.7 [SBN 76]).

Hume's account of probable reasoning has until recently received relatively little attention in the secondary literature.[29] Many of his commentators have overlooked his account of general rules, and of the rules for probable reasoning, often while criticizing Hume for failing to offer any standards for rational or justified belief.[30] Others have considered some more limited aspect of this discussion without recognizing its larger context in his thought.[31] For example, Stove has insisted that Hume is an inductive skeptic, who believes that "all predictive-inductive inferences are unreasonable." However, Stove also confesses in an appendix that he is puzzled by Hume's account of general rules, and never mentions his rules for probable reasoning.[32]

---

29. Several earlier exceptions to this observation include Church, *Hume's Theory of the Understanding*, 213–17; MacNabb, *David Hume*, 84–100; and Passmore, *Hume's Intentions*, 51–64.

30. See Hendel, *Studies;* Flew, *Hume's Philosophy of Belief*, 106–7, and *David Hume*, 14–15, 52–60, and 109–21; and Stroud, *Hume*.

31. See, for example, Laird, *Hume's Philosophy of Human Nature*, 91–92 and 139–43; Kemp Smith, *Philosophy of David Hume*, 99–102, 382–88; Ayer, *Hume*, 70–74; Wright, *Sceptical Realism*, 161 and 226–33; Fogelin, *Hume's Skepticism*, 60–63; Pears, *Hume's System*, 96–97; and Johnson, *Mind of David Hume*, 188–99 and 220–26.

32. Stove, *Probability and Hume's Inductive Scepticism*, 30–34 and 118–25. For a similar criticism of Stove, see Garrett, *Cognition and Commitment*, 93–94.

The last several decades have seen a more extensive consideration of Hume's treatment of philosophical probable reasoning, beginning with two articles by Thomas Hearn on his account of general rules.[33] Hume's discussion of general rules and the rules for probable reasoning has since been increasingly recognized as a central theme in his theoretical philosophy.[34] In addition, many further studies have turned to the role of general rules in other areas of his thought, especially in his moral, political, and aesthetic theories.[35] Finally, an increasing series of studies, including those by Beauchamp and Rosenberg, Wilson, Garrett, and Falkenstein, have called attention to the constructive role of Hume's rules for judging causes and effects in his account of scientific reasoning, challenging the view that Hume is a skeptic about induction.[36] In light of these studies and the preceding discussion, we may therefore reconsider several criticisms of Hume that have been prevalent since the early decades of the twentieth century.

First, many of his critics have charged that Hume cannot distinguish justified from unjustified belief, or science from superstition. For example, Bertrand Russell states that Hume "started out with a belief that scientific method yields the truth, the whole truth, and nothing but the truth," and ended "with the conviction that belief is never rational, since we know nothing." Similarly, Flew maintains that according to Hume's own "official position" there cannot be any question "of better or worse reasoning about matters of fact," since nothing in his philosophy enables us "to choose in point of rationality between science and superstition." Finally, Bennett argues that according to Hume causal beliefs "cannot be supported by reasons," and are therefore "unreasonable."[37]

A similar criticism appears in the allegation that Hume does not distinguish logic from psychology. In an influential statement of this view, Kemp Smith has argued that in Hume's account "psychology, as exposing the mechanisms through which belief is causally produced, usurps upon logic, as defining the conditions under which it can be intelligently regulated." This view is echoed by Passmore, in his claim that Hume rejects the contrast between normative logic and descriptive psychology, so that "'Right reasoning' has no legislative force" in his philosophy. Similarly, Flew criticizes Hume for attempting to replace logical standards with "psychologically based discriminations between the

---

33. See especially Hearn, "General Rules in Hume's *Treatise*," 405–22.

34. See Noxon, *Hume's Philosophical Development*, 81–90; Capaldi, *David Hume*, 44–48, 110–17, and 125–29; and Baier, *Progress of Sentiments*, 54–100.

35. See, for example, Jones, *Hume's Sentiments;* Livingston, *Hume's Philosophy of Common Life;* Whelan, *Order and Artifice;* and Baier, *Progress of Sentiments.*

36. Beauchamp and Rosenberg, *Hume and the Problem of Causation*, 33–170; Wilson, *Hume's Defence of Causal Inference*, 111–241; Garrett, *Cognition and Commitment*, 76–117, 142–62, and 226–27; Falkenstein, "Naturalism, Normativity, and Scepticism," 29–72; Owen, *Hume's Reason*, 197–223. For a critical discussion of this interpretation, see Penelhum, *David Hume*, 107–13.

37. Russell, *History of Western Philosophy*, 671; Flew, *Hume's Philosophy of Belief*, 79; Bennett, *Locke, Berkeley, Hume*, 300.

somehow commendable products of firm and durable principles of the understanding and the less worthy results of flightier and more capricious propensities," and then concludes that he "fails to achieve complete consistency in this
heroic but misguided enterprise."[38]

A further charge, that Hume is a skeptic about induction, has been developed especially by Popper. While Popper agrees with Hume that there is no
ultimate justification for reasoning from experience, he rejects what he considers to be Hume's attempt to formulate a psychological solution to the problem
of induction as resting upon a naive theory of habit and repetition, but without
providing any account of scientific testing.[39] In another version of this criticism,
Stove accuses Hume of confusing the recognition that inductive inferences
are not deductive arguments, with the separate and unfortunate view that such
inferences are "unreasonable," in his alleged acceptance of the hidden "deduc-
tivist thesis" that "all invalid arguments are unreasonable."[40]

Finally, Russell argues that Hume's "self-refutation of rationality" led to a
"great outburst of irrational faith," and to the "growth of unreason" from the
nineteenth to at least the middle of the twentieth century, which Russell
describes as "a natural sequel to Hume's destruction of empiricism." Popper
also testifies to these alleged consequences by stating that Hume reduced knowledge to "rationally indefensible belief," and thus to "irrational faith."[41]

In this chapter I have shown, on the contrary, that although Hume rejects
any absolute *a priori* or *a posteriori* justification for our causal judgments, he also
attempts to establish a relative distinction between "philosophical" and "unphilosophical" probable reasoning, by arguing that we may be guided in our
causal judgments by a set of rules for judging causes and effects, which we
develop through reflection upon our ordinary causal judgments. I have also
shown that he presents these principles of probable reasoning as a system of
inductive logic, in contrast the spontaneous psychological principles of association, and that he recommends this set of rules as the basis for distinguishing
science from superstition. Hume therefore provides us with the principles for
evaluating and correcting our causal judgments, and for excluding both superstition and rationalism from our empirical knowledge in the natural and human
sciences.[42]

38. Kemp Smith, *Philosophy of David Hume*, 387; Passmore, *Hume's Intentions*, 19; cf. 18–41; Flew, *Hume's Philosophy of Belief*, 265.
39. Popper, *Logic of Scientific Discovery*, 27–34, and *Objective Knowledge*, 3–7, 23–24 and 85–101.
40. Stove, *Probability and Hume's Inductive Scepticism*, 27–45 and 49–52. See also Glossop, "In Defence of David Hume," 59–63, and Garrett, *Cognition and Commitment*, 77 and 93–94.
41. Russell, *History of Western Philosophy*, 673; Popper, *Objective Knowledge*, 5.
42. Garrett and Dicker have both recently argued that Hume distinguishes between the absolute justification of induction itself through rational argument and the relative justification of the standards of reasoning that we formulate within the context of our inevitable presupposition of the legitimacy of induction.

I maintain that Hume's account of philosophical probable reasoning should be regarded as a key to his writings. That is, Hume initially provides a general account of the nature, origin, and justification of the principles of scientific reasoning, and their application to various subjects within the natural and human sciences. He then applies these rules in his own further inquiries into psychology, the social sciences, ethics, aesthetics, history, and religion. In other words, I have shown here that Hume develops a critical, constructive, and consistent defense of the principles of scientific inquiry, against the various portrayals of him as a thoroughgoing skeptic by Russell, Popper, and Stove; as an uncritical naturalist by Kemp Smith and Stroud; and as an inconsistent philosophical mongrel by Flew, Bennett, and Passmore. On the other hand, Hume's endorsement of the principles of philosophical probable reasoning is also circumscribed by his commendation of intellectual modesty: a recommendation arising from his skeptical arguments, as these are presented especially in Book 1, Part 4 of the *Treatise*. We will consider the skeptical dimension of Hume's epistemology in Chapter 5.

Since many of these criticisms of Hume's philosophy turn on the use of words related to "reason," it will be useful to conclude this section by considering some of the individual terms from this family used by Hume and by his critics.[43]

In his most general use of the terms "reason" and "reasoning," Hume characterizes "all kinds of reasoning" as consisting in "nothing but a *comparison*, and a discovery of those relations, either constant or inconstant, which two or more objects bear to each other." He later states that "reason is the discovery of truth or falshood," or in other words the "agreement or disagreement" of our judgments, "either to the *real* relations of ideas, or to *real* existence and matter of fact" (T 1.3.2.1, 3.1.1.9; cf. 2.3.10.2 [SBN 73, 458; cf. 448]). He accordingly divides the two types of "reasoning" into mathematical demonstrations and causal judgments (cf. T 1.3.11.2, 2.3.3.1–10 [SBN 124, 413–18]; EHU 4.1–4, 4.18 [SBN 25–27, 35]).

Elsewhere, however, Hume applies the terms "reason" and "reasoning" to more specific types of mental activity, in usages that are often at variance with each other, although even this seeming carelessness still reflects a consistent pattern. First, he applies the term "reasoning" to the activity of causal inference,

---

On this view, we may regard particular causal judgments as more or less justified or rational, relative to the principles of philosophical probable reasoning, even if the practice of induction cannot be ultimately justified by either demonstrative or probable arguments. See Garrett, *Cognition and Commitment*, 91–95, and Dicker, *Hume's Epistemology and Metaphysics*, 75–76 and 91–98, along with Strawson, *Introduction to Logical Theory*, 256–58, and Wilson, *Hume's Defence of Causal Inference*, 19.

43. For further discussions of Hume's own use of the word "reason" and related terms, see Price, *Hume's Theory of the External World*, 7; Árdal, "Some Implications," 91–106; Norton, *David Hume*, 208–38; Garrett, *Cognition and Commitment*, 94–95; Wilson, *Hume's Defence of Causal Inference*, 5 and 33; and Owen, *Hume's Reason*.

in his references to "probable reasoning," to "reasonings from causes or effects," to "reasonings from causation," and to "reasonings concerning existence" (T 1.3.8.12, 1.3.4.1, 1.3.7.3, 1.3.14.36 [SBN 103, 82, 95, 172]; cf. EHU 4.1–4, 4.14–18 [SBN 25–27, 32–35]). On the other hand, he also asserts that our causal inferences are ultimately dependent, not upon "reasoning," but on custom and experience (T 1.3.6.4–8, 1.3.14.31, 1.3.14.36 [SBN 88–90, 170, 172]; EHU 4.5–11, 5.4–5 [SBN 27–30, 42–43]). Finally, he also argues that we are never "determin'd by reason" in our judgments concerning causes and effects, that causal judgments never arise from "reasonings *a priori,*" and that our causal judgments are "*not* founded on reasoning" (T 1.3.6.4 [SBN 88–89]; EHU 4.6, 4.15 [SBN 27, 32]).

Many of Hume's critics have overlooked these variations in his usage, and have further interpreted his claim that causal inferences are not "determin'd by reason" as asserting that these inferences can never be "rational." However, these readings have overlooked his own description of philosophical probable reasoning as a "reasonable" foundation for belief and opinion, and his presentation of the rules for probable reasoning as the principles of "logic" which can be applied in our reasonings concerning causes and effects, in order to counteract the influence of prejudice and other unphilosophical forms of probable reasoning (T 1.3.13.1, 1.3.15.11 [SBN 143, 175]).

In order to establish a relatively unified terminology for discussing Hume's thought, which is also consistent with his own usage, I would first recommend following his usage by applying the verb form "reasoning" both to processes of causal inference and to mathematical demonstration. However, I would recommend limiting our use of the noun "reason" to the faculty that performs the *a priori* activity of mathematical demonstration, and also perhaps (as indicated in Chapter 2) of valid deduction from self-evident principles. Accordingly, in Hume's view a causal judgment is a type of "reasoning" or inferential process, which however ultimately arises, not from "reason," but from the influence of repeated observation upon the imagination.

Finally, Hume's rejection of the view that our causal inferences are founded upon reason is often taken to deny that our causal judgments can be "rational." However, this overlooks his own preferred use of the word "reasonable" for those causal inferences which conform to the standards of philosophical probable reasoning, since he states that these inferences provide us with "reasonable foundations of belief and opinion" (T 1.3.13.1 [SBN 143]). Elsewhere Hume occasionally uses the word "rational" as a synonym for "reasonable," for example in referring to "rational arguments" and to philosophers who are "rational and modest" (T 1.4.1.12 [SBN 186]; EHU 4.12 [SBN 30]). However, he also uses the word "rational" for the ability to use language or to engage in any kind of inferential process, as in referring to "rational discourse" and to the "rational faculties" of a hypothetical first human being (EHU 4.4, 4.6 [SBN 27]). I would recommend that, in considering or applying Hume's account of philosophical probable reasoning, we should describe any conclusions supported by a preponderance of evidence, according to his standards of scientific judgment, as "reasonable" rather than "rational," especially since the former term preserves the more modest tone of Hume's analysis.

NATURAL SCIENCES

Although Hume was primarily interested in the general principles of cognition and in the moral or human sciences, he also took a sustained interest in "natural philosophy" or the natural sciences.[44] Indeed, he served from 1751 until the early 1760s as joint secretary of the Edinburgh Philosophical Society, an association devoted to advancing the study of the natural sciences in Scotland.[45] His responsibilities in this capacity are reflected most notably in his 1762 letter to Benjamin Franklin acknowledging the receipt of Franklin's paper on a new method of "preserving houses from thunder" (L 1.357–58). Hume's own contributions to the natural sciences were largely indirect, consisting mainly in his attempt to account for the fundamental concepts and principles of reasoning in the modern natural sciences, and to locate these within the larger context of human cognition.[46] Thus, although he excludes the natural sciences from the domain of his inquiry in the *Treatise,* Hume maintains that even natural philosophy depends upon the "science of MAN" for the examination and justification of its first principles (T Int.4; cf. 1.1.2.12, 1.2.5.4 [SBN xv; cf. 8, 55]).

At the beginning of the *Treatise* Hume notes that in the natural sciences, unlike the moral sciences, we may arrange our experiments "purposely" and even "with premeditation" by placing an object in a particular situation and observing the results (T Int.7, Int.10 [SBN xvi–xvii, xix]). Later, in describing the application of his rules for judging causes and effects to natural subjects, he argues that every "phænomenon in nature" is "compounded and modify'd by so many different circumstances," that in order to discover causes and effects in nature "we must carefully separate whatever is superfluous, and enquire by new experiments, if every particular circumstance of the first experiment was essential to it" (T 1.3.15.11 [SBN 175]).

---

44. For Hume's background and interest in the natural sciences, see Barfoot, "Hume and the Culture of Science," 151–90, and Force, "Hume's Interest in Newton and Science," 166–216. See also Emerson, "Science and Moral Philosophy," 11–36.

45. Mossner, *Life of David Hume,* 257–58.

46. For a survey of Hume's contribution to the development of the philosophy of science, see Rosenberg, "Hume and the Philosophy of Science," 64–89.

Once we have acquired relatively extensive experience in judging causes and effects, Hume argues that we may be able to base new judgments on the observation of a few events or even a single event. In other words, he finds that both in scientific investigation and in ordinary life we often attain knowledge of a particular cause "merely by one experiment, provided it be made with judgment, and after a careful removal of all foreign and superfluous circumstances," or that we may even justifiably "build an argument on one single experiment, when duly prepar'd and examin'd" (T 1.3.8.14, 1.3.12.3 [SBN 104, 131]; cf. EHU 9.5n20 [SBN 107n1]). He later refers to the Baconian conception of an *experimentum crucis,* or a single experiment that "points out the right way in any doubt or ambiguity" (EPM 5.17 [SBN 219]). This argument for the evidential value of a single, well-designed scientific experiment qualifies his observation that we can never build a causal argument on "one instance or experiment" (EHU 7.27 [SBN 74]). A controlled experiment in the context of an established habit of causal expectation isolates a single variable as the only possible cause of the effect in question, and gives the idea of this variable an extra force and vivacity. On the other hand, in his later rejection of miracles and his criticism of the design argument Hume maintains that we cannot derive any causal inferences from a succession of events in which either the objects or their conjunctions are considered to be unique (EHU 10.12–13, 11.30 [SBN 114–16, 148]; DNR 2.149).

Hume offers a more direct account of the purpose and methods of the natural sciences in the first *Enquiry.* Here he argues that the goal of the study of nature is "to reduce the principles, productive of natural phænomena, to a greater simplicity, and to resolve the many particular effects into a few general causes" by reasoning from "analogy, experience, and observation" (EHU 4.12 [SBN 30–31]). However, these advances require not only a successful use of the appropriate techniques but also the ability to recognize and to compare unexpected phenomena and operations in nature. We thus find that the greatest obstacle to progress in the investigation of nature is "the want of proper experiments and phænomena, which are often discovered by chance, and cannot always be found, when requisite, even by the most diligent and prudent enquiry" (EHU 7.2 [SBN 61]).

Although he rejects the claim that we have an impression, or a positive idea, of a general causal power in nature, which operates in all instances of causation, Hume notes in the *Treatise* "that there may be several qualities both in material and immaterial objects, with which we are utterly unacquainted," and adds that "if we please to call these *power* or *efficacy,* 'twill be of little consequence to the world" (T 1.3.14.27 [SBN 168]). However, it is not entirely clear what he means by "qualities" in this passage. On the one hand, these might be qualities with which we are as yet unacquainted because they lie beyond the present range of our observation, although we may presume that these as-yet unobserved qualities also belong to objects and are regularly conjoined with certain effects. On the other hand, he might be identifying the causal tendencies of objects as "powers" in a positive sense, and then denying that we can attain any knowledge of these powers apart from constant conjunctions between the observable qualities of objects. In this case, if we are attempting to discover the "original and ultimate principle" that binds the cause of every phenomenon to its effect, we will be "disappointed" to learn that "this connexion, tie, or energy lies merely in ourselves," as a determination of the mind arising from custom (T 1.4.7.5 [SBN 266–67]).

In his later works Hume refers more freely and frequently to the possible operation of "secret powers" in nature, apparently as the hidden active qualities in objects which enable them to produce their effects. He thus states in the *Enquiry* that nature allows us "only the knowledge of a few superficial qualities of objects," while concealing "those powers and principles, on which the influence of these objects entirely depends." This conclusion arises from our recognition that we cannot discover any ultimate reason why bread should provide nourishment, or why a moving body should continue to move, even though "we always presume, when we see like sensible qualities, that they have like secret powers." Hume even apparently suggests that we may formulate a concept of the "ultimate springs and principles" in nature connecting qualities to their effects, although these supposed powers are "totally shut up from human curiosity and enquiry," since they are not given directly through our senses, and since there is no known "connexion between the sensible qualities and the secret powers" that we can discover beyond the bare observation of a constant conjunction between qualities and effects (EHU 4.16, 4.12, 4.21 [SBN 32–33, 30–31, 36–37]). In other words, in attributing a causal relation to two objects that have been regularly conjoined in our experience, we suppose there to be "some power in the one, by which it infallibly produces the other," and which operates "with the greatest certainty and strongest necessity" (EHU 7.27 [SBN 75]).

On the other hand, Hume brackets this discussion of hidden powers in the *Enquiry* by a pair of footnotes, in which he argues that the concept of a power, like that of a cause, is merely a relative idea, since both refer entirely "to an effect, or some other event constantly conjoined with the former." We accordingly have no idea of a power apart from "the *unknown* circumstance of an object, by which the degree or quantity of its effect is fixed and determined," and no means of observing a power apart from its effects, or of characterizing a power other than in terms of these effects (EHU 7.29n17; cf. 4.16n7 [SBN 77n1; cf. 33n1]). For example, Hume argues that our concept of inertia arises from our repeated observations of the fact "that a body at rest or in motion continues for ever in its present state, till put from it by some new cause; and that a body impelled takes as much motion from the impelling body as it acquires itself." However, in characterizing inertia as a "power," we can "only mark these facts, without pretending to have any idea of the inert power," just as "when we talk of gravity, we mean certain effects, without comprehending that active power" (EHU 7.25n16 [SBN 73n1]). Hume anticipates this analysis of the idea of a "power" in the *Treatise*, where he renounces any attempt to explain how motion can occur in a plenum, since this would require an explanation of "the nature of bodies" and the "secret causes of their operations" that would extend beyond the scope of his project and even perhaps "beyond the reach of human understanding." Instead, we can never claim to know anything about bodies "otherwise than by those external properties, which discover themselves to the senses" (T 1.2.5.26 [SBN 64]).

Several recent studies have cited Hume's references to these "secret powers" in objects as evidence that he defends a version of causal realism, or the view that causal regularities arise from antecedently existing powers in objects, although he believes that these powers are inaccessible to human inquiry and that we only attribute them to objects on the basis of the regular conjunctions we observe between them. By contrast, the critics of this interpretation have called attention to Hume's sustained rejection of any claim that we have a positive idea of causal powers in objects, arguing instead that his references to the "secret powers" of objects actually express the relative idea, either of some deeper and as-yet unobserved qualities in objects, or of the causal relation itself.[47]

I contend that in Hume's view the idea of a causal power is a relative idea that we derive as a secondary projection, from our primary projection of a necessary connection onto objects that have been regularly conjoined in our experience.[48] In this secondary projection, we locate the source of the causal connection within the objects themselves, thereby producing a useful theoretical construct for scientific inquiry and explanation. For example, we attribute an inertial or gravitational force to the objects themselves, and then treat these

---

47. For proponents of this interpretation, see Wright, *Sceptical Realism,* 2–3, 123–86, and Strawson, *Secret Connexion;* as well as Costa, "Hume and Causal Inference," 141–59, and "Hume and Causal Realism," 172–90. See also Livingston, *Hume's Philosophy of Common Life,* 155–67. For critics of this view, see Winkler, "The New Hume," 52–87, and Waxman, *Hume's Theory of Consciousness,* 191–99. Additional essays on this discussion are included by Read and Richman in *The New Hume Debate.* Falkenstein provides a further discussion of criticisms of the idea of "causal powers" in both Hume and Kant, in "Hume's Answer to Kant," 331–60.

48. Here I am expanding upon the account by Livingston, who is often included among those who interpret Hume as a causal realist, but whose reading of Hume is, I believe, closer to the interpretation that I have indicated here. However, in contrast to Livingston, I would regard Hume's discussion as a direct and deliberate treatment of the use of theoretical language in the natural sciences. See Livingston, *Hume's Philosophy of Common Life,* 155–60.

Hume's references to the history of science begin with the Copernican revolution in astronomy. Hume argues that Copernicus developed the heliocentric model of the solar system, not merely to account for new data, but also to formulate a simpler theory of planetary motion. In other words, the Copernican system arose in part from the application of the principle of simplicity, or the maxim "that nature acts by the simplest methods, and chooses the most proper means to any end." By contrast, the Ptolemaic astronomers had "contriv'd such intricate systems of the heavens, as seem'd inconsistent with true philosophy," by inventing "a new principle to every new phænomenon, instead of adapting it to the old" (DNR 12.214; T 2.1.3.7 [SBN 282]; cf. E Sc.164–65).

In the introduction to the *Treatise* Hume describes the development of "experimental philosophy" since the seventeenth century, especially in England, and gives particular credit to Francis Bacon for introducing the experimental method into natural philosophy (T Int.7 [SBN xvii]). However, in the *History of England* he notes that Bacon "pointed out at a distance the road to true philosophy," but did not recognize the possibilities in applying mathematics to physics and astronomy, and was in this respect "inferior to his cotemporary Galileo" and "perhaps even to Kepler." Hume then departs momentarily from his national history in order to describe Galileo's contribution to the revival of geometry and to praise his achievement as "the first that applied it, together with experiment, to natural philosophy" (H V.App.4.153). Hume includes a further discussion of Galileo in the *Dialogues,* in the context of a discussion of the principles of simplicity and analogy. Here Philo appeals to the example of Galileo, who sought to demonstrate "that there was no foundation for the distinction commonly made between elementary and celestial substances." More specifically, Galileo sought to show that the moon is similar "in every particular" to the earth, and that both are similar to the planets, allowing scientists "to extend the same arguments and phenomena from one to the other" (DNR 2.151). In his essay "Of the Middle Station of Life," Hume indeed identifies Galileo, along with Newton, as two figures in the history of philosophy who appear "so far to excel all the rest, that I cannot admit any other into the same Class with them" (E MS.550).

In the *History of England* Hume also considers the discovery by Harvey of the circulation of the blood, as well as the founding of the Royal Society, and the achievements of its members. He gives particular attention to Robert Boyle, not only for his discoveries in pneumatics, chemistry, and hydrostatics; but also for contributing to the general rise of "mechanical philosophy," which "by discovering some of the secrets of nature, and allowing us to imagine the rest, is so agreeable to the natural vanity and curiosity of men" (H 6.62.153–54; H 6.71.540–41).

Finally, in the *History of England* Hume singles out Isaac Newton as "the greatest and rarest genius that ever arose for the ornament and instruction of the species."[52] He especially praises Newton for being "cautious in admitting no principles but such as were founded on experiment; but resolute to adopt every such principle, however new or unusual." Thus, while Newton seemed to "draw off the veil from some of the mysteries of nature," he also revealed the "imperfections" of mechanical philosophy, and thereby restored "her ultimate secrets to that obscurity, in which they ever did and ever will remain" (H 6.71.541). In the *Enquiry* he further praises Newton for leading astronomy beyond merely describing the movements of the heavenly bodies by discovering "the laws and forces, by which the revolutions of the planets are governed and directed" (EHU 1.15 [SBN 14]).

In addition to Newton's rules for scientific reasoning, which we have considered above, Hume offers several further reflections concerning the Newtonian method. For example, he criticizes both the Cartesian philosophers and some of Newton's followers for maintaining that all motion should be attributed to the direct action of the deity, since "it was never the meaning of Sir ISAAC NEWTON to rob second causes of all force or energy." Indeed, Newton proposed the existence of "an etherial active fluid to explain his universal attraction," although recognizing with his characteristic caution and modesty that this was "a mere hypothesis, not to be insisted on, without more experiments" (EHU 7.25n16 [SBN 73n1]; cf. LG 28–29). Hume presents his own attempts to explain the idea of a vacuum as consistent with "the *Newtonian* philosophy," which maintains "a modest scepticism to a certain degree, and a fair confession of ignorance in subjects, that exceed all human capacity" (T 1.2.5.26n12 [SBN 639]).

Many studies have examined Newton's influence on Hume, and have offered different interpretations of this influence.[53] The simplest of these is the argument that Hume sought to extend the principles and discoveries of Newtonian physics to the moral sciences by developing a mechanistic account of perceptions and of human action.[54] However, I would argue that Hume's philosophy should instead be regarded as an attempt to examine and justify the foundations of Newtonian physics by tracing its explanatory principles and its central concepts of space, time, causation, and external objects to their origins in sensation and imagination. Hume's philosophy may thus be regarded as one among a number of attempts, including those of Reid and Kant, to formulate a philosophical account of the principles of Newtonian science. Finally, Hume also attempts to apply the resulting Newtonian principles of explanation to the distinctive

52. For an inventory and discussion of Hume's various references to Newton, see Force, "Hume's Interest in Newton and Science," especially 169–78.

53. For various discussions of Hume's "Newtonianism" see Capaldi, *David Hume*, 49–70; Hurlbutt, *Hume, Newton, and the Design Argument;* Barfoot, "Hume and the Culture of Science," 151–90; Force, "Hume's Interest in Newton and Science," 181–206; McIntyre, "Hume: Second Newton of the Moral Sciences," 3–18; and Sapadin, "Note," 337–44.

54. See, for example, Kemp Smith, *Philosophy of David Hume,* 53–76 and 549–53.

types of description and explanation that are required in moral philosophy or the human sciences, as we will see in subsequent chapters of this study.[55]

Hume even calls attention in the *Dialogues* to the value of studying the history of science. Here Philo observes "the modern system of astronomy is now so much received by all enquirers, and has become so essential a part even of our earliest education, that we are not commonly very scrupulous in examining the reasons upon which it is founded." Accordingly, although we might initially be inclined to treat the works of earlier scientists as a "mere curiosity," it is useful "to study the first writers on that subject, who had the full force of prejudice to encounter, and were obliged to turn their arguments on every side, in order to render them popular and convincing." He especially encourages his companions to read the works of Galileo, in order to appreciate the discoveries which, by their own time, were taken for granted as the foundations of modern physics and astronomy (DNR 2.150–51).

Finally, it might not be amiss to note that although Hume was not a practicing scientist, his writings seem to have been important influences for several crucial lines of development in the history of the modern natural sciences. For example, his imaginative account in the *Dialogues* of various theories by which we might explain the apparent order in nature not only anticipates the development of evolutionary theories in nineteenth-century geology and biology, but may indeed have influenced Charles Darwin through his grandfather, the eccentric poet and scientist Erasmus Darwin (DNR 6.170–81).[56] In addition, Hume's account of space and time in the *Treatise* was cited by Albert Einstein as an important influence on his thought.[57]

TESTIMONY

Hume applies his account of philosophical probable reasoning not only to the natural sciences but also, and indeed more extensively, to the explanation of human action, as we will see in later chapters. However, in concluding this chapter, I would like to consider his preliminary reflections in Book 1, Part 3 of the *Treatise* concerning the role of human testimony in our causal reasonings.

Hume includes the beliefs arising from human testimony within the system of reality that rests upon causal judgments. For example, we may develop "an

55. McIntyre has indeed argued that one of Hume's main targets in metaphysics as well as ethics was Samuel Clarke, and that Hume was challenging Clarke's interpretation and application of Newtonian principles. See McIntyre, "Hume: Second Newton of the Moral Sciences," 3–18. On the other hand, Russell regards Hume's challenge to Clarke as also a challenge to Newtonianism: see "Hume's *Treatise*," 108–9.

56. See Monteiro, "Hume, Induction and Natural Selection," 299–301.

57. See Einstein, *Autobiographical Notes*, 51, and Zabeeh, *Hume*, 1–2.

idea of ROME," and a belief in its history, through the ideas which we receive "from the conversation and books of travellers and historians" (T 1.3.9.4 [SBN 108]). More specifically, once we have acquired "a confidence in human testimony," we can expand our individual experience by receiving further information through "books and conversation" (EHU 9.5n20 [SBN 107n1]). However, he also observes that testimony may exercise an unphilosophical influence over causal reasoning, through the natural tendency among human beings toward "CREDULITY, or a too easy faith in the testimony of others." Indeed, our trust in human testimony "arises from the very same origin as our inferences from causes to effects, and from effects to causes." However, while experience is "the true standard of this, as well as of all other judgments," we also find in human beings "a remarkable propensity to believe whatever is reported," arising partly from our delight in novelty and partly from our sympathy with others. This even extends to include reports "concerning apparitions, enchantments, and prodigies, however contrary to daily experience and observation" (T 1.3.9.12 [SBN 112–13]; cf. 2.1.11.9 [SBN 320]; EHU 10–16 [SBN 117]). In order to help us counteract this unphilosophical tendency toward credulity, Hume advises us to develop principles for the evaluation of human testimony. He accordingly directs us to consider such factors as the number, reliability, and motives of the original witnesses, and of any subsequent participants in the chain of transmission (T 1.3.4.2, 1.3.13.5 [SBN 83, 145–46]; EHU 10.5–8 [SBN 111–13]). Thus, although human testimony is a legitimate and valuable source of information concerning matters of fact, it is also subject to typical forms of distortion and error; and should be evaluated according to the principles of judgment appropriate to the moral sciences, derived from the standards of philosophical probable reasoning. We will consider Hume's general account of the interpretation of human action in Chapter 7, and his more particular account of the principles which should govern the evaluation of human testimony in Chapter 13.

Hume also introduces the subject of education in his discussion of human testimony. Here he notes that an idea which is frequently brought before the mind through an external influence gradually acquires a "facility and force" until it comes to maintain itself "by its firm hold and easy introduction" against any new and unusual ideas. This tendency, especially when reinforced by sympathy, accounts for the influence of "EDUCATION," by which "all those opinions and notions of things, to which we have been accustom'd from our infancy" have become so deeply rooted that it seems almost impossible "by all the powers of reason and experience, to eradicate them." Indeed, Hume speculates "that upon examination we shall find more than one half of those opinions, that prevail among mankind, to be owing to education," outweighing the opinions "owing either to abstract reasoning or experience." However, since its precepts are "frequently contrary to reason," and since education is "an artificial and not a natural cause," its influence is often neglected by philosophers, even though it is built "on the same foundation of custom and repetition as our reasonings from causes and effects" (T 1.3.9.16–19 [SBN 115–17]). In other words, the convictions arising from education are derived from human testimony, and are subject to the same principles of critical evaluation as any form of testimony, although the critical evaluation of the presuppositions established in childhood is especially difficult for most of us, as a result of the combined influence of long habit and the remembered sympathies of childhood with our teachers and caregivers. However, Philo suggests in the *Dialogues* that the influence of education is "much diminished" in the modern world, since people now enjoy "a more open commerce of the world" and have learned to "compare the popular principles of different nations and ages" (DNR 1.139).

Hume presents a more consistently optimistic view of education in his moral and political writings. For example, later in the *Treatise* he argues that "private education and instruction" play a crucial role in developing respect for the principles of justice, since our parents recognize "that a man is the more useful, both to himself and others, the greater degree of probity and honour he is endow'd with," and that these principles "have greater force, when custom and education assist interest and reflection" (T 3.2.2.26 [SBN 500]). In the *Essays* he argues that moral conduct arises, not from the precepts of philosophy or religion, but instead from "the virtuous education of youth" through "wise laws and institutions" (E PG.55).

Finally, with this preliminary treatment of Hume's account of testimony and education, we may return briefly to his discussion of custom. In this chapter we have seen that custom occupies a central place in his account of philosophical probable reasoning. Many studies of Hume's social and political philosophy have also emphasized the role of custom in these areas of his writings.[58] Indeed, several authors have described Hume's account of custom as one of the central constructive and unifying themes in his philosophy.[59] In light of our larger interest here in the social and historical aspects of Hume's thought, we may wish to consider whether the word "custom" does indeed perform this unifying function.

As we have seen, in his general analysis of human cognition Hume tends to use the word "custom" in the strictly individualistic sense, which, as he indicates, is synonymous with "habit" (cf. T 1.3.8.10 [SBN 102]; EHU 5.5 [SBN 43]). Hume also occasionally uses the word "custom" to refer to an established social or cultural practice, although he generally restricts this usage to his moral

58. Bryson, *Man and Society*, 124–25, 156–59, 243, and 267; Acton, "Prejudice," 323–36; and Swinge-wood, "Origins of Sociology," 169–70.

59. Livingston, *Hume's Philosophy of Common Life*, 276; Whelan, *Order and Artifice*, 333; Phillipson, *Hume*, 148; Baier, *Progress of Sentiments*, 32 and 288.

philosophy and studies of history and social life (T 3.2.10.9n82 [SBN 559n2]; EPM D.43–50 [SBN 339–40]; E RC.366–76). Indeed, he often refers in this sense to the "manners and customs" of a particular culture or a period in history (EPM D.18 [SBN 330]; E ST.246, E Mo.290). However, Hume himself does not develop any connection between "custom" in the individualistic sense and in its social and cultural sense, and indeed appears to separate these two uses from each other deliberately in his various writings. Accordingly, Kemp Smith's attempt to conflate these two senses of "custom" in Hume's usage, by contrasting a causal inference derived from custom, as the "heavy fly-wheel" which tends to perpetuate the beliefs of a society, to the inferences derived from reflective reasoning, is a distortion of Hume's usage and his argument.[60]

However, while Hume does not specifically use the word "custom" as a unifying theme in his writings, he later expands upon his initial account of general rules, in order to consider the social processes by which we develop the rules that govern various types of social activity. This appears especially in his discussion of "artifices" and "conventions," in Book 3 of the *Treatise* and in the second *Enquiry*, which we will consider in Chapter 8. Hume's later discussion of the development of artifices or conventions might invite us to consider the possibility that the rules for probable or scientific reasoning also emerge through a process of social coordination. As we have seen, he describes the history of these rules indirectly, in his account of the development of the methodological principles of modern science by its leading figures. In other words, Hume calls attention to the historical dimension of probable reasoning, not only by discussing testimony and education, but also in his references to the development of the standards of critical reflection in the modern natural sciences, which will be applicable to both the investigation of nature, and the explanation of human action and the evaluation of human testimony.

---

60. Kemp Smith, *Philosophy of David Hume*, 386; cf. 383–88, and 539–40.

4

Metaphysics

In the initial presentation of his theory of ideas, Hume identifies perceptions, including impressions of sensation, impressions of reflection, and ideas, as the contents of all our conscious states. In the course of the *Treatise* Hume argues that the principles of traditional metaphysics, or the ideas which serve to structure our ordinary experience, including our ideas of space, time, causation, external existence, and personal identity, are constructed by the mind through various types of imaginative extrapolation from our impressions of sensation and reflection. In the *Abstract* and the first *Enquiry* Hume focuses his attention upon the idea of causation, and sharply curtails or even dispenses with his analysis of our ideas of space, time, external existence, and personal identity.

In this chapter I will consider Hume's analysis of our ideas of space and time in Book 1, Part 2 of the *Treatise,* and our ideas of external existence and personal identity in Book 1, Part 4. This order of presentation, and indeed Hume's own organization of Book 1, might seem to be problematic, since not only space and time, but also external existence and even personal identity are presuppositions of his analysis of causation. More specifically, Hume argues that the idea of causation is superimposed upon sets of external objects by the mind as a result of its memory of a series of conjunctions in space and time between similar objects.[1]

1. For a further discussion of Hume's order of presentation, see Price, *Hume's Theory of the External World,* 6–8, 17–18, and 116–17.

I have already provided a preliminary consideration of Hume's account of our idea of space in Chapter 2, in relation to his discussion of geometry. However, I have postponed his treatment of space and time to the present chapter in order to trace the continuity between this theory and his analysis of our ideas of external objects and the self. I will consider his examination of the preceding systems of metaphysics and the various forms of skepticism in Chapter 5.

SPACE AND TIME

In Book 1, Part 1 of the *Treatise* Hume initially presents spatial and temporal contiguity as natural relations, and relative locations in space and time as philosophical relations that are given directly through observation (T 1.1.4.1, 1.1.5.5, 1.3.2.1–2 [SBN 11, 14, 73–74]). He examines our "abstract ideas" of space and time in Part 2 (T 1.2.3.5–6 [SBN 34–35]). Many of Hume's critics have regarded his analysis of space and time as obviously unsatisfactory, or indeed even as incoherent.[2] I contend, however, that Hume provides a thoughtful and intriguing account of the origin of our ideas of time and space, as arising from the mind's recognition of the arrangement of its perceptions in inner and outer experience.

As we have already seen in Chapter 2, Hume argues that our ideas of space and time, and therefore also space and time themselves, are composed of indivisible parts he calls "points" and "moments." However, he also argues that these indivisible parts of space and time must be filled with something perceptible in order to be either perceived or imagined. First, the "atoms" occupying the minimal points of space must be colored or solid, and hence visible or tangible. For their part, the indivisible moments of time must be filled with "some real object or existence" drawn from "our perceptions of every kind," including not only our inner and outer impressions, but also our ideas (T 1.2.3.5–7, 1.2.3.17 [SBN 34–35, 39]).

In applying his first principle to our abstract ideas of space and time, Hume finds that these ideas do not arise from any "primary distinct impression" that is either "mix'd up" with other impressions or can appear to the mind apart from any other impression (T 1.2.3.10; cf. 1.2.3.1, 1.2.5.28 [SBN 36–37; cf. 33, 64–65]). Instead, he argues that our ideas of space and time arise from the ideas of extension and duration, which we in turn derive, as distinctions of reason, by comparing the arrangements, or what he calls the "manner of appearance," which we discover among our perceptions (T 1.2.3.4–5, 1.2.3.10 [SBN 34, 37]).

2. For surveys of recent assessments of Hume on space and time, see Johnson, *Mind of David Hume*, 81–107, and Frasca-Spada, *Space and the Self*, 57–58. See also Jacquette, *David Hume's Critique of Infinity*, 11–13.

Through the propensity of the imagination to continue its operation, we then project our ideas of extension and duration beyond any immediate series of perceptions, in order to formulate our abstract ideas of space and time.[3]

First, in considering the origin of our idea of space, Hume argues that our impressions of sensation, for example in the visual appearance of a table, do not provide a separate impression of extension, but present themselves merely as "impressions of colour'd points, dispos'd in a certain manner." However, when we compare this collection of colored points to various other collections of colored points in our visual field, we are able to overlook their differences in color and formulate an abstract idea of extension founded "merely on that disposition of points, or manner of appearance, in which they agree." In addition, we discover a resemblance between the arrangement of these colored points and our impressions of touch, since the latter are "found to be similar to those of sight in the disposition of their parts" (T 1.2.3.4–5 [SBN 34]). The concept of extension is thus formulated through a distinction of reason, in which we attend to a specific type of resemblance: a resemblance in the configuration or "manner of appearance," first among, and then also between, our visual and tactile sensations (cf. T 1.4.2.11–12, 1.4.5.9 [SBN 191–92, 235]).

Next Hume turns to the idea of time, which is derived from the concept of duration.[4] Here he argues that time never appears to the mind as an impression, either alone or in the perception of any unchanging object. Instead, the idea of time is conveyed to the mind "by some *perceivable* succession of changeable objects," and "arises altogether from the manner, in which impressions appear to the mind." For example, "five notes play'd on a flute give us the impression and idea of time," not indeed as a separate perception, but when the mind, through a distinction of reason, "takes notice of the *manner,* in which the different sounds make their appearance." The abstract idea of this arrangement, or this succession of different perceptions, is the concept of duration (T 1.2.3.7–10; cf. 1.2.5.28, 1.4.2.29 [SBN 35–37; cf. 64–65, 200]).

While the idea of spatial extension arises from the arrangement of only our visual and tactile sensations, our idea of temporal duration arises from "the succession of our perceptions of every kind," including "ideas as well as impressions, and impressions of reflection as well as of sensation." Accordingly, the idea of time "comprehends a still greater variety than that of space," and is "for ever present with us" in the continuous series of perceptions in our minds.

3. For studies of Hume's account of our idea of space and time in the context of his general theory of ideas and cognition, see Church, *Hume's Theory of the Understanding,* 57–64; Maund, *Hume's Theory of Knowledge,* 210–26; Waxman, *Hume's Theory of Consciousness,* 116–17; Garrett, *Cognition and Commitment,* 52–57 and 168–69; Frasca-Spada, *Space and the Self;* Falkenstein, "Space and Time," 179–201; and Jacquette, *David Hume's Critique of Infinity,* 43–128.

4. On Hume's examination of time, see Johnson, "Time and the Idea of Time," 205–19, and Costa, "Hume, Strict Identity, and Time's Vacuum," 1–16.

In other words, the idea of time is more encompassing than the idea of space, and is also more immediately and continually present to the mind (T 1.2.3.6, 1.2.5.29 [SBN 34–35, 65]).

Hume thus presents our ideas of extension and duration as abstract ideas, or concepts, in which we associate a general term with many particular images of extended or changing objects, according to the resemblances that we discover in the "manner of their appearance." However, these abstract ideas of extension and duration are always represented in the mind by some particular image which has "a determinate quantity and quality" (T 1.2.3.4–6 [SBN 34–35]).

Since our ideas of space and time do not arise directly from distinct impressions, but are merely ideas "of the manner or order, in which objects exist," Hume argues that we cannot form any image of space apart from material objects, or any image of time apart from a succession of changing objects. In other words, we cannot formulate a positive idea of either empty space or empty time. However, the claim that "we can form no idea of a vacuum, or space, where there is nothing visible or tangible" seems to be contradicted, not only by our apparent experiences of both observing and imagining spaces between bodies, but also by the arguments of many natural scientists, who claim that we must presuppose the idea of empty space in order to account for the motion of bodies (T 1.2.4.2, 1.2.5.1–4, 1.2.5.24 [SBN 39–40, 53–55, 63]).

Hume responds to the apparent arguments for the possibility, and the existence, of a vacuum by arguing that our idea of empty space is derived from our idea of extension. According to his analysis, I develop the idea of empty space only by seeing or touching separated bodies, and finding that I can place other bodies between them, or move my hand from one to the other. Since the supposed empty distance between bodies can be converted into a composition of extended points by receiving another body, and since this distance affects the senses in ways that are similar to the distance of an extended body, Hume concludes that the idea of empty space is derived from the idea of extension by an association of ideas, according to the natural relations of causation and resemblance. Accordingly, our idea of empty space, such as the space in an empty room, is a "fictitious distance," or the merely derivative idea of an invisible and intangible gap in an arrangement of visible and tangible objects, which we regard as capable of receiving other objects (T 1.2.5.21–23 [SBN 61–62]).[5]

Hume initially concludes this argument in the *Treatise* by disavowing any intention to explain how material objects can be separated by invisible and intangible distances that have the capacity to receive other bodies. Indeed, he describes this as a question that lies outside his own investigation, and even

5. See also Garrett, *Cognition and Commitment,* 49 and 54–57; Frasca-Spada, *Space and the Self,* 157–93; and Jacquette, *David Hume's Critique of Infinity,* 57–99.

beyond the range of our experience and understanding, since we can never know any of the properties of bodies "otherwise than by those external properties, which discover themselves to the senses" (T 1.2.5.26; cf. 1.2.5.3, 1.2.5.23–26 [SBN 64; cf. 54–55, 62–64]). He expands upon this in a footnote added in the Appendix, where he notes that if we seek to move beyond the "*appearances* of objects to our senses," and to discover the "real nature and operations" of these objects, our efforts are likely to end in "scepticism and uncertainty." He applies this argument in particular to the question of whether the apparent space between bodies must be filled with some type of body in order to account for separation and motion. In response, he states that "the *Newtonian* philosophy" asserts the existence of a vacuum only by affirming that bodies may be so distributed as to receive other bodies between them. However, at least in his view, Newtonian physics does not attempt to determine whether the intervening distance is filled with "something or nothing," or to describe "the real nature of this position of bodies," apart from their effects on our senses (T 1.2.5.26n12 [SBN 638–39]).[6]

Similarly, Hume argues that we cannot derive an idea of empty time, or of "time without a changeable existence," either from a distinct impression of time, or by observing an unchanging object. Instead, we apply the concept of duration to a static object only through a "fiction," by regarding this object as coexisting with a changing object, or in other words, a changing series of perceptions, such as the moving hands of a clock. We also regard an unchanging object as capable of changing in a given period of time, and we recognize that the qualities of a static object vary in our memory in the same degrees as those of a changing object. Our idea of time thus arises from a succession of changing perceptions and can be applied to an unchanging object only "by a fiction of the imagination, by which the unchangeable object is suppos'd to participate of the changes of the co-existent objects" (T 1.4.2.29; cf. 1.2.5.29 [SBN 200–201; cf. 65]).

Although he maintains that we cannot formulate a positive idea of empty space or empty time, Hume concedes that we may apply our concepts of extension and duration to the apparent spaces between bodies and to unchanging objects. He describes these extrapolated ideas of extension and duration in both cases as a "fiction," or an idea produced by the inertial propensity of the imagination when it projects the ideas derived from our impressions, including the abstract idea of the manner of their distribution, beyond the arrangement of a given set of sensible points or a given succession of perceptions (T 1.2.3.11, 1.2.5.23, 1.4.2.29 [SBN 37, 62, 200–201]).

---

6. On the relation of Hume's argument to various discussions among his predecessors and contemporaries, see Frasca-Spada, *Space and the Self,* 157–93, and Jacquette, *David Hume's Critique of Infinity.*

Finally, Hume also considers our systematic extrapolation and application of these "fictitious" ideas of extension and duration through various types of reasoning. For example, he finds that we project our ideas of space and time beyond the range of our perceptions through causal reasoning, which gives us information concerning "such existences, as by their removal in time and place, lie beyond the reach of the senses and memory" (T 1.3.9.4 [SBN 108]). He also identifies location in space and time as philosophical relations, or relations in which we judge the relative situations of objects by "an infinite number of comparisons, such as *distant, contiguous, above, below, before, after,* &c." We may even divide extension and duration into units and use these to measure and to calculate extensions in space and time according to the philosophical relation of "proportions in quantity or number," although Hume maintains that "we ought not to look for the utmost *precision* and exactness" in these applications of mathematical reasoning to extended objects (T 1.1.5.6, 1.3.1.2, 1.2.4.17 [SBN 14–15, 70, 45]). Hume accordingly indicates that, by engaging in causal reasoning and using various systems of measurement, we can extend our ideas of extension and duration beyond our direct field of perception in order to situate other inferred objects within a continuous spatial and temporal framework (cf. T 1.2.1.5 [SBN 28]). He thus interprets the Newtonian conceptions of absolute time and space, not as positive ideas of empty time and space, but rather as imaginative extrapolations of our concepts of extension and duration into unfolding fields of possible perception, which we project in order to accommodate any objects whose existence we may infer beyond the immediate range of our senses (cf. T 1.2.5.23–29, 1.2.5.26n12 [SBN 62–65, 638–39]).[7]

After his analysis of our ideas of space and time in Book 1, Hume also considers the influence of space and time on the human passions in Book 2 of the *Treatise.* In this context he examines various characteristics of space and time from the standpoint of human existence, such as the division of time into past, present, and future (T 2.3.7.1–2.3.8.13 [SBN 427–38]). We will return to this discussion in Chapter 6, in which we will consider the human passions and the human attitude of concern within a physical and social environment.

EXTERNAL EXISTENCE

The longest section in Book 1 of the *Treatise* is devoted to our idea of the existence of external objects. In this chapter I consider Hume's analysis of our ordinary idea of external existence in Part 4, Section 2, and its relation to his

---

7. See Price, *Hume's Theory of the External World,* 174–77; Kuhns, "Hume's Republic," 73–95; and Wright, *Sceptical Realism,* 100–105.

earlier account of our ideas of existence and substance. In the next chapter I will turn to his critical assessment of the ordinary idea of external existence and his discussion of the alternative proposals offered by the "antient" and "modern" systems of philosophy, as presented in Sections 2–4.

As we have seen, Hume maintains that "nothing is ever really present with the mind but its perceptions or impressions and ideas," and that "the only existences, of which we are certain, are perceptions," since only these are "immediately present to us by consciousness" (T 1.2.6.7, 1.4.2.47 [SBN 67, 212]).[8] He even indicates that perceptions may be identified as substances, according to the definition of a substance as whatever may be "consider'd as separately existent, and may exist separately" and has "no need of any thing else" to support its existence (T 1.4.5.5; cf. 1.4.5.24, 1.4.6.3 [SBN 233; cf. 244, 252]).[9]

In Part 2 Hume further characterizes a perception as an "object of thought," or simply as an "object," and distinguishes an object in this sense from "external objects," which are known to us "only by those perceptions they occasion" (T 1.2.6.2–7 [SBN 66–67]). However, in the course of Book 1 he also uses the word "object" noncommittally, or even with a deliberate equivocation, for both perceptions and external objects (cf. T 1.1.5.1–10, 1.2.3.1–17 [SBN 13–15, 33–39]). He finally explains this apparent ambiguity in Part 4. Here he notes that the "vulgar," among whom he includes "almost all mankind, and even philosophers themselves, for the greatest part of their lives," identify their perceptions with external objects and suppose "that the very being, which is intimately present to the mind, is the real body or material existence" (T 1.4.2.38 [SBN 206]; cf. EHU 12.6–8 [SBN 151–52]).[10] He then stipulates that he will distinguish in his philosophical analysis between an "object," or an external object, and a "perception." However, he warns us that when he is considering our ordinary idea of external existence, he will revert to the undifferentiated usage of the vulgar by supposing that there is "a single existence, which I shall call indifferently *object* or *perception*" (T 1.4.2.31; cf. 1.4.2.46 [SBN 202; cf. 211]).[11]

8. For two valuable discussions of Hume's account of perceptions, see Bricke, *Hume's Philosophy of Mind,* especially 150–53, and Waxman, *Hume's Theory of Consciousness,* 210–22.

9. For different assessments of this assertion, see Bricke, *Hume's Philosophy of Mind,* 67–71, and Johnson, *Mind of David Hume,* 280–81 and 307–8. Since Hume repeatedly asserts the autonomy of perceptions in similar terms (cf. T 1.4.2.39, 1.4.6.16 [SBN 207, 259–60]), I would regard this characterization of perceptions as a serious proposal. I indeed agree with Bricke that Hume is distinguishing between two uses of the word of "substance": the traditional use of this term for a substratum, and his use of this term for a perception. See Bricke, *Hume's Philosophy of Mind,* 59–62.

10. In Part 3 Hume distinguishes the "wise," or those who rely on philosophical probable reasoning, from the "vulgar," who often do not (T 1.3.13.12 [SBN 150]). However, in Part 4 he uses the term "vulgar" interchangeably with "common" and "popular" for the opinions of the "generality of mankind," including "all of us, at one time or other," in contrast to the opinions we reach through philosophical reflection (T 1.4.2.31, 1.4.2.36, 1.4.2.56–57 [SBN 202, 205, 217–18]).

11. For a further discussion of Hume's usage, see McRae, "Nature of Mind," 150–67.

Indeed, he maintains that it is impossible for us to conceive of any external objects as "any thing but exactly the same with perceptions" (T 1.4.2.56; cf. 1.2.6.6–9 [SBN 218; cf. 67–68]).

Hume presents a separate discussion of the idea of existence in Book 1, Part 2. Here he notes that we might expect to derive the concept of existence directly from our impressions and ideas, since all of these are "conceiv'd as existent." However, he argues that we encounter several problems in attempting to explain our idea of existence. First, the idea of existence is not derived from any distinct impression that attends every perception. Next, we cannot derive the idea of existence by comparing a perception that exists to a perception that does not exist, since every perception, as such, necessarily exists. Instead, Hume argues that the idea of existence is already itself the same as "the idea of what we conceive to be existent" (T 1.2.6.2–4; cf. App.2 [SBN 66–67; cf. 623]).[12]

However, at the end of this discussion Hume distinguishes between the idea of existence that applies to our perceptions, which I will call "absolute existence," and the idea of "external existence," or the existence which we attribute to external objects. Here he argues that although we cannot formulate a positive idea of anything which would be "specifically different from ideas and impressions," we can form a "relative idea" of the existence of external objects, by which we do not suppose these objects to be "specifically different" from our perceptions, "but only attribute to them different relations, connexions and durations" (T 1.2.6.1–9 [SBN 66–68]). That is, we regard external objects as continuing to exist apart from our perceptions, or as composed, in effect, of unobserved and connected perceptions. Hume considers this "relative idea" of external existence in Part 4 and elsewhere in his writings in terms that reinforce the contrast between external existence and his account of absolute existence in Part 2. In the first *Enquiry* he argues that "whatever *is* may *not be,*" and "the non-existence of any being, without exception, is as clear and distinct an idea as its existence." As a result, two propositions affirming its existence or non-existence are equally intelligible, even though only one can be true; and the existence of any being "can only be proved by arguments from its cause or its effect," which are "founded entirely on experience" (EHU 12.28–29 [SBN 164]). Similarly, the relative idea of external existence seems to be reflected in Cleanthes' claim that "whatever we conceive as existent, we can also conceive as

---

12. Wilson argues that, in Hume's view, the idea of existence is not a distinction of reason but a species-concept, which applies to all of our perceptions but is not derived either from a separate impression or from a quality in which they resemble one another. See Wilson, "Hume on the Abstract Idea of Existence," 167–201. For other attempts to explain Hume's arguments on the concept of existence, see Cummins, "Hume on the Idea of Existence," 61–82; Tweyman, "Some Reflections," 137–49; and Johnson, *Mind of David Hume,* 108–16.

non-existent," and that there is no being "whose non-existence implies a contradiction" (DNR 11.189). We will return to Hume's account of the concept of existence and of external existence in the course of the present section.

In Part 4 Hume examines the causes of our ordinary belief in the existence of "body," or external objects.[13] He begins by dividing our idea of external existence into two constituent ideas: the idea of a "CONTINU'D existence" of objects, when they are not immediately present to the senses, and of an "existence DISTINCT from the mind and perception." He then divides the idea of distinct existence into two further ideas: those of their "situation" and "relations," or "their *external* position as well as the *independence* of their existence and operation" (T 1.4.2.2; cf. 1.4.2.23, 1.4.2.44 [SBN 188; cf. 199, 210]).

Next, Hume examines the three possible sources for the ideas of continued and distinct existence: the senses, reason, and imagination. First, the senses cannot provide the idea of the continued existence of an object, since it is precisely the interrupted character of our sensations that initiates the problem of continued existence, and since the continued existence of objects could only be given through the senses if we suppose that the senses continue to operate "even after they have ceas'd all manner of operation," which is a "contradiction in terms." Nor can the senses give us any idea of the distinct existence of objects, since sensations do not indicate in their immediate appearance whether they are the representations of external objects or merely subjective states of consciousness (T 1.4.2.3–4 [SBN 188–89]).

Second, Hume argues that our ideas of continued and distinct existence cannot arise from reason. Here he appeals to the evidence provided by children, common people, and even animals, who all believe in the continuing and distinct existence of body, but do not have a sophisticated ability to reason. On the contrary, reason shows us, through "a very little reflection and philosophy," that "every thing, which appears to the mind, is nothing but a perception, and is interrupted, and dependent on the mind" (T 1.4.2.44, 1.4.2.14 [SBN 210, 193]; cf. EHU 12.8–16 [SBN 151–55]). Here Hume is referring to the evidence put forward by many ancient and modern philosophers, and also by contemporary natural scientists, to show that our impressions of sensation appear to be relative to the condition of our sense organs, nerves, and "animal spirits." Hume refers to several of these observations, including the discovery that we can induce double vision by pressing our eyeballs, or recognizing the effects of distance or illness on our sensations (T 1.4.2.45; cf. 1.4.4.3–4 [SBN 210–11; cf. 226–27]). Several critics have objected that Hume is begging the question here, since his argument allegedly requires us to presuppose the continued

13. The most thorough discussion of this analysis is Price's study, *Hume's Theory of the External World*. Several valuable recent studies include Pears, *Hume's System*, 152–97; Waxman, *Hume's Theory of Consciousness*, 238–65; Wilson, *Hume's Defence of Causal Inference*, 84–98; and Collier, "Filling the Gaps," 155–70.

existence and distinct operation of our sense organs and nervous system when we are not perceiving them.[14] However, Hume's larger argument does not rest upon the supposition of the distinct and continued existence of our sensory apparatus, since his main concern is to argue that perceptions are dependent on the mind or consciousness, prior to any determination regarding the existence of body, including my own body. On Hume's view, our scientific belief in the continued and distinct existence of our sensory apparatus arises from the same principles as our vulgar and philosophical beliefs in the existence of external objects, since I regard even my own body as an object that is exterior to my mind, and since I learn about the interior of my own body through the study of other human bodies. In this passage Hume is merely noting that once we have accepted the existence of an external and internal sensory apparatus, scientific reasoning shows us that our sensations are correlated to the observed states of this apparatus.

Hume further argues that we cannot derive our belief in external objects from causal reasoning, since causal reasoning only arises from the conjunction of two observed objects and leads us to expect the conjunction of similar observable objects. This type of inference can never lead us beyond the field of observation to infer the existence of an unobserved object from the appearance of a perception, since we cannot observe a conjunction between an unobserved object and a perception (T 1.4.2.14, 1.4.2.47 [SBN 193, 212]).

Having eliminated the senses and reason as candidates, Hume provisionally concludes that our idea of the distinct and continued existence of sensible objects must be "entirely owing to the IMAGINATION" (T 1.4.2.14 [SBN 193]).

To trace the role of the imagination in producing our idea of external existence, Hume suggests that we should begin by reconsidering the apparent division of our impressions into two types. The first includes "our pains and pleasures, our passions and affections," while the second contains those other impressions, including "colours, tastes, smells, sounds, heat and cold," along with "figure, bulk, motion and solidity." Of these two types of impressions, we regard the former as "internal and perishing" and the latter as qualities of external objects. Next, in a more differentiated account of the second set of impressions, Hume notes that the "vulgar" believe that the secondary qualities of color, taste, and sound, as well as the primary qualities of shape, solidity, and motion, have a "distinct continu'd existence," while philosophers ascribe a distinct and continued existence only to primary qualities (T 1.4.2.12, 1.4.2.15–16; cf. 1.4.4.3–4 [SBN 192, 194; cf. 226–27]; EHU 12.15 [SBN 154–55]). However, he notes that sounds, tastes, and smells, while "commonly regarded by the mind

---

14. For discussions of this passage, see Price, *Hume's Theory of the External World,* 7–9 and 115–20; Waxman, *Hume's Theory of Consciousness,* 220–21 and 254–62; and Johnson, *Mind of David Hume,* 264–65.

as continu'd independent qualities," appear, in contrast to color and shape, "not to have any existence in extension, and consequently cannot appear to the senses as situated externally to the body" (T 1.4.2.9; cf. 1.4.6.13 [SBN 191; cf. 258]). Finally, neither the vulgar nor philosophers attribute a continued distinct existence either to pains and pleasures, or to the passions (T 1.4.2.12 [SBN 192]).

In a later discussion of nonspatial objects Hume argues, against the view he attributes to many other metaphysicians, "that an object may exist, and yet be no where," and even that "the greatest part of beings do and must exist after this manner." Among these nonspatial objects or perceptions he includes tastes, smells, and sounds; desires, passions, and moral reflections; and indeed "all our perceptions and objects, except those of the sight and feeling." He then argues that the impressions of taste and smell cannot exist in a "local conjunction" with extended objects, and that our idea of this conjunction arises indirectly from other relations. That is, we attribute taste or smell to an object when we discover that a conjunction between an extended object and certain organs of our body regularly produces a specific impression of taste or smell in that organ. The imagination is led by these relations of contiguity and causation to suppose a "conjunction in place" between the smell or the flavor and the extended object. We therefore suppose that the taste of an olive exists in the object; and even that this flavor exists "in such a manner, that it fills the whole without extension," yet also subsists "entire in every part without separation" (T 1.4.5.10–13; cf. 1.4.2.10, 2.1.5.6 [SBN 235–38; cf. 191, 287]).

In response to Hume's assertion that neither the vulgar nor philosophers attribute a continued distinct existence to the passions (T 1.4.2.12; cf. 1.4.2.20 [SBN 192; cf. 195]), Price has argued that we often regard our passions as continuing to exist even after an interruption. This view is also affirmed by Hume in his own discussion of the passions, where he attributes to human beings "certain calm desires and tendencies," which produce "little emotion in the mind, and are more known by their effects than by the immediate feeling or sensation." Indeed, he argues that such a disposition tends to operate as a "settled principle of action" or a "predominant inclination of the soul," although its influence can be interrupted by a momentary passion (T 2.3.3.8–2.3.4.1 [SBN 417–19]). Hume also describes the "characters and disposition" of a person as a set of tendencies in that person "that is durable or constant," since it is made up of "durable principles of the mind, which extend over the whole conduct" (T 2.3.2.6, 3.3.1.4 [SBN 411, 575]). Price describes this theory of affective dispositions, which Hume appears to presuppose in his later discussion, as an "introspective naive realism," corresponding to the perceptual naive realism of the vulgar, and suggests that Hume can also account for our belief in latent affective traits on the basis of his analysis of our idea of continued existence.[15] However, Price's suggestion that this application of Hume's theory must also entail the distinct existence of the passions seems less plausible, since an affective disposition would presumably have a continued existence within the mind, and not apart from it.[16]

Indeed, Hume's analysis of the passions calls attention to an interesting problem in his account of external existence, which is his failure to explain the concept of "distinct existence." As we have seen, Hume argues that our idea of the "existence of body" consists in the ideas of continued, external, and independent existence, with the second and third together comprising the idea of distinct existence. That is, we regard something with an independent external existence as distinct "from the mind and perception" (T 1.4.2.2 [SBN 188]). However, Hume also recognizes that we often attribute a continued and independent, although not an external, existence to many of our sensations (such as tastes, smells, and sounds), and a continued, but not an independent or external, existence to some of our impressions of reflection (for example, to our calm passions or dispositions).[17] In other words, although we attribute a *continued* existence to many impressions apart from those which we regard as distributed in space, we attribute *external* existence only to impressions of color and touch, through a process which Hume has indeed already considered in his account of our idea of extension. Accordingly, it would seem that in Part 4, Hume is actually presenting an account of our idea of the continued existence, and perhaps also the independent existence, of any entity, which might be either mental or corporeal; while his account of our idea of external or corporeal existence is instead presented in Part 2. Hume appears to recognize this later in Part 4, in noting that the imagination cannot attribute spatiality to any perceptions "except those of the sight and feeling" (T 1.4.5.10 [SBN 235–36]; cf. EHU 12.15 [SBN 154]). Indeed, Hume surreptitiously replaces his analysis of externality in Part 4 with an account of the independence of body, thereby abandoning any more specific discussion of spatiality, at least in this context (T 1.4.2.4–5, 1.4.2.9–10 [SBN 189, 191]). Finally, as Hume himself indicates, any account of our belief in external existence, even in the external existence of the objects of sight and touch, must include an account of the self to which these objects

15. Hume's account of the enduring existence of affective mental dispositions might also be applied to our cognitive abilities, such as reason and the imagination, when we regard these as faculties that have a continued existence even when we are not using them (cf. T 1.4.2.2, 1.4.2.32–35 [SBN 188, 202–4]).

16. See Price, *Hume's Theory of the External World*, 27–29 and 69–70; cf. 19–20. For further views of the status of mental dispositions in Hume's philosophy, see Bricke, *Hume's Philosophy of Mind*, 46–58; Johnson, *Mind of David Hume*, 296–300; Garrett, *Cognition and Commitment*, 170–71; Wilson, *Hume's Defence of Causal Inference*, 36; and Frasca-Spada, *Space and the Self*, 157–93.

17. We can apparently imagine that a passion could have an independent as well as a continued existence, if a passion can be imagined as intruding itself from outside into the conscious life of an individual, for example in certain types of alleged psychic abilities. However, we need not require Hume to consider this possibility, since it does not belong to our everyday understanding of the passions.

are exterior. This requires either an account of the mind, which Hume has not yet provided, or an account of the idea of our own body, which must apparently be explained in the same terms as our idea of any other corporeal object (T 1.4.2.4–10 [SBN 189–91]).[18]

With this consideration of the problem of independence and externality we may now turn to the central concern of Hume's discussion: his account of our idea of the continued existence of objects.

First, Hume argues that in many of our attributions of continued existence to objects we are guided by a "peculiar *constancy*" among our impressions, whenever these present themselves "in the same uniform manner, and change not upon account of any interruptions in my seeing or perceiving them." As examples of constancy, or of exact resemblance among the perceptions in an interrupted series, we may consider "these mountains, and houses, and trees, which lie at present under my eye," along with "my bed and table, my books and papers," which "when I lose sight of them by shutting my eyes or turning my head, I soon after find them return upon me without the least alteration" (T 1.4.2.18 [SBN 195–96]). As we will see, this exact resemblance between our interrupted perceptions leads us to regard these perceptions as "individually the same," even though they are different from each other, and to further suppose the continued existence of these perceptions even when we do not perceive them (T 1.4.2.24 [SBN 199]).

Second, we often attribute a continued existence to objects on the basis of a series of perceptions that do not exactly resemble each other. In these cases Hume finds that the changes in the series of perceptions "preserve a *coherence, and have a regular dependence on each other*," providing the foundation for "a kind of reasoning from causation" which also produces the idea of continued existence. In his example, my visual impressions of the merry blaze in my fireplace might be very different after I have been away from the room for an hour. However, I attribute a continued existence to the fire because I remember a certain sequence of changing perceptions during an interval of time similar to the one that elapsed while I was away (T 1.4.2.19 [SBN 195]). This recognition

18. Pears also objects to Hume's account of distinct existence, though for different reasons. According to Pears, Hume mistakenly attributes to the vulgar the view that "the object of his perception" has a continued and independent existence, but not an existence in physical space. This interpretation can be criticized on several grounds. First, Hume includes externality in our idea of distinct existence, and also argues that the vulgar believe that their perceptions exist as objects in space: or externally, as well as independently from the mind. Next, while Pear asserts that the vulgar, according to Hume, do not ask themselves whether their "objects" are physical or mental, Hume evidently maintains that the vulgar do indeed identify a subset of their perceptions with physical objects, and do not regard these perceptions as mind-dependent entities (T 1.4.2.12–13, 1.4.2.31, 1.4.2.36, 1.4.2.40–41 [SBN 192–93, 202, 205, 207–9]). Hume thus is not committed to the view that the idea of external existence entails belief in the double existence of perceptions and objects. Instead, on his view, the vulgar believe in the external existence of certain perceptions as external objects, but not in the double existence of perceptions and objects. See Pears, *Hume's System*, 155–67.

of a coherence among our perceptions, arising from our projection of a remembered causal sequence onto an interrupted series of perceptions, enables us to form an idea of, and belief in, a changing world as the cause of our individual impressions. This allows me to account for the movement of a messenger through the door and into the room behind me, and for the arrival of a letter written to me by a friend in a foreign country and delivered by means of "posts and ferries." We are thus led to suppose "the effects and continu'd existence" of objects according to our "memory and observation," and to "connect their past and present appearances" according to the changes we have found by experience "to be suitable to their particular natures and circumstances." As a result, we regard the world "as something real and durable," which continues to exist even when not present to our senses (T 1.4.2.20 [SBN 195–97]; cf. EHU 12.7–8 [SBN 151–52]).

Hume argues that the imagination produces our idea of the continued existence of external objects by generating a "supposition" or "fiction," which extends our idea of an object beyond our immediate perceptions (T 1.4.2.29, 1.4.2.36, 1.4.2.43 [SBN 200–201, 205, 209]). He presents this supposition as another product of the inertial propensity of the imagination, whose activity he has traced in our idea of an exact standard of equality in geometry (T 1.4.2.22; cf. 1.2.4.23–26 [SBN 198; cf. 47–49]). In attributing external existence to a constant series of interrupted perceptions, the mind is attempting to resolve a conflict between their exact resemblance, which gives us an idea of their perfect identity, and the real difference between them that arises from their interruption. To overcome this conflict, the imagination disguises the interruption by supposing its perceptions to be connected by "a real existence, of which we are insensible." Similarly, in observing a coherent series of changes in an interrupted series of perceptions, we discover that this coherence is "much greater and more uniform, if we suppose the objects to have a continu'd existence" (T 1.4.2.22–24 [SBN 198–99]). This supposition of a continued existence acquires the character of a "belief" through the combined forcefulness of the individual impressions of sensation, enhanced by the lively satisfaction we receive from uniting our "broken impressions." Finally, once we have developed the propensity to attribute a continuing existence to a series of impressions, we tend to ascribe persistence to similar sequences of perceptions, even before we have had a comparable experience of their constancy or coherence. In these cases the resemblance we discover between various constant and coherent sequences among our perceptions become "a source of reasoning and analogy," which enables us to attribute "the same qualities to the similar objects" (T 1.4.2.24, 1.4.2.42 [SBN 199, 208–9]).

In sum, the constancy or coherence we discover among our successive impressions arouses the inertial "propension" of the imagination and leads it to generate a "fiction" by which we regard these sequences of impressions as objects that continue to exist even when the series is interrupted (T 1.4.2.36 [SBN 205]).[19]

Finally, Hume adds that our belief in the "*distinct* or *independent* existence" of objects apart from the mind is a "necessary consequence" of our belief in their continued existence. In his own words, this belief appears "wherever the mind follows its first and most natural tendency," even though "the doctrine of the independent existence of our sensible perceptions is contrary to the plainest experience" (T 1.4.2.44 [SBN 210]). Here he is echoing his initial assertion that the continued and the distinct existence of objects will mutually entail each other. However, he now apparently reduces "distinct" to "independent" existence, thereby implicitly conceding, as I have suggested, that he has not specifically explained our idea of external or spatial existence in Part 4 (T 1.4.2.2; cf. 1.4.5.10 [SBN 188; cf. 235–36]).

We may now return to Hume's general account of our idea of existence. As we have seen, Hume suggests that the idea of existence in the strict sense, or what I have called the absolute idea of existence, is derived from the existence of our perceptions, which, however, cannot be compared to any nonexistent perceptions. He then argues that we can only form a "relative idea" of the existence of external objects, or of objects "suppos'd *specifically* different from our perceptions," when we "attribute to them different relations, connexions and durations" than we attribute to perceptions themselves (T 1.2.6.9 [SBN 68]). In Part 4 he shows that this "relative idea" of external existence arises from the imagination, which attributes durations and connections to our perceptions by supposing that they continue to exist when they are not perceived, or by supposing that they are connected to unperceived impressions. Through these propensities, the imagination produces our idea of an external object and our belief in its existence.

Once we have formulated the relative idea of an external object, Hume indicates that we may also develop the idea of a nonexistent external object, or an object that does not have the appropriate set of connections to the objects we believe to exist, as well as the idea of an unobserved object. We may formulate the idea of a nonexistent object in two ways. First, the idea of a nonexistent object may be a deliberate product of the creative fancy, in which case it is not an object of belief. Second, the idea of a nonexistent object may be an extrapolation from a series of impressions that, upon a more careful or a complete survey, does not display a very compelling constancy or coherence, in which case we regard our initial belief in the object as mistaken. In cases of the latter type,

---

19. Price has proposed a more streamlined version of Hume's argument by suggesting that constancy and coherence are both types of "gap-indifference," with constancy as the limiting case of coherence; see *Hume's Theory of the External World,* 37–38 and 59–71.

in which we mistakenly believe in the existence of some particular external object, we have allowed our imagination to be guided by our hasty judgments of the causal relations between our perceptions: judgments which we may correct by appealing to the philosophical principles of causal reasoning. In other words, Hume argues that we may draw inferences from "the coherence of our perceptions," to distinguish, for example, between those impressions conjured by poetry or madness, and those which we should regard as real objects, by relying upon "reflection and *general rules*" (T 1.3.5.2, 1.3.10.11 [SBN 84, 631]).

According to Hume's analysis, we thus rely on causal reasoning, not only to attribute external existence to a changing series of impressions, but also to distinguish those sequences of perceptions we identify as external objects from those sequences we regard as fictions or illusions (cf. T 1.2.6.9, 1.4.2.45, 1.3.10.11–12 [SBN 68, 210–11, 632]). Similarly, we can account for our idea of and our belief in an unobserved object, such as an object distant in space or remote in time, as a further supposition produced by the imagination, under the guidance of analogy and causal reasoning, to explain a set of present perceptions (T 1.3.9.4 [SBN 108]).[20] Hume argues that causal reasoning cannot be the source of our idea of external existence, since we cannot perceive any cause of our perceptions that is separate from our perceptions (T 1.4.2.21 [SBN 197–98]). However, we rely upon the habit of causal reasoning in order to form the idea of any particular changing object, to distinguish a real object from an illusion, and to posit the existence of unobserved objects. Hume is accordingly referring to external existence, or the relative idea of existence, when he claims that "whatever is may not be," and when he asserts that the existence of a being "can only be proved by arguments from its cause or its effect" which are "founded entirely on experience" (EHU 12.29 [SBN 164]; cf. DNR 11.189).

Hume concludes that this activity of the imagination in producing a "supposition" or a fiction is the source of our common or vulgar idea of separate and enduring objects, which "are seen, and felt, and become present to the mind," and are considered to be "sometimes present to the mind, and sometimes absent from it, without any real or essential change" (T 1.4.2.40 [SBN 207–8]; cf. EHU 12.8 [SBN 151–52]). However, he argues that this opinion of the continued and distinct existence of our perceptions as external objects is shown by "a very little reflection and philosophy" to be false (T 1.4.2.44 [SBN 210]). These arguments have led philosophers develop a distinction between perceptions and objects: a distinction which Hume examines at the end of his discussion, and which I will consider in Chapter 5.

20. See Price, *Hume's Theory of the External World*, 164–75 and 216, and Wilson, *Hume's Defence of Causal Inference*, 41–70.

In concluding this section I would like to examine two key principles in Hume's account of our idea of external existence: the concept of identity, and the concept of a fiction.

Hume introduces the concept of identity in Part 2 as a philosophical relation that we first ascribe, "in its strictest sense," to "constant and unchangeable objects," and then also, in a derivative sense, "to every being, whose existence has any duration" (T 1.1.5.4 [SBN 14]). He further includes identity among those relations of fact immediately given to the senses (T 1.3.2.1–2 [SBN 73–74]). In Part 4 he offers a more detailed analysis of the concept of identity, as a relation that we attribute to external objects and our own mind. He initially argues that a single object or perception can give rise only to an idea of "unity," and rejects the use of the word "identity" for the supposed relation of an object to itself, since the alleged proposition that "an object is the same with itself" does not include a distinct subject and predicate, and would accordingly "mean nothing." On the other hand, we cannot derive the concept of identity from a "multiplicity" of objects, since the mind regards each object as a separate individual. The concept of identity therefore cannot be derived either from one perception or object, or from a collection of these (T 1.4.2.26–27; cf. 1.4.6.6 [SBN 200; cf. 253–54]).

In order to account for our idea of identity, and its relation to both unity and number, Hume returns to his account of time. As we have seen, in Part 2 Hume argues that the concept of duration is derived from a changing succession of perceptions, and then attributed to unchanging objects by a "fiction of the imagination." He now suggests that this fiction, when applied to an uninterrupted sequence of unchanging objects, produces the concept of identity, in which we regard a number of distinct momentary perceptions as a single object enduring through time. In our attributions of identity we accordingly judge, in effect, that "the object existent at one time is the same with itself existent in another." In other words, identity is "a medium betwixt unity and number," or more properly "either of them, according to the view, in which we take it," since in our attributions of identity we regard a multiplicity of perceptions as forming a unity through a "suppos'd variation of time" (T 1.4.2.29–30 [SBN 200–201]).

Hume argues that we may attribute identity "in its strictest sense," or "perfect identity," only to "constant and unchangeable objects," or in other words, to a perception enduring through time without an interruption or a change. This would presumably be an uninterrupted view of an unchanging object (T 1.1.5.4, 1.4.2.33; cf. 1.4.6.6 [SBN 14, 203; cf. 254]). However, we also have the propensity to ascribe identity to an interrupted succession of exactly resembling perceptions, and even to successive perceptions that do not resemble each other very closely but are regularly conjoined in certain ways. In other words, the imagination continues the same "smooth and uninterrupted progress" when it recognizes "a succession of related objects" as in considering "the same invariable object," and tends to confuse "the succession with the identity" (T 1.4.2.34 [SBN 203–4]). He accordingly states that all the objects "to which we ascribe identity, without observing their invariableness and uninterruptedness" consist in a succession of perceptions that are related to each other by "resemblance, contiguity, or causation" (T 1.4.6.7 [SBN 255]).[21] This type of identity, which we attribute to objects from an interrupted series of resembling perceptions, or a coherent series of changing perceptions, may be called "imperfect" identity (T 1.4.6.9 [SBN 256]).

Finally, Hume considers the principles by which we attribute this "imperfect" identity to changing objects. First, we generally attribute a continued identity to any "mass of matter" after a very small part has been added or removed, usually distinguishing a small change from a change in the identity of an object "by its *proportion* to the whole." Thus, in his examples, "the addition or diminution of a mountain wou'd not be sufficient to produce a diversity in a planet," although a change in "a very few inches wou'd be able to destroy the identity of some bodies." Next, we regard a "mutual dependence," or a "reciprocal relation of cause and effect," within a series of perceptions, even in their "actions and operations," as grounds for attributing identity. This is especially apparent in the case of organic bodies, which we regard as maintaining their identity through a series of changes even while "their form, size, and substance" are "entirely alter'd," and even when the body does not preserve "one particle of matter, or figure of its parts the same." Finally, we may also regard the human ability to direct each in a series of changing objects toward a "*common end* or purpose" as a basis for attributing identity to a sequence of perceptions as a single object. This is evident, for example, in the case of "a ship, of which a considerable part has been chang'd by frequent reparations." Indeed, Hume finds that many attributions of identity are determined by human artifices or conventions as these apply to a causal sequence. This appears, for example, when we say, after an old brick church has fallen into ruin, that "the parish rebuilt the same church of free-stone, and according to modern architecture," even though "neither the form nor materials are the same, nor is there any thing common to the two objects, but their relation to the inhabitants of the parish." We may even consider a "republic or commonwealth" to maintain its identity through all of the "incessant change of its parts," including not only

---

21. Price has argued that, on Hume's account, even the identity of a supposedly unchanging and uninterrupted object arises from our attribution of duration to a series of spatial minima and/or temporal minima: see his *Hume's Theory of the External World*, 46–50, and also Waxman, *Hume's Theory of Consciousness*, 203–7.

new generations of inhabitants, but also changes in its "laws and constitutions" (T 1.4.6.9–13, 1.4.6.19 [SBN 255–58, 261]).[22]

In cases of very close resemblance and very familiar causal relations in a sequence of perceptions, Hume argues that the constitutive activity of the imagination "almost universally takes place," producing a spontaneous agreement among human observers in our judgments of identity (T 1.4.2.29 [SBN 201]). In other cases our attributions of identity require a more specialized experience with similar objects, and judgments drawn through philosophical probable reasoning concerning the regular sequence of changes in this type of object under various conditions. In other words, an Indian prince would not judge a pool of ice to be identical to a pool of water without experience of the tendency of water to freeze in cold temperatures (cf. EHU 10.10 [SBN 113–14]). Finally, in attributing identity to objects on the basis of human purposes, or human conventions, we must apply the standards of identity that are implicitly recognized for that type of object within the life of a community, or even explicitly prescribed by an institution, as in the case of a ship or a parish church. However, Hume observes that we do not always have a precise standard in every case for determining the identity of the object through every possible change; and for this reason he concludes that many of our disputes over the identity of an object might seem to be "merely verbal," although the parties in these disputes appeal to the philosophical concept of identity insofar as "the relation of parts gives rise to some fiction or imaginary principle of union" (T 1.4.6.21; cf. 1.4.6.7 [SBN 262; cf. 255]).[23]

Hume thus indicates that we may develop standards for attributing identity to certain types of objects according to our philosophical or scientific principles of probable reasoning, and in some cases according to the social conventions that govern the attribution of identity to certain types of objects (cf. 1.3.10.11–12 [SBN 631]). That is, we appeal to the philosophical principles of probable reasoning to distinguish those products of the imagination which are "permanent, irresistible, and universal" from those which are "changeable, weak, and irregular," or the "trivial suggestions of the fancy" from the "general and more establish'd properties of the imagination" that we call the "understanding" (T 1.4.4.1, 1.4.7.7 [SBN 225, 267]). Our concept of identity is, therefore, a construction of the imagination, which we may judge to be applicable to an object in any given case according to the standards of critical reflection provided by Hume in his account of probable reasoning and his later discussion

22. See Noxon, "Senses of Identity," 367–84, and Ashley and Stack, "Hume's Theory of the Self and its Identity," 239–54.

23. On the linguistic and philosophical aspects of Hume's account of identity, see Penelhum, "Hume on Personal Identity," 213–39; Robison, "In Defense of Hume's *Appendix*," 89–99; and Waxman, *Hume's Theory of Consciousness*, 324n22. See also Henze, "Linguistic Aspect of Hume's Method," 121.

of the conventional standards for various types of judgment in social and political life.[24]

Hume introduces the concept of a fiction in Book 1, Part 2, where he observes that our ideas "always represent the objects or impressions, from which they are deriv'd, and can never without a fiction represent or be apply'd to any other." His example in this context is the idea of duration, which arises from a series of changing perceptions but is also applied to unchanging objects (T 1.2.3.11; cf. 1.2.5.29 [SBN 37; cf. 65]). We also apply a fictitious extension to distances between objects, even though this distance is not filled with visible or tangible objects (T 1.2.5.23 [SBN 62]). Our supposed idea of a standard of equality in geometry is also "a mere fiction of the mind," along with our supposed ideas of precise colors or musical notes, by which we suppose that we can judge "an exact comparison and equality beyond the judgments of the senses" (T 1.2.4.24 [SBN 48–49]).

In Part 4 Hume again argues that we can apply the idea of time to an unchanging object "only by a fiction of the imagination" (T 1.4.2.29 [SBN 200–201]). He also describes our idea of an object when it does not appear to the senses as the "fiction of a continu'd existence" (T 1.4.2.36; cf. 1.4.2.42, 1.4.6.6–7 [SBN 205; cf. 209, 254–55]). In other words, the idea of continued existence is a fiction produced by the imagination in order to unite a series of related but interrupted perceptions. As we will see, the identity of the mind is also a "fictitious" identity, which is produced by the imagination in order to unite our remembered perceptions as a subjective succession (T 1.4.6.15; cf. 1.4.6.21 [SBN 259; cf. 262]).

Many commentators have regarded Hume's account of fictions as a skeptical, dismissive, or despairing conclusion to his analyses of space, time, external existence, and personal identity. This is reflected, for example, in Bennett's statement that, according to Hume, the vulgar belief in external objects is merely "another worthless fiction."[25] Other studies have suggested that Hume intends to present a more positive view of fictions, as the principles by which the imagination constructs both the physical and the mental world, and even the social world with its "fictional" artifices and conventions, which we will consider in later chapters.[26]

Hume himself presents a multileveled approach to the question of whether and in what sense the fiction of external existence is justified as a principle of

24. For further discussions of Hume's view of the relative justification of our judgments of identity, see Price, *Hume's Theory of the External World*, 139–40, 144, 160–64, and 215–17; Baier, *Progress of Sentiments*, 119–21; and Garrett, *Cognition and Commitment*, 214–15.

25. Bennett, *Locke, Berkeley, Hume*, 349.

26. See Wilson, *Hume's Defence of Causal Inference*, 90–98; Sokolowski, "Fiction and Illusion," 189–225; Traiger, "Impressions, Ideas, and Fictions," 381–99; and Baier, "Hume's Account of Social Artifice," 757–78. See also Whelan, *Order and Artifice*, 17, 58, 98–101, 131–34, and 308–9, and Strawson, *Secret Connexion*, 49–67.

cognition. First, he repeatedly states that this fiction is "really false," and that we can only extend an idea beyond our immediate perceptions by an "error" or "mistake" of the imagination (T 1.4.2.43–44, 1.4.6.6–7 [SBN 209–10, 254–55]). He reaffirms this assessment in considering the skeptical implications of his analysis, which we will consider in Chapter 5. However, Hume also maintains that these fictions are "very natural" and "almost universally take place," leading Kemp Smith and others to describe them as spontaneous, unreflective, and unavoidable "natural beliefs" (T 1.2.4.24, 1.4.2.29 [SBN 48, 201]).[27] On the other hand, although any attribution of external existence involves a fiction of the imagination, Hume argues that we may distinguish dreams, hallucinations, and poetic images from the objects of sensation and memory. In other words, we may apply the standards of causal reasoning in order to judge which of these apparent external objects possess "truth and reality" (T 1.3.10.6 [SBN 121–22]; cf. 1.3.5.4, 1.3.10.10–12 [SBN 85, 630–32]; EHU 5.10–13 [SBN 47–50]). Accordingly, when we judge the spatial and temporal location of objects, their identity through time, and even the identity of a human person, we are guided not merely by the promptings of the imagination, but also by the philosophical or scientific principles of causal reasoning. In this respect Hume regards the fictions of space and time, external existence, and personal identity not merely as unavoidable and nonrational beliefs arising from the imagination, but also as principles of judgment whose application in every individual case is subject to critical evaluation and correction.

Finally, several critics have objected to Hume's account of fictions by arguing that Hume cannot account for the idea of a fiction within his "copy theory" of ideas. For example, Williams has criticized Hume's account of fictions as a departure from the copy theory, while Traiger has instead suggested that "what is commonly called Hume's theory of impressions and ideas ought to be called the theory of impressions, ideas, *and fictions*."[28] However, I would argue that, on Hume's view, the idea of a fiction is the idea of that propensity of the imagination by which we attribute extension to an empty distance, duration to unchanging objects, continued existence to an interrupted series of perceptions, and the unity of belonging to a single mind to a series of perceptions. On this view, the derivation of the idea of a fiction is parallel to the derivation of the idea of a necessary connection between a cause and its effect. According to Hume, the idea of a necessary connection is derived from an impression of necessity, which is itself a disposition of the mind, arising in this case from a custom or habit produced by repeated observations. We then project our idea of this necessity onto sets of objects or sequences of events, which we regard as

27. Kemp Smith, *Philosophy of David Hume*, 124–27, 454–58, and 485–87.

28. Williams, "Hume's Criterion of Significance," 290–91; Traiger, "Impressions, Ideas, and Fictions," 381. See also Johnson, *Mind of David Hume*, 261.

necessarily connected to one another (T 1.3.14.22 [SBN 165–66]). Similarly, our idea of a fiction, such as the fiction of external existence, is an idea of the felt propensity of the mind to posit a series of unperceived perceptions, or an unperceived object, to connect our perceptions. Here again, the idea arises from the disposition of the mind to project the products of the imagination outward, and to suppose, in this case, the independent existence of a series of perceptions which we then call the object.[29] This view is reflected in Hume's assertions that we have "no idea" of space, time, external objects, or the self, if these are supposed to arise from any positive image derived from any particular impression (cf. T 1.2.3.16, 1.2.5.28, 1.4.5.6, 1.4.6.1–2 [SBN 39, 64, 234, 251–52]). However, we may form relative ideas of various arrangements of our perceptions, as these arrangements are projected beyond our perceptions by the imagination.[30]

PERSONAL IDENTITY

In Book 1, Part 4 of the *Treatise* Hume also presents an account of our idea of the mind or self. He returns to the topic of personal identity in the Appendix, where he appears to direct a searching criticism against his earlier analysis, although the precise nature and extent of his later reservations are matters of considerable controversy.

In the course of his discussion, Hume distinguishes between the analysis of personal identity "as it regards our thought or imagination," and personal identity as it pertains to "our passions or the concern we take in ourselves." He addresses the first question in Book 1, while apparently deferring his discussion of "our identity with regard to the passions" to Book 2 (T 1.4.6.5, cf. 1.4.6.19 [SBN 253; cf. 261]). I will consider Hume's account of the self as an object of our thought and imagination in the remainder of this chapter, and his account of the self as the subject of passion and volition in Chapters 6 and 7.[31]

Hume introduces his analysis by rejecting the view that we can receive any impression of the self through our senses, or indeed that the senses "can ever distinguish betwixt ourselves and external objects." On the contrary, the question of personal identity is among the most abstruse in philosophy, and can only be addressed through "the most profound metaphysics" (T 1.4.2.6 [SBN 189–90]). He then anticipates his later argument that "what we call a *mind,* is

29. See Wilbanks, *Hume's Theory of Imagination,* 80–84, and Wright, *Sceptical Realism,* 106–7.
30. See Flage, "Hume's Relative Ideas," 65.
31. For additional discussions, see Penelhum, "Hume on Personal Identity," 571–89; Noxon, "Senses of Identity," 367–84; Ashley and Stack, "Hume's Theory of the Self and Identity," 239–54; Vesey, *Personal Identity;* Bricke, *Hume's Philosophy of Mind;* Pears, *Hume's System,* 120–51; Baier, *Progress of Sentiments,* 122–28; Biro, "Hume's New Science of the Mind," 47–58; Waxman, *Hume's Theory of Consciousness,* 203–37; Johnson, *Mind of David Hume,* 285–310; and Stevenson, "Humean Self-Consciousness Explained," 95–129.

nothing but a heap or collection of different perceptions" which are "united together by certain relations, and suppos'd, tho' falsely, to be endow'd with a perfect simplicity and identity." Finally, external objects are said to become "present to the mind" when they attain "such a relation to a connected heap of perceptions," as to influence these perceptions "very considerably in augmenting their number by present reflections and passions, and in storing the memory with ideas" (T 1.4.2.39–40 [SBN 207]).[32]

Next, Hume responds to those philosophers who "pretend that we have an idea of the substance of our minds," and that we cannot account for our perceptions without some "material or immaterial substances, in which they suppose our perceptions to inhere."[33] Here he reaffirms his earlier argument that we have no impression or idea of a substance apart from our perceptions nor of either a material or an immaterial substance in which these perceptions are supposed to inhere. However, he also adds that we may describe perceptions themselves as substances, according to the definition of a substance as "something which may exist by itself," since perceptions are "distinct and separable, and may be consider'd as separately existent, and may exist separately, and have no need of any thing else to support their existence" (T 1.4.5.2–5 [SBN 232–34]; cf. 1.1.6.1–2 [SBN 15–16]; E 1S.591–92).

In presenting his constructive account of our idea of personal identity in Section 6, Hume begins by rejecting the popular belief among philosophers that "we are every moment intimately conscious of what we call our SELF; that we feel its existence and its continuance in existence; and are certain, beyond the evidence of a demonstration, both of its perfect identity and simplicity." On the contrary, he claims on the basis of introspection that we cannot find any single, constant, and invariable impression of a self among our perceptions; and thus do not have "any idea of *self*, after the manner it is here explain'd." Instead, he reports that "when I enter most intimately into what I call *myself*, I always stumble on some particular perception or other," such as "heat or cold, light or shade, love or hatred, pain or pleasure," and can never catch "*myself* at any time without a perception, and can never observe any thing but the perception." Accordingly, while a few metaphysicians might claim to discover a separate impression of themselves, he ventures to affirm for himself and the rest of the human species that we are each of us "nothing but a bundle or collection of different perceptions, which succeed each other with an inconceivable rapidity,

32. Waxman has indeed argued that Hume's account of personal identity is a necessary presupposition for his complete account of external existence, although this is obscured by his order of presentation in the *Treatise*; see *Hume's Theory of Consciousness*, 238–44.

33. McIntyre and Russell both argue that the most immediate target of Hume's criticism of the view of the soul as an immaterial substance is Samuel Clarke. See McIntyre, "Hume: Second Newton of the Moral Sciences," 3–18, and Russell, "Hume's *Treatise* and the Clarke-Collins Controversy," 95–115.

and are in a perpetual flux and movement." In order to account for the idea of the self, we must therefore explain our propensity "to ascribe an identity to these successive perceptions, and to suppose ourselves possest of an invariable and uninterrupted existence thro' the whole course of our lives" (T 1.4.6.1–5 [SBN 251–53]).

Hume's main focus in his discussion of personal identity, both in the original text and in the Appendix, is upon the idea of the mind. As indicated above, he argues that the mind consists entirely in a sequence of perceptions that are distinguishable and separable from each other. Since we cannot discover any "real bond" or "real connexion" between our perceptions, he argues that it is the imagination which attributes identity to the mind, based on the relations of resemblance and causation that we discover within this sequence of perceptions (T 1.4.6.16 [SBN 259–60]).[34] However, Hume's account of the influence of these relations on this activity of the imagination is rather obscure, and indeed he himself appears to have become dissatisfied with his own analysis, judging by his reconsiderations in the Appendix.

In the original text of Section 6 Hume first argues that our memory-images resemble our past perceptions, and that "the frequent placing of these resembling perceptions" in our train of thought conveys the imagination from one to the other, giving the entire sequence the appearance of identity. While we are only able to discover these resemblances among our own perceptions, he argues that we would also recognize these resemblances if we could "see clearly into the breast of another, and observe that succession of perceptions, which constitutes his mind or thinking principle."[35] Next, he reminds us of his earlier argument that "impressions give rise to their correspondent ideas, and these ideas in their turn produce other impressions," in what we regard as a series of causal relations. Accordingly, "the true idea of the human mind, is to consider it as a system of different perceptions" which are "link'd together by the relation of cause and effect." Finally, memory is the faculty that discloses both the succession of our perceptions and the relations of resemblance and causation between them. Hume therefore maintains that memory "not only discovers the identity, but also contributes to its production," and should thus be regarded as the "source of personal identity" (T 1.4.6.18–20 [SBN 260–62]).

---

34. Hume excludes contiguity from his account of mental identity as having "little or no influence in the present case" (T 1.4.6.17 [SBN 260]). Waxman has accordingly noted that the spatial contiguity of perceptions seems irrelevant to Hume's account of the identity of the mind: see *Hume's Theory of Consciousness*, 228. However, since the natural relation of contiguity includes both spatial and temporal contiguity (T 1.1.4.1 [SBN 11]), we may still ask why Hume does not consider the possible influence of the temporal contiguity of perceptions in contributing to the identity of the mind, especially given the importance of memory in his theory. This application of the principle of temporal association might indeed have anticipated Kant's account of time as the form of inner sense, including empirical self-consciousness.

35. See Bricke, *Hume's Philosophy of Mind*, 85–91, and Waxman, *Hume's Theory of Consciousness*, 326n29.

Hume accordingly maintains that the identity we ascribe to the mind is "only a fictitious one." The imagination initially applies this identity to a given series of changing perceptions (T 1.4.6.15 [SBN 259]). However, to disguise any interruptions in this series of perceptions, we then extend this fiction by supposing the existence "of a *soul,* and *self,* and *substance,*" which is supposed to be endowed with a "perfect identity and simplicity" (T 1.4.6.6, 1.4.6.1; cf. 1.4.6.22 [SBN 254, 251; cf. 263]). This supposition is reflected especially in the doctrine of the soul as an immaterial substance, which Hume has already criticized in Section 5. By contrast, he maintains that our successive perceptions alone "compose" or "constitute the mind," and that apart from these perceptions we have no idea "of the place, where these scenes are represented, or of the materials, of which it is compos'd" (T App.20, 1.4.6.4 [SBN 635, 253]; cf. A 28 [SBN 657–58]; DNR 2.146, 4.158–59).

However, this concept of the mind, as a system of perceptions disclosed by memory, does not yet give us our complete idea of personal identity. Although we derive the idea of our identity from our remembered perceptions, we also extend this idea to include "the identity of our persons beyond our memory." Indeed, we regard this extension as including the greater part of our lives. In order to account for this extended concept of personal identity, Hume argues that once we have developed an idea of our mind from the memory of our successive perceptions, we continue to trace "the same chain of causes" beyond the direct reach of our memory. This allows us to project the "identity of our persons" through many other "times, and circumstances, and actions, which we have entirely forgot, but suppose in general to have existed." In other words, we suppose our continuing identity, during those intervals of time which we do not remember, through causal reasoning, by which we judge that we were probably present during various past events which we judge to have occurred from the evidence now available to us. In this extension of our idea of personal identity, Hume concludes that memory accompanied by causal reasoning "does not so much *produce* as *discover* personal identity" (T 1.4.6.20 [SBN 261–62]).

We may also ask whether Hume includes the idea that we each have of our own bodies in his account of personal identity. One response to this question is suggested by Ayer's statement that Hume "equates personal identity with the identity of the mind, and defines this without any reference to the body."[36] In Book 2 of the *Treatise,* Hume alludes to the discussion among his predecessors over whether the body should be regarded "as a part of ourselves" or "as something external" (T 2.1.8.1 [SBN 298]). He presents his own view earlier in Book 1, Part 4, by arguing that although we might expect to discover through the

36. Ayer, *Hume,* 51. See also Bricke, *Hume's Philosophy of Mind,* 92–94; Flew, *David Hume,* 3–5 and 90–108; and Pears, *Hume's System,* 121, 129–34, and 145–49.

senses that "our own body evidently belongs to us," and that many other objects are "exterior to the body," we discover upon a more careful consideration that "properly speaking, 'tis not our body we perceive, when we regard our limbs and members, but certain impressions, which enter by the senses." Our idea of our own body is an idea of an object which we perceive through our senses, and must be explained in the same way as our idea of any other external object (T 1.4.2.9 [SBN 190–91]). This body, which we regard as a corporeal object through sensation, causal reasoning, and imaginative supposition, presumably provides a further ground for the attribution of personal identity. This is because we suppose that the body continues to exist during an interval of publicly measured time, through the interruptions of our perception and memory, as in sleep or other periods of unconsciousness. We are also led by causal reasoning to attribute a series of changes to this body, such as its development from infancy to maturity (T 1.4.6.20, 1.4.6.3, 1.4.6.12 [SBN 261–62, 252, 257]).

Hume also considers the problem of the apparent interaction between the mind and body. In Section 5 he endorses the view that thought and extension are "wholly incompatible, and never can incorporate together into one subject." More specifically, thought can never exist in a "local conjunction" with extension, since thought is not given to us as distributed in space. Accordingly, he rejects the view of "materialists, who conjoin all thought with extension" (T 1.4.5.7, 1.4.5.11–15 [SBN 234–35, 236–39]). On the other hand, we also discover, through observation and causal inference, that various types of impressions are conveyed to the mind by the organs of our body, that our capacity to receive impressions is influenced by the condition of the body, and that it is interrupted by sleep and terminated by death (T 1.4.2.12, 1.4.2.45, 1.4.5.12, 1.4.6.3 [SBN 192, 210–11, 237, 252]; E IS.596–98). In addition, we discover constant conjunctions between our perceptions and the movements of objects, and also between our thoughts and the movement of our own bodies. Hume argues that these constant conjunctions are the necessary and sufficient conditions for affirming both the possibility and the actuality of a causal interaction between thought and matter, as in the case of any other causal connection, even if we cannot explain this conjunction at any deeper level. In other words, although "thought and motion are different from each other," we also find that they are "constantly united," and may conclude "that motion may be, and actually is, the cause of thought and perception," (T 1.4.5.30 [SBN 248]). Through our experience of their constant conjunction, we also find that thought and volition may be the causes of physical action, as we will see at greater length in Chapter 7 (T 1.4.5.30, 2.3.1.1–4 [SBN 248, 399–401]; EHU 8.1–36, 12.29n35 [SBN 80–103, 164n1]; DNR 4.160).[37]

37. For a further discussion of this argument, see Bricke, *Hume's Philosophy of Mind,* 25–45, and Cummins, "Hume as Dualist and Anti-Dualist," 47–55.

Hume therefore provides us with the materials for regarding our idea of our own bodies as a product of the imagination, which is produced in the same way as our idea of any other external object. However, he also indicates that we discover, through causal reasoning, that this body has a distinctive relation to the remembered succession of perceptions which constitutes our mind. In particular, we find that our sensations arise from the organs of the body, and that our volitions can cause various actions of the body.[38] Hume returns to this discussion in Book 2, in which he considers our ideas of the various qualities of our minds and bodies, along with our experience and our conception of voluntary action.

Hume's reflections concerning personal identity in the Appendix have been regarded by many commentators as a retraction of his analysis of personal identity in the original text of the *Treatise*.[39] However, while his later reflections are perhaps even more obscure than his original account of the relations between our perceptions, Hume's departure in the Appendix from his earlier discussion may be less extreme than suggested by many of his critics.

In the original text Hume assures his readers that "the intellectual world," or the mind, "tho' involv'd in infinite obscurities, is not perplex'd with any such contradictions, as those we have discover'd in the natural," in considering our idea of external existence (T 1.4.5.1 [SBN 232]). However, in the Appendix he admits that "upon a more strict review of the section concerning *personal identity*," he finds himself "involv'd in such a labyrinth" that he doubts his ability to defend a consistent position. While he reaffirms his argument against "the strict and proper identity and simplicity of a self or thinking being," he now questions his earlier account of the "principle of connexion" that is supposed to bind our perceptions and give us an idea of their "real simplicity and identity." He still maintains that "no connexions among distinct existences are ever discoverable by human understanding," and instead that "we only *feel* a connexion or a determination of the thought, to pass from one object to another." However, he is apparently dissatisfied with his failure to provide a more specific account of "the principles, that unite our successive perceptions in our thought or consciousness," and is unable to offer any satisfactory theory of these principles. He is thus left with two allegedly inconsistent propositions, "that all our distinct perceptions are distinct existences, and that the mind never perceives

---

38. For more on the role of the body in Hume's account of personal identity, see Baier, *Progress of Sentiments*, 130–42; Frasca-Spada, *Space and the Self*, 194–98; Williams, *Cultivated Reason*, 129–66; and Stevenson, "Humean Self-Consciousness Explained," 120–22.

39. See Pears, "Hume on Personal Identity," 289–98, and *Hume's System*, 135 and 145–47; along with Dicker, *Hume's Epistemology and Metaphysics*, 31–32. For other assessments, see McIntyre, "Is Hume's Self Consistent?" 79–88; Robison, "In Defense of Hume's *Appendix*," 89–100; Bricke, *Hume's Philosophy of Mind*, 95–98; Swain, "Being Sure of One's Self," 107–19; Loeb, "Causation," 219–31; Waxman, "Hume's Quandary Concerning Personal Identity," 233–53; and Garrett, *Cognition and Commitment*, 163–86. Garrett also includes an excellent survey of various recent approaches to the interpretation of the Appendix.

any real connexion among distinct existences" (T App.10, App.20–21 [SBN 633, 635–36]). The problem for his readers is to find what he means here by a "real connexion," and why he now regards his initial failure to give an account of this connection as a difficulty for his analysis. In his original discussion, Hume did not appeal to a strict connection between our perceptions to account for personal identity, instead presenting the relations of resemblance and causation as the "uniting principles" which lead the imagination to formulate the idea of personal identity. He even reminds us that all our judgments of causation, even those that contribute to our idea of personal identity, rest on a "customary association of ideas" rather than any "real connexion" (T 1.4.6.16 [SBN 259–60]).

Hume never explains why he has come to regard the absence of any explanation of the "real connexion" between our perceptions as a difficulty for his earlier theory of mental identity. However, it seems evident that in the Appendix he is acknowledging the inadequacy of some aspect of his general theory of perceptions, including their relations according to the natural principles of association, for supporting a satisfactory theory of the mind.

Several commentators have suggested that in recognizing a problem in his analysis Hume is anticipating Kant's theory of the transcendental unity of apperception, in which we find the unity of the mind to be presupposed by any activity of combining perceptions according to any principles of relation. This comparison is perhaps supported by Hume's own indication that the "self or person" may be characterized as "that to which our several impressions and ideas are suppos'd to have a reference" (T 1.4.6.2 [SBN 251]).[40]

Whatever might be the precise character of the difficulty that he is attempting to address in the Appendix, it seems clear that Hume does not regard this difficulty as a threat to his larger philosophical argument in the *Treatise*. As we have seen, he initially hopes that his account of the mind will not be "perplex'd" with such contradictions as those in his discussion of external existence (T 1.4.5.1 [SBN 232]). While he abandons this hope in the Appendix, he also reminds his readers that this new difficulty is only another of the many "contradictions, and absurdities" which have already been "abundantly supplied" in the *Treatise* (T App.10 [SBN 633]). Hume is therefore cheerfully prepared to accommodate the difficulty he has discovered in his analysis of personal identity, whatever this problem might be, within his larger philosophical project. We will consider his further account of the implications of these contradictions for his philosophical project in the following chapter, where we will turn to his discussion of skepticism.

40. See Robison, "Hume on Personal Identity," 181–93; Waxman, "Hume's Quandary Concerning Personal Identity," 244–45, and *Hume's Theory of Consciousness*, 326–27n32; and Brook, *Kant and the Mind*, 192–94. See also Garrett, *Cognition and Commitment*, 169–71.

We have thus seen that in Book 1, Part 4 Hume extends his account of the philosophical principles of probable reasoning in order to account for the standards by which we determine the distinct and continued existence of external objects, the identity of the mind, and the relation of the mind to a particular body. These judgments of identity involve an imaginative extrapolation beyond our perceptions and are therefore "false" in the strict sense, but they may also be more or less justified individually, according to the relations of resemblance and causation we discover between our perceptions, as directed by the rules for judging causes and effects, and in some cases by the standards of identity established in the culture and institutions of a community. In other words, Hume defends the relative legitimacy and value of our standards of identity for persons and objects, both in ordinary life and in the natural and human sciences.[41]

However, Hume's analysis of external existence and personal identity, along with his further reflections concerning causal reasoning, are all presented within the larger context of his discussion of skepticism in Part 4. In order to defend the present interpretation of his analysis as a constructive account of human cognition, we must therefore turn to his discussion of the various forms of skepticism, and their relation to our everyday opinions and to various systems of philosophy.

41. Several commentators have indeed described Hume's account of the identity and nature of physical objects as a version of critical realism that is intended to provide a justification for the modern natural sciences. See especially Wright, *Sceptical Realism;* along with Wilson, "Was Hume a Subjectivist?" 247–82; "Is Hume a Sceptic with Regard to the Senses?" 49–73; and *Hume's Defence of Causal Inference,* 90–98. For a discussion of this view, see Livingston, "A Sellarsian Hume?" 281–90; Wilson, "Hume's Critical Realism," 291–96; and Winkler, "The New Hume," 52–87.

5

Skepticism

Hume's overarching theme in Book 1, Part 4 of the *Treatise* is his account of skepticism, which he explicitly introduces in the first two sections, develops along with a consideration of different systems of philosophy in the next four sections, and completes in the seventh section. This examination of skepticism, and his final characterization of his own philosophical position, is the culmination of his account "Of the understanding" in Book 1, and the point of departure for his further inquiries belonging to the moral or human sciences in Books 2 and 3. He later reaffirms these skeptical arguments in the *Abstract* and the *Letter from a Gentleman to his Friend in Edinburgh,* offers a further account of the different types of skepticism in Section 12 of the first *Enquiry,* and introduces skepticism in the *Dialogues Concerning Natural Religion* as the starting point for his examination of natural theology.

Hume's consideration of skepticism was immediately recognized as a central theme in his writings, and the skeptical implications of his philosophy were highlighted in the earliest reviews and discussions of his works.[1] The subsequent interpretation of Hume's philosophy has been dominated by discussions of the nature and extent of his skepticism. Many critics have echoed

---

1. See Mossner, *Life of David Hume,* 116–33, 225–27, 294–300, and 577–88; as well as Hume's response to an anonymous critic in his *Letter from a Gentleman* (LG 3–4, 17–21).

his earliest reviewers by regarding Hume as an extreme skeptic.[2] However, an increasing number of studies have argued that Hume is presenting a version of skepticism that is not intended to subvert our reasonings in the sciences and in ordinary life, but rather to explain the principles of cognition presupposed by these reasonings, and to examine their limitations, while also considering the practical context and the purposes of human cognition.[3] In this chapter I show that Hume consistently defends a moderate version of skepticism, in contrast to the alternatives of both extreme skepticism and uncritical naturalism.[4] I also consider his assessment of the implications of mitigated skepticism for our investigations in the natural and human sciences.

EXTREME SKEPTICISM

Many readers of Book 1 of the *Treatise* have attempted to identify skeptical arguments prior to Hume's explicit discussion of skepticism in Part 4. However, Hume himself refers to skepticism only once in the original text of Parts 1–3. This reference appears in Part 3, where, in considering our ability to correct judgments arising from general rules by judgments according to other general rules, he notes that "the sceptics may here have the pleasure of observing a new and signal contradiction in our reason" (T 1.3.13.12 [SBN 150]).[5] In the introduction, where he is inviting his prospective readers to accompany him in his "metaphysical reasonings," he even states that an aversion to metaphysics among professed scholars can arise only from "the most determin'd scepticism, along with a great degree of indolence" (T Int.3 [SBN xiv]).[6] Finally, in a footnote on the Newtonian theory of space added to Part 2 in the Appendix, he remarks that nothing is more suited to Newtonian philosophy "than a modest

2. See the Introduction and Chapter 3 of this book.

3. See Norton, *David Hume;* Wright, *Sceptical Realism;* Livingston, *Hume's Philosophy of Common Life* and *Philosophical Melancholy and Delirium;* Fogelin, *Hume's Skepticism;* Tweyman, *Scepticism and Belief;* Pears, *Hume's System,* vii–viii; Baier, *Progress of Sentiments,* 57–59 and 287–88; Penelhum, *David Hume,* 1–38; Waxman, *Hume's Theory of Consciousness,* 5–18 and 266–79; Garrett, *Cognition and Commitment,* 204–5 and 232–41; Wilson, *Hume's Defence of Causal Inference,* 193–94; and Falkenstein, "Naturalism, Normativity, and Scepticism," 29–72. Note, however, that these studies do not agree in their specific interpretations of the relation between Hume's skeptical arguments and his constructive philosophical or scientific views.

4. My approach here has been influenced by Livingston's argument that Hume's various discussions of skepticism have a dialectical structure which we may trace as an unfolding progression in his various texts: see *Hume's Philosophy of Common Life,* 9–59, 272–84; and *Philosophical Melancholy and Delirium,* 17–52. See also Coleman, "Hume's Dialectic," 139–55; Waxman, *Hume's Theory of Consciousness,* 18 and 266–79; and Williams, *Cultivated Reason,* 21–60.

5. Hume does not explicitly describe his analysis of our idea of causation as "sceptical" until the first *Enquiry* (SBN 4.1, 5.1 [SBN 25, 40–41]).

6. For a discussion of Hume's strategy in his depiction of skepticism in the Introduction to the *Treatise* and the Conclusion of Book 1, see Cummins, "Hume's Diffident Skepticism," 43–65.

scepticism to a certain degree, and a fair confession of ignorance in subjects, that exceed all human capacity" (T 1.2.5.26n12 [SBN 639]).

Hume's first explicit discussion of skepticism emerges in Book 1, Part 4 of the *Treatise,* which is entitled "Of the sceptical and other systems of philosophy." In Section 1 he considers "scepticism with regard to reason," or the skeptical implications of his examination of probable reasoning; and in Section 2 he turns to "scepticism with regard to the senses," or the skeptical implications of analyzing our idea of external existence. In the next three sections he considers the prevailing systems of ancient and modern philosophy, including the ancient doctrine of substance and accident, the modern doctrine of primary and secondary qualities, and modern approaches to the doctrine of the soul, and seeks to expose their unrecognized skeptical implications. Finally, he develops his own version of skepticism in the "Conclusion of this book," where he explores the effects of these skeptical arguments in the intellectual and emotional life of a philosopher and establishes the point of departure for his further study of human nature in Books 2 and 3.

Hume begins his discussion of skepticism in Part 4, Section 1, by considering the skeptical implications of his analysis of demonstrative and probable reasoning in Part 3. First, in the case of demonstrative reasoning, he argues that although the rules of mathematical reasoning may in themselves be "certain and infallible," we find through experience that in applying these rules "our fallible and uncertain faculties are very apt to depart from them, and fall into error." We must therefore evaluate any conclusion reached through demonstrative reasoning by a further judgment of its probable accuracy, according to "our experience of the veracity or deceitfulness of our understanding, and according to the simplicity or intricacy of the question." In other words, we may consider our efforts in demonstrative reasoning as "a kind of history," and compare those occasions in which "our understanding has deceiv'd us" to others when its testimony was "just and true," in order to identify the causal circumstances that tend to influence our mathematical reasonings. On the basis of this experience we may even develop procedures for improving the accuracy and assurance of our mathematical reasonings, such as "artificial" accounting methods, repeated calculations, and submitting our conclusions to other skilled mathematicians for checking and confirmation. However, all of these methods can only serve to enhance the probable accuracy of our mathematical reasonings. Hume concludes that, in practice, the "knowledge" arising from demonstrative reasoning actually "resolves itself," or "degenerates," into probability (T 1.4.1.1–4 [SBN 180–81]).

With this account of the merely probable character even of our mathematical judgments, considered as the products of human cognitive activity, Hume returns to the different degrees of assurance in our causal reasonings (cf. T 1.3.12.1–20 [SBN 130–55]). As a further and alarming "species of probability," he now argues that each of our probable judgments is subject to "a new uncertainty" derived from the weakness of our faculties of judgment. In other words, from our experience in reasoning we each recognize that we have committed "many errors in the past, and must still dread the like for the future." Hume accordingly argues that every causal judgment is subject to a further judgment concerning its probable accuracy as a particular operation of our understanding, which, even if one can ascribe it a high degree of probability, still weakens the probability of the original judgment. Next, since the second judgment is also an operation of the understanding, it is attended by a similar doubt, and requires a further judgment of its probable accuracy. This leads us to an infinite regress, in which each judgment further diminishes the probability of the original judgment. Accordingly, Hume maintains that the force of the original evidence for any particular opinion is diminished by every successive evaluation of our own cognitive activity: a process that, by "all the rules of logic," must eventually produce "a total extinction of belief and evidence" (T 1.4.1.5–6 [SBN 181–83]; cf. 1.4.7.7 [SBN 267–68]; EHU 12.17–23 [SBN 155–59]).[7]

However, if asked whether, in presenting this argument, the author is revealing himself as "one of those sceptics, who hold that all is uncertain, and that our judgment is not in *any* thing possest of *any* measures of truth and falshood," Hume answers that "neither I, nor any other person was ever sincerely and constantly of that opinion." Instead, we find that "nature, by an absolute and uncontroulable necessity has determin'd us to judge as well as to breathe and feel." Accordingly, after one or two judgments of this diminishing probability, our cognition becomes "forc'd and unnatural," and our assurance of this infinite regress is weakened "in proportion to the efforts, which the imagination makes to enter into the reasoning."[8] In other words, "nature breaks the force of all sceptical arguments in time, and keeps them from having any considerable influence on the understanding." By contrast, the "dogmatical" pretensions of reason, if pursued consistently, lead to an extreme skepticism that would subvert not only these dogmatic pretensions, but also the skeptical arguments arising

7. For discussions and criticisms of this argument, see Raynor, "Hume's Scepticism," 103–6; Imlay, "Contrasting Themes," 121–33; Fogelin, Hume's Skepticism, 17–20; DeWitt, "Hume's Probability Argument," 125–36; Morris, "Hume's Scepticism About Reason," 39–60; Johnson, Mind of David Hume, 230–38; Dauer, "Hume's Scepticism with Regard to Reason," 211–29; Garrett, Cognition and Commitment, 222–28; Wilson, Hume's Defence of Causal Inference, 242–68; and Owen, Hume's Reason, 175–96.

8. In Part 3 Hume examines a similar argument, that a consideration of the causal chain in the transmission of historical testimony seems to diminish our belief in any historical event to the vanishing point. However, he argues that this decay of belief is counteracted by the extra vivacity generated by the resemblances between our ideas of the successive "printers and copists" whom we imagine as comprising this chain of transmission (T 1.3.13.4–6 [SBN 144–46]). See Wilson, Hume's Defence of Causal Inference, 249–53; and DeWitt, "Hume's Probability Argument," 125–36.

from these pretensions, as well as undermining ordinary human understanding. Fortunately, nature breaks this cycle and allows us to return to "common judgments and opinions." Hume concludes that neither he, nor anyone else, can seriously be a member of "that fantastic sect" which supposedly defends *"total scepticism."* His own purpose in developing these arguments is rather to reinforce his conclusion that all causal reasonings arise from custom, and that "belief is more properly an act of the sensitive, than of the cogitative part of our natures." In other words, "the sceptic still continues to reason and believe, even tho' he asserts, that he cannot defend his reason by reason" (T 1.4.1.7–1.4.2.1 [SBN 183–85]).

PHILOSOPHICAL SYSTEMS

We have already considered Hume's account of our ordinary or "vulgar" idea of external existence. In the middle of Part 4, Section 2, he offers a philosophical criticism of the popular view, and in Sections 3 and 4 he considers two contrasting theories in the history of philosophy concerning the nature and qualities of bodies. These theories are the doctrine of substance and accident in the "antient" or the Aristotelian and Scholastic tradition, and the "modern" theory of primary and secondary qualities. Hume argues that both of these systems arise from the same principles of the imagination as the ordinary idea of external existence, and are subject to the same and further criticisms.

As we have seen, Hume argues that the vulgar tend to "confound perceptions and objects, and attribute a distinct continu'd existence to the very things they feel or see." For them, "those very sensations, which enter by the eye or ear," are the "true objects," and they are not ready to believe "that this pen or paper, which is immediately perceiv'd, represents another, which is different from, but resembling it" (T 1.4.2.14, 1.4.2.31 [SBN 193, 202]; cf. EHU 12.8 [SBN 151–52]). This identification of perceptions with objects, combined with the general tendency of the imagination to disguise any interruptions and changes in a series of perceptions, leads the vulgar to develop the fiction of a distinct and continued existence. This is the idea of external existence maintained by "the unthinking and unphilosophical part of mankind," which includes "all of us, at one time or another" (T 1.4.2.36 [SBN 205]).

However, Hume reminds us that we may challenge this ordinary view of external existence through "a very little reflection and philosophy," based on various experiences such as inducing double vision by pressing our eyes, or considering the effects of distance on vision. Such experiments indicate that these perceptions, which we identify as objects in our vulgar moments, are instead "dependent on our organs, and the disposition of our nerves and animal spirits," and do not have "any distinct or independent existence" (T 1.4.2.44–45 [SBN 210–11]; cf. T 1.4.4.3–4 [SBN 226–27]; EHU 12.6–9 [SBN 151–52]). Philosophers thus agree that "nothing is ever really present with the mind but its perceptions," and further, that everything which appears before the mind "is interrupted, and dependent on the mind" (T 1.2.6.7, 1.4.2.14 [SBN 67, 193]). In other words, philosophers recognize that the fiction of external existence is "really false," and arises from an "error" or "mistake" of the imagination (T 1.4.2.43, 1.4.6.6–7 [SBN 209–10, 254–55]).[9]

However, although philosophers have denied the distinct and continued existence of our perceptions, they are reluctant to give up entirely the idea of continued existence. Instead, to accommodate these competing impulses toward affirming both the dependence and the continuity of our perceptions, philosophers have developed a distinction between perceptions and objects. On this view, perceptions are "interrupted, and perishing, and different at every different return," while objects are thought to be "uninterrupted, and to preserve a continu'd existence and identity." These philosophers then maintain that our perceptions are caused by objects, and that perceptions resemble the objects which produce them. This philosophical theory is identified by Hume as the hypothesis of a "double existence of perceptions and objects" (T 1.4.2.46 [SBN 211]; cf. EHU 12.11 [SBN 152–53]).

In spite of its apparently philosophical credentials, however, Hume argues on several grounds that this "new system" of double existence is "only a palliative remedy" that has "no primary recommendation, either to reason or to the imagination." First, this theory cannot arise from sensation or causal reasoning, since we can never observe any causal relations between our perceptions and supposed but unperceived objects. Second, as a product of the imagination, the fiction of the separate object is less immediate than the ordinary supposition of the vulgar that "our perceptions are our only objects, and continue to exist even when they are not perceiv'd" (T 1.4.2.46–48 [SBN 211–13]). Indeed, Hume argues that the theory of a double existence of perceptions and objects is ultimately derived from the ordinary or vulgar or idea of the continued existence of our perceptions, as this is generated by the imagination.

As we have seen, the theory of double existence arises from the discovery by philosophers of the "dependence and interruption" of our perceptions, and the

9. Collier has argued that Hume's skeptical conclusions regarding the conflict between the philosophical analysis of our perceptions and the propensity of our imagination in the analysis of our idea of external existence arises from Hume's failure to recognize that the activity of the imagination is justified by completing a series on the basis of memory to produce the "best fit." However, it seems to me that the central point in Hume's analysis, whether compelling or not, is that any theory of the imaginative generation of a supposed perception to fill a gap in a sequence is opposed to the philosophical account of a perception as dependent on the mind, or in other words as existing only when present to consciousness. See Collier, "Filling the Gaps," 155–70.

impulse to suppose the existence of continuous objects as the source of these perceptions. However, Hume argues that in positing a separate object, the philosopher is adopting the ordinary supposition of "an independent and continu'd existence," which has taken "such deep root in the imagination, that 'tis impossible ever to eradicate it," since it appears to be "natural and obvious." Although in moments of "calm and profound reflection," we may indeed set aside the vulgar conception of the distinct and continued existence of our perceptions by recognizing that our perceptions are fleeting and depend on the mind, the imagination reasserts itself when we "relax our thoughts," and leads us to suppose the existence of a continuing object separate from our perceptions. This hypothesis of a double existence allows philosophers to satisfy the demands of both "reflection and fancy" by enabling us to assign the interruption and continuation respectively to "different existences," in other words "the *interruption* to perceptions, and the *continuance* to objects" (T 1.4.2.51–52 [SBN 214–15]). Since it is impossible for us to develop a genuine idea of objects that are different from our perceptions, Hume describes these supposedly separate objects as "a new set of perceptions," which are invented by philosophers to accommodate their ideas of independent and continuous existence (T 1.4.2.56 [SBN 218]). In other words, we develop the theory of double existence only after we have accepted "the common hypothesis of the identity and continuance of our interrupted perceptions," or the ordinary idea of a separate object which continues to exist in spite of the interruptions in our perceptions (T 1.4.2.46 [SBN 211]).[10] This "new fiction" of a double existence seeks to reconcile the fleeting perceptions disclosed by reason with the idea of an enduring object produced by the imagination. In other words, the philosophical system is "the monstrous offspring of two principles, which are contrary to each other, which are both at once embrac'd by the mind, and which are unable mutually to destroy each other." The doctrine of double existence allows us to "set ourselves at ease as much as possible, by successively granting to each whatever it demands" (T 1.4.2.52 [SBN 215]). However, this system perpetuates the errors of the popular system by supposing entities that continue to exist when they are not perceived. Even more egregiously, the philosophical system "at once denies and establishes the vulgar supposition" by summarily inventing "a new set of perceptions," which are supposed to exist even though they are not perceived, and are further supposed, without any evidence, to resemble and cause our perceptions (T 1.4.2.56 [SBN 217–18]).

After this general discussion of the philosophical system of double existence, Hume considers two theories in the history of philosophy concerning the

---

10. For a further discussion of Hume's view of the dependence of philosophical systems on common opinion, see Livingston, *Hume's Philosophy of Common Life*, 9–33, and *Philosophical Melancholy and Delirium*, 17–52. See also Williams, *Cultivated Reason*, 21–60.

nature of objects, in order to show that both of these theories are products of the activity of the imagination. These are the "antient" doctrine of substances and the "modern" theory of primary and secondary qualities.[11]

As we have seen, Hume includes modes and substances, along with relations, among the "complex ideas" he identifies earlier in the *Treatise* as "the common subjects of our thoughts and reasoning." He then argues that we have "no idea" of a substance or a mode, apart from "a collection of simple ideas, that are united by the imagination, and have a particular name assign'd them." Accordingly, the idea of a substance is really the idea of a "principle of union" between a number of causally related qualities, although it is commonly extended to include the "fiction" of an "unknown *something,* in which they are suppos'd to inhere." Similarly, the idea of mode is the idea of a set of qualities in an individual, such as those comprising beauty, or the idea of a condition supervening upon a collection of individuals, such as a dance. In any given case, our ideas of a "substance" or a "mode" are thus derived by the imagination from simple ideas. However, these ideas are then extended by the imagination into ideas of a supposed external object and its qualities, which are further supposed to be distinguishable from each other (T 1.1.4.7, 1.1.6.1–2 [SBN 13, 15–17]; cf. E IS.591).

Hume turns more specifically to what he calls the "antient" system of philosophy, or the theory of substance and accident in the Aristotelian and Scholastic tradition, in Part 4. Here he argues that the idea of substance was developed by philosophers in order to accommodate the conflicting demands of the philosophical discovery that our idea of a particular body arises from a collection of sensible qualities, and the impulse of the imagination to regard such a collection of sensible qualities as a "compound object" that continues to maintain its identity even after changes in these qualities. Philosophers in the "antient" or peripatetic tradition have supposed the existence of an "unintelligible something" which is "perfectly homogeneous in all bodies," and have called this "substance, or original and first matter." Next, these philosophers have developed the idea of a "substantial form" as the principle of individuation, and the source for the particular qualities of each species of object. Finally, this tradition has characterized the perceived qualities of objects as "accidents," and has supposed that these must be supported by a substance, which is their "subject of inhesion." Hume maintains that this system is "entirely incomprehensible," since it depends upon the "unintelligible chimera" of a "substance." However, he also argues that this theory has "a very intimate connexion with the principles of human nature," since it arises from the same principles as our ordinary

11. For a systematic reconstruction of Hume's view of the history of philosophy, see Livingston, *Philosophical Melancholy and Delirium,* especially 80–101 and 119–42.

idea of external objects. In other words, the "fictions of the antient philosophy," which may seem to be "unreasonable and capricious," are products of the same activity of the imagination as our ordinary conception of external existence (T 1.4.3.1–8 [SBN 219–22]).

Hume applies a similar analysis to the Scholastic treatment of causation. In this case he argues that the idea of "occult qualities" in objects, as the sources of their causal powers, arises from the discovery by philosophers that we cannot identify any causal powers in objects merely by examining their "nature and qualities." This discovery is then combined with the popular view that there must be a "natural and perceivable connexion" between the qualities of an object and its effects. Accordingly, instead of developing causal explanations by observing regular conjunctions between similar objects, the peripatetic philosophers have argued "that any phænomenon, which puzzles them, arises from a faculty or an occult quality," thereby forestalling "all dispute and enquiry upon the matter." Hume concludes that nature "has not neglected philosophers more than the rest of the creation," but provides them "a consolation amidst all their disappointments and afflictions," consisting principally "in their invention of the words *faculty* and *occult quality*" (T 1.4.3.8–10 [SBN 222–24]; cf. DNR 4.162–63). Philosophers in the Scholastic tradition are also "guided by every trivial propensity of the imagination" to explain various natural operations as arising from "*sympathies, antipathies,* and *horrors of a vacuum.*" The peripatetics, like children and poets, thus tend to personify external objects and their qualities, although this is hardly an appropriate activity for philosophers (T 1.4.3.11 [SBN 224–25]; cf. NHR 3.29–30).

Hume's criticism of the "antient" system of philosophy is consistent with the attack on Scholastic philosophy by the Cartesian and Lockean traditions in modern philosophy. However, in the next two sections Hume applies his analysis of our idea of external existence to several of the central doctrines of "modern" philosophy, including the Cartesian theory of the soul as an immaterial substance, and the theory of the primary and secondary qualities of matter, as this arose from modern physics and was affirmed by both Descartes and Locke.

In Section 5 Hume extends his criticism of the idea of a substance to various attempts by modern philosophers to prove the existence of the soul, as the "material or immaterial" substance in which our perceptions are supposed to inhere. Here he initially argues that we do not require a substratum to account for the existence of our perceptions, since these are immediately given to us without any indication of a supposed ground of inhesion. Indeed, perceptions may themselves be regarded as substances, according to the definition of a substance as "something which may exist by itself" (T 1.4.5.1–5 [SBN 232–34]). He then examines the "infamous" doctrine proposed by Spinoza that there must be "one simple substance in the universe" which is "the support or *substratum* of everything." In a rather mischievous turn, however, he argues that this "hideous hypothesis" is an inevitable consequence of the doctrine of the immateriality of the soul, as this is defended by most theologians, leading both Spinoza and his critics to a "dangerous and irrecoverable atheism" (T 1.4.5.17, 1.4.5.25, 1.4.5.19, 1.4.5.26 [SBN 240–41, 244–45]).

However, the focus of Hume's discussion of "modern philosophy," as this is presented in Section 4, is the modern theory of matter and its primary and secondary qualities. In this section Hume initially distinguishes between those principles of the imagination which appear to be "permanent, irresistible, and universal; such as the customary transition from causes to effects, and from effects to causes," and those which are "changeable, weak, and irregular," such as the operation of the imagination in generating the fictions of Scholastic philosophy. The principles of the first type are "the foundation of all our thoughts and actions," without which "human nature must immediately perish and go to ruin." By contrast, the second type are neither unavoidable, necessary, nor even useful in the conduct of ordinary life. In an echo of his distinction in Part 3 between the philosophical and unphilosophical forms of probable reasoning, he concludes that the former principles of the imagination are "receiv'd by philosophy, and the latter rejected" (T 1.4.4.1; cf. 1.3.13.1, 1.3.13.13 [SBN 225; cf. 143, 150]). Modern philosophers might agree that the ancient fictions are the products of principles that "however common, are neither universal nor unavoidable in human nature." However, these philosophers have supposed their own theory to be "entirely free from this defect, and to arise only from the solid, permanent, and consistent principles of the imagination" (T 1.4.4.2 [SBN 226]). Hume therefore sets out to examine the modern system in order to consider whether there are any grounds for this confidence.

Hume divides all our sensory impressions into three types: (1) "the figure, bulk, motion and solidity of bodies," which modern philosophers identify as primary qualities; (2) "colours, tastes, smells, sounds, heat and cold," which they identify as secondary qualities; and (3) "pains and pleasures, that arise from the application of objects to our bodies." Philosophers agree with the vulgar that pains and pleasures are "merely perceptions," which are fleeting and dependent on the mind. In contrast to pleasures and pains, the vulgar believe that the impressions identified as primary and secondary qualities both have "a distinct continu'd existence." This view is partially rejected by modern philosophers, who place secondary qualities "on the same footing" with pain and pleasure, while agreeing with the vulgar that the primary qualities of "figure, bulk, motion and solidity" have a distinct and continuous existence in external objects (T 1.4.2.12 [SBN 192–93]). In response to this view, however, Hume maintains that we cannot develop any idea of primary qualities apart from perceptions of secondary qualities, and that the differences between these two types of qualities arise neither from sensation nor from reason, but from the imagination (T 1.4.2.13 [SBN 192]).

According to Hume, the modern system of philosophy is based on the "fundamental principle" that secondary or sensible qualities, including "colours, sounds, tastes, smells, heat and cold," are "nothing but impressions in the mind" which are "deriv'd from the operation of external objects," but do not have "any resemblance to the qualities of the objects." This conclusion arises from the discovery that the secondary qualities we attribute to objects are found to vary with the circumstances or condition of the perceiver. Accordingly, if we assume that all of our impressions resemble a quality in the object, we are obliged to accept the incoherent view that every object possesses a set of mutually exclusive qualities. On the other hand, if we reject this view, but have no reason to single out any particular impressions as resembling actual qualities of the object, we must conclude that our impressions of secondary qualities are merely "internal existences" arising from causes "which no ways resemble them." This is the view that has been adopted by modern philosophers. Finally, once we have rejected the external existence of secondary qualities, we are left with the primary qualities of "extension and solidity," and their modifications such as "figure, motion, gravity, and cohesion," as "the only *real* ones, of which we have any adequate notion" (T 1.4.4.3–5 [SBN 226–27]).

In criticizing this theory, Hume draws upon the argument developed by Berkeley and others to show that primary qualities can be reduced to secondary qualities, and are accordingly also dependent upon the mind.[12] More specifically, he argues that the theory of primary and secondary qualities leads to "the most extravagant scepticism" concerning external objects, since if we maintain that sensible qualities are "merely perceptions," we cannot conceive of anything else, even including primary qualities, which could possess "a real, continu'd, and independent existence" (T 1.4.4.6 [SBN 228]). He defends this claim through an analysis of three primary qualities: motion, extension, and solidity. First, the idea of motion depends on the idea of a body that is moving, and may therefore be resolved into extension and solidity. However, as he has shown in Part 2, the idea of extension itself arises from sensations of vision and touch, or from the perceptions of "colour or solidity." Since modern philosophy has excluded color "from any real existence," we must suppose that our concept of extension arises from the idea of solidity. However, in the final stage of his argument, Hume shows that we cannot formulate any idea of solidity without

12. See Berkeley, *Principles of Human Knowledge* (1.9–15), in *Works*, 2:44–47; and *Three Dialogues* (First Dialogue), in *Works*, 2:187–94. This argument was originally stated by Simon Foucher in response to Malebranche, and further developed by Bayle in his article "Pyrrho," note B. See Bayle's *Historical and Critical Dictionary*, 197–98, and the editorial notes by Popkin in this edition.

already having an idea of extended objects. First, he rejects the initially plausible view that our idea of solidity arises directly from the sensation of touch, arguing that the sense of touch only provides impressions of texture and resistance, which do not represent any further qualities of external objects. Next, he indicates that we attribute solidity to any bodies that are supposed to exert pressure against each other and to exclude each other from their respective locations. That is, the idea of solidity requires the idea of an encounter in space and time between two bodies, which are both supposed to maintain a distinct and continued existence. This idea of external existence, as we have seen, is ultimately an imaginative projection from the arrangements of visible and tangible objects. However, since these secondary qualities have been excluded from our analysis, Hume maintains that the modern system leaves us "no just nor satisfactory idea of solidity." We therefore have no positive idea of matter in the modern sense, since any attempt to describe the primary qualities of matter either "returns in a circle" or relies upon an appeal to secondary qualities (T 1.4.4.7–10 [SBN 228–29]).

Hume therefore concludes that the modern system of philosophy cannot claim to be any more plausible than the Scholastic system, since "instead of explaining the operations of external objects by its means, we utterly annihilate all these objects, and reduce ourselves to the opinions of the most extravagant scepticism concerning them" (T 1.4.4.6 [SBN 228]).

Hume states his preliminary answer to extreme skepticism in Section 2 by observing that the skeptic must acknowledge the existence of the external world, even if this belief cannot be supported by any philosophical arguments, since "nature has not left this to his choice, and has doubtless esteem'd it an affair of too great importance to be trusted to our uncertain reasonings and speculations." Thus, although we may investigate the causes that lead to our belief in the existence of body, we cannot investigate whether body exists or not, since "that is a point, which we must take for granted in all our reasonings" (T 1.4.2.1 [SBN 187]).

However, once he has criticized both the popular and philosophical theories of external existence, Hume reconsiders the apparently skeptical implications of his argument. Although he had begun this analysis "with premising, that we ought to have an implicit faith in our senses," he now finds instead that, "to be ingenuous, I feel myself *at present* of a quite contrary sentiment," and "more inclin'd to repose no faith at all in my senses, or rather imagination, than to place in it such an implicit confidence." First, considering our ordinary idea of external existence, we must deny that "such trivial qualities of the fancy, conducted by such false suppositions, can ever lead to any solid and rational system." However, the theory of double existence not only arises from the same principles but absurdly "at once denies and establishes the vulgar supposition," first by rejecting the distinct and continued existence of perceptions, and then by inventing unperceived "objects" to which we may attribute these qualities (T 1.4.2.56 [SBN 218]). Accordingly, it is "impossible upon any system to defend either our understanding or senses," and "a profound and intense reflection on those subjects" only leads to a skeptical doubt that is "a malady, which can never be radically cur'd." Hume concludes that "carelessness and in-attention alone can afford us any remedy," and he is now prepared to rely entirely upon these, trusting, whatever may be his or his reader's opinion at this present moment, "that an hour hence he will be perswaded there is both an external and internal world" (T 1.4.2.57 [SBN 218]).

Hume provides the following summary of the skeptical implications of the system of modern philosophy:

> Thus there is a direct and total opposition betwixt our reason and our senses; or more properly speaking, betwixt those conclusions we form from cause and effect, and those that perswade us of the continu'd and independent existence of body. When we reason from cause and effect, we conclude, that neither colour, sound, taste, nor smell have a continu'd and independent existence. When we exclude these sensible qualities there remains nothing in the universe, which has such an existence. (T 1.4.4.14 [SBN 231]; cf. 1.4.7.4 [SBN 265–66]; EHU 12.9–16 [SBN 152–55])

The fictions of the peripatetic tradition, and presumably the fiction of double existence in modern philosophy, allow philosophers to "set themselves at ease," and arrive by an illusion "at the same indifference, which the people attain by their stupidity, and true philosophers by their moderate scepticism" (T 1.4.3.10 [SBN 224]).

Hume therefore introduces "moderate scepticism," which he also describes as the opinion of "true philosophers," as an alternative not only to extreme skepticism, but also to the various types of "false" or "dogmatical" philosophy in both the ancient and modern traditions (T 1.4.3.9–10, 1.4.7.13–14; cf. 1.4.1.12, 1.4.7.15 [SBN 222–24, 271–73; cf. 187, 274]).

MODERATE SKEPTICISM

Hume concludes his discussion of the "sceptical and other systems of philosophy" in Part 4, and indeed his general discussion of the understanding in Book

1 of the *Treatise,* with the "Conclusion of this book" in Section 7, in which he traces the intellectual and emotional progress of the philosopher through the various types of skepticism.[13] Since Section 7 is narrated as an introspective monologue, this section has often been regarded as the autobiographical account of a personal crisis that Hume passed through while confronting the skeptical implications of his own philosophy.[14] On this reading, Hume's monologue is a continuation of his description, in a letter he drafted to a physician in 1734, of the various physical and psychological complaints arising from his philosophical studies in his early twenties (L 1.12–18; cf. ML xxxiii).[15]

In contrast to this reading, I would argue on several grounds that Hume is adopting the literary structure of a confession, not for direct and spontaneous self-expression, but rather to guide his readers through an expected series of intellectual and emotional reactions to his skeptical arguments. His purpose is to secure their concurrence to the mitigated skepticism with which he ends the conclusion, and which also provides the basis for his further inquiries in Books 2 and 3. First, Section 7 is not an excerpt from a private diary, but a discourse that has been crafted for publication, as a coherent and integral part of a larger work. Next, we will see that Hume's initial account of the various stages of skeptical despair is carefully balanced by his discussion of the remedies provided by nature, which tend to support his moderate skepticism. He also frames his expression of skeptical despair by statements of his intention to continue his larger project of developing the science of man in the *Treatise.* These appear at the end of Section 6 (T 1.4.6.23 [SBN 263]), and in the concluding pages of Section 7 (T 1.4.7.12–15 [SBN 270–74]). In other words, in Section 7 Hume considers not only the intellectual and emotional difficulties arising from his skeptical arguments but also their apparent resolution; and he explores not only the theoretical but also the emotional and practical basis for further intellectual inquiry, which he reaffirms in its concluding pages. Hume's strategy in Section 7, leading to his final affirmation of moderate skepticism, has been obscured by those commentators who have focused their attention upon his preliminary

13. Baier regards this concluding section as a microcosm of book 2 and indeed a key to the *Treatise* as a whole: see *Progress of Sentiments,* 1–27.

14. This autobiographical interpretation of *Treatise* 1.4.7 appears in Hendel, *Studies,* 251; Mossner, *Life of David Hume,* 115–16; Noxon, *Hume's Philosophical Development,* 14, 22; and Siebert, *Moral Animus,* 170–74.

15. It seems to me that in this letter Hume is describing the symptoms, both physical and psychological, of excessive studying and a lack of recreation, as he himself suggests in citing the remedies from which he has already benefited. The most distressing psychological symptom he reports is a difficulty in concentrating, which he fears might jeopardize his intellectual pursuits. The only indication of any melancholy following from the content of his studies is his reference to a tendency toward moral self-examination that he had already renounced by the time of writing this letter. Hume does not express any melancholy arising from his recent unspecified discoveries in theoretical philosophy, but rather a pleasurable excitement in his project. For discussions of this letter to an unnamed physician see Greig, *David Hume,* 76–83; Mossner, *Life of David Hume,* 66–88; and Stewart, "Hume's Manuscripts," 270–76.

account of the crisis of extreme skepticism, while overlooking the details of its resolution.[16]

Hume begins by pausing, in the wake of his skeptical arguments and before continuing on to "those immense depths of philosophy, which lie before me," in order "to ponder that voyage, which I have undertaken," requiring "the utmost art and industry to be brought to a happy conclusion." Since he now recognizes "the wretched condition, weakness, and disorder" of his cognitive faculties, he compares himself to a traveler who after many dangers is determined "to put out to sea in the same leaky weather-beaten vessel," and is almost resolved to surrender and "perish on the barren rock, on which I am at present," rather than venturing into the unbounded expanse ahead (T 1.4.7.1 [SBN 263–64]). In addition to the despair produced by recognizing his intellectual condition, the skeptical thinker is also "affrighted and confounded" by the "forlorn solitude, in which I am plac'd in my philosophy." Indeed, he feels like "some strange uncouth monster" who is expelled from all human society, since he has not only separated himself from the unthinking crowd, but exposed himself to the contempt and ridicule of other philosophers (T 1.4.7.2 [SBN 264–65]).

In this state of melancholy, Hume reviews the skeptical arguments set forth in the earlier sections of Part 4.[17] Here he reminds us that that probable reasoning tends to subvert itself by diminishing our confidence in each of our particular judgments (T 1.4.7.7 [SBN 267]), that we cannot discover any causal powers in nature (T 1.4.7.5 [SBN 266–67]), that "memory, senses, and understanding" are all "founded on the imagination, or the vivacity of our ideas" (T 1.4.7.3 [SBN 265]), and that causal reasoning and belief in external existence are directly contrary to each other (T 1.4.7.4 [SBN 266]). We are saved from "total scepticism" only by that "singular and seemingly trivial property of the fancy," which makes it difficult for us to sustain these "remote views of things" for any length of time (T 1.4.7.7 [SBN 267–68]).

However, this conclusion is not immediately consoling to the philosopher, who appears to be confronted with a perpetual choice of accepting or rejecting all "refin'd and metaphysical" reasonings, which must lead in either case to renouncing any pretensions to the consistent use of reason, and consequently all science and philosophy. In other words, the philosopher is left with no choice "but betwixt a false reason and none at all" (T 1.4.7.7 [SBN 268]). The "*intense* view" of these contradictions and imperfections in his own reason leaves the

---

16. See Popkin, "Critique of Pyrrhonism," 62–70, and Wilson's response in *Hume's Defence of Causal Inference*, 242–44 and 327. On this view of *Treatise* 1.4.7 as providing philosophical guidance to the reader, see also Livingston, *Hume's Philosophy of Common Life*, 37–39; Box, *Suasive Art of David Hume*, 96–111; and Baier, *Progress of Sentiments*, 1–27.

17. For a more detailed analysis of Hume's skeptical arguments in the *Treatise* as summarized here, see Garrett, *Cognition and Commitment*, 208–32.

philosopher "in the most deplorable condition imaginable, inviron'd with the deepest darkness, and utterly depriv'd of the use of every member and faculty" (T 1.4.7.8 [SBN 268–69]).

However, nature does not abandon the skeptical philosopher, but provides a cure even for this "philosophical melancholy and delirium, either by relaxing this bent of mind," or providing "some avocation, and lively impression of my senses, which obliterate all these chimeras." These solitary remedies are enhanced by the natural influence of human sociability: "I dine, I play a game of back-gammon, I converse, and am merry with my friends; and when after three or four hour's amusement, I wou'd return to these speculations, they appear so cold, and strain'd, and ridiculous, that I cannot find in my heart to enter into them any farther" (T 1.4.7.9 [SBN 269]). The previously isolated and distraught thinker is now "absolutely and necessarily determin'd to live, and talk, and act like other people in the common affairs of life," and is tempted to burn all his books and papers in his resolution "never more to renounce the pleasures of life for the sake of reasoning and philosophy." However, this impulse arises from his "spleen and indolence," and is eventually dispelled by calm reflection and the gradual return of a "serious" but "good-humour'd disposition": "At the time, therefore, that I am tir'd with amusement and company, and have indulg'd a *reverie* in my chamber, or in a solitary walk by a riverside, I feel my mind all collected within itself, and am naturally *inclin'd* to carry my view into all those subjects, about which I have met with so many disputes in the course of my reading and conversation" (T 1.4.7.11–12 [SBN 270]). Refreshed by these intervals of sociability and solitary reflection, the philosopher gradually finds that he "cannot forbear having a curiosity" regarding various topics of intellectual inquiry, such as the principles by which we judge truth and falsehood, good and evil, beauty and deformity, the causes of the passions, and the nature of government. Indeed, he is troubled to find that he has been formulating these judgments without knowing the principles upon which he proceeds. He is also distressed by the "deplorable ignorance" of the learned world regarding these principles, and wishes to contribute to the education of humanity, and to enjoy the reputation and honor that would arise from these endeavors. These, at least, are the sentiments that "spring up naturally in my present disposition," so that if he were to banish them by any other pursuit or distraction "I *feel* I shou'd be a loser in point of pleasure." Hume accordingly presents the sentiments of curiosity, benevolence, and ambition, which have now superseded his intellectual melancholy, as "the origin of my philosophy" (T 1.4.7.12 [SBN 270–71]).[18]

18. David Owen argues that, on Hume's view, our approval of philosophical probable reasoning follows the same principles as our approval of the virtues: its results are useful or agreeable, or both, to the self or others. See Owen, *Hume's Reason*, 217–23.

Next, he reaffirms the value of philosophical or scientific reasoning for those thinkers who have passed through the dark night of total skepticism to this renewed interest in intellectual pursuits. Here he writes that it is almost impossible for the human mind to rest "in that narrow circle of objects, which are the subject of daily conversation and action." However, since we may be tempted by the even bolder systems of superstition, he suggests that we should instead follow the "safest and most agreeable" principles in our abstruse inquiries, including the methods by which we attempt to assign "new causes and principles to the phænomena, which appear in the visible world." In other words, he recommends philosophy in preference "to superstition of every kind or denomination." More specifically, he advises us to pursue a "just" philosophy, which encourages only "mild and moderate sentiments," and by which we may hope to establish "a system or set of opinions," which, even if we cannot know them to be true, "might at least be satisfactory to the human mind, and might stand the test of the most critical examination." He describes this as the view of the "true sceptic," who is "diffident of his philosophical doubts, as well as of his philosophical conviction," and distinguishes this view not only from the "false and extravagant" forms of systematic philosophy, but also from the view of the extreme skeptic, who is led by his "doubts and scruples" to abandon philosophy (T 1.4.7.13–15 [SBN 271–73]). Hume has already identified the outlook of "true philosophers" with "moderate scepticism" (T 1.4.3.10 [SBN 224]), and he now identifies this as the view of the "true sceptic," which he defends as the conclusion of his examination of the understanding (T 1.4.7.14–15 [SBN 273–74]).

With this conclusion, Hume also reaffirms his larger project as stated in the introduction to the *Treatise*. As a newly revealed moderate skeptic, he now hopes to "contribute a little to the advancement of knowledge" by showing his readers that "Human Nature is the only science of man," thereby giving "a different turn to the speculations of philosophers, and pointing out to them more distinctly those subjects, where alone they can expect assurance and conviction" (T 1.4.7.14 [SBN 273]). He also implicitly anticipates his moderate skepticism in the introduction, by indicating that once we have attained the "utmost extent of human reason" in applying the experimental method to the study of human nature, we may rest contented with our conclusions, even though we are "perfectly satisfy'd in the main of our ignorance," and cannot provide any further reason for our "most general and refin'd principles, beside our experience of their reality" (T Int.9 [SBN xviii]).[19]

Finally, Hume turns from this supposed personal journey to offer an invitation to those who have accompanied him thus far: "If the reader finds himself

---

19. For a further discussion of Hume's strategy in his presentation of skepticism in the Introduction to the *Treatise* and in the Conclusion of Book 1, see Cummins, "Hume's Diffident Skepticism," 43–65.

in the same easy disposition, let him follow me in my future speculations. If not, let him follow his inclination, and wait the returns of application and good humour" (T 1.4.7.14 [SBN 273]).

We have accordingly seen that Hume concludes his account of the different systems of skepticism and philosophy in Book 1 of the *Treatise* by defending a version of skepticism that concedes the cogency of the arguments of extreme skepticism, and also recognizes the influence of "nature" in breaking their force, but moves beyond extreme skepticism and uncritical naturalism by defending the standards of critical judgment that emerge from our reasonings in the sciences, and ultimately from our reasonings in ordinary life. This affirmation of scientific judgment, in the context of moderate skepticism, is already anticipated in the introduction, where he presents the application of the "experimental method" to human nature as the basis for an examination of the principles of investigation in both the natural and human sciences. He then carries out this project in the *Treatise,* by examining the principles of probable or scientific reasoning in Book 1, and by applying these principles in Books 2 and 3 to psychology, moral theory, and political theory.

Hume's characterization of his own view as "moderate scepticism" is further reflected in the various shorter works in which he summarizes and defends the *Treatise.* In the *Abstract* he describes his philosophy as "very sceptical," by which he means that it "tends to give us a notion of the imperfections and narrow limits of human understanding." In his first identification of extreme skepticism with the ancient Pyrrhonian school, he adds that philosophy would leave us "entirely *Pyrrhonian,* were not nature too strong for it," and that we employ our reason "only because we cannot help it" (A 27 [SBN 657]). In the *Letter from a Gentleman* Hume rejects the characterization of his philosophy as "universal Doubt" or Pyrrhonian skepticism, which it is "impossible for any Man to support." Instead he maintains that "*Modesty* then, and *Humility,* with regard to the Operations of our natural Faculties," are the appropriate and enduring results of his skeptical arguments (LG 19).

Hume's defense of moderate skepticism also pervades the *Enquiry Concerning Human Understanding.* In the opening section of the *Enquiry* he suggests that while abstract philosophy might seem to be "the inevitable source of uncertainty and error," we may also cultivate a "true metaphysics" by examining the nature of human understanding, in contrast to the various forms of "abstruse philosophy and metaphysical jargon" which have become "mixed up with popular superstition," and also to a skepticism which is "entirely subversive of all speculation, and even action" (EHU 1.11–14 [SBN 11–14]). He later calls attention to the skeptical implications of his analysis of causation by presenting his argument that causal beliefs are not founded on reason as "Sceptical Doubts concerning the Operations of the Understanding" (Section 4), and then describes his view that these beliefs arise from habit as a "Sceptical Solution of these Doubts" (Section 5). He also presents this solution as consistent with the view that he now calls "ACADEMIC or SCEPTICAL philosophy" (EHU 4.1, 5.1 [SBN 25, 40]).

In the concluding Section 12 of the first *Enquiry*, "Of the Academical or Sceptical Philosophy," Hume develops a systematic account of different versions of skepticism. Here he distinguishes between antecedent or Cartesian skepticism, consequent or Pyrrhonian skepticism, and mitigated or academic skepticism. He then considers the implications of these philosophical positions for scientific inquiry, and ends with a defense of mitigated skepticism.[20]

First, Hume describes Cartesian skepticism as "a species of scepticism, *antecedent* to all study and philosophy," which has been proposed as a "sovereign preservative against error and precipitate judgement." This type of skepticism recommends "an universal doubt, not only of all our former opinions and principles, but also of our very faculties," and then attempts to establish the reliability of our faculties through a "chain of reasoning" from "some original principle, which cannot possibly be fallacious or deceitful." Hume argues that even if we could discover such a principle, we would never be able to advance beyond it except by those very faculties whose reliability had been called into question. A complete antecedent skepticism is thus unattainable and would be incurable. However, he endorses a moderate version of Cartesian doubt, which recommends a careful examination of our presuppositions and the stages in our reasoning, as a valuable maxim for philosophical and scientific investigation (EHU 12.3–4 [SBN 149–50]).

Next Hume considers "excessive" skepticism, which he attributes to the Pyrrhonian tradition. This type of skepticism is "*consequent* to science and enquiry," and is propounded "when men are supposed to have discovered, either the absolute fallaciousness of their mental faculties," or at least their inability to reach any satisfactory conclusions "in all those curious subjects of speculation, about which they are commonly employed." Accordingly, extreme skepticism challenges all of the apparent evidence of our senses, and casts the "maxims of common life" into the same doubt as "the most profound principles or conclusions of metaphysics and theology" (EHU 12.5, 12.21–34 [SBN 150, 158–65]). Hume illustrates this type of skepticism by recalling many of the skeptical arguments that he had already presented in the *Treatise,* including his paradoxical conclusions regarding space and time, and his analysis of our idea of external existence (EHU 12.6–23 [SBN 151–59]).

20. Many studies have indicated that Hume has confused the two classical traditions of "Pyrrhonian" and "academic" skepticism, perhaps by relying upon Bayle's depiction of Pyrrho as an extreme skeptic and Cicero's moderate version of academic skepticism. See Popkin, "Critique of Pyrrhonism," 53–98; Raynor, "Hume's Scepticism," 105–6; Norton, *David Hume,* 266–69 and 277–79; Penelhum, *David Hume,* 23; and Livingston, *Philosophical Melancholy and Delirium,* 7–11.

Once again, however, Hume finds that while it might be impossible to refute this extreme type of skepticism, its influence tends to be dispelled by the "more powerful principles of our nature," whenever we leave our speculations and are confronted "by the presence of real objects, which actuate our passions and sentiments." In other words, the "great subverter" of Pyrrhonian skepticism is "action, and employment, and the occupations of common life" (EHU 12.21 [SBN 158–59]). In addition, as the "chief and most confounding objection to *excessive* scepticism," Hume maintains that its principles cannot offer any enduring benefit to society, since if they were to prevail "all discourse, all action would immediately cease," and people would remain in a "total lethargy, till the necessities of nature, unsatisfied, put an end to their miserable existence." The only lasting effect of Pyrrhonism is to demonstrate "the whimsical condition of mankind," since we are obliged to "act and reason and believe," even though we are unable to provide any ultimate cognitive justification for these activities (EHU 12.23 [SBN 159–60]).

Finally, Hume offers his own defense of "academical" skepticism, in contrast to both Cartesian and Pyrrhonian skepticism, as the culmination of his argument in the *Enquiry*. In his analysis of causation Hume has already recommended "ACADEMIC or SCEPTICAL philosophy," which calls for "doubt and suspence of judgement," and encourages us to impose "very narrow bounds" on our inquiries by renouncing "all speculations which lie not within the limits of common life and practice." He thus advises us to oppose both the "lofty pretensions" and the "superstitious credulity" of human cognition, and limit our inquiries to "common life," or the realm of action and scientific pursuits (EHU 5.1 [SBN 41]).

In Section 12 Hume argues that this "*mitigated* scepticism, or ACADEMICAL philosophy" arises from Pyrrhonian skepticism, when the doubts of the latter are, "in some measure, corrected by common sense and reflection." This type of skepticism is "thoroughly convinced of the force of the PYRRHONIAN doubt," and recognizes that only the "strong power of natural instinct" can free us from this doubt, while also affirming the usefulness and value of the reasonings arising from this instinct within common life. Accordingly, academic skepticism tends to moderate the tendency toward dogmatism in human reasoning, and to promote the degree of "doubt, and caution, and modesty, which, in all kinds of scrutiny and decision, ought for ever to accompany a just reasoner." This philosophy recommends that we confine our inquiries "to such subjects as are best adapted to the narrow capacity of human understanding," and encourages us to develop "a correct *Judgement*," which avoids "all distant and high enquiries" and instead limits itself "to common life, and to such subjects as fall under daily practice and experience." In other words, the academic skeptic recognizes that "philosophical decisions are nothing but the reflections of common life, methodized and corrected" (EHU 12.24–25 [SBN 161–62]).

Hume concludes his account of academic skepticism by offering a survey of the "proper subjects of science and enquiry," which are disclosed through a study of the "natural powers of the human mind" and our experience in the "reflections of common life." These subjects are divided into mathematics, which is the only proper object of "knowledge and demonstration," and the various natural and moral sciences founded upon "moral" or causal reasoning, including certain approaches to ethics, aesthetics, and perhaps theology (EHU 12.25–34 [SBN 163–65]). Hume therefore maintains that mitigated or academic skepticism supports our inquiries in the demonstrative, natural, and human sciences, as these investigations emerge from the systematic correction and extension of our reasonings in ordinary life, or from "daily practice and experience" (EHU 12.25 [SBN 162]).

In the *Dialogues Concerning Natural Religion* Hume develops a further discussion of skepticism by juxtaposing the views of his three characters. First, Cleanthes rejects skepticism in order to defend the use of reason, both in general and especially in natural theology. Next, Demea defends a version of negative theology that appeals to skepticism in order to justify its reliance upon revelation against the pretensions of natural theology. Finally, Philo defends a more limited account of reason and its proper use in natural philosophy, while developing a skeptical critique of natural theology.

In Part 1 of the *Dialogues* Philo apparently endorses Demea's view that the education of young people should help them recognize what Philo calls the "weakness, blindness, and narrow limits of human reason," as these appear in the "errors and deceits" of our senses, and also in the contradictions arising from our ideas of "matter, cause and effect, extension, space, time, motion." In response, Cleanthes challenges the extreme version of skepticism which he believes Philo to be mischievously defending, since Philo has not renounced his senses and experience in the ordinary activities of life, but rather exhibits "the firmest reliance on all the received maxims of science, morals, prudence, and behaviour." Indeed, Cleanthes argues that it is impossible for anyone to maintain a "total scepticism" in thought and conduct for even a few hours: since "external objects press in upon him: Passions solicit him: His philosophical melancholy dissipates," and even the violent distortion of his natural inclinations "will not be able, during any time, to preserve the poor appearance of scepticism" (DNR 1.131–32, 1.137).

Philo responds to Cleanthes' criticism of extreme skepticism by defending a moderate, mitigated or academical version of skepticism, as presented in the *Treatise* and the *Enquiry*. He initially concedes that "to whatever length any one may push his speculative principles of scepticism, he must act, I own, and live, and converse like other men," and is not obliged to give any reason for this other than the "absolute necessity" of doing so. However, Philo argues that the

philosophical skeptic may continue his investigations even beyond the immediate concerns of ordinary life, by general inquiries into "natural or moral subjects." The skeptic is encouraged in this pursuit by finding that "every one, even
in common life, is constrained to have more or less of this philosophy," since
from our childhood and throughout our lives, we are all continually advancing
"in forming more general principles of conduct and reasoning." Philo maintains that "what we call *philosophy* is nothing but a more regular and methodi-
cal operation of the same kind," and that we may expect "greater stability, if not
greater truth" from philosophy than from our reasonings in common life only
by "its exacter and more scrupulous method of proceeding." We may accordingly investigate "trade, or morals, or politics, or criticism" by appealing to
"common sense and experience," against the objections that might arise from
"very subtile and refined" reasonings. However, we have no evidence from either
experience or common life that can support the arguments of natural theology,
since its objects are "too large for our grasp," and its arguments "run wide of
common life" (DNR 1.134–35).

Philo's project through the rest of the *Dialogues* is to apply the standards of
experience and common life to natural theology, in order to show that its conclusions are not supported by philosophical probable reasoning. For example,
since we have little or no evidence of the general "œconomy of a universe," we
can imagine "no conjecture" concerning the origin of evil "however wild, which
may not be just; nor any one, however plausible, which may not be erroneous."
The proper aim of human understanding is to be "sceptical, or at least cautious,"
in admitting of any hypothesis, "much less, of any which is supported by no
appearance of probability" (DNR 11.205). This is the view of "philosophical
sceptics," who, "from a natural diffidence of their own capacity," are prepared
to suspend judgment concerning such extraordinary and sublime topics as the
divine attributes. Philo concludes that one who has been "seasoned with a just
sense of the imperfections of natural reason, will fly to revealed truth with the
greatest avidity." He ends the discussion in the *Dialogues* by asserting provocatively that "to be a philosophical sceptic is, in a man of letters, the first and most
essential step towards being a sound, believing Christian" (DNR 12.227–28).

Hume's 1742 essay "The Sceptic" is less useful as a direct expression of his
views for two reasons. First, this essay is more directly concerned with human
motives and conduct than with metaphysical and epistemological issues. Second, the four essays in the set, which also includes "The Platonist," "The
Stoic," and "The Epicurean," are written in assumed voices rather than as direct
expressions of the views of their author, in order to illustrate the relation
between different philosophical views and different types of human temperament. However, we may note that the speaker in this essay is criticizing the
pretensions of philosophers, while affirming that human beings are almost

entirely guided by their individual "constitution and temper," rather than by reasoning. Indeed, rather than defending extreme skepticism, he affirms that there seems to be "a real, though often an unknown standard, in the nature of things" which determines the truth or falsity of our judgments concerning matters of fact (E Sc.169, 164).[21]

We may therefore trace a dialectical development between two types of skepticism in each of Hume's philosophical works. The first is the total, "excessive," or "Pyrrhonian" version of skepticism, which emerges as the inevitable consequence of our philosophical reasonings, but is subverted by the propensities of the imagination and the activities and concerns of common life. The second is the moderate, mitigated, or "academical" version of skepticism, which Hume identifies in the *Treatise* as the view of "true sceptics" and "true philosophers," and which Philo calls "philosophical scepticism." This view recognizes the legitimacy of the arguments of extreme skepticism, and acknowledges the influence of nature in breaking their force. However, it also recommends a new role for philosophy: the articulation of the principles of critical reflection that we rely upon in our ordinary reasonings. Hume defends this version of skepticism in Book 1 of the *Treatise,* in the *Abstract,* in the first *Enquiry,* and in the *Dialogues* through the character of Philo. In other words, he presents moderate or mitigated skepticism as the outcome of his examination of human cognition, and defends this view as his own philosophical position and as the basis for his further inquiries.[22]

With these reflections we may return to the various interpretations of Hume's philosophy that have emerged from the ongoing discussion of his skepticism. First, those who regard his philosophy as a version of extreme skepticism have emphasized his examination of the arguments that support extreme skepticism, while overlooking his conclusions concerning the influence of nature and common life in breaking their force, or dismissing these conclusions as a half-hearted addition to his discussion. In its turn, the naturalistic interpretation calls attention to the role of "nature" in subverting the skeptical arguments and providing us with unreflective and unavoidable beliefs about the world. However, at least in Kemp Smith's version, this interpretation tends to overlook Hume's account and his relative justification of the standards of probable or scientific reasoning, and its importance for his further inquiries into the

---

21. For a further account of Hume's "mitigated scepticism" in his various writings, and of the consistency of his conclusions, see Norton, "How a Sceptic May Live Scepticism," 119–39. For a further discussion of "The Sceptic," see Williams, *Cultivated Reason,* 19, 33–34, 44, and 61–91.

22. This interpretation suggests that Hume is contributing to the tradition of constructive or mitigated skepticism in early modern Europe that has been identified and traced especially by Richard Popkin, a continuity that is obscured by Popkin's emphasis on the Pyrrhonian and naturalistic interpretations of Hume. See Popkin, *History of Scepticism,* 129–50, and *High Road to Pyrrhonism;* along with Van Leeuwen, *Problem of Certainty;* Norton, *David Hume,* 208–38; and Ferreira, *Scepticism and Reasonable Doubt.*

science of man. By contrast, I have shown that Hume intends to move beyond both extreme skepticism and uncritical naturalism by providing an account of the standards of critical reflection that may be applied in the natural and human sciences, as these emerge from the systematic examination of our ordinary concepts and reasonings. I have also shown that he presents this philosophical position as the view of the moderate or mitigated skeptic who is engaged in studying the presuppositions and principles of human cognition. With this conclusion, which has emerged from a study of Book 1 of the *Treatise* and Hume's related writings, we may turn in the rest of this study to consider his application of these principles to various dimensions of human life, in Books 2 and 3 of the *Treatise* and in his later writings.

6

The Passions

In Book 2 of the *Treatise* Hume examines the passions, along with sympathy and the will. He later restates his discussion of the will in the *Enquiry Concerning Human Understanding,* his account of sympathy in the *Enquiry Concerning the Principles of Morals,* and his analysis of the passions in "On the Passions," published in the *Four Dissertations* of 1757.[1]

Until recently, Hume's analysis of the passions received little attention in the secondary literature, and the prevailing opinion has generally been dismissive. For example, Selby-Bigge and Kemp Smith both describe Book 2 as the least successful major division of the *Treatise,* and "Of the Passions" as the worst of Hume's writings.[2] Book 2 of the *Treatise* has also been described as lengthy, mechanistic, and dreary, while "Of the Passions" has been charged with presenting an even more desultory, dry, and uninspired version of the argument in Book 2.[3]

Hume's theory of the passions is not only a contribution to the philosophical discussion of the passions but also an integral

1. "Of the Passions" was given the title "A Dissertation on the Passions" by Green and Grose, and is often known by that title. The edition by Green and Grose, which is cited here, was until recently the only reprint available. For a welcome facsimile reprint of the 1757 edition of "Of the Passions," see Hume, *Four Dissertations,* page sequence 1, 119–81.

2. Selby-Bigge, "Editor's Introduction," xxi–xxii; Kemp Smith, *Philosophy of David Hume,* 160 and 535–36.

3. For examples of these criticisms, see Passmore, *Hume's Intentions,* 128; Noxon, *Hume's Philosophical Development,* 23; and Flew, *David Hume,* 144.

part of his philosophy as a "science of man," or a study of the principles of human nature.[4] Hume also presents his first sustained view of the social and historical dimension of human existence in Book 2, in his rich and engaging depiction of the human subject as an emotional, active, and social being, and in his observations concerning the human passions and the role of sympathy in human existence.

PASSIONS

In his initial classification of perceptions in Book 1 of the *Treatise,* Hume identifies our "passions, desires, and emotions" as "impressions of reflection," and indicates that these, unlike our impressions of sensation, are derived "in a great measure from our ideas." Accordingly, in arranging the *Treatise* he reverses the order that might at first seem to be "most natural," by offering "a particular account of ideas, before we proceed to impressions" (T 1.1.2.1 [SBN 8]). He further characterizes impressions of reflection as "internal impressions," in contrast to the outward impressions conveyed through the senses (T 1.2.3.2 [SBN 33]; cf. EHU 2.9 [SBN 22]; DNR 3.156).

In Book 2 Hume reformulates this contrast by distinguishing "original" from "secondary" impressions. Of these, "original" impressions, or sensations, arise from physical states of the body and the influence of external objects on our senses, while "secondary" or reflective impressions "proceed from some of these original ones, either immediately or by the interposition of its idea" (T 2.1.1.1 [SBN 275]). These secondary impressions include "the passions, and other emotions resembling them." Next, Hume distinguishes between "calm" and "violent" passions. In his initial discussion he identifies the aesthetic and moral sentiments as examples of "calm" passions, while characterizing as "violent" those sentiments which we ordinarily call "passions," such as "love and hatred, grief and joy, pride and humility." That is, he first distinguishes calm and violent passions by type rather than degree. However, he also concedes that this distinction is inexact, and that his own use of the apparently relative terms "calm" and "violent" might in some cases be misleading, since "the raptures of poetry and music frequently rise to the greatest height; while those other impressions, properly call'd *passions,* may decay into so soft an emotion, as to become, in a manner, imperceptible" (T 2.1.1.3 [SBN 276]). Indeed, later in Book 2 he applies the phrase "calm passions" to affective dispositions, in

4. For more favorable assessments of Hume's work on the passions, see Laing, *David Hume,* 160–73; Laird, *Hume's Philosophy of Human Nature,* 188; Árdal, *Passion and Value;* Dietl, "Hume on the Passions," 554–66; Capaldi, "Hume's Theory of the Passions," 172–90; McIntyre, "Personal Identity and the Passions," 545–57; Baier, *Progress of Sentiments,* 1–27 and 129–51; and Rorty, "From Passions to Sentiments," 165–79.

contrast to occurrent affective states, and suggests that calm and violent passions are distinguished by their intensity rather than their distinctive quality. Here he argues that an initially intense or "violent" passion may become "a settled principle of action" through custom, after which it "commonly produces no longer any sensible agitation," although it is likely to have a stronger effect on the will than a momentary intense passion (T 2.3.4.1; cf. 2.3.8.12 [SBN 418–19; cf. 437]). Hume considers our vivid occurrent affective states, or "violent" passions in Book 2, Parts 1 and 2, of the *Treatise* and in "Of the Passions." He develops his account of affective dispositions while examining volition in Book 2, Part 3, of the *Treatise* and turns to the moral and aesthetic sentiments in Book 3 of the *Treatise,* in the second *Enquiry,* and in his essays on aesthetics.

In tracing the origin of the passions, Hume begins with the perceptions of pleasure and pain that accompany our impressions of sensation and our ideas. In Book 1 he suggests that the "perception" of pleasure or pain is an original principle "implanted in the human mind," which appears to be "the chief spring and moving principle of all its actions" (T 1.3.10.2 [SBN 118]; cf. 1.1.2.1, 3.3.1.2 [SBN 8, 574]; EPM App.1.18–19 [SBN 293]). On the other hand, he also finds that the conscious states we regard as pleasurable or painful include a variety of sensations and sentiments, so that "under the term *pleasure,* we comprehend sensations, which are very different from each other," and may indeed have "only such a distant resemblance, as is requisite to make them be express'd by the same abstract term" (T 3.1.2.4 [SBN 472]). These include, most obviously, the physical sensations of pleasure or pain arising from the condition of our bodies and from the effects of external objects on our senses (T 1.4.2.12–16, 2.1.1–2 [SBN 192–94, 275–76]; OP 1.1.139; EPM App.2.12 [SBN 301–2]). However, our feelings of pleasure also include the enjoyment we receive from music or fine wine; from company; and from considering the actions and characters of other people (T 3.1.2.4, 2.2.4.4 [SBN 472, 352–53]; EPM 9.25 [SBN 283–84]). Hume indeed provides what seems to be a list of some of his own favorite pleasures in a recently discovered manuscript fragment on evil. In this fragment he states that someone "in good Health & in good Humour" experiences more "small Pleasures" than instances of pain. This is because such a person receives satisfaction from "every common Incident of Life," including eating and drinking, hearing the news, performing his business, the weather, and even "a Fiddle, a warm Bed, a Coffee-house Conversation." On the other hand, since these pleasures are often slight, fleeting, and even trivial, they have less effect on the imagination than the pains that afflict human life (FE 166–67; cf. T 1.4.7.9).[5] Hume further examines the susceptibility of individuals to different types of pleasure in his essays on the temperaments of the Epicurean, the

5. On this fragment, see Stewart, "An Early Fragment on Evil," 160–70, and my own discussion in Chapter 12.

Stoic, the Platonist, and the Sceptic (E Ep.138–45, E St.146–54, E Pl.155–58, E Sc.159–80).⁶

The perceptions of pleasure or pain may accompany our impressions of sensation, our impressions of reflection, and the ideas of these produced by memory and imagination (T 1.1.2.1, 1.3.10.2, 2.2.5.4 [SBN 7–8, 118–19, 358]). However, Hume argues that every type of passion is itself a distinct or "peculiar" sensation of pleasure or displeasure, arising in the mind in response to the idea of an object as a remembered or imagined source of pleasure or displeasure (T 2.1.5.4 [SBN 286]; cf. 2.1.8.2 [SBN 298–99]; EPM App.2.12 [SBN 301]). The impressions of pleasure and pain are the sources for our ideas of good and evil, in the original or non-moral sense of these terms (T 1.3.10.2, 2.1.1.4, 2.3.1.1, 2.3.9.1–8 [SBN 118, 276, 399, 438–39]; OP 1.1–2.139). Hume later distinguishes this hedonic conception of good and evil from the moral conception of good and evil (cf. T 3.1.1.2–3 [SBN 456]; EPM 2.17 [SBN 180]). Finally, he indicates that the goal of human action is happiness, which consists in the pleasures arising from the satisfaction of our various passions (EHU 3.4; EPM 9.14–25 [SBN 278–84]; NHR 2–3.26–32, 15.74–76).

The most thorough discussion of pain in Hume's writings appears in the *Dialogues*. Here Philo considers the view that the purpose of pain is to "excite all creatures to action" and make them "vigilant in the great work of self-preservation" (D 11.205). However, Philo argues that all motives for action could also arise from the prospect of increased pleasure, and that even if pain were required to promote self-preservation, the amount of pain experienced by animals and human beings far exceeds what is needed for this purpose (cf. DNR 10.193–202, 11.205–12; FE 166). Thus, while, the ability to feel pain is a natural disposition in human beings and animals, this capacity also provides the most powerful argument against the existence of an omnipotent and benevolent creator.

Hume appears to present two lines of approach for examining the individual passions. On the one hand, he maintains that the passions are "simple and uniform impressions," which makes it impossible for anyone to give "a just definition of them."⁷ He describes these introspective or phenomenological qualities of the passions as "sensations" or "peculiar emotions," which appear to "our very feeling." These are each "an original quality" of the mind that constitutes the "very being and essence" of the individual passion (T 2.1.2.1,

---

6. See Hudson, "Humean Pleasures Reconsidered," 545–62; Sutherland, "Concept of Pleasure," 218–24; Siebert, *Moral Animus,* 187–94; and Livingston, *Philosophical Melancholy and Delirium,* 97–100, 137–40, and 168–71.

7. As we will see, Hume indicates that various passions may be conjoined or even mixed in different ways, which might seem to yield exceptions to his usual pattern of identifying passions as simple and uniform impressions. On the other hand, even if these compound passions can be resolved into simpler passions, these simple passions remain indefinable.

2.1.5.4; cf. 2.3.10.1, 3.1.2.4 [SBN 277, 286; cf. 448, 472]). We may note that in using the word "sensation" for the distinctive and indefinable character of each of the passions, Hume is departing from his initial use of the word "sensations" for the impressions that arise from the condition of our bodies and the influence of external objects on our sense organs.[8] Hume accordingly indicates that we can only formulate a positive idea of the passions through introspection, or by producing the image of an impression.

On the other hand, Hume also argues that we may develop a "description" of each of the various passions. First, by recognizing the types of circumstances in which I tend to experience each of these passions, and the physical manifestations of the passions in my own body, I am led to attribute the same passions to other people. Thus, whenever I observe the "external signs" or "effects" of any passion "in the voice and gesture of any person," my mind passes "from these effects to their causes" and produces "a lively idea of the passion," which I then attribute to the other person (T 2.1.11.2–3, 3.3.1.7; cf. 1.3.13.14 [SBN 317, 576; cf. 151]).[9] He describes this process as "a kind of *presentation;* which tells us what will operate on others, by what we feel immediately in ourselves" (T 2.2.1.9 [SBN 332]). Indeed, Hume argues that "we never remark any passion or principle in others" which does not have "a parallel in ourselves," and maintains that "the minds of all men are similar in their feelings and operations" (T 2.1.11.5, 3.3.1.7 [SBN 318, 575–76]). In the first *Enquiry* he adds that there are "few or no instances" of a human individual who has never felt, or is incapable of feeling, all the passions that belong to the human species (EHU 2.7 [SBN 20]). In the *Natural History of Religion* he describes various human passions as arising "from an original instinct or primary impression of nature," which we find to be "absolutely universal in all nations and ages" (NHR Int.21). Finally, Philo notes in the *Dialogues* that the outward expressions of the passions in human beings and animals "contain a universal language" (DNR 3.153). We will return in Chapter 7 to Hume's view of the universality of the passions, and its relation to the question of the uniformity of human nature.

Next, the resemblances between the types of circumstances in which we as human beings find ourselves physically expressing the various passions, and our resulting belief in the universality of the passions, is the basis for our ability to apply the same words to these passions. Hume accordingly states that,

8. For the issues arising from Hume's description of a passion as a "simple and uniform" impression, see Árdal, *Passion and Value*, 7–16; Hawkins, "Simplicity, Resemblance and Contrariety," 24–38; and Brand, *Hume's Theory of Moral Judgment*, 9–17.

9. In these passages Hume considers the role of these characteristic bodily expressions in our ideas of the passions, contrary to the criticisms in Kenny, *Action, Emotion and Will,* 26, and Gardiner, "Hume's Theory of the Passions," 38–39. For other discussions of Hume's view of the role of the body in expressing the passions, see Árdal, *Passion and Value*, 42–45; Farr, "Hume, Hermeneutics and History," 307–10; and Brand, *Hume's Theory of Moral Judgment*, 71–82.

in encountering the terms in common use for the different passions, "every one, of himself, will be able to form a just idea of them, without any danger of mistake," and that their distinctive sensations are all "sufficiently known from our common feeling and experience" for us to engage in a shared discourse concerning the passions (T 2.1.2.1, 2.2.1.1; cf. 2.3.1.2 [SBN 277, 329; cf. 399]).

Finally, we may develop a description of each passion by "an enumeration of such circumstances, as attend them," and may even hope, by this method, to identify the "distinguishing characteristic" of each passion (T 2.1.2.1, 2.1.3.3 [SBN 277, 280]).

In his subsequent examination of the passions Hume attempts to provide a description, or an analysis, of the individual passions, or the distinctive modifications of pleasure and displeasure which tend to arise within a conscious human subject in response to certain types of objects and relations, as these are recognized by the given subject.[10] The passions are distinguished from each other especially by "the mixture of different views and reflections," according to the "situation of the object," or a "turn of thought," or the variations in our idea of a given object "according to the light in which it is surveyed" (T 2.3.9.31 [SBN 447–48]; OP 1.1.139).

With this preliminary account of the passions, Hume introduces the basic principle of his system of classification for the individual passions: the distinction between direct and indirect passions.[11] Of these, the direct passions such as "desire, aversion, grief, joy, hope, fear, despair and security" arise in the mind "immediately from good or evil, from pain or pleasure." By contrast, the indirect passions of "pride, humility, ambition, vanity, love, hatred, envy, pity, malice, generosity, with their dependants" arise "from the same principles, but by the conjunction of other qualities" (T 2.1.1.4 [SBN 276–77]; cf. OP 2.1.144).

Hume presents a relatively brief discussion of the direct passions both in the *Treatise* and in "Of the Passions."[12] The basic direct passions are desire and aversion, which arise merely from considering an object as pleasurable or painful, or in other words as good or evil. He regards the passions of desire and aversion, like the capacity for perceiving pleasure and pain, as original principles of the

---

10. Following the usage that is more common in our own day, I will refer to the human individual who experiences a passion as its "subject." As we will see, Hume uses the word "subject," in his analysis of the "causes" of the indirect passions, for the object in which the pleasant or unpleasant qualities that give rise to these passions are supposed to inhere (cf. T 2.1.2.6 [SBN 279]). For reasons that I indicate in this chapter, I will refer to the "cause," including the "subject" and its relevant "qualities," as the "secondary object" of the indirect passion.

11. McIntyre provides a valuable discussion of Hume's distinction and its originality: see "Hume's Passions," 77–86.

12. McIntyre argues that the relatively brief treatment of the direct passions is actually a reflection of Hume's view that in human beings the direct passions are subordinate to the indirect passions of pride, humility, love, and hatred. See McIntyre, "Hume's Passions," 77–86.

human mind, since "the mind by an *original* instinct tends to unite itself with the good, and to avoid the evil" (T 2.3.9.2 [SBN 438–39]; cf. OP 1.2.139). The other direct passions, such as "grief and joy, hope and fear," arise as modifications of desire and aversion, according to our ideas of the various circumstances in which we may encounter an object that we regard as a possible source of pleasure or pain. These circumstances are diversified as the object "changes its situation, and becomes probable or improbable, certain or uncertain, or is consider'd as out of our power for the present moment" (T 3.3.1.2 [SBN 574]). For example, "when good is certain or probable, it produces JOY," while a probable or certain evil arouses "GRIEF or SORROW," and an evil or good which is less certain produces "FEAR or HOPE," in proportion to the probability we assign to its occurrence (T 2.3.9.5–6 [SBN 439]; OP 1.2.139). A more precise specification of the probability of an event gives rise to the further modifications of fear and hope, such as "terror, consternation, astonishment, anxiety," which are all "nothing but different species and degrees of fear" (T 2.3.9.31 [SBN 447]). Hume's most thorough treatment of any of the direct passions is indeed his discussion of fear and hope, which includes a further account of probability and its effect on the imagination. We will return to this discussion in the final section of this chapter, where we will consider his account of the relation between the passions and cognition.

Hume devotes the first and longest division of Book 2 to the indirect passions—pride and humility, love and hatred, and their modifications. These passions arise when we associate the idea of an object of a specific type (that is, a person) with the idea of an object of another specific type (that is, a quality or an external object), such that a direct passion toward the second object inspires a distinct but parallel passion toward the first object. In other words, the indirect passions arise from a "double relation of ideas and impressions" in which the idea of an object or a quality as tending to produce pleasure or pain, and thus as the object of a direct passion, is associated with the idea of a person, who becomes the object of the indirect passion, as a distinct but correspondingly pleasurable or painful impression of reflection (T 2.1.5.5; cf. 2.2.2.3 [SBN 286–87; cf. 333]). In this analysis Hume extends his theory of association to our passions, which may be associated with each other either by our tendency to associate the ideas of their objects, or directly through their resemblance to each other in their pleasurable or painful qualities (T 2.1.4.1–5 [SBN 282–84]).[13] He traces this network of associations in his examination of the indirect passions, beginning with pride and humility, then turning to love and hatred, and finally considering the various modifications of these passions.[14]

13. See Hawkins, "Simplicity, Resemblance and Contrariety," 24–38.
14. Hume's passion of "humility" is the passion that we would more usually call "shame" (cf. T 2.2.10.6 [SBN 391]). He identifies love more specifically as "*Love* or *Friendship*" in "Of the Passions" (OP 2.1.144), and

In considering the two ideas that are associated with each other in producing an indirect passion, Hume distinguishes between the "cause" and the "object" of the indirect passions, or "that idea, which excites them, and that to which they direct their view, when excited." Each of the indirect passions may be described by identifying the "object" and the "cause," along with the pleasurable or painful character of the direct passion aroused by the cause. From a survey of the examples of the indirect passions in our ordinary experience, we discover that the "object" of an indirect passion is always the idea of a person. For pride and humility this object is the self, while for love and hatred the object is another person. However, each of the indirect passions also has a "cause" distinct from the object. This cause is a thing, a quality, or a circumstance that produces an impression of pleasure or pain in the subject, and is therefore the object of a direct passion. Finally, when the idea of the cause is associated by the subject with the idea of the object, that is, the self or another person, this association produces an indirect passion directed toward that person (T 2.1.2.3–4 [SBN 277–78]).

Hume also refers to the "object" and the "cause" together as the "two objects" involved in the production of an indirect passion (T 2.1.6.5 [SBN 292]).[15] To clarify his terminology, we might identify what he calls the "cause" as the intentional object of a direct passion and the "object" as the intentional object of the indirect passion. It would even perhaps be more accurate to identify the "cause" of the indirect passion as the subject's belief that these two objects stand in a certain type of relation to each other.[16] In the present study I will refer to the "object" and the "cause" respectively as the "primary" and "secondary" objects of an indirect passion, so that a person is its primary object, while the occasioning thing, quality, or circumstance is its secondary object. We will see in a moment that the secondary objects of the indirect passions are considerably more varied than their primary objects, although Hume argues that even these secondary objects can be divided into several types through empirical observation. Finally, the two indirect passions of pride and love are both modifications of pleasure, since they arise from the association of the primary object with a secondary object which is itself regarded as a source of pleasure, while humility and hatred are both modifications of aversion.

Next, Hume considers whether the different objects of the indirect passions are either "natural" or "original" to the human mind. First, he argues that the primary objects of these passions are determined by principles of the mind that

---

provides a separate discussion of the "amorous passion" in both texts, as we will see (T 2.2.11.1–6 [SBN 394–96]; OP 3.7.158).

15. Baier notes this in *Progress of Sentiments,* 133.

16. For a further discussion of beliefs as the causes of the indirect passions, see Davidson, "Hume's Cognitive Theory of Pride," 755–57.

are both "natural" and "original." On the one hand, the self and other persons
are "natural" objects of the indirect passions, because of the "constancy and
steadiness" with which the passions of pride or humility, and love or hatred, are
directed respectively toward the self or another person. However, this determination is also an "original" principle of the mind, since their direction toward
the self or another person is the "distinguishing characteristic of these passions"
(T 2.1.3.2–4 [SBN 280]). Hume characterizes pride, for example, as a "certain
disposition" implanted in the mind by nature, which tends to produce a certain type of reflective impression directed toward the idea of the self (T 2.1.5.6
[SBN 287]). Hume thus includes the indirect passions and their intentional
direction among the instincts or principles that may be traced to the "primary
constitution of the mind," along with the direct passions, and their intentional
directedness toward objects as anticipated sources of pleasure or pain (T 2.1.5.3
[SBN 286–87]; cf. 1.3.10.2, 2.3.9.1–3, 3.3.1.2 [SBN 118, 438–39, 574–75];
OP 1.1.139).

In turning to the "causes" or secondary objects of the indirect passions,
Hume finds that these are also "natural," since these passions are consistently
directed to certain types of objects "in all nations and ages," and since we are
generally able to recognize, explain, and even predict the causes of these passions in others. However, the causes of the indirect passions, unlike their
objects, do not appear to be "original," or determined individually "by a particular provision, and primary constitution of nature." On the contrary, in addition to their "prodigious number," we find that "many of them are the effects
of art, and arise partly from the industry, partly from the caprice, and partly
from the good fortune of men." It seems unreasonable to suppose that "every
new production of art" which might become the source of pride or humility
is already anticipated by a specific principle implanted in the mind. On the
other hand, by considering a number of examples, we may find some common
characteristics among the secondary objects of these passions, allowing us to
identify the types of objects that tend to become the occasioning causes of the
indirect passions (T 2.1.3.4–7 [SBN 280–82]). As an addition to his initial
analysis, he now argues that the secondary object, in the case of pride or humility, is made up of a "subject," or some entity related to the self, such as "parts
of ourselves, or something nearly related to us," and a "quality" belonging to
that subject, which is the source of pleasure or pain, and thus the immediate
object of our desire or aversion (T 2.1.5.1–3 [SBN 285–86]).[17]

Hume finds, by introspection and observation, that we may divide the
secondary objects of pride and humility into three types. First, these objects
include "every valuable quality of the mind," or of "imagination, judgment,

17. See note 10.

memory or disposition," such as "wit, good-sense, learning, courage, justice, integrity." Next, these objects include qualities of the body, so that "a man may be proud of his beauty, strength, agility, good mien, address in dancing, riding, fencing, and of his dexterity in any manual business or manufacture." Finally, pride and humility may be aroused by any external object related to ourselves: "Our country, family, children, relations, riches, houses, gardens, horses, dogs, cloaths" may all become causes of pride or humility (T 2.1.2.5 [SBN 279]). In other words, the secondary objects of pride and humility may be divided into qualities of the mind, qualities of the body, and external objects (cf. T 2.2.1.4– 5, 3.3.5.1 [SBN 330, 614]).

In the case of love and hatred, the primary object is clearly "some sensible being external to us." However, Hume maintains that love and hatred are also indirect passions, in that they also have a cause or a secondary object distinct from, but related to, the person who is their primary object. Further, the same types of qualities or attributes that arouse pride or humility in ourselves are also the occasioning causes for our love or hatred toward others: these are, again, qualities of mind and character, bodily attributes and achievements, and external possessions or circumstances. These qualities, when attributed to another person, accordingly render him or her the object of "love and esteem, or hatred and contempt" (T 2.2.1.2–4 [SBN 329–30]; OP 3.1.155–56).

Thus, although we cannot present a "just definition" of the passions, Hume indicates that we may formulate a description or an analysis of each indirect passion by characterizing its primary and secondary objects, the subject's belief concerning his or her relation to these objects, and the subject's response to these objects as sources of pleasure or displeasure (T 2.1.2.2, 2.1.3.1–3 [SBN 277, 280]). We may accordingly state that "all agreeable objects, related to ourselves, by an association of ideas and of impressions, produce pride, and disagreeable ones, humility." We may also say of love and hatred that "the cause of both these passions is always related to a thinking being" and produces a "separate pleasure" in the case of love and a "separate uneasiness" in cases of hatred (T 2.1.6.1, 2.2.1.6 [SBN 290, 331]; cf. OP 2.5.146, 3.1.156).

Hume also considers several further judgments that contribute to the production of the passions. As we have seen, the indirect passions arise within the mind of a subject from a judgment concerning the relation between the secondary and primary objects: a judgment that ultimately depends upon the association of ideas (T 2.1.5.5, 2.2.2.16 [SBN 286, 339–40]). Hume also finds, however, that for any secondary object to arouse pride or humility, its relation to the self must also be regarded as relatively close, exclusive, enduring, and obvious to others. Pride and humility require an additional series of judgments on the part of the subject concerning his or her relation to some specific mental, bodily, or external attribute; and also concerning the recognition of this relation by others (T 2.1.6.1–10 [SBN 290–94]; cf. OP 2.11.153–55). Similarly, love and hatred require a further series of judgments concerning other persons, including judgments of their intentions, actions, and character (T 2.2.3.4–5, 2.2.7.1–6, 2.2.8.12–20, 2.2.10.1–8 [SBN 347–65, 368–71, 377–80, 389–93]).

Hume also considers a number of other passions that are related to the basic indirect passions. First, he identifies several variations of love and hatred arising from our tendency to compare our own circumstances to those of other people. For example, an idea of the sufferings of others may produce a sympathetic pain and give rise to pity, or enhance our self-satisfaction and give rise to malice. Similarly, the good fortune of others may produce envy, by increasing our dissatisfaction with our own circumstances, or esteem, which is a "species of love," if it does not turn our attention toward our own dissatisfactions (T 2.2.7.1– 2.2.8.20, 2.2.5.1–21 [SBN 368–81, 357–65]).[18] Hume also considers various passions that can be conjoined with other passions. As we have seen, he argues that not only our ideas but also our passions can be associated with each other according to the principle of resemblance (cf. T 2.1.4.1–5 [SBN 282–84]). This applies not only to the internal structure of the indirect passions but also to the relation between the indirect passions and various other passions. For example, he argues that benevolence and anger, which consist respectively in a desire for the happiness or the misery of another person, are distinct from love and hatred, although regularly conjoined with them (T 2.2.6.3–6 [SBN 367–68]). On the other hand, Hume suggests that some passions may be "susceptible of an entire union" through their association, producing a distinctive impression, or "compound" passion, which is a mixture of the original passions (T 2.2.3.1, 2.2.6.1, 2.2.9.1 [SBN 347, 366, 381]). For example, respect is a mixture of love and humility, while contempt is a mixture of pride and hatred (T 2.2.10.1–3 [SBN 389–90]). In addition, Hume describes the "amorous passion, or love betwixt the sexes," as a passion that arises from the mixture of three more basic passions: the enjoyment of beauty, the "bodily appetite for generation," and what he initially calls a "generous kindness or good-will," and later, in "Of the Passions," "friendship or affection" (T 2.2.11.1 [SBN 394]; OP 3.7158; cf. FE 166).

As we have seen, Hume initially appears to present two separate approaches to the examination of the passions. First, we recognize each passion in ourselves by its distinctive phenomenological character, which would be described in the "just definition" of a given passion. He maintains, however, that it is impossible to formulate a "just definition" of any passion, since every passion is a simple and uniform impression without any parts that could be enumerated in a definition. Accordingly, he does not attempt to offer definitions of the individual

18. For further discussions of our tendency to compare our own situation to that of others, and its role in generating various passions, see Árdal, *Passion and Value,* 59–61; Baier, *Progress of Sentiments,* 146–51; and Brand, *Hume's Theory of Moral Judgment,* 82–90.

passions, or even to describe their distinctive sensations. Instead, he presents a description of the individual passions by identifying their "nature, origin, causes and objects," or in other words the particular objects, circumstances, and relations that gives rise to each passion, as a specific modification of pleasure or pain (T 2.1.2.1, 2.2.1.1 [SBN 277, 329]).

Many critics of Hume's theory of the passions have criticized what appears to be his initial reduction of the passions to distinctive feelings, while overlooking his further discussion of the individual passions as intentional states, which are not only directed toward objects, but also arise from a cognitive evaluation of the object and its qualities in relation to the self. For example, according to Kenny, Hume holds that "it is because our minds happen to be made as they are that the object of pride is self, not because of anything involved in the concept of *pride*," and that "a passion can be, and be recognized as, pride before the idea of its object comes before the mind." Similarly, Gardiner argues that "on Hume's view of the matter it would appear to be at least *intelligible* to talk of a man feeling proud of something which bore no special relation to himself," because of Hume's allegedly "entire treatment of the passions as the isolable contents of a direct introspective awareness," which, as "mere impressions or 'inward' sensations," may be described "without reference to the objects towards which they are directed and in distinction from any of the forms of outward expression in which they typically manifest themselves." More concisely, Neu asserts that for Hume emotions are "essentially feelings" to which thoughts are "incidentally attached."[19]

In this section, however, we have seen that Hume rejects any attempt to characterize the passions through a "just definition," or a description of their phenomenological feeling-qualities based purely upon introspection. On the contrary, he attempts to describe the various passions as intentional states that are directed toward an object, and arise from the evaluation of this object and its relation to the self. According to his analysis, every evaluation of an object as a potential source of good or evil within the context of such a subjectively judged relation produces a distinctive feeling within the human subject which is a modification of pleasure or displeasure. These feelings are then often expressed through characteristic gestures and speech; and we are able to attribute these passions to other people on the basis of similarity between us in these public types of expressions. Hume therefore develops an analysis of the passions as intentional states of consciousness, consisting in distinctive inner sensations that are caused by and directed toward objects on the basis of a cognitive assessment of these objects, through our judgments of their nature and their relation

19. Kenny, *Action, Emotion and Will,* 24–25; Gardiner, "Hume's Theory of the Passions," 38–39; Neu, *Emotion, Thought and Therapy,* 1. See also Bedford, "Emotions," 281–304; Pitcher, "Emotion," 326–46; Mercer, *Sympathy and Ethics,* 20–44; and Mounce, *Hume's Naturalism,* 63–64 and 71–73.

to ourselves. Finally, he also indicates that we apply names to the passions by recognizing the similarities in how they are publicly expressed, as we observe these expressions in ourselves and in other people.[20] There are several passages in Hume's account of the passions that are often cited in order to support the purely introspective, nonintentional, and non-cognitive interpretation of his analysis. However, each of these is consistent with the present interpretation of his approach as an intentional and cognitive analysis of the passions as directed toward certain types of objects on the basis of various types of beliefs. We have already encountered the first of these, which is presented in his opening account of pride and humility:

> The passions of PRIDE and HUMILITY being simple and uniform impressions, 'tis impossible we can ever, by a multitude of words, give a just definition of them, or indeed of any of the passions. The utmost we can pretend to is a description of them, by an enumeration of such circumstances, as attend them: But as these words, *pride* and *humility,* are of general use, and the impressions they represent the most common of any, every one, of himself, will be able to form a just idea of them, without any danger of mistake. (T 2.1.2.1; cf. 2.2.1.1 [SBN 277; cf. 329])

While the opening sentence of this passage is often cited as evidence that Hume presents a purely introspective and noncognitive theory of the passions, the second sentence presents his further proposal for a "description" of the passions in terms of their objects and the circumstances of our encounter with these objects, as an alternative to an unattainable "definition" or statement of their introspected sensations. He also suggests here that our shared experience of the passions, as this is reflected in our ordinary linguistic usage, allows us to form a "just idea" of any passion for the purposes of discussion, since these public terms remind us of our own subjective experiences of these passions. If we further extend his apparent distinction between "just" and "relative" ideas to his account of the passions, we might suppose that in Hume's view we produce the "just idea" of a passion by remembering its appearance in our experience, while any conscious beings who do not experience the full range of human passions might be able to formulate a "relative idea" of a given passion from its description, or by observing those who do experience it. In other words, Hume proceeds in this passage from our recognition of the passions as introspected conscious

---

20. For other arguments against a purely introspective, nonintentional, and noncognitive view of Hume's analysis of the passions, see Dietl, "Hume on the Passions," 560–64; Árdal, *Passion and Value,* 27–28; Davidson, "Hume's Cognitive Theory of Pride," 755–57; Baier, "Hume's Analysis of Pride," 29; Sutherland, "Morality and the Emotions," 14–23, and "Hume and the Concept of Pleasure," 218–23; and Russell, *Freedom and Moral Sentiment,* 88–96.

states to an account of their public identification through a common language, and then states his intention to provide a description of the passions, as they are publicly recognized and identified, in the rest of his discussion.

Another passage often cited in order to support the nonintentional interpretation of Hume on the passions is his claim that "a passion is an original existence, or, if you will, modification of existence, and contains not any representative quality, which renders it a copy of any other existence or modification. When I am angry, I am actually possest with the passion, and in that emotion have no more a reference to any other object, than when I am thirsty, or sick, or more than five foot high" (T 2.3.3.5; cf. 3.1.1.9 [SBN 415; cf. 458]). Hume's assertion here that any passion is an "original" modification of existence that does not contain "a reference to any other object" has often been regarded as stating that we can recognize and characterize the passions apart from any object: for example, that I could be angry without any object for my anger.[21] Indeed, Penelhum has described this passage as a "wildly implausible denial of the intentionality of the passions."[22] However, in this passage Hume is not denying the intentional direction of the passions, but rather that a passion may "represent" or "copy" other impressions, and be judged true or false by a comparison with any object. Instead, it is "ideas" or propositions that may be judged to be true or false, according to their agreement with the objects they are supposed to represent (T 3.1.1.9, 1.3.7.5n20 [SBN 458, 96n1]). In other words, Hume is using the word "reference" here for the relation of "copying" or representation between an idea and its object. His denial of this type of relation to the passions does not preclude other types of relation between a passion and its objects, any more than he precludes other types of relations in his examples. On the contrary, thirst is causally produced by physical states of the body, and is the desire for a certain type of object; while being more than five feet tall is judged by applying a system of measurement using the appropriate tool (cf. T 2.1.5.7 [SBN 287]). All of these states involve various types of relations to other objects, which may perhaps be described as forms of "reference" in a broader sense, but not as a "copy" of "any other existence or modification."

A third passage that might seem to support a nonintentional interpretation of Hume's theory of the passions appears in his account of the contingent relations between such passions as love and benevolence, or hatred and anger:

> According as we are possess'd with love or hatred, the correspondent desire of the happiness or misery of the person, who is the object of

---

21. Indeed, Hume does not provide any specific discussion of the apparently objectless passions that we would call "moods," such as cheerfulness, melancholy, or irritability.

22. Penelhum, "Hume's Moral Psychology," 128; see also Baier's remarks on this "silly paragraph" in *Progress of Sentiments*, 160–62.

these passions, arises in the mind, and varies with each variation of these opposite passions. This order of things, abstractedly consider'd, is not necessary. Love and hatred might have been unattended with any such desires, or their particular connexion might have been entirely revers'd. . . . I see no contradiction in supposing a desire of producing misery annex'd to love, and of happiness to hatred. (T 2.2.6.6 [SBN 368])

Here, however, we must distinguish between the intentional character of the indirect passions and a conjunction between distinct passions. As we have seen, Hume presents the relation between a passion and its objects as an intentional relation, in which a passion is inherently directed toward a certain type of object as it is perceived and judged under certain specific sets of circumstances. In this passage, however, he is considering the relation between different passions, and asserting their independence from each other. He thus argues that love and hatred "may express themselves in a hundred ways, and may subsist a considerable time, without our reflecting on the happiness or misery of their objects." Indeed, he presents this observation as proof "that these desires are not the same with love and hatred, nor make any essential part of them," although they may be regularly or even constantly conjoined with these passions (T 2.2.6.5 [SBN 367–68]).[23] That is, the conjunctions between these passions are contingent, while the direction of a passion toward a certain type of object, on the basis of its idea, is an essential part of its distinctive sensation and should be included in its description.

Finally, Hume indicates that the social and historical context contributes to determining the particular objects of the passions for any individual human subject. That is, he shows that our evaluation of an object as a potential source of pleasure or displeasure is often influenced by the prevailing assessment of objects in our cultural environment.[24] First, he argues that the secondary objects of the indirect passions are "natural" but not "original," since many of these objects are "the effects of art, and arise partly from the industry, partly from the caprice, and partly from the good fortune of men" (T 2.1.3.5 [SBN 281]). Next, he observes that these secondary objects, including attributes of the body, attributes of mind and character, and external possessions or circumstances, become sources of pleasure and occasions for pride and love insofar as they are "useful, beautiful or surprising" (T 2.1.8.5 [SBN 300]). Finally, he indicates that the utility, beauty, and novelty of an object or personal attribute are at least partly determined by the cultural context in which they appear. For example,

23. Árdal challenges Hume on this point by maintaining that the connection between love and benevolence "is in fact a logical one." See *Passion and Value*, 72.

24. For a further discussion of the social dimension of the indirect passions, see Whelan, *Order and Artifice*, 136–88. This aspect of Hume's discussion is overlooked by Berry in "Hume on Rationality," 239–43.

beauty is "an order and construction of parts" which gives a peculiar type of pleasure to the observer "either by the *primary constitution* of our nature, by *custom*, or by *caprice*" (T 2.1.8.2 [SBN 299]). Similarly, the usefulness of various objects or qualities is at least partly determined by particular social and historical circumstances. For example, such qualities as generosity, pride, and honor may be better suited to the "circumstances of one age than those of another," and may thus have "different *utilities*" in different contexts (EPM D.40; EPM 3.33 [SBN 337, 196]).[25] We will find in later chapters that those external possessions and advantages which may become the secondary objects of our indirect passions, including family relationships, property, social status, and nationality, are attributed to any given individual through a combination of individual and historical memory, social convention, and legal prescription.[26] We may also trace the influence of social and historical circumstances in determining the secondary objects of human pride and humility by comparing these to the causes of the same passions in nonhuman animals. In doing so, we find that since other animals cannot formulate any concepts of mental qualities, and do not have extensive memories of family relations or conceptions of property, they are only able to regard the immediately useful or agreeable qualities of their own bodies, such as beauty or strength, as occasions for pride (T 2.1.12.4–5 [SBN 326–27]).[27]

Hume's account of the social and historical dimension of the indirect passions receives its most explicit statement in his reference to the role of custom and general rules in establishing the causes of the indirect passions in a given setting. He thus observes, in a fanciful moment, that "if a person full-grown, and of the same nature with ourselves" were suddenly to be "transported into our world," this person "wou'd be very much embarrass'd with every object, and wou'd not readily find what degree of love or hatred, pride or humility, or any other passion he ought to attribute to it." However, as participants in a community we find that "custom and practice have brought to light all these principles, and have settled the just value of every thing," giving us "general establish'd maxims" for recognizing "the proportions we ought to observe in preferring one object to another" (T 2.1.6.9 [SBN 293–94]; cf. OP 2.11.155). We accordingly find that "custom," in the social and historical sense of the term, tends to determine the causes and the objects of the passions in any given cultural setting.[28]

25. See Cohen, "Notion of Moral Progress," 109–27.

26. See also Livingston, *Hume's Philosophy of Common Life*, 101–5 and 146–48.

27. It seems debatable to me whether the swagger of a male peacock, or the raptures of a dog who has been praised by its owner, are accurately described as pride, although we might be able to explain these as expressing some other passion that we share with animals. I find it easier to extend Hume's account of love and hatred to nonhuman animals than his analysis of pride and humility.

28. On the role of custom in the indirect passions, see also Hearn, "General Rules in Hume's *Treatise*," 414–16; Miller, *Philosophy and Ideology*, 44–45; and Whelan, *Order and Artifice*, 184–87.

SYMPATHY

In the course of examining the passions, Hume also introduces his account of sympathy, which will be further developed in the *Treatise* and elsewhere in his writings.[29]

In the *Treatise* Hume does not apply the word "sympathy" to a particular passion, such as a generous concern for the welfare of others—a passion he prefers to call "benevolence" or "humanity."[30] Instead, he uses the word "sympathy" to denote the disposition to "receive by communication" the "inclinations and sentiments" of others (T 2.1.11.1–2; cf. 3.3.3.4 [SBN 316, 604]). This is yet another process involving the association of our impressions and ideas. As we have seen, Hume argues that while we cannot feel the passions of others, we may recognize a passion in another person "by those external signs in the countenance and conversation, which convey an idea of it." He then argues that the idea of a passion may attain "such a degree of force and vivacity, as to become the very passion itself" and thus be "converted into an impression" (T 2.1.11.3 [SBN 317]). He accordingly concludes that the sympathetic communication of a passion is "nothing but a lively idea converted into an impression" (T 2.2.9.13 [SBN 385–86]).[31]

Indeed, this sympathetic diffusion of a passion also occurs among certain animals when they observe the expression of a passion among other members of their own species. We thus find that fear, anger, courage, and grief are "frequently communicated from one animal to another, without their knowledge of that cause, which produc'd the original passion." For example, "the howlings and lamentations of a dog produce a sensible concern in his fellows," and hounds are more animated "when they hunt in a pack, than when they pursue their game apart" (T 2.2.12.6 [SBN 398]).

In human beings, however, sympathy is often mediated by judgment, and may even operate only after "a great effort of imagination." Accordingly, we may sympathize with the expected passions of others by considering their present circumstances, or even by anticipating their future circumstances, without directly observing the signs of the passion in that person (T 2.2.9.13–14; cf. 3.3.1.7 [SBN 385–86; cf. 576]).[32] The operation of sympathy in human beings

---

29. For a study of Hume's account of sympathy and its role in his ethics, aesthetics, political theory, and historical writings, see Herdt, *Religion and Faction*.

30. For further discussions of Hume on sympathy, see Árdal, *Passion and Value*; Mercer, *Sympathy and Ethics*; Butler, "T and Sympathy," 1–20; Farr, "Hume, Hermeneutics and History," 285–310; Capaldi, *Hume's Place in Moral Philosophy*, 177–235; and Brand, *Hume's Theory of Moral Judgment*, 82–90.

31. Waxman argues that Hume's account of this process as "transforming" an idea into an impression is problematic, and that he might more accurately describe this process as an impression of reflection or passion "supplanting" the received idea of the passion. See Waxman, *Hume's Theory of Consciousness*, 30–31 and 40–41.

32. For further discussions of the role of the imagination in sympathy, see Farr, "Hume, Hermeneutics and History," 295–96 and 308, and Herdt, *Religion and Faction*, 82–167.

is also influenced by any resemblances between the subject and the observed person, for example in character, circumstances, or cultural context. That is, "any peculiar similarity in our manners, or character, or country, or language" beyond the "general resemblance of our natures" serves to facilitate the sympathetic arousal of a passion, so that "we sympathize more with persons contiguous to us" than those who are distant, and with acquaintances and countrymen, rather than strangers or foreigners (T 2.1.11.5, 3.3.1.14 [SBN 318, 581]). Indeed, the effort to develop a sympathetic response to the passions of a person of a different character or culture often requires a deliberate attempt to identify the objects of the particular passions for that person, a process we will consider at greater length in Chapter 7 (cf. EPM D.18–51 [SBN 330–41]; E ST.239–40).[33]

Many studies have argued that Hume renounced his earlier account of sympathy after the *Treatise,* especially in the second *Enquiry,* where he seems to identify sympathy with universal benevolence, or a "sentiment of humanity" (EPM 9.5; EPM App.2.5n60; EPM App.3.2 [SBN 271–72, 298n1, 303]).[34] However, elsewhere in the second *Enquiry* he reaffirms his earlier discussion of sympathy, for example by stating that anything which "presents us with the view of human happiness or misery" is likely to produce "a sympathetic movement of pleasure or uneasiness" in the observer, or to "infuse" an observer with the same passion (EPM 5.23, 5.18 [SBN 221, 220]). Hume's theory of sympathy is also reflected in several of his essays. He thus observes that our predominant dispositions give us each "a peculiar sympathy" with writers who resemble us (E ST.244). He also considers the role of "sympathy," or a "contagion" of passions, manners, and inclinations, in the formation of national characters (E NC.204). These passages indicate that Hume retains his theory of the sympathetic communication of the passions in his later writings, although he uses the term less rigorously.[35]

Hume notes that the sympathetic communication of any passion is in itself a source of pleasure for human beings. He initially finds that the mind is "insufficient, of itself, to its own entertainment," and therefore "naturally seeks after foreign objects, which may produce a lively sensation, and agitate the spirits." This is expressed in a variety of pursuits and in our engagements with a variety of objects. However, human company is more "rejoicing" than any of these, since it gives us "the liveliest of all objects, *viz.* a rational and thinking

---

33. Cohen argues that, on Hume's view, sympathy enables us to discover the common human dispositions underlying the apparent historical and cultural diversity of human life: see "Notion of Moral Progress," 109–27.

34. See Selby-Bigge, "Editor's Introduction," xxvi; Kemp Smith, *Philosophy of David Hume,* 150–52 and 533–34; Passmore, *Hume's Intentions,* 129; and Capaldi, *David Hume,* 180–87, and *Hume's Place in Moral Philosophy,* 237–67.

35. For further discussions of the continuity in Hume's view of sympathy, see Stewart, *Moral and Political Philosophy,* 329–38; Norton, "Hume's Common Sense Morality," 542n11; and Altmann, "Hume on Sympathy," 133–35.

being like ourselves, who communicates to us all the actions of his mind," or his thoughts and feelings toward objects and events in our shared world (T 2.2.4.4 [SBN 352–53]). We thus find that while a "general survey of the universe" will disclose the "force of sympathy thro' the whole animal creation," its influence "is still more conspicuous in man, as being the creature of the universe, who has the most ardent desire of society, and is fitted for it by the most advantages." Indeed, Hume finds that we can formulate "no wish, which has not a reference to society," and that solitude may be "the greatest punishment we can suffer." He concludes in a moment of particular eloquence: "Let all the powers and elements of nature conspire to serve and obey one man: Let the sun rise and set at his command: The sea and rivers roll as he pleases, and the earth furnish spontaneously whatever may be useful or agreeable to him: He will still be miserable, till you give him some one person at least, with whom he may share his happiness, and whose esteem and friendship he may enjoy" (T 2.2.5.15 [SBN 363]). Thus, according to Hume, a sympathetic reception of the passions of others, and the assurance of a sympathetic response from them to our own passions, are among the fundamental sources of pleasure in human life, and thereby serve to facilitate social cooperation and cohesion.

Yet on the other hand, sympathy also exacerbates the divisions and conflicts in a society by promoting the cohesion of groups in opposition to each other. In the second *Enquiry* Hume finds that "popular sedition, party zeal, [and] a devoted obedience to factious leaders" are "some of the most visible, though less laudable effects of this social sympathy in human nature" (EPM 5.35 [SBN 224]). Hume especially examines the divisive effects of sympathy in religion and politics, for example in his historical writings, where he describes the sympathetic diffusion of improbable or socially harmful beliefs or dispositions throughout a sect, faction, or group as a "contagion" (cf. E IC.523, H 5.45.12, H 5.53.258, H 5.53.280).[36] The force of sympathy may even override the independent judgment of the individual in the activities of ordinary life, since even people of the "greatest judgment and understanding" often find it difficult to persist in any desires or judgments opposed by "that of their friends and daily companions" (T 2.1.11.2 [SBN 316]; cf. NHR 15.76).

Sympathy plays an important role in many areas of Hume's thought. In this section I consider his view of its role in the passions, in our concepts of the passions and characters of other people, in promoting similar qualities among individuals in various social groups, and in the communication of opinions through testimony and education. I consider the role of sympathy in other areas of his thought later in this study.

---

36. For a further discussion of sympathy as a source of social division and conflict, see Herdt, *Religion and Faction.*

Hume introduces his discussion of sympathy as an important but belated supplement to his account of pride and humility, while examining our "love of fame." In this context he identifies the "opinions of others" as a subordinate cause of pride and humility, since our assessment of an object has little effect in occasioning pride or humility unless it is "seconded by the opinions and sentiments of others" (T 2.1.11.1 [SBN 316]). Love is also furthered by the "easy sympathy and correspondent emotions" that we experience with our friends and relations (T 2.2.4.7 [SBN 353–54]). Many of our other passions are feelings of pleasure or pain that arise from our sympathetic response to the passions of others and are then differentiated by a "particular turn of thought and imagination." For example, compassion is a displeasure arising from our sympathetic recognition of the suffering of another person, while "esteem" is a pleasure that is aroused by the "rich and powerful," in part from a sympathetic appreciation of their happiness (T 2.2.7.1; cf. 2.2.7.1–6, 2.2.5.1–14 [SBN 368–70; cf. 357–62]). Even envy and malice require a sympathetic recognition of the passions of other persons, although in both cases our sympathetic response to their happiness or misery is reversed in its pleasurable or painful quality, as a result of our tendency to contrast our own situation to that of the other person (T 2.2.8.1–20 [SBN 372–80]). Hume concludes that sympathy is the "soul" or the "animating principle" of all the passions, since none of these would have any force if we were to "abstract entirely from the thoughts and sentiments of others" (T 2.2.5.15 [SBN 363]).[37]

Sympathy also allows us to formulate our ideas of the passions and characters of other people. As we have seen, Hume indicates that we attribute the various passions to other people by observing a resemblance between their behavior and our own under similar circumstances, and by ascribing to the other person the subjective impression we experience in these cases (T 2.1.11.2–3, 2.2.1.9, 3.3.1.7 [SBN 317, 332, 576]). We may also attribute a disposition toward any specific passion to an individual by observing regular patterns in his or her behavior. Hume identifies this observable tendency to act in certain ways under certain circumstances as a "calm passion," and as a "settled principle of action" or even a "predominant inclination of the soul" (T 2.3.4.1; cf. 2.3.1.10, 2.3.2.6 [SBN 419; cf. 403, 411]). Finally, we derive the concept of the "character" of a human individual from our ideas of the set of calm passions or dispositions by which that individual tends to be motivated. We may accordingly classify the various actions of individuals as expressing either the "*general* character" or the "*present* disposition" of the person: that is, as arising either from the "calm passions" and dispositions of the person, or else from an immediate and perhaps

---

37. For discussions of the role of sympathy in the indirect passions, see Farr, "Hume, Hermeneutics and History," 289; Whelan, *Order and Artifice*, 167–84; and McIntyre, "Hume's Passions," 77–86.

uncharacteristic violent passion (T 2.3.3.10 [SBN 418]). In other words, the character of a person is the set of prevailing passions or dispositions that we attribute to that person as the causes of their actions, on the basis of observation or other evidence concerning their actions through time. This notion of character is reflected in Hume's own characterizations of a number of contemporary and historical figures in his writings. Examples of these appear in his essay on Sir Robert Walpole (E RW.574–76), and in the *History of England,* where he examines the character of each of the important English monarchs and other figures at appropriate intervals in his narrative, as in the cases of William the Conqueror, Thomas More, and Lady Jane Gray (H 1.4.225–27, H 3.31.215–16, H 3.36.402 and 419–21). I will return to Hume's notion of character in Chapters 7 and 8, in order to consider its role in his account of the interpretation of human action and in his moral theory.[38]

Sympathy also contributes to establishing the unity and even the "character" of social groups. Hume indeed argues that sympathy, in contrast to the other influences proposed in the eighteenth century, such as "soil and climate," accounts for "the great uniformity we may observe in the humours and turn of thinking of those of the same nation" (T 2.1.11.2 [SBN 316–17]). We may indeed depict the "character" of a given nation by describing the uniformities of thought and temperament that are expressed in the prevailing character traits, or the patterns of behavior and "peculiar set of manners," among its inhabitants (T 2.3.1.10 [SBN 403]; cf. E NC.197–98]).

Finally, the sympathetic diffusion of passions among human beings tends to facilitate the communication of opinions through language. Indeed, Hume observes that the "correspondence of human souls" is "so close and intimate" that a partner in conversation often "diffuses on me all his opinions, and draws along my judgment in a greater or lesser degree," so that even if I do not change my own opinion, the "easy course" of my thought is disturbed (T 3.3.2.2; cf. 2.3.6.8 [SBN 592; cf. 427]). We are thus drawn to embrace the opinions of others "both from *sympathy,* which renders all their sentiments intimately present to us; and from *reasoning,* which makes us regard their judgment, as a kind of argument for what they affirm." He concludes that "these two principles of authority and sympathy influence almost all our opinions" (T 2.1.11.9 [SBN 320–21]).[39]

We have seen that in Book 1 of the *Treatise* Hume regards testimony and education as in many cases "unphilosophical" sources of opinion (T 1.3.9.16–19 [SBN 115–17]). He notes in the *Treatise,* and also in a 1761 letter to Hugh Blair

---

38. See also McIntyre, "Character," 193–206; Baier, *Progress of Sentiments,* 134 and 174–97; Russell, *Freedom and Moral Sentiment,* 58–70 and 95–136; and Purviance, "Indirect Passions," 195–212.

39. For the epistemological significance of Hume's understanding of sympathy for the human sciences, see Farr, "Hume, Hermeneutics and History," 292 and 296.

on the debate concerning miracles, that children "implicitly embrace every opinion propos'd to them" through sympathy with their caregivers (T 2.1.11.2 [SBN 316]; cf. L 1.349). However, sympathy also prompts the acceptance of testimony by adults. We may explain the "remarkable propensity" in human beings "to believe whatever is reported, even concerning apparitions, enchantments, and prodigies" as resulting not only from agreeable emotions of "*surprize* and *wonder*," but also from a sympathetic response to the signs of passion in the reporter (T 1.3.9.12 [SBN 113]; EHU 10.16 [SBN 117]). The influence of sympathy in the communication of opinions, like the association of ideas, is spontaneous and unreflective, but may be counteracted through the disciplined activity of reasoning according to the rules for philosophical probable reasoning, as these are applied to the evaluation of human testimony. I will consider Hume's account of the evaluation of human testimony at greater length in Chapter 13 (cf. T 1.3.4.2, 1.3.13.5–6 [SBN 83, 145–46]; EHU 10.5–10 [SBN 111–13]).[40]

In another vivid description of sympathy Hume observes that "the minds of men are mirrors to one another," so that our sentiments and opinions are reflected back to us, along with those of others, through a continuous process of reverberation (T 2.2.5.21 [SBN 365]). The desire to communicate our emotions though sympathy is a central motivation for social life and facilitates our collective activities, although it also tends to promote the development of socially disruptive passions and the opposition of social groups to each other. In other words, sympathy tends to enhance both cooperation and conflict among human beings.

CONCERN

In the preceding chapters of this study I have considered Hume's account of ideas and concept formation; of demonstrative and causal reasoning; and also of our ideas of space, time, external existence, and personal identity. In accordance with his own approach, I have initially considered these activities and products of the understanding and imagination apart from any of the practical activities and emotional engagements of human life. However, in Book 2 of the *Treatise* Hume explores the practical context of the various activities of the understanding, as this is provided by the emotional and volitional dimensions of human life, within which the activities of our cognitive faculties are directed by "concern" (T 1.4.6.5, 2.2.9.9, 2.3.7.4, 2.3.10.7–8 [SBN 253, 384, 429,

---

40. For further reflections on the relation between sympathy, custom, and education in Hume's thought, see Stewart, *Moral and Political Philosophy*, 48, 65–66, and 147–48, and Whelan, *Order and Artifice*, 277–80.

451–52]; NHR 2–3.27–32, 8.47).[41] In this section I examine Hume's account of the role of the passions in stimulating us to form our ideas of the self, external objects, and space and time, and also in motivating us to engage in various activities of reasoning.

In Book 1 of the *Treatise* Hume distinguishes between the idea of the self or personal identity "as it regards our thought or imagination" and the idea of our identity "as it regards our passions or the concern we take in ourselves" (T 1.4.6.5; cf. 1.4.6.19, 3.1.1.26 [SBN 253; cf. 261, 469]). In Book 2 he examines the second aspect of personal identity, by exploring the role of the passions, sympathy, and the will in our formulation of the particular ideas we have of ourselves as empirical subjects.[42]

Hume first returns to the concept of the self in his account of the passions of pride and humility, in which he argues that these passions are directed toward the self as a result of our association of the idea of our self with the idea of some thing or quality that is the object of a separate passion. He also maintains that the idea of the self is itself singled out as the object of pride and humility by a "natural" and "original" principle of the mind (T 2.1.2.1–4, 2.1.3.1–3, 2.1.5.4–5, 2.2.1.2 [SBN 277–78, 280, 286, 329]).

Hume begins by restating his analysis of the self in Book 1 as "that succession of related ideas and impressions, of which we have an intimate memory and consciousness" (T 2.1.2.2 [SBN 277]). However, he then indicates that the particular conceptions we each have of ourselves arise from our recognition of the various qualities of our own minds and bodies. That is, we learn to recognize and judge our own mental activities, including our "imagination, judgment, memory or disposition," through the motivation provided by these passions and by our concern for the opinions of others (T 2.1.2.5; cf. 2.1.7.1–8, 3.1.1.26 [SBN 279; cf. 295–98, 469]). We also trace the history of the qualities of our own minds through our memory, as these qualities are reflected not only in our subjective states but also in our "actions and manners," to form the idea of "our personal character" (T 2.1.5.2 [SBN 285]). Hume concludes that the idea of the self is, in this sense, "produced" by pride, since pride "turns our

41. In drawing upon Hume's occasional use of the term "concern," I am also suggesting a comparison between Hume's account in Book 2 of the human subject, as finding itself located within a spatio-temporal sphere of emotional engagements with objects and other persons, and Heidegger's account of the general attitude of *Dasein* as care or concern; see Heidegger, *Being and Time*, 83–84. However, in contrast to Heidegger's arrangement of his text, Hume's discussion of the existing subject is preceded rather than followed by his examination in Book 1 of theoretical cognition, as this emerges from our primordial existence within a world.

42. For other discussions of the continuity in Hume's account of our idea of the self in Books 1 and 2 of the *Treatise*, see Baier, "Hume on Heaps and Bundles," 285–95, and *Progress of Sentiments*, 129–51; Henderson, "Personal Identity and the Indirect Passions," 33–44; Penelhum, "The Self of Book I and the Selves of Book II," 281–92; McIntyre, "Personal Identity and the Passions," 544–57, and "Character," 193–206; Garrett, *Cognition and Commitment*, 168–69; Purviance, "Indirect Passions," 195–212; Frasca-Spada, *Space and the Self*, 77 and 194–98; and Stevenson, "Humean Self-Consciousness Explained," 95–129.

view to ourselves, and makes us think of our own qualities and circumstances" (T 2.1.5.6 [SBN 287]).[43]

Accordingly, in Book 2 Hume maintains that we have a further concept of the self, not merely as a succession of impressions and ideas, but as the supposed subject of the particular attributes, experiences, dispositions, and actions that we trace in our memories and then ascribe to ourselves as comprising our personal histories and characters. The concept of the self therefore emerges, not only from reflecting upon the sequence of perceptions that is disclosed to us by our memories, but also from the activities of the imagination and understanding, by which we identify the qualities of our minds in our remembered engagements with persons and objects in the world. The self is also the object of our "concern," since we are each interested in our own impressions, especially of pleasure and pain, not only as these are given to us in the present, but as they are remembered in the past and anticipated as possible in the future (T 1.4.6.19, 3.1.1.26 [SBN 261, 469]). In other words, although we do not have a simple impression or idea of the self, each of us develops a complex idea of our self, which includes ideas of our own body, mind, and history, from the sequence of perceptions that is disclosed by the memory and which we expect to continue into the future. Hume concludes that this discussion of our identity, "as it regards our passions or the concern we take in ourselves," serves to "corroborate" his analysis of the idea of the self "with regard to the imagination" (T 1.4.6.5, 1.4.6.19 [SBN 253, 261]).

However, in a rather perplexing apparent shift from his argument in Book 1, Hume also states in Book 2, in the context of his discussion of pride, that "the idea, or rather impression of ourselves is always intimately present with us." Indeed, he maintains that "our consciousness gives us so lively a conception of our own person" that this idea communicates its vivacity to the idea of anything we regard as related to ourselves (T 2.1.11.4; cf. 2.2.4.7, 2.3.7.1 [SBN 317; cf. 354, 427]).[44] Hume's reference to an "idea" of the self here might consistent with his account of the idea of the self as a complex idea of a bundle of particular perceptions that are connected by the memory and imagination. However, his further reference to an "impression" of the self seems to endorse

---

43. Hume's statement here is inconclusive, but it would seem that the idea of the self must precede the appearance of pride, since the idea of the secondary object must be associated with the idea of the self for pride to appear in the first place. He might therefore be stating here, not that pride produces our first idea of the self, but that pride is always directed toward the idea of the self, or that pride contributes to the production of our idea of the empirical self as the subject of various particular attributes. For other discussions of the contribution of pride to the idea of the self, see Baier, "Hume on Heaps and Bundles," 285–95; Rorty, "Pride Produces," 255–69; Henderson, "Personal Identity and the Indirect Passions," 33–44; McIntyre, "Personal Identity and the Passions," 544–57, and "Character," 193–206; and Purviance, "Indirect Passions," 195–212.

44. For two critical discussions of this statement, see Kemp Smith, *Philosophy of David Hume,* 74 and 555–58, and Penelhum, "Hume's Moral Psychology," 134 and 141.

the view, which he had vigorously rejected in Book 1, that a distinct impression of the self is always present to our consciousness. Yet several commentators have sought to argue that even this may be rendered consistent with Hume's larger analysis. For example, Waxman argues that belief in the self, on Hume's view, transforms the complex idea of the self into an impression of reflection, while Garrett suggests that the "impression" of the self referred to here is really the remembered sequence of impressions in our own conscious history, and Stevenson suggests that the self in this statement refers to the "felt unity" of the amalgam of the body and mind which is the concern of the passions in Book 2.[45]

Indeed, Hume describes human self-consciousness in Book 2 as "that succession of related ideas and impressions, of which we have an intimate memory and consciousness" (T 2.1.2.2 [SBN 277]). He further notes that "we are at all times intimately conscious of ourselves, our sentiments and passions," and that we identify ourselves as "that identical person, of whose thoughts, actions, and sensations we are intimately conscious," in contrast to other persons "of whose thoughts, actions, and sensations we are not conscious" (T 2.2.2.15, 2.2.1.2 [SBN 339, 329]). In these passages he seems to suggest that self-consciousness consists in our memory of our own sensations and passions, and our recognition of their immediacy as conscious states. In describing the special vivacity of the "idea, or rather impression of ourselves" which "is always intimately present with us," Hume may thus be referring, not in fact to any idea or impression of the self, but rather to the "intimacy," or immediacy, in our consciousness of our own perceptions (T 2.1.11.4 [SBN 317]).[46]

From this consideration of Hume's various discussions of the self in Books 1 and 2, we may conclude that a complete idea of our self consists, not merely in our idea of a succession of remembered impressions and ideas as a series of detached perceptions, but also in our ideas of the various qualities of our own minds and bodies, which we discover and trace, in our memories and by the activity of our understanding and imagination, in those actions, thoughts, and sentiments of which we are "intimately conscious." This action of my understanding, in producing my idea of myself as an individual with various particular characteristics, is motivated by the passions of pride and humility, which direct my attention to the qualities of my own mind and body, and also by my concern for my own enjoyment of pleasure and avoidance of pain, which leads me to project my continued existence as I anticipate the pleasure or pain that may be produced in me by possible but uncertain events in the future. However, the idea of the self may also become the subject of philosophical reflection

45. See Waxman, *Hume's Theory of Consciousness,* 325n25, and Garrett, *Cognition and Commitment,* 168–69.
46. For a further discussion of Hume's view of self-consciousness, see Stevenson, "Humean Self-Consciousness Explained," 95–129.

and criticism, in which we discover that the idea of the self is a "fiction" projected by the imagination to provide a continuous and unifying substratum for the series of perceptions disclosed to us by memory.

In Book 2 Hume argues that human beings have a disposition toward activity, including various ways of engaging with external objects (T 2.2.2.17, 2.2.4.4 [SBN 340, 352–53]). Indeed, we regard almost every object with some emotion, but especially those objects which may be "esteem'd of consequence in life" (T 2.2.10.9 [SBN 393]). We discover through observation that external objects have a positive "consequence" or value for human life when they are regarded as "useful, beautiful or surprizing," since these qualities are sources of pleasure; and a negative value if we regard them as inconvenient, ugly, dangerous or boring, since these are sources of pain (T 2.1.10.2; cf. 2.2.5.3, 2.1.8.3–6 [SBN 311; cf. 358, 300–301]). In the second *Enquiry* he describes our ability to evaluate objects by aesthetic or moral "taste" as a "productive faculty," which "raises, in a manner, a new creation" by "gilding or staining all natural objects" with qualities arising from the passions. However, the activity of reasoning, by which we consider objects "as they really stand in nature," is initiated and directed through motives provided by the passions (EPM App.1.21 [SBN 294]).[47] External objects are thus regarded as good or evil on the basis of the tendency of their various qualities to produce pleasure or pain, and may accordingly become primary objects of the direct passions and secondary objects of the indirect passions.

In Book 1 Hume indicates that we are guided in formulating our ideas of particular external objects, including their identity over time and through any change, by our practical activities and emotional engagements with the sequences of perceptions that we regard as enduring objects. As examples of external objects, he considers the furnishings of his study, the fire in his fireplace, and the letter from a distant friend that is brought by a porter (T 1.4.2.9, 1.4.2.18–20 [SBN 190–91, 194–97]). His account of our ideas of external objects in Book 1, like his treatment of personal identity, is supplemented in Book 2 by his account of external objects as the intentional objects of our passions and concern, since our affective states and dispositions provide us with our initial motivation to trace a series of perceptions through time, and to connect these by the fiction of a distinct, continued, and changing existence, producing the idea of an external object that endures through time and change.

In this context we may also return to Hume's account of abstract ideas. In Book 1, he argues that we formulate abstract ideas by recognizing resemblances between objects, but also suggests that this process proceeds in an "imperfect manner" which is directed toward serving the "purposes of life," especially in

47. Hume offers some further reflections concerning the role of the passions in our ideas of objects in "The Sceptic" (E Sc.159–80). For related discussions see Baier, "Hume on Heaps and Bundles," 285–95; Sawyier, "A Mark of the Growing Mind," 315–25; and Stroud, "Gilding or Staining," 253–72.

"reflection and conversation" (T 1.1.7.7, 1.1.7.2 [SBN 20, 18]). He implicitly considers the larger context of this activity in Book 2, by indicating that it is the passions that turn our attention toward the qualities of objects, and guide us in "collecting" various examples of objects that resemble each other and associating these with a certain term. In other words, the passions provide the "purposes of life," which not only direct our interest and concern toward particular objects, but also lead us to classify objects in order to facilitate our reasoning and communication.

Finally, Hume also returns to the topics of space and time in Book 2, by considering the spatial and temporal dimensions of human existence and their influence over our passions and volition.

As we have seen, in Book 1 Hume presents an account of space and time as "fictions" generated by the imagination to encompass and extend the conceptions of distance and duration arising from our consideration of the arrangement of our perceptions. However, in Book 2 Hume considers space and time from the perspective of the emotions and activities of a human subject, who projects these spatial and temporal intervals as the relative distances of objects and events within his or her sphere of interest and activity.

Hume initially observes in Book 2 that we are perpetually reminded of the "points of space and time, in which we are existent" by our "passions and senses," which continually direct our attention to the immediate present. From this central point of consciousness, we then regard objects and events as variously situated in space and time in relation to ourselves, ranging from those which appear to be "contiguous to us," to those which are "distant and remote." He then argues that the idea of a contiguous object has greater force and vivacity than the idea of a remote one, and thus a greater influence on our imagination, passions, and volition. As a result, we are generally more concerned about nearby objects than remote ones (T 2.3.7.1–3 [SBN 427–28]; cf. DNR 12.220).

After this preliminary analysis, which applies to both space and time, Hume considers the differences between spatial and temporal distance in their influence on the human imagination, the passions, and volition. Hume initially argues that the imagination apprehends distant objects by recognizing and "passing thro'" all of the points between the self and the object. Since this process requires an effort of the imagination, such a distance tends to diminish the vivacity of our ideas of these objects as these objects become more remote (T 2.3.7.2 [SBN 428]). Hume uses this argument to explain, first, the different effects of space and time and, then, the effects of different directions in time, upon our passions and cognition.

First, Hume examines the "different properties" of space and time, to determine why a distance in time usually has more effect in diminishing the vivacity of an idea than a distance in space, except in cases of very great distances in space or time, which we will consider separately. Here he finds that the points of space are coexistent, and may be "at once present to the sight or feeling," while points of time are separated from each other in a succession. He then argues that the imagination moves more easily through coexistent points of space than through successive points in time. However, in the example he uses to illustrate this argument, Hume also indirectly indicates that there are other possible sources of the difference between the effects of spatial and temporal distance on human passions and volition. In this example he observes that a *"West-India* merchant" in Britain is probably more concerned about present events in Jamaica than most of us are about remote future events (T 2.3.7.5 [SBN 429]).[48] While this may indeed be a result of the easy movement of the imagination through coexisting points in space, the concern of the merchant for whatever is now occurring in Jamaica also arises from his recognition that these events might have an effect upon his resources and investments in the future, and might even require some action on his part in order to protect or promote his interests. In other words, the effect of an idea of these events on his imagination and passions arises from the further idea of his present interests, and his recognition that current events in Jamaica might affect those interests in the future.[49] This discussion of the effects of a distance in space accordingly leads us to Hume's account of the influence of time on the passions and volition.

Next Hume attempts to explain why the idea of a moderate distance in the future tends to have more effect on the imagination, and thus on the passions and will, than a similar distance in the past.[50] When we consider something in the future, Hume argues that the imagination is able to follow the natural progression of time, which increases the vivacity of the idea of the object by a kind of momentum. By contrast, when the imagination considers any past object or event, it moves backward "in opposition to the natural course of the succession," and thereby weakens the vivacity of our idea of the object. These tendencies are enhanced by our view of "the future as flowing every moment nearer us, and the past as retiring," so that we regard our distance from a past event as "continually encreasing," and a distance in the future as "continually

<hr>

48. The phrase "West-India merchant" is changed to "East-India merchant" in the first printing of the Oxford Philosophical Text edition of the *Treatise.* However, the original phrase will be restored in the Clarendon edition and in any future printings of the OPT edition. For a discussion of the relevant considerations, see Norton and Norton, "Substantive Differences," 272–73.

49. Other discussions of Hume's account of spatiality and human existence are provided in Baier, *Progress of Sentiments,* 48–52; Frasca-Spada, *Space and the Self,* 194–98; and Jacquette, *David Hume's Critique of Infinity,* 307–33.

50. This discussion of Hume's approach to the temporal dimension of the passions is especially indebted to Livingston's account of the "temporal passions" in *Hume's Philosophy of Common Life,* 112–30. See also McIntyre, "Personal Identity and the Passions," 544–57; Baier, *Progress of Sentiments,* 48–52; and Magri, "Natural Obligation," 231–53. For a related discussion of Hume's account of time in Book 1, see Bossert, "Hume and Husserl," 44–52.

diminishing" (T 2.3.7.8–9 [SBN 430–32]). Accordingly, the idea of a future event receives greater vivacity than the idea of a past event, either from the momentum of the imagination in moving toward the event, or by our view of its approach. Finally, this increased vivacity, according to either explanation, is the source of our tendency to react more passionately to the idea of a future event than that of a past event.

However, Hume also implicitly considers another aspect of the difference between past and future events in their influence on the will. This appears in his observation that "as none of our actions can alter the past, 'tis not strange it shou'd never determine the will" (T 2.3.7.6 [SBN 430]). He also develops this theme in his discussion of the direct passions, in which he gives particular attention to hope and fear and their modifications. Hope and fear arise from the basic passions of desire and aversion, which are directed toward good and evil objects considered simply in themselves. These passions become modified as hope and fear when the occurrence of their object is regarded as "only probable and uncertain" (T 2.3.9.9 [SBN 439–40]). Accordingly, in Book 2 Hume extends his earlier account of probable reasoning by considering the effects of uncertainty or conflicting evidence on our passions. He now argues that conflicting evidence concerning the future occurrence of a good or evil event produces in us momentary impressions of grief and joy, in proportion to the evidence in either direction. These are fused into a single passion, once we have judged the probability of the event, of fear or hope, depending on the judgment. We also distinguish different degrees of hope and fear according to the degree of probability that we assign to the event, and then introduce other terms, such as "consternation," "anxiety," and "terror," to signify the modifications of hope and fear according to the "different situation of the object" (T 2.3.9.31 [SBN 447]). Finally, we are moved by hope or fear, or the desire or aversion directed toward the possible occurrence of a future event, to act in order to attain a desired object or avoid an undesirable one (T 2.2.9.13, 2.3.3.3 [SBN 385–86, 414]; EHU 3.4).

In this discussion Hume indicates that we may account for the distinctive influence of the idea of futurity on our passions as a result of our recognition of the imminence, the uncertainty, and the possibly pleasurable or painful effects of any future events. This recognition produces in us the passions of hope and fear, which are aroused only by the anticipation of future events, and are more vivid than the passions aroused in us by past events. In other words, the anticipation of any future but uncertain event which we regard as desirable or undesirable produces the passion of hope or fear, according to our judgment of the probable occurrence of the event. The passions of hope and fear then influence the will by moving us to act in such a way as to further increase or decrease the likelihood of the event. Accordingly, it is the uncertainty of future good or evil events, and our ability to act in such a way as to promote or to prevent their occurrence, which distinguishes the effects of our ideas of past and future events on our passions.[51]

Hume also considers other aspects of the influence of the past on the passions and volition in the concluding sections of Book 2. First, our personal histories clearly influence our passions and actions, since custom or repetition give the individual "a facility to perform any action," although the past cannot influence the will by providing ideas of events that can be prevented or promoted by our actions (T 2.3.5.5, 2.3.7.6 [SBN 424, 430]). Hume also observes that our idea of a very great distance in the past tends to have a more powerful effect on the imagination and the passions than our idea of a distance in space, or even of the same distance in the future. This is apparent in our admiration for ancient artifacts, such as "a *Greek* medal" or "ancient busts and inscriptions," and also in the veneration we may feel for our distant ancestors. Hume explains the tendency of a very great distance to produce this feeling of reverence as an example of the invigorating effect upon the mind of any contemplation of vastness. As we will see in Chapter 11, when we turn to his discussion of the sublime, the effort that is required to contemplate any great distance "enlarges the soul" and thereby produces "a sensible delight and pleasure." Finally, since we may receive this pleasure from contemplating a great distance in space, or a distant future, as well as a distant past, Hume argues that our peculiar respect for an ancient object arises from the extra difficulty encountered by the imagination in moving backward through time in order to consider the origin and history of the object (T 2.3.8.2–5, 2.3.8.11 [SBN 432–33, 436]).

Thus, in addition to his analysis of our ideas of space and time in Book 1 of the *Treatise,* Hume also examines the influence of our ideas of various spatial and temporal distances on our imagination, passions, and volition in Book 2, where he considers the human being, not merely as a cognitive subject, but also as an emotional and active one.

In this section we have seen that in Book 2 of the *Treatise* Hume expands his discussion of our ideas of space, time, external existence, and personal identity, or places them within their larger context, by considering the human subject as a cognitive, emotional, and active being that locates itself within a spatial and temporal world of persons and objects. As human subjects, we formulate the idea of our own identities and our own individual characteristics by reflecting upon the succession of our own sensations, thoughts, and passions. In addition, we regard ourselves as surrounded at various distances in space, and various distances in the two directions of time, by other persons, objects, and events that

---

51. McIntyre also notes the role of probability judgments in the generation of the direct passions: see "Hume's Passions," 85.

can be sources of pleasure or displeasure. Finally, we also regard ourselves as able to engage in various activities within this spatial and temporal framework in order to influence these persons, objects, and events in the future. In other words, our sphere of emotional engagement and practical activity provides us with the initial context and motivation for the development of our abstract ideas of time, space, the self, and external objects.

In the concluding section of Book 2 Hume turns to the passion of "curiosity, or the love of truth." As we have already seen, in the concluding section of Book 1 Hume guides us through false or dogmatic philosophy, extreme skepticism, and a retreat into common life, until we arrive at the moderate skepticism that sustains and directs our reasonings in the sciences and ordinary life. He resumes this discussion at the end of Book 2 by considering "that love of truth, which was the first source of all our enquiries," in order to show "its origin in human nature" (T 2.3.10.1 [SBN 448]).

Hume begins by reminding us that there are two types of truth, corresponding to the two types of reasoning and knowledge. These are "the discovery of the proportions of ideas, consider'd as such" and "the conformity of our ideas of objects to their real existence" (T 2.3.10.2; cf. 3.1.1.9 [SBN 448; cf. 458]). Next, since the pursuit of truth is an activity, and since all human activity arises from the desire to pursue pleasure and avoid displeasure, he sets out to discover the nature of the pleasure that we receive from the pursuit of truth.

First, Hume finds that truth is not a source of pleasure when considered simply in itself, since we do not receive any pleasure merely from compiling "easy and obvious" truths. Indeed, the pursuit of truth is often painful rather than pleasurable, as in the attempt to solve a difficult algebraic problem, or in the case of philosophers who have "consum'd their time, have destroy'd their health, and neglected their fortune" by pursuing their investigations. Accordingly, the discovery of truth is a source of pleasure to us only if we regard the truth that we seek, or the process of discovering the truth, as "endow'd with certain qualities," which we must examine to discover our motives for intellectual inquiry (T 2.3.10.2–4 [SBN 448–49]).

Many of the types of pleasure that can motivate us to engage in the pursuit of truth arise from qualities that are common to both demonstrative and probable reasoning (T 2.3.10.11 [SBN 452–53]). In the first place, these include "the genius and capacity, which is employ'd in its invention and discovery" (T 2.3.10.3 [SBN 449]). More specifically, we enjoy exercising our mental faculties in the pursuit of interesting objects (T 2.2.4.4, 2.3.5.2 [SBN 352–53, 422–23]), and we admire mental abilities or achievements, in ourselves or in others, which we regard as distinctive or surprising (T 2.1.2.5, 2.1.8.5, 2.2.1.4 [SBN 279, 300–301, 330]). For example, we may enjoy tracing the "demonstrations of mathematicians," because we admire the intricacy of their reasonings, and also because we may find the "exercise of genius" this requires on our part to be a "pleasant and agreeable" activity of the mind (T 2.3.10.3–4 [SBN 448–49]).

However, Hume argues that a truth must also have some "importance" or value for human life for its pursuit to become a source of pleasure. Indeed, even in their pursuit of very abstract or obscure studies, scientists and philosophers are generally convinced of the value of their inquiries for human life, even if these persons seem to have only a "remote sympathy" with the "interests of mankind" (T 2.3.10.4–6 [SBN 449–50]). In other words, the possible usefulness of a discovery, as this is recognized either directly or by sympathy with others, is a source of pleasure. Hume has already noted that the study of mathematics is useful in "almost every art and profession." Similarly, our motives for probable reasoning concerning causes and effects arise largely from the "prospect of pleasure or pain" associated with an object, since we are never concerned to know the causes and effects of objects that are "indifferent to us" (T 2.3.3.2–3 [SBN 413–14]). In the *Enquiry* he adds that knowledge of causes is the most "instructive" type of knowledge, since it alone enables us "to controul events, and govern futurity" (EHU 3.9).

Hume concludes his general account of the motives for intellectual inquiry by comparing it to two other types of activity, hunting and gambling, since in these cases we enjoy the activity and also receive a separate pleasure from the results (T 2.3.10.8–10 [SBN 451–52]).

Hume also identifies a further set of motives for our study of human life. As we have seen, human beings are especially interested in other people, who enliven, intrigue, and reassure us by their resemblance to ourselves (T 2.2.4.4–7, 2.2.5.4, 2.3.1.15 [SBN 352–54, 359, 405]). We thus find, even in ordinary life, that "some people have an insatiable desire of knowing the actions and circumstances of their neighbors, tho' their interest be no way concern'd in them," and indeed even when "they must entirely depend on others for their information." This curiosity about other people is also reflected in our general reasonings in the moral or human sciences concerning human action, which Hume considers in the *Treatise* and in his later writings. For example, we are likely to take a particular interest in the history of our own nation, in the history and manners of a nation we have visited, or in a historical era that is described in an interesting way (T 2.3.10.11–12 [SBN 453]; RH 378). We are also interested in understanding the actions of others with whom we expect to engage in any interaction, since this understanding helps us predict their future actions. As we will see in the next chapter, we do this by observing the actions of other people and developing a concept of their dispositions or character, which enables us to predict their actions in various future circumstances (T 2.3.1.15–17, 2.3.3.2–3 [SBN 404–6, 414]; EHU 8.17–19 [SBN 89–91]). The general principles by which we explain human actions are in turn the basis for the various moral or human sciences, as we will see in the remaining chapters of this study.

In the introduction to the *Treatise* Hume states his intention to consider the sciences that "more intimately concern human life," along with the sciences we pursue out of "pure curiosity." He also expects his study of human nature to be a source of pleasure to the reader, as well as the author (T Int.6, Int.9 [SBN xvi, xvii–xviii]). Similarly, in the concluding section of Book 1, he guides us through his skeptical arguments and the passions of melancholy, spleen, and indolence, to a renewed curiosity and a desire to pursue various types of intellectual inquiry. This renewed curiosity arises partly from recognizing the value of intellectual inquiry for himself and humanity; partly from ambition, or the hope of taking pride in his own contributions to learning; and partly from a desire for interesting activity (T 1.4.7.11–14 [SBN 270–73]). In the first *Enquiry* he describes his study of "the nature of human understanding" as a more attainable goal and as a better starting point for the sciences than any other forms of speculation, including superstition and false philosophy; and argues that careful reasoning is "fitted for all persons and all dispositions" (EHU 1.12 [SBN 12]). He also observes that "the ACADEMIC or SCEPTICAL philosophy" serves to moderate every passion "except the love of truth," which "never is, nor can be, carried to too high a degree" (EHU 5.1; cf. 12.24 [SBN 41; cf. 161–62]).

In sum, Hume presents the human desire to engage in intellectual inquiry, or the passion of "curiosity" or the "love of truth," as including a set of more particular desires—including the desires to engage in absorbing and challenging activities, to invent or discover things that might be useful to ourselves or others, to learn interesting things about other human beings, to interact effectively with others, and to take pleasure and pride in our own achievements. He also argues that curiosity is especially compatible with the outlook of the moderate skeptic, who recognizes the value of intellectual inquiry in the various sciences, but also accepts that our inquiries must be limited to the realm of experience. Curiosity is therefore an important motive for emerging from the abyss of extreme skepticism into the busy and sociable world of mitigated skepticism and its pursuit of scientific inquiry.

Hume accordingly argues that we are motivated by a variety of passions to discover the relations between ideas, the causes of natural events, and the reasons for human actions. He also indicates that it is these passions and concerns which lead us to theoretical reflection, through which we may improve the ordinary reasonings of common life by developing the procedures of mathematical demonstration, the rules for probable reasoning, and the standards of judgment in the various moral sciences. Finally, it is these motives and principles of reasoning which provide the basis for his further investigations into human nature, in the *Treatise* and in his later writings.

7

Human Action

Hume's study of the principles of human action serves as the bridge between his general philosophy, or his epistemology and metaphysics, and his writings in the various branches of the human sciences. Since his reflections concerning human action are widely dispersed throughout his writings, his critics have often overlooked the unity in his account of human action.

Hume initially examines volition, along with the passions, in Book 2 of the *Treatise,* after his analysis of our idea of causation in Book 1, and before turning to his moral theory in Book 3. He later separates the main topics in this discussion by considering the problem of freedom and determinism in the first *Enquiry,* the relative influence of reason and emotion over the will in "Of the Passions," and the relation between voluntary action and morality in the second *Enquiry.*

Hume also examines the principles governing the interpretation of human action at various intervals in his writings. He offers a preliminary account of these principles while developing his analysis of volition in the *Treatise* and *Enquiries.* He then extends his theoretical discussion of these principles in his essays and historical writings. Finally, he also applies these principles throughout his works to the study of particular actions, including both individual and collective actions, in various cultural and historical settings.

THE WILL

Hume introduces his discussion of the will in Book 2, Part 3 of the *Treatise* in the context of his discussion of the direct passions. As we have seen, he argues here that the direct passions are targeted toward pleasurable or painful objects by "an *original* instinct" of the human mind, which "tends to unite itself with the good, and to avoid the evil." We also find that these passions are frequently accompanied by the will, which "exerts itself, when either the good or the absence of the evil may be attain'd by any action of the mind or body" (T 2.3.9.2, 2.3.9.7 [SBN 438, 439]; cf. OP 1.2.139). In the first *Enquiry* he observes that since the human individual "is a reasonable being and is continually in pursuit of happiness," which we attain by gratifying our passions, a human being "seldom acts or speaks or thinks without a purpose and intention" (EHU 3.4). The disposition to act according to motives and purposes is thus given to human beings as a part of our natural constitution.

Hume initially presents the will as a further impression of reflection which is distinct from the passions, and more specifically as "the internal impression we feel and are conscious of, when we knowingly give rise to any new motion of our body, or new perception of our mind" (T 2.3.1.2 [SBN 399]). He then disclaims any intention to describe the subjective character of volition, since this subjective character, as in the case of the passions, is impossible to define, but is also familiar to everyone through introspection and indicated by our common use of the relevant terms.[1] Indeed, Hume offers even less information about the phenomenological character of volition than of the passions. While he describes the passions as modifications of pleasure and pain according to the situation of their object, he merely describes volition as a distinctive impression that appears in our consciousness whenever we "knowingly" perform any action of mind or body.[2] In this sense, volition and voluntary action are contrasted to movements in which the body is compelled by an external force, since such movements are not accompanied by this impression (cf. EHU 8.23 [SBN 95]).

While he does not attempt to describe the subjective quality of the impression of volition as such, Hume does seek to explain the relation between the occurrence of this impression within the subjective consciousness of an agent and the performance of a voluntary action by that agent. In an addition to the *Treatise* in the Appendix he criticizes the assertion that when we perform a

1. On Hume's view of the impression of volition, see Kemp Smith, *Philosophy of David Hume*, 435–36; Árdal, *Passion and Value*, 81–85; Stalley, "The Will in Hume's *Treatise*," 41–53; Russell, *Freedom and Moral Sentiment*, 111; and Bricke, *Mind and Morality*, 49–59.
2. Stalley suggests on the contrary that our condition in "knowingly" producing an action should be understood, not as an impression, but as the special type of knowledge we have of our own volition: see "The Will in Hume's *Treatise*," 48–49.

voluntary action "we feel an energy, or power, in our own mind," which we directly recognize as the source of "the motions of our body, and the thoughts and sentiments of our mind." Instead, he argues that the impression of volition "has no more a discoverable connexion with its effects, than any material cause has with its proper effect," since this connection is not directly given to the senses or to reason in either case. Indeed, he reminds us that many philosophers have found the causal connection between actions of the mind and the body to be even less explicable than causal connections between physical events. As an alternative to the preceding view, he argues that our attributions of causal efficacy to our impressions of volition arise from our experience of a constant conjunction between this subjective feeling of volition and the movements of our body or succession of our ideas (T 1.3.14.12 [SBN 632–33]). In the first *Enquiry* he further notes that a person who is "suddenly struck with a palsy in the leg or arm, or who had newly lost those members" often claims to feel an impression of volition when attempting to move the paralyzed or missing limb. Thus, although the influence of the will on our actions is "a matter of common experience," since we each recognize the regular succession between our impressions of volition and our voluntary actions, we must conclude that the "power or energy by which this is effected" is just as "unknown and inconceivable" as the power involved in the production of any physical event (EHU 7.13–15; cf. 7.9–12, 8.21 [SBN 66–67; cf. 64–65, 92]).

Although he considers both actions of the mind and movements of the body as effects of the will, Hume's discussion in Book 2 is largely concerned with the relation between volition and bodily movement. Indeed, I show in this chapter that his application of his analysis of volition to the inner operations of the mind is problematic, as a result of his appeal in his general analysis of the causal relation to the point of view of an observer, since this point of view is unavailable to us when we are attempting to account for the influence of one mental state on another.

LIBERTY AND NECESSITY

Hume opens his analysis of voluntary action by examining "that long disputed question concerning *liberty and necessity*," especially in response to the "scholastic doctrine of *free-will*" (T 2.3.1.2, 2.1.10.5 [SBN 399, 312]). As his own contribution to this debate, he mainly considers the question of whether human actions are free or determined by natural causes, although he also briefly examines the theological question of whether human freedom is compatible with divine omniscience and omnipotence (T 1.4.5.31 [SBN 248–49]; EHU 8.31–36 [SBN 99–103]). Although he rejects the "fantastical system of liberty," or the doctrine of absolute human freedom, Hume also considers the various senses in which both "liberty" and "necessity" may be attributed to the human will. Accordingly, in the *Enquiry* he describes his overall approach to the question of liberty and necessity as a "reconciling project" (T 2.3.1.15, 2.3.2.1–2 [SBN 404, 407–9]; EHU 8.23 [SBN 95]).[3]

Hume develops his criticism of the doctrine of absolute freedom by applying his general analysis of causal necessity in Book 1 to human action. In other words, he argues that if our judgments concerning human actions are causal judgments which arise from the "constant union" of two ideas and an inference from one to the other, then we must attribute necessity to human actions, since these inferences would then have the same origin and structure as our other causal judgments. We must accordingly discover whether there are any subjective states that are regularly conjoined with those actions we regard as voluntary human actions, or in other words, if there is a "constant union in the actions of the mind" corresponding to the constant conjunctions which we observe in the operations of matter (T 2.3.1.4; cf. 2.3.2.4, 1.3.14.31 [SBN 400–401; cf. 409–10, 169–70]).

In response to this challenge, Hume invites us to agree, on the basis of our observation of ourselves and of ordinary human life, "that our actions have a constant union with our motives, tempers, and circumstances." He then argues that these regularities provide the basis both for our ordinary and for our philosophical or scientific inferences concerning human action (T 2.3.1.4 [SBN 401]; cf. 2.3.1.11–12 [SBN 403–4]; EHU 8.22 [SBN 94]). He sets forth this threefold scheme of motives, temperament, and circumstances in both the *Treatise* and the first *Enquiry,* although he does not offer a detailed account of its structure. However, he presents the idea of a motive, in effect, as the central explanatory principle involved in the interpretation of human action; and then indicates that this may be supplemented by the concepts of character and circumstances.

In the *Treatise* Hume argues that the passions determine the will and are the ultimate motives for human action (T 2.3.3.1–10 [SBN 413–18]). Indeed, he describes motives as "impelling" or "actuating" passions (T 3.2.1.18, 3.2.5.6 [SBN 483, 518]). Since he also maintains that the "chief spring and moving principle" of human action is the desire to attain pleasure and avoid pain (T 1.3.10.2, 3.3.1.2 [SBN 118, 574]), we might first suppose that a motive is

3. Hume's argument has generally been regarded as a classic statement of compatibilism: or the view that a plausible theory of human freedom is compatible with a deterministic theory of human action, and also, in many versions of this view, that both are compatible with moral responsibility. See Penelhum, "Hume's Moral Psychology," 129–32, and Garrett, *Cognition and Commitment,* 118–36. However, Paul Russell argues, against the "classical" interpretation, that on Hume's view our attributions of responsibility are derived from moral sentiment rather than from any theoretical defense of freedom: see *Freedom and Moral Sentiment,* especially 3–5, 11–84, and 176–85.

nothing but a particular passion of desire or aversion, directing us toward an object we regard as good, or away from an object we regard as evil.

However, in Hume's view, the motive for an action also includes two types of cognition. As we have already seen, he initially argues that the passions arise in response to the idea of an object or, more specifically, to a conception of the object, a belief in its existence, and a judgment of its relation to the self. He now indicates, though less explicitly, that the motive for any action also includes a judgment by the agent that the proposed action is likely to be effective in attaining or avoiding the object. He thus indicates that motives involve the "views" as well as "sentiments" of the agent, and identifies the causes of human action as the "designs, and projects, and views of men" (T 1.3.15.11, 2.3.2.1, 3.1.2.9 [SBN 175, 407, 474]). He also occasionally refers to a motive as the "reason" for an action (T 3.2.1.9 [SBN 479]). Finally, in considering a particular example of a motive, he observes that the residents of a civil society are dissuaded by "motives of interest or safety" from injuring their neighbors. These motives apparently include not only the desire to avoid pain but also the judgment that the civic authorities are likely to inflict pain on those who harm their neighbors (T 2.1.10.6 [SBN 312]). Hume also indicates the role of these two types of cognition in the motive for any action by considering the two types of mistaken judgments that may influence our actions: a mistaken judgment regarding the existence or nature of an object, or a mistaken judgment concerning the effectiveness of the projected action (T 2.3.3.1–10, 3.1.1.12 [SBN 413–17, 459–60]).

In Hume's view, the motive for a given action accordingly consists in a pleasurable or painful passion toward a particular object, which arises from a series of judgments concerning the existence and nature of the object and concerning its relation to the agent, and is accompanied by a judgment concerning the efficacy of the action for attaining or avoiding the object.[4]

Hume apparently regards a motive in this sense, or the combination of a desire with a set of beliefs, as the immediate cause of voluntary action in human beings. This is reflected in his frequent references to the conjunction between motive and action, without any further allusion to circumstances and character, as the guiding principle for explaining human action (T 2.1.10.6–7, 2.3.1.14 [SBN 313, 404]; A 32 [SBN 661]; EHU 8.7 [SBN 83]). In the first *Enquiry* he argues that by studying the "actions, expressions, and even gestures" of individual human beings, we may attain knowledge of their "inclinations and motives," and that we may also "descend to the interpretation of their actions" from our conception of their motives. He accordingly describes these principles as the "clue" for untangling the "intricacies" of human nature (EHU 8.9 [SBN 85]).

---

4. For a further account of a Humean motive as consisting in a primary desire and a set of subordinate beliefs, see Bricke, *Mind and Morality*, 5–34.

Next, Hume supplements his analysis of motivation by showing that a consideration of the character and situation of a human agent enables us to develop a more extensive understanding of the motives of that agent. Our concepts of the character and the circumstances of an agent consist respectively in our ideas of the distinctive passions and beliefs of a given agent, and our ideas of the physical and cultural context of a given agent as it further influences his or her beliefs and passions.

As we have seen, in the *Treatise* Hume identifies the idea of "character" with our idea of the prevailing passions and dispositions of an individual, as these are expressed in the actions of that person.[5] He further identifies the settled passions or dispositions that comprise the character of a person as "calm passions," in contrast to the "violent" passions that may be aroused by the immediate appearance of a pleasurable or painful object (T 2.3.1.10, 2.3.2.6, 2.3.3.8–10 [SBN 403, 411, 417–19]). In the *Enquiry* he applies the term "character" to the patterns of motivation, or sets of dispositions, we attribute to human beings on the basis of their actions. He thus invites us to consider the "diversity of characters" that tends to appear in different social and historical contexts, among the two sexes, and at different stages in the human life cycle, as well as the temperaments or dispositions "peculiar to each individual." He even refers to the distinctive judgments, or the "prejudices" and "opinions" of individuals, as if these were to be included in our concept of their character (EHU 8.10–11 [SBN 85–86]).

Several of Hume's essays are concerned with describing different types of character, such as those prone to a "delicacy" of taste or of passion (E DT.3–8), and to the different temperaments he attributes to the Epicurean, the Stoic, the Platonist, and the Sceptic (E Ep.138–45, E St.146–54, E Pl.155–58, E Sc.159–80). He also recommends the study of literature and history as a means for enhancing our ability to judge the "characters of men" by widening our experience of human life (E DT.6–8; E SH.567–68).

Hume therefore argues that we may improve our judgments concerning the motives for any particular human action by considering the "character" of the agent: that is to say, the distinctive set of beliefs, desires, and passions in that individual. More specifically, the study of the character of an individual agent may help us recognize the motives of that individual by discovering the distinctive passions and beliefs that lead that individual to regard various objects as sources of pleasure or displeasure and various courses of action as effective for either attaining or avoiding these objects.

Finally, Hume observes that we often consider the "circumstances" or "situation" of an agent as it influences his or her motives for performing a particular

---

5. See also McIntyre, "Character," 193–206; Baier, *Progress of Sentiments*, 134 and 174–97; Russell, *Freedom and Moral Sentiment*, 58–70 and 95–136; and Purviance, "Indirect Passions," 195–212.

action. He initially applies the term "situation" to the context of an action within a particular state of affairs as this is explicitly recognized and evaluated by an agent. For example, the "situation" of living in civil society provides a motive for restraint to the potential aggressor and a motive for confidence to potential victims (T 2.1.10.7 [SBN 312–13]). However, a variety of circumstances—including the particulars of "sexes, ages, governments, conditions, or methods of education"—may influence the motives and character, and consequently the actions, of any given individual without having been consciously recognized by that agent. These circumstances include the natural or biological conditions of human life, as we might arguably find in the cases of age or sex, and the customs and traditions of a given society, since these tend to impart particular beliefs and desires to individuals (T 2.3.1.5–7 [SBN 401]; EHU 8.10–11 [SBN 85–86]). In the next section of this chapter I will consider Hume's more extensive account of the influence of social and historical conditions on human motives in "A Dialogue" at the end of the second *Enquiry,* in which he argues that the passions which belong universally to human nature are directed by the individual toward specific objects according to the historical and cultural context of that person (EPM D.1–57 [SBN 324–43]).

To summarize, Hume argues that we may explain the voluntary actions of human beings as effects of the motives, characters, and circumstances of the human individual. The motive for an action consists in the beliefs and desires that are the immediate source of the action, and these may, in turn, be explained as products of the character and circumstances of the agent. He further affirms the variety of human characters and circumstances in the *Dialogues,* in Philo's observation that the causes of human thought "never operate in two persons after the same manner," or in the same way throughout the life of one person. On the contrary, we never find "two persons, who think exactly alike," or one who thinks "exactly alike at any two different periods of time," since human thought is influenced by "a difference of age, of the disposition of his body, of weather, of food, of company, of books, of passions" (DNR 4.161).

In his philosophical writings Hume offers us no detailed account of the relation between motive, character, and circumstances in any particular example of human action. Instead, he merely argues that this conjunction is apparent from "a very slight and general view of the common course of human affairs." More specifically, he argues that if we consider the various similarities and differences among human actions, especially when these are correlated with age, sex, nation, class, profession, and historical circumstances, we find in these patterns "the same uniformity and regular operation of natural principles" we discover in matter. Accordingly, we expect to explain the distinctive "sentiments, actions and manners" that tend to appear in different social and historical groups as the effects of uniform principles operating through the different characters and circumstances of individuals (T 2.3.1.5–9 [SBN 401–2]). However, he provides many more specific examples of explaining human actions in terms of motives, character, and circumstances in his essays and in the *History of England,* as we will see in Chapter 13.

Hume concludes that our regular observation of a conjunction between an apparent type of motive and a given type of behavior generates our idea of a connection between motives and human actions. It also produces our belief in the necessity of this connection, by *"determining* us to infer the existence of one from that of another" (T 2.3.1.14 [SBN 404]). This determination of the mind to infer actions from motives, and motives from action, is expressed in our judgments concerning the causes of human action, as these are reflected in our practical activities as well as in the moral or human sciences.

First, in considering the practical activities of everyday life, Hume observes that since "nothing more nearly interests us than our own actions and those of others, the greatest part of our reasonings is employ'd in judgments concerning them." Indeed, he provides examples of some of the ways in which human beings rely upon their ability to predict the actions of others: "A prince, who imposes a tax upon his subjects, expects their compliance. A general, who conducts an army, makes account of a certain degree of courage. A merchant looks for fidelity and skill in his factor or super-cargo. A man, who gives orders for his dinner, doubts not of the obedience of his servants" (T 2.3.1.15 [SBN 405]). This type of reasoning, from motive, character, and circumstances to action, and then back again, "runs thro' politics, war, commerce, œconomy," and indeed "mixes itself" so thoroughly in human affairs that it would be impossible to act in society without it (T 2.3.1.15 [SBN 405]). In the first *Enquiry* Hume observes that the dependence of human beings upon each other in society is so great that "scarce any human action is entirely compleat in itself, or is performed without some reference to the actions of others." For example, even a solitary craftsman expects to be protected by the civic authorities and to receive reasonable payment for his products on the market. Human beings thus anticipate the actions of other human beings, by reasoning from our past experiences of human actions "in the same manner as in their reasonings concerning external objects," and this type of reasoning is presupposed "in every deliberation of our lives, and in every step of our conduct and behavior" (EHU 8.17, 8.22 [SBN 89, 94]).

Indeed, Hume points out that even those philosophers who defend the freedom of human volition accept "moral evidence," or judgments concerning the "actions of men" which are derived from considering their "motives, temper and situation," as a distinct type of probable reasoning. In Book 1 of the *Treatise* Hume maintains that philosophical probable reasoning provides us with "reasonable foundations for belief and opinion." He now argues in Book 2 that moral evidence is generally regarded by philosophers as providing a "reasonable foundation" for both "speculation and practice" (T 2.3.1.15, 1.3.13.1 [SBN 404, 143]; cf. A 32–33 [SBN 661]). This account also confirms his statement in Book I that the rules for judging causes and effects may be applied in moral philosophy or the human sciences, as well as in natural philosophy (T 1.3.15.11 [SBN 175]). In the first *Enquiry* he describes the study of human action as a type of probable reasoning that offers "more or less degrees of certainty," in proportion to "our experience of the usual conduct of mankind in such particular situations." He also provides a survey of the "speculative parts of learning" that rest upon this type of reasoning, including history, politics, morals, and criticism (EHU 8.18–20 [SBN 89–91]; cf. 12.28–34 [SBN 163–65], T Int.4–5 [SBN xv–xvi]). In "Of National Characters" he considers the nature of "*moral* causes," or those circumstances "which are fitted to work on the mind as motives or reasons, and which render a peculiar set of manners habitual to us." These moral causes are the causes of the distinctive "character," or the typical customs and manners that we might call the culture of a nation. These moral causes of the character of a particular nation include, on Hume's view, its form of government, its economic conditions, and its domestic and foreign policies. Hume presents this view especially in contrast to Montesquieu's theory that national characters are influenced mainly by physical causes, such as "qualities of the air and climate," that work "insensibly" upon the temperament (E NC.198).

We thus find that in our reasonings concerning the "moral causes" of human actions, in our ordinary lives as well as in the human sciences, we are committed to believing in the necessity of human action. However, in accordance with his general analysis of causation, Hume maintains that we do not directly perceive this necessary connection, either in the agent or as a quality of the action. Instead, this necessity is a determination of the mind "in any thinking or intelligent being, who may consider the action" (T 2.3.2.2 [SBN 408]). This view of the necessity of human action, as consisting in a customary transition in the mind of an observer from the idea of a motive to an expectation of some particular action, has several implications for Hume's account. First, as Hume himself points out, this analysis indicates that the necessity of human action is more properly recognized by an observer than by the agent.[6] In fact, he concedes that as agents we generally feel a "false sensation" of liberty in our actions, although "a spectator can commonly infer our actions from our motives and character," or at least expects to be able to do so if he or she were "perfectly

---

6. Garrett overlooks this distinction between the perspective of the agent and the view of an observer, although it appears to be an important source of the ambivalence which he describes in our ordinary and philosophical views concerning the liberty of human action; see *Cognition and Commitment*, 118–36. For further discussions of the role of the observer in Hume's account of the necessity of human action, see Árdal, *Passion and Value*, 88; Baier, *Progress of Sentiments*, 152–54; and Russell, *Freedom and Moral Sentiment*, 53–55.

acquainted with every circumstance of our disposition and character" (T 2.3.2.2 [SBN 408–9]; EHU 8.22n18 [SBN 94n1]). In other words, we apparently attribute necessity, as observers, to the actions of others, but not to our own. Hume does not consider the process by which we ascribe motives and dispositions to ourselves, although this discussion would have supplemented his account in Book 2 of our concepts of our own qualities of mind and character (T 2.1.5.1–2, 2.1.9.2 [SBN 285, 303]).

Hume's account of this necessity in our judgments of human actions is also problematic as applied to his claims regarding the supposed necessary connection between the mental states of an individual, since in this case the agent is the only possible observer of the connection. Indeed, Hume's own discussions elsewhere of the succession of human thought are inconclusive regarding the determinacy or indeterminacy of this sequence.[7]

First, we may ask whether either the determinacy or the indeterminacy of human thought is disclosed in our immediate self-consciousness. As we have seen, Hume maintains that the will is an internal impression that we "feel and are conscious of," whenever we "knowingly give rise" to any "new perception of our mind," as well as a movement of our body (T 2.3.1.2 [SBN 399]; cf. A 26 [SBN 657–57]). In the paragraph added in the Appendix, he asserts that, as in the case of the voluntary movements of our body, we do not directly perceive any connection between any individual idea and the preceding impression of volition. On the contrary, the "empire of the will over our mind" is no more intelligible than the influence of the will on the body, since even in the voluntary succession of our thoughts, the thought that is the effect is "distinguishable and separable from the cause, and cou'd not be foreseen without the experience of their constant conjunction."[8] In addition, he notes that we have command over the activities of our mind only "to a certain degree, but beyond *that* lose all empire over it," and that we cannot discover "any precise bounds" between these voluntary and involuntary actions of our mind without consulting experience (T 1.3.14.12 [SBN 632–33]). Unfortunately, he does not provide any further account of the evidence from experience that shows a distinction between the voluntary and involuntary course of our thoughts, either by providing examples, or by considering any phenomenological distinction between a voluntary and an involuntary course of thoughts.

7. For further discussions of the problem of the determination of human thought, see Russell, *Freedom and Moral Sentiment*, 33–34, and Garrett, *Cognition and Commitment*, 169–73.

8. One might object here that while I recognize that my impression of volition and the corresponding bodily movement are distinct and separable by considering the case of willing to move a missing limb, I cannot separate the impression of volition from the intended idea, since immediately upon willing to produce an idea, I am already producing that idea. However, David Norton has pointed out to me that we encounter this separability when we think of one aspect of an object and then attempt unsuccessfully to think of another aspect, for example in trying to recall the name of a person or the first line of a song.

In light of this further discussion, we may return to Hume's initial statement that "nothing is more free than the imagination," and that the principles of association are "not to be consider'd as an inseparable connexion: for that has been already excluded from the imagination" (T 1.1.4.1 [SBN 10]; cf. EHU 2.4–5, 7.15–20 [SBN 18–19, 67–69]). In this context Hume appears to indicate that the principles of association operate deterministically, whenever they do operate. However, he also maintains that the activities of the imagination are "free," and even that this freedom of the imagination is able to override any apparent determination of our thoughts. On the other hand, he does not indicate how, or if, we can distinguish the succession of ideas according to the principles of association from the free activities of the imagination. We are thus left with three competing assertions concerning the question of whether the succession of our thoughts, as this is given to us through introspection, is free or determined: that the imagination is free; that it is determined by the principles of association; and that the course of our thoughts is sometimes voluntary and sometimes involuntary. However, while he may be implicitly appealing in the paragraph added in the Appendix to our common experience of appearing to control some of our thoughts and not others, Hume does not provide us with any clear evidence that the apparently voluntary course of our thoughts is really free, or ultimately determined by the principles of association, which are otherwise given such a pervasive role in his account of the operations of the human mind.

Hume also considers the view of human thought that would be given to us if we were able to observe the perceptions in another mind. Interestingly, he argues that if we could "see clearly into the breast of another, and observe that succession of perceptions, which constitutes his mind or thinking principle," and if we suppose that this succession "always preserves the memory of a considerable part of past perceptions," we would expect to observe resemblances between these impressions and the subsequent ideas. This series of resemblances would prompt us to attribute identity to the entire sequence as a single unified mind. Finally, he notes that this would be the case "whether we consider ourselves or others" (T 1.4.6.18 [SBN 260–61]). Here he is apparently asserting that we can discover regular connections of resemblance between our own impressions and ideas through introspection, at least in the past succession of our perceptions as disclosed to us through our memory.

Hume provides a further discussion of this issue in the *Dialogues*. In considering the supposed nature of the divine mind, Philo argues that "a mental world or universe of ideas requires a cause as much as does a material world or universe of objects." We may trace the influence of causes in both worlds by observing, respectively, the operations of our own minds and the physical processes in organic bodies. On the basis of "experience," he then argues that "we never find two persons, who think exactly alike," or even one person who thinks "exactly alike at any two different periods of time." By comparing many such cases, we find that the "curious machinery of thought" is influenced by a number of "delicate" causes, such as "a difference of age, of the disposition of his body, of weather, of food, of company, of books, of passions," and so on (DNR 4.160–61). Unfortunately for our purposes, Philo's reference here to considering "our own mind" is ambiguous: he could be referring to the results of introspection, or to conclusions concerning the minds of other human beings derived from observing their behavior. Philo's usage suggests introspection, but his examples are drawn from observations of other people. On the other hand, Philo also claims that experience only shows us that the ideas within a human mind "by an unknown, inexplicable œconomy, arrange themselves so as to form the plan of a watch or house." This passage indicates that there is "an original principle of order in mind," but does not provide any further indication of its source, or any indication of whether this principle is to be regarded as an expression of the freedom or determination of the mind (DNR 2.146).

To conclude, Hume never definitively establishes, on the basis of introspection, whether the succession of thoughts in the human mind is free or determined. He apparently intends to affirm the freedom of the imagination in Book 1, Part 1 of the *Treatise,* and the causal determination of our ideas and thoughts in his later addition to Part 3 and in the *Dialogues,* but does not offer a conclusive discussion of either alternative. Finally, he concedes that we cannot directly observe the succession of thoughts in another person (T 1.4.6.18 [SBN 260]). Thus, in spite of his assertion (T 2.3.1.2 [SBN 399]) that we must ascribe necessity to the actions of the human mind, as well as to external human behavior, it seems that I as a subject can only acquire an idea of necessity from observing the regular connection between the motives and the bodily actions of another person. On the other hand, I cannot derive the idea of a necessary succession from the sequence of thoughts in the human mind, either in myself through introspection, or in another mind through observation.

In defending his analysis of the necessity attributed to the actions of others, Hume considers the objection that human actions do not display any such regularities, but are instead notoriously "inconstant" and "capricious," and often seem "irregular and uncertain" to an observer, especially compared to the operations of matter. In response to this objection, he reminds us that we often encounter irregularities in a series of physical events, and that, when reasoning philosophically, we regard such unexpected events as effects of "contrary and conceal'd causes," which are only hidden from us "on account of our imperfect knowledge." Similarly, in the case of human action, whenever we are unable to identify the motive for a particular action, we generally assume that the action arose from a motive that is not immediately apparent to us. Indeed, we tend to expect that even the most "irregular and unexpected" actions of individuals may be explained "by those, who know every particular circumstance of their character and situation" (T 2.3.1.12 [SBN 403–4]; EHU 8.15 [SBN 88]; cf. T 2.3.2.2 [SBN 408–9]; EHU 8.22 [SBN 93–94]). Hume further attributes the same continuous range of variation through degrees of probability to our judgments concerning human actions as our judgments concerning natural events, extending from judgments of a "strong motive," to cases in which we find an equal balance of evidence, to irregular actions whose causes are hidden or unknown (T 2.1.10.5–7, 2.3.1.12 [SBN 312–14, 403–4]). Finally, in an essay on explaining "remarkable customs," Hume argues that it might be easier to account for any "irregular and extraordinary appearances" in the "moral" than the "physical world," since any surprising human actions are still explained by "springs and principles, of which every one has, within himself, or from observation, the strongest assurance and conviction" (E RC.366). This view of our greater ease in explaining human actions echoes his earlier characterization of the regular connection between actions and motives as the "intelligible quality" of human action, which is the model for any intelligibility that we might attribute to the operations of matter (T 2.3.2.4 [SBN 410]).

Hume concludes that "*natural* and *moral* evidence cement together, and form only one chain of argument betwixt them," since both are "of the same nature, and deriv'd from the same principles." This reaffirms his assertion in Book 1 "that there is but one kind of *necessity*, as there is but one kind of cause," and that "the common distinction betwixt *moral* and *physical* necessity is without any foundation in nature" (T 2.3.1.17, 1.3.14.33; cf. 1.3.15.11 [SBN 406, 171; cf. 175]). In the *Enquiry* he asserts that "the conjunction between motives and voluntary actions is as regular and uniform, as that between the cause and effect in any part of nature." He also maintains that this conjunction has never been disputed, either in philosophy or in common life. Accordingly, since actions display a "regular conjunction with motives and circumstances and characters," and since "we always draw inferences from one to the other," he concludes that we should acknowledge, as philosophers, the determination of human action that we implicitly recognize "in every deliberation of our lives, and in every step of our conduct and behaviour" (EHU 8.16, 8.22 [SBN 88, 94]).[9]

In addition to his account of its determination, Hume also examines the sense in which we may attribute liberty to the human will. In the *Treatise* he distinguishes between the "liberty of *spontaneity*" and the "liberty of *indifference*," and argues that only the first may be ascribed to any human actions. In the *Enquiry* he describes the first type of liberty as the "power of acting or not acting, according to the determinations of the will," which is "universally

9. For a discussion of Hume's view of "moral causal explanations," as compared to causal explanation in the natural sciences, see Livingston, *Hume's Philosophy of Common Life,* 187–209.

allowed to belong to every one who is not a prisoner and in chains." Liberty, in this sense, is freedom from external constraint, or the ability to act upon our own beliefs and desires. This, in Hume's view, is the only type of liberty that we may coherently attribute to the human will, and this is indeed our ordinary concept of human freedom (T 2.3.2.1 [SBN 407–8]; EHU 8.23 [SBN 95]). By contrast, a "liberty of indifference" would be the supposed ability of an agent to perform actions that have no connection to the beliefs and desires of that agent. Such actions would be performed without any motivation, and would thus be completely arbitrary. In other words, the doctrine of a "liberty of indifference" would be "a negation of necessity and causes," or an affirmation that human actions can arise from chance, or without any motive on the part of the agent. As we have seen, Hume maintains in general that chance is "nothing real in itself," but "merely the negation of a cause," which we attribute to any event for which we cannot find the cause. He now argues that any appeal to chance in our approach to human action has also been excluded by our inferential practice of explaining human actions as the effects of motives, and our expectation that irregular actions may be regarded as the effects of unknown motives in the agent. He thus rejects any positive attribution of chance to human action, as well as to events in the natural world (T 2.3.2.1, 1.3.11.4 [SBN 407, 124–25]; EHU 8.25 [SBN 95–96]).

The most dramatic apparent case of a "liberty of indifference" in human action is the case of "mad-men," who might seem on Hume's analysis to have "no liberty," since their actions have less "regularity and constancy" than those of other human agents. On the other hand, we might also be tempted to regard their actions as more free than those of other human beings, since these actions seem to be more irregular than those of other human agents, and often do not appear to arise according to regular pattern from motives in the agent (T 2.3.1.13 [SBN 404]). Indeed, Philo describes madness as a system of thought that has "no order" at all (DNR 4.162). On the other hand, in the *Enquiry* Hume compares the uncharacteristic actions of a person who is driven by a "sudden and unknown frenzy" to perform murder and theft, to an unexpected natural event, such as an earthquake, which has an unknown physical cause (EHU 8.20 [SBN 91]).

Although he rejects the "liberty of indifference," or the absolute freedom of the human will, Hume does attempt to explain the popularity of this doctrine among philosophers. First, the rejection of necessity in human action arises from a tendency among philosophers to confuse the connection between motive and action with the necessity of an external compulsion. This is thought to include a "force, and violence, and constraint" that does not appear in our immediate consciousness of our voluntary actions, even if we recognize that we were indeed "influenc'd by particular views and motives" in performing these actions (T 2.3.2.1 [SBN 407]). Indeed, we seem to feel a "false sensation" of a liberty of indifference in our own actions, which we then regard as evidence for a real liberty of indifference. The source of this false sensation is our discovery, through introspection, that when we imagine any courses of action other than those which we have pursued in the past, the will "moves easily" in these alternative directions, and allows us to imagine ourselves following a different course of action. We may even attempt to perform "capricious and irregular actions" to prove our absolute freedom, either to ourselves or others. However, Hume argues that these capricious actions would in such a case arise from the "fantastical desire of showing liberty," which, as "the motive of our actions," would provide yet another example of the causal connection between motive and action (T 2.3.2.2 [SBN 408–9]; EHU 8.22n18 [SBN 94n1]).

While the doctrine of necessity is often regarded as a threat to morality, Hume maintains, on the contrary, that the doctrine of necessity as presented in his account is "essential to religion and morality." That is, he argues that we do not blame human beings for particular actions, but for the qualities of character which led them to perform these actions. Accordingly, any judgments of moral responsibility must presuppose the causal relation between motives and actions denied by the "hypothesis of liberty," as we will see in Chapter 8 (T 2.3.2.5–6 [SBN 410–11]).

To summarize, Hume maintains that we already attribute "necessity" to the connection between motive and action in our reasonings concerning human actions. However, we may also attribute a "liberty of spontaneity" to all human actions that are not determined by external constraints, but instead arise directly from the motives of the agent. In other words, human actions are free in the only possible sense when they are not subjected to external coercion; but, on the basis of experience, we regard such actions as determined by the beliefs and desires that constitute the motives of the agent, as these are influenced by circumstances and character.

Hume concludes that the controversy over liberty and necessity has largely amounted to a verbal dispute, since both of the contending parties implicitly accept the same view, which is also the view that he himself defends, of the connection between motives and human action. In the *Treatise* he traces this debate to "confus'd ideas and undefin'd terms," and suggests that it can be addressed properly only if the participants agree in their terminology, especially in the definition of "necessity" (T 2.3.1.13, 2.3.1.18 [SBN 404, 407]). In the *Enquiry* he introduces his account of liberty and necessity by considering the effects in general of linguistic disputes in the history of philosophy. He then argues that, since all the participants in this debate have always attributed both liberty and necessity, in his own sense of these two terms, to human agents, "a few intelligible definitions," such as his own, should put an end to the controversy (EHU 8.2 [SBN 81]).[10]

THE INTERPRETATION OF HUMAN ACTION

As we have seen, Hume traces our belief in the necessary connection between motives and actions to our observation of regular patterns of behavior in human beings and our resulting ability in many cases to explain and to predict human actions. In this section I consider two criticisms that have been directed specifically against Hume's account of the interpretation of human action. One is the criticism that Hume is reducing the problem of understanding human actions to discovering empirical regularities in these actions, without recognizing the distinctive character of intentional action or, consequently, the distinctive type of explanation belonging to the human sciences. The other criticism is the allegation that Hume presupposes and reinforces the assumption that there is a "uniform human nature," which we may study, in our reasonings concerning human conduct, apart from any consideration of the influence of a particular social, historical, and cultural context on a given individual. Both of these criticisms reflect important features of his analysis of voluntary action, but also overlook certain aspects of his discussion.

Hume's approach to the explanation of voluntary conduct has often been described as a mechanistic or reductionist view that denies any intentional character to human action and instead explains human conduct strictly as the result of physical operations. This view seems to be supported by his own statements that natural and moral evidence are "of the same nature, and deriv'd from the same principles," and that "the common distinction betwixt *moral* and *physical* necessity is without any foundation in nature" (T 2.3.1.17, 1.3.14.33 [SBN 406, 171]). For example, Zabeeh characterizes Hume's discussion as reducing "moral necessity to physical necessity," while Flew charges him with failing to recognize that explanations in the natural and the human sciences are of "two irreducibly different logical types," appealing respectively to "necessitating causes" and "motivating reasons." Similarly, Berry finds in Hume an empirical or causal rather than an intentional account of human action; and Burns argues that Hume regards covering-law explanations as the only valid form of explanation and therefore fails to recognize the distinctive character of intentional explanations.[11]

---

10. For a criticism of Hume's view of this debate as a merely verbal dispute, see Steinberg, "Hume on Liberty," 113–37.

11. Zabeeh, *Hume*, 170; Flew, *David Hume*, 133 and 139; Berry, *Hume, Hegel and Human Nature*, 93–94; Burns, *The Great Debate on Miracles*, 161–63, 177–80, and 196–215. See also Broiles, *Moral Philosophy of David Hume*, 62–68.

In the present discussion we have seen, on the contrary, that Hume gives a central role to motives in the explanation of human action. That is, although he argues that all judgments of causation arise from our observation of a regular conjunction between similar sets of events, he also distinguishes between the physical causes that we discover by observing the operations of matter; and motives, consisting in the beliefs and desires that we attribute to others on the basis of introspection, observation, and sympathy; and he identifies these motives as the causes of human action. In other words, he specifically distinguishes between the types of causes that we examine in the natural and in the human sciences, though he maintains that our causal explanations have the same origin and structure, and arise from the same principles in both cases. This is reflected in his later distinction in Book 3 between the "will or choice," which determines human action, and the "laws of matter and motion" that determine the growth of an oak tree (T 3.1.1.24 [SBN 467]).

However, in this context we may also consider how Hume would assess the materialist reduction of these beliefs and desires to physiological states of the human body, specifically to states of the central nervous system, and the ensuing reduction of the mental causes of bodily motion to physical causes. We have already considered his evaluation of the evidence for both mental-to-physical and physical-to-mental causation, in which "we find by the comparing their ideas, that thought and motion are different from each other, and by experience, that they are constantly united." We may thus conclude that "motion may be, and actually is, the cause of thought and perception." Indeed, thought and motion may be "constantly united" in either order, and may thus be regarded as causes of change in each other, although he is specifically interested here in the influence of physical causes on mental events (T 1.4.5.29–30 [SBN 246–48]). In this discussion Hume maintains that the mind and body, or mental events and physical events, are distinguishable in idea, and are thus distinct in reality. He then argues that any specific judgments concerning the causal connections between mental and physical states are matters of experience.

Accordingly, to eliminate any distinct mental causes from the explanation of human behavior on Humean grounds, we would presumably be required to show that certain specific physical events in the brain are constantly conjoined with certain bodily movements apart from these mental events. However, it would apparently be impossible to carry out this project, either through introspection, in which we cannot avoid experiencing our mental states, or by observing other people, whose mental states we can never experience, although we may indeed find that their actions are determined by their observable physiological states. On the other hand, in order to eliminate any distinct physical causes from actions of the body, and to isolate a mental cause, we would be required to distinguish a mental event, which is only accessible to us in our own case and only through introspection, from any physical event, and to identify this mental event as the cause of an action in our body, on the basis of repeated observation. Thus, according to this application of Hume's view, the irreducibility of consciousness to a physical state for each of us individually in our own case prevents us from reducing mental states to physical states. On the other hand, the evidence of introspection in our own case discloses the reality and thus also the possibility of physical-to-mental causation and mental-to-physical causation, which we then ascribe to others through observation and sympathy, although not with the same immediacy of evidence. The only way to decide, through a Humean observation of constant conjunctions, whether the causes of bodily movement are mental or physical, is to find some way for me to observe both my mental states and the physical states that appear to be correlated with these states, and to discover whether they are separable and distinguishable. Apart from this achievement, my impressions of volition will always seem to be the causes of my actions, although I might be led by the advances in modern science and technology to regard observable physical states in the central nervous systems of others as the causes of their actions.

Hume's account of explanation in the human sciences has been claimed as a predecessor of many recent lines of development in the philosophy of action and also in the philosophy and methodology of the social sciences. For example, according to James Farr, Hume's account of sympathy, of attributing motives to other human beings, and of explaining of human action anticipates of the *Verstehen* tradition of Dilthey and Weber, and its subsequent development in philosophical hermeneutics and the interpretative approach to the social sciences.[12] On the other hand, Davidson challenges the distinction between reasons and causes in the philosophy of action by arguing, with Hume, that the explanation of an action by a "primary reason," consisting in "a belief and an attitude," satisfies our ordinary and philosophical standards for causal explanation. Similarly, Beauchamp and Rosenberg have attributed to Hume a deductive-nomological, or covering-law, approach to the explanation of human action, in which we derive our explanation of a particular action from a generalization concerning the motives of the agent, arising from our previous observation of the actions of that person.[13] Finally, Donald Livingston has claimed to find, in Hume's writings as a whole, examples of both covering-law and covering-reason approaches to the interpretation of human action, reflecting various methods belonging to the different disciplines included in the human sciences.[14]

12. See Farr, "Hume, Hermeneutics and History," 285–310, and "Humean Explanations," 57–76.
13. Davidson, "Actions, Reasons, and Causes," 685–700; Beauchamp and Rosenberg, *Hume and the Problem of Causation,* 320–27. See also Bricke, *Mind and Morality,* 5–34.
14. Livingston, *Hume's Philosophy of Common Life,* 187–246. For a study of covering-law and intentional explanations that may be usefully considered in this context, see Roberts, *The Logic of Historical Explanation.*

These studies offer different views of the proper role of empirical general-izations in the explanation of human action, and different assessments of Hume's commitment to the use of lawlike generalizations in the human sciences. How-ever, all of these studies recognize that Hume assigns a distinctive role to beliefs and desires, and to motives, character, and circumstances, in the understanding and explanation of human action. I will return to this discussion in the remain-ing chapters by examining Hume's various discussions of the principles of explanation belonging to the different disciplines included in the moral or human sciences.[15]

The second criticism of Hume's approach to the interpretation of human action is that his theory rests upon an unhistorical view of a "uniform human nature" which is supposed to be the same in all ages and nations. According to his critics, in accepting this view Hume is in effect relying upon the assump-tions and the standards of his own cultural setting to understand and explain all human actions. In an influential version of this criticism, Black argues that Hume was "dominated, as indeed were all the eighteenth-century *philosophes,* by the belief that human nature was uniformly the same at all times and places." Collingwood offers an even more forceful statement of this objection: "Hume never shows the slightest suspicion that the human nature he is analyzing in his philosophical work is the nature of a western European in the early eighteenth century, and that the very same enterprise if undertaken at a widely different time or place might have yielded widely different results."[16]

These criticisms are directed especially against Hume's account of the neces-sity of human action in the first *Enquiry.* In this text Hume indeed states that there is "a great uniformity among the actions of men, in all nations and ages," and that "human nature remains still the same" across historical eras and geo-graphic regions. He also argues that we may draw upon our observations of modern European life in order to understand the "sentiments, inclinations, and course of life of the GREEKS and ROMANS." Indeed, the study of history discloses "the constant and principles of human nature," by showing that "the same motives always produce the same actions " (EHU 8.7 [SBN 83]). In the *Treatise* he argues in similar terms that "like causes still produce like effects," in human action as well as the operations of matter (T 2.3.1.5 [SBN 401]).

Black, Collingwood, and other critics have cited these passages as evidence for Hume's belief in a uniform human nature, and also for his tendency to attribute the beliefs and motives typical of his own eighteenth-century European

15. For further discussions, see Wallis, "David Hume's Contribution to Social Science," 358–71; along with Bryson, *Man and Society;* Swingewood, "Origins of Sociology," 164–77; and Capaldi, "Hume as Social Scientist," 99–123.

16. Black, *Art of History,* 86; Collingwood, *Idea of History,* 83. See also Berry, *Hume, Hegel and Human Nature,* 1–20 and 57–68, and "Hume on Rationality," 234–47.

culture to human beings in all times and places. In response to this criticism, however, several more recent studies have argued that Hume is presenting a more focused account of the universal dispositions in human nature, which is also intended to provide the principles for explaining the variations in human motives and actions among different cultures and historical periods. In particular, Forbes, Wertz, and Cohen argue that the uniform principles in Hume's account of human nature are the general structures of motivation, including the general relation of ideas and desires in the production of the various passions, the conjunction of passions and beliefs in the production of a motive, and the role of motives in the determination of human actions. The attribution of these general principles of motivation and action to all human beings is not equivalent to the claim that any specific beliefs and desires, or any actions arising from these beliefs and desires, must be the same in every cultural and historical setting.[17] Thus, although he states that human nature is the same everywhere "in its principles and operations," Hume also argues that history discloses these "universal principles of human nature" by presenting human life, not as a fixed scene, but "in all varieties of circumstances and situations," providing us with a series of "experiments," or observations, in which we may discover "the regular springs of human action and behavior." Through the study of human beings in different times and places, we find that "ambition, avarice, self-love, vanity, friendship, generosity, public spirit" have always been the sources of human action. However, Hume is not identifying any universal causes of these passions, or finding that they always give rise to precisely the same actions (EHU 8.7 [SBN 83]).

As we have seen, Hume identifies the passions as the "springs and principles" of human action (T 2.2.12.1 [SBN 397]). He also regards the intentional structure and characteristic feeling of each passion as determined by universal dispositions in human nature, although he argues that many of the objects of the passions are determined by "custom and practice" within a given historical and cultural setting (T 2.1.6.9 [SBN 293–94]). On Hume's view, the uniformity of human nature, as this is reflected in human actions, consists in the universal disposition to form beliefs, a universal susceptibility to the same set of passions, and a universal propensity to act in response to these beliefs and passions. He thus argues that the basic passions, such as ambition, greed, and friendship, have been "the source of all the actions and enterprizes, which have ever been observed among mankind." Indeed, we would probably doubt anyone who claims to have discovered a country whose inhabitants were entirely free from any of these passions (EHU 8.8 [SBN 83–84]). Similarly, in the *Treatise*

17. See Wertz, "Hume, History, and Human Nature," 481–96, and *Between Hume's Philosophy and History*, 19–34; Forbes, *Hume's Philosophical Politics*, 102–21; and Cohen, "Notion of Moral Progress," 109–27; along with Farr, "Humean Explanations," 74–76, and Livingston, *Hume's Philosophy of Common Life*, 214–25.

he maintains that the study of human life, in all its social, cultural, and historical variety, shows us "the same uniformity and regular operation of natural principles" in the human passions and the motives for our actions (T 2.3.1.5 [SBN 401]).

However, Hume also develops his own sustained criticism of the assumption that there is any uniformity among nations, or even among individuals, in their specific beliefs or principles of conduct. In the *Treatise* he argues that we must take into account the differences in "sexes, ages, governments, conditions, or methods of education" in order to trace the "uniformity and regular operation" of the underlying principles of human action (T 2.3.1.5 [SBN 401]). In the *Enquiry* he rejects the view "that all men, in the same circumstances, will always act precisely in the same manner." Instead, in our attempts to understand human actions, we must consider "the diversity of characters, prejudices, and opinions." We must also consider the different "manners of men" in "different ages and countries," and indeed "the great force of custom and education, which mould the human mind from its infancy, and form it into a fixed and established character" (EHU 8.10–11 [SBN 85–86]). In "Of the Standard of Taste" he calls attention to the "great variety of Taste, as well as of opinion," among human beings, and even the "great inconsistence and contrariety" in taste that appears if we compare the artistic preferences of "distant nations and remote ages." Here again, however, he finds that this variety arises from "the different humours of particular men," and from "the particular manners and opinions of our age and country" (E ST.226–27; E ST.243; cf. E Sc.163). In other words, the differences in our actions may be traced to differences among the beliefs and temperaments of individuals, and also to the differences in our beliefs and attitudes toward particular objects arising from our historical and cultural setting.

Accordingly, Hume's attempt to identify the uniform principles of human action is not a claim that the actions of all human beings should be understood and judged by their conformity to eighteenth-century European manners and morals. Instead, it is a claim, and even a methodological stipulation, that we must refer to the general system of the passions, and to the general structure of human motivation, in order to understand and explain any human actions, including the actions we encounter in very different historical or cultural contexts.

Hume offers a restatement of these principles for explaining human actions, and a vivid application of these principles, in the excursus titled "A Dialogue" at the end of the *Enquiry Concerning the Principles of Morals*. In this dialogue Hume presents a fictional conversation between himself as the narrator and his adventurous friend Palamedes, who opens the dialogue by describing his visit to a country called Fourli, whose inhabitants "have ways of thinking, in many things, particularly in morals, diametrically opposite to ours" (EPM D.2

[SBN 324]). He then recounts a series of anecdotes from Fourli in which compliments are regarded as offensive, assassination and parricide are honored, marriages are contracted between siblings, and homosexuality is condoned and promoted. Hume insists that Palamedes must be joking, since "such barbarous and savage manners" are not only opposed to civilized life but are indeed "scarcely compatible with human nature." However, his friend replies that Hume is now "speaking blasphemy" against "the GREEKS, especially the ATHENIANS," along with the inhabitants of other ancient nations, whom Palamedes has described under this unfamiliar name (EPM D.12–13 [SBN 328]). Hume then offers a similar account of the fashionable manners and morals of modern French society, which holds adultery and abject subservience to the monarch in high esteem, while regarding ordinary raillery as a deadly insult. These customs, he says, would have been just as contemptible among the ancient Athenians as they are to eighteenth-century Britons (EPM D.19–24 [SBN 330–32]).

In evaluating their discussion, Hume argues that Palamedes' approach to describing human actions is fundamentally misleading, since it deliberately presents the conduct of the ancient Greeks and Romans as absurd and offensive, and indeed even employs "a little art or eloquence" to misrepresent their actions. As an alternative, he recommends that we attempt to understand the actions of others as arising from the beliefs, values, and practices of their time and place, rather than explaining and judging all actions according to our own manners and morals. Thus, instead of judging any specific actions of the ancient Greeks or Romans according to English common law, we should consider how these actions would be judged by their own principles, since the most "innocent or reasonable" human actions "may be rendered odious or ridiculous, if measured by a standard, unknown to the persons" (EPM D.19 [SBN 330]).

Accordingly, whenever we would like to explain human actions from another culture or historical period, Hume suggests that we should examine the "first principles, which each nation establishes, of blame or censure." In other words, we must presuppose the universal system of the passions and the structure of motivation, and then attempt to discern the particular beliefs and desires that comprise the motive for any given action by a specific individual within a given historical context. In an elaboration of his earlier metaphor describing the passions as the "springs" of human action, he thus observes that "the RHINE flows north, the RHONE south; yet both spring from the *same* mountain, and are also actuated, in their opposite directions, by the *same* principle of gravity. The different inclinations of the ground, on which they run, cause all the difference of their courses" (EPM D.26 [SBN 333]). Hume therefore argues in "A Dialogue" that all human actions can be explained according to "the most universal, established principles of morals," which are the universal passions and structures of motivation, even though the actions arising from these motives might be incomprehensible or offensive to an observer from another cultural setting (EPM D.27 [SBN 334]).

Finally, Hume applies these general principles of explanation to his preceding discussion with Palamedes. For example, the "GREEK loves" arose from "a very innocent cause," which was "the frequency of the gymnastic exercises among that people," and were recommended as a source of friendship and fidelity, which are "esteemed in all nations and all ages." Next, the modern French value for attachments of "gallantry" between the sexes arises from a preference for the "sociable pleasures" over domestic pleasure: a motive that might perhaps be appreciated even by the English, although they profess to prefer "a strict fidelity and constancy." Hume also examines several other ancient and modern customs, such as the marriage of half-siblings, infanticide, dueling, and suicide, to show that "the principles upon which men reason in morals are always the same; though the conclusions which they draw are often very different" (EPM 28–32, 36 [SBN 334–36]).[18]

A number of studies have indicated that Hume fails to understand sympathetically the actions, motives, and circumstances of individuals in certain groups, especially ancient Anglo-Saxons and modern Africans.[19] However, in his account of the methodological principles for the interpretation of human action, especially in "A Dialogue," Hume articulates the standards by which we may diagnose and criticize his own deficiencies in sympathy and understanding as failures to apply his own principles consistently. I will consider this topic at greater length in Chapter 13.

REASON AND THE PASSIONS

After presenting his general account of human action in the *Treatise,* Hume considers the "influencing motives of the will," or the relative influence of reason and the passions on human action. Here he criticizes the view that there is a conflict between reason and the passions in the determination of human action, and the corresponding tendency among moral philosophers and even in public discourse "to give the preference to reason, and assert that men are only so far virtuous as they conform themselves to its dictates" (T 2.3.3.1 [SBN 413]). Instead, he argues that the passions are the immediate sources of all human

18. Hume provides a further explanation of his arguments in this text in a 1751 letter to his friend Gilbert Elliot (L 1.150–53). For further discussions of "A Dialogue," see Forbes, *Hume's Philosophical Politics,* 102–21, and Livingston, *Hume's Philosophy of Common Life,* 214–25. See also Beauchamp's "Introduction" to the *Enquiry Concerning the Principles of Morals,* xvii.

19. On Hume's discussions of "barbarians" and different races, see Livingston, *Hume's Philosophy of Common Life,* 235–46; Popkin, "Hume's Racism," 251–66, and "Hume's Racism Reconsidered," 64–75; Immerwahr, "Hume's Revised Racism," 481–86; and Palter, "Hume and Prejudice," 3–23.

action, that the influence of reason is subordinate to the passions, and that the role traditionally accorded to reason in the determination of human action actually belongs to those dispositions which he calls the "calm passions."

As we have seen, Hume argues that the "chief spring and moving principle" in the human mind is the perception of pleasure and pain (T 1.3.10.2 [SBN 118]). These two impressions give rise, first to the passions of desire and aversion, and then to the various other passions, which are all modifications of desire and aversion. Finally, the will is roused to activity when we recognize that an object which might give us pleasure or pain can be attained or avoided by the actions of our mind or body (T 2.3.9.1–7 [SBN 438–39]).

In considering the possible influence of reason on the will, Hume first reminds us that, according to his argument in Book 1, the word "reasoning" can be applied only to the inferential discovery of numerical proportions and causal relations. He now maintains that neither type of reasoning can in itself be the cause of any action. He also argues more generally that reason is not the faculty by which we feel pleasure or pain, and that objects consequently cannot "affect us" through reason. Accordingly, "reason alone can never produce any action, or give rise to volition," and can never oppose the passions in their influence over the will. Indeed, nothing can oppose the influence of a passion over volition but a "contrary impulse" arising from another passion. Hume concludes that reason "can never be a motive to any action of the will" and "can never oppose passion in the direction of the will," since it is "inactive" or "inert," in contrast to the passions, which are principles of action (T 2.3.3.1–4, 3.1.1.7–8 [SBN 413–15, 457–58]).

As support for this argument, Hume reviews the different types of reasoning in order to show that every particular activity of reasoning is initiated by a passion that directs us toward a source of pleasure or away from a source of displeasure. First, Hume argues that the activity of demonstrative reasoning is directed by the desire to intervene in the natural world or in human affairs. For example, mechanical engineers use mathematical reasoning to find proportions in the "influence and operation" of matter, which helps them regulate "the motions of bodies *to some design'd end or purpose*," while merchants use mathematical reasoning to assign debts and credits, through which they elicit certain actions from others. The activity of demonstrative reasoning is thus directed toward enabling us to act causally, either in the natural world or in society, and is therefore subordinate, as a practical activity, to probable reasoning. Next, in the case of probable reasoning, Hume argues that whenever we expect to receive pleasure or pain from any object, our passions also direct our attention toward those objects that we have found through experience to be connected with the original one "by the relation of cause and effect." We may then attempt to attain or avoid the object by intervening in a similar causal sequence. In other words, we are moved to engage in any type of reasoning by the desire to attain pleasure or avoid pain, and would never engage in any process of reasoning if its objects were "indifferent to us" (T 2.3.3.2–3 [SBN 413–14]).

Hume's account of the subordination of reason to the direction provided by the passions is reinforced by his surveys in the *Treatise* of our motives for intellectual activity. Here, as we have seen, he argues that the pursuit of truth can be a source of pleasure for human beings, not only by helping us to discover the methods for attaining the objects of our various desires, but as an exercise of our talents, and even as a means for gaining public admiration. In these sections he again indicates that the pursuit of pleasure is in one way or another the motive for intellectual inquiry, even though the ultimate source of the pleasure any individual receives from his or her research may not always be immediately obvious to others (T 1.4.7.12–15, 2.3.10.1–12 [SBN 270–74, 448–54]).[20]

In contrast to the supposed motivating power of reason, Hume argues that the goals of human actions are determined by the passions, which, by responding to objects as the sources of pleasure or pain, indicate which objects are to be regarded as good or evil in the natural sense, or in other words as either desirable or undesirable. Indeed, we often find that "a trivial good may, from certain circumstances," produce a desire which is "superior" to the desire arising "from the greatest and most valuable enjoyment." In these cases, he argues that the strength of the desire in the agent establishes the subjective value of the object for the agent, and that reason cannot affect the evaluation of the object, or criticize the ends of human action when these ends are considered simply as objects of the passions. Accordingly, it is not contrary to reason for me to prefer "the destruction of the whole world to the scratching of my finger," or on the other hand to choose "my total ruin, to prevent the least uneasiness of an *Indian* or person wholly unknown to me." More generally, it is not contrary to reason for me to prefer "my own acknowledg'd lesser good to my greater," if this preference reflects "a more ardent affection for the former than the latter" (T 2.3.3.6 [SBN 416]). In the second *Enquiry* he states that the "ultimate ends" of human action can never be "accounted for by *reason*," but instead appeal "entirely to the sentiments and affections of mankind" (EPM App.1.18 [SBN 293]). He concludes that we are not speaking "strictly and philosophically" when we refer to a conflict between reason and the passions. Instead, he maintains that "reason is, and ought only to be the slave of the passions, and can never pretend to any other office than to serve and obey them" (T 2.3.3.4 [SBN 415]).

20. For a systematic study of the various types of judgments that appear in Hume's analysis of motivation, see Kydd, *Reason and Conduct*. For further discussions of the relative role of reason and the passions in motivation, see Falk, "Hume on Practical Reason," 1–18; Baier, *Progress of Sentiments*, 157–66; Magri, "Natural Obligation," 231–53; and Radcliffe, "Generation of Motives," 101–22.

Within the framework of this analysis, however, Hume argues that since the passions that serve as motives are accompanied by judgments, and since these judgments can be erroneous, we may be moved by a passion to perform an action that is inadequate for attaining our goal. In such cases he concedes that we may loosely describe the passion as "unreasonable." He illustrates this "obvious and natural" principle by considering two types of circumstances in which our actions may be influenced by a mistaken judgment. First, a passion can arise from a "supposition of the existence of objects, which really do not exist," or a mistaken judgment concerning the qualities of an object, as when I desire a piece of fruit which I believe has "excellent relish" but which is really sour or rotten. Second, I may perform an action that is "insufficient for the design'd end," as the result of a mistaken judgment concerning the causes that may be expected to produce the desired effect. In both cases, however, he argues that "even then 'tis not the passion, properly speaking, which is unreasonable, but the judgment" (T 2.3.3.6–7; cf. 3.1.1.12 [SBN 416–17; cf. 459–60]). He thus concedes that reason may indeed be a "mediate cause" of an action, but only "by prompting, or by directing a passion" (T 3.1.1.16 [SBN 462]).[21]

However, Hume also indicates that our passions may respond, not only to the idea of an immediate good or evil, but also to the idea of a future good or evil. The former ideas are more vivid and tend to arouse the violent passions, while the latter are less vivid and tend to arouse calmer passions (T 2.3.4.1, 2.3.7.3–5 [SBN 418–19, 428–30]).

In order to explain the widespread conviction that reason may conflict directly with the passions, Hume argues that whenever we regard reason as a motive, we are actually confusing reason with "certain calm desires and tendencies" which he calls "calm passions." These passions produce little or no disturbance in the mind, especially compared to the violent passions, and are indeed more likely to be recognized by their effects than their inward sensations.[22] In this regard, the calm passions resemble the calm sensations that accompany the activities of reasoning, since reason generally "exerts itself without producing any sensible emotion" and "scarce ever conveys any pleasure or uneasiness." Since the feelings that accompany both reasoning and the calm passions are similar to each other, and differ from the forceful sensations belonging to the violent passions, the calm passions are easily mistaken for "determinations of reason" (T 2.3.3.8 [SBN 417]; cf. EPM 6.15 [SBN 239]).

In the opening pages of Book 2 Hume suggests that the calm passions are different from the violent passions in kind, since he characterizes as "calm" such

---

21. See also Árdal, "Some Implications," 91–106.

22. On Hume's account of the "calm passions," see Árdal, *Passion and Value,* 93–105 and 128–29; Shaw, "Hume's Theory of Motivation," 163–83, and "Hume's Theory of Motivation—Part II," 19–39; Magri, "Natural Obligation," 231–53; and McIntyre, "Hume's Passions," 77–86.

distinctive passions as "the sense of beauty and deformity," or our moral and aesthetic sentiments (T 2.1.1.3 [SBN 276]). He initially reaffirms this analysis in Part 3 by identifying certain specific passions, such as benevolence, resentment, love of life, and kindness to children, as calm passions. However, he also describes the calm passions here as dispositions toward various passions, including those that may appear as violent passions. Indeed, while he describes the calm passions cited above as "instincts" that are "originally implanted in our natures," he argues subsequently that any passion may become a calm passion if it becomes established as "a settled principle of action" within the mind or character of an individual. In other words, a violent passion may be converted into a calm passion through repeated experience or custom, which can instill in us a "*tendency* or *inclination*" toward an object, and thereby transform an initially violent passion into a settled disposition (T 2.3.3.8, 2.3.4.1, 2.3.5.1 [SBN 417, 419, 422]). Thus, in addition to the calm instincts that seem to be innate and universal in human beings, the calm passions also include settled dispositions in the characters of individuals toward any of the different passions.

After establishing this distinction between the calm and violent passions, Hume turns to consider their relative influence on the human will. The violent passions might seem to have the most powerful motivating influence on the will, since these are more forceful and are obviously aroused in us by the sudden appearance of an object of our intense desire or aversion. However, since a calm passion operates as "a settled principle of action," or a "predominant inclination of the soul," Hume argues that this type of passion has a more pervasive influence on the will, as seen in our actions over time, than the "momentary gust" of a violent passion. In other words, a calm passion may be stronger than a violent passion as a motivating force, while a violent passion may be relatively weak in its overall effect (T 2.3.4.1 [SBN 418–19]).

Hume concludes that any supposed cases of conflict between reason and the passions are really conflicts between a calm and a violent passion. Such conflicts arise when these are directed toward different objects of desire and aversion, or toward different qualities of these objects, or toward different aspects of its situation in relation to ourselves. When this occurs, we are moved by our competing desires to consider several incompatible courses of action. For example, an object "when near, will cause a violent passion, which, when remote, produces only a calm one," while a violent desire for an immediate object may conflict with our calm desire for a distant but more highly valued object. In these cases, the decision to pursue a greater but more remote good is properly described as the victory of an enduring calm passion in determining the will over the temporary effects of a violent passion. However, since the calm passions resemble the activity of reasoning in their subjective feeling-quality, the triumph of a calm passion over a violent one is easily, though mistakenly, regarded as the conquest of a passion by reason (T 2.3.4.1 [SBN 418–19]; cf. 2.3.8.13 [SBN 437–38]; EPM 6.15 [SBN 239]).

According to Hume, we follow the general principles governing our interpretation and the explanation of human actions when we attribute calm passions to individuals, and explain their actions as products of either calm or violent passions. In other words, we discover the influence of the calm or violent passions in any given case by considering the "*general* character or *present* disposition of the person*," as this is discerned by observing their actions over time. However, he also notes that the more usual influence of several passions on the decisions of any individual "diversifies human life," not only by distinguishing one human individual from another, but also by exhibiting the complexity in every individual character, as well as the changes in individual character over time. Indeed, the diversity, complexity, and variability of character are among the leading sources of our difficulties in attempting to explain and predict human actions (T 2.3.3.10, 2.3.8.13 [SBN 418, 438]).

Hume therefore concludes that any alleged conflict between reason and the passions is more properly described as a conflict between calm and violent passions, since reason cannot operate as an independent source of motivation. However, he also recognizes and affirms an important, though subordinate, twofold role for reason in any analysis of the motives for human action: in our judgments concerning the qualities of objects, and in our judgments concerning the effectiveness of various actions for attaining these objects. He even concedes that human actions can be described as more or less "reasonable" as attempts to attain a goal, if these two judgments conform to the philosophical standards for demonstrative and probable reasoning. However, he maintains that, apart from the passions, reason can neither determine the goal, nor provide the motivating impulse for any action.[23] Hume's affirmation of the subordinate but crucial role for reason in human action stands as a response to those who criticize his discussion for denying any role for reason in human action, or for its alleged inconsistency, either internally or in relation to his account of reasoning in Book 1.[24] We will return to the issues involved in Hume's account of the relation between reason, the passions, and human action in the next chapter, in which we turn to his moral theory.

23. See also Shaw, "Hume's Theory of Motivation," 163–83, and "Hume's Theory of Motivation—Part II," 19–39, as well as his "Reason and Feeling," 349–68.
24. See, for example, Broiles, *Moral Philosophy of David Hume*, 27–70; Mercer, *Sympathy and Ethics*, 67–81; Tweyman, *Reason and Conduct*, 122–38; Harrison, *Hume's Moral Epistemology*, 5–26; and Stroud, *Hume*, 167–70.

8

Moral Theory

Hume presents two major statements of his moral theory: in Book 3 of the *Treatise,* titled "Of Morals," and in the *Enquiry Concerning the Principles of Morals.* In both versions he begins by comparing the influence of reason and sentiment in morals, and then considers the various qualities of character that we call "virtues," ending with a further account of the moral sentiments in the final section of the *Treatise* and in the first Appendix of the second *Enquiry.*

Hume expected his ethical theory to be the most interesting and engaging part of his philosophical project for the general reader. He presented Book 3 of the *Treatise* as "in some measure independent of the other two," and as accessible to "ordinary readers" even apart from his inquiry into the understanding and passions (T Adv.3; cf. 3.1.1.1 [SBN 454; cf. 455–56]). In the concluding section of the *Treatise* he hopes that his theory has exhibited "the *happiness,* as well as the *dignity* of virtue," and that it will also contribute to "practical morality" by showing popular moral instruction how to become "more correct in its precepts, and more perswasive in its exhortations" (T 3.3.6.6 [SBN 620–21]). Finally, in "My Own Life" he describes the *Enquiry Concerning the Principles of Morals* as "incomparably the best" among his writings (ML xxxvi). By emphasizing the accessibility of his writings in moral philosophy, he is clearly hoping to help improve the public understanding of morality, as well as contributing to the lively debate contemporary among philosophers concerning the foundations of morals.[1]

For much of the twentieth century Hume's account of moral evaluation was seen as a version of emotivism, in which moral statements are regarded as non-cognitive expressions of the emotional states of individuals; or subjectivism, in which moral statements are regarded as cognitive reports of the sentiments, either of a given individual, or of a majority of individuals in a given society.[2] In this chapter I will show that Hume establishes a role for cognition in moral assessment and motivation, and that he also seeks to establish objective standards for moral judgment, although he maintains that the underlying basis for our ability to make moral distinctions ultimately lies in our passions or sentiments. More specifically, I will show that, in Hume's view, our recognition of moral distinctions arises from our ability and disposition to consider the harmful or beneficial effects of the actions and characters of individuals upon society, through our sympathy with the pleasure or pain of others, and to articulate principles of conduct on the basis of this perspective. These principles, according to Hume, then receive an objective formulation in two stages: first, in the different historical systems of popular morality; and second, in the critical principles we derive from a philosophical examination of these systems, which may then be used to criticize a given system of morality. Accordingly, both a popular system of morality and the philosophical principles of morality allow us to derive particular judgments of moral evaluation and obligation from a set of moral rules, although these rules ultimately arise from our sentiments.

MORAL SENTIMENTS

In both of his main ethical works, Hume presents the ordinary concern for morality as the point of departure for moral reflection. In Book 3 of the *Treatise* he argues that our concern for the "peace of society" makes our moral reasonings appear more "real and solid" than the abstract speculations of Books 1 and 2 (T 3.1.1.1 [SBN 455–56]). In the second *Enquiry* he criticizes all of those "disingenuous disputants" who deny the reality of moral distinctions but "really

---

1. For discussions of Hume's context in the history of moral theory, especially in early modern Britain, see Norton, *David Hume*, 21–191, and his introduction to the *Treatise*, 74–97; and Beauchamp's introduction to the *Enquiry Concerning the Principles of Morals*, xviii–xxii.

2. For surveys of the interpretation of Hume's moral philosophy, see Botwinick, *Ethics, Politics and Epistemology*, 45–67; Capaldi, *Hume's Place in Moral Philosophy*, 131–52; Snare, *Morals, Motivation and Convention*, 1–6; and Garrett, *Cognition and Commitment*, 187–91. For a lively interpretation of Hume as a moral realist, in contrast to the prevailing approaches indicated above, see Norton, *David Hume*, 43–54 and 94–151, and "Hume's Moral Ontology," 189–214.

do not believe the opinions they defend." On the contrary, even such critics still retain the tendency to distinguish between "RIGHT and WRONG," which we find in ourselves and observe in other human beings through history and across cultures (EPM 1.2; cf. 1.10 [SBN 169–70; cf. 173–74]).

Hume introduces his moral theory in the *Treatise* by arguing that since moral judgments are a type of mental state or activity, and since "nothing is ever present to the mind but its perceptions," moral judgments must be classified as perceptions, along with "seeing, hearing, judging, loving, hating, and thinking." Accordingly, the next question raised by this classification is whether we distinguish between moral good and evil "by means of our *ideas* or *impressions*," or in other words, on the basis of reason or sentiment (T 3.1.1.2–3; cf. 1.3.7.5n5 [SBN 456; cf. 96n1]).

In approaching this question, Hume first considers the rationalist approach to ethical theory among his predecessors such as Wollaston, Clarke, and Balguy, who held that "morality, like truth, is discern'd merely by ideas, and by their juxta-position and comparison," or that "virtue is nothing but a conformity to reason," or that there are "eternal fitnesses and unfitnesses of things, which are the same to every rational being that considers them." In response, Hume seeks to demonstrate that it is impossible "from reason alone, to distinguish betwixt moral good and evil" (T 3.1.1.4 [SBN 456–57]; cf. EPM 1.3–9, App.1.1–21 [SBN 170–73, 285–94]).

Hume derives what he regards as an immediately conclusive refutation of the rationalist view of morality from his general theory of motivation, which we have considered in Chapter 7. Here he argues, first, that moral exhortations are regarded, both in a common view and by moral theorists, as intended to influence human actions, and second, that these exhortations often succeed in this purpose, since we find in "common experience" that people are frequently moved to act or refrain from action by considerations of duty and obligation. However, since he has shown that we must be moved by a passion to perform any action, while "reason of itself is utterly impotent in this particular," he concludes that these moral precepts must be the products of moral distinctions that ultimately arise from the passions. The passions which provide the grounds for moral distinctions are "original facts and realities, compleat in themselves," which unlike ideas, cannot enter into relations of "agreement or disagreement" with any other objects. Human actions may thus be "laudable or blameable," but cannot be "reasonable or unreasonable" in the strict sense of these terms; and we therefore cannot simply identify moral conduct with "reasonable" conduct (T 3.1.1.5–10 [SBN 457–58]; cf. EPM 1.9, App.1.21 [SBN 172, 294]).[3]

---

3. For discussions of these arguments, see Harrison, *Hume's Moral Epistemology*, 5–26; Mackie, *Hume's Moral Theory*, 52–55; Snare, *Morals, Motivation and Convention*, 34–144; Bricke, *Mind and Morality*, 79–86; and Garrett, *Cognition and Commitment*, 191–93.

In response to the possible objection that reason might contribute "obliquely" to the production of an action, Hume recalls his earlier discussion of the two senses in which reason may be described as the "mediate cause" of human action. That is, probable reasoning may inform us of the existence and nature of objects, or discover the appropriate means for attaining a particular end. He now argues that we may characterize an action as "unreasonable," although only in a "figurative and improper way of speaking," if it arises from a mistaken judgment concerning the object, or concerning the means we expect to be effective for attaining a desired end. However, we do not morally blame someone for pursuing an object from a mistaken view of its desirable qualities, or for "foolish conduct" in attempting to attain an object. We thus do not regard actions that may be called "unreasonable" in either of these senses to be, as such, immoral (T 3.1.1.11, 2.3.3.1–10 [SBN 459–60, 413–18]; cf. 3.1.1.16 [SBN 462–63]; EPM App.1.2 [SBN 285–86]).

Hume also rejects the claim that moral distinctions can be grounded in, or recognized by, or "conformable" to reason, even apart from any question of their motivating power.[4] As he has indicated in Book 1, reason is "the discovery of truth or falshood," which consists in discovering the "agreement or disagreement" of our ideas "either to the *real* relations of ideas, or to *real* existence and matter of fact." If moral distinctions could be recognized through reason, or by "thought and understanding," virtue and vice would consist in a relation that is evident to us either by intuition as a relation of ideas or as a matter of fact discovered by observation (T 3.1.1.9, 3.1.1.18 [SBN 458, 463]). However, he then examines and rejects both versions of moral rationalism.[5]

First, Hume considers the possibility that virtue and vice can be discovered by examining the relations among our ideas, and that morality is "susceptible of demonstration," and may even be brought "to an equal certainty with geometry or algebra." Against this view, he argues that we cannot locate moral distinctions or relations among the four relations of resemblance, contrariety, degrees in quality, or proportions in quantity, and that no one has offered a satisfactory account of any separate moral relations discerned through the comparison of ideas. Finally, Hume observes that, while we regard various types of relations as morally culpable when they arise from a human action, we do not blame nonhuman behaviors that produce the same relations in nature. His examples here are parricide and incest, which we do not condemn as immoral

---

4. By contrast, Snare has argued that Hume systematically confuses the question of moral evaluation with the question of moral motivation: see *Morals, Motivation and Convention*, 11–33. For other views of Hume's consideration of this distinction, see Capaldi, *Hume's Place in Moral Philosophy*, 286–308, and Penelhum, *David Hume*, 138–42.

5. For discussions of Hume's arguments that moral distinctions cannot be derived from reason, see Tweyman, *Reason and Conduct*; Harrison, *Hume's Moral Epistemology*, 47–67; Mackie, *Hume's Moral Theory*, 55–61; Bricke, *Mind and Morality*, 86–105; and Garrett, *Cognition and Commitment*, 191–93.

or vicious when they occur among animals or plants (T 3.1.1.18–25 [SBN 463–68]; cf. 3.1.1.4 [SBN 456–57]; EPM App.1.6–13 [SBN 287–91]).

Although Hume apparently regards this last argument as decisive, it does not appear to directly refute the doctrine that morality consists in relations of ideas, since incest and parricide, according to his own analysis, are not relations of ideas, or philosophical relations at all. Instead, these are actions that include in their definition a certain type of causal relation between the agent and an object. Indeed, Hume himself complains here of the tendency among moral philosophers to use the word "relation" without any clear meaning. Thus, although they apparently intend to claim that the moral quality of a state of affairs is a relation that is discovered through reason, these philosophers actually hold a more modest version of rationalism, asserting that an action arising from or bringing about a certain type of empirical relation can, as such, be subjected to moral evaluation through reason (T 3.1.1.19n69 [SBN 464n1]; EPM App.1.7–8 [SBN 288]).

Accordingly, Hume next considers the possibility that morality consists in a matter of fact we discover through observation. Here he initially argues that we do not observe any distinct quality properly called "vice," either in human actions or among the "passions, motives, volitions, and thoughts" we regard as the causes of human action. However, while "the vice entirely escapes you, as long as you consider the object," he maintains that "you never can find it, till you turn your reflection into your own breast, and find a sentiment of disapprobation, which arises in you, towards this action." This sentiment, he concedes, is a matter of fact: but this fact is "the object of feeling, not of reason," since by characterizing an action as immoral you mean "that from the constitution of your nature you have a feeling or sentiment of blame from the contemplation of it." We then describe the agent toward whom we feel these sentiments of approval or disapproval as virtuous or vicious; and finally, we identify virtue and vice as qualities of the agent. Hume thus argues that moral qualities are similar to aesthetic qualities and to secondary qualities such as "sounds, colours, heat and cold, which, according to modern philosophy, are not qualities in objects, but perceptions in the mind" (T 3.1.1.26–27, 3.2.8.8n80 [SBN 468–70, 547n1]).

Hume concludes his rejection of any rationalist derivation of morality in the *Treatise* with a paragraph that is generally regarded as a classic statement of the distinction between statements of fact and statements of value:

> In every system of morality, which I have hitherto met with, I have always remark'd, that the author proceeds for some time in the ordinary way of reasoning, and establishes the being of a God, or makes observations concerning human affairs; when of a sudden I am surpriz'd

to find, that instead of the usual copulations of propositions, *is,* and *is not,* I meet with no proposition that is not connected with an *ought,* or an *ought not.* This change is imperceptible; but is, however, of the last consequence. For as this *ought,* or *ought not,* expresses some new relation or affirmation, 'tis necessary that it shou'd be observ'd and explain'd; and at the same time that a reason shou'd be given, for what seems altogether inconceivable, how this new relation can be a deduction from others, which are entirely different from it. But as authors do not commonly use this precaution, I shall presume to recommend it to the reader; and am perswaded, that this small attention wou'd subvert all the vulgar systems of morality, and let us see, that the distinction of vice and virtue is not founded merely on the relations of objects, nor is perceiv'd by reason. (T 3.1.1.27 [SBN 469–70])

While the is-ought paragraph has received extensive attention in recent moral philosophy as well as among Hume scholars, it has been difficult to determine exactly what Hume is arguing here.[6] All of his commentators agree that Hume is criticizing any existing moral theory that moves directly to moral exhortation from statements of theological or anthropological fact without attempting to account for the transition. Beyond this, however, they have offered several different interpretations of his argument. First, according to the prevailing view in the first half of the twentieth century, Hume is rejecting any transition from "is" to "ought" statements as unjustified, and is thus establishing an absolute distinction between statements of fact and statements of moral value.[7] More recently, however, a number of studies have argued that Hume is criticizing as unsatisfactory all preceding attempts to derive ethical from factual statements, but is not explicitly claiming that such a derivation can never be justified.[8] Finally, Capaldi has argued that Hume is rejecting the traditional conception of a moral "ought" altogether, an interpretation that he also attributes to Thomas Reid and T. H. Green.[9]

6. Many contributions to this discussion are included in Chappell's collection of critical essays, *Hume,* and in Hudson's *Is-Ought Question.* For additional surveys of this debate, see Moonan, "Hume on Is and Ought," 83–98; Yalden-Thomson, "Hume's View of 'Is-Ought,'" 89–93; Capaldi, *Hume's Place in Moral Philosophy* 80–94; and Martin, "Explaining the Nature of Morality," 277–89.

7. For a discussion of the history of this interpretation, see MacIntyre, "Hume on 'Is' and 'Ought,'" 35–50. For more recent defenses of this interpretation, see Flew, "On the Interpretation of Hume," 278–86; Hudson, "Hume on *Is* and *Ought,*" 295–307; and Harrison, *Hume's Moral Epistemology,* 69–70.

8. See MacIntyre, "Hume on 'Is' and 'Ought,'" 240–64; Hunter, "Hume on *Is* and *Ought,*" 59–63, and "A Reply to Professor Flew," 70–72; Yalden-Thomson, "Hume's View of 'Is-ought,'" 90–93; Mackie, *Hume's Moral Theory,* 61–63; Martin, "Explaining the Nature of Morality," 277–89; and Garrett, *Cognition and Commitment,* 189 and 200–201.

9. See Capaldi, "Hume's Rejection," 126–37, and *Hume's Place in Moral Philosophy,* 55–80 and 116–19, where he further argues that Hume reduces moral obligation to natural obligation.

We can at least say that in the is-ought paragraph Hume is criticizing one approach to deriving statements of moral obligation from factual statements, without offering any alternative or indicating whether he intends to provide such an alternative. Unfortunately, he does not clarify or even restate this argument in his later writings. Given these difficulties, I would argue that we must attempt to interpret the is-ought paragraph by considering its context within Hume's moral philosophy as a whole, rather than regarding it as a key for the interpretation of his moral theory.

In accordance with this principle, many recent discussions of the "is-ought" passage have regarded Hume's moral theory as an attempt to formulate a new and legitimate derivation of moral obligation from the appropriate type of factual statement, such as statements about the interest of society or the happiness of others,[10] or statements about our own sentiments of approval and disapproval.[11] In this chapter I will show that, although he never explicitly reaffirms the argument in the is-ought paragraph, Hume subsequently argues that statements concerning moral evaluation and obligation are derived from certain types of factual statements. Specifically, he derives them from statements about human sentiments concerning various qualities of human character, when considered from a certain perspective.

In contrast to the rationalist view that moral distinctions are discovered through reason, Hume maintains that moral distinctions arise from our passions or sentiments. First, as we have seen, moral precepts evidently "produce or prevent actions," and must therefore arise from the passions. Second, the only matter of fact that can provide the basis for a moral judgment is "a feeling or sentiment" of blame or approval, which arises in us from the contemplation of certain actions and characters. Hume also argues, apparently by a disjunctive syllogism, that if moral distinctions are not discovered through reason, they must be determined by "some impression or sentiment." He concludes that morality is "more properly felt than judg'd of," since it is discerned by the passions rather than cognition (T 3.1.1.6, 3.1.1.26, 3.1.2.1 [SBN 457, 468–69, 470]).

Hume initially introduces the term "sentiment" here as an alternative for "impression," and thus includes the moral sentiments of approval and disapproval more precisely among the "passions, desires, and emotions" he has already identified as "impressions of reflection" (T 3.1.2.1, 1.1.2.1; cf. 2.1.1.2 [SBN 470, 7–8; cf. 275–76]). Hume also offers us several further indications that moral sentiments are included among the passions.[12] First, moral sentiments

---

10. See MacIntyre, "Hume on 'Is' and 'Ought,'" 240–64.

11. See Hunter, "Hume on *Is* and *Ought*," 59–63, and "A Reply to Professor Flew," 70–72; Martin, "Explaining the Nature of Morality," 277–89; and Garrett, *Cognition and Commitment,* 189, 200–201.

12. On Hume's account of the moral sentiments, see Árdal, *Passion and Value,* 109–211; Hearn, "General Rules and Moral Sentiments," 57–72; Boatright, "Hume's Account of Moral Sentiment," 79–90; Loeb,

arise "in a great measure from our ideas," specifically from our ideas of various qualities belonging to human character when these are considered from a particular perspective, as we will see. Next, moral sentiments are modifications of pleasure or pain, since "the impression arising from virtue" is "agreeable," while "that proceeding from vice" is "uneasy." Third, the sentiments of moral praise or blame are each distinctive sensations we can recognize and identify through introspection, and which we may describe by enumerating their causes, although these sensations cannot be defined. That is, a moral perception is "a pleasure or uneasiness of a particular kind," since "to have the sense of virtue, is nothing but to *feel* a satisfaction of a particular kind from the contemplation of a character." We may also characterize our moral sensations as calm passions, since a moral sentiment "is commonly so soft and gentle, that we are apt to confound it with an idea" (T 1.1.2.1, 3.1.2.1–3; cf. 3.3.1.18 [SBN 7–8, 470–71; cf. 583–84]). Finally, Hume argues that the moral sentiments, like the other passions, are implanted in the human mind by the "primary constitution of nature" (T 2.1.7.5; cf. 2.1.5.6, 3.1.2.8 [SBN 296; cf. 287, 474]).

In the subtitle of the relevant section of the *Treatise,* Hume further indicates that moral distinctions are "deriv'd from a moral sense" (T 3.1.2.1 [SBN 470]). He occasionally refers to a "sense of morals," or "moral sense," in the main text of the *Treatise,* and describes this faculty as "a principle inherent in the soul," and as a "moral taste" (T 3.1.1.10, 3.3.1.25, 3.3.6.3, 3.3.1.15 [SBN 458, 588, 619, 581]). In the final section of Book 3, he endorses the effort by other moral philosophers to "resolve the sense of morals into original instincts of the human mind." He then offers his own argument, that the moral sense arises from an "extensive sympathy with mankind," as a further contribution to this project (T 3.3.6.3; cf. 2.1.7.2–6 [SBN 619; cf. 295–96]).

In the second *Enquiry,* Hume initially proposes what appears to be the more conciliatory opinion that "*reason* and *sentiment* concur in almost all moral determinations and conclusions." However, he also indicates that the ultimate source of these distinctions might turn out to be an "internal sense or feeling, which nature has made universal in the whole species" (EPM 1.9 [SBN 172–73]). He returns to this discussion in Appendix 1, "Concerning Moral Sentiment." Here he argues, consistently with the *Treatise,* that reason is in itself "no motive to action," but can only direct the impulses arising from "appetite or inclination" by directing us to the means by which we may attempt to attain happiness and avoid misery. Instead, the "first spring or impulse to desire and volition" is the sentiment or "taste" which distinguishes pain from pleasure, and which thereby

"Hume's Moral Sentiments," 395–403; Mackie, *Hume's Moral Theory,* 64–75; Norton, *David Hume,* 94–151; Capaldi, *Hume's Place in Moral Philosophy,* 153–267; Brand, *Hume's Theory of Moral Judgment,* 91–98; Stewart, *Opinion and Reform,* 109–51; Russell, *Freedom and Moral Sentiment,* 87–94; and Bricke, *Mind and Morality,* 106–68.

"constitutes happiness or misery" (EPM App.1.1, App.1.21 [SBN 285, 294]). That is, he argues in accordance with his analysis in the *Treatise* that reason is unable to discover moral properties or to provide any motive for moral action.

Hume has occasionally been criticized for presenting moral sentiments as another set of simple, irreducible, and indefinable "feelings," which like the other passions can be identified only through introspection.[13] However, as in his general discussion of the passions, Hume indicates that we can describe the moral sentiments as impressions of reflection, which arise within us in response to certain types of ideas. More specifically, the sentiments of blame and approval are painful or pleasurable responses to the idea of a certain type of intentional object, when this object is considered from a certain perspective in relation to the self. In order to examine the moral sentiments, we must therefore begin by considering our ideas, first of these objects, and then of the situation from which we regard these objects with moral approval or disapproval.

In considering the possible objects of the moral sentiments, Hume finds that although we might seem to blame or praise individual actions, the ultimate objects of the moral sentiments are dispositions of human character. We attribute these to individual human beings by regarding the actions of individuals as signs: first of immediate motives, and then of enduring qualities of character within the agent. Thus, in praising actions, we are really praising "the motives that produc'd them," without attributing moral worth to the action itself. These motives, when they are regarded as "principles in the mind and temper," then become "the ultimate object of our praise and approbation." In other words, we consider human actions to be "virtuous or vicious" only when these actions arise from "durable principles of the mind, which extend over the whole conduct, and enter into the personal character." On the other hand, those actions which do not reflect enduring qualities of the agent "are never consider'd in morality" (T 3.2.1.2, 3.3.1.4 [SBN 477, 575]). Here Hume is confirming his earlier argument that moral judgment presupposes belief in the necessity of human action, since a moral evaluation is always directed toward "some cause in the characters and disposition of the person, who perform'd them," regarded as a "durable or constant" principle of action in the agent.[14] By contrast, since the "hypothesis of liberty" denies that human actions have any connection to our motives or qualities of character, this doctrine absolves us from all moral responsibility, even for what seem to be the most heinous crimes. Indeed, the intensity of our moral sentiments tends to vary according to our judgment concerning the degree of connection between an action and a principle of character within the individual. For example, we do not blame agents for harmful

13. See, for example, Foot, "Hume on Moral Judgement," 67–76.
14. See Norton, *David Hume*, 108–20 and 142–45; McIntyre, "Character," 193–206; Baier, *Progress of Sentiments*, 134 and 174–97; and Russell, *Freedom and Moral Sentiment*, 95–136.

actions performed in ignorance, and we blame them more for actions arising from "thought and deliberation" than for those committed "hastily and unpremeditately" (T 2.3.2.6–7 [SBN 410–12]).[15] The intentional objects of the moral sentiments are therefore the enduring motives or qualities of character in human beings that we call "virtues" and "vices" (T 3.2.1.1–7 [SBN 477–79]). In the *Enquiry* Hume considers "that complication of mental qualities" which we call "PERSONAL MERIT," by examining the dispositions he had classified as virtues in the *Treatise*. However, he only gradually applies the term "virtue" to these qualities in the *Enquiry;* and he considers the concept of virtue itself only in the fourth Appendix (EPM 1.10; cf. 8.1n50, App.4.1–22 [SBN 173; cf. 261n1, 312–23]).

As we have seen, Hume argues that the passions are "diversify'd" by our assessment of the pleasure or pain we expect to receive from an object, and of our "situation" in relation to an object of desire or aversion. For example, the object may be more or less attainable or avoidable, or it may be associated either with the self or another person (T 3.3.1.2 [SBN 574]). Our moral sentiments also follow from a judgment concerning the "situation" of a given quality of character in relation to the self. However, while the other passions arise within us in response to our ideas of objects as possible sources of pleasure or pain to ourselves, the sentiments of praise and blame arise within us "when a character is consider'd in general, without reference to our particular interest" (T 3.1.2.4 [SBN 472]). That is, we feel the moral sentiments of approval or blame when we consider the character of an agent by adopting a general point of view, on behalf of other possible subjects, toward the qualities of character in this agent. This perspective is the distinctive "situation" of the self, in relation to an intentional object, which gives rise to the moral sentiments, and distinguishes these sentiments from the other modifications of pleasure and pain in Hume's system of the passions. We thus find that everything in human action that gives us uneasiness upon a "general survey" is called vice, while "whatever produces satisfaction, in the same manner" is called virtue (T 3.2.2.24 [SBN 499]).

Next, Hume attempts to discover the origin of the moral sentiments, or to determine "Why any action or sentiment upon the general view or survey, gives a certain satisfaction or uneasiness" (T 3.1.2.11 [SBN 475]).

In Book 3 of the *Treatise* Hume argues that our moral sentiments do not arise simply in themselves, but from our sympathy with the pleasure or pain of others.[16] As we have seen, he describes sympathy in Book 2 as the tendency

---

15. See Johnson, "Hume's Theory of Moral Responsibility," 3–18.

16. Hume's account of the role of sympathy in our moral sentiments is often overlooked by those who confine their attention to the first two sections of Book 3 of the *Treatise* and do not recognize the reaffirmation of sympathy in the second *Enquiry*. See Stevenson, *Ethics and Language,* 273–76, and Harrison, *Hume's Moral Epistemology,* 104–5. For a more complete view of sympathy in the *Treatise,* see Árdal, *Passion and Value,*

of a human or animal to "receive" the emotions of others, upon observing the characteristic expressions of this emotion in other members of its species (T 2.1.11.2 [SBN 316]). He now describes moral approval and disapproval as distinctive feelings of pleasure or uneasiness that arise in us when we consider the effects of human actions on others, through "a sympathy with those, who have any commerce with the person we consider" (T 3.3.1.18 [SBN 583]). The operation of sympathy is enhanced by our ability to consider by "reflection," or probable reasoning, the effects of human actions upon remote or unknown individuals. Our sympathy is also broadened by our ability to imagine the usual effects of a disposition on others, even when circumstances prevent the agent from acting upon this disposition, since we agree that "virtue in rags is still virtue," and we continue to esteem a virtuous person who is trapped in "a dungeon or desart" (T 3.3.1.19 [SBN 584–85]).[17]

According to Hume, sympathy establishes the perspective, or the situation, from which we take the "general survey" of human character traits, and recognize their tendency to benefit or harm others. In this sense, he even argues that sympathy "produces our sentiment of morals" (T 3.3.1.10; cf. 3.2.2.24 [SBN 577–78; cf. 499]). In the final section of Book 3 he further maintains that "sympathy is the chief source of moral distinctions." Indeed, he argues that while we might wish to include the "sense of morals" among the "original instincts of the human mind," the moral sentiments themselves actually arise from our propensity to sympathy, which is an even more basic disposition in human nature (T 3.3.6.1–3 [SBN 618–19]).[18]

Hume strictly distinguishes the operation of sympathy from the passion of universal benevolence, which he rejects as a possible source of moral sentiment. Indeed, in the *Treatise* he argues that human beings do not feel any such passion as universal benevolence, or a "love of mankind" considered "merely as such," apart from our consideration of "personal qualities, of services, or of relation to ourself." Moreover, a supposed passion of universal benevolence would be "too remote and too sublime to affect the generality of mankind," especially in opposition to our selfish desires or personal affections. On the contrary, the principles of morality are intended to counteract our limited generosity and would not be required if we were already motivated by a passion of universal benevolence. However, while he denies any passion of universal benevolence to human nature, Hume finds that human beings have an extensive capacity for sympathy, since

---

41–69; Capaldi, *Hume's Place in Moral Philosophy*, 195–241; Baier, *Progress of Sentiments*, chaps. 6–9; Brand, *Hume's Theory of Moral Judgment*, 70–136; and Bricke, *Mind and Morality*, 128–48.

17. For a discussion of the role of the imagination in our moral sentiments and judgments, see Brand, *Hume's Theory of Moral Judgment*, 134–36.

18. For a discussion of the role of sympathy in Hume's moral theory, see Herdt, *Religion and Faction*, 17–81.

there is no image of "happiness or misery," when encountered in our own species or in other animals, which "does not, in some measure, affect us, when brought near to us, and represented in lively colours" (T 3.2.1.11–12; cf. 3.2.7.1 [SBN 480–81; cf. 534]). He accordingly presents sympathy in the *Treatise* as the only possible source for that "extensive concern for society" which is expressed in our moral sentiments (T 3.3.1.11 [SBN 579]).

In the second *Enquiry* Hume apparently reverses this argument, by attributing a passion called "general benevolence" or "humanity" to human beings, and by presenting this as the source of our moral sentiments. However, as I have shown in Chapter 6, the passion of benevolence, as described in the *Enquiry*, arises from the mechanism of sympathy (cf. EPM 2.1–5, App.2.5n60 [SBN 176–78, 298n1]). Indeed, in his Index to the second *Enquiry*, Hume identifies sympathy, rather than benevolence, as "the great Source of moral Sentiment" (EPM Ind.292, 288).

Thus, according to Hume, our moral feelings, or our "sentiments of right and wrong," are distinctive passions that we feel toward qualities of character in human beings, when we consider the tendency of these qualities to give pleasure or pain to others (EPM 9.10 [SBN 276]; cf. T 3.2.2.23 [SBN 498]). These sentiments, like the indirect passions, are "new impressions," arising from our sympathy with the passions of those who might be affected by the character of the agent (cf. T 2.3.9.3 [SBN 439]). Finally, the moral sentiments are "calm" passions, or settled principles of action, which may exert a pervasive and enduring influence on our actions, at least in some individuals (T 2.1.1.3, 3.3.1.18 [SBN 276, 583–84]).[19]

In the next two sections I will consider Hume's account of the "artificial" and "natural" virtues, and his derivation of our moral approval of these dispositions. According to Hume, we approve of the artificial virtues because they support a system that tends to promote "the good of mankind," and more specifically because we receive "a lively idea" of the pleasure that others receive from actions in accordance with this system. This idea "affects us by sympathy," and is thus converted into an impression of pleasure (T 3.3.1.14 [SBN 580]). By contrast, we approve of the natural virtues because they contribute directly to the happiness of individuals: either of the agents themselves, who may receive pleasure from qualities in their own character, or of other persons, who may receive pleasure from qualities of character in other agents. Indeed, we may even sympathize with the happiness of many individuals, as the "happiness of mankind," or the "interest" or "good" of society (T 3.3.1.27, 3.3.1.9, 3.3.1.11 [SBN 589–90, 577, 579]). Similarly, in the *Enquiry* he argues that what he calls

---

19. For a further examination of Hume's view of moral motivation as it is developed in his subsequent discussion, see Brown, "From Spectator to Agent," 19–35; and Radcliffe, "Motivating Sentiments," 37–58.

the "usefulness" of the different virtues is "only a tendency to a certain end," which is in this case the "happiness of society" or the "happiness of mankind," which we appreciate through sympathy (EPM 5.17, App.1.3 [SBN 219, 286]).[20]

Several important questions have been left open in Hume's discussion of the moral sentiments so far. One of these is our experience of the variability of sympathy. In his account of the artificial virtues, Hume argues that benevolence is confined to our close associates by the "limited generosity" of human nature. However, he then suggests that we may develop a concern, through sympathy, for others beyond our immediate acquaintance (T 3.2.1.12–19, 3.2.2.23–24 [SBN 481–89, 498–500]). On the other hand, in his account of the natural virtues he suggests that even the operation of sympathy is limited initially to our own intimate circle, and that our sentiments of blame or praise first arise in response to their interests (T 3.3.1.13–16 [SBN 580–82]). This raises the problem of accounting for our ability to establish a general point of view, by which these sentiments on behalf of our intimates may be elevated into moral sentiments. Second, Hume indicates that our ideas of the effects of various character traits arise partly from the imagination and probable reasoning. We may thus consider the extent to which the imagination and reasoning are involved in moral approval and disapproval (T 3.3.1.15–21, 3.3.1.27 [SBN 581–85, 589–90]). Finally, even though he argues that moral distinctions arise from sentiments, Hume introduces his discussion of moral theory with the problem of accounting for moral "judgments." However, he does not immediately indicate whether these are different from moral sentiments and if so, how moral sentiments and moral judgments are related to each other (T 3.1.1.2 [SBN 456]). We will return to these questions, which all pertain to Hume's view of the role of reason in our moral distinctions, after we have considered his account of the artificial and natural virtues.

ARTIFICIAL VIRTUES

Hume organizes his classification of the virtues in the *Treatise* by considering whether, and in what sense, we may regard the sentiments of morality as "natural." Here he considers three senses of the term "natural," on the basis of three possible opposites of the term: the miraculous, the "rare and unusual," and the artificial. First, the moral sentiments are "natural" as opposed to miraculous, since they apparently arise without supernatural intervention. They are also "natural" in the second sense, since they are found among human beings in

20. On Hume's use of the terms "usefulness" and "utility," and his relation to the later utilitarian tradition, see Glossop, "Is Hume a 'Classical Utilitarian'?" 1–16; Long, "'Utility' and the 'Utility Principle,'" 12–39; and Darwall, "Invention of Utilitarianism," 58–82. See also Whelan, *Order and Artifice*, 211–18.

236 · *David Hume: Reason in History*

different historical and cultural contexts. In the third sense, however, we might regard human actions as "artificial," as opposed to "other principles of nature," since they are "perform'd with a certain design and intention." However, although all voluntary actions may be described as "artificial" in this sense, Hume distinguishes between those qualities of character that we approve naturally, and those which arise and become the objects of moral evaluation only as a result of conventions within the context of a social order. In light of this distinction, he argues that "our sense of some virtues is artificial, and that of others natural." However, he rejects any simple characterization of virtue as "natural" and vice as "unnatural," in any of his three senses (T 3.1.2.7–10 [SBN 473–75]; cf. EPM App.3.9 [SBN 307]).[21]

In the *Treatise* Hume identifies the "artificial virtues" as including the virtues of "justice" or respect for property rights, fidelity to promises, and allegiance to government. He argues that these virtues cannot be accounted for by any of the natural motives for moral conduct suggested by his predecessors, such as self-interest, or personal affection and benevolence, or a general love for humanity. On the contrary, "the sense of justice and injustice" arises in us "artificially, tho' necessarily from education, and human conventions." Hume traces the genealogy of these virtues by pursuing two questions: first, the origin of the rules that govern these practices; and second, the origin of their moral obligation (T 3.2.1.10–19 [SBN 480–84]). Hume applies the word "justice" here specifically to the virtue of respect for property (cf. T 3.2.1.12–17, 3.2.3.28 [SBN 481–83, 501]; EPM 3.22–23 [SBN 192–93]). However, for the sake of clarity I will refer to the rules of property and promises collectively as the "rules of justice" or "principles of justice."

In considering the origin of the rules governing property and promises, Hume observes that although human beings, compared to other animals, are relatively weak and unable to provide for ourselves individually, we have developed society to overcome many of our individual deficiencies by cooperation and specialization (T 3.2.2.1–3 [SBN 485]). The first impulse in human beings toward social living arises from the "natural appetite betwixt the sexes," which serves to establish a bond between individuals "till a new tye takes place in their concern for their common offspring." We learn the benefits of social existence from family life, which shows to children "the advantages, which they may reap from society" and prepares them for a larger social life "by rubbing off those rough corners and untoward affections, which prevent their coalition." Finally, the benefits of society are reinforced by the pleasure we derive from "company and conversation" (T 3.2.2.4, 3.2.2.9 [SBN 486, 489]). Since human beings

21. In a footnote Hume considers two further senses of "natural": as opposed to "civil," in describing human life apart from participation in a political order, and as opposed to "moral," in describing the domain of natural philosophy in contrast to the realm of human life (T 3.1.2.9 n70 [SBN 475n1]).

are already drawn together by the bonds of affection between family members, Hume maintains that in their "very first state and situation" human beings "may justly be esteem'd social," and that the notion of a human "state of nature" apart from society, is "a mere philosophical fiction" (T 3.2.2.14 [SBN 493]; cf. 3.2.7.1 [SBN 534]; EPM 3.15–16 [SBN 189–90]).

While these impulses toward social life are natural and original to the human species, Hume finds that other aspects of our "natural temper," combined with certain aspects of our "outward circumstances," are a constant threat to social existence. First, our passions lead us to prefer not only our own interests but also the interests of our family and friends to the interests of strangers: a preference which appears in our "natural uncultivated ideas of morality." Second, our material circumstances are characterized by the "instability," or easy transfer, of external goods, and by their scarcity compared to our needs and desires. Accordingly, the "*selfishness* and *limited generosity*" of human beings, combined with the instability and scarcity of external goods, are pervasive threats to human social existence that cannot be effectively opposed by any of the supposedly natural motives for morality (T 3.2.2.5–8, 3.2.2.16 [SBN 486–89, 494]; cf. EPM 3.1–14 [SBN 183–89]).

The institution of property arises, both in the family and within the early history of the human species, as we come to recognize both the advantages of society and the threats to social existence arising from our nature and circumstances (T 3.2.2.14 [SBN 493]). The institution of property is originally developed as a "convention" in a community of human beings, by which we "bestow stability" upon the possession of external goods, ensuring for everyone "the peaceable enjoyment of what he may acquire by his fortune and industry" (T 3.2.2.9 [SBN 489]). Hume argues that a convention in this sense is not a promise, but an explicit or even implicit agreement between individuals "to regulate their conduct by certain rules" out of "a general sense of common interest." For example, "two men, who pull the oars of a boat, do it by an agreement or convention, tho' they have never given promises to each other." Similarly, the convention of property also "arises gradually, and acquires force by a slow progression, and by our repeated experience of the inconveniences of transgressing it" (T 3.2.2.10 [SBN 490]).

Hume describes both the institution of property and the disposition to respect property rights as "artificial," since they arise from a convention. However, the institution of property is "natural" in another sense. That is, since "mankind is an inventive species," any human invention which is both common and necessary may be regarded as "natural" to the species, as properly as actions arising "from original principles, without the intervention of thought or reflection" (T 3.2.1.19 [SBN 484]). In addition, while the principles of justice are developed by the "judgment and understanding" to remedy what is "irregular and incommodious in the affections," the activity of the understanding is itself motivated by the passions of self-interest and private affection. We may thus conclude that the rules of justice are "the real offspring of those passions, and are only a more artful and more refin'd way of satisfying them" (T 3.2.2.9, 3.2.6.1 [SBN 489, 526]).[22] Hume even adopts the terminology of the natural law tradition by observing that we may refer to the artifices governing property and promises, when considered as general principles apart from any specification through civil laws, as "laws of nature," since they are "common to," and even "inseparable from," the human species (T 3.2.1.19 [SBN 484]: cf. EPM App.3.6 [SBN 305]).[23]

Hume argues that our initial motivation to obey the rules of justice is the recognition of our own self-interest. Thus, although "single acts of justice may be contrary, either to public or private interest," we recognize that "the whole plan or scheme is highly conducive, or indeed absolutely requisite, both to the support of society, and the well-being of every individual." As a result, we may expect that "every individual person must find himself a gainer, on ballancing the account." This gives each of us a "natural" or "interested" obligation to obey the rules of justice (T 3.2.2.22–23 [SBN 497–98]; EPM 9.14 [SBN 278]; cf. T 3.3.1.12 [SBN 579–80]).[24] On the other hand, the imaginations and passions of human beings tend to be more powerfully affected by the ideas of nearby than of distant objects. Accordingly, once we enter into civil society, our natural obligation to obey the rules of justice is reinforced by the power of government to punish us for disobeying these rules, as we will see in Chapter 9 (T 3.2.7.1–4, 3.2.8.4–8 [SBN 534–36, 543–44]). However, we may still ask whether actions that support the system of justice will always be more conducive to our happiness than actions arising directly from our self-interest, apart from the additional motive provided by the threat of punishment. Indeed, Hume concedes that it might be impossible to convince a sensible knave that what we might secure by a secret crime will always be outweighed by our interest in justice. Instead, Hume can only suggest that we may include the pleasure of "a satisfactory review of our own conduct," and a secure enjoyment of the "trust and

---

22. For Hume's account of artifices and the artificial virtues, see Hayek, "Legal and Political Philosophy," 335–60; Cherry, "Nature, Artifice and Moral Approbation," 265–82; Cottle, "Justice as Artificial Virtue," 457–66; Ponko, "Artificial Virtue," 46–58; and Baier, "Hume's Account of Social Artifice," 757–78. See also Mackie, *Hume's Moral Theory*, 76–129; Whelan, *Order and Artifice*, 189–293; Snare, *Morals, Motivation and Convention*, 176–309; and Bricke, *Mind and Morality*, 169–232.

23. For discussions of Hume's relation to the natural law tradition in medieval and early modern philosophy, see Forbes, *Hume's Philosophical Politics*, 3–58; Stewart, *Opinion and Reform*, 13–108; Westerman, "Hume and the Natural Lawyers," 83–104; Haakonssen, *Natural Law and Moral Philosophy;* and Herdt, *Religion and Faction*, 17–81.

24. For a discussion of Hume's account of natural obligation as part of an implicit account of prudential rationality in his writings, see Magri, "Natural Obligation," 231–53.

confidence" of others, among the natural motives for justice, especially since the enjoyment of conversation and society are among the highest pleasures of human life (EPM 9.22–25 [SBN 282–84]; cf. T 3.3.6.6 [SBN 620]).[25]

After considering our "interested" obligation to obey the rules of justice, Hume turns to our idea of the moral obligation attending this obedience. Here he observes that the benefits of a system of justice might be directly and immediately obvious in a small society, whose members are all directly acquainted with each other. However, in a larger society, where most people are strangers to each other, acts of justice can affect us only through sympathy, which gives us "a pleasure from the view of such actions as tend to the peace of society, and an uneasiness from such as are contrary to it" (T 3.2.6.11 [SBN 533]). That is, our sentiments of moral approval toward the artificial virtues arise from our recognition of, and sympathy with, the benefits that others receive from a disposition to obey the rules of justice. It is this regard for the "public interest," arising from sympathy, which produces our "*moral* approbation" of the artificial virtues (T 3.2.2.23–24; cf. 3.3.6.1 [SBN 498–500; cf. 618]).[26] However, although the virtue of conforming to the rules of justice can only arise with the development of these rules, and is "artificial" in this sense, our moral approbation of any disposition to obey them, and our sense of their moral obligation, "follows *naturally,* and of itself" from our sympathy with the interest of others, and may in this sense be described as "natural" (T 3.2.6.11 [SBN 533]).[27]

This natural sense of the morality attending obedience to the rules of justice, arising from sympathy, may also be reinforced by the "artifice of politicians," and by "private education and instruction," both of which "assist nature" in producing the moral sentiments (T 3.2.2.25–26 [SBN 500–501]). In Book 1 Hume views education as the leading source of human opinions, but also finds that its teachings are often inconsistent and even "contrary to reason," and are thus regarded with suspicion by philosophers (T 1.3.9.16–19 [SBN 115–17]). However, he now offers a more positive account of moral education, especially in the family, although he also calls attention in his essays to the influence of "wise laws and institutions" in promoting the moral development

25. See Postema, "Hume's Reply to the Sensible Knave," 23–40; Gauthier, "Artificial Virtues and the Sensible Knave," 401–27; and Baier, "Artificial Virtues," 429–39.

26. Taylor and Gill both argue that in tracing the development of moral motives as arising from non-moral motives through the operation of sympathy, Hume is presenting a progressive view of morality and human nature, as opposed to the static view among the earlier British moralists of the origin of morality in human nature. See Taylor, "Justice and the Foundations of Social Morality," 5–30, and Gill, "Hume's Progressive View of Human Nature," 87–108.

27. On Hume's view of obligation, see Haakonssen, "Hume's Obligations," 7–17; Pitson, "Hume on Promises and their Obligation," 176–90; Norton, "Hume, Human Nature, and the Foundations of Morality," 168–71; Darwall, "Motive and Obligation in Hume's Ethics," 415–48; and Brown, "From Spectator to Agent," 19–35.

and "virtuous education of youth" (T 3.2.2.26 [SBN 500–501]; E PG.55; cf. E RA.270–75). This interest in moral education is also apparent in Hume's presentation of his own ethical theory as a contribution to the task of "practical morality," which is intended for a more general audience (T 3.3.6.6 [SBN 621]).

On the other hand, as we will see in Chapters 9 and 12, Hume maintains and recommends some suspicion toward the influence of politicians and religious leaders in moral education. He notes that public figures in both domains often tend to promote principles of action in others that serve their own purposes, and that systems of exhortation arising from political interest or religious enthusiasm often violate and even distort the natural sentiments of morality. Since human beings require a process of socialization to develop and transmit the principles of justice, Hume argues that system of the artificial virtues arises "artificially, tho' necessarily from education, and human conventions" (T 3.2.1.17 [SBN 483]). However, he rejects the view that our ability to recognize moral distinctions could have been created by the "artifice of politicians," if we did not already have a natural disposition to recognize moral distinctions (T 3.2.2.25 [SBN 500]).

As we have seen, Hume begins his examination of the rules of justice by considering the rule of the stability of possession, which is the basic principle of property and the first "law of nature." He turns next to the rules by which particular objects are assigned to specific individuals in a given social order. Here he argues that while the principles governing the distribution of property might indeed emerge through a sympathy with the public interest, particular property laws are "principally fix'd by the imagination" according to regular patterns of association among our ideas (T 3.2.3.4n71 [SBN 504n1]). By examining common practice through history, we find that property is initially assigned by "present possession," or by the rule "that every one continue to enjoy what he is at present possess'd of." This rule arises from our association of the idea of an object with the idea of the person who physically controls it. Next, we also recognize a right of property either by "first possession" or "occupation," or by "long possession" or "prescription," on the basis of a repeated association between our idea of an object and our idea of the person who has physically controlled it. Finally, we also tend to recognize a right to property on the basis of various causal relations, such as the right of "accession," by which we are entitled to the "fruits of our garden" or the "offspring of our cattle," and the right of "succession," since "we are naturally directed to consider the son after the parent's decease, and ascribe to him a title to his father's possessions" (T 3.2.3.4–11 [SBN 503–13]; cf. EPM 3.22–35 [SBN 192–98]).

Hume provides a similar account of the laws applying the general principle of the transfer of property by consent, which he identifies as the second "law of nature" and the basic principle of commercial exchange. In the simplest cases, a transfer of property is effected by delivering the object into the physical control of the recipient. However, we often find that such a delivery is impracticable or even impossible, and that property, "when taken for something real, without any reference to morality, or the sentiments of the mind" is difficult to imagine, being "perfectly insensible, and even inconceivable." Accordingly, a transfer of property rights over an object is often effected by the "*symbolical* delivery" of a related object, which assists the imagination in forming an idea of the trans-action. For example, "giving the keys of a granary is understood to be the deliv-ery of the corn contain'd in it," while "the giving of stone and earth represents the delivery of a mannor" (T 3.2.4.2; cf. 3.2.6.3 [SBN 515; cf. 526–27]).

The third artificial virtue on Hume's list is the "performance of promises," which serves the "necessities and interests of society" by facilitating our exchange of goods and services. Since human beings are "naturally selfish, or endow'd only with a confined generosity," we find that we rarely perform benefits for strangers unless we can expect a reciprocal benefit. However, we also find that these "mutual performances" often cannot be "finish'd at the same instant," and in these cases we have little incentive to perform the first action unless we have an advance guarantee of the "mutual commerce of good offices" (T 3.2.5.8 [SBN 519–20]). This "interested" reciprocation of goods and services is secured by the invention of "a certain form of words," by which we may commit our-selves to performing an action in the future. By pronouncing this formula, the agent not only expresses his intention to perform the action, but also "subjects himself to the penalty of never being trusted again in case of failure," and is by this means "immediately bound by his interest to execute his engagements" (T 3.2.5.10 [SBN 522]). Hume argues that while the obligation of a promise might appear to arise from an action of the mind or will, it is actually derived from the public use of a specific form of words. The use of this formula is indeed "the principal part of the promise," and is regarded as binding even if the speaker secretly gives "a different direction to his intention" by withholding his assent privately when pronouncing the formula. Indeed, Hume notes that the obligatory force of a promise also requires the use of this formula in a context that is recognized as appropriate by the participants; since someone who uses the formula without understanding its meaning, or with clear signs that he is speaking "in jest only" and without any "serious intention of binding himself," is not usually considered to have placed himself under the indicated obligation (T 3.2.5.13; cf. 3.2.5.3 [SBN 523–24; cf. 516–17]).[28]

The rules of justice accordingly consist, not only in the general principles governing the distribution of property, the transfer of property, and the perform-ance of promises, but also in a network of supporting practices that originally

28. For studies comparing Hume's account of promises to other historical and recent views, see Árdal, "Promise, Intention and Obligation," 47–69; Baier, *Postures of the Mind,* 174–204; Snare, *Morals Motivation and Convention,* 266–76; Pitson, "Hume on Promises and their Obligation," 176–90; and Vitek, *Promising.*

arise as conventions through the association of ideas. These practices may then be instituted as the traditional rules or laws of a particular society, depending upon its stage of political development, and are enforced by the customary sanctions of the community or legal authority of the state. These rules may further prescribe the use of certain symbolic words or actions, which are initially suggested by the imagination, to exhibit publicly the assignment of these rights and obligations. Hume describes this use of symbolism as "a kind of superstitious practice in civil laws," resembling the *"Roman Catholic* superstitions in religion," in which ritual formulas, objects, and gestures are used to represent "the inconceivable mysteries of the *Christian* religion, and render them more present to the mind." A promise is thus a "mysterious and incomprehensible operation," similar to *"transubstantiation,* or *holy orders,"* in which the statement of "a certain form of words, along with a certain intention, changes entirely the nature of an external object, and even of a human creature." The main difference, according to Hume, is that while the rules of justice are "absolutely requisite to the well-being of mankind and existence of society," the rituals of Catholicism "have no public interest in view," and are on the contrary "frivolous, useless, and burdensome." Similarly, apart from their contribution to the public interest, "nothing can appear more whimsical, unnatural, and even superstitious, than all or most of the laws of justice and of property" (T 3.2.4.2, 3.2.5.14 [SBN 515–16, 524]; EPM 3.35–38 [SBN 197–99]).[29]

In addition to the rules of justice, Hume argues that modesty in female comportment is an artificial virtue. In other words, the "exterior modesty" required "in the expressions, and dress, and behaviour of the fair sex" is not given by nature, but is developed within society as an "artifice," to sustain the "union of male and female" that is necessary to secure provision and care for their children. Although family unity is generally sustained by natural affection, Hume notes that this cohesion would usually be threatened if either of the two adults were to doubt their own biological relation to the children. However, by a "trivial and anatomical observation," we find that it is "utterly impossible" for a woman to be mistaken in her children, but almost impossible for the man to be certain of his paternity. This discrepancy, according to Hume, accounts for all the differences of "education and duties" between the sexes. Thus, although he concedes that the temptation to infidelity is just as strong in women as in men, Hume argues that the interest of society in family life

---

29. Hume provoked considerable controversy as a result of using the word "artificial" in his moral theory. In a letter to Francis Hutcheson in 1739, regarding the draft of the third book of the *Treatise,* he responds to criticism by distinguishing "artificial" from "unnatural" (L 1.33). His description of certain aspects of morality as "artificial" was cited as an objection to his candidacy for the chair in moral philosophy at the University of Edinburgh (LG 18, 30–32). Accordingly, as belated cautions, he uses the word "artifice" in the second *Enquiry* only in a footnote to the third Appendix, and avoids the term in his related discussion in "Of the Original Contract" (EPM App.3.10n64 [SBN 307–308n2]; E OC.479–80).

requires greater restraint in the sexual activity of women. This restraint is most effectively secured by "the punishment of bad fame or reputation," arising from "surmizes, and conjectures, and proofs, that wou'd never be receiv'd in any court of judicature." The threat of such a condemnation produces in women "a preceding backwardness or dread" toward all forms of expression and behavior which might suggest a tendency toward infidelity. It is this "dread" which determines the principles of modest comportment. Finally, these principles are applied general rules to women even beyond their reproductive years, from childhood through old age. Hume adds that society also has an interest in restraining the sexual liberty of men, but in this case that the interest and moral obligation are both weaker, judging at least by "the practice and sentiments of all nations and ages" (T 3.2.12.1–9 [SBN 570–73]).

Hume provides several intriguing further discussions of marriage in his essays. In "Of Polygamy and Divorces" he considers a variety of marriage customs, through history and across cultures, as these reflect the needs of a society in a given place and time. He pronounces these to be "equally lawful, and equally conformable to the principles of nature; though they are not all equally convenient, or equally useful to society" (E PD.183). Then, comparing the practices of polygamy, temporary monogamy, and permanent monogamy, he finds that both polygamy and divorce tend to be harmful to men, women, and children, and that lifelong monogamy is generally the best, for all the members of a family and for society as a whole (E PD.181–90). In this essay, and also in "Of Love and Marriage," he describes a good marriage as an equal partnership in which the spouses are joined by a mutual love that is founded on friendship, prudence, and pleasure, reflecting his analysis of amorous love as combining sexual desire, an appreciation of beauty, and kindness or friendship (E PD.184, 188–89; E LM.557–62; T 2.2.11.1–6 [SBN 394–96]; OP 3.7.158).[30]

Hume even includes good manners among the artificial virtues, by noting that "we establish the *rules of good-breeding,* in order to prevent the opposition of men's pride, and render conversation agreeable and inoffensive." Good manners may thus be regarded as "a kind of lesser morality" for securing "the ease of company and conversation" (T 3.3.2.10 [SBN 597–98]; EPM 4.13 [SBN 209]). Many of the rules of "GOOD MANNERS or POLITENESS" arise directly from attempts to avoid conflicts in conversation, including the rules by which "a mutual deference is affected: Contempt of others disguised" and "attention

---

30. There has been considerable discussion since the 1970s over Hume's views of sexuality and gender roles, and whether his views may be regarded as progressive, from a modern feminist standpoint, relative to other authors of his day. For a series of works illustrating the range of opinion, see Burns, "The Humean Female," 415–24; Marcil-Lacoste, "Hume's Position Concerning Women," 425–40; Baier, "Good Men's Women," 1–19; and Levey, "Under Constraint," 213–26. For a collection of essays reflecting recent directions in feminist thought on Hume, see Jacobson, *Feminist Interpretations of David Hume.*

given to each in his turn," to ensure "an easy stream of conversation" without any vehemence, excessive interruption, "eagerness for victory," or "airs of superiority." However, many other rules of courtesy are "arbitrary and casual," although they generally follow some principle of association. For example, "A SPANIARD goes out of his own house before his guest, to signify that he leaves him master of all," while in many other countries "the landlord walks out last, as a common mark of deference and regard" (EPM 8.1–2 [SBN 261–62]; cf. E RP.126–34).

Thus, according to Hume, the artificial virtues such as respect for property, fidelity to promises, feminine modesty, and good manners are dispositions to obey a set of general rules established to regulate our interactions in society. These dispositions arise from our recognition of the benefits that we and others receive from the stability of property, the exchange of goods and services, the plausible assurance of paternity, and enjoyable conversation. In order to secure the benefits provided by these social systems, we accept these rules as "unchangeable by spite and favour, and by particular views of private or public interest." We also accept these rules as peculiarly inflexible and exact in their application, which further indicates that they are not the "immediate offspring of any natural motive or inclination" (T 3.2.6.9 [SBN 532]).[31] Finally, our moral approval of a disposition to obey these rules cannot arise either from self-interest or from the natural virtue of generosity, since any action conforming to the rules of justice might violate our own interests and even our inclinations of private benevolence. Instead, our moral approval of the artificial virtues arises from our sympathy with others, whom we expect to benefit from a general obedience to the rules of justice.

Hume's discussion of artifices and conventions has been regarded as perhaps the most original aspect of his moral and political philosophy, and also as an important theme in other areas of his thought.[32] I will therefore return to his account of conventions at the conclusion of this chapter.

NATURAL VIRTUES

In the preceding section we have considered Hume's account of the artificial virtues, or the dispositions of human beings to obey the rules of conduct

31. On Hume's account of general rules and standards in his moral philosophy, see Hearn, "General Rules and Moral Sentiments," 57–72; and Atkinson, "Hume on the Standard of Morals," 25–44; Norton, *David Hume*, 95, 127–33; Livingston, *Hume's Philosophy of Common Life*, 136–49 and 272–84; Whelan, *Order and Artifice*, 196–213; Snare, *Morals, Motivation and Convention*, 176–309; and Brand, *Hume's Theory of Moral Judgment*, 38–65 and 112–33.

32. See Hayek, "Legal and Political Philosophy," 335–60; and Baier, "Hume's Account of Social Artifice," 757–78.

belonging to a system that tends as a whole to benefit the individuals in a society. By contrast, Hume identifies those dispositions of human character that we regard with moral approval, but that are not specifically directed toward supporting any social institutions, as "natural virtues." As in the case of the artificial virtues, he argues that our moral approval of these dispositions arises from a sympathy with others, once we recognize the tendency of these "qualities and characters" to promote "the interest of society." However, while actions conforming to the rules of justice may individually be contrary to the "public good," even though the system as a whole is advantageous to society, we recognize that the happiness of others is directly promoted by "every single act" arising from a natural virtue. Since the actions arising from natural virtues tend to benefit particular individuals, these virtues have a more vivid influence on our imagination, and thus inspire warmer and livelier sentiments of approval than the artificial virtues (T 3.3.1.11–12 [SBN 579–80]).

Hume develops a systematic account and classification of the natural virtues by examining the various qualities of character that we generally regard with approval, either in domestic or in public life. The most obvious are those qualities, such as *"generosity* and *humanity,"* which tend to benefit others.[33] However, we also approve of those character traits that enable their possessors to pursue their own interests effectively: these qualities include "prudence, temperance, frugality, industry, assiduity, enterprize, dexterity." In his first set of natural virtues, Hume thus includes those qualities of character that are "useful," either to others, or to their possessor. We also approve of character traits that are "immediately agreeable" to others or to the self. Of these, the qualities that are agreeable to others include wit, ingenuity, and cheerfulness, while qualities that are agreeable to the self include courage and philosophical tranquillity (T 3.3.1.24 [SBN 587–88]; EPM 9.1–2 [SBN 268–69]).

Accordingly, Hume argues that our moral approval of the natural virtues is a sentiment of pleasure, arising from sympathy, toward those qualities of human character that we recognize as tending to promote the happiness, or the "interests and pleasures" of individual human beings (T 3.3.1.30 [SBN 591]). These include those qualities of character which tend to produce pleasure directly, and are therefore "immediately agreeable," and qualities which are "useful," or which tend to promote the "interest," or the long-term pleasure or happiness, of others or the self.[34]

33. In the second *Enquiry* Hume indicates that the artificial virtues may be included among the qualities that are useful to others, thereby producing a single system of the virtues (cf. EPM 1.11, 3.1 [SBN 175, 183]).

34. Hume's discussion of the principles of utility and agreeableness would thus provide the standards for practical judgment corresponding to the rules for probable reasoning, filling what Bricke regards as a serious deficiency in his moral philosophy; see *Mind and Morality,* 247–48.

Hume offers several vivid descriptions of the tendency of the natural virtues to promote happiness. First, we praise a benevolent or generous man for the "happiness and satisfaction" his actions diffuse over all the individuals associated with him, since he is "an easy friend, a gentle master, an agreeable husband, or an indulgent father" (T 3.3.3.9 [SBN 606]; cf. EPM 2.6 [SBN 178]). We also praise every character trait which "capacitates a man best for the world, and carries him farthest in any undertaking." These give to their possessor "the prospect of elevation, advancement, a figure in life, prosperous success, a steady command over fortune, and the execution of great or advantageous undertakings," all of which tend to promote the happiness of the agent (EPM 6.17, 6.3 [SBN 241, 234]). Third, we approve of qualities that are agreeable to the agent, such as a "due degree of pride," which makes us "sensible of our own merit, and gives us a confidence and assurance in all our projects and enterprizes." In other words, a proper pride or confidence tends to please others through sympathy, if we are careful to regulate the expression of our pride by the rules of good breeding (T 3.3.2.8–11 [SBN 596–99]). Finally, wit and sociability tend to produce "a lively joy and satisfaction" in almost all observers, and are thus agreeable to others (EPM 8.3, 9.18 [SBN 262, 280]). Hume offers an especially engaging portrait of the natural virtues in the second *Enquiry* by describing the character of an ideal son-in-law, whose generosity, professional ability, sociability, and philosophical serenity combine to provide "a model of perfect virtue" (EPM 9.2 [SBN 269–70]).

According to Hume, our initial approval of the natural virtues arises from the benefit or pleasure that we receive directly from these qualities of character, in ourselves or in other persons. However, as in the case of the artificial virtues, he also attempts to explain the distinctively moral approbation that we extend to these qualities of character, even when they do not provide any pleasure or benefit to ourselves. Here again he appeals to sympathy, although he indicates that our moral approval of the natural virtues arises only indirectly from the operation of sympathy. As we have seen, Hume regards sympathy as a remedy produced by nature for our natural tendency to prefer our own happiness, and the happiness of our close associates, to the happiness of strangers. The operation of sympathy leads us to regard with approval the system of justice that tends to promote the happiness of the members of a society. However, in his discussion of the natural virtues, he discovers a variation in our sympathy in response to character traits that does not appear in our moral judgments. More specifically, he finds that although we often feel a greater sympathy with our compatriots, we extend "the same approbation to the same moral qualities in *China* as in *England*." In other words, he distinguishes between our initial sentiments of praise and blame, which may vary "according to our situation of nearness or remoteness, with regard to the person blam'd or prais'd," and our moral sentiments of approval and disapproval (T 3.3.1.14–16 [SBN 581–82]).[35]

In order to distinguish the operation of sympathy in itself from its role in the generation of our moral sentiments, Hume argues that our distinctively moral approval of the natural virtues arises from the development, through sympathy, of a "general" or "common point of view." Hume finds that, as social beings, we are impelled to develop "some *steady* and *general* points of view," transcending our assessment of persons and characters on the basis of our own perspectives and interests. This impulse arises from our discovery that it would be impossible for us to converse "on any reasonable terms" if each of us were merely to consider "characters and persons, only as they appear from his peculiar point of view." As individuals, we formulate this common point of view by sympathizing with those persons whom we imagine to be directly affected by the qualities of an agent's character, while overlooking any personal benefit or injury that we might receive from the agent. This common point of view enables us to "correct" our self-interested or partial sentiments of praise or blame, and to avoid the "continual *contradictions*" which would otherwise disrupt any conversations about human characters and their effects. Thus, by interacting with others, we tend to develop a "more *stable* judgment of things," which we may adopt in our assessment of any character, "whatever may be our present situation" (T 3.3.1.15, 3.3.1.30 [SBN 581–82, 591]; cf. EPM 9.5–8 [SBN 271–74]).[36] This common point of view allows us to take the "general survey" of different human characters that is required for moral assessment (cf. T 3.1.2.4, 3.1.2.11, 3.2.2.24 [SBN 472, 475, 499]).

Hume also indicates that this common point of view is formulated and expressed within a community through the development of a common moral language and moral standards. First, he argues that although our individual sentiments tend to vary with our situation, we also formulate and transmit a set of moral terms, through our interactions with each other, to express this shared point of view. That is, our sympathy with others "soon teaches us this method of correcting our sentiments, or at least, of correcting our language, where the sentiments are more stubborn and inalterable." Hume compares this correction of our sentiments to the "correction of appearances" in our judgments concerning the objects of perception, which occurs when we learn to recognize that external objects have different appearances, according to location and the

---

35. For other views of the variability of sympathy in Hume, see Brand, *Hume's Theory of Moral Judgment*, 96–98, 115–19, and Bricke, *Mind and Morality*, 128–48.

36. On Hume's account of the "moral point of view," see Taylor, "Hume's Views of Moral Judgments," 64–68; Stewart, "The Moral Point of View," 177–87; Baier, *Postures of the Mind*, 157–73; Brand, *Hume's Theory of Moral Judgment*, 96–98 and 112–34; and Sayre-McCord, "On Why Hume's 'General Point of View' Isn't Ideal," 202–28.

conditions under which we perceive them. Indeed, he argues that a correction of our sentiments is required for all thought and conversation, and that we could not "make use of language, or communicate our sentiments to one another" if we did not "correct the momentary appearances of things, and overlook our present situation." We are thus led to develop moral terms, or a moral language, in order to express sentiments of approval and disapproval from a general perspective, without regard to our own individual interests (T 3.3.1.16 [SBN 582]; EPM 5.41–42, 9.6–8 [SBN 227–29, 272–74]).[37]

With the development of a common moral language, a society can also develop a "general inalterable standard," or a "standard of merit and demerit," by which we "approve or disapprove of characters and manners." We may then apply this standard individually in our judgments, even though "the *heart* does not always take part with those general notions, or regulate its love and hatred by them" (T 3.3.3.2, 3.3.1.18 [SBN 603, 583]). In other words, on Hume's view, we can derive moral judgments from a moral rule or standard, even when our sentiments do not conform to this standard. However, this standard itself arises obliquely, through sympathy and a process of social agreement, from our sentiments of morality.

As we will see, Hume argues that the different systems of morality which arise in different historical contexts all reflect, to some degree, the "standard of virtue and morality" that is recognized by common opinion as well as by philosophers. That is, these systems tend to approve of those qualities of human character that promote the happiness of individuals within the given society, and to condemn those that promote unhappiness. In this sense, the standards of morality arise "from the general interests of the community" (T 3.3.1.31 [SBN 591]; EPM 5.42 [SBN 228]).

Thus, by adopting the common or moral perspective that is reflected in the moral language and moral standards of a community, "the imagination adheres to the *general* views of things, and distinguishes betwixt the feelings they produce, and those which arise from our particular and momentary situation." This enables us to reconcile "the *extensive sympathy,* on which our sentiments of virtue depend," with the "limited generosity" which belongs to human nature (T 3.3.1.23 [SBN 586–87]).

Hume's account of the role of common terms and standards in moral evaluation is also reflected in his view of the sense of duty, which he regards as a substitute for the natural virtues. Here he argues that when a virtuous motive is "common in human nature," a person who does not feel this passion "may hate himself upon that account," and act according to this virtue "from a certain sense of duty," either to cultivate the motive, "or at least, to disguise to him-self, as much as possible, his want of it." This indicates that we may derive statements of moral obligation, as well as moral evaluation, from a set of virtues or rules, even if we do not feel the corresponding sentiments in a given case. We thus find that since "a man naturally loves his children better than his nephews, his nephews better than his cousins, his cousins better than strangers," the sense of duty follows the "common and natural course of our passions," by prescrib-ing our obligations in this order, even in the absence of the usual passions (T 3.2.1.8, 3.2.1.18; cf. 3.2.5.6, 3.3.3.2 [SBN 479, 483–84; cf. 518–19, 603]).

Hume's account of the role of a social perspective in our approval of the natural virtues might lead us to reconsider his basic distinction between the natural and artificial virtues. As we have seen, he argues that our moral approval of the natural virtues requires not only sympathy but also the perspective afforded by a "general survey" of actions and characters from a "common point of view." We develop this common point of view through our interactions with others and by considering their interests, and this point of view allows us to collectively evaluate the qualities of character in human individuals according to their tendency to contribute to the pleasure or interest of others, apart from any consideration of our own advantage. Finally, this common point of view is instituted in a given society through the development of a set of moral terms, moral standards, and a catalog of virtues. In other words, the principles by which we approve of the natural virtues are developed through a process of mutual accommodation that is similar to the process by which we establish the principles of justice and the artificial virtues (cf. T 3.2.2.10 [SBN 490]; EPM App.3.7 [SBN 306]). We thus find that there is an element of "artifice" involved even in our assessment of the natural virtues (cf. T 3.2.1.19 [SBN 484]).[38]

Finally, especially in his writings after the *Treatise,* Hume indicates that our lists of various qualities as virtues and vices often reflects a particular historical context, since different qualities of human character are often found to be useful or agreeable in relation to a specific cultural setting. In other words, differences in the "customs and manners" of different societies may alter the usefulness, and consequently the merit, of human qualities. For example, courage is regarded as the "predominant excellence" of character in all "uncultivated nations," which have never had "full experience of the advantages attending beneficence, justice, and the social virtues." Indeed, the ancients would have regarded the "humanity,

---

38. Taylor argues that the development of the conventions underlying the artificial virtues also produces the social perspective from which we approve of the natural virtues, and that this explains Hume's ordering of his treatment of the virtues in the *Treatise.* See Taylor, "Justice and the Foundations of Social Morality," 5–30. McIntyre provides a parallel discussion of the role of a social perspective in Hume's ordering of his analysis of the passions in "Hume's Passions," 77–86. For other formulations of the view that Hume's analy-sis tends to assimilate the natural to the artificial virtues, see Mackie, *Hume's Moral Theory,* 120–25, and Baier, *Progress of Sentiments,* 178–79.

clemency, order, tranquillity, and other social virtues" which have been attained by modern civilizations as "romantic and incredible," if indeed they could have formulated "a fair representation of them." Similarly, honor and military glory tend to be especially valued under a monarchy, while the qualities that promote industry and commerce are more valued in a republic (EPM 6.20, 7.15–18, 6.35 [SBN 241, 255–57, 248–49]; cf. CMH 58–60; E RP.111–37; E ST.245–46).[39]

Hume even traces the modern conception of morality to a particular historical origin. In his view, the "distinction of voluntary or involuntary," which would become the foundation for most modern moral theories, was largely overlooked by classical authors, who did not distinguish natural abilities from moral virtues. For example, ancient moralists made "no scruple of placing prudence at the head of the cardinal virtues." Indeed, Hume argues that modern popular opinion agrees in this respect with ancient rather than modern moral theory. In other words, we approve of natural talents, and even the advantages of body and fortune, by the same principles by which we approve of what modern moralists call the moral virtues: by recognizing the pleasure they give to others through their useful or agreeable tendencies. Accordingly, he argues that the term "virtue" is properly applied to any quality of character, whether voluntary or involuntary, which we recognize as useful or agreeable to its possessor or to others. By contrast, Hume traces the modern view, that virtues are distinguished from natural abilities because they are expressed in voluntary actions, to the influence of the Christian theological tradition. This tradition extends the principles of civic law to morality, and holds that all morality is "guarded by the sanctions of reward and punishment." Subsequent philosophers, "or rather divines under that disguise," have accordingly regarded the distinction between voluntary and involuntary action as "the foundation of their whole theory" (EPM App.4.20–21 [SBN 321–22]; T 3.3.4.3–4 [SBN 608–10]).

In his criticism of this modern conception of morality, Hume reminds us that no human actions can be regarded as absolutely free, as we have seen in Chapter 7. Instead, whenever we praise or blame actions, we are regarding these actions as the necessary expressions of motives and dispositions, rather than as spontaneous events with no ground in the character of the agent. On the other hand, Hume distinguishes between actions arising from motives in the character of the agent, which are often preceded by a process of deliberation, and actions that are uncharacteristic or accidental. Here he argues that when we praise or blame any action, we generally consider the "intention" of the agent, to determine whether the action is deliberate, arising from "fore-thought and design," or whether it is instead "casual and involuntary," arising from a sudden

---

39. On Hume's approach to understanding moral values within their cultural context, see Herdt, *Religion and Faction*, 117–67; Taylor, "Justice and the Foundations of Social Morality," 5–30; and Cohen, "Notion of Moral Progress," 109–27.

passion. In other words, Hume himself distinguishes between actions arising directly from motives in the agent, which are called "voluntary" by modern moralists, and "involuntary" actions, or those committed unintentionally.[40] Finally, he concedes that only intentional actions give rise to moral sentiments in the observer (T 2.2.3.3–6; cf. 2.3.2.7 [SBN 348–51; cf. 411–12]). He thus appears to acknowledge that our moral sentiments and judgments are directed only toward those qualities of character that receive expression in what we generally call voluntary actions.[41] However, he concludes that the difference between virtues and natural abilities is largely a verbal dispute; and he suggests that it is "the business of *philosophers*" to account for the sentiment of morals, but of "*grammarians* to examine what qualities are entitl'd to the denomination of *virtue*" (T 3.3.4.3–4; cf. 2.3.2.3–8 [SBN 409–12]; EPM App.4.1–22 [SBN 312–23]).

In accordance with his own analysis of the virtues as those qualities of character that are agreeable to the self or to others, Hume favors the classical virtues over the Christian system of morality, and especially over the "monkish virtues" of "celibacy, fasting, penance, mortification, self-denial, humility, silence, solitude" (EPM 9.3 [SBN 270]). For example, he defends the classical virtue of "pride" against the Christian virtue of humility by arguing that a recognition of our own valuable qualities is useful and agreeable to ourselves, and hence morally praiseworthy, since it "gives us a confidence and assurance in all our projects and enterprizes." Indeed, all the actions of heroism and nobility which we admire in history arise from "a steady and well-establish'd pride and self-esteem," or "greatness and elevation of mind" (T 3.3.2.7–13; cf. 2.1.7.8 [SBN 596–600; cf. 297–98]). By contrast, the ascetic or "monkish" virtues are "every where rejected by men of sense," because "they serve to no manner of purpose," but instead "cross all these desirable ends; stupify the understanding and harden the heart, obscure the fancy and sour the temper." Indeed, since these qualities are harmful and disagreeable, we may even "transfer them to the opposite column, and place them in the catalogue of vices" (EPM 9.3 [SBN 270]; cf. NHR 10.52).[42]

40. On the basis of Hume's moral philosophy, Paul Russell has developed the argument that individuals are held responsible for their character, even though this character is not acquired voluntarily. In other words, we are considered responsible for what we do with the dispositions we find in ourselves, once we have developed an adult capacity for moral feelings and judgments: see *Freedom and Moral Sentiment*, 95–153. See also Bricke, *Mind and Morality*, 233–48, and Purviance, "Indirect Passions," 195–212.

41. For other discussions of Hume's apparent inconsistency in attempting to deny any distinctive place for the recognition of voluntary action in morality, see Mackie, *Hume's Moral Theory*, 127–29, and Russell, *Freedom and Moral Sentiment*, 124–28.

42. For a defense of these qualities as possible virtues on Humean grounds, at least in some contexts, see Davie, "Hume on Monkish Virtue," 139–53. Davie argues that Hume's target is really asceticism directed toward pleasing a deity, and that various ascetic practices may be useful or agreeable to the individual or others in both religious and nonreligious contexts. In fact, as Davie notes, the life of a secular scholar often requires at least some of these qualities.

Hume returns to the ascetic virtues at the end of "A Dialogue," where Palamedes asks how we can account for the "*artificial*" lives and manners," or idiosyncratic principles of conduct, adopted by many ancient philosophical schools and modern religious sects. He specifically calls attention to Pascal, who was clearly a man of "parts and genius," and might have been a model of virtue if he had followed his natural sentiments rather than the ascetic practices of the Catholic Jansenist movement. In response, Hume argues that these idiosyncratic systems of conduct are adopted under the influence of "religious superstition or philosophical enthusiasm." Where these interfere, the "natural principles" of the human mind "play not with the same regularity, as if left to themselves," and our sentiments, and even our use of moral terms, may be "warped from their natural course" (EPM D.53–57, App.4.21 [SBN 341–43, 322]; cf. CMH 57). We may thus distinguish between the moral standards of common life, arising from the moral sentiments produced by sympathy, and those principles of conduct adopted under the influence of philosophical speculation or religious enthusiasm, especially if these principles do not conform to the standards of what is useful and agreeable.[43]

Hume provides another example of an "artificial" moral system in the essay "Of Moral Prejudices."[44] Here he depicts the imaginary case of "a young Lady" of good birth, fortune, and "Philosophic Spirit" who rejects "the receiv'd Maxims of Conduct and Behaviour" because of her "refin'd Search after Happiness or Perfection." In her view, the best possible life could only be achieved by remaining single and yet having a child. She accordingly entered into intimate relations with an attractive young man, whom she then dismissed when she achieved her purpose. However, it is difficult to determine from Hume's account what precisely he is regarding as objectionable in her conduct, unless it is the distress of the estranged father (E MP.542–44).[45]

In presenting his moral theory, Hume therefore offers us an account of both the various historical systems of morality, and the critical philosophical principles by which we may evaluate any given system of morality. First, he argues that we feel moral sentiments when we consider various qualities of human character from a general point of view, which we may attain individually, through sympathy, by recognizing the tendency of a given disposition to give pleasure or pain to others. However, this sympathetic correction is attained and

<hr/>

43. On Hume's discussion of "artificial lives," see MacIntyre, *After Virtue*, 228–32; Baier, *Postures of the Mind*, 246–62; King, "Hume on Artificial Lives," 53–88; and Herdt, *Religion and Faction*, 168–218.

44. This essay was one of several that Hume withdrew from publication after their first appearance in 1742, perhaps because he regarded them as too frivolous. Hume gives this as a reason for withdrawing several of his other essays in a letter to Adam Smith in 1752 (L 1.168).

45. Baier adopts this essay as the point of departure for her collection *Moral Prejudices;* see x–xi. See also Livingston, *Philosophical Melancholy and Delirium*, 130–35. This essay is also relevant to feminist assessments of Hume; see Jacobson, *Feminist Interpretations of David Hume*.

extended through our interaction with others in the context of a historical community, and this tends to produce conventional systems of morality consisting in sets of moral terms, rules of conduct, and catalogs of virtues. These arise in a given society from an implicit agreement concerning the actions and qualities of character likely to give pleasure or displeasure to others in that society. Accordingly, these systems may be expected to differ according to variations in their cultural context. For example, military virtues are more valued in a monarchy, while commercial virtues are more highly valued in a republic. In other words, the type of government, "by varying the *utility* of those customs, has commonly a proportionable effect on the sentiments of mankind," and thus upon the catalog of the virtues in a society (EPM 6.35 [SBN 248–49]). Yet the standards of morality in a community may be distorted by religious, philosophical, or political systems of belief and conduct, which are promoted by individuals or groups, and may be manipulated by public figures in pursuit of their own self-interest, as we will see in Chapters 9 and 12.

Finally, in response to these possible distortions of our sentiments of praise or blame, Hume presents our ability to recognize the tendency of various qualities of character to promote pleasure and happiness as the "standard of virtue and morality." That is, the standard of utility and agreeability is discovered through philosophical reflection to be the implicit principle in the common conception of virtue. This standard may accordingly be used to judge the adequacy of any particular catalog of virtues within its historical context (T 3.3.1.30 [SBN 591]; cf. EPM D.37–51 [SBN 336–41]). As a result, various systems of conduct, such as the "monkish virtues," may be rejected from the catalog of virtues in a given society, and even be classified as vices.[46]

MORAL JUDGMENTS

With this survey of the virtues, we may return to the issue of the influence of reason in morals. In the *Treatise* Hume introduces his moral theory by considering the basis of our "moral distinctions," or "those judgments, by which we distinguish moral good and evil." He then argues that these distinctions are derived, not from reason, but from a "moral sense," or the distinctive sentiments of approval or disapproval arising from our sympathy with the pleasure or pain of others, so that morality is "more properly felt that judg'd of" (T 3.1.1.1–2, 3.1.2.1 [SBN 456–57, 470]). In this preliminary discussion he

---

46. Alasdair MacIntyre criticizes Hume's moral theory as a typically modern rejection of the synthesis of classical virtue theory with biblical doctrines of divine law and human freedom, in *After Virtue* and *Whose Justice? Which Rationality?* In response, Baier has defended the modern relevance of Hume's virtue theory, and its continuity with the Aristotelian tradition, in *Postures of the Mind*, 246–62.

appears to exclude reason from our moral judgments, and even implicitly to deny the possibility of these judgments as cognitive functions that can be distinguished from the immediate promptings of sentiment.[47]

On the other hand, in his subsequent examination of the artificial and natural virtues, Hume establishes and defends the possibility of moral judgments as cognitive functions that may be derived from a system of principles, even though these principles are ultimately grounded in sentiment. In the case of the artificial virtues, he argues that, as members of a human community, we collectively invent the rules of justice through our "judgment and understanding," first for the sake of self-interest, and then for their tendency to promote the happiness of others, which we appreciate through sympathy. We then treat the rules of justice as "inflexible either by spite or favour" in applying them, through judgments, to particular cases (T 3.2.2.9, 3.2.3.3 [SBN 489, 502–3]). In the case of the natural virtues, we are guided by the perspective of a common point of view, generated by our sympathy and interaction with others, to correct by "reflection" our self-interested or partial sentiments of approval toward various qualities of human character (T 3.3.1.15–18 [SBN 581–83]). Once the common point of view is established in a given society, through the development of a moral vocabulary, moral rules, and a catalog of virtues, we may derive moral judgments from these principles as they apply in any particular case, even apart from our individual sentiments (cf. T 3.3.1.30 [SBN 591]). Finally, Hume also indicates that our moral appraisal of the different qualities of character requires us to engage in probable reasoning concerning the likely effects of these qualities on others (T 3.1.1.11–16, 3.3.1.19 [SBN 459–63, 584–85]). In the *Treatise* Hume thus ascribes an important role to reason in moral approval and disapproval, although he regards the contribution of reason as subordinate to the passions or sentiments, which provide the ultimate basis for our moral distinctions and the motives for moral action.

Hume offers a similar view of the relative influence of reason and sentiment over morality in the second *Enquiry.* In this text, however, he argues explicitly and systematically that "*reason* must enter for a considerable share" in all our moral decisions, since reason is required "to instruct us in the tendency of qualities and actions, and point out their beneficial consequences to society and to their possessor." This is especially evident in applying the rules of justice, where "a very accurate *reason* or *judgement* is often requisite, to give the true determination," although reasoning is also required to discover the beneficial tendencies of the natural virtues. Thus, in any type of moral evaluation we find "that much

---

47. For the relation between moral sentiments and judgments in Hume, see Glossop, "Hume's Ethics," 527–36; Hearn, "General Rules and Moral Sentiments," 67–68; Árdal, "Hume's Account of Moral Evaluation," 405–19; Norton, *David Hume,* 94–151; Capaldi, *Hume's Place in Moral Philosophy,* 97–153; and Brand, *Hume's Theory of Moral Judgment.*

reasoning should precede, that nice distinctions be made, just conclusions drawn, distant comparisons formed, complicated relations examined, and general facts fixed and ascertained." Accordingly, our moral decisions are often corrected by "argument and reflection" (EPM App.1.2; EPM 1.9 [SBN 285–86, 173]).

Reasoning thus plays a role in Hume's account of moral evaluation at several levels. First, moral approval and disapproval, like other passions, arise in response to ideas, in this case our ideas of the pleasure or pain of others, and from our judgments concerning the probability that others will experience pleasure or pain as a result of actions arising from the character of a given agent. Next, Hume indicates that our sentiments of moral approval and disapproval are directed toward particular qualities of character by the moral institutions developed by human beings within a given community, on the basis of their sympathy with the pleasure and pain of others. These institutions include not only the rules of justice, which assign rights and obligations, but also a system of natural virtues, codified in the moral terminology, the standards of moral conduct, and the catalog of virtues in a given community. The system of morality in a given society, including both the rules of justice and the list of natural virtues, enables individuals in that society to engage in moral evaluation and conform to moral principles, even when they are not feeling the appropriate moral sentiments. In these cases, the members of a society are able to derive moral judgments from the general principles of morality. Finally, Hume indicates that we can derive a "standard of virtue and morality," through philosophical "speculation," from the discovery that our moral sentiments and moral judgments are directed toward qualities of human character that are sources of pleasure or pain to others. Once we have recognized this principle as the underlying standard of morality, we may correct our own sentiments, the judgments we derive from a conventional system of morality, and even this popular system of morality itself, by determining whether the actions arising from any given quality of character are likely to promote the pleasure or pain of others. However, we must ultimately feel a sentiment of morality in order "to give a preference to the useful above the pernicious tendencies" (T 3.3.1.30 [SBN 591]; EPM App.1.3 [SBN 285–86]).[48]

Several recent studies have indicated that Hume's account of sentiment, sympathy, and reason includes a theory of moral progress. According to this view, Hume recognizes that the socially recognized standards of morality may be developed toward an improved tendency to promote qualities that are genuinely useful and agreeable, as human beings develop an improved appreciation

---

48. For a classic study of Hume's account of reason in human action, including moral evaluation and moral motivation, see Kydd, *Reason and Conduct*, 164–89. See also Mackie, *Hume's Moral Theory*, 51–63; Norton, *David Hume*, 94–151; Capaldi, *Hume's Place in Moral Philosophy*, 97–131; Brand, *Hume's Theory of Moral Judgment*; Shaw, "Reason and Feeling," 349–68; and Garrett, *Cognition and Commitment*, 202–4.

256 · David Hume: Reason in History

of what is useful and agreeable, an improvement which he regards as a result of the advance of civilization.[49] For example, as previously discussed, he notes that courage is regarded as the highest virtue in all "uncultivated nations, who have not, as yet, had full experience of the advantages attending beneficence, justice, and the social virtues" (EPM 7.15 [SBN 255]). He also indicates that the development of industry and commerce tend to promote the happiness of a greater number of individuals than had been possible under earlier economic conditions (E Co.253–67; E RA.268–80). He even allows for the possibility of future improvement, by observing that we do not know "what degree of refinement, either in virtue or vice, human nature is susceptible of; nor what may be expected of mankind from any great revolution in their education, customs, or principles" (E CL.87–88). However, even in this passage, Hume does not regard the process of historical change as guaranteed to advance toward such an improvement, as we will see in Chapter 13.

We may conclude this section by considering Hume's approach to "practical morality," or moral education and exhortation, as presented both in his philosophical works and elsewhere in his writings (T 3.1.1.5–6, 3.3.6.6 [SBN 457, 620–21]). In Hume's view, the two central tasks for practical morality are to expand our sympathetic recognition of the pleasures and pains of others, and to motivate us to cultivate the virtues, or those qualities of character which promote the happiness of society by being useful or agreeable to others or ourselves.

First, as methods for expanding our range of sympathy, Hume advises us to study history and literature, and also attempts in his own essays and historical writings to examine the beliefs, dispositions, beliefs, and motives of various real or imaginary characters. These inquiries are intended to promote a deeper understanding of the passions and motives of others in relation to their circumstances, and thereby to improve our sympathy with these agents. In his political essays on various controversial issues, he seeks to promote a sympathetic receptiveness on each side to the views of their opponents (cf. E DT.3–8; E SH.567–68; E PG.64–72; E CP.493–501). By this means, as we will see in Chapter 9, he hopes to diminish political partisanship, and to promote instead a sympathy with the beliefs and concerns of others, which is required for moral sensitivity and moral conduct within the larger community.

Second, in order to promote the cultivation of virtue, Hume challenges the views that there must be a conflict between pursuing our immediate goals as opposed to our long-term happiness, or our own happiness as opposed to the happiness of others. Indeed, the task of the practical moralist, in his view, consists precisely in persuading us that the most enduring pleasures for human

---

49. See Taylor, "Justice and the Foundations of Social Morality," 5–30; Gill, "Hume's Progressive View of Human Nature," 87–108; and Cohen, "Notion of Moral Progress," 109–27.

beings arise from a balance of activity and leisure, and of solitude and sociability, guided by a prudent regard for our future happiness, and combined with a generous concern for others (EPM 9.14–25 [SBN 278–84]; T 3.3.6.6 [SBN 620–21]). He pursues this project most notably in his essays on the four temperaments, represented by four ancient philosophical schools, in which he indicates that the cultivation of virtue produces happiness, not only for the cerebral Stoic and Platonist, but also for the more sensual Epicurean and Sceptic (E Ep.141–43; E St.151–54; E Pl.158; E Sc.159–80).

Hume accordingly seeks to improve the morals of contemporary British society by encouraging individuals in the prudent pursuit of their long-term interest, the enjoyment of enduring pleasures, the expansion of sympathy, and the cultivation of sociability, all of which he expects to increase their own happiness and the happiness of society. By contrast, he criticizes the artificial systems of morality that are generated by religious superstition and enthusiasm, as tending to detract from the happiness of agents and those around them (EPM 9.3; EPM D.53–57 [SBN 270, 341–43]). Finally, he seeks to encourage the development of those character traits which may be expected to promote the advance of industry, commerce, prosperity, civic order, civility, and the arts and sciences, all of which, in his view, tend to further the happiness of the individuals within a modern society.[50]

CONVENTION

As we have seen, the idea of a "convention" plays a central role in Hume's discussion of the artificial virtues. In this discussion, however, he suggests that conventions emerge in many other forms of cooperative human activity and provide the basis for other social practices and institutions.

According to Hume, a convention is an agreement between individuals to engage in cooperative behavior, so that each can secure greater benefit than would be attained through solitary or uncoordinated activities.[51] In such a convention, the actions of each "have a reference to those of the other, and are perform'd upon the supposition, that something is to be perform'd on the other

50. For further discussions of Hume's approach to practical morality, see Price, *David Hume;* Siebert, *Moral Animus;* Danford, *Problem of Reason,* 155–63; Baier, *Progress of Sentiments;* Immerwahr, "The Anatomist and the Painter," 1–14, and "Hume on Tranquillizing the Passions," 293–314; Martin, "Hume on Human Excellence," 383–99; Sayre-McCord, "On Why Hume's 'General Point of View' Isn't Ideal," 202–28; and Wertz, *Between Hume's Philosophy and History,* 67–87.

51. For the classic recent discussion of conventions as solutions to problems of coordination in game theory, whose author acknowledges a debt to Hume, see Lewis, *Convention,* 3. Other discussions of Hume's theory of conventions in relation to game theory include Snare, *Morals, Motivation and Convention,* 202–4 and 246–309, and Bricke, *Mind and Morality,* 195–232.

part." This ability to coordinate our behavior arises from sympathy and reasoning, which allow us to recognize the motives and anticipate the actions of others. Sympathy also diffuses a pleasing camaraderie over our cooperative activities. A convention often arises from "a general sense of common interest," which is "mutually express'd" by the participants, and "induces them to regulate their conduct by certain rules." However, as in the rowing example cited previously, a convention may also arise tacitly through a process of observation and accommodation between agents, even without a verbal agreement.

Indeed, language itself arises from a process of mutual accommodation, so that "speech and words and language are fixed, by human convention and agreement" (T 3.2.2.10 [SBN 490]; EPM App.3.8 [SBN 306]). While many of our conventions seem to be arbitrary, Hume indicates that they are often suggested by habits, by convenience, or by association. As examples of these, Hume considers the principles governing the right of way in traffic, according to which a lighter vehicle gives way to a heavier one, and those going toward the capital have precedence over those leaving it (EPM 4.19n16 [SBN 210n1]). Regardless of its initial basis, Hume argues that "whatever is advantageous to two or more persons, if all perform their part," but "loses all advantage, if only one perform," cannot arise from any principle other than that of convention (EPM App.3.8 [SBN 306]).

The simplest type of convention is a tacit and temporary agreement, as in the example of rowing a boat. However conventions may also develop as informal practices or traditions that are honored by many members of a community. This is found, for example, in the case of language, along with the principles governing traffic in Hume's day, which were tacitly recognized by "waggoners, coachmen, and postilions." The conventions governing certain types of cooperative activity may also be explicitly formulated and enforced by a mutually recognized authority, as in the medieval "court or parliament of love," which decreed and enforced the rules of "gallantry," or in "societies for play," which determine the rules of their games (EPM 4.17–19 [SBN 210]). Finally, since the conventions governing property and contracts are "absolutely requisite, both to the support of society, and the well-being of every individual," these conventions are codified and enforced by the sovereign power within a state (T 3.2.2.22; cf. 3.2.6.8 [SBN 497; cf. 538–39]).

Hume's account of conventions and their role in various types of human activity also provides an indirect contribution to his general account of cognition in Book 1 of the *Treatise*, in at least three respects. First, this discussion adds an important element to his account of abstract ideas. In Book 1, Hume presents the process of forming abstract ideas as the individual activity of an isolated subject, who associates various resembling images with other images and also with a term, and is then able to recall these images to fulfill the requirements of any particular case (T 1.1.7–18 [SBN 20–25]). According to this account, I might invent a word and apply it to a series of images apart from any existing language. However, in Book 3 Hume indicates that the public use of language requires a conventional assignment of words to objects and qualities, so that these words may be used and understood by many individuals (T 3.2.2.10; cf. 3.3.1.16 [SBN 490; cf. 582]). We might thus expect, although Hume does not explicitly draw this conclusion, that the individuals in a given linguistic community will generally assign words to images by learning the conventional uses of these words within their community.[52] Next, Hume's account of conventions also accounts for at least some attributions of identity. As we have seen, for example, in the cases of ships, buildings, and states, many of our attributions of identity to specific types of objects through a series of changes are determined by rules formulated in the context of a social institution. Accordingly, many of our attributions of identity ultimately arise from conventions (T 1.4.6.11–19 [SBN 257–61]). Finally, Hume's account of conventions might also be applied to the rules that govern scientific inquiry. According to the account presented in Book 1 of the *Treatise,* it would seem that the rules for judging causes and effects might in principle be newly formulated by each individual scientist working in isolation. However, a study of the history of science, as indicated by Hume's references to the methodological contributions of Bacon, Galileo, Boyle, and Newton, shows that the principles of investigation within the natural sciences were formulated gradually, through a series of individual innovations and collective agreements among scientists concerning the most effective rules for empirical investigation. In this sense, we might even regard the rules of "philosophical" or scientific reasoning as a set of conventions, developed in order to regulate and coordinate the activities of individual scientists.[53]

In sum, Hume traces all coordinated activities between two or more individuals to conventions, or the implicit or explicit agreement to follow a rule. Conventions range in their duration and force from temporary arrangements, through traditions, to the rules of a social institution, and finally to laws established and enforced by state authority. We find examples of conventions in collaborative projects, the public use of symbols, the principles of etiquette, the rules governing property and contracts, the rise of government, the acceptance and transfer of sovereignty, the ritual practices of religious communities, and even in games. Many conventionally established rules of conduct might appear to be frivolous, whimsical, or even superstitious. However, at least regarding

---

52. For discussions of Hume's account of language, see Árdal, "Convention and Value," 51–68, and "Language and Significance," 779–83; along with Wilson, "Hume and Derrida on Language and Meaning," 99–121.

53. See Chapter 3 above; and also Noxon, *Hume's Philosophical Development,* 130–32.

conventions that are beneficial to the members of a society, Hume argues that although they are "artificial" in their origin, they are no longer "arbitrary," once they are accepted and established as rules of conduct (T 3.2.1.19 [SBN 484]).

Hume's attention to conventions in many areas of human life has led many commentators to regard this analysis as a central theme in his writings. For example, Mossner has described the idea of a convention as a "structural idea" that gives unity to Hume's writings, while Livingston identifies "convention" as perhaps the most important technical term in his philosophy. In addition, Snare has described Hume's theory of conventions as an individualistic and naturalistic basis for the analysis of institutional facts, which is especially valuable for research in the social sciences.[54] In the later chapters of this study I will consider Hume's treatment of conventions in other areas of human life, including political institutions, economic behavior, aesthetic judgment, and religious belief and practice.

---

54. See Mossner, "An Apology for David Hume," 681; Livingston, *Hume's Philosophy of Common Life*, 66; and Snare, *Morals, Motivation and Convention*, 4 and 202–4, 282. For a relevant discussion of institutional facts, see Searle, *Construction of Social Reality*.

9

Political Theory

Hume sets forth the basic principles of his political theory in the context of his moral theory in Book 3 of the *Treatise* and in the second *Enquiry*. Many of his essays are concerned with current issues in the government and political culture of contemporary Britain. Hume also devotes several essays to the "science" of politics, or the empirical study of the actions of individuals in the context of social and political groups, as this study might be used to improve the structure and policies of government.[1] In the *History of England* he traces the history of the English constitution, partly as background for understanding the eighteenth-century system of government in Great Britain.[2] Finally, Hume

---

1. After many centuries of turbulent relations, a century of interlacing royal lines, and several decades of increasing economic rivalry, the governments of England and Scotland were combined by mutual agreement to create the United Kingdom of Great Britain by the Act of Union in 1707. By this union, the political institutions of Scotland were in effect absorbed by the English government. Hume was Scottish by birth, education, and accent, but also lived in England from time to time and had extensive connections there. He was thus inclined to view the history and political life of England as either an outsider or an insider, depending on the context. See Phillipson, *Hume*, 29–34; Baier, *Progress of Sentiments*, 255–76; Stewart, *Opinion and Reform*, 227–30 and 310–17; and Ainslie, "Problem of the National Self," 289–313.

2. The English constitution, and subsequently the British constitution, was not a single document but a collection of legal documents and common-law practices. The precise history and character of the English constitution, as we will see in the present chapter, had been a matter of considerable controversy in England, especially during the century preceding Hume's birth. See Miller, "Hume on Liberty," 53–103.

offers a personal commentary on a variety of contemporary political events in his letters, especially after the British victory in the Seven Years' War in 1763, which confronted the British government with new ventures and challenges overseas and new levels of social, economic, and political tension at home.

THE ORIGIN AND NATURE OF GOVERNMENT

In Book 1 of the *Treatise* Hume includes an inquiry into the "nature and foundation of government" among the subjects we might wish to address after surmounting the crisis of extreme skepticism (T 1.4.7.12 [SBN 271]). He turns to this topic in Book 3, in which he develops an account of government as arising from human conventions to counteract the disruptive effects of self-interest and limited benevolence. He reaffirms his analysis of government in the *Enquiry Concerning the Principles of Morals,* and also in several of his essays, especially "Of the First Principles of Government," "Of the Origin of Government," and "Of the Original Contract."

As we have seen, Hume rejects the view that human beings could ever have existed in a "state of nature" envisioned as a "perpetual war of all against all." Instead, already in our natural state we are drawn into cooperative relationships by sexual attraction, family affection, and the desire for companionship. We thus find that all human beings are "necessarily born in a family-society, at least," where they are "trained up by their parents to some rule of conduct and behaviour" (EPM 3.15–16 [SBN 189–90]; cf. T 3.2.2.14 [SBN 493]). As the next stage of human sociability, several families join together, forming a "small uncultivated society" for cooperation, protection, and company. Such a society might exist for a long time without any formal government, since in this society "the possessions, and the pleasures of life are few," and individuals have little or no temptation to violate the rules of justice. Indeed, Hume maintains that a small society without a government is "one of the most natural states of man" (T 3.2.8.1–3 [SBN 539–41]; cf. EPM 3.21 [SBN 192]).[3] However, even in families or tribal societies, a set of rules based on the principles of justice is enforced through rewards and sanctions, even apart from the authority of a government. Thus, while any real "distinction of property" among the members of a family is diminished or obliterated by their "mutual benevolence," most families find themselves obliged to formulate certain rules of property, such as those allocating playthings among the children (EPM 3.6 [SBN 185]; T 3.2.2.5–6, 3.2.2.14 [SBN 487, 493]).

---

3. For a comparison of Hume's view of human sociability to those of his predecessors and contemporaries, see Forbes, *Hume's Philosophical Politics,* 3–90, and Stewart, *Opinion and Reform,* 152–93.

Since the system of justice ultimately benefits every member of society, each of us has a "natural" or self-regarding interest in upholding the rules of justice, or an "interested obligation" to obey them (T 3.2.2.22–24 [SBN 497–99]). This interested obligation may indeed be apparent immediately to members of a small society. However, in a larger and more complex society we find that individuals often act against this interest by violating the rules of justice. This occurs when agents are more powerfully affected by the idea of nearby objects of desire than by the idea of the benefits secured to them by acting justly. In other words, individuals "often act in contradiction to their known interest," by preferring "any trivial advantage" in the present to the remote good of upholding the order of society by obeying the rules of justice (T 3.2.7.3 [SBN 535]; cf. 2.3.3.8–2.3.4.1, 2.3.6.1–9 [SBN 417–19, 424–32]).

However, the socially disruptive tendencies in human nature are counteracted through the "consent of men," by our invention of an artificial system that provides a motive for each of us to prefer obeying the rules of justice over any advantage we might expect to gain by violating these rules. Since we cannot secure a preference for justice by changing "any thing material in our nature," this is achieved by changing our "circumstances and situation," by means of a "voluntary convention." This convention consists in giving to certain individuals an immediate interest in constraining everyone else to obey the rules of justice, by the status and other benefits attending their performance of this function. These persons, "whom we call civil magistrates, kings and their ministers, our governors and rulers," are accordingly invested with the authority to enforce the "laws of nature," or principles of justice, within a community (T 3.2.7.6, 3.2.10.2 [SBN 537, 554]; cf. E OG.37–39, E OC.467–69). That is, once we find that in "large and polish'd societies" we cannot guarantee the obedience of others to the rules of justice on the grounds of interest or morality, we consent to the "new invention" of government, whose main purpose is to punish those who disobey these rules. Our initial motive for allegiance to government is the "natural" obligation of self-interest, although this is again supplemented by moral obligation, which we recognize through our sympathy with others (T 3.2.8.5–7 [SBN 543–46]).

The general principles of justice, or "laws of nature," are given a particular formulation by the sovereign of each state in a set of positive laws (T 3.2.8.5, 3.2.10.14 [SBN 543, 561]). In the second *Enquiry* Hume notes that civil laws are established to "extend, restrain, modify, and alter the rules of natural justice, according to the particular *convenience* of each community." These civil laws "have, or ought to have" a constant reference to the government, manners, climate, religion, commerce, and situation of each given society. Finally, the positive laws of a state are determined by "statutes, customs, precedents, analogies, and a hundred other circumstances," through reason and the associative processes of the imagination (EPM 3.34–35, 3.42–45; cf. App.3.10 [SBN 196–97, 202–3; cf. 308–9]).[4]

The main purpose of government is to enforce obedience to the laws of nature, as these are codified in the positive laws of a particular state. However, Hume also observes that once a government is established, it may extend its "beneficial influence" into other areas of activity, for example, by organizing cooperative projects that are useful to the members of the society but difficult to arrange without the initiative and planning of a central authority. It is thus through the "care of government," from its interest in promoting the welfare of the state and its population, that "bridges are built; harbours open'd; ramparts rais'd; canals form'd; fleets equipp'd; and armies disciplin'd." In light of these functions, Hume describes government as "one of the finest and most subtle inventions imaginable" (T 3.2.7.8 [SBN 538–39]).

However, Hume rejects the view that every human society must have a government. As we have seen, he argues that families, and even societies arising from the cooperation of several families, may recognize and even enforce the rules of justice without establishing a regular system of government. Indeed, since family life, according to his view, does not require any strict central authority, he rejects the theory that the concept and the institution of political sovereignty originally arise "from patriarchal government, or the authority of a father" (T 3.2.8.2 [SBN 541]; cf. EPM 3.21 [SBN 192]).[5] Indeed, he maintains that government would not arise spontaneously within a tribal society as a result of merely internal developments (T 3.2.8.1; cf. 3.2.8.4 [SBN 539–40; cf. 543]). Instead, he argues that government first arises from the experience of wartime leadership, which shows the members of a society what can be achieved by a central authority. This type of authority is subsequently found to be a remedy for conflicts between individuals within that society, once the amount of "riches and possessions" has so increased, through plunder, trade, or industry, "as to make them forget, on every emergence, the interest they have in the preservation of peace and justice." Accordingly, Hume argues that "camps are the true mothers of cities," and that monarchy, as the earliest type of government, is modeled on military leadership rather than patriarchal authority (T 3.2.8.1–2 [SBN 539–41]; cf. E OG.39–40, E OC.468–69). Hume provides an example of this process in his *History of England,* where he traces the haphazard emergence of rulers and political institutions among the Saxon tribes, during their conquest and settlement of England (H 1.1.15–16; H 1.App.1.160–65).

---

4. For a further discussion of Hume's contribution to the philosophy of law, see Hayek, "Legal and Political Philosophy," 335–60, and Beitzinger, "The Place of Hume," 20–37.

5. For an intriguing account of Hume's view of the family in relation to his own experience of family life, see Baier, "Hume's Account of Social Artifice," 757–78, and *Progress of Sentiments,* 256–57.

Hume offers his analysis of political obligation as an alternative to the prevailing version of the social contract theory, derived from Locke, which by the middle of the eighteenth century had become what he describes as the "creed" of the ruling Whig party in Britain, and accordingly the "foundation of our fashionable system of politics." According to the Whig view, government is instituted when a number of individuals agree, "either expressly or tacitly," to establish a civil authority by individually promising their allegiance, so that the moral obligation of obedience to government is based on our duty to keep a promise. Hume maintains that the popularity of this theory arises from the view that a promise is binding through a natural rather than an artificial moral obligation, and can therefore provide a natural basis for our moral obligation of political obedience. In contrast to this view, Hume maintains that promises and government both arise from conventions, and that obedience to each is regarded as obligatory on the basis of the same two principles: self-interest, which gives us a natural obligation of obedience in both cases, and sympathy with the welfare of others, which leads us to regard obedience in both cases as a moral obligation. We are thus led to regard allegiance to government as a duty by "our own interest," or by "that of the public, which we partake of by *sympathy*." The obligation to keep a promise cannot, in other words, be more basic or secure than our direct motives for obedience to government. Hume also maintains that our natural and moral obligations to obey the government are both distinct from any obligations that might arise from a promise. That is, even if our duty of allegiance to government were first established through a promise, this duty "immediately takes root of itself, and has an original obligation and authority." Both the natural and the moral obligation of allegiance instead arise from the tendency of government to maintain "order and concord in society," which is directly beneficial to ourselves and to others, even apart from any promises T 3.2.8.3–5, 3.2.8.7 [SBN 541–46, 671]; cf. 3.2.9.2, 3.2.11.41 [SBN 550–51, 569]; E FP.32–34; E OC.480–81).

Finally, Hume appeals to the "universal consent of mankind," to confirm that the duty of obedience to government does not arise from any promises on the part of the subjects. Indeed, he maintains that in politics, as well as in morals, popular opinion has a particular authority, and may even be regarded as "infallible." First, he rejects the argument that the successors to those who supposedly gave their promise of allegiance in the original contract are bound by a "tacit promise" to obey the government, since these succeeding generations have neither indicated nor apparently willed such a promise. On the contrary, he argues that if we ask "the far greatest part of the nation, whether they had ever consented to the authority of their rulers, or promis'd to obey them," they would "think very strangely of you," and reply "that the affair depended not on their consent, but that they were born to such an obedience." Common

266 · David Hume: Reason in History

opinion also denies to those born and raised within a state the right to decide for themselves, upon reaching adulthood, whether to promise allegiance to its government. Hume also rejects the claim that the continued residence of an individual in a state implies a tacit promise of allegiance to its government, since this view assumes that "a poor peasant or artizan has a free choice to leave his country, when he knows no foreign language or manners, and lives from day to day, by the small wages which he acquires" (T 3.2.8.8–9 [SBN 546–49]; E OC.475, 486–87). Hume concludes that obedience to the government is usually regarded as obligatory for the inhabitants of a given state without regard to any promise, implicit or explicit. This would be the case even if a government originally arose through a convention, and even if the present inhabitants have implicitly or explicitly consented to this government.[6]

The next problem is to determine "whom we are to regard as our lawful magistrates" (T 3.2.10.2 [SBN 554]). Here we find that, since "the private interest of every one is different," and tends to produce an "endless confusion" among our opinions concerning the best rulers and types of government, the same interest that calls us to submit to government makes us renounce "the choice of our magistrates, and binds us down to a certain form of government, and to particular persons, without allowing us to aspire to the utmost perfection in either." Instead, public opinion is guided in assigning sovereignty by rules that are similar to those determining the distribution of property. That is, we acknowledge the legitimacy of a particular government on the basis of long possession, present possession, conquest, succession, and also the "positive laws" by which a legislative body establishes "a certain form of government and succession of princes" (T 3.2.10.3, 3.2.10.14 [SBN 555, 561]; cf. E OC.465–87). Hume indeed notes that the study of history soon teaches us "to treat very lightly all disputes concerning the rights of princes," since the principles that determine the assignment of civil authority to any particular person arise from the patterns of association among our ideas, and thus "hold less of reason, than of bigotry and superstition" (T 3.2.10.15 [SBN 562]).

In his essays Hume repeatedly states that while the authority of government rests upon popular opinion, public support for government does not require and need not be expressed in a promise, either explicit or implicit. Since numbers are "always on the side of the governed," he argues that the legitimacy of any particular government is ultimately derived from public opinion. This applies not only to representative or participatory systems but even to the "most despotic and most military governments," which at least require the support of the armed forces (E FP.32–33). However, in contrast to the view that

6. Hampton presents a further development of Hume's theory of political obligation, as an alternative to traditional versions of the social contract theory, in her *Political Philosophy;* see especially 70–117.

government must be founded upon the prior consent of the governed in order to be legitimate, he argues that the present acquiescence of a large part of the population determines this legitimacy, regardless of its origins of that government (E OC.465–87; E CP.498–500; E IC.512). Similarly, in a 1764 letter to the Whig historian Catherine Macaulay, he states that he considers all types of government, from the monarchy in France to the democracy in some of the Swiss cantons, "to be equally legal, if established by custom and authority" (NL 81). That is, "time and custom give authority to all forms of government," and may even confer it retroactively upon a line of succession founded by what historians might describe as an act of usurpation (T 3.2.10.19; cf. 3.2.10.4–9 [SBN 566; cf. 556–59]). Hume concludes in his historical writings that "the only rule of government, which is intelligible or carries any authority with it, is the established practice of the age," which is "prevalent, and universally assented to" (H 2.23.525; cf. E CP.498–99).

Hume's criticism of the Lockean version of the social contract theory, especially as the foundation of the current English political system and the creed of the Whig party, is a response to a peculiar set of historical circumstances. The Whig and Tory parties had emerged during the Restoration period under Charles II, in the aftermath of the Civil War and the Puritan Republic. Both parties had subsequently participated in deposing James II, the Catholic brother of Charles II, in the Glorious Revolution of 1688; in establishing the new constitutional settlement under William and Mary in 1689; and in securing the Protestant succession by confirming the Hanoverian line in 1701 and 1714. The Whigs had justified the Glorious Revolution by appealing to the social contract theory. According to this theory, since the obligation of allegiance rests on a promise of obedience given in return for a promise of "protection and security," our duty of allegiance is suspended if our government, by an "egregious tyranny," fails to uphold or violates this agreement. Any severe oppression of its subjects by a government would thus provide a justification for rebellion (T 3.2.9.1 [SBN 549]).

Hume argues that the Whig account of the right of resistance to government is derived from a mistaken conception of political obligation, although the principle itself is "perfectly just and reasonable," and may indeed be secured "on more reasonable principles" by his own analysis of political authority. According to Hume's theory, since the primary function that we attribute to government is to establish "the security and protection, which we enjoy in political society," we have a natural obligation to obey the government only as long as this interest is met. The moral obligation of allegiance extends at least a little further, since common opinion holds that we should obey the government even when we individually believe that it has ceased to serve its expected function. However, even the moral obligation of allegiance is suspended by "the more flagrant instances of tyranny and oppression," once common opinion agrees in concluding that the government has failed to fulfill its purpose, and in supporting the right of rebellion. He therefore argues that the right of resistance is justified directly by his account of the nature and purpose of political authority, without appealing to any violation of a supposed contract (T 3.2.9.1–4 [SBN 549–52]).

Hume thus agrees with the Whig social contract theorists in rejecting the Tory doctrine of "passive obedience," or the duty of unconditional submission to government. Indeed, he regards the latter doctrine as an "absurdity" which has never been accepted "in all our notions of morals." He even points out in his essays that the doctrine of passive obedience cannot be defended with any consistency by the Tory or "high monarchical party," which had itself participated in the uprising against James II in 1688 (T 3.2.9.4 [SBN 549–52]; E PGB.70–71; E PO.490). However, while he defends the right of resistance to tyranny, Hume argues that the limits of our duty of allegiance cannot, and should not, be specified in advance, either by philosophers or by political leaders. In the *Treatise* he states that although the right of resistance is authorized by common opinion and universal practice, it is impossible "for the laws, or even for philosophy, to establish any *particular* rules, by which we may know when resistance is lawful." As a result, while he praises the constitutional settlement emerging from the Revolution of 1688, Hume declines to judge whether the institutions of English government had really been "threaten'd with the utmost danger" under James II, although he professes to doubt, though perhaps disingenuously, that this question "admits of controversy." However, his description of the process by which the succession was settled, and his own lukewarm endorsement of the Hanoverian line, reflects more directly his deflationary analysis of the principles by which we determine the legitimacy of any government (T 3.2.10.16–19 [SBN 563–67]).

Hume also emphasizes the indeterminacy of the right of resistance in his later writings. In "Of Passive Obedience" he argues that it is generally better to teach the duty of obedience than to attempt to identify in advance "all the cases, in which resistance may be allowed" (E PO.490). In the *History of England* he affirms this principle in considering an earlier case of resistance to government: the execution of Charles I. Since government is established "to restrain the fury and injustice of the people," and is "always founded on opinion, not on force," he maintains that it is dangerous to weaken "the reverence, which the multitude owe to authority, and to instruct them beforehand, that the case can ever happen, when they may be freed from their duty of allegiance." However, we need not fear that this warning will reduce humanity to "a state of abject servitude," since even where an exception has not been "previously expected and descanted on," an egregious tyranny will be "so obvious and undisputed, as to remove all doubt, and overpower the restraint, however great, imposed by teaching the general doctrine of obedience" (H 5.59.544). That is, the limits in our duty of allegiance to government are determined, not in advance by the reasonings of politicians and philosophers, but by public opinion during a time of immediate crisis. Resistance is accordingly justified when a large part of the population unites to oppose an extreme abuse of power, without regard to any theories concerning the extent and limits of political obligation.

In sum, Hume derives a dual obligation of political obedience from our recognition of the tendency of government to preserve the "peace and order" of society. These consist in a natural obligation arising from self-interest, and a moral obligation to support the public interest, which we recognize and accept through sympathy with other agents (T 3.2.11.5, 3.2.8.8 [SBN 569, 545]). These two principles of natural and moral obligation are generally regarded as the source of the legitimacy of government; and these principles also provide the standard by which the value of maintaining any particular government is decided by public opinion. A given population generally regards its system of government as legitimate, even if this system does not approximate what might be regarded as an ideal form of government. However, the population may be expected to actively reject a government that does not provide a minimal level of peace and order.

Hume recognizes that different governments may be more or less successful in preserving the peace of a society, and in enhancing its prosperity and happiness. In his view, three conditions are crucial for the success of a government, especially in the modern world. These are its constitutional structure, its legislative and administrative activity, and public support for and participation in the government, or what we might call the political culture of the nation. While the eighteenth-century British system of government was a source of pride for its subjects and widely admired throughout Europe, Hume also recognized that it might be made more effective in a number of areas. As a political essayist, Hume accordingly seeks to improve the government, policies, and political culture of contemporary Britain. We will return to his activities as a practical political writer later in this chapter, after considering his account of the study of politics as a branch of the social sciences.

POLITICS AS A SCIENCE

We have already considered Hume's account of the interpretation of individual human actions in Chapter 7. In this section of the present chapter I consider his further references to the principles involved in explaining developments within and collective actions by social groups. These discussions appear especially in his essays, often as the theoretical background for his treatment of various particular developments in social, economic, political, or cultural life.[7]

Hume includes "politics" in the Advertisement to the *Treatise* among the topics that he hopes to address in his study of human nature. In the introduction he describes politics as the science in which we consider human beings "as united in society, and dependent on each other" (T Adv.1, Int.5; cf. 1.4.7.12 [SBN xii, xv–xvi; cf. 271]). He later indicates that causal reasoning "runs thro' politics, war, commerce, œconomy," both as practical activities and as subjects of inquiry among moral philosophers (T 2.3.1.15; cf. 1.3.15.11 [SBN 405; cf. 175]). In the first *Enquiry* he characterizes politics as a study of the "uniform influence" of "laws and forms of government" in human society. He also describes politics, natural philosophy, medicine, and chemistry as sciences that "treat of general facts," or in other words "the qualities, causes, and effects of a whole species of objects," unlike the sciences of history, geography and astronomy, which study particular facts (EHU 8.18, 12.31 [SBN 90, 164–65]).

Hume develops several further discussions of the "science" of politics in his *Essays*. In these passages he describes politics as a discipline that examines the patterns of behavior we discover in our historical and cross-cultural studies of human life, especially as these appear to be influenced by different types of government.[8]

In several of his essays Hume specifically defends the value of "general reasonings," in politics, economics, and other areas of human activity. Thus, although a study of the "general course of things" might appear to be the "chief business of philosophers," this study is also the "chief business of politicians," since the task of promoting "the public good, which is, or ought to be their object," requires them to understand "the concurrence of a multitude of causes" (E Co.254). He accordingly describes political inquiry as the science "which, of all others, contributes most to public utility," as well as to the "private satisfaction of those who addict themselves to the study of it" (E CL.87).

In light of this affirmation of the value of the study of politics, we may consider Hume's account of the principles for explaining collective actions or developments in human society. In "Of the Rise and Progress of the Arts and Sciences" he observes that one of the central problems in the explanation of human affairs is "to distinguish exactly what is owing to *chance*, and what proceeds from *causes*." He then defends the twofold hypothesis that "what depends upon a few persons is, in a great measure, to be ascribed to chance, or secret and

7. See Wallis, "David Hume's Contribution to Social Science," 358–71; Bryson, *Man and Society;* Swingewood, "Origins of Sociology," 164–77; and Capaldi, "Hume as Social Scientist," 99–123.
8. See Conniff, "Hume's Political Methodology," 88–108; Forbes, *Hume's Philosophical Politics*, 224–30; Warner and Livingston, "Introduction," xiv–xviii.

unknown causes," while on the other hand "what arises from a great number, may often be accounted for by determinate and known causes." For example, it is easier to explain the gradual changes in the domestic life of a nation than the sudden changes in its foreign relations, and to account for "the rise and progress of commerce in any kingdom, than for that of learning" (E RP.111–13).

While this hypothesis might seem to contradict his rejection of an appeal to "chance" in any causal explanation, Hume is actually using the word "chance" here rather misleadingly, to describe the influence of "particular" as opposed to "general" causes in human affairs. In a more accurate statement of his view, the science of politics attempts to explain the "general facts" of human action, or the "causes and effects" of many human actions as "a whole species of objects," rather than the unique actions of individuals. In other words, the science of politics attempts to trace the similar circumstances and motives for similar actions that are performed by a number of individuals (EHU 12.30–31 [SBN 164–65]). Historians, who study the "particular facts" in human life, may attempt to explain particular actions in history by identifying the motives of individual agents. However, such unique actions may be set aside by the generalizing social scientist as instances of "chance," if they do not belong to a large set of similar actions in the given society, which can be explained as "general facts." The "science" of politics, along with the other social sciences such as economics, sociology, and demographics, is accordingly directed toward the study of social trends, or the similar actions of many individuals. By contrast, Hume finds that the study of art, literature, science, scholarship, and international events may be more effectively pursued through a study of a unique series of causes and effects. In other words, we may explain unique historical events through "*particular* deliberations" in which we consider "the caprices of a few persons," while attempting to explain larger social developments through "*general* reasonings" concerning similar actions by many individuals (E Co.255). Finally, the "grosser and more stubborn" causes operating in a given society, especially when reinforced by sympathy, tend to promote the predominant "inclination or passion" that we often find "at a certain time, and among a certain people." This predominant passion moves many individuals to similar actions, even though we also find that "many individuals may escape the contagion, and be ruled by passions peculiar to themselves" (E RP.112; cf. E NC.202–4).

Hume's apparent distinction between "chance" and causes in human affairs may thus be described more accurately as a demarcation between two methods for explaining human actions: a particular account of a unique series of actions, and a general account of the resembling actions of many agents. However, this distinction is relative rather than absolute for several reasons. First, both of these methods appeal to the same basic principle of explanation by regarding human actions as the effects of motives, or of particular beliefs and desires, as these are determined by the character and circumstances of the agent. However, while history is concerned with tracing the motives and actions of particular individuals, the generalizing social sciences are concerned with tracing the influence of similar beliefs, desires, passions, and circumstances on similar actions by many individuals. In addition, while the "sciences" of history and politics are respectively concerned with particular or general facts in human life, Hume also regards history in a broader sense as the collective experience of the human species, and thus the single and unified object of both types of study. In other words, through the study of history we may "glean up" further experiments to supplement the "cautious observation" of contemporary life, which provides the data for the science of man (T Int.10 [SBN xix]; cf. E SH.565–68). Indeed, Hume draws upon his own study of history to provide the empirical data for his social and political generalizations in several of his essays. On the other hand, as we will see in Chapter 13, Hume also incorporates a continuous account of general social, economic, and cultural trends in English and European history into his *History of England,* woven into his narrative account of the unique individuals and events of English political history.

Hume also addresses this relative distinction between explaining unique historical actions and general patterns of development in "Of Some Remarkable Customs." In this essay he considers the principles by which we might attempt to explain those "irregular and extraordinary appearances" that we often find "in the moral, as well as in the physical world" (E RC.366). He then examines three surprising political practices, in order to show that when such actions do not conform to any general principles of politics, they can often be explained instead as the effects of particular historical circumstances. The first is the ancient Athenian law permitting the criminal prosecution of the sponsor of any legislation that was accepted by the general assembly but later judged to have been harmful to the public interest. This law seems to violate the general principle that an "entire liberty of speech" is necessary for the proceedings of a legislative body. However, Hume argues that this law arose from the distinctive Athenian system of government. Since a direct democracy is especially susceptible to the influence of demagogues, and since the Athenians were "averse to checking themselves by any rule or restriction," they sought to protect themselves in advance from being persuaded into dangerous undertakings by irresponsible or self-serving leaders (E RC.366–70). As other examples of "remarkable customs," Hume considers the coexistence of two legislative bodies in ancient Rome, and the extralegal practice of "impressing" or kidnapping sailors for the navy by the modern English government. In both of these cases, he argues that while each of these customs might be an exception to a "general maxim" in politics, each can also be explained as a result of the beliefs and desires arising within a particular society, in response to a distinctive set of historical circumstances, and in contrast to the motives and actions that might appear under more typical circumstances (E RC.370–76; cf. CMH 59–60).

In light of the difficulties in identifying the motives for individual human actions, and in tracing the influence of circumstances on any resembling sets of actions by many individuals, Hume indicates "that all general maxims in politics ought to be established with great caution" (E RC.366). Indeed, he observes that "the world is still too young to fix many general truths in politics," since three thousand years of historical experience have not yet perfected the "art of reasoning" in this domain, nor provided "sufficient materials upon which we can reason." He thus expects many of his own conclusions concerning social and political developments to be "refuted by further experience, and be rejected by posterity" (E CL.87, 89). He also notes that first appearances are often deceitful in the science of politics, since this science offers us "few rules, which will not admit of some exception, and which may not sometimes be controuled by fortune and accident" (E OC.477). Finally, he warns us that the social sciences do not provide a basis for secure predictions. In other words, even though we might in many cases explain human actions in retrospect, it is often "fully as impossible for human prudence, before-hand, to foresee and foretel them" (E RC.366; cf. E BG.47).

Hume's most impressive application of the generalizing methods of the social sciences to a particular area of human life appears in his essay "Of the Populousness of Ancient Nations," in which he compares the population levels of the ancient and modern worlds, mainly in Europe and the Mediterranean region, using two interrelated arguments.[9] First, and more important for our present discussion, he examines the causes that are likely to produce an increase or decrease in population, and finds that these would indicate a greater population in modern Europe than in the ancient world (E PA.377–421). Second, based on his analysis of the documentary evidence, he rejects the fashionable view among many of his contemporaries that Europe and the Mediterranean region were in fact more populous in antiquity and hence, by implication, offered better living conditions for human beings (E PA.421–64).

In considering the causes of different population levels, Hume initially observes that certain "physical causes," such as disease, might contribute to differences in population levels between one nation or historical period and another. However, he attributes more importance to the "moral causes" of different population levels, or in other words to the social conditions that are likely to influence the population rate by influencing the motives and actions of many

---

9. For discussions of Hume's essay on population, see Rotwein's introduction to his *David Hume: Writings on Economics*, lxxxviii–xc, and the notes by Miller in his edition of the *Essays Moral Political and Literary* (E PA.377–464).

people (E PA.380; cf. E NC.198). He divides the moral causes of an increase or decrease in population into two types: those belonging to the domestic life of a given people, and those belonging to their political circumstances (E PA.383). First, in considering the domestic causes of demographic trends, he argues that the widespread practice of slavery in antiquity tended to maintain a lower population. That is, the desire of the owners to limit the number of nonworking slaves would motivate them to prevent pregnancies and births among their slaves, especially if they could easily purchase adult slaves. Accordingly, procreation would have been more limited in the ancient than the modern world (E PA.386–98). Next, Hume identifies several political causes in the ancient world that might have contributed to population growth, such as the relatively small size of ancient nations, and the relative equality of wealth among individuals. However, he also identifies three political sources for a higher level of population in the modern world. These include the ancient style of war, which tended to be more destructive than eighteenth-century warfare; the ruthless civil strife of antiquity; and the modern expansion of trade, industry, and civic order, which by enhancing the general prosperity have also encouraged prospective parents to have larger families (E PA.400–421).

Hume sets forth a more direct study of the operations and effects of political institutions in "That Politics May Be Reduced to a Science." In this essay he attempts to determine whether the quality of a government depends upon the personalities and actions of individual rulers, or instead upon its constitutional structure, which would allow us to compare and evaluate different systems of government. He then argues that while the quality of an absolute monarchy depends largely upon the character of the individual ruler, a "republican and free government" specifically includes a system of "checks and controuls" in its constitution which are designed to reduce the influence of individual characters in the administration of government. A "wisely constituted" republican government thus engages the interests "even of bad men, to act for the public good," while a poorly designed republican government may become "the source of all disorder, and of the blackest crimes," as in the case of the later Roman republic. Hume therefore argues that the influence "of laws, and of particular forms of government" on the motives and actions of the ruler, in contrast to the unbridled "humours and tempers of men," is so powerful and extensive "that consequences almost as general and certain may sometimes be deduced from them, as any which the mathematical sciences afford us" (E PR.14–16).

Next, by examining the various patterns of motivation and action that are likely to arise under different types of government, and also by considering several historical examples, Hume proposes a threefold generalization as a "universal axiom in politics." This is the principle that "an hereditary prince, a nobility without vassals, and a people voting by their representatives, form the best MONARCHY, ARISTOCRACY, and DEMOCRACY," especially in contrast to an elective monarchy, a feudal nobility, and a direct democracy. He then proposes several further "general truths" in politics, which also arise from the constitution of a government rather than the characters of its rulers or subjects. First, while "free" or republican governments provide more liberty for their own populations, they also tend to be more "ruinous and oppressive" toward their colonies than monarchical governments. For example, the Roman provincial governors and their contacts under the republican bureaucracy connived in despoiling the conquered territories in order to profit from their temporary terms of office, while the Roman emperors were lenient and generous toward conquered populations because of their interest in maintaining the long-term loyalty of their provincial subjects. Hume finds a similar pattern in the relatively benevolent rule of the modern French monarchy over Corsica, as compared to the rule of Parliament over Ireland under the English constitutional system. As a third principle, he finds that a gentle government tends to give the greatest security to both rulers and subjects. Since these and other effects arise from the legal and administrative structure of a government, he concludes that legislators should not trust "the future government of a state entirely to chance," but should instead establish "wise regulations," or "a system of laws to regulate the administration of public affairs to the latest posterity," as "the most valuable legacy that can be left to future ages" (E PR.18–24). In "Of National Characters" he considers the effects of various systems of government on national culture, along with the effects of geographic distribution; different ethnic, religious, or linguistic traditions; social classes; and economic activities (E NC.204–7).

Hume argues that the expansion of the rule of law in the modern state, rather than the development of any particular system of government, has been the most important "change for the better" in modern politics. This development has in fact reduced the sharp contrast between monarchial and republican government, so that we may now affirm "of civilized monarchies, what was formerly said in praise of republics alone, *that they are a government of Laws, not of Men.*" A modern monarchy, under the rule of law, is "susceptible of order, method, and constancy," so that "property is there secure; industry encouraged; the arts flourish; and the prince lives secure among his subjects, like a father among his children" (E CL.93–94). However, Hume argues that every government must combine elements of both liberty and authority, and maintain a balance between them, so that any differences between "free" and monarchial governments in this respect are relative rather than absolute. The success of a government thus depends less on its type than upon the quality of its laws and

276 · David Hume: Reason in History

constitution, and upon their ability to promote the welfare of the population under its given social and economic conditions (E OG.40–41; cf. E. CL.94–96).[10] Hume emphasizes the value of wisely formulated laws throughout his writings. Indeed, he regards the development of constitutional government as the greatest achievement of the modern republican movement. A republican government, in spite of what he calls its barbarian origins, "necessarily, by an infallible operation, gives rise to LAW," and thereby establishes the security required for the development of the arts and sciences (E RP.118). An absolute monarchy is denied this security; but a civilized monarchy can borrow its "laws, and methods, and institutions, and consequently its stability and order" from the republican form of government (E RP.124–26). Thus, among those who "distinguish themselves by memorable achievements," even in the arts and sciences, Hume gives the greatest honor "to LEGISLATORS and founders of states, who transmit a system of laws and institutions to secure the peace, happiness, and liberty of future generations" (E PG.54; cf. E PR.25–27).[11] In the *History of England* he praises the Saxon kings Ethelbert and Alfred the Great for developing written codes of law, and also identifies the rediscovery of Justinian's *Pandects* during the twelfth century as the central event in the intellectual and cultural reawakening of Europe (H 1.1.32; H 1.2.78–79; H 2.23.520–21). Hume's regard for a wise system of law is also echoed by his Stoic philosopher, who considers "liberty and laws" to be "the source of human happiness," and regards the effort to guard and preserve the law for the "most distant posterity" as the noblest endeavor of the human mind (E St.152–53).

Hume therefore presents the study of politics as a science that is of interest, not only to the moral philosopher and the reflective person in private life, but also to those responsible for the government of a state, who have an interest in promoting the welfare and prosperity of the nation through their own legislative and administrative functions. The scientific study of politics may enhance the ability of legislators and rulers to anticipate the probable effects of their laws on the motives and actions of the population, and to judge how these laws are likely to influence the welfare of the nation, or the "happiness and virtue" of the people (E PA.382; cf. E PG.54–55; E RA.280). Finally, the social scientist who is also a practical moralist may help legislators in this task by tracing the influence of various laws and policies on the population, by recommending specific laws and administrative policies, and even by engaging public support for civic laws and institutions. Hume himself pursues all of these projects in

10. For discussions of Hume's comparison of different political systems, see Forbes, *Hume's Philosophical Politics*, 140–67; Livingston, *Hume's Philosophy of Common Life*, 266–67; Whelan, *Order and Artifice*, 352–53; and Stewart, *Opinion and Reform*, 171.

11. On Hume's view of wise legislators, see Forbes, *Hume's Philosophical Politics*, 224–30 and 315–23; Whelan, *Order and Artifice*, 348–57; and Danford, *Problem of Reason*, 123–35.

own writings as a practical political philosopher, especially in his reflections concerning the structure of British government, the tendencies in English political culture, and the economic policies of the British government.

SPECULATIVE SYSTEMS OF GOVERNMENT

Hume applies the principles he derives from his theoretical analysis of politics to a distinctive aspect of modern political life in his critique of speculative systems of government, or what we might call political ideology.[12] This critique emerges in three areas of his writings: his general examination of political parties in the *Essays,* his account of seventeenth-century English political history in the *Essays* and the *History of England,* and his observations concerning the "Wilkes and Liberty" movement in a number of his letters after 1763.[13]

Hume introduces his account of speculative political principles in his earliest volume of essays, especially in "Of Parties in General," and "Of the Parties of Great Britain," in which he combines a historical survey of the different types of political parties with a social-scientific account of their origins in human nature. He returns to this discussion in a later essay, "Of the Coalition of Parties," in which he attempts to specify the proper place of the two parties in English political life.

Hume initially observes that human beings have a propensity to divide themselves into parties or factions, which promote "the fiercest animosities among men of the same nation." He then develops a classificatory system for different types of parties by examining the types of factions that have appeared through history. First, he distinguishes between "PERSONAL" and "REAL" factions. Personal factions arise from "personal friendship or animosity," especially in small republics, while real factions arise from "some real difference of sentiment or interest." Real factions may in turn be divided into three further types of parties: "from *interest,* from *principle,* and from *affection.*" The first of these, parties of interest, are "the most reasonable, and the most excusable," since they arise when the members of a particular social group, such as merchants or landowners, recognize that they can cooperate to attain a variety of common ends. By contrast, parties of affection emerge from "different attachments of

12. Here I am using the term "ideology" for any system of political doctrines, and not in the more specific sense derived from Marxist theory, in which a system of political beliefs is regarded as the disguised expression of the economic interests of a social class. For a useful history of this concept, see Goldie, "Ideology," 266–91.

13. In this section I am following the analysis presented especially by Letwin in *Pursuit of Certainty,* 1–123, and by Livingston in *Hume's Philosophy of Common Life,* 272–342, and *Philosophical Melancholy and Delirium,* 217–66.

men towards particular families and persons, whom they desire to rule over them." Parties of affection thus resemble personal factions, although they do not rest upon any direct personal acquaintance between their leaders and followers (E PG.55–63).

While the three preceding types of parties appear in almost every nation, Hume argues that "parties from *principle,* especially abstract speculative principle, are known only to modern times." Indeed, he describes the modern party of political principle as "the most extraordinary and unaccountable *phænomenon,* that has yet appeared in human affairs." Unlike the other kinds of factions, modern parties of principle embrace "opposite views" against each other concerning the "essentials of government," leaving "no room for any compromise or accommodation." This absolute opposition promotes a powerful cohesion within each party and an extreme antagonism between them, tendencies which are especially dangerous to society, since they may lead to political stalemate, to factional violence, and even to civil war (E PG.60–63; E CP.493).

Hume explains the development and proliferation of these "parties of principle" within a given society by appealing to his discussion of sympathy. Since the human mind is "wonderfully fortified by an unanimity of sentiments," but "shocked and disturbed by any contrariety," we as human beings generally respond with affection to those who agree with us, and with "impatience" toward those who oppose us "even in the most speculative and indifferent opinions" (E PG.60–61). Sympathy encourages us to seek agreement with our close associates and to seek unanimity in our own groups against groups with other opinions. The diffusion of abstract opinions is thus promoted by sympathy, whose operation in this context may be compared to a "contagion" or "infection" (cf. H 5.53.258; E IC.523). This desire for unanimity among the members of a party is also reinforced by shared interests, and a shared affection toward "party-zealots" (E PR.27–28; cf. E IP.42–43). Hume accordingly includes "popular sedition, party zeal, [and] a devoted obedience to factious leaders" among "the most visible, though less laudable effects of this social sympathy in human nature" (EPM 5.35 [SBN 224]).[14]

Historically, Hume traces the original emergence of this type of absolute opposition to differences in religious opinions. Here he finds that, unlike two people passing each other on the road, "two men, reasoning upon opposite principles of religion, cannot so easily pass, without shocking," even if there seems to be room enough for each one to pursue his own course without disturbing the other. Hume argues more specifically that this type of absolute opposition initially arose from the combination of Christianity with philosophy. Since Christianity arose in a culture that was hostile to it and also pervaded by

14. For a further discussion of Hume's account of factions, see Herdt, *Religion and Faction.*

philosophy, its leaders sought to defend their teachings by developing a "system of speculative opinions" and cultivating a "keenness in dispute" in their apologetics. This disposition toward contention continued as Christianity was divided into different sects, whose leaders sought to promote "a mutual hatred and antipathy" between their "deluded followers." As a result of these conflicts, Christianity has "engendered a spirit of persecution" wherever it has become established, "which has ever since been the poison of human society, and the source of the most inveterate factions in every government" (E PG.60–63). Hume also traces the opposition between "SUPERSTITION" and "ENTHUSIASM" as another type of factional division in Christianity, beginning with the conflict between the Catholic church and Protestant sects during the Reformation, and including the conflict between the High Church and Puritan movements in the Church of England during the sixteenth and seventeenth centuries (E SE.73–79; H 1.Var.xiv–xviii; H 3.29.134–42).[15]

According to Hume, the Tory and Whig parties in Britain initially developed from the parties of interest and affection among the court nobility and the country gentry. This division between a court party and a country party is a natural product of the British system of government, and of the differences in "men's passions and prejudices," since "those of mild tempers, who love peace and order" tend to favor the monarchy, while those of a more bold and expansive outlook tend to become "passionate lovers of liberty" (E PGB.63–64). However, during the early seventeenth century the court and country parties respectively developed the conflicting political doctrines of royal absolutism and republicanism, and also adopted the opposing religious systems of High Anglicanism and Puritanism. After the Civil War and the Restoration these parties, now called Tories and Whigs, continued to assert their principles of passive obedience on the one hand and resistance to tyranny on the other. However, these ideological pretensions were subverted by the participation of both parties in the revolution and constitutional settlement of 1688–89, when the Tories helped to depose a monarch, and the Whigs helped to establish a new government without seeking the consent of the population (E PGB.64–71; E OC.472–73; E CP.494–501). In spite of these derelictions, both parties continued to defend their opposing principles and programs under the very different political conditions of the eighteenth century. Thus, since "no party, in the present age" can sustain itself "without a philosophical or speculative system of principles, annexed to its political or practical one," each faction in eighteenth-century British political life "reared up a fabric," drawn from its earlier system of doctrines, "to protect and cover that scheme of actions, which it pursues" (E OC.465; cf. H 6.68.381; H 6.71.523–30).

15. See Haakonssen, "Hume's Political Theory," 182–221.

As a remedy for this tendency in contemporary English political culture, Hume seeks to undermine the absolute conflict between the Whig and Tory positions in several of his essays by showing that neither party is "fully supported by reason," in its principles or its policies (E CP.494). The Tories depict government as a divine institution to render it inviolate, while the Whigs regard government as dependent upon popular consent to reserve the right of resistance. In response, Hume argues that "both these *systems* of speculative principles are just; though not in the sense, intended by the parties," and also that "both the *schemes* of practical consequences are prudent; though not in the extremes, to which each party, in opposition to the other, has commonly endeavoured to carry them" (E OC.466). As a mediating view, he presents his own theory, in which, as we have already seen, government arises from consent but acquires an independent authority once it is established, and the people retain a right of resistance, the extent of which, however, cannot be exactly determined in advance (E OC.465–87; E PO.488–92).

Hume also considers the opposing Whig and Tory interpretations of two crucial events in recent English history by reconstructing the debates over the constitutional crisis of the 1640s, and the succession in 1714. Here he attempts to show that there were sound precedents, cogent arguments, and good intentions on both sides (cf. E CP.494). First, after comparing the royal and parliamentary claims that led to the Civil War, he argues that "the event, if that can be admitted as a reason, has shown, that the arguments of the popular party were better founded," although "according to the established maxims of lawyers and politicians" the royalist view would have appeared at the time to be "more solid, more safe, and more legal" (E CP.500). In considering the succession crisis, he argues that although there were advantages and disadvantages in establishing either the Catholic Stuart or Protestant Hanoverian line at the time, the Protestant line has since become so secure and popular, as to have acquired a legitimate claim to universal acceptance (E PS.510–11).[16] In these essays Hume attempts to persuade his readers that a thoughtful view of these events does not exclusively support the interpretation of either party, and that the resulting system of government is entitled to the support of both parties.

Hume traces the development of these two competing speculative theories of government in the two *History of England* volumes on the seventeenth century, which he indeed later described as the period in which "the misrepresentations of faction began chiefly to take place" (ML xxxvi). In fact, Hume wrote the two volumes on the Stuart period before he decided to examine the earlier history of England, first in two Tudor volumes, and then in two medieval volumes

16. The legitimacy of the Hanoverian settlement in 1714 was still a delicate issue during Hume's lifetime, with several abortive but disruptive Jacobite rebellions in Scotland on behalf of the Stuart line, culminating in the final Jacobite uprising of 1745. See Mossner, *Life of David Hume*, 177–86.

extending the narrative back to Celtic and Roman Britain. These four volumes are largely concerned with examining the earlier history of the English constitution, in response to the "misrepresentations of faction" in the seventeenth century and in his own day.

Hume begins his account of the Stuart period by describing the rapidly increasing pace of social, economic, intellectual, and cultural change in England and elsewhere in Europe during the fifteenth century. By 1600 this "universal fermentation" had produced "a general, but insensible revolution" in English thought, in which "the ideas of men enlarged themselves on all sides," and many medieval traditions of government, "which seem to have lain long unactive," were revived and came into conflict with each other. This "rising spirit" had been restrained during the "severe though popular, government of Elizabeth," but with the accession of James I, a "less dreaded and less beloved" monarch from the Scottish Stuart line, "symptoms immediately appeared of a more free and independent genius in the nation." Hume argues that the conflict between Parliament and the Stuart kings arose from these underlying tensions rather than any immediate complaint, since "the grievances, under which the English laboured," apart from these disputed constitutional issues, "scarcely deserve the name," and were indeed neither "burthensome on the people's properties, or anywise shocking to the natural humanity of mankind" (H 5.45.18–19; H 5.52.249).

During the reign of James I, a few "men of genius and of enlarged minds" began to develop various elements of the English political tradition into "principles of liberty." These principles were adopted by many in the House of Commons, but were as yet "pretty much unknown to the generality of the people." At the same time the king, who was already "jealous of regal, because conscious of little personal authority," was developing in his own mind "a speculative system of absolute government" (H 5.45.18–19; H 5.NoteC.550). However, both sets of principles were only tenuously related to the actual circumstances of seventeenth-century English government. On the one hand, the despotism of the monarch was "more speculative than practical," while on the other hand the increasing independence of the House of Commons was "too new and recent to be as yet founded on systematical principles and opinions" (H 5.46.45).

Hume traces the development of these two opposing theories of government in a series of confrontations between the first two Stuart monarchs and the House of Commons, leading to the Civil War and the overthrow of the monarchy. Throughout this narrative, he maintains that there were legitimate claims on both sides, and that the tradition of the English government afforded "a variety of precedents," so that "no party or both parties" were equally to blame for the conflict (H 5.48.96). In other words, both theories of government could be justified, though on different grounds. On the side of the monarchy, "appearances were sufficiently strong in favor of the king to apologize for his following such maxims," while on the side of Parliament, public liberty would have been "so precarious under this exorbitant prerogative" that opposition was "not only excuseable, but laudable, in the people" (H 5.52.236). However, Hume argues that this political conflict would not have led to civil war without an associated conflict over religion, emerging within the Church of England, in which the supporters of parliamentary rights were drawn to Puritanism, while the court was increasingly identified with the episcopal polity and Arminianism. These "theological or metaphysical controversies" infused the political conflict with the zeal of religious antagonism, and produced the "factions, convulsions, and disorders" of the Civil War, ending in the capture and execution of Charles I (H 5.51.214; H 5.NoteW.570; cf. E PGB.67–69; H.5.51.211–13; H 5.57.441–42).

In his account of the Puritan Commonwealth, Hume shows that the same "fanatical spirit" that had emerged from the conflict between the king and Parliament also fragmented the republican movement, as various individuals and sects began to promulgate different systems of religion and government. With the dissolution of all civic and ecclesiastical authority "by which the nation had ever been accustomed to be governed," the "spirit of refinement and innovation" spread in the Puritan and republican ranks, until "every man had framed the model of a republic," and had "adjusted a system of religion," founded upon their own "supposed inspiration," rather than a traditional authority or "any principles of human reason." These individuals and sects, such as the Levellers, millenarians, and even proto-anarchists, attempted to impose their "fantastical" systems on others, through persuasion or force (H 6.60.3; cf. 5.55.380; 5.59.532). Even the republicans who "adopted not such extravagancies, were so intoxicated with their saintly character" that they claimed "peculiar privileges," and exempted themselves from oaths, laws, and contracts. As a result "the bands of society were every where loosened; and the irregular passions of men were encouraged by speculative principles, still more unsocial and irregular" (H 6.60.4). This process of disintegration was finally ended by Cromwell, who used the support of the army and his reputation for piety to establish his own "unlimited authority" as the Protector, and to govern as a military dictator (H 6.60.5; H 6.61.63–65). Thus, in Hume's view, the political and religious fanaticism of the Puritan movement led to a new type of absolutism, which was much more dangerous than the Stuart monarchy had been, since it operated through the direct exercise of military force in a chaotic setting without any of the traditional restraints.

By 1660, public dissatisfaction with Puritan rule and a decline in republican leadership facilitated the reconvening of Parliament and the unconditional restoration of the monarchy in the person of Charles II. However, under his

Catholic brother and successor, James II, a renewal of religious and political tensions between the king and Parliament led to the deposition and exile of the king in the Glorious Revolution of 1688. The recurring conflict between the king and Parliament was finally resolved by the Declaration of Rights accepted upon their coronation by William and Mary in 1689. In this document "all the points, which had, of late years, been disputed between the king and people, were finally determined," and royal prerogative was "more narrowly circumscribed and more exactly defined, than in any former period of the English government." Hume concludes that the resulting political system, as bequeathed to eighteenth-century Britain, is, if not perhaps "the best system of government," at least "the most entire system of liberty, that ever was known amongst mankind" (H 6.71.530–31).

Hume traces the earlier development of the English constitution in the other volumes of his *History,* especially challenging the Whig view that the English government before 1600 had consisted in a "regular plan of liberty" (ML xxxviii). In his account of the Tudor period, he shows that even Queen Elizabeth, who was especially admired by Whig historians and politicians, took the principles of royal absolutism for granted, although she was a more talented ruler and enjoyed more popular support than her Stuart successors (H 4.App.3.354–70). He also shows that the balance of power between the monarch and other social groups had shifted repeatedly in the English government during the medieval period, from the relative democracy of the Saxon tribes, to the aristocracy in the Anglo-Saxon kingdoms, toward the king under early Norman rule, and again toward the feudal nobility with the signing of the Magna Carta. He also points out that the House of Commons in Parliament is a relatively late development, and that the lower classes did not benefit from the liberties secured by the feudal nobility. On the contrary, these privileges allowed the nobility to subject the commoners to their own increasingly arbitrary power. This was only restrained as the monarchy began to develop an "authority almost absolute" during the later medieval period, in which the kings were enabled "to pull down those disorderly and licentious tyrants," and to establish "that regular execution of the laws, which, in a following age, enabled the people to erect a regular and equitable plan of liberty" (H 2.23.525; cf. 4.App.3.355nl; H 1.App.2.461–72). In other words, the House of Commons arose, not from a struggle between the monarch and the entire population, but through an alliance between the monarch and an emerging middle class against the feudal nobility (H 2.12.34–40; H 2.13.100–110; E CP.497–98).

As a result of his historical study, Hume criticizes both the republican movement of the seventeenth century and the Whig leadership of his own day for appealing to the supposed "original plan" of the "ancient constitution" as a basis for defending civil liberty against the privileges claimed by the monarchy.

Not only is this view of the constitution illusory, but earlier English governments are, in any case, "by reason of the greater barbarity of the times," inappropriate models for a contemporary system of government. Instead, the success of the present political system in Britain, as "the most perfect and most accurate system of liberty that was ever found compatible with government," is its own best justification (H 2.23.525; H 4.App.3.355nl).[17]

As we will see in the next section, Hume has been repeatedly criticized, from the time of the publication of the first Stuart volume to the present, for the alleged Tory bias of his political narrative in the *History of England*. Much of this criticism has coincided with the Whig interpretation of English constitutional history, which dominated English historiography from his own day until the mid-twentieth century.[18] However, Stockton has shown that the development of a sustained challenge to the Whig historiographical tradition in the twentieth century has led historians to develop an account of the history of the English constitution that is very close to Hume's.[19] Like Hume, this interpretation contrasts the actual character of feudal government to the Whig conception of the "ancient constitution," examines the conflicting precedents in the English political tradition, and presents the modern English constitution as the unintended result of a struggle between the kings and Parliament. As a result, the general outline of Hume's history of the English constitution is reflected in many recent textbook accounts of the history of England.[20]

In a number of letters from the 1760s, Hume extended his critique of speculative systems of government to the "New Whig" movement, which had developed under William Pitt during his popular leadership in the House of Commons, and became especially visible in the "Wilkes and Liberty" movement.[21] John Wilkes was an ambitious Member of Parliament associated with Pitt's circle, who was arrested and imprisoned briefly by the Crown in 1763 for seditious libel after he published an attack on the conciliatory peace policy of the royal ministry, then led by Lord Bute, a Scottish Tory. His arrest was carried out under the controversial legal expedient of a general warrant, in spite of his status as a Member of Parliament. In the ensuing legal and political conflict Wilkes presented himself as the champion, not only of the traditional rights

17. For further discussions of the idea of the "ancient constitution" in English political history, see especially Pocock, *Ancient Constitution;* Forbes, *Hume's Philosophical Politics,* 233–60; and Stewart, *Opinion and Reform,* 256–57.

18. Herbert Butterfield presents a survey and a critique of this approach to the English constitution in his *Whig Interpretation of History.*

19. Stockton, "Historian of the English Constitution," 277–93. See also Forbes, "Introduction," 7–54.

20. See, for example, Dunn, *The Age of Religious Wars,* 164–78 and 189–98, and Kenyon, *Stuart England.*

21. For a concise history of the Wilkes affair, see Jarrett, *Britain,* 266–94. For Hume's reaction to the Wilkes movement, see Letwin, *Pursuit of Certainty,* 112–19; Forbes, *Hume's Philosophical Politics,* 128–35 and 187–92; and Livingston, *Hume's Philosophy of Common Life,* 269–71 and 323–29, and *Philosophical Melancholy and Delirium,* 266–89.

and liberties of Members of Parliament, but also of the interests of the middle and lower classes. This appeal to public opinion continued as he extended his conflict with the government to the House of Commons, which repeatedly disqualified him for membership between 1763 and 1774, when he was allowed to take his seat and returned to traditional political methods. During his period of suspension from Parliament, Wilkes led what was, in effect, the first popular political movement in English history, by claiming to defend the liberties secured by the British constitution, in terms that also seemed to promote improved living conditions for both the voting middle classes and the disenfranchised lower classes in London. Both of these groups were distressed by economic uncertainty and felt an increasing stake in the political process and in British public life, making them receptive to Wilkes as an apparent champion of their interests. The Wilkes movement also promoted English nationalism, imperialism, and anti-Scottish agitation, and was accompanied by sporadic violence on both sides.

Hume and Wilkes had met in Edinburgh in 1754, when Wilkes was seeking election to the parliamentary seat for nearby Berwick-upon-Tweed. In fact, during the course of that year Hume sent Wilkes two cordial letters and a copy of the first volume of the *History of England,* in which Wilkes had expressed an interest (L 1.194–95; L 1.205–6). Accordingly, writing in 1763 to his London publisher and fellow Scot, Andrew Millar, Hume censures Wilkes as "very blameable" in his publicly anti-Scottish sentiments, which are "low, vulgar, & ungenerous, and come with a bad Grace from him, who conversd so much with our Countrymen" (L 1.382–83). As a resident of London in 1768, Hume describes the "ferment" around the repeated Wilkes elections in a letter to the Marquise de Barbenane in Paris, adding that "these mutinies were founded on nothing, and had no connexion with any higher order of the state" (L 2.178). In 1769 he writes to his friend the Scottish cleric Hugh Blair that "this Madness about Wilkes," after raising his indignation and apprehension, had now continued "to such a Height, that all other Sentiments with me are bury'd in Ridicule" (L 2.197). Writing in the same year to Strahan, another Scot, he wishes that the police would be directed to take firmer measures against this new attempt by politicians to exploit the "violence of the Mob" for their own ends, since "Open Violence gives such a palpable Reason for the severe Execution of the Laws" (L 2.213). Finally, in a letter of 1771 to Strahan, he concludes a list of the political effects of the Wilkes movement by asking, "For God's sake, is there never to be a stop put to this inundation of the Rabble?" (L 2.245).

In explaining Hume's reactions to the Wilkes and Liberty movement, Livingston and others have pointed out that Hume was troubled by, among other things, how Wilkes and his supporters used the word "liberty." As we have seen, Hume considers the development of rights or liberties to be a valuable

286 · *David Hume: Reason in History*

part of the English political tradition, and he regards the success of the modern constitution in securing these rights as an important part of its achievement. However, and indeed for these very reasons, he is critical of the abstract appeal to liberty that emerged during the seventeenth century in the period leading up to the Civil War, and which still persisted in the rhetoric of the Whig party against the Crown.

Hume expresses his reservations over the misuse of the word "liberty" in a number of his letters. In a 1764 letter to Catherine Macaulay, he remarks that although "the cause of liberty, which you, Madam, with the Pyms and Hampdens have adopted, is noble and generous," many proponents of this cause in the seventeenth century "disgraced it, by their violence, and also by their cant, hypocrisy, and bigotry, which, more than the principles of civil liberty, seem to have been the motive of all their actions" (NL 81). In a letter to Turgot in 1768 concerning the Wilkes movement he writes that the London public has been "thrown into Disorders," though he hopes not dangerous ones, "merely from the Abuse of Liberty, chiefly the Liberty of the Press." All of this has occurred "without any Grievance, I do not only say, real, but even imaginary; and without any of them being able to tell one Circumstance of Government which they wish to have corrected." On the contrary, "they roar Liberty, tho' they have apparently more Liberty than any People in the World; a great deal more than they deserve; and perhaps more than any men ought to have" (L 2.180). He even maintains to Strahan in 1769 that "so much Liberty is incompatible with human Society," and hopes that Britain can escape from these public agitations "without falling into a military Government, such as Algiers or Tunis" (L 2.210).

In other words, Hume regards the popular demand for "liberty" as a demand for "license," or dispensation from law, rather than for any specific liberties to be secured through the legal and political institutions of Britain. In a 1772 letter to Strahan he indeed expresses the hope "that People do not take a Disgust at Liberty," since he finds that "men of Sense are sick at the very mention of it," and adds that "I hope a new term will be invented to express so valuable and good a thing" (NL 196). He also maintains that genuine liberty requires a stable political order. Indeed, writing in 1775 to his nephew, David Hume the younger, he argues provocatively that one of the advantages of a republican government, as compared to the "mixt Monarchy" of Great Britain, is that a system of republican rule would "considerably abridge our Liberty, which is growing to such an Extreme, as to be incompatible with all Government." He directs this argument especially against the "Fools" who "perpetually cry out Liberty: and think to augment it, by shaking off the Monarchy" (L 2.306).[22]

---

22. Hume's nephew, David Hume (1757–1839) would eventually become a Professor of Scots Law at Edinburgh, and later Baron of the Exchequer. I have followed Greig's reconstruction of several phrases in this letter.

Hume never refers to Wilkes by name in his published writings, but he addresses some of the issues raised by the Wilkes movement in his essays. In "Of the Origin of Government," he argues that all governments are subject to "a perpetual intestine struggle, open or secret, between AUTHORITY and LIBERTY." While on the one hand "a great sacrifice of liberty must necessarily be made in every government," on the other hand "the authority, which confines liberty, can never, and perhaps ought never, in any constitution, to become quite entire and uncontroulable." Hume concludes that "liberty is the perfection of civil society," although authority should be preferred in cases of extreme conflict, since order is essential to its very existence (E OG.40–41). Hume's reaction to the Wilkes movement is also reflected in his final revision to "Of the Liberty of the Press." In the versions of this essay published from 1741 to 1768, he argues that a free press is "attended with so few inconveniences" that it may be claimed as the "common right of mankind," and should be granted "almost in every government." However, in his final revisions, which were included in the 1777 edition, he concludes that a free press, although especially valuable in a constitutional monarchy, is also "one of the evils, attending those mixt forms of government" (E Var.604; E LP.13).

Hume therefore regards the word "liberty" as properly referring to the rights that are granted to various individuals within a state by its political traditions and institutions.[23] By contrast, he regards the Wilkian demand for liberty as an empty appeal to a speculative principle, which was intended to rally popular sentiment against the ordinary procedures and authority of government, without any specific demand or genuine grievances, and although the institutions and the authority of government are themselves the sources of civil liberty. Hume was also critical of the Wilkes movement for encouraging other harmful popular sentiments such as aggressive nationalism and militarism. Accordingly, the Wilkes movement, in Hume's view, was not an attempt to improve the government or political culture of Britain, but rather an attempt to promote the ambitions of one rather disreputable politician, supported by a disorderly element in the London population. In other words, Hume is not criticizing any specific political demands, or even a new conception of liberty put forward as a guiding principle for constitutional reform, but the use of the word "liberty" as an empty, self-serving, and manipulative political slogan.

Subsequent historians have regarded the Wilkes movement as the product of both the increasing social, economic, and political tensions in English society after 1750, and the new style of political activity and discourse emerging

---

23. For a further discussion of Hume's view of liberty, see the essays in Capaldi and Livingston's *Liberty in Hume's History of England,* along with Forbes, *Hume's Philosophical Politics,* 186–92; Livingston, *Hume's Philosophy of Common Life,* 323–29; Whelan, *Order and Artifice,* 356–63; Danford, *Problem of Reason,* 109–63; and Stewart, *Opinion and Reform,* 184–87 and 230–57.

with a popular national culture. Together, these and other developments would generate a successful movement in nineteenth-century Britain and elsewhere in the modern world toward an expansion of civic rights and political enfranchisement. Hume of course did not anticipate, and might not have supported, these developments. Instead, he assumes that the task of government belongs to the monarchy, aristocracy, and gentry, as he indicates in a 1769 letter to Strahan (L 2.210), although he also expects improvements in government and a rising prosperity to benefit the entire population of Britain. We might therefore plausibly regard Hume's reaction to the Wilkes and Liberty movement as expressing and reinforcing the interest of the gentry, from the perspective of a self-supporting younger son of a landed family, against any political activity by the lower classes. Indeed, as we will see below, Greig and others have regarded Hume's social and political views as conservative or reactionary on these grounds.[24]

On the other hand, Livingston has pointed out that if we regard the popular movements of late-eighteenth-century Britain as a step toward universal enfranchisement, we are also in effect following Hume's approach to the study of seventeenth-century English political thought. That is, we are tracing another "universal fermentation," or a "general, but insensible revolution," in which "the ideas of men enlarged themselves on all sides." During this period the Wilkes movement and other events led to new interpretations and applications of the English political tradition, including the concept of liberty, which were subsequently developed into "systematical principles and opinions" as a program for reform, and finally incorporated into the existing constitution, as an improvement on the preceding system of government (H 5.45.18; H 5.46.45; cf. 6.71.530–31). In evaluating Hume's response to the Wilkes and Liberty movement, we may also consider his indications that historical agents cannot understand all the underlying conditions that influence their actions, or foresee the consequences of their actions. Indeed, as we will see in Chapter 13, Hume argues that the historical significance of the conflict between the Stuart kings and Parliament was only dimly recognized at the time by its participants (cf. E CP.495; E PS.507).[25] We may thus follow Hume's example by distinguishing his own view of the Wilkes movement from the appreciation of its place in a process of development that would become possible from the vantage point of the historian. Finally, as we have seen, Hume allows for the possibility of moral progress by indicating that we can learn the advantages of greater benevolence, justice, and general prosperity in a society (EPM 7.15 [SBN 255]; cf. E Co.265), and that we cannot predict "what degree of refinement, either in virtue or vice, human nature is susceptible of," or what can arise from any "great revolution"

24. Greig, David Hume, 375–76.
25. See Livingston, Hume's Philosophy of Common Life, 269–71.

in our "education, customs, or principles" (E CL.87–88).[26] We may also note that Hume disliked the nationalistic and imperialistic tendencies of the Wilkes movement and was personally distressed by its anti-Scottish sentiment. Finally, whatever his private reactions to "this Madness about Wilkes," Hume did not publicly attack the movement or publicly call for its suppression.[27]

POLITICAL PRACTICE

In the preceding section we considered Hume's criticism of the ideological tendencies in the political parties and political movements of Great Britain. In this section I explore his account of the contemporary constitutional order and political culture of Britain, and the measures he proposed for their improvement.

Hume regards the modern system of government of Great Britain as perhaps the most perfect guarantor of liberty so far in European history, although he does not accept the view held by some Whigs that the British constitution is a perfect government, or even the uniquely legitimate form of government. He describes the modern British government as a "limited monarchy," or as a "mixed form of government," since it includes both a monarch and a "republican" legislative branch (E IP.46; E LP.10). He also characterizes this type of system as a "free government," because its power is divided between these branches and is exercised through "general and equal laws" (E OG.40–41). In his view, it is this "balance of power" by a system of "checks and controuls," rather than any particular institution of government, which establishes and protects civil liberty (E CL.93; E PR.15).[28] The liberties of British subjects depend on the authority of government, as this is exercised and restrained by the balance of power between the monarchy and Parliament. Hume therefore warns that any significant threat to this balance would undermine the ability of the government to preserve the constitutional liberties of the people.

In his political essays Hume especially considers three areas of possible improvement in contemporary British politics: the administration of government, public political discourse, and economic policy. First, he recommends measures to counteract what he regards as a current trend toward an increase in parliamentary power at the expense of the monarchy, to maintain a balance between

---

26. See Taylor, "Justice and the Foundations of Social Morality," 5–30; Gill, "Hume's Progressive View of Human Nature," 87–108; and Cohen, "Notion of Moral Progress," 109–27.

27. Ainslie points out that the types of speculative ideology and enthusiasm which Hume regarded as a danger in religion and party politics would become associated with nationalism in the nineteenth century: see "Problem of the National Self," 305–7.

28. For Hume's assessment of the British system of government, see Forbes, *Hume's Philosophical Politics,* 167–86, and Stewart, *Opinion and Reform,* 230–57.

them. Second, he attempts to replace the rhetoric of absolute opposition with a style of political discourse in which the relative oppositions of interest and affection are discussed with moderation and civility. I consider both of these projects in the present section. Finally, he also recommends a number of economic policies to the British government, which I will consider in Chapter 10.

In justifying his proposals for the improvement of government, Hume notes that "some innovations must necessarily have place in every human institution." A nation is fortunate when these changes are guided by reason, when they tend to expand liberty and justice, and when they are pursued gradually, rather than as a sudden challenge to its established political traditions and institutions (E OC.477). Since he regards the existing British government as especially stable and successful (E PS.508), his own proposals for reform are relatively minor, and are directed toward improving the effective operation, rather than the constitutional structure of the government.

During the eighteenth century, any supposed opposition of principles between the Whigs and Tories was subverted, not only by their earlier cooperation in the Revolution of 1688 and in the Hanoverian settlement, but also by the tendency of the monarchy to draw upon Parliament for its ministerial appointments. The resulting Whig domination of both the royal administration and Parliament shifted the balance of power toward Parliament and the Whigs, especially from 1721 until 1760, when George III sought to revive the constitutional prerogatives of the Crown.

In his political essays of the 1740s, Hume attempts to promote a more level balance by proposing measures to strengthen the monarchy. In "Of the Independency of Parliament" he argues that while the British constitution is intended to maintain a balance between the king and Parliament, the constitutional division of power actually favors Parliament, since its control over legislative initiatives and government finances tends to limit the legislative and executive powers of the monarchy. To counterbalance these constraints, the monarchy seeks to attain influence in Parliament by appointing members of Parliament to the royal ministry. This practice had been criticized by many outside the Whig establishment as a form of "corruption" that would reduce Parliament to "dependence." However, Hume defends this practice as a necessary measure for the effective functioning of government, and encourages both sides to recognize that the Crown will always have some degree of influence in Parliament (E IP.42–46). Next, in "Of the First Principles of Government" he considers the attempt by critics of the royal administration to force members of Parliament to follow the exact "instructions" of their constituencies. He regards this as another attempt to promote opposition between Parliament and the monarchy, by denying members of Parliament any latitude for negotiating with the ministry. Instead, he presents the obligation of representatives to follow the instructions of the electorate as a matter of degree (E FP.35–36; E Var.606–7). Finally, in "That Politics May be Reduced to a Science" he rebukes both the Whig leadership and its critics for their preoccupation with the personal character of Robert Walpole, the first Prime Minister, and thus for failing to recognize that the quality of a government is determined by the quality of its constitution (E PR.27–31).[29]

Hume's larger concern in his political writings is to encourage moderation in the public discussion of political issues and to counteract the extremes of party rhetoric in British political discourse. In the preface to his first volume of essays he indeed explicitly presents this as his intention: "Public Spirit, methinks, shou'd engage us to love the Public, and to bear an equal Affection to all our Country-Men; not to hate one Half of them, under Pretext of loving the Whole. This PARTY-RAGE I have endeavour'd to repress, as far as possible; and I hope this Design will be acceptable to the moderate of both Parties; at the same Time, that, perhaps, it may displease the Bigots of both."[30] He thus attempts to counteract the polarization of British political discourse, and to promote an effective working relationship between the parties, by striving to prevent "all unreasonable insult and triumph" of one over the other, and to promote "moderate opinions" on both sides. To this end, he attempts to show "the proper medium in all disputes," by persuading each side "that its antagonist may possibly be sometimes in the right" (E CP.494). As we have seen, he pursues this project in the essays in which he considers both sides of the various speculative, historical, and practical controversies between the Whig and Tory parties. In this way he hopes to encourage members of both parties to replace "declamation" with "calm enquiry," and to regard the differences in their opinions as relative rather than absolute (E IP.45). He also indicates that "the surest way of producing moderation in every party is to increase our zeal for the public," or the nation as a whole. Accordingly, while he seeks to present "a lesson of moderation with regard to the parties, into which our country is at present divided," this moderation is not intended "to abate the industry and passion, with which every individual is bound to pursue the good of his country." Indeed, he hopes to encourage his contemporaries to defend "with the utmost ZEAL" the institutions of government "by which liberty is secured, the public good consulted, and the avarice or ambition of particular men restrained and punished" (E PR.26–27).[31]

29. For Hume's response to the political situation of the 1720s–40s in Britain, see Forbes, *Hume's Philosophical Politics*, 193–223; Miller, *Philosophy and Ideology*, 177–81; Phillipson, *Hume*, 17–23 and 55–75; Stewart, *Opinion and Reform*, 230–57; and Haakonssen, "Introduction," ix–xxx.

30. Reprinted in Green and Grose, *Philosophical Works of David Hume*, 3:41–42.

31. For an account of Hume's political project in relation to the concern for civility or politeness in the literary culture of his day, see Phillipson, *Hume*, 23–33 and 53–55.

While he rejects using speculative systems of government as the basis for political activity, Hume regards the attempt to design an ideal system of government as a valuable project, which might even be of assistance in improving an existing system of government or creating a new one. In his essay on the "Idea of a Perfect Commonwealth," he indeed rejects the suppositions that a government can be created out of nothing, that we can replace an older model if a new one seems more "accurate and commodious," or that we can adopt a new system on a trial basis. On the contrary, he argues that an existing government "has an infinite advantage, by that very circumstance of its being established," since the general population tends to accept the authority of government from a respect for antiquity rather than through arguments. Accordingly, he asserts that a wise statesman will never "tamper" or "try experiments" with a government on the basis of any "supposed argument and philosophy." Instead, a wise politician or legislator will "bear a reverence to what carries the marks of age," and adjust "improvements for the public good . . . as much as possible, to the ancient fabric, and preserve entire the chief pillars and supports of the constitution." However, he also observes that since some governments are more successful than others, we might also find it interesting and useful to imagine a perfect form of government. By providing this model, we might also help the legislators of an existing state to improve their own government through "gentle alterations and innovations." Indeed, in case of the dissolution of one government and the "combination of men to form a new one," this model might even be used to develop a new and better constitution (E IC.512–14). Hume's own sketch of a perfect system of government depicts a republic with several levels of representation, and a division of the executive and legislative functions between two elective bodies, to minimize both oppression and factionalism. In contrast to the widespread view among the political theorists of his own day, Hume argues that a representative government could operate effectively even in a large state. Finally, he proposes several modifications to the British system of representation in order to more closely approximate another ideal, "the most perfect model of limited monarchy," thereby moving from his imaginative account of a perfect government to proposals for improving an existing government (E IC.514–29; cf. E BG.52–53).

In his letters after 1763 Hume identifies a number of new and interrelated threats to the stability and effectiveness of the British government. These included the growing influence of the London public in domestic and foreign affairs, an aggressive English nationalism, the imperialistic trend of British foreign policy, and the increasing public debt.[32] As we have seen, he also saw

---

32. For more on Hume's reaction to developments in British political life after 1763, see Letwin, *Pursuit of Certainty*, 112–22; Forbes, *Hume's Philosophical Politics*, 125–34 and 186–92; Miller, *Philosophy and Ideology*, 181–84; Stewart, *Opinion and Reform*, 302–310; and Livingston, *Philosophical Melancholy and Delirium*, 256–313.

the popular movements inspired by Pitt and later by Wilkes as a threat, not only to the balance of power between the Crown and Parliament, but also to the authority of the government in general. Indeed, in a 1769 letter to Strahan he almost expects an outbreak of violence between the royal administration and the "abandon'd Faction" in the Commons, unless the king could persuade its leaders to "either acquiesce or return to the ordinary, parliamentary Arts of Opposition" (L 2.212–13). He also foresaw harmful consequences from the growing public debt as the British government sought to finance its expanding foreign operations (E PC.349–65; cf. E CL.95–96). Finally, he watched with dismay as all sides in the British political establishment increasingly catered to the nationalistic and militaristic sentiments of the London public. Indeed, unlike many of his contemporaries, he saw war as generally harmful rather than beneficial to the economic and social life of a nation (1768 letter to Turgot, L 2.181; 1771 letter to Strahan, L 2.234–35).[33]

In an extension of these views, Hume predicted and supported the independence of the American colonies before many of his contemporaries in Britain. In his letters he discusses the unrest in the American colonies over the Stamp Tax (1766 letter to the Earl of Hertford, L 2.18–23, L 2.43), and was soon mischievously hoping for a revolt (1768 letter to Elliot, L 2.184; 1769 letter to Strahan, L 2.210). In a letter to Strahan in 1771 and again in 1774, he observes more seriously that the existing relation between Britain and its colonies in America could not be sustained much longer, although he doubted that the colonies were ready for independence (L 2.237; L 2.288). By 1775 he was arguing, against many of his friends, that granting the colonies independence would be preferable to any attempt to suppress them, for several reasons: their independence would have little effect on the British economy; subjugation would require an expensive military campaign that would destroy their liberties and democratic institutions; and the government had no realistic plan for effectively governing them after this suppression (1775 letter to Strahan, L 2.300–305; 1775 letter to John Home, L 2.307–8). Indeed, this view of the situation in the colonies reflects his earlier arguments that the authority of a limited monarchy cannot be upheld for long at a distance; that free governments are often more "ruinous and oppressive" toward their provinces than absolute governments; and that extensive conquests tend to undermine every form of government, especially a republican one (E PR.18–21; E IC.529).

Hume offers a general summary of his reaction to the developments in English foreign policy and domestic politics after 1763 in several of his letters. Writing to Strahan in 1769, he seems to carry his reservations about some of

33. On Hume's view of commerce as tending to promote peace, and his efforts in his economic writings to promote policies directed toward securing peace and stability, see Manzer, "The Promise of Peace?" 369–82, and Soule, "Hume on Economic Policy and Human Nature," 143–57.

the tendencies in contemporary British political life to an ironical extreme, although the serious principles of his criticism are still evident: "Notwithstanding my Age, I hope to see a public Bankruptcy, the total Revolt of America, the Expulsion of the English from the East Indies, the Diminution of London to less than a half, and the Restoration of the Government to the King, Nobility, and Gentry of this Realm" (L 2.210; cf. 1768 letter to Elliot, L 2.184). Here Hume is clearly criticizing an interrelated set of destructive tendencies in British political life, including the public debt; the intrusive and costly mismanagement of the American and Indian colonies; and the influence of the London public over British foreign and domestic policy.

Hume's *History of England* was frequently denounced, in his own day and subsequently, as a work of Tory propaganda. Although he intended to avoid partisanship, Hume indicated to Strahan in 1755 after the publication of the first Stuart volume that he had been attacked by Whig loyalists as "a Jacobite, Passive Obedience Man, Papist, & what not," and to Clephane in 1757 that he had been charged with "Paganism, and Jacobitism, and many other wretched *isms*" (L 1.222; L 1.263). In his own view, the *History* supported various aspects of both the Whig and Tory interpretations of English history. For example, he judged his account of the early Stuarts to have "a little of a Tory Aspect," while his account of the later Stuarts was more inclined to the Whig view (1754 letter to Strahan, L 1.217). He also describes his account of *"things,"* or of political events and institutions, as "more conformable to Whig principles," while his "representations of *persons'"* was perhaps closer to "Tory prejudices" (1756 letter to Clephane, L 1.237). In "My Own Life" he traces the response to his *History,* beginning with the publication of the first volume, which was "assailed by one cry of reproach, disapprobation, and even detestation" from all sides for its sympathetic portrayal of Charles I; through the favorable reception of the second Stuart volume among Whigs; to a renewed outcry from every party against his portrayal of the Tudor period, and especially of the popular Queen Elizabeth (ML xxxvii–xxxviii).

In addition to this assessment of Hume's *History* as a work of Tory propaganda, Hume's political philosophy in general has often been regarded as a conservative defense of the existing political order. The classic statement of this view is the assertion by Leslie Stephen that Hume's skepticism in philosophy led him to adopt a "cynical conservatism" in politics.[34] On the other hand, Hume's political philosophy has been appropriated for a wide range of positions across the political spectrum. Many studies have presented Hume's political philosophy as a version of liberalism. Indeed, Hayek identifies Hume as "the outstanding philosopher of liberal political and legal theory," while Forbes has

34. Stephen, *History of English Thought,* 2:157.

described his view as a "scientific" or "skeptical" Whiggism, in contrast to "vulgar Whiggism."[35] Hume also influenced the development of radical and socialist thought in Britain, largely through Godwin.[36] Several commentators have accordingly described Hume's political thought as a distinctive combination of conservative, liberal, and radical elements. For example, Miller argues that Hume provides a revolutionary basis for an establishment Whig ideology, while Whelan describes his view as a conservative utilitarianism that offers conditional support to liberal political institutions; and Stewart finds in his works a program of reform, which recommends the use of cautiously conservative methods to perfect a liberal social and political order.[37] These apparent conflicts within Hume's political thought, or at least in the secondary literature, are highlighted in the question posed by his biographer, J. Y. T. Greig, in the early part of the twentieth century: "How could he defend the Colonists in North America for their resistance to the arbitrary power of king, ministers, and venal House of Commons and yet attack the Old Whigs, and Patriots, and Wilkites, and democratic radicals of every sort, for trying to resist the same agencies at home?"[38] Greig traces these apparent inconsistencies in Hume's political opinions to the psychological conflicts allegedly resulting from Hume's rejection of his Calvinist upbringing. However, I have shown here that Hume presents a consistent view of the basis and nature of political authority, the dynamics of political culture, and of contemporary events, which also foreshadows many important elements of later conservative, liberal, and radical theories.

Many of the recent interpretations of Hume's political thought as a type of conservatism have located the distinctive character of his conservatism in his criticism of speculative systems of government. On this view, Hume's conservatism is a philosophically, historically and social-scientifically grounded critique of the emerging tendency toward "metaphysical abstraction" in modern political thought, which has also been characterized as political "rationalism" or as the "totalistic imagination" of revolutionary intellectuals and political leaders.[39] Hume advises his readers against any appeal to abstract principles of government in the political process, not only because these principles tend to be unrealistic, but also, and even importantly, because they tend to become tools of the authoritarian pursuit of self-interest by individuals and political parties. Instead, he regards an existing political tradition as the appropriate court of

35. Hayek, "Legal and Political Philosophy," 341, and Forbes, *Hume's Philosophical Politics*, 134–40.

36. Plamenatz, *The English Utilitarians*, and Halévy, *Growth of Philosophic Radicalism*, 11 and 191–203.

37. Miller, *Philosophy and Ideology*, 187–205; Whelan, *Order and Artifice*, 348–73; Stewart, *Opinion and Reform*, 3–12 and 224–317.

38. Greig, *David Hume*, 375–76.

39. See Burke, *Reflections on the Revolution in France*, 151; Oakeshott, *Rationalism in Politics and Other Essays*, 1–36; and Jay, *Marxism and Totality*, 13.

appeal for the political life of a given community, since this tradition is collectively recognized; and he recommends drawing upon this tradition in any attempt to modify its system of government. This is seen in his view that the English political tradition includes a "variety of precedents" through which this tradition has been adapted to the constantly changing circumstances of English political life. He also argues that those who develop a new government after the "dissolution of some old government," or the "combination of men to form a new one," must appeal to an existing political tradition, and preserve a recognizable continuity with the preceding political and social order, if it is to be accepted by its new subjects (H 5.48.96; E IC.512–14).[40]

Indeed, many of these commentators have argued that Hume, rather than Burke, should be regarded as the founder of the conservative tradition in modern political thought, since Hume traced the emergence of speculative principles of government already in seventeenth-century English political culture, and criticized their legacy, well before Burke's reaction to the French Revolution. In addition, some of Hume's sympathizers have suggested that he provides the principles for a conservative approach to the criticism, improvement, and reform of a given set of political institutions.[41] On this view, Hume presents a more systematic and flexible challenge to political rationalism than the arguably more quiescent and romantic conservatism of Burke.[42]

I would therefore propose the following characterization of Hume's political position, in the terms of subsequent political discourse. First, Hume presents a philosophically grounded and historically informed conservative account of the nature of political authority as a product of tradition operating on popular opinion through custom, in which allegiance to an existing political tradition and its institutions is justified, as both a natural and moral obligation, for its tendency to maintain order within a given society. However, Hume also considers the perfection of a government to consist in its extension of law toward securing the greatest amount of liberty for its subjects that is compatible with civic order. In these respects he defends a liberal political order.[43] Finally, by describing political institutions as human creations, and the happiness of

40. See Marshall, "David Hume and Political Scepticism," 247–57; Wolin, "Hume and Conservatism," 239–56; Letwin, Pursuit of Certainty, 1–123; Livingston, Hume's Philosophy of Common Life, 272–342; and Haakonssen, "Hume's Political Theory," 196.

41. For discussions of the implications in Hume's political theory for the criticism and reform of political, social, and economic institutions, see Marshall, "David Hume and Political Scepticism," 255; Livingston, Hume's Philosophy of Common Life, 334–42; Whelan, Order and Artifice, 364–73; and Stewart, Opinion and Reform, 194–317.

42. This comparison between Hume and Burke is developed especially in Letwin, Pursuit of Certainty, 118–23; Marshall, "David Hume and Political Scepticism," 247–57; Wolin, "Hume and Conservatism," 239–56; and Livingston, Hume's Philosophy of Common Life, 272–342.

43. Whelan, Order and Artifice, 357–63; Stewart, Opinion and Reform, 3–12, 224–317; and Danford, Problem of Reason, 109–12 and 136–63.

society as the ultimate aim of government, Hume provides a basis for the critique and reform of existing political institutions, although he would presumably advise any reformers to adopt a conservative method, by appealing to precedents within the existing political tradition.[44]

Finally, we may briefly consider Hume's influence on the subsequent history of political events and institutions in America and France. As we have seen, Hume took an increasing interest in events in the American colonies after the 1760s, and was privately expressing support for their independence by 1771. Although Locke's version of the social contract theory was more popular among the leaders of the American Revolution and the Constitutional Convention, several of Hume's essays contributed to the development of American political thought, especially his essays on economics, political parties, and his account of the ideal commonwealth, in which he described a government for a large republic. These essays appear to have been important sources for Madison in preparing the tenth *Federalist* paper. On the other hand, the leaders of the American Revolution were critical of Hume's allegedly Tory perspective, and Jefferson even promoted John Baxter's "republicanized" version of Hume's *History of England,* over Hume's original version, for use by American intellectuals and educational institutions.[45]

Hume's account of English political history was also profoundly influential in French political life and thought during the revolution. The *History of England* was already popular among both *philosophes* and conservatives, though for different reasons, before 1789. With this initial popularity, the *History of England* became a point of reference for both sides during the unfolding events of the French Revolution, which followed, almost uncannily, a parallel course to Hume's depiction of the English civil war. As a result, Hume's *History of England* provided inspiration to the early revolutionary leaders; consolation to the imprisoned Louis XVI, who read and reread Hume's account of the courage and nobility of Charles I while awaiting his own execution; and support for an emerging spirit of self-criticism among some of the original revolutionaries, including those, such as de Maistre, who became conservative critics of the Revolution after the beginning of the Reign of Terror in 1793.[46]

44. Stewart in particular argues that Hume's historical, political, and economic writings should be regarded as a program for reform; see *Opinion and Reform,* 5–8 and 315–16.

45. On Hume's view of America, see Pocock, "Hume and the American Revolution," 325–43. For a discussion of Hume's influence in American political thought, see Werner, "David Hume and America," 439–56, and Livingston, *Philosophical Melancholy and Delirium,* 317–32. For his influence on Madison, see Adair, "That Politics May Be Reduced to a Science," 404–17. On Jefferson's view of Hume, see Walton, "Hume and Jefferson," 389–403.

46. For a study of Hume's influence in France during the revolutionary period, see Bongie, *David Hume.* See also Popkin, "Condorcet and Hume and Turgot," 76–89.

10

Economics

Although Hume has been mainly known to later generations as a philosopher or a historian, he was first widely recognized during his own lifetime as the author of the *Political Discourses* (1752), a volume of essays on economic subjects.[1] Indeed, the *Political Discourses* sold out and went into a second edition within a year, and Hume singles out this volume in "My Own Life" as "the only work of mine that was successful on the first publication." The *Political Discourses* was quickly translated into French and German, and soon also into Italian, Spanish, and Dutch, and was thus "well received" both at home and abroad (ML xxxvi).[2]

Hume develops the underlying principles of his economic theory in the *Treatise* and the *Enquiries,* where he considers our ideas of external objects; our desires, passions, and motives; the principles for explaining human action; and the rules for exchanging goods and services, which initially emerge as conventions and are then legislated and enforced by government in a civil society.[3] In his essays, especially those included in the

1. Hume's so-called early memoranda contain a number of notes concerning political economy: see Mossner, "Hume's Early Memoranda, 1729–1740," 492–518; and Stewart, "Hume's Manuscripts," 276–88. Stewart has challenged Mossner's dating of these notes, arguing that they reflect Hume's preliminary research, probably after the *Treatise,* for his essays of the 1740s and early 1750s.

2. See Jessop, *Bibliography,* 23–26; Mossner, *Life of David Hume,* 224–29; and Ikeda, *David Hume,* 1–181.

3. Forbes has pointed out that in Hume's account a political society is primarily an

Political Discourses, he offers a more specific discussion of economics as a science and recommends a number of economic policies to the British government in response to contemporary conditions and debates.[4] He also pursues these debates in his letters to other economic theorists and elsewhere in his correspondence.[5] Finally, Hume includes an account of British and European economic developments in his *History of England,* especially in the appendices and "miscellaneous transactions" with which he concludes each major period and reign in English history.[6]

Hume is one of the few figures in the history of economic thought to have also written substantial works in both philosophy and history. In this chapter we will see that his philosophy, his moral and political concerns, and his historical interests are also reflected in his economic writings, and that his approach to economics reflects many of the principles we have traced in other areas of his thought.[7]

ECONOMIC ACTIVITY

In the introductory essay to the *Political Discourses,* "Of Commerce," Hume argues that "every thing in the world is purchased by labour," and identifies our passions as "the only causes of labour" (E Co.261). The most obvious motivating passion for labor is avarice, or the desire to attain physical control and property rights over particular objects. We desire objects as property both as anticipated sources of direct pleasures and also in many cases to attain the admiration of others and enhance our own pride (E CL.93; E RP.113; T 2.1.9.1, 2.1.10.1–12 [SBN 303, 309–16]). However, among the motives for economic activity Hume also includes our desire for a balanced combination of "action, pleasure, and indolence," since all of these appear to be required for human happiness, although the desired balance may vary with the temperament of the individual. Indeed, in the first *Enquiry* he describes the human individual as a

economic society regulated by government: see *Hume's Philosophical Politics,* 86–90, and Stewart, *Opinion and Reform,* 122 and 152–59.

4. On the eighteenth-century Scottish context of Hume's writings in economics, see Hont and Ignatieff, *Wealth and Virtue;* Saville, "Scottish Modernisation," 6–23; and Fry, "Commercial Empire," 53–69.

5. Hume's various writings on economics have been conveniently assembled by Rotwein in *Writings on Economics.*

6. On Hume's account of economic history, see Forbes, *Hume's Philosophical Politics,* 320–23; Stockton, "Economics and the Mechanism of Historical Progress," 296–320; and Danford, "Hume's *History,*" 155–94, and *Problem of Reason,* 109–35.

7. The most thorough general study of Hume's economic writings is the "Introduction" by Rotwein to his edition of *Writings on Economics,* ix–cxi. See also Johnson, *Predecessors of Adam Smith,* 161–81; Rostow, *Theorists of Economic Growth from David Hume to the Present;* McGee, "The Economic Thought of David Hume," 184–204; and Skinner, "David Hume: Principles of Political Economy," 222–54.

reasonable, sociable, and active being, who thrives upon a "mixed kind of life" in which all of these capacities are exercised (E RA.269–70; EHU 1.6 [SBN 9]; cf. T 1.4.7.9–14 [SBN 269–73]).[8] Hume thus includes the desire for activity, and even for novelty and lively sensations, among the basic human motives that are reflected in economic activity (T 2.1.10.2, 2.2.4.4, 2.3.10.1–12 [SBN 311, 352–53, 448–54]).[9]

In contrast to many of his contemporaries, Hume believes that members of the poor and working classes are motivated by the same passions and desires as those above them in the social hierarchy. While he agrees that members of the lower classes often appear to engage in irrational types of social and economic behavior, he explains this behavior as a result of the frustration and discouragement of these universal desires produced by their external circumstances.[10] In other words, since human beings seem to have a universal desire for "exercise and employment," a lack of satisfying activity often leads individuals, whether rich or poor, to pursue harmful but immediate pleasures. A man who is deprived "of all business and serious occupation" might thus run restlessly "from one amusement to another" and not consider "the ruin which must follow him from his immoderate expences" (E In.300–301). Hume also regards "the plenty or penury in which the people live" as one of the causes of human action and sources of national character, since "poverty and hard labour debase the minds of the common people, and render them unfit for any science and ingenious profession" (E NC.198). Similarly, both extreme necessity and exorbitant taxes tend to "destroy industry" by "producing despair" (E Var.635; cf. E Ta.345).

In both the *Treatise* and the first *Enquiry* Hume includes commerce among the types of human activity that depend on moral reasoning, or the use of probable reasoning to discover the causes of human action (T 2.3.1.15 [SBN 405]; EHU 8.17 [SBN 89]). He seeks to promote the study of commerce in his first two volumes of essays in the 1740s, where he calls attention to both the novelty and the value of the study of commerce, noting that "trade was never esteemed an affair of state till the last century; and there scarcely is any ancient

8. On Hume's discussion of economic motivation, see Rotwein, *Writings on Economics*, xxxii–liii; Hundert, "The Achievement Motive in Hume's Political Economy," 139–43; and Soule, "Hume on Economic Policy and Human Nature," 143–57.

9. Recent studies have offered widely diverging views of Hume's conception of the good life in relation to economic activity. For example, Rostow finds in Hume an Aristotelian view of happiness as the full exercise of human powers, while MacIntyre attributes to Hume a modern bourgeois value for status and consumption at the expense of the Aristotelian model of the good life. Finally, Danford argues that Hume revises the Aristotelian account of virtue and the good life for a modern commercial society, while Siebert describes his system as a "worldly morality." See Rostow, *Theorists of Economic Growth*, 33–34; MacIntyre, *Whose Justice? Which Rationality?* 298–303; Danford, *Problem of Reason*, 161 and 193; and Siebert, *Moral Animus*, 136–69.

10. Rotwein, *Writings on Economics*, xlviii–xlix; Hundert, "The Achievement Motive in Hume's Political Economy," 141–43; Arkin, "Economic Writings of David Hume," 145; and Soule, "Hume on Economic Policy and Human Nature," 143–57.

writer on politics, who has made mention of it" (E CL.88). He also argues that economic developments, such as the rise of commerce, are relatively easy to explain, since these consist in the activities of a large number of people (E RP.113). In the *Political Discourses* he observes that politicians should be especially interested in the study of commerce, since this would assist them in promoting the public good, "which is, or ought to be their object" (E Co.254).

In the course of his essays Hume traces the history of human economic activity and the associated division of society into different economic classes. The earliest types of economic behavior are such activities as hunting and fishing, through which human beings sustained themselves before they had developed an extensive network of property. The first genuine economic system arises with the "arts of agriculture." In the agrarian system, land is appropriated as property, and society is divided into manorial landowners, private farmers, and agricultural laborers. Next, since the genius of human beings leads them to discover ways to use other natural materials, the superfluity of labor in a prosperous agrarian society produces another class of workers who can devote their labor to the "finer arts" (E Co.256). These are "artisans," who develop the skills to manufacture various types of objects, and can then trade some of their products while retaining others "for their own use and subsistence." Commerce originates in the exchange of agricultural goods, raw materials, and artifacts within an immediate geographic region. However, as agrarian workers and craftsmen increase their productivity, and consumers expand their desires and purchasing power, trade is extended to include items from a wider geographic range, produced by the variety of "soils, climates, and geniuses" in different nations. This exchange of commodities is facilitated by the new class of merchants, who indeed become "one of the most useful races of men" by conveying information as well as goods from one region to another (E In.299–300; E BT.324). The development of commerce also encourages the invention and use of money, which is more convenient than a direct exchange of commodities. The use of money, in turn, promotes the development of financial institutions, the banking profession, and the techniques of financial management. Finally, a commercial society also tends to produce other professionals, such as lawyers and physicians, who offer services in exchange for a fee (cf. E Co.256–67; E In.297–302; T 3.2.4.1 [SBN 514]).

In contrast to Rousseau and many others among their contemporaries, Hume argues that the advance of industry and commerce, including what he variously calls "luxury" or "refinement in the arts," tends to promote both the greatness of a state and the happiness of its subjects.[11] Hume traces the origin and spread

11. See Rotwein, *Writings on Economics,* xci–civ; Venning, "Hume on Property," 79–92; and Soule, "Hume on Economic Policy and Human Nature," 143–57.

of the "arts of luxury" to the superfluous labor that becomes available in a society through the increasing efficiency of its agriculture. The employment of this superfluous labor in the manufacture of luxury goods gives to many individuals "the opportunity of receiving enjoyments, with which they would otherwise have been unacquainted" (E Co.255–56). The development of industry and commerce also tends to strengthen the military readiness of the state, even without any direct military investment, since a state with extensive trade and manufactures has a reserve of labor that can be directed toward military industries in times of need. Accordingly, Hume rejects the view that the "luxury of individuals" tends to threaten the interests of a state or the ambitions of its rulers (E Co.256–60).

Hume offers a further defense of the consumer market in an essay that he originally called "Of Luxury," but later retitled "Of Refinement in the Arts." Here he argues that "refinement in the gratification of the senses" should not as such be regarded with disapproval, although we may distinguish an "innocent" indulgence in luxury from one which is "blameable" by considering "the age, or country, or condition" of the agent in question (E RA.268–29; cf. EPM D.41 [SBN 337]). First, we may regard a luxury as "foolish" if the agent could reasonably expect to be harmed by the indulgence. Second, we may consider a luxury "vicious" if it is pursued in violation of the rules of justice, or even "at the expence of some virtue, as liberality or charity," by depriving the agent of enough resources to perform "such acts of duty and generosity as are required by his situation and fortune" (E RA 268–69, 279). Hume therefore regards the pursuit of pleasure as "blameable" if it tends to harm oneself or others, and includes among the latter the harm of depriving many people of the necessities that could easily be provided by sacrificing a trivial but expensive pleasure. On the other hand, the spread of "innocent" luxury, or a taste for "refinement in the arts," promotes virtue by encouraging the increase of industry, the cultivation of sociability and benevolence, the advance of learning, and the expansion of civil liberty (E RA.268–80). Indeed, in response to the supposed historical example of the harmful effects of luxury, cited by many critics of the expanding modern trade in consumer goods, Hume argues that the decline of the Roman republic resulted not from the spread of luxury, but from "an ill modelled government, and the unlimited extent of conquests" (E RA.276).

Hume maintains that the benefits of modern industry and commerce should be diffused throughout a society, both on ethical grounds and to stimulate further economic expansion and promote political stability. Indeed, he argues that "a too great disproportion among citizens weakens any state," and that "every person, if possible, ought to enjoy the fruits of his labour, in a full possession of all the necessaries, and many of the conveniences of life." This is desirable on moral grounds because "such an equality is most suitable to human nature, and diminishes much less from the *happiness* of the rich than it adds to that of the poor." An equitable distribution of wealth also tends to increase the power of the state, by ensuring that "any extraordinary taxes or impositions be paid with more chearfulness." In such a case, "when the riches are dispersed among multitudes, the burthen feels light on every shoulder, and the taxes make not a very sensible difference on any one's way of living." On the other hand, when the riches of a nation are concentrated "in few hands, these must enjoy all the power, and will readily conspire to lay the whole burthen to the poor, and oppress them still farther, to the discouragement of all industry." Indeed, unlike many of his contemporaries, Hume recommended that the working classes should be allowed to receive higher wages, both on moral grounds and to promote the growth of a consumer economy by enabling every person to enjoy not only the necessities but also a share of the "conveniences" available on the market.[12] While he recognizes that a higher price of labor in England might be somewhat disadvantageous to the export trade, he maintains that, "as foreign trade is not the most material circumstance, it is not to be put in competition with the happiness of so many millions." He even appears to approve of "conspiracies" among underpaid laborers to raise their wages, though he does not expect these to be successful; and denounces efforts by the rich to "conspire against *them*" by shifting the whole tax burden to the poor (E Co.265–66; cf. E Ta.347). In other words, Hume advocates not only a basic level of subsistence, but also the possibility of an increasing level of prosperity for the working classes, both as a moral end and in order to promote political stability and a flourishing national economy.

Many historians of economic theory, drawing upon the prevailing interpretations of Hume's philosophy as a form of skepticism, or as a version of empiricism narrowly concerned with the principles of the natural sciences, have supposed that there is a discontinuity between his general philosophy and his economic thought. For example, Schumpeter accepts the view of Hume's philosophy as an introspective associationist psychology that overlooks the social and historical aspects of human life, and concludes that his philosophy has nothing to do with his economic theory.[13] However, other studies have traced the continuity between Hume's philosophical, historical, and economic writings as providing the basis for a unified account of the psychological, historical, and sociological aspects of economic behavior. For example, Rotwein has indicated

---

12. In advocating a fair wage for workers, Hume is rejecting the contemporary "utility of poverty" thesis, according to which both employers and the state had an interest in keeping wages low. The proponents of this doctrine held that a lower wage provided a greater incentive to work than a higher wage, and that higher wages would encourage profligacy and harm productivity. See Hundert, "The Achievement Motive in Hume's Political Economy," 139–43; and Soule, "Hume on Economic Policy and Human Nature," 143–57.

13. Schumpeter, *History of Economic Analysis*, 125–26, 135, and 447n4.

that Hume's systematic treatment of psychology and history serves to connect his philosophical and economic writings, while Rostow locates Hume's contribution to economic theory "in his insistence on placing economic analysis in this broad human and societal setting and keeping it there."[14] Indeed, such studies have contrasted Hume's contextual approach with the ahistorical model of human behavior that developed in economic theory after Hume, beginning with his own contemporary and friend, Adam Smith, which became a standard model as the study of economics was increasingly focused upon quantitative analysis.[15] Hume's approach to the study of economic activity therefore anticipates recent efforts to promote a more interdisciplinary approach to economics, by considering the psychological, social, and cultural context of economic activity.[16]

ECONOMIC POLICY

Hume's recommendations concerning British economic policy arise from his account of economic motivation and are directed toward encouraging the expansion of economic activity. He therefore judges economic policies according to their tendency to promote industry and trade and to diffuse the benefits of industry and trade through society.[17]

We may begin with Hume's views on monetary policy. In his philosophical writings he describes money as a "convention" through which materials such as gold and silver "become the common measures of exchange, and are esteem'd sufficient payment for what is of a hundred times their value" (T 3.2.2.10 [SBN 490]; cf. EPM App.3.8 [SBN 306]).[18] We therefore desire money for the power it gives us to acquire property rights over objects, and other sources of pleasure (T 2.1.10.3; cf. 2.1.10.9 [SBN 311; cf. 314]). In "Of Money" he describes currency as "the instrument which men have agreed upon to facilitate the exchange of one commodity for another" by its "representation of labour and commodities." In other words, money is not an object of commerce for its own sake,

14. Rotwein, *Writings on Economics,* xvi–xvii and cv–cxi; Rostow, *Theorists of Economic Growth,* 18.

15. For an account of Hume's influence on Smith, and on another contemporary economist and friend, James Steuart, see Skinner, "David Hume: Principles of Political Economy," 245–49.

16. See Rotwein, *Writings on Economics,* cvi–cxi; Arkin, "Economic Writings of David Hume," 141–60; Hundert, "The Achievement Motive in Hume's Political Economy," 139–43; Lyon, "Notes on Hume's Philosophy of Political Economy," 457–61; Rostow, *Theorists of Economic Growth,* 16, 33–47, 51–52, and 480–82; Skinner, "David Hume: Principles of Political Economy," 246–49; and Soule, "Hume on Economic Policy and Human Nature," 143–57.

17. For studies of Hume on political economy, see Rotwein, *Writings on Economics,* liv–xc; and McGee, "The Economic Thought of David Hume," 184–204.

18. Hume defends this view in a 1767 letter to the French economist, the Abbé Morellet, who instead identified the value of currency with the value of its constituent material as a commodity (L 2.204–5).

but is instead the "oil" which renders the motion of the wheels of trade "more smooth and easy" (E Mo.281, 285; cf. E In.297).

In contrast to the prevailing mercantilist theory, Hume argues that the quantity of money in a given state is irrelevant to the condition of its domestic economy, since wages and prices tend to adjust themselves automatically to the amount of money in circulation. That is, prices depend "on the proportion between commodities and money" in a nation: and not even on their absolute proportions, but upon the number of commodities "which come or may come to market," and the amount of money which is in circulation. According to Hume, the effects on a national economy that are supposed to follow from the abundance or scarcity of money are instead determined by the "manners and customs of the people," as these are expressed in their economic activity (E Mo.290–91). For example, a "simple manner of living," consisting mainly in a local exchange of necessities, harms the economy of a nation "by confining the gold and silver to few hands, and preventing its universal diffusion and circulation" throughout the population. By contrast, "industry and refinements of all kinds incorporate it into the whole state," and every economic transaction, until "no hand is entirely empty of it." Hume maintains that a mere lack of money "can never injure any state within itself," since the workers and commodities "are the real strength of any community." However, he notes that a gradual increase in the supply of gold or silver tends to stimulate economic activity by their "thorough concoction and circulation through the state." Thus, for example, the sudden influx of gold and silver from the New World had little long-term effect on the Spanish economy, where it was confined to a few hands; but it stimulated commerce in the rest of Europe once it began to circulate outside Spain. On the other hand, he maintains that a gradual increase in the supply of money tends to raise prices and wages, and thus to restore the original equilibrium between them (E Mo.293–94; cf. 286–87).

In his essay "Of Interest" Hume endorses the general opinion that a low rate of interest is a sign of the "flourishing condition" of a nation. However, he maintains that the interest rate is determined, not by the amount of money in the nation, but again by the manners and customs of the population. In other words, all of the causes that tend to lower the interest rate, including a greater amount of ready wealth, lower demand for borrowing, and lower individual profits, arise from an expanding commerce and industry, and thus from the "habits and way of living" of the people. The decline of interest rates is therefore not a direct effect of the absolute supply of money, but a collateral effect of an increase in economic activity (E In.295, 298).

Several of Hume's most important economic essays are concerned with promoting free trade between nations. In the opening essay of the *Political Discourses,* he argues that foreign trade stimulates the growth of the domestic economy and tends to promote both the power of the state and the happiness of its subjects (E Co.263–64). In two further essays he argues that the development of international trade, and even of foreign industries, will tend to stimulate rather than discourage the expansion of British industry. In "Of the Balance of Trade," he argues that the balance in foreign trade has less effect on the prosperity of a nation than the condition of its domestic economy. Again in response to mercantilism, which encouraged nations to develop "a strong jealousy with regard to the balance of trade, and a fear, that all their gold and silver may be leaving them," he argues that this is "almost in every case, a groundless apprehension," since we need not fear "that money should abandon a kingdom in which there are people and industry." Instead, we should work to "carefully preserve these latter advantages" without worrying about the balance of trade. More specifically, Hume points out that a sudden decrease in the amount of money circulating within a nation tends to lower the prices of its goods and labor, thus giving a temporary advantage to its export trade that tends to restore the monetary supply. Similarly, any sudden increase in the amount of money in circulation will lead to an increase in its consumer expenditures on imported goods, until the balance is again restored. In other words, the market adjustment tends to maintain a supply of money that is generally proportioned to the levels of industry among different nations (E BT.309–13).[19] This analysis of what has come to be called the "price-specie-flow mechanism" is generally regarded as Hume's central contribution to economic theory. On the basis of this principle, Hume criticized the protectionist policies of the eighteenth-century mercantilist nations, especially British restrictions on French imports, by arguing that the "barriers and obstructions" placed on foreign trade only serve "to check industry, and rob ourselves and our neighbors of the common benefits of art and nature" (E BT.315, 324). On the other hand, as a partial exception to this principle of free trade, he recommends an import tax on certain luxury items, both as an especially convenient source of government revenue, and also to stimulate domestic manufactures. He concludes, however, that while a government "has great reason to preserve with care its people and its manufactures," it may leave the adjustment of its monetary supply "to the course of human affairs" (E BT.324–26). In "Of the Jealousy of Trade" he argues that any increase of "riches and commerce" within a nation "instead of hurting, commonly promotes the riches and commerce of all its neighbors." The more productive nation offers a greater variety of goods for exchange, which tends to promote the domestic industry of the neighboring states. Finally, if any state seems to be deprived of its preeminence in a particular industry by another state, Hume

---

19. Hume had already developed and defended this view in a 1749 letter to Montesquieu (L 1.136–38); and a 1750 letter to James Oswald (L 1.142–44).

maintains that such a loss of advantage should be blamed on "their own idleness, or bad government, not the industry of their neighbors" (E JT.328, 330). A further example of Hume's study of economic motivation, and his recommendation of policies that are designed to promote economic activity, appears in "Of Taxes." In this essay he considers the influence of various forms of taxation on the "manners and customs" of a people, and thus upon the industry, commerce, and prosperity of a nation. Here he argues that the most desirable kind of government levies are moderate taxes on consumer goods, which, when they are "laid on gradually, and affect not the necessaries of life," tend to stimulate industry (E Ta.343). The best kind of taxes are those on luxury goods, which are "least felt by the people," since this type of tax is paid "gradually and insensibly" and is even "in some measure, voluntary; since a man may chuse how far he will use the commodity which is taxed." In fact, taxes on luxury goods "naturally produce sobriety and frugality, if judiciously imposed." In addition, a luxury tax also "checks itself" by discouraging purchases when rates become too high, so that it is in the interest of the nation to maintain a limit on the rate, and consumers are unlikely to be "altogether ruined by such taxes." The only disadvantage of a sales tax , which is however a considerable one, is that it is "expensive in the levying." By contrast, property taxes are the least expensive to collect, but have "every other disadvantage." Hume further rejects the view shared by Locke and the French Physiocrats that all taxes are ultimately derived from land and should therefore be directly levied as property taxes. Instead, he maintains that luxury taxes are more equitably distributed than property taxes among the different social classes.[20] Finally, Hume denounces arbitrary levies as "the most pernicious of all taxes," since they discourage industry and fall unequally on different members of the population. The worst type of tax is the poll tax, or a universal tax at a flat rate on every individual, which is not only unequal, but can also be increased without any limit by the government until it becomes "altogether oppressive and intolerable." Hume indeed argues that the substitution of a poll tax by Constantine for all other methods of taxation was one of the main causes of the fall of the Roman Empire, and that imposition of a "new and unusual tax" of three groats on every adult by Richard II was the immediate cause of the Peasants' Revolt in 1381 (E Ta.345–46; H 2.17.289). He concludes that the regularity and equity of a system of taxation is more important than the amount levied, and that "a pound, raised by a general imposition" is less harmful to the economy and society of a nation than a shilling taken in an "unequal and arbitrary" manner (E Ta.348). In an almost prophetic moment, he especially criticizes the arbitrary system of

20. Hume also pursues this discussion in an exchange of letters in 1766 with the French Physiocrat Anne Robert Turgot, who would later attempt unsuccessfully to reform the French economy during his brief tenure as controller-general (1774–76) under Louis XVI (L 2.76, 93–94).

taxation in contemporary France: "The greatest abuses, which arise in FRANCE, the most perfect model of pure monarchy, proceed not from the number or weight of the taxes, beyond what are to be met with in free countries; but from the expensive, unequal, arbitrary, and intricate method of levying them, by which the industry of the poor, especially of the peasants and farmers, is, in a great measure, discouraged, and agriculture rendered a beggarly and slavish employment." Accordingly, he hopes that the French system of taxation will be reformed by a ruler or a minister with "sufficient discernment to know his own and the public interest," and a "sufficient force of mind to break through the ancient customs" (E CL.95). This hope was, of course, perceptive but fruitless.[21]

As the most important policy issue confronting the British economy, Hume directs his attention in "Of Public Credit" toward the growing national debt, which had been amassed by the British government through the sale of securities, to finance its military operations overseas.[22] In fact, he regards the increase in the public debt as the greatest source of potential instability for the contemporary British government (E CL.95–96). While he concedes that public credit might provide a slight stimulation to commerce and industry, Hume maintains that any such benefit is outweighed by its harmful effects in drawing people and wealth to the capital, extending paper credit, increasing the tax rates, allowing foreign control of national industries, and supporting a class of idle and unproductive stockholders who have "no connexions with the state" and may indeed spend their income "in any part of the globe in which they chuse to reside" (E PC.354–55, 357). The shift of economic power from the landed and middle classes to a class of government shareholders also weakens the most important barrier against an arbitrary increase of royal power (E PC.357–60; cf. E RA.277–78). The expanding national debt also renders the nation increasingly vulnerable to foreign conquest (E PC.361–65).

Hume considers three possible consequences of the continuing expansion of public credit, by which "either the nation must destroy public credit, or public credit will destroy the nation." First, he considers the superficially appealing proposal that the debt should be repaid all at once through a single property tax and rejects this plan as falling disproportionately on the poor and landowners. More specifically, he argues that since the working poor "could not advance, at once, a proportional part of the sum required," and since the "property in money and stock in trade" of bankers and merchants is easily "concealed or disguised," it is the "visible property in lands and houses" which would "really at last answer

21. Hume does not consider the possibility of an income tax, which was first proposed and briefly instituted in Great Britain in the 1790s, during the Napoleonic Wars.
22. On Hume's discussion of the public debt, and the history of the public debt in Britain, see Laursen and Coolidge, "David Hume and Public Debt: Crying Wolf?" 143–49.

for the whole." This, or any other ineffective method of payment, would lead public credit to "die of the doctor." Second, in what Hume describes as the "natural death" of public credit, the government could ruin its creditors by repudiating the debt. However, he acknowledges that the government is more likely to protect the interests of its stockholders than to declare a voluntary bankruptcy. Finally, a continuing increase in the public debt will lead to the deterioration of the national economy and render the entire nation vulnerable to foreign conquest, which would produce the "violent death" of the national debt (E PC.360–65). In a letter to Strahan in 1771 he describes the possible ruin of the government stockholders as a "great Calamity," which would however be of little importance compared to the ruin of the nation. He expects, however, that since the creditors "fill all the chief Offices and are the Men of the greatest Authority in the Nation," the debt will not die a "natural death" through government default, and will instead gradually undermine the national economy (L 2.237).

Most commentators have regarded Hume as an advocate of free-market economic theory, although some have argued that he combines elements of mercantilism with liberal and free-trade principles.[23] However, I would argue that Hume's main concern in his economic writings is not to defend any particular theory of economic development, but to promote a set of economic goals: specifically, the development of industry and trade, and the diffusion of their benefits throughout a national population. However, his account of the methods by which these goals may be attained is flexible and pragmatic.[24] In other words, he presents the empirical study of human motivation as the basis for economic policy, and then recommends measures that are likely to enhance the productive activity and prosperity of the inhabitants of a nation. While he promotes the free operation of national and international markets, he does so in the expectation that they will tend to increase the productivity and prosperity of each individual nation, judging by the provisional results of his empirical study, rather than by an *a priori* commitment to a theory of economic development.[25]

23. See, for example, Johnson, *Predecessors of Adam Smith,* 161–81; and Roll, *A History of Economic Thought,* 117–20.

24. Danford has argued that Hume's *History of England* should be regarded as a lesson in the superiority of a "liberal commercial society," or a free market economy, against critics of free trade and as a model for Third World development. See Danford, "Hume's *History,*" 178–82, and *Problem of Reason,* 2, 112–15, and 136–55. In contrast to this view, I argue here and in Chapter 13 that Hume regards eighteenth-century British civilization as a product of a series of social, cultural, economic, and political developments that we do not find automatically replicated in any other nation. A practical economist in the Humean tradition might indeed wish to promote the expansion of commerce, the arts and sciences, and the rule of law in other nations, but would also recognize that attempts to promote economic development in a given nation must take into account the distinctive manners and customs of the population, and the history and institutions of that nation. Hume's attention to social institutions and their influence on economic activity is also emphasized by Skinner in "David Hume: Principles of Political Economy," 235 and 248–49.

25. See also Stockton, "Economics and the Mechanism of Historical Progress," 305–6; and Skinner, "David Hume: Principles of Political Economy," 243–44.

Hume's flexibility concerning the means for achieving a specified set of economic goals is especially apparent in his view of the role of government in economic life. As we have seen, the main function of government, according to Hume, is to secure the general peace and stability of society, especially by providing a secure framework for its economic activities. However, he also indicates that government may undertake measures to promote the economic development of the nation. In the *Treatise* he assigns to government the task of directing public projects, such as the construction of bridges and canals, which the members of a society would be unable to carry out without a central authority (T 3.2.7.8 [SBN 539]). In his essays he recommends a system of taxation that will not only provide revenue, but also encourage productivity by promoting an adequate level of subsistence, and even the possibility of an increasing prosperity, among the working classes. He even suggests that a ruler should encourage industriousness by building up public stores of grain, cloth, and armaments. This policy will not only maintain a reserve supply of these goods, but also ensure a "stock of labour" which is experienced in peacetime production but can also be drawn upon in times of war (E RA.262).[26] On the other hand, in the *History of England* he indicates that any attempts by government to regulate prices, as in the famine of 1315, or to regulate trade, wages, and various conditions of labor, as under Henry VII, have tended to be ill-judged and counterproductive. Instead, he believes that these are better left to market forces (H 2.14.177; H 3.26.77–80).[27]

Hume's writings in economics reflect an optimism founded upon two centuries of moderate but sustained commercial and industrial expansion in Britain, but preceding the dramatic changes of the Industrial Revolution. During the next century, new technologies and new types of economic organization would produce, not only a dramatic increase in productivity, but also new levels of poverty, social dislocation, dehumanization, and environmental degradation unforeseen by Hume or his contemporaries. Instead, Hume expected the expanding prosperity of his day to steadily improve the condition of the entire population. This view was widely held in Europe until the revolutions of 1848, when the conflict between unregulated industrial capitalism and the welfare of the poor and working classes became obvious to perceptive observers.[28]

From the perspective provided by our vantage point in the postindustrial economic order, I would argue that there are grounds in Hume's economic and

26. On Hume's view of the value of commerce for promoting the military strength of a nation, see Manzer, "The Promise of Peace?" 373–76; and Soule, "Hume on Economic Policy and Human Nature," 143–57.
27. Rotwein, *Writings on Economics*, lxxix–lxxx.
28. Ibid., ix–xi; Rostow, *Theorists of Economic Growth*, 16–31, 42, and 93–94; and Soule, "Hume on Economic Policy and Human Nature," 143–57.

political writings to support a more extensive role for government than he envisions in order to ensure at least a minimal level of economic security, and even the possibility of economic advance, for the poor and working classes. [29] In other words, Hume's endorsement of free-market liberalism in the eighteenth century need not entail an endorsement of the unregulated industrial capitalism of the nineteenth century. Some of the grounds for this view appear in his own policy recommendations, as in his suggestion that a system of taxation should be designed to reward laborers for their industry and to prevent extreme poverty. However, a more general defense of this role for government in economic activity may also be derived from his account of the nature and purpose of government. As we have seen, Hume argues that the main function of government is to legislate and enforce a set of rules directing the distribution and exchange of goods and services and to secure a basic level of order and stability in a given society. This analysis might also indicate that the government should legislate and enforce other rules, such as regulations for working conditions, to maintain the peace and stability of society against inequitable and destabilizing economic trends, and to enable workers to participate as consumers in the operation of the market (cf. E Co.262).

Several recent studies have gone further, by asking whether it is possible to formulate a theory of distributive justice on Humean grounds. [30] Hume indeed concedes that there are moral arguments in favor of the "rule of equality." However, he specifically rejects any schemes for the redistribution of wealth according to either merit or need, since he considers such schemes to be impracticable and even dangerous in their political effects: "Render possessions ever so equal, men's different degrees of art, care, and industry will immediately break that equality. . . . The most rigorous inquisition too is requisite to watch every inequality on its first appearance; and the most severe jurisdiction, to punish and redress it" (EPM 3.26 [SBN 194]; cf. T 3.2.3.2 [SBN 502]; H 2.27.290). Instead, Hume maintains that property must be distributed according to fixed and obvious rules provided by the principles of justice, as expressed in the positive laws of individual nations, and allowing for some degree of inequality in this distribution, which may be beneficial in stimulating economic activity (cf. EPM 3.27 [SBN 194]). However, he also affirms the moral obligation of the rich to help ensure that the poor are provided with the necessities of life (T 3.2.1.14, 3.2.5.6 [SBN 482, 518]; E RA.269, 279). In his economic essays he further indicates that

29. See also Lyon, "Notes on Hume's Philosophy of Political Economy," 459–61; Hundert, "The Achievement Motive in Hume's Political Economy," 139–43; and Velk and Riggs, "David Hume's Practical Economics," 154–65.

30. Hiskes, "Has Hume a Theory of Social Justice?" 72–93. See also Mackie, *Hume's Moral Theory*, 93–96; Macleod, "Rule-Utilitarianism and Hume's Theory of Justice," 74–84; and Stewart, *Opinion and Reform*, 179–84.

self-interest and the principles of morality both direct us toward promoting an adequate level of subsistence and the possibility of an increasing prosperity for all of the inhabitants of a nation. He expects this steady increase to be achieved mainly through the natural expansion of trade and industry. However, he also indicates that the interest of a nation and its government in the expansion of prosperity may justify the legislation of various economic policies, especially to promote the creativity and industriousness of the working classes by ensuring an adequate return for their labor.

In sum, Hume rejects any proposal for an equal distribution of wealth. However, he also indicates that it is in the interest of a nation to enact policies to counteract any tendencies toward extensive or extreme poverty within its population, since these conditions tend to undermine the stability and overall prosperity of a society. He also indicates that such policies should be based on an understanding of the "manners and customs" of the community, and a judgment concerning the probable effects of the proposed rule on the motives and actions of its inhabitants. Finally, such policies should facilitate the wide diffusion of prosperity within a society by promoting the economic activities of its inhabitants, both as workers and as consumers, through a reinforcement of the motives for economic activity arising from their historical and cultural context.

11

Aesthetics

In "My Own Life," Hume tells us that he was "seized very early with a passion for literature," by which he meant all genres of humanistic writing, from history to poetry to philosophy; and that this remained the "ruling passion" of his life (ML xxxii–xxxiii). In the Advertisement describing his overall project in the *Treatise,* which he published in Book 1, he indicates that he intends to include a discussion of "criticism" in a later volume of the *Treatise,* along with his examination of morals and politics (T Adv.1 [SBN xii]). As it turned out, Hume did not include a direct treatment of criticism in the *Treatise,* although he considers several themes belonging to what we now call aesthetics in both the *Treatise* and the *Enquiries,* such as the poetic imagination and the appreciation of beauty. He does not examine criticism, or the theory of art and taste, at any length until his essays, where he addresses these topics especially in two works originally published in his *Four Dissertations* of 1757, "Of Tragedy" and "Of the Standard of Taste." He also includes a brief critical history of European literature in the *History of England* (H 5.App.4.149–55; H 6.62.149–54; H 6.72.542–45).[1] In this chapter, I will use the modern term "aesthetics" for the study of the sentiments and critical judgments involved in our

---

1. See Mossner, "An Apology for David Hume," 679. For facsimiles of the first edition of these two essays, see Hume, *Four Dissertations and Essays on Suicide and the Immortality of the Soul,* page sequence 1, 183–240.

appreciation of nature and the fine arts, as these are treated by Hume in his various writings.[2]

Hume's own aesthetic tastes generally reflect the prevailing neoclassicism of the upper classes in Britain at the middle of the eighteenth century.[3] However, the importance of his discussion of aesthetics does not lie in his discussion of any particular works of art, or in his defense of any particular aesthetic standard, but rather in his general theory of aesthetic appreciation, including his theory of the aesthetic sentiments and his account of criticism and taste.[4] These indeed point beyond the limitations of his own aesthetic preferences and direct our attention, both to the possibility of a broader range of aesthetic values, and toward a consideration of the social and historical dimensions of the aesthetic sentiments and aesthetic judgment.

AESTHETIC SENTIMENTS

In both the *Treatise* and the second *Enquiry,* as well as in "Of the Standard of Taste," Hume presents his discussion of aesthetic appreciation as a parallel to his account of the moral sentiments and moral judgments.

Hume introduces his discussion of the aesthetic sentiments in Books 2 and 3 of the *Treatise* with a discussion of beauty, as one of the qualities in objects which inspire pride or love (T 2.1.2.5, 2.1.8.1–9 [SBN 279, 298–303]).[5] In Book 1 he identifies the idea of beauty as an idea of a mode, in this case a set of properties making up a condition of an object (T 1.1.6.3 [SBN 17]). In Book 2 he further describes beauty as an "order and construction of parts" in an object, when this ordering is suited "either by the *primary constitution* of our nature, by *custom,* or by *caprice*" to give "a peculiar delight," or a distinctive "pleasure and satisfaction to

2. The term "aesthetics" was first applied to the philosophical study of taste or criticism by the German philosopher Alexander Baumgarten: an innovation Kant notes in the *Critique of Pure Reason*, 156n (A 21n / B35n).

3. For a discussion of Hume's own references to and acquaintance with various works of art, see Jones, "Hume's Literary and Aesthetic Theory," 255–60. Townsend has emphasized that Hume was more open to innovation in the arts, as seen in his interest in the novels of Fielding, than a strict neoclassicism might have allowed: see *Hume's Aesthetic Theory,* 208.

4. For general studies of Hume's aesthetics, see Brunet, *Philosophie et Esthétique;* Brunius, *David Hume on Criticism;* Jones, *Hume's Sentiments,* and "Hume's Literary and Aesthetic Theory," 255–60; Cohen, "Hume's Literary Enquiries," 97–115; and Townsend, *Hume's Aesthetic Theory.* Carabelli's *On Hume and Eighteenth-Century Aesthetics* is perhaps better described as an evocative interpretation of Hume than as a systematic study of his aesthetics.

5. On Hume's discussion of beauty, see Halberstadt, "A Problem in Hume's Aesthetics," 209–14; Korsmeyer, "Hume and the Foundations of Taste," 201–15; and Townsend, *Hume's Aesthetic Theory,* 105–16. See also various works by Jones, including "Cause, Reason and Objectivity in Hume's Aesthetics," 323–42; "Hume's Aesthetics Reassessed," 48–62; *Hume's Sentiments,* 123–32; and "Hume's Literary and Aesthetic Theory," 261–64.

the soul." That is, the enjoyment of beauty is a specific type of pleasure, which, like other passions, is identified in ourselves by recognizing its distinctive feeling-quality, and in other individuals by recognizing its characteristic expressions and the circumstances under which these tend to appear. He further describes the enjoyment of beauty as "a taste or sensation," or as a "sentiment" in the mind (T 2.1.8.1–2 [SBN 298–99]; EPM App.1.13–15 [SBN 291–93]). When considered as an attribute of an object, beauty is a "power" in the object, belonging to its form, to produce this distinctive pleasure in a human observer. The impression of beauty is thus a perception in the mind that we then regard as a quality of the object in a process that is parallel to our attribution of secondary qualities and moral properties to objects (T 2.1.8.1–2; cf. 3.1.1.26, 3.1.2.3 [SBN 298–99; cf. 468–69, 471]). In both "The Sceptic" and the second *Enquiry* Hume indicates that beauty is an "effect" produced in the mind by an object. In other words, the perception of beauty is a distinctive sentiment arising in the mind in response to an object, resulting from the nature and structure of the object and from the "peculiar fabric or structure" of the mind (E Sc.164; EPM App.1.14 [SBN 291–92]). Finally, Philo notes in the *Dialogues* that "beauty of all kinds" gives pleasure to human beings (DNR 10.198–99).

In the *Treatise* Hume argues that our attributions of beauty to objects arise mainly from our perception of the utility of their forms, or the "fitness" of a given form for the purposes we attribute to the object. For example, "that shape, which produces strength, is beautiful in one animal," while "a sign of agility" is beautiful in another, and "the order and convenience of a palace are no less essential to its beauty, than its mere figure and appearance." This response to a utility of form is also found in our aesthetic appreciation of the human body, since the outward signs of health, energy, and sexual promise in a human body all contribute to our appreciation of its beauty (T 2.1.8.2; cf. 2.2.5.16, 3.3.5.1–6 [SBN 299; cf. 363–64, 614–17]). Indeed, he observes that while a plain which is "overgrown with furze and broom, may be, in itself, as beautiful as a hill cover'd with vines or olive-trees," it would never appear so to anyone "who is acquainted with the value of each," since the fertility of a field contributes more to its beauty than any other quality. By contrast, an uncultivated plain can only have a beauty of "imagination," which has "no foundation in what appears to the senses" (T 2.2.5.18 [SBN 364]).

The perception of utility accounts more broadly for our aesthetic appreciation of balance and proportion in the objects of vision. For example, the "rules of architecture require, that the top of a pillar shou'd be more slender than its base," since "such a figure conveys to us the idea of security, which is pleasant," while the opposite proportion "gives us the apprehension of danger, which is uneasy." By the same principle, the rules of painting require "ballancing the figures, and placing them with the greatest exactness on their proper centers of gravity," so as not to convey "ideas of its fall, of harm, and of pain" (T 2.1.8.2, 2.2.5.19 [SBN 299, 364]; cf. EPM 6.25 [SBN 244–45]). Hume does not consider our aesthetic appreciation of other elements of the visual arts, such as color or texture; however, his remarks on proportion suggest that our appreciation of other visual qualities is derived from our ordinary experience of these characteristics in natural objects, as signs of their utility, either to human beings or in some cases to the organisms that possess them.[6]

Finally, the appreciation of beauty that arises from a recognition of utility in the form of an object often involves the operation of sympathy. For example, the qualities of a house belonging to someone else can please us only through our sympathy with the owner, by which "we enter into his interest by the force of imagination, and feel the same satisfaction, that the objects naturally occasion in him." Similarly, we generally regard the signs of "health and vigour" in the human body as beautiful, through our sympathy with the benefits of health and energy to that person (T 2.2.5.16–20; cf. 3.3.1.13–31 [SBN 363–65; cf. 580–91]).

As we have seen, Hume argues that while beauty depends on "the proportion, relation, and position of parts" in an object, beauty does not consist in these relations. Instead, beauty consists in the effect produced by these relations in the human mind, which is rendered "susceptible of such sentiments" by its "peculiar fabric or structure." Accordingly, the beauty of a column lies in its effect upon an observer, so that "till such a spectator appear, there is nothing but a figure of such particular dimensions and proportions: From his sentiments alone arise its elegance and beauty" (EPM App.1.13–15 [SBN 291–92]; cf. E Sc.163–66). Hume thus attributes a general uniformity to the aesthetic sentiments of human beings: a uniformity that he traces to the structure of the human mind, as this is reflected in our tendency to respond in similar ways to specific objects.

On the other hand, Hume also calls attention to the variability among human individuals in whether we regard an object as beautiful. Indeed, he indicates that our sentiments of beauty may be influenced not only "by the *primary constitution* of our nature" but also "by *custom,* or by *caprice*" (T 2.1.8.2 [SBN 299]). Many of these differences might be expected to arise from the "different utilities" of objects in different cultural and historical contexts (cf. EPM D.42 [SBN 337]). Hume does not immediately offer a detailed account of the influence of custom and caprice in our appreciation of beauty, either in natural objects or in works of art. However, he considers examples of the influence of custom and caprice elsewhere, in his remarks concerning the Gothic style of ornamentation and the conceits of Renaissance and Baroque poetry (CMH 58;

---

6. Korsmeyer suggests this in "Hume and the Foundations of Taste," 206–9.

E SR.192–93; H V.App.4.149–53). His discussion of the pleasure we derive from familiarity on the one hand, and from novelty on the other, might also support his view of the influence of both custom and caprice in the appreciation of beauty (T 2.2.4.1–13, 2.1.8.5, 2.1.10.3 [SBN 351–57, 300–301, 311]).

A striking expression of Hume's broadly neoclassical view of beauty, as especially valuing simplicity and order, is found in his remarks concerning Shakespeare. In the *History of England* he criticizes Shakespeare for the "many irregularities, and even absurdities" that often "disfigure" his dramatic scenes, although "at the same time, we perhaps admire the more those beauties, on account of their being surrounded with such deformities." In Shakespeare we indeed find vivid sentiments and picturesque expressions, but without any "purity or simplicity of diction," so that he combines a "great and fertile genius" with a "want of taste," in both his tragic and comic works (H 5.App.4.151). For this reason, Hume indicates to his friend, the dramatist John Home, in a letter of 1754, that Shakespeare should be admired and enjoyed, but perhaps not emulated (L 1.215). Hume's general neoclassicism is also reflected in his two main ventures into literary criticism: his assessment of Home's tragedy *Douglas,* and his letters on behalf of the *Epigoniad,* a Homeric epic by William Wilkie. These efforts also reflect his desire to promote contemporary Scottish authors, a desire which was loyal and generous, but not always very discerning.[7]

In addition to his reflections concerning the enjoyment of beauty, Hume also considers another aesthetic sentiment: our appreciation of the sublime, which arises from the perception of a great magnitude and from the influence of this perception on the imagination and the passions. For example, in our response to an ocean or a mountain range, we find that "the mere view and contemplation of any greatness, whether successive or extended, enlarges the soul" and gives "a sensible delight and pleasure." Indeed, such an object surpasses "every thing, however beautiful, which accompanies not its beauty with a suitable greatness" (T 2.3.8.2 [SBN 432]).

In explaining our appreciation of the sublime, Hume initially argues that our view of every minimally sensible part of an object produces a separate emotion. Since our view of a very large object consists in a large number of minimal perceptions, it is attended by the conjunction of all these emotions. Finally, the combined force of these emotions produces in the mind an "admiration," which is itself "one of the most lively pleasures, which human nature is capable of enjoying" (T 2.2.8.4 [SBN 373–74]). However, he later indicates that the

7. Hume's writings on behalf of *Douglas* include a letter to Spence in 1754 (L 1.204); and his 1757 dedication of the *Four Dissertations* to John Home, reprinted in Green and Grose, *Philosophical Works of David Hume,* 4: 439–41. His writings on behalf of the *Epigoniad* include a letter to Elliot in 1757 (L 1.253) and a letter to the *Critical Review* in London, published in 1759 (LW 425–37). See also Mossner, *Life of David Hume,* 356–69 and 383–86.

pleasure we derive from contemplating an object as having reached us by passing through a vast distance, in either time or space, arises from the opposition
and challenge that the contemplation of any vastness presents to the imagination and passions. This difficulty "invigorates and enlivens the soul," or the
activity and range of these faculties, an effect we find pleasurable (T 2.3.8.1–9
[SBN 432–36]). This is especially apparent in our contemplation of an immense
height, or of a present object as having originated in the remote past, both of
which require the imagination to oppose our customary tendency to look down-
ward and forward (T 2.3.8.8–12 [SBN 434–37]).[8]

Hume's discussion of these two aesthetic sentiments is reflected in a letter
written while on a journey through Europe to his brother, also named John
Home, in 1748. Here he describes the scenery along the banks of the Rhine and
expresses both his appreciation of beauty and his admiration of the sublime. He
thus admires not only the "open, beautiful, well cultivated Plains," but also the
"high Mountains" which are "so steep, that they are obligd to support the Earth
by Walls, which rise one above another like Terrasses, to the length of forty or
fifty Stories." Indeed, he describes this landscape as a unique assemblage of
"wild & cultivated Beauties in one Scene" (L 1.120–21).[9]

The possibility of other aesthetic values beyond the neoclassical appreciation of beauty and the sublime is indicated by Hume in two unpublished essays
from the last decade of his life, in which he appears to describe the rough
grandeur of medieval art as an aesthetic value, although inferior to modern aesthetic values. In writing his *History of England* he had found little or no evidence
for artistic achievement among the Anglo-Saxons; and he disdained also the
later medieval or "Gothic" style (H 1.App.1.185; H 2.23.518–19; E SR.192–
93). However, in his unpublished 1773 review of Robert Henry's *History of
Great Britain* he notes that, according to Henry, the Anglo-Saxons seem to have
cultivated the arts of poetry and music, at least, "with much assiduity, and
no contemptible success" (RH 385).[10] Next, in his unpublished essay "Of the
Poems of Ossian," from around 1775, he observes that the "Lapland and Runic
odes" have "a savage rudeness, and sometimes grandeur, suited to those ages."
On the other hand, the so-called poems of Ossian, which he correctly regarded
as eighteenth-century forgeries, display "an insipid correctness, and regularity,
and uniformity," which are among the worst characteristics of second-rate modern poetry. These signs indicated that their author was "a man without genius,"

8. On Hume's discussion of the sublime, see also Hipple, *The Beautiful, the Sublime, and the Picturesque,*
42–44; Kallich, *Association of Ideas,* 83–84; and Jacquette, *David Hume's Critique of Infinity,* 307–33.
9. On Hume's aesthetic reflections concerning the various scenes and objects encountered in his travels,
see Siebert, *Moral Animus,* 141–48.
10. Hume's review of Robert Henry's *History of England* was submitted to the *Edinburgh Magazine and
Review* in 1773, but withheld by its editor, who instead published his own unfavorable review. See Mossner,
"Hume as Literary Patron," 361–82, and Norton and Popkin, *David Hume: Philosophical Historian,* 377.

who was so restricted to the "productions of civilized nations, and had his imagination so limited to that tract, that it was impossible for him even to mimic the character which he pretended to assume" (PO 392–93). In these passages Hume appears to express some appreciation for the unclassical aesthetic qualities of "barbarous" poetry, which may also be reflected in his view that even "the most vulgar ballads are not entirely destitute of harmony or nature," although they will generally appear rough and uninteresting to those accustomed to "superior beauties" (E ST.238). I will return to Hume's discussion of the Ossian poems in Chapter 13.

Hume also occasionally describes "wit" in terms similar to those he uses to describe the appreciation of beauty. For example, he indicates that true wit produces a pleasure, and false wit an uneasiness, which we cannot explain or describe, but can only judge by taste, according to an implicit standard (T 2.1.7.7, 2.2.5.3 [SBN 297, 358]).

In addition to the distinctively aesthetic sentiments—the appreciation of beauty and the admiration of the sublime—which we feel in response to objects in nature, Hume also considers the ordinary emotions we feel when responding to works of art. These ordinary emotions are especially apparent in our response to the representational arts, such as painting, sculpture, and imaginative literature. Accordingly, in this context he also considers the nature and purpose of the fine arts, especially imaginative literature.

Hume introduces his account of artistic creativity in Book 1 of the *Treatise*, where he describes "the fables we meet with in poems and romances" as products of the imagination (T 1.1.3.4 [SBN 10]). As we have seen, he then distinguishes between belief and the imagination by describing belief as arising from a relatively greater "force and vivacity" in our ideas. For example, two people may read the same narrative as either a "romance" or a "true history." However, the reader who regards the narrative as a history, or an object of belief, will have livelier ideas of its characters and incidents than a reader who regards it as a fiction. The latter has a more "faint and languid" conception, and can indeed "receive little entertainment" from the story apart from "the style and ingenuity of the composition" (T 1.3.7.8 [SBN 97–98]). Accordingly, poets often refer to historical events to give "an air of truth to their fictions" (T 1.3.10.5 [SBN 121–22]).

On the other hand, Hume also suggests in the *Treatise* that the intention of the artist is to provide vivid depictions of objects and events, in order to elicit from their audience an analogue of belief. Indeed, authors of imaginative literature develop "what they call a poetical system of things," such as the characters and events derived from classical mythology, which is "believed neither by themselves nor readers," but is "commonly esteem'd a sufficient foundation for any fiction," especially when developed according to clear and consistent patterns of association (T 1.3.10.6 [SBN 121]). Hume even indicates that in the "warmth of a poetical enthusiasm," the poet has "a counterfeit belief," which is communicated to the reader through a "blaze of poetical figures and images." These are similar to the images produced by "madness or folly," except that neither poets nor their audiences confuse these images with reality. On the contrary, "the least reflection dissipates the illusions of poetry, and places the objects in their proper light" (T SBN 123).[11] Hume's renewed account of belief in the Appendix implicitly reaffirms his discussion of imaginative literature as depicting a separate "system of reality," and as eliciting a "counterfeit belief." Here he again concedes that poetic images may be conceived with a greater vivacity than memories, which are the objects of belief. However, poetic images still do not produce belief, or "the same *feeling*," as when we reason even on "the lowest species of probability" (T 1.3.10.10 [SBN 630–31]).

Hume also indicates in the Appendix that we may distinguish the feelings aroused by objects of belief from the passions inspired by imaginative literature. Although indeed "there is no passion of the human mind but what may arise from poetry," we find that "the *feelings* of the passions are very different when excited by poetical fictions" than by "belief and reality." For example, "A passion, which is disagreeable in real life, may afford the highest entertainment in a tragedy, or epic poem." Hume concludes that the distinctive vivacity of a fiction depends on the "poetry and eloquence" in its presentation, rather than its relation to reality (T 1.3.10.10 [SBN 630–31]). As we will see, in his essays on eloquence and on tragedy Hume develops his account of our enjoyment of fiction as involving a counterfeit belief and counterfeit feelings, produced by the "poetry and eloquence" of the writer.

In the second *Enquiry* Hume indicates that "no passion, when well represented, can be entirely indifferent to us," since there is none "of which every man has not, within him, at least the seeds and first principles." He then describes the goal of poetry as "to bring every affection near to us by lively imagery and representation, and make it look like truth and reality" (EPM 5.30 [SBN 222–23]). The "great charm of poetry" accordingly lies in its ability to give us "lively pictures" of various human emotions. These include the "sublime passions" such as magnanimity, courage, and fortitude, and "tender affections" of love and friendship, by which the poet seeks to "warm the heart, and diffuse over it similar sentiments and emotions." However, he notes that even disagreeable passions, such as grief and anger, "when excited by poetry," as in the case of a tragic drama, are discovered "to convey a satisfaction, from a mechanism of nature" which is not easily explained (EPM 7.26 [SBN 259]).

---

11. This paragraph was replaced by three new paragraphs on belief and poetry in the Appendix to the *Treatise* (T 1.3.10.10–12 [SBN 630–32]).

Hume approaches this problem by considering the effects of rhetorical artistry on the human passions, which he addresses in a number of his writings. In the *Treatise* he observes that "nothing is more capable of infusing any passion into the mind, than eloquence, by which objects are represented in their strongest and most lively colours." The eloquence of an orator or poet can accordingly give further appeal, interest, and value even to ordinary objects such as cider, as in the poem *Cyder*, by John Philips (1708) (T 2.3.6.7, 2.2.5.3 [SBN 426–27, 358]). Hume also refers to the "the figures of poets and orators" as examples of the tendency of the human mind to confuse ideas associated by resemblance, contiguity, or causation (T 1.2.5.21 [SBN 61]). In "Of the Standard of Taste" he offers a more specific account of a variety of rhetorical devices in imaginative literature, observing that many beauties of poetry and eloquence "are founded on falsehood and fiction, on hyperboles, metaphors, and an abuse or perversion of terms from their natural meaning." Indeed, it is "contrary to the laws of criticism" for poetry to "submit to exact truth," since the results are often "insipid and disagreeable" (E ST.231).

In "Of Eloquence" Hume indicates that the task of rhetoric is to arouse the passions of the audience, and then compares the ancient and modern styles of rhetoric. He concludes that the greatest of the ancient orators, such as Demosthenes and Cicero, not only possessed "elegance, and subtilty, and force of argument," but were also skilled in using the "pathetic and sublime" to influence the passions and resolutions of their audience: a combination of qualities he finds more among writers than public speakers in modern Britain (E El.107–8). In "Of Simplicity and Refinement in Writing" he considers the proper balance between simplicity and the use of wit or ornament, which he calls "refinement," in writing. He first argues that a completely natural style of writing, such as in a transcript of ordinary conversation, would be insipid and even distasteful. Instead, elegant writing should depict "nature drawn with all her graces and ornaments," and even "low life" with "strong and remarkable" strokes, in order to convey "a lively image to the mind." On the other hand, too much refinement, especially when it emphasizes the "merely surprising, without being natural," is a blemish in any art. For example, too many "uncommon expressions, strong flashes of wit, pointed similies, and epigrammatic turns" disfigure rather than embellish a discourse, just as the "multiplicity of ornaments" in a Gothic building tends to distract the eye from appreciating its overall structure. In both cases, the mind is soon "fatigued and disgusted with the constant endeavor to shine and surprize" (E SR.192–93). The passions are also more easily aroused by a direct simplicity than by excessive wit, which tends to distract us from the central theme of a discourse (E SR.195). In the *History of England* he denounces the "glaring figures of discourse, the pointed antithesis, the unnatural conceit, the jingle of words" in Roman and Baroque literature. By contrast, Greek poetry and oratory express the "genuine movements of nature and passion" and enduring beauties of "solid sense and lively passion." He apparently did not find these natural and enduring types of beauty among English writers, at least before the eighteenth century (H 5.App.4.149–50; cf. E SR.193; H 6.62.149–54; H 6.71.542–45; LW 483).[12]

Hume's most thorough discussion of the aesthetic sentiments and of artistic creativity is presented in "Of Tragedy," where he considers the problem of why we enjoy tragic drama.[13] He initially addresses this problem in the *Treatise*, where he suggests that we indeed feel unpleasant passions of fear and terror while viewing a dramatic performance, from our sympathy with the passions of the characters depicted by the author. However, these passions are softened by the "want of belief in the subject," so that they instead exercise the "agreeable effect of enlivening the mind, and fixing the attention." He later adds that the viewer of a tragic drama "passes thro' a long train of grief, terror, indignation, and other affections," and may even feel a "fictitious joy as well as every other passion" if it ends happily (T 1.3.9.15, 2.2.7.3 [SBN 115, 369]). As we have seen, the passions aroused by tragedy and epic poetry are the same as those arising from real events, but have a different "feeling," which is enjoyable rather than disagreeable (T 1.3.10.10 [SBN 630–31]).[14] He notes in the second *Enquiry* that all of the human passions, "even the most disagreeable, such as grief and anger," can be aroused by poetry and "convey a satisfaction" through an operation of the mind which invites explanation (EPM 7.26 [SBN 259]).

In "Of Tragedy" Hume accordingly seeks to explain the "unaccountable pleasure, which the spectators of a well-written tragedy receive from sorrow, terror, anxiety, and other passions, that are in themselves disagreeable and uneasy." Indeed, "they are pleased in proportion as they are afflicted, and never are so happy as when they employ tears, sobs, and cries to give vent to their sorrow, and relieve their hearts, swoln with the tenderest sympathy and compassion" (E Tr.216–17). He then considers two recent attempts by French literary theorists to explain our enjoyment of tragedy. According to Jean Baptiste Dubos, the human mind seeks any activity, even disagreeable passions, to avoid the "insipid langour, which arises from perfect tranquillity and repose." Hume holds that this theory cannot account for the pleasure we receive from tragic drama, since similar events in real life would cause "the most unfeigned uneasiness,"

12. For a discussion of Hume's literary influences, and his favorite contemporary authors, see Box, *Suasive Art of David Hume,* 20–25.

13. See Hipple, "The Logic of Hume's Essay 'Of Tragedy,'" 43–52; Cohen, "Transformation of Passion," 450–64; Paton, "Hume on Tragedy," 121–32; White, "Some Remarks," 287–91; and Herdt, *Religion and Faction,* 82–116.

14. This passage has often been overlooked in the discussion of Hume's theory of tragedy. See Cohen, "Transformation of Passion," 450–51, and White, "Some Remarks," 287.

rather than pleasure (E Tr.217–18). Instead, he agrees with Bernard de Fontenelle that the pleasure arising from a tragedy is derived from our awareness that we are witnessing a dramatic performance. On this view, the painful emotions aroused by a tragic drama are converted into pleasure when we "comfort ourselves, by reflecting, that it is nothing but a fiction" (E Tr.218–19). Hume seeks to improve upon this theory by considering the effects of artistry on the emotions.

In the case of oratory, Hume finds that when we read the trial speeches of Cicero, we enjoy his literary ability, even though he is describing events that are both real and distressing. Accordingly, the source of our pleasure must be the rhetorical artistry of the speaker, or "that very eloquence, with which the melancholy scene is represented." In other words, we admire "the genius required to paint objects in a lively manner, the art employed in collecting all the pathetic circumstances, the judgment displayed in disposing them," along with "the force of expression, and beauty of oratorial numbers." By these skills, "the uneasiness of the melancholy passions is not only overpowered and effaced" by a stronger and opposite feeling, "but the whole impulse of those passions is converted into pleasure, and swells the delight which the eloquence raises in us" (E Tr.219–20).

Hume argues that our enjoyment of tragedy also arises from this enjoyment of eloquence, combined with our enjoyment of imitation. Accordingly, the pleasure we receive from tragedy is a result of "the force of imagination, the energy of expression, the power of numbers, the charms of imitation," which are "naturally, of themselves, delightful to the mind," and especially "when the object presented lays also hold of some affection." He specifically describes our enjoyment of tragedy as arising from a "conversion" of the passions, in which a distressing passion that would be aroused in real life is "smoothed, and softened, and mollified" by the "finer" literary arts, and instead produces a "uniform and strong enjoyment" (E Tr.222–23, 220). To confirm this analysis, he notes that our enjoyment is diminished if the artist is too successful in imitating the distressing event, and that those who have experienced a painful situation similar to one depicted in a speech or a tragedy will not derive pleasure from the production. At the other extreme, a poorly written tragedy tends to arouse other emotions, which may indeed overwhelm and extinguish the original passion. For example, bloody and grotesque scenes produce uneasiness instead of pleasure, while a mere depiction of "plaintive virtue" suffering under a "triumphant tyranny" is not an enjoyable spectacle. Instead, "the virtue must either convert itself into a noble courageous despair, or the vice receive its proper punishment" (E Tr.224).

Several recent studies have suggested that in "Of Tragedy" Hume is developing a theory of representational art, not primarily as an imitation of nature, but as a new creation of the artist. On this view, the artist imposes a form on materials drawn from nature in a production that the audience recognizes as a separate imaginative world. The audience then enjoys this production through an emotional response that is converted into pleasure through a detached admiration.[15] This interpretation of his theory is supported by his account in the *Treatise* of the "poetical system of things" as eliciting a "counterfeit belief," and of the passions inspired by imaginative fiction as characterized by a distinctive feeling produced by the "poetry and eloquence" of the author (T 1.3.10.6–10 [SBN 121–23, 630–31]). This view of representational art is also anticipated in his early essay "On Chivalry and Modern Honour," where he considers the tendency of the human imagination to raise up "a new set of Passions, Affections, Desires, Objects, & in short a perfectly new World of its own, inhabited by different Beings, & regulated by different Laws, from this of ours." Examples of these imaginary worlds range from different systems of religion and philosophy to the literary traditions of the "Grecian poets" and "Romantick Chivalry or Knight-Errantry" (CMH 57–59).

Hume further examines the systematic character of literary creativity in his discussion of narrative principles in the first *Enquiry*.[16] In this discussion he argues that works of imaginative literature and history are both organized by their authors according to some "plan or design," or a "united view" of the subject. More specifically, both are structured according to the principles of association. Since a work of imaginative literature is especially intended to influence the passions of the audience, the rules of poetry and drama, such as the unity of action, are intended to guide authors in using the principles of association within a story to enhance its effect on the passions of the audience (EHU 3.4–18). He then indicates by an example that a critic's task may include explaining the principles of connection in a literary work. Thus, on his account, the three central events in Milton's *Paradise Lost*—the creation of the world, the angelic rebellion, and the fall of man—are united by resemblance, since they involve supernatural events and other parallels; and also by contiguity, since all of these events are supposed to have happened in the prehistory of the human race. However, the causal connections between these events are either too general, or too intricate, to provide a satisfactory structure for an epic poem (EHU 3.17). He also indicates, in his letter on Wilkie's *Epigoniad,* that an epic may be based upon a relatively simple story. Indeed, the story is "the least essential part of it," since the merits of a poem are found in "the force of the versification, the

---

15. See Cohen, "Transformation of Passion," 461; Paton, "Hume on Tragedy," 125–26; Hill, "Delightful Tragedy Problem," 319–26; and Herdt, *Religion and Faction,* 82–116.

16. This passage appeared in Section 3, "Of the Association of Ideas," and in all editions of the first *Enquiry* that Hume published during his lifetime. However, he removed it in his final revision of this work, and it did not appear in the posthumous edition of 1777.

vivacity of the images, the justness of the descriptions," and "the natural play of the passions." By contrast, a "prosaic novelist" is more dependent upon the "design" of his or her work, which presumably consists in an intricate and engaging story.

AESTHETIC JUDGMENT

Hume designates the study of our appreciation of the arts, and especially of literature, as "criticism." In the *Treatise* he expects his "science of MAN" to provide the foundation, not only for mathematics, natural philosophy, and natural religion, but also for logic, morals, criticism, and politics (T Int.4–5; cf. Adv.1 [SBN xv–xvi; cf. xii]). He later includes criticism among the studies a philosopher might wish to resume after overcoming the crisis of skepticism (T 1.4.7.12 [SBN 271]). In his concluding survey of the various intellectual disciplines in the first *Enquiry*, he observes that "morals and criticism are not so properly objects of the understanding as of taste and sentiment," but may be the subjects of reasoning insofar as they refer to a fact, such as "the general taste of mankind" (EHU 12.33 [SBN 165]). In the second *Enquiry* he argues that although natural beauty may indeed receive our immediate "affection and approbation," our appreciation of beauty in the arts may require "much reasoning," and even "argument and reflection," to correct a false taste (EPM 1.9 [SBN 173]).

Hume presents his main discussion of the principles of criticism in "Of the Standard of Taste." In this essay he considers the problem of justifying a standard of taste as the basis for criticism, in response to the possibility of a complete aesthetic relativism, which, as he himself recognizes, might seem to be implicit in his account of the aesthetic sentiments.[17] He describes aesthetic relativism in "The Sceptic" as the view that all opinions of "beauty and worth" depend entirely on "the sentiment of that mind which blames or praises," and should thus be considered "merely of a relative nature," since they arise from "the peculiar structure and constitution of that mind" (E Sc.163). In the second *Enquiry* he summarizes the arguments for moral and aesthetic relativism as holding that taste, the principle of judgment in both domains, is not disputable. Thus, while in the case of cognitive truth, "what exists in the nature of things is the standard of our judgement," in morals and aesthetics it might seem that "what each man feels within himself is the standard of sentiment" (EPM 1.5 [SBN 171]).

---

17. For a discussion of the historical background to Hume's "Of the Standard of Taste," see Jones, *Hume's Sentiments*, 93–123, and "Hume's Literary and Aesthetic Theory," 255–76; Herdt, *Religion and Faction*, 117–67; and Townsend, *Hume's Aesthetic Theory*, 12–85. See also Cassirer, *Philosophy of the Enlightenment*, 297–312.

In "Of the Standard of Taste" Hume begins by indicating that "the great variety of Taste, as well as of opinion, which prevails in the world, is too obvious not to have fallen under every one's observation." Indeed, even people of "confined knowledge" are likely to notice "a difference of taste in the narrow circle of their acquaintance," even among those who have been "educated under the same government, and have early imbibed the same prejudices." In addition, however, "those, who can enlarge their view to contemplate distant nations and remote ages, are still more surprized at the great inconsistence and contrariety." The variety of taste is even more apparent when we consider particular aesthetic opinions, since the common use of evaluative terms tends to obscure individual differences in taste. We thus find that "every voice is united in applauding elegance, propriety, simplicity, spirit in writing; and in blaming fustian, affectation, coldness, and a false brilliancy." However, "when critics come to particulars, this seeming unanimity vanishes; and it is found, that they had affixed a very different meaning to their expressions." We are "apt to call *barbarous* whatever departs widely from our own taste and apprehension," but this "epithet of reproach" may also be directed by others against our own aesthetic preferences (E ST.226–27).

This discovery of the variety in our aesthetic opinions leads to a "species of philosophy" which denies that we can or should develop a standard of taste. Instead, this view holds that "all sentiment is right," and "a thousand different sentiments, excited by the same object" are equally right, because none of them refer to anything in the object or beyond themselves. Indeed, since beauty is not a property of objects themselves, but is projected onto the object as a result of an operation of the mind, we might suppose that "each mind perceives a different beauty," and that one person "may even perceive deformity, where another is sensible of beauty." As a result of both common observation and skeptical philosophy, we seem forced to conclude that "every individual ought to acquiesce in his own sentiment, without pretending to regulate those of others" (E ST.229–30).

However, there is also a "species of common sense" which opposes this argument, or "at least serves to modify and restrain it," by recognizing our tendency to seek agreement with others in our aesthetic judgments. We accordingly find that "whoever would assert an equality of genius and elegance between OGILBY and MILTON, or BUNYAN and ADDISON," would be dismissed as defending an "extravagance." While some may indeed "give the preference to the former authors," no one else "pays attention to such a taste; and we pronounce without scruple the sentiment of these pretended critics to be absurd and ridiculous" (E ST.230–31).

Since the appeal to an aesthetic standard appears to be implicit in our ordinary aesthetic judgments, Hume argues that "it is natural for us to seek a *Standard of Taste*" according to which "the various sentiments of men may be reconciled," or by which we may at least reach a decision "confirming one sentiment, and condemning another" (E ST.229). However, he also maintains that "none of the rules of composition are fixed by reasonings *a priori,*" or derived as "abstract conclusions of the understanding, from comparing those habitudes and relations of ideas, which are eternal and immutable." Instead, these rules are derived from "experience," or the history of the reception and appreciation of various works of art. The "rules of art" are therefore "general observations, concerning what has been universally found to please in all countries and in all ages," as these are discovered "either by genius or observation" (E ST.231–33).

Hume also argues that the rules of art reflect the "common sentiments of human nature," which he regards as inherent in the human mind. This conclusion follows from our discovery that "amidst all the variety and caprice of taste, there are certain general principles of approbation or blame" which we may trace in all "operations of the mind" involving aesthetic appreciation. As a result of this study, we find that "some particular forms or qualities, from the original structure of the internal fabric, are calculated to please, and others to displease," and that "if they fail of their effect in any particular instance, it is from some apparent defect or imperfection in the organ" (E ST.232–33). These principles appear in all works of real artistic genius, and have made them popular as classics, through a variety of changes in the "climate, government, religion, and language" of ages and nations. Indeed, the general approval of these works is a reflection of "an entire or a considerable uniformity of sentiment among men," from which we may derive "an idea of the perfect beauty" (E ST.233–34). Finally, from these common sentiments, and the common idea of beauty, we may develop "general rules of beauty." With these we may correct a bad critic by indicating to that person "an avowed principle of art," illustrated by examples that, "from his own particular taste, he acknowledges to be conformable to the principle," and demonstrating "that the same principle may be applied to the present case, where he did not perceive or feel its influence" (E ST.235–37).

However, instead of describing the characteristics of a beautiful work of art, or stating the rules of art, or examining classic works in the history of art, Hume devotes the rest of his essay to considering the principles that appear to guide a cultivated aesthetic taste, in contrast to an unrefined aesthetic enjoyment. In other words, he considers the distinguishing characteristics of a good critic.[18] Some of these principles reflect his presentation of the standard of taste as a set of rules derived from considering a canon of recognized classics. However, other aspects of his description of a good critic point beyond such an established aesthetic tradition toward the possibility of cultivating an enjoyment of a wider variety of artistic works.

18. For a related treatment of this discussion, see Townsend, *Hume's Aesthetic Theory,* 206–13.

The first characteristic of a good critic, according to Hume, is a delicacy of imagination and sentiment. He describes this delicacy as the ability to discern the merits of a work of art, or the subtle qualities in a given work that are "fitted by nature" to produce aesthetic sentiments, even if these qualities are minute, or "mixed and confounded with each other." This power of discernment may be compared to a delicacy of palate, or the ability of a connoisseur of food or wine to discern ingredients and flavors. However, Hume maintains that a delicate taste in the appreciation of art is cultivated by studying and applying the rules of beauty, which are "drawn from established models, and from the observation of what pleases or displeases, when presented singly and in a high degree," or from "those models and principles, which have been established by the uniform consent and experience of nations and ages" (E ST.234–35, 237).

The second and third characteristics of a good critic, according to Hume, are practice in the study of art and experience in comparing works of art. However, in order to gain practice and experience, the aspiring critic or connoisseur is still directed to study and to compare recognized models, or classics, belonging to the given genre. In this regard, the aspiring critic is again presumably guided by the opinion of established critics (E ST.237–38).

By contrast, in turning to the final two characteristics of a good critic, namely good sense and freedom from prejudice, Hume implicitly sets forth the principles for an expanded range of aesthetic appreciation. In considering these two characteristics, although he himself only partially recognizes this, he in effect provides the principles by which a critic or a connoisseur may move beyond a given canon or set of rules.

First, in recommending freedom from prejudice, Hume argues that a good critic should not allow anything to influence his response to a work of art but "the very object which is submitted to his examination." The critic should also approach the production from the appropriate perspective, since "every work of art, in order to produce its due effect on the mind, must be surveyed in a certain point of view," and "cannot be fully relished by persons, whose situation, real or imaginary, is not conformable to that which is required by the performance." As an example of attempting to attain the appropriate point of view, Hume considers the principles involved in the interpretation and aesthetic evaluation of historical texts, especially of orations. An effective speaker must have considered the "particular genius, interests, opinions, passions, and prejudices" of his audience, and attempted "to conciliate their affection, and acquire their good graces" before presenting the substance of his discourse. The reader must take these original conditions into account, especially if they are historically and culturally remote from his or her situation. In other words, "a critic of a different age or nation, who should peruse this discourse, must have all these circumstances in his eye, and must place himself in the same situation as

the audience, in order to form a true judgment of the oration." Also, to counteract any contemporary sources of prejudice, Hume recommends that any
critic of current literature who feels a personal affection or animosity toward a
given writer must put these feelings aside in order to appreciate and judge the
works of that author adequately. By contrast, someone who is guided by prejudice "obstinately maintains his natural position, without placing himself in
that point of view, which the performance supposes." Such a critic makes no
allowances, in a foreign text, for the "peculiar views and prejudices" of different ages and nations; or in the contemporary case, never forgets his own interest "as a friend or enemy, as a rival or commentator." Otherwise, the sentiments
of this critic are "perverted," and "his taste evidently departs from the true standard; and of consequence loses all credit and authority" (E ST.239–40).[19]
    The most effective method for counteracting prejudice toward an artist,
whether grounded in distance or in self-interest, is to follow the principles of
sound reasoning, or "good sense," in judging the circumstances of the author
and the original audience. Indeed, Hume argues that although reason is not an
"essential part of taste," it may contribute in several ways to the generation of
our aesthetic sentiments. First, reason may discover the unity and purpose of a
work of art, since every artistic production has "a mutual relation and correspondence of parts" and requires that we "comprehend all those parts, and compare them with each other, in order to perceive the consistence and uniformity
of the whole." Every artistic work also has "a certain end or purpose, for which
it is calculated," and is considered "more or less perfect," as we judge it to be
"more or less fitted to attain this end." Finally, in the case of a literary work,
reason enables the reader to follow the "chain of propositions and reasonings,"
which appears in "every kind of composition, even the most poetical." For
example, the characters depicted "in tragedy and epic poetry, must be represented as reasoning, and thinking, and concluding, and acting, suitably to their
character and circumstances." This literary verisimilitude requires "judgment,
as well as taste and invention" on the part of the poet, and a corresponding
series of judgments by the audience and the critic (E ST.240; cf. EHU 3.9–15).
    Since the cultivation of good taste in the arts depends partly on the study
of classics and partly on the exercise of reason, Hume indicates that a person
of good sense and understanding, who also has experience in studying works of
art, will usually be a good critic. In other words, a good critical judgment requires "strong sense, united to delicate sentiment, improved by practice, perfected by comparison, and cleared of all prejudice." Because it is difficult to
meet all of these conditions consistently, he expects that only a few people will

---

19. On the role of sympathy in Hume's account of the aesthetic sentiments and aesthetic judgment, see
Herdt, *Religion and Faction,* 117–16, and Townsend, *Hume's Aesthetic Theory,* 99–105.

be qualified "to give judgment on any work of art, or establish their own sentiment as the standard of beauty." We may, however, regard the joint verdict of these critics as "the true standard of taste and beauty" (E ST.241).

Finally, Hume asks how such critics are to be found: a question that seems to return us to the problem of relativism in our aesthetic preferences. Hume maintains that the identification of critics is, however, a matter of fact rather than of sentiment. This question is decided by measuring the judgments of an aspiring critic against the established principles and models in the history of art, and assessing the adequacy of his or her judgments concerning these classics. Indeed, since the "beauties of eloquence and poetry" hold "an universal, undisputed empire over the minds of men," we find a natural tendency in society for "men of delicate taste" to acquire a position from which they may provide guidance in appreciating works of "true genius," as others seek out their opinions (E ST.242–43).

However, Hume notes that there are two sources of variation in taste, which are likely to remain even after these conditions are met, producing "a certain degree of diversity in judgment," even among cultivated critics. The first is the difference between individuals in their "humours" and circumstances, which leads us to prefer writers who echo our own experience or disposition. For example, a young person "whose passions are warm" is especially drawn toward "amorous and tender images," while someone who is "more advanced in years" may derive more pleasure from "wise, philosophical reflections concerning the conduct of life and moderation of the passions." Differences in temperament also lead individuals to prefer different genres, such as comedies, tragedies, satires, or odes. We accordingly choose "our favourite author as we do our friend, from a conformity of humour and disposition." The resulting preferences are "innocent and unavoidable, and can never reasonably be the object of dispute," because in these cases "there is no standard, by which they can be decided" (E ST.243–44).

The other source of an innocent and unavoidable variation in critical taste is the influence of "the particular manners and opinions of our age and country." Hume observes that individuals tend to prefer "pictures and characters" resembling those of our own time and place to those that represent a "different set of customs." However, he maintains that anyone who has the benefit of "learning and reflection" will make allowances for the "peculiarities of manners" in a different age or nation. On the other hand, a "common audience" will never "divest themselves so far of their usual ideas and sentiments, as to relish pictures which no wise resemble them" (E ST.243, 245).

However, Hume maintains that the critic should not overlook serious violations of our philosophically corrected moral standards, even in works of art that are products of another time and place. Thus, in judging a foreign work of art, a good critic should distinguish between both "innocent peculiarities in manners" and differences in speculative opinions, on the one hand, and any moral deficiencies on the other. First, any "innocent" peculiarities in customs and manners should be accepted in a work of art, and a rejection of these is "an evident proof of false delicacy and refinement." Next, a difference in speculative opinions should not diminish our regard for a work of art, since a production from another time or place requires only "a certain turn of thought or imagination to make us enter into all the opinions, which then prevailed, and relish the sentiments or conclusions derived from them." However, Hume argues that when "the ideas of morality and decency alter from one age to another, and where vicious manners are described," without any blame and disapproval, we may regard this as tending to "disfigure the poem, and to be a real deformity." For example, the "want of humanity and of decency" in the characters depicted by many of the ancient poets, including Homer and the tragic dramatists, "diminishes considerably the merit of their noble performances, and gives modern authors an advantage over them," since we "cannot prevail on ourselves" to enter into the sentiments of the author, or to feel any affection toward his characters. Indeed, we are justified in refusing to engage in any such attempt, since morality depends on sentiment and is cultivated by habit. As a result, when one is "confident of the rectitude of that moral standard, by which he judges, he is justly jealous of it, and will not pervert the sentiments of his heart for a moment, in complaisance to any writer whatsoever" (E ST.245–47; cf. LW 434).

Finally, the influence of religion in a work of art may be judged by whether it is morally innocent or blamable. Hume maintains that speculative errors arising from religion are the "most excusable" in works of literature, and that we should avoid judging "the civility or wisdom of any people, or even of single persons, by the grossness or refinement of their theological principles." In our enjoyment and assessment of ancient poetry we should thus overlook the "absurdities of the pagan system of theology," just as our own posterity "must have the same indulgence to their forefathers." On the other hand, since religious fanaticism and superstition tend to "confound the sentiments of morality, and alter the natural boundaries of vice and virtue," these may be seen as "eternal blemishes," which cannot be excused by the "prejudices and false opinions of the age."[20] Finally, religious references and images may be said to disfigure a work of art if they are used inappropriately or hyperbolically, and may indeed have seemed ridiculous in these cases even to contemporaries of the author (E ST.247–49). Hume further notes in his letter on Wilke's *Epigoniad* that "the Christian religion, for many reasons, is unfit for the fabulous ornaments of

20. For a further discussion of the role and the limitations of sympathetic understanding in appreciating representation in art of different moral and religious systems, see Herdt, *Religion and Faction*, 117–67.

334 · David Hume: Reason in History

poetry," and that the system of the "heathen Gods" is more suited to depiction in epic poetry (LW 435).

In "Of the Standard of Taste" Hume therefore defends the view, anticipated in his earlier works, that we can judge "a *right* or a *wrong* taste" in beauty and eloquence (T 3.2.8.8n80; cf. 1.4.7.12 [SBN 547n1; cf. 271]). That is, although aesthetic appreciation ultimately arises from "taste and sentiment," its conclusions may also be subjected to reasoning, insofar as they may be compared to "the general taste of mankind" (EHU 12.33 [SBN 165]), which is expressed in the opinions of critics, the rules of art, and a canon of classics. By appealing to these standards, we may even resort to "reasoning," or "argument and reflection," to correct a false taste (EPM 1.9 [SBN 173]).

Hume also considers the purpose of criticism in several of his essays, in which he suggests that cultivating a delicate aesthetic taste benefits individuals and a society in ways that cannot be achieved by an uncultivated enjoyment of the "obvious beauties" in nature and art. For example, he distinguishes between an excessive "*delicacy* of *passion*," or a sensitivity to our own circumstances, by which individuals may be rendered "extremely sensible to all the accidents of life," and a "*delicacy* of *taste*," which instead produces a sensitivity to beauty. Both types of delicacy tend to enlarge "the sphere both of our happiness and misery," and make us sensitive "to pains as well as pleasures, which escape the rest of mankind." However, a delicacy of taste is less troublesome and inconvenient than an extreme delicacy of passion, and "improves our sensibility for all the tender and agreeable passions," while rendering the mind "incapable of the rougher and more boisterous emotions." A delicacy of taste also enables us to appreciate the "nobler arts," enhances our understanding of human nature, and even moderates our passions (E DT.3–6; cf. E Sc.171). In "Of the Standard of Taste" he argues that "a delicate taste of wit or beauty" produces "the finest and most innocent enjoyments" in human life. The task of the critic is to help others cultivate an appreciation of beauty, so that they can also enjoy these pleasures (E ST.236; cf. EPM 7.28 [SBN 260]). Finally, the cultivation of the arts may promote the development of civilization, especially by fostering the civic and sociable virtues (E CL.87–96; E RP.111–37; E Co.253–67; E RA.268–80).[21] However, he observes that refined taste does not always coincide with good manners or virtue. For example, the ancient Greeks had better taste than the modern English in rhetoric and poetry, but were less advanced in civility and humanity (E RP.127–31; E NC.209).

Hume examines the influence of social and historical conditions on the development of artistic talent as well. He argues that artistic genius is not supernatural, but "only runs along the earth; is caught from one breast to another;

21. On Hume's view of the personal and social functions of art, see also Jones, "'Art' and 'Moderation' in Hume's Essays," 161–79; Herdt, *Religion and Faction*, 82–167; and Williams, *Cultivated Reason*, 161–65.

and burns brightest, where the materials are best prepared, and most happily disposed." In other words, artists are influenced by the "spirit and genius" of their own age and nation, which is also reflected in other aspects of its cultural life (E RP.114). More specifically, he observes that "Nature must afford the richest Genius that comes from her Hands; Education and Example must cultivate it from the earliest Infancy; And Industry must concur to carry it to any Degree of Perfection" (E MS.549). He concludes that natural genius, a favorable setting, and individual effort are all generally required for artistic flourishing. By contrast, the "Epicurean" considers artistic talent entirely a product of nature, and the "Stoic" regards it as entirely a product of industry and effort (E Ep.139; E St.146–47).

As we have seen, Hume begins his discussion of aesthetics by acknowledging the variety among human beings in our aesthetic reactions to particular objects. However, he then attempts to account for the patterns of intersubjective agreement among our aesthetic sentiments, and for our tendency to establish standards of aesthetic judgment to express and coordinate this agreement within the context of an aesthetic tradition. Instead of endorsing complete relativism in aesthetic appreciation, he thus maintains that human beings are naturally inclined to compare the objects of their aesthetic sentiments, and to seek agreement concerning the aesthetic merits of objects. This agreement is expressed in a standard of taste, which may then be used to judge the aesthetic value of other works, and to help us improve our aesthetic appreciation of objects. Finally, this aesthetic appreciation provides a delicate and wholesome source of pleasure; promotes the exercise of our imagination, emotions, and reasoning; moderates our passions; and cultivates virtue.

However, in the course of this discussion Hume indicates that the process of discerning and promoting agreement in our aesthetic judgments actually leads us to develop several types of standards. First, these standards include the "rules of art," which serve as guiding principles for the creative process in the various artistic genres, and for analyzing and evaluating works of art. Next, these standards include a canon of classics, or a set of works that are widely approved as objects of aesthetic enjoyment. Finally, these standards include the judgments of critics, or those connoisseurs who have cultivated their talents for discerning merit in particular works of art. It would thus seem that, in Hume's view, the combination of a set of rules, a canon of classics, and the opinions of critics together provide a standard according to which individual works may be judged more or less effective in their ability to arouse a delicate aesthetic enjoyment, and thus to promote the various nonaesthetic benefits of aesthetic appreciation.

In his theory of criticism, Hume assumes that his task is to account for the development of a single standard of taste in a cultural tradition: specifically, the broadly neoclassical standard of his own day. However, his analysis of the process by which a standard of taste is developed in a given cultural tradition can also be applied to other aesthetic standards, including not only the various standards of different ages and cultures, but even the variety of standards belonging to the different aesthetic subcultures of a pluralistic community. Indeed, Hume's theory of the development of a standard of taste is borne out by observing that every successive medium of mass communication in modern culture tends to become a forum for aesthetic discussion. We thus find that even the aesthetic subcultures of our own society have a tendency to develop conventions for works of art in their traditions, to identify a canon of classics, and to seek talented critics who can guide the members of that community in discussing new works in their tradition. Hume's account of the standard of taste is thus also a contribution to the history and sociology of art, in its description of the process by which a standard of taste is developed within a particular aesthetic tradition.[22]

Hume's account of the standards of aesthetic judgment is a parallel to his discussion of the standards of moral judgment in several important respects. In both cases, the standard of judgment consists in a general point of view, which is formulated through sympathy, articulated and applied through a distinctive terminology, and codified in the rules of approbation within a given community. However, in the case of moral judgments, he maintains that the standards of approval within a given culture are themselves subject to critical assessment. The principle for this philosophical criticism of an existing moral tradition is the recognition that the tendency of various qualities of human character to promote happiness, by being useful or agreeable, is the underlying standard for any system of morality.

By contrast, in his theory of criticism Hume does not attempt to formulate any specific principles of aesthetic judgment as precise as either the conventional precepts or the philosophical standard of morality.[23] On the other hand, in his account of the characteristics of a good critic, Hume implicitly allows for the possibility of correcting the standard of taste within a given community. On his view, a good critic has the task, not only of appreciating works of art in the existing canon, but also of recognizing the merits of new or previously unappreciated works and commending them to the public. This new appreciation of an existing work of art can arise either from an increased delicacy in

22. On Hume's contribution to the sociology of art, see Brunius, *David Hume on Criticism,* 87–88, and Brunet, *Philosophie et Esthétique,* 796–850. On his view of the historical and cross-cultural dimension of aesthetics, see Brunet, *Philosophie et Esthétique,* 98–108, and Atkins, *English Literary Criticism,* 379.

23. For Hume's view of the relation between aesthetics and moral theory, see Brunius, *David Hume on Criticism,* 33–79; Brunet, *Philosophie et Esthétique,* 221–66; Árdal, *Passion and Value,* 122–23; Jones, "Another Look," 53–59; and Townsend, *Hume's Aesthetic Theory,* 137–57.

discerning its nuances, or from a deeper understanding of its context and intention, especially where previous critics or audiences have been influenced by
prejudice (E St.234–41).[24] Indeed, although he might not in general be the
most direct spokesman for Hume in the *Dialogues,* Cleanthes expresses this view
by noting that some beauties in literature "gain the affections, and animate the
imagination," although they seem to be "contrary to rules," and indeed to "all
the precepts of criticism, and to the authority of the established masters of
art" (DNR 3.155).

Many studies of Hume's aesthetic theory have criticized Hume for appealing variously to a set of established rules of art, a canon of exemplary works,
the judgments of respected critics, and even to a consensus in public opinion,
without identifying any of these as the final court of appeal in controversies concerning the merits of any given work of art. As a result, many of his commentators have argued either that he implicitly defends the primacy of one of these
sources, or that his argument is either infinitely regressive or viciously circular.[25] However, as another possibility, Jones and Townsend have both suggested
that Hume is not attempting to identify any ultimate court of appeal in judgments of taste. Instead, Hume is calling our attention to the dynamic character
of the aesthetic and critical tradition of a given community, as involving an
ongoing consideration of particular works of art, continuing attempts to articulate the rules of art, a recognition of the changing opinions of critics, and the
developing aesthetic sentiments of the general public.[26] I would further argue
that, on Hume's view, the larger purpose of aesthetic criticism is not to establish final judgments concerning the merits of particular works of art, but to
help the general public to discern, enjoy, and discuss the merits of artistic creations. In other words, Hume does not intend to articulate a specific standard
of taste in any detail. Instead, he is encouraging his readers to participate in the
ongoing social process of developing standards for judging aesthetic merit, and
applying these to individual works of art. Finally, he indicates that the best way
for his readers to participate in this process is by familiarizing themselves with
the rules and the classics of their aesthetic tradition, and by recognizing and
cultivating, in others or in themselves, the characteristics of a good critic.

---

24. See Brunet, *Philosophie et Esthétique,* 765–88; Jones, *Hume's Sentiments,* 106–135; Livingston, *Hume's Philosophy of Common Life,* 69 and 118–20; and Townsend, *Hume's Aesthetic Theory,* 208–12.

25. For several contributions to this discussion, see Brown, "Hume's Theory of Taste," 193–98; Cohen, "Hume's Experimental Method," 270–89; Noxon, "Hume's Opinion of Critics," 157–62; Kivy, "Hume's Standard of Taste," 63–65; Talmor, "Forgotten Classic," 15–18; Carroll, "Hume's Standard of Taste," 181–94; Weiand, "Hume's Two Standards of Taste," 129–42; and Wertz, *Between Hume's Philosophy and History,* 59–66.

26. Jones, "Hume's Literary and Aesthetic Theory," 274; Townsend, *Hume's Aesthetic Theory,* 213–16.

12

Religion

Among his contemporaries, including not only the reading public, but also his circles of acquaintance in Edinburgh, London, and Paris, Hume was known above all as a skeptic concerning religion.[1] In a larger historical perspective, Hume has been considered one of the most wide-ranging, creative, and thorough critics of religion in the history of European thought. In this regard, he anticipates — and indeed influenced — both the examination and critique of religion in the nineteenth-century German philosophical tradition and the scientifically grounded attack on religion by the logical positivists in twentieth-century Europe and America.

Hume develops several lines of analysis in his critical examination of religion, which he presents as separate in principle, but that often overlap in his writings.[2] First, he criticizes a number of contemporary attempts to justify religion through reason, especially the argument from miracles as evidence for Christianity, and the argument for the existence of God from the analogy between the system of nature and works of human artifice.

1. For Hume's acquaintance with religion, and his privately expressed views on religion, see Mossner, *Life of David Hume,* and Gaskin, *Hume's Philosophy of Religion,* 219–31.

2. There are several general studies of Hume's writings on religion, including Kemp Smith's "Introduction" to his edition of the *Dialogues Concerning Natural Religion,* 1–75; Gaskin, *Hume's Philosophy of Religion,* and "Hume on Religion," 313–44; Yandell, *Hume's "Inexplicable Mystery"*; and Penelhum, *Themes in Hume,* 177–282.

The first criticism is presented in Section 10 of the first *Enquiry*, "Of Miracles"; the second is introduced in Section 11, "Of a Particular Providence and a Future State," and developed in the *Dialogues Concerning Natural Religion*. Hume also develops a social-scientific account of the origin and development of religion, especially in *The Natural History of Religion*, and examines the history of Christianity in his essays and the *History of England*. He also examines two Christian doctrines in essays that were withheld from publication during his life, "Of Suicide" and "Of the Immortality of the Soul" (E SU.577–89; E IS.590–98).[3] Finally, he considers the influence of religion in human psychology, morals, social life, and politics, especially in the *Natural History of Religion* and the *Dialogues Concerning Natural Religion*. In these texts Hume combines a thinly veiled skepticism concerning religious belief and a lack of religious sentiment with an extensive knowledge of classical and contemporary works on religion and a sustained interest in the "ænigma" of religion (NHR 15.76).

In his writings concerning religion Hume often professes views that appear to be inconsistent, either within a single work, or from one text to another, or with his private views as evidenced by his letters and contemporary anecdotes. Many of his affirmations of theism may be accounted for as expressions of caution, irony, or both at once; others may be explained as expedient measures for separating one line of inquiry from another in order to focus on only one in a given context. However, some of Hume's enigmatic statements, especially in the *Dialogues*, are less easily explained in these ways, and still present ongoing problems of interpretation for his readers. I will attempt to address some of these questions of interpretation in the course of my discussion.

REASON AND RELIGION

In the *Natural History of Religion* Hume states that there are two especially important questions in the study of religion, "that concerning its foundation in reason, and that concerning its origin in human nature" (NHR Int.21). According to this text, the main attempt to provide a rational foundation for religion is the argument from design, which he was examining concurrently in the initial draft of the *Dialogues Concerning Natural Religion*. However, Hume had already presented his examination of miracles in the *Enquiry Concerning Human Understanding* as a response to those "dangerous friends or disguised enemies to the CHRISTIAN religion, who have undertaken to defend it by the principles of human reason," by appealing to the evidence supposedly provided by the

3. For a discussion of the history of these essays, see Mossner, *Life of David Hume*, 319–35. For facsimiles of these two essays, from the posthumous 1783 edition, see Hume, *Four Dissertations and Essays on Suicide and the Immortality of the Soul*, page sequence 2, 1–66.

biblical miracles (EHU 10.40 [SBN 130]). He thus criticizes two attempts to establish a foundation in reason for religion: the attempt to justify Christianity as a revealed religion by appealing to the evidence of reported miracles, and the attempt to justify deism through "natural theology" or the argument from design.

Before we proceed, it will be useful to consider the terminology that is often used in discussing Hume's arguments concerning natural and revealed religion. In accordance with the usage of our own day in many discussions of this topic, I will use the word "deist" for someone who affirms the existence of a divine being on the basis of the design argument, but denies any particular revelation.[4] Some deists might also conclude from the design argument that God acts providentially, by distributing rewards and punishments to souls in the after-life, although other deists might deny this.[5] I will use the word "theist" for someone who affirms the existence of a deity mainly on other grounds, such as scriptures, *a priori* proof, or personal revelation; although a theist might incidentally accept the design argument. The "religious philosophers" mentioned in Part 11 of the first *Enquiry,* along with Cleanthes in the *Dialogues,* are deists of the type who affirm not only the existence, but also the moral attributes and providential intentions of God from the design argument. By contrast, Demea, who is called the "orthodox" character in the *Dialogues,* is a theist who accepts an *a priori* argument for the existence of God, and also presumably the Christian scriptural revelation (EHU 11.10 [SBN 135]; DNR PH.128; DNR 2.141–43, 9.188–89).

This use of the words "deist" and "theist" differs from Hume's own usage in several respects. In the *Natural History of Religion* Hume uses the word "theism" more specifically for "monotheism," in contrast to polytheism (NHR 6.41–42, 9.50). According to my usage, both monotheism and polytheism would be types of theism, if they are founded on any grounds other than the design argument. However, in Hume's own place and time most of the professed theists, or believers in religion on traditional grounds, were of course monotheists. Hume also refers here to a "genuine Theism" which is founded on the design argument:

4. Samuel Clarke provides a valuable contemporary survey of different types of deism in his Boyle Lectures of 1705: see his *Works,* 2: 600–608. On the history of the deist movement in England, and its role in controversies over the evidence for Christianity, see Stephen, *History of English Thought,* 1: 74–277; Mossner, "Deism," 326–36, and *Life of David Hume,* 112–13; Burns, *The Great Debate on Miracles,* 13–14 and 70–95; Reventlow, *Authority of the Bible,* 289–410; and Beiser, *Sovereignty of Reason,* 220–65. For a related study of the arguments over natural theology between Scholastic and Cartesian theologians in sixteenth-century France, see Kors, *Atheism in France.*

5. The doctrine of what Hume calls a "particular providence" is usually held to assert that God acts in history, and that God rewards and punishes human beings in the afterlife. As we will see, Hume considers both of these doctrines in various contexts (cf. SBN Sections 10 and 11 [SBN 109–48]; NHR 6.42; E SU.581–86; DNR 12.219–28).

a view that in my usage would be called "deism" (NHR Int.21). Similarly, in the *Dialogues* he describes someone who professes monotheism on the basis of the design argument as a "philosophical theist." From this we may coin the phrase "philosophical theism" as a more precise expression in Hume's own terms for "deism" (D 12.226). Hume himself uses the term "deists" in the *History of England* for a group of radical republicans who "denied entirely the truth of revelation," and consequently the political claims of all the other factions during the Puritan period, although he does not indicate their grounds for believing in a deity. Finally, he notes that "many of the ingenious men" of the Restoration period were accused of being deists, and that many Whig leaders in his own day were "*deists* or profest *latitudinarians*" (H 6.61.59–60; H 6.71.539; E SE.78–79).[6]

Hume's first sustained discussion of any argument for religious belief is his examination of human testimony to miracles in Section 10 of the first *Enquiry*. He apparently developed his first version of this argument in a section titled "Reasonings concerning Miracles" in the original draft of the *Treatise*. However, as he indicates in a 1737 letter to Henry Home, he removed this section to avoid giving offense, especially to the Anglican philosopher and theologian Joseph Butler, whom he hoped would be supportive of the *Treatise*. Indeed, he regrets that he is cutting out the "noble Parts" of the *Treatise* and blames himself for his cowardice, although he defends the prudence of his action (L 1.24–25). The manuscript of this discussion of miracles has not survived, and we have no definite evidence regarding its original placement in the *Treatise*, or its relation to Section 10 of the *Enquiry*. However, Hume describes the deleted section as rather diffuse in style, and as more accessible to a popular audience than the rest of the *Treatise*: an assessment that also applies to "Of Miracles."[7]

In this text, Hume is contributing to the debate on miracles that had emerged in the controversies between the deists and Anglican theologians during the preceding fifty years.[8] Hume's essay has endured as the most famous contribution to this debate, although it was nearly upstaged at its initial publication in 1748 by the simultaneous publication of a study by Conyers Middleton of the alleged miracles in the early history of the Catholic Church (cf. ML xxxv).[9]

6. For a useful survey of Hume's unpublished references to deism, see Gaskin, "Hume's Attenuated Deism," 167–68.

7. The textual history of Hume's essay on miracles is examined in Mossner, *Life of David Hume*, 112; Burns, *The Great Debate on Miracles*, 131–41; Nelson, "Burial and Resurrection," 57–76; and Wootton, "Hume's 'Of Miracles,'" 191–229.

8. For discussions of the historical context of Hume's essay on miracles, see Burns, *The Great Debate on Miracles*; Gaskin, *Hume's Philosophy of Religion*, 143–52; Wootton, "Hume's 'Of Miracles,'" 191–229; and Stewart, "Hume's Historical View of Miracles," 171–200. On the responses to Hume's essay, see Mossner, *Life of David Hume*, 227, 232, 286–88, and 290–94.

9. Middleton's study indeed complements Hume's essay by presenting a history of miracle reports in the post-Apostolic church and a naturalistic account of their origin, which is intended to undermine the claims

Hume approaches the evaluation of miracles through three main arguments.[10] The first of these is often referred to as his *a priori* argument against the possibility of miracles, although he himself does not describe it in these terms. The second is a general argument that the probable evidence from human testimony for the occurrence of a miracle can never outweigh the *a priori* evidence against the occurrence of a miraculous event. The third consists in a series of *a posteriori* arguments intended to show that all known cases of miracle reports fail to attain even a moderate degree of probability. Instead, these reports can themselves be explained as arising from human passions, desires, and intentions.

Hume avoids considering any Old Testament or New Testament miracles directly until the end of his discussion, where he reaches his ostensibly fideistic conclusion that Christianity, or "our most holy religion," is and must be founded upon faith rather than reason. At this point he also applies his analysis to the miracle stories of the Pentateuch, purportedly to criticize misguided attempts by recent Christian theologians to regard the Old Testament as accurate historical testimony (EHU 10.40 [SBN 130]). He alludes to the central New Testament miracles only indirectly, although unmistakably, by using a report of a person who has been raised from the dead as an example of a miracle story (EHU 10.12–13, 10.37 [SBN 115–16, 128]). Interestingly enough, many rationalist criticisms of various aspects of Christian belief had emerged from controversies between the various confessional traditions arising from the Reformation. Hume contributes to this tendency by presenting his thesis in "Of Miracles" as a generalization of an argument by an Anglican cleric, John Tillotson, against the Catholic doctrine of the real presence (EHU 10.1 [SBN 109]). Indeed, he indicates in a letter of 1762 to George Campbell, an unusually courteous critic of his argument in "Of Miracles," that he had originally developed his argument in response to the miracles allegedly performed among the Jesuits at La Flèche, where he had lived from 1735–37 while writing the *Treatise.* He then notes, no doubt disingenuously, that one of his acquaintances among the Jesuits had objected that this argument "operated equally against the Gospel as the Catholic miracles; — which observation I thought proper to admit as a sufficient answer" (L 1.361). By contrast, he presents his analysis in "Of Miracles" as applying, more broadly, to any and all miracle stories, whether religious or secular (EHU 10.2 [SBN 110]).

---

of the Roman Catholic church and various other Christian sects, and to affirm the principles and value of historical scholarship. See Middleton, *Free Inquiry,* 228–31, and Stephen, *History of English Thought,* 1: 253–77.

10. For studies of the argument in "Of Miracles," see Flew, *Hume's Philosophy of Belief,* 166–213; Burns, *The Great Debate on Miracles,* 176–246; Beckwith, *David Hume's Argument Against Miracles;* Levine, *Hume and the Problem of Miracles;* Yandell, *Hume's "Inexplicable Mystery,"* 315–38; and Johnson, *Hume, Holism, and Miracles.*

Hume's first argument, in which he apparently asserts *a priori* the impossibility of any miraculous event, has generally been regarded as the most unsatisfactory point in his analysis. Hume initially defines a "miracle" in this text as "a violation of the laws of nature." He later offers a second and apparently more complete definition in a footnote, where he states that "a miracle may be accurately defined, *a transgression of a law of nature by a particular volition of the Deity, or by the interposition of some invisible agent*" (EHU 10.12, 10.12n23 [SBN 114, 115n1]; cf. T 3.1.2.7 [SBN 474]). However, with reference to the first definition of a miracle as "a violation of the laws of nature," he argues that since "a firm and unalterable experience has established these laws, the proof against a miracle, from the very nature of the fact, is as entire as any argument from experience can possibly be imagined." In other words, by this very definition there must be a "uniform experience against every miraculous event," which amounts "to a direct and full *proof,* from the nature of the fact, against the existence of any miracle" (EHU 10.12 [SBN 124–25]).

This argument is puzzling in several respects. First, it appears to depart from both his general analysis of causation, as a relation that we attribute to sets of objects as a result of habit, and his account of the laws of nature, as generalizations from experience. These aspects of his theory of causation do not seem to justify his more ambitious present appeal to an "unalterable experience" that has established the laws of nature. However, Hume appears here to be merely reminding us of his earlier claim, that by observing regularities, we tend to develop a habit of expecting the types of conjunctions we have observed in the past to occur in the future (cf. EHU 4.14–21 [SBN 32–36]). Indeed, in introducing his analysis in "Of Miracles," he reaffirms his argument that our judgments positing the laws of nature can arise only from our experience of regular conjunctions between events (EHU 10.3–4 [SBN 110–11]).

Accordingly, in Hume's view, a miracle is not a violation of a general law known antecedently to operate inexorably in nature. Instead, a miracle is an "extraordinary" event, which does not conform to any regular conjunction that we have previously observed, and is indeed regarded as an exception to any experienced patterns of conformity. Since we appeal to inferences from causation, or from constant conjunction, in all our reasonings concerning matters of fact, Hume maintains that our "uniform experience" as human observers is sufficient evidence against any miracle report (EHU 10.8, 10.12; cf. 10.28–38 [SBN 113, 115; cf. 125–29]). Although this is argument often described as an *a priori* argument against miracles, Hume himself describes it as a "proof," a term that he uses elsewhere for those probable reasonings that have the highest degree of evidential force. Indeed, he maintains that his conclusion, "from the very nature of the fact," is "as entire as any argument from experience can possibly be imagined" (EHU 10.12 [SBN 114]; cf. T 1.3.11.2 [SBN 124]; DNR

9.188–92). If this reasoning is to be described as an *a priori* argument, it must therefore be an argument from our concepts of experience and miracle, rather than from any reasoning apart from experience (cf. DNR 9.188–92).

We have seen, however, that Hume's own initial definition of a miracle is incomplete. As he himself indicates in his later footnote, according to the more complete theological definition a miracle is not a spontaneous event that violates the laws of nature by occurring without a natural cause. Instead, a miracle is a deliberate transgression of the laws of nature by the "interposition" or the "particular volition" of an "invisible agent," who is regarded as a supernatural being (EHU 10.12n23 [SBN 115n1]). In response to this possible explanation of an extraordinary event, Hume argues that we have no knowledge of the "attributes or actions of such a Being, otherwise than from the experience which we have of his productions, in the usual course of nature." In other words, we have no evidence that these events are actions of a divine being, especially apart from any evidence of the existence of such a being (EHU 10.38 [SBN 129]).

On the other hand, defenders of the evidential value of miracles for proving the existence of God might argue, on Humean grounds, that they are explaining a series of otherwise inexplicable events according to the same principles by which we attribute deliberate actions to human agents. That is, a miraculous event is an action that expresses the character and will of an invisible agent. This analysis would be consistent with the view that a miracle is to be regarded, not merely as a random event without a natural cause, or even as an arbitrary action of a completely mysterious invisible being, but rather as a "sign" that reveals a divine character to human beings. For example, according to Clarke's definition in 1705, a miracle is an unusual event produced by a divine intervention in nature "for the proof or evidence of some particular doctrine, or in attestation to the authority of some particular person."[11] It would seem possible, on Humean grounds, to judge that a given event is a violation of the laws of nature arising from the direct action of an invisible being, if we cannot find a physical cause for the event, but can instead regard it as an expression of the intentions and character of an invisible agent. This would be analogous to attributing certain types of events to invisible or unknown human agents. However, this explanation would also require us to establish antecedently the probable existence, character, and intentions of such a being, either through an *a priori* demonstration or through an accumulation of probable evidence beyond any single event, alternatives Hume criticizes here and in the *Dialogues*.

11. Clarke, *Works*, 2: 701. The first part of Clarke's definition is cited by Kemp Smith as combining the two "methods of definition" used by Hume. However, Kemp Smith does not refer to the further element of Clarke's definition that I have quoted here. See Kemp Smith's "Introduction" to the *Dialogues*, 48n4.

The other two arguments in "Of Miracles" concern the evaluation of testimony. First, Hume argues that the evidential value of any human testimony to a miracle, however compelling in any given case, can never outweigh the improbability of the event. As we have seen, a miracle is defined as a violation of the laws of nature; and since these laws are established through uniform experience, any miracle must be judged to be at least highly improbable. We also learn by experience that while human testimony can be truthful, mistaken testimony can also arise from such causes in human nature as error, credulity, or deliberate deception. Accordingly, in the case of a miraculous event, it is always more probable that the testimony is mistaken than that the event took place (EHU 10.13, 10.35–38 [SBN 115–16, 127–29]).[12]

Finally, Hume presents a series of arguments that are intended to show that no example of testimony to a miracle in the historical record has ever reached even a moderately high degree of probability. First, the witnesses to a supposed miracle have never been shown to be sufficiently reasonable and honest to compel belief. Second, the spread of miracle stories can be explained by considering the natural passions and cognitive tendencies of human beings. For example, these reports tend to be accepted and circulated in a religious context, where passions and imaginations have already been enlivened and are especially receptive to mysterious and paradoxical teachings. In addition, the proponents of miracle stories in a religious context may even be led, by generous zeal, by ambition, or by vanity, to circulate stories that they know to be false. Third, such stories tend to appear in "ignorant or barbarous nations." Finally, miracle are found in all religions, and also in civic or national histories, often conforming to certain general patterns. From this observation, Hume maintains that wherever miracle stories are used to establish the unique legitimacy of a particular religious tradition, these claims cancel each other out in a case of equal probability, both as grounds for believing in the specific events, and as warrants for the larger tradition (EHU 10.14–39 [SBN 116–29]). Accordingly, Hume concludes that no testimony has ever had, or can ever have, "such force" as to justify belief in a miracle, to the degree that is required for it to provide a "just foundation" for a "system of religion" (EHU 10.35 [SBN 127]).

Hume does not thoroughly examine every possible justification for regarding an event as a miracle in "Of Miracles." First, he has not ruled out the possibility of consistent and convincing testimony to the occurrence of an event that appears to violate the laws of nature (EHU 10.35–36 [SBN 127–28]). Second, he has not ruled out the possibility that we might regard a series of events

---

12. For discussions of the type of probable reasoning that Hume relies on in his argument concerning miracles, see Sobel, "On the Evidence of Testimony for Miracles," 166–86; Owen, "Hume 'Versus' Price," 187–202; Dawid and Gillies, "A Bayesian Analysis," 57–65; Wilson, "Logic of Probabilities," 255–75; and Gower, "Probability of Miracles," 17–32.

as highly probable evidence for the intervention of an invisible agent in the natural order. Finally, he does not address the question of how I as an individual would, or should, evaluate the evidence of my own senses if I were ever to be an eyewitness to an apparent miracle. All of these questions are raised, however, in an intriguing passage of the *Dialogues*. Here Cleanthes asks Philo what he would conclude if he were to hear an "articulate voice" speaking from the clouds, and if he were then to receive reports of the same voice giving wise and benevolent instruction at the same time to all nations in their own languages. Cleanthes maintains that in such a case we would be obliged to attribute this voice to a divine Being. This discussion leaves Philo "a little embarrassed and confounded" (DNR 3.152–55).[13] However, since he does not acknowledge any compelling examples of such testimony, Hume apparently considers these limitations in his argument to be outweighed by the historical evidence for the human origin of miracle reports, and by the inadequacy of any existing miracle reports to support the cognitive pretensions of any specific religious tradition.

Hume's second target in his criticism of the supposed foundations of religion in reason is "natural religion," or natural theology, as represented by the argument from design. The design argument had been developed during the preceding century, partly from the success of the new sciences in explaining the natural world, but also from debates in theology over the traditional proofs for the existence of God.[14] The design argument begins by arguing that the order in nature is analogous to the order that is evident in products of human craftsmanship. It then argues, from this analogy, that a creator, who is invisible and much more intelligent and powerful, must have designed the world. Beyond this preliminary conclusion, however, the design argument could be taken to support several different versions of deism or theism: (1) a minimal deism, arguing for a creator who has created matter and prescribed the laws of nature, but does not interfere in their subsequent operations; (2) a providential deism, which also infers, from the order in nature, the moral qualities and providential intentions of the creator; or (3) a version of traditional theism, in which the design argument is regarded as supplementing, but not replacing, the testimony of a scriptural tradition or some other testimony to the existence of a deity.

Hume offers what appear to be several endorsements of the design argument in his early writings. In a footnote to the *Treatise,* added in the Appendix, he intimates that "the order of the universe proves an omnipotent mind," which is

13. For a discussion of these analogies, see Wadia, "Philo Confounded," 279–90; Tweyman, *Scepticism and Belief,* 47–65; and Wootton, "Hume's 'Of Miracles,'" 215–17.

14. For the English background and context of the design argument, see Hurlbutt, *Hume, Newton, and the Design Argument;* Jeffner, *Butler and Hume on Religion;* and Reventlow, *Authority of the Bible.* Kors provides an intriguing study of its earlier background in the debates within French Catholicism in "The French Context of Hume's Philosophical Theology," 221–36.

indeed all that is required for "the foundations of religion" (T 1.3.14.12n30 [SBN 633n1]). He presents the argument for natural theology at greater length in the *Letter from a Gentleman,* which he circulated anonymously to defend the *Treatise* against his critics during his candidacy for the chair of Ethics and Pneumantical Philosophy at the University of Edinburgh. Here he states that "all the solid Arguments for Natural Religion retain their full Force upon the Author's Principles concerning Causes and Effects," so that "Wherever I see Order, I infer from Experience that *there,* there hath been Design and Contrivance." Finally, this "obliges me to infer an infinitely perfect Architect, from the infinite Art and Contrivance which is display'd in the whole Fabrick of the Universe" (LG 24–26).

However, these early endorsements, which, especially in the *Letter from a Gentleman,* might also be seen as prudential attempts to mitigate the implications of his philosophy for the criticism of religion, are counterbalanced or superseded by the earliest document reflecting Hume's sustained criticism of the design argument. This is a manuscript fragment with the intriguing heading "Sect. 7, Fourth Objection," which has only recently come to light, and has been published with an editorial discussion by M. A. Stewart as a "fragment on evil." In this fragment, Hume apparently moves from a lost series of arguments against "the Intelligence of the Deity" to an argument "against his moral Attributes," since both types of attributes are "equally essential to the System of Theism." He then responds to any attempts to prove the benevolence of a divine creator from the "Phænomena," or evidence of nature, by citing as counter-evidence the ubiquity, and indeed the very existence, of "evil," or pain, in human and animal consciousness, an argument which would later be developed by Philo in the *Dialogues* (FE 165–66; DNR 10.193–202, 11.205–12). This objection was apparently one among several in a systematic analysis and criticism of the design argument, beginning with three objections to the attempt to prove "the Intelligence of the Deity" from the evidence of nature, and moving to the moral attributes of the deity, an order which Hume would again follow in the *Dialogues.* Stewart traces this fragment to the late 1730s or early 1740s, based on the evidence of the paper and the handwriting; and he argues that it is an excerpt either from an early draft of the *Treatise,* where it might have been part of the material that was removed to avoid giving offense to Butler, or a separate and otherwise unknown expository work that was concerned, in whole or in part, with the design argument.[15] In either case, between the late 1730s and early 1740s Hume apparently worked out a systematic criticism of the design argument in which he initiated some of the themes that he would later develop in his various dialogues on religion. Since the manuscript

15. Stewart, "An Early Fragment on Evil," 160–70.

was neither published nor preserved by Hume among his papers, it would seem that he decided by the late 1740s, for whatever reason, to abandon this expository approach and instead adopt the dialogue form in his subsequent treatment of the design argument.[16]

Hume presents his first published examination of the design argument in Section 11 of the first *Enquiry,* "Of a Particular Providence and of a Future State." Here he argues, using the devices of a dialogue and an imaginary speech, that speculative disputes in theology and philosophy are both irrelevant to the "peace of society and security of government" (EHU 11.9 [SBN 135]).[17] The two characters are Hume and an unnamed friend, who composes a speech that the philosopher Epicurus might have addressed to the Athenian assembly in defense of the freedom of inquiry. I will accordingly call his friend "the Epicurean."

The Epicurean begins his speech by observing that many recent "religious philosophers" have sought to advance beyond the traditional religion of their community and establish religion upon "principles of reason," by arguing that "the chief or sole argument for a divine existence" is derived from the "order of nature." The Epicurean disclaims any need in this context to consider the "justness of this argument," and also affirms with apparent reverence the traditional religious teachings of his community. The issue that brings him before the Assembly is his denial, on the basis of his philosophical inquiries, of "a providence and a future state," or a divine plan of future rewards and punishments for human beings. In response to his accusers, he argues first that he is not undermining the foundations of society, and second, that his conclusions are consistent with the arguments of these religious philosophers (EHU 11.10 [SBN 135]).

First, the Epicurean argues that the design argument cannot justify any inferences to the perfection or moral attributes of the creator. On the contrary, the "rules of just reasoning" do not allow us to ascribe any qualities to a cause beyond "what are precisely requisite to produce the effect," as these are discovered through experience and observation. Since the world, as given to our observation, is not perfect, we can infer the existence only of an imperfect creator, who lacks either the power or the benevolence to make a perfect world (EHU 11.13–18, 11.22, 11.26n31 [SBN 136–39, 141–42, 145n1]). In response to the charge that this rejection of providence would undermine morality and civil order, the Epicurean argues that morality is better justified through experience,

16. Hume was also influenced in his use of the dialogue form for writing about religion by the dialogue *De Natura Deorum* by Cicero, who was one of his favorite authors. See Fosl, "Doubt and Divinity," 103–20.

17. This section was in fact titled "Of the Practical Consequences of Natural Theology" in the first edition of the *Enquiry:* see Beauchamp's editorial appendix in his edition of Hume's *Enquiry Concerning Human Understanding,* 263.

and should be presented as the course of life most likely to produce happiness. Indeed, Hume regards this justification of morality as more compelling than the argument for a divine distribution of rewards and punishments in the after-life, which is less well supported by any evidence (EHU 11.20–23, 11.27 [SBN 140–42, 146–47]; cf. E 1S.592–96).

The Epicurean also considers several problems in the design argument itself, such as the weakness of the analogy between an imperfect human craftsman and a creator who is invisible and perfect, and the recognition that we have no other analogy for a supreme being, for the world as a whole, or for the creation of a world by such a being. Indeed, Hume notes that since our judgments of causation arise from observations of regular conjunctions between "two *species* of objects," it is impossible to form "any conjecture or inference at all" concerning the cause of a unique effect, such as the universe in its entirety (EHU 11.23–25, 30 [SBN 142–44, 147–48]).

Hume presents his most sustained account of the argument from design in the *Dialogues Concerning Natural Religion*. The *Dialogues* were written and revised intermittently over a period of twenty-five years, from about 1751 to 1776, and published posthumously, after negotiations between Hume and several friends and relatives during the last months of his life over which of them would be willing to take responsibility for its publication. He also periodically discussed the manuscript of the *Dialogues* in letters to several of his friends, where he not only solicits their advice, but also laments their attempts to dis-suade him from publishing.[18]

Judging at least by one standard, its compelling presentation of more than one side in a philosophical controversy, Hume's *Dialogues Concerning Natural Religion* is among the most successful dialogues in the history of philosophy, since two of its three characters, Cleanthes and Philo, have been plausibly regarded by various readers as representing the author himself.[19] We find some intriguing evidence, both for Hume's own view and for his care in presenting opposing arguments, in a letter of 1751, in which he asks his friend Gilbert Elliot to help him strengthen the arguments put forward by Cleanthes. Since Elliot was a theist who was also sympathetic to the design argument, Hume expects him to welcome this commission, and even attempts to lure him by describing Cleanthes as the "Hero of the Dialogue." On the other hand, Hume expects Elliot to agree that he himself will be able to articulate the views of Philo "naturally enough" (L 1.153–54). However, this letter has not been re-garded as decisive evidence for Hume's view, and we will see that a number of

---

18. For a discussion of the manuscript evidence for the various stages in the writing of the *Dialogues,* see Stewart, "Hume's Manuscripts," 288–308.

19. For a useful survey of the debate over which of the characters, if any, represents Hume himself, see Gaskin, *Hume's Philosophy of Religion,* 209–18.

further questions concerning Hume's intentions are raised by several surprising turns in the discussion.[20] The first question in the interpretation of the *Dialogues* is if, and to what extent, any of the characters can be regarded as directly presenting Hume's own view of the argument from design. A second is the problem of Philo's apparent reversal in Part 12, where he appears to endorse a version of the design argument (DNR 12.214–28). A third problem is the use of a letter from Pamphilus, the pupil of Cleanthes, as a framing device for the *Dialogues*. Pamphilus offers his friend Hermippus an introduction to the conversation, and a concluding assessment in which he favors the arguments of Cleanthes (DNR PH.127–29, 12.228). In the present discussion I will offer and defend my own proposals regarding these controversial points of interpretation in the *Dialogues*, while developing my account of Hume's argument and overall intention of the text.

Pamphilus describes the perspectives brought to the *Dialogues* by its three characters as "the accurate philosophical turn" of Cleanthes, the "careless scepticism" of Philo, and the "rigid inflexible orthodoxy" of Demea (DNR PH.128).[21] However, these sketches are misleading, since we soon find that the reasonings of Cleanthes are not so accurate, those of Philo not so careless, and those of Demea not so clearly orthodox, at least in any sectarian sense, as these remarks seem to indicate. The three characters actually provide more helpful characterizations of each other, in describing Demea as a "mystic," Cleanthes as an "anthropomorphite," and Philo as a "philosophical sceptic" (DNR 4.158, 12.227–28).[22]

The initial topic of conversation in the *Dialogues* is the appropriate method for religious instruction (DNR 1.130). However, this question leads to a further inquiry, not supposedly into "the *being* of a God," which Pamphilus, Demea, and Philo all claim to regard as self-evident, but into "the *nature* of that divine Being," or in other words "his attributes, his decrees, his plan of providence" (DNR PH.128; cf. 2.141–42). However, the arguments developed by Cleanthes and Demea are in fact mainly directed toward proving the existence of God. Each of their arguments is then criticized by Philo and the other character, both as proofs for the existence of God, and in their implications for the nature and attributes of God.

---

20. On the argument in the *Dialogues*, see Kemp Smith's "Introduction" to his edition of the *Dialogues Concerning Natural Religion*, 1–75; Pike, "Hume on the Argument from Design," 128–238; Tweyman, *Scepticism and Belief*, and "Hume's Dialogues on Evil," 74–85; and Yandell, *Hume's "Inexplicable Mystery,"* 131–278.

21. Baier calls particular attention to Hume's use of the word "careless," and its significance for his conception of philosophy, in *Progress of Sentiments*, 1–27.

22. Several studies have suggested that Demea represents the views of Samuel Clarke, apparently as supplemented by an endorsement of skepticism and negative theology; and that Cleanthes presents those of Joseph Butler, perhaps as supplemented by the arguments of the Newtonian apologists Colin Maclaurin and George Cheyne. See Mossner, "The Enigma of Hume," 334–49; Hurlbutt, *Hume, Newton, and the Design Argument;* Jeffner, *Butler and Hume on Religion;* Gaskin, "Introduction," xx–xxiii; and Penelhum, *Themes in Hume*, 244–60.

As the first speaker in the *Dialogues,* Demea recommends a plan of religious instruction that begins by attempting to instill an "early piety" and a "habitual reverence for all the principles of religion" by precept and example. This should be followed by a course of study in the secular sciences, and only then by philosophy and "natural theology." He expects this examination of human knowledge to conclude in skepticism, which he endorses as an appropriate starting point for contemplating "the greatest mysteries of religion" (DNR 1.130–31). He further argues that the attributes of God are "altogether incomprehensible and unknown to us," and that we should not attempt the "impiety" of inquiring into the nature and decrees of God. Instead, we should merely "adore in silence his infinite perfections," a view he attributes to Christian theologians and philosophers from the early church to Malebranche (DNR 2.141–42, 3.155–57). Demea accepts the appellation of "mystic" from Cleanthes, in that he denies any similarity between the Deity and the human mind (DNR 4.158–59). He also presents what he calls an "argument *a priori*," in contrast to the design argument, that is intended to prove both the existence of God and "the INFINITY of the divine attributes." This is the argument that the series of natural causes that we observe in the universe must have a first cause, which must be "a necessarily existent Being, who carries the REASON of his existence in himself" (DNR 9.188–89). However, after the criticism of this argument by Cleanthes and Philo, he maintains that each person feels "the truth of religion" from "a consciousness of his imbecility and misery, rather than from any reasoning." This leads each of us "to seek protection from that Being, on whom he and all nature is dependent," hoping for consolation in the afterlife, and in the meantime addressing the deity "by prayers, adoration, and sacrifice" (DNR 10.193). Demea leaves the company at the end of Part 11, after recognizing that Philo, with whom he had apparently agreed over the inadequacy of human reason and the reality of human misery, is "a more dangerous enemy than CLEANTHES himself," once Philo had proceeded to argue that the first cause of the world must also be the cause of evil (DNR 11.212–13).

The central theme of the *Dialogues* is presented by Cleanthes, who begins by dismissing extreme skepticism as both impractical and insincere (DNR 1.132–40), and then states the design argument as an inference from analogy that is justified by experimental reasoning. He accordingly argues that "the curious adapting of means to ends, throughout all nature, resembles exactly, though it much exceeds, the productions of human contrivance." Since these effects resemble each other, we are led "by all the rules of analogy" to infer that "the Author of nature is somewhat similar to the mind of man; though possessed of much larger faculties, proportioned to the grandeur of the work, which he has executed." Cleanthes claims to have proven "by this argument *a posteriori* . . . the existence of a Deity, and his similarity to human mind and intelligence"

(DNR 2.143; cf. 3.154–55, 12.224). He cheerfully allows the others to call him an "anthropomorphite," affirming that the first cause must be a divine mind resembling the human mind, "for I know of no other," and that a mind without distinct and successive acts, sentiments, and ideas, or with "no thought, no reason, no will, no sentiment, no love, no hatred . . . is no mind at all" (DNR 4.158–59; cf. 5.166, 11.203). He defends this conclusion in response to Philo's sustained attempt to show that this appeal to analogy also allows theories of the origin of the universe that are unacceptable to the theist, including the theories that this order is generated by matter (DNR 4.162), that the world has been created by an infant deity, an aging deity, or a committee of deities (DNR 5.167–69), that the world is a product of vegetation or animal generation (DNR 6.170–81; cf. NHR 4.35), and that the order in the world arises from the random motion of atoms (DNR 8.182–85). In response to Demea, Cleanthes asserts the impossibility of proving any matter of fact *a priori,* and maintains that there is no Being "whose non-existence implies a contradiction," and whose existence is therefore necessary (DNR 9.189–91; cf. 8.182–83). Finally, in contrast to both Demea and Philo, he rejects the claim of a preponderance of misery over happiness in human life, partly as a result of his cheerful temperament, but also because he intends to establish the moral as well as the natural attributes of God by the argument from analogy, and finds that "the only method of supporting divine benevolence" which is consistent with this argument "is to deny absolutely the misery and wickedness of man" (DNR 10.200; cf. 12.224). He also concedes that if we renounce traditional panegyrics and suppose "the Author of nature to be finitely perfect, though far exceeding mankind," we may account for the natural and moral imperfections of the world without abandoning the design argument (DNR 11.203).

Finally, Philo emerges in the *Dialogues* as a sometime ally of both Demea and Cleanthes, but more decidedly as a thinly disguised religious skeptic, who criticizes the design argument presented by Cleanthes, as well as Demea's *a priori* argument and "mystical" attribution of infinite perfections to God. Against the criticism by Cleanthes of a ridiculous and insincere form of extreme skepticism, Philo defends a version of skepticism that is consistent with the moderate skepticism of the *Treatise* and first *Enquiry,* by affirming the "uncertainty and narrow limits of reason," the influence of nature in limiting our ability to sustain extreme skepticism, the principles of philosophical probable reasoning arising from the common life, and the benefit and pleasure we derive from applying these in the natural and moral sciences (DNR 1.133–36). In other words, he endorses the account of experimental or scientific reasoning that Hume has already developed in his philosophical works. He then appeals to these principles by arguing, against Cleanthes, that the design argument is not even "the most certain and irrefragable" argument of that kind, since any departure from a similarity in the effects tends to weaken the analogy and diminish the evidence (DNR 2.144). Accordingly, he examines a number of considerations that undermine the analogy between a human craftsman and a supposed creator of the world as envisioned in the design argument.

Philo appears to find himself at a loss only once in the *Dialogues,* in his reaction to the two thought experiments presented by Cleanthes: a marvelous event (a voice speaking from the clouds) and a marvelous example of natural order (books growing from plants). According to Cleanthes, these two imaginary cases indicate that it would be possible to regard certain events as compelling evidence for a divine artificer, although Cleanthes considers the evidence in these cases to be less compelling than the evidence actually provided by many ordinary structures in nature (DNR 3.152–55).[23] However, it is difficult to judge from Pamphilius's report whether Philo is perplexed by these examples as serious possibilities, or by Cleanthes' strategy in inviting him to compare an imaginary example of order to our ordinary experience of the world, since only the latter is directly relevant to the design argument.

Philo also joins Cleanthes in criticizing *a priori* arguments for the existence of God. As a supplement to Cleanthes' answer to Demea, he adds that *a priori* arguments have been convincing only to those who are interested in metaphysics and mathematics. Otherwise, even those who are inclined to religion always feel that there is "some deficiency in such arguments," even if they are not able to specify where it lies. This is a "certain proof" that human beings "derive their religion from other sources than from this species of reasoning" (DNR 9.192). On the other hand, Philo endorses Demea's view of the prevalence of pain over happiness in human life, and then argues against Cleanthes that the existence of any pain or misery at all, while it may be compatible in some hidden and unknown way with the power and goodness of God, undermines any attempt to prove these supposed attributes from experience (DNR 10.193–95, 10–11.198–211; cf. FE 165–68). Indeed, he argues that religious beliefs and sentiments tend to arise from human misery, hope, fear, and even from the tendency of human beings to "raise up" for themselves "*imaginary* enemies" (DNR 10.195; cf. 10.193, 11.213, 12.224–26). He concludes that the most probable inference concerning the moral qualities of any supposed first cause is that this agent has "neither goodness nor malice," an intimation that drives Demea to his final outburst and departure (DNR 11.212–13; cf. T 1.4.5.31 [SBN 249]; EHU 8.31–36 [SBN 99–103]).

Philo's views are thus consistent with Hume's mitigated skepticism in the *Treatise* and the first *Enquiry,* his disjunction between natural theology and morality in the first *Enquiry,* and his account of the psychological origins of religion

23. See Wadia, "Philo Confounded," 279–89, and Tweyman, *Scepticism and Belief,* 47–65.

in the *Natural History of Religion*. I would therefore maintain that Hume is presenting through Philo his own criticism of the design argument, in opposition to the combination of negative theology and *a priori* argumentation presented by Demea, and the conclusions concerning the nature of God drawn by Cleanthes from the design argument.[24] This attribution is supported by Hume's own remark to Elliot in 1751 that the "Character of Philo" was the one that he himself could support "naturally enough" in composing the *Dialogues* (L 1.154).

However, this interpretation must also account for Philo's apparent endorsement of the design argument in Part 12, once Demea has left and the other two have settled into a more comfortable conversation. Philo now asserts that, in spite of his freedom in thought and argument, "no one has a deeper sense of religion impressed on his mind, or pays more profound adoration to the divine Being, as he discovers himself to reason, in the inexplicable contrivance and artifice of nature." Indeed, he maintains that one can only be an atheist nominally and in jest (DNR 12.214, 12.218). Giving a conciliatory turn to the discussion, he declares that any disagreement over the design argument amounts to a "dispute of words," since any observer is likely to recognize both similarities and differences between the "works of nature" and "productions of art." Accordingly, while theists and atheists might agree that there is probably a first cause, and even agree to call this "a GOD or DEITY," they might not agree in regarding it as a "*mind* or *intelligence*" by analogy to the human mind (DNR 12.216–17). Philo then declares his own "veneration for true religion," or religion of the "philosophical and rational kind," although this stops short of an avowal (DNR 12.219–20, 12.223). On the other hand, he rejects "vulgar superstitions" as combining absurdity with impiety, and exerting a harmful influence on morality and on social and political life (DNR 12.219–24). He concludes that "the whole of natural theology" can be justly resolved into the admittedly vague proposition "that the cause or causes of order in the universe probably bear some remote analogy to human intelligence." However, this conclusion does not justify further inferences concerning the nature of this cause, or any other inference "that affects human life, or can be the source of any action or forbearance" (DNR 12.227). At this point, in presenting what we may call his preliminary conclusion, Philo appears to be endorsing the view that I have called "minimal deism."

Finally, however, Philo adds that a "well-disposed mind" will naturally look for "some more particular revelation to mankind," and "fly to revealed truth with the greatest avidity," unlike the "haughty dogmatist," who pretends to build

24. Stewart has also argued, on the basis of the various revisions to the manuscript of the *Dialogues*, that Philo should be regarded as the spokesman for Hume: see "Hume's Manuscripts," 303–4.

a complete theological system through philosophy. Philo thus recommends to Cleanthes, and his student Pamphilius, the principle that "to be a philosophical sceptic is, in a man of letters, the first and most essential step towards being a sound, believing Christian" (DNR 12.227–28).[25]

I would suggest that we may account for Philo's apparent endorsement of minimal deism, and for Pamphilius's concluding observation that the arguments of Cleanthes are "still nearer to the truth" than those of Philo, by considering the interpersonal considerations that are likely to have influenced Hume in preparing the *Dialogues* for publication. Hume had at least two reasons to conciliate his anticipated critics among the theistic readers of the *Dialogues*. The first was a desire to avoid a charge of atheism based on this text. For his own sake, this could only, at best, have minimized a reputation that was already well entrenched by 1751.[26] However, during his illness in 1776, when he made the last additions and corrections to the *Dialogues,* he was also considering the interests and concerns of persons other than himself. Once he had realized that his illness was likely to be terminal, he devoted a great deal of his attention to securing the consent of one of his friends to carry out the posthumous publication of the *Dialogues.* Judging by his letters, he was keenly aware of their concern that any apparent impiety in the *Dialogues* might be held against the executor. Hume may have been addressing these fears in his final additions, although without sacrificing his own arguments.[27]

A second reason for Philo's apparent reversal in Part 12, and for the preference given by Pamphilius to the arguments of Cleanthes, applies to the original composition of the *Dialogues* in the 1750s. This is the motivation to adopt a more conciliatory approach to religion, which might have emerged from Hume's friendly contacts with a circle of liberal theists after he had settled in Edinburgh in 1751. These included not only Elliot, who was an advocate by profession, but also many rising figures in a scholarly and urbane group of moderate Presbyterian clergymen. From these friendships Hume apparently derived, if not a different view of religion, at least a stronger desire to seek areas of agreement in theological discussions, and to persuade his theistic readers

25. Philo's concluding references to "our Faith" are among the very few indications in the *Dialogues* that any of the speakers are Christian or specifically concerned with Christianity. To be sure, Demea presents his views as continuous with the Christian theological tradition (DNR 2.141–42), and all three refer to the history of Christian theology in its relation to philosophy (cf. DNR 1.138–39, 4.160). All three also profess to agree that religious education is desirable, and that it should include both traditional piety and philosophical theology. However, there is nothing in the text to indicate whether Cleanthes, in particular, is a deist or a Christian theist who also accepts the design argument.

26. See also Stewart, "Hume's Manuscripts," 288–302.

27. Stewart argues that this paragraph is the only addition that Hume made during his last illness in 1776. See Stewart, "Hume's Manuscripts," 302. For an account, with the relevant texts, of Hume's negotiations with his friends concerning the publication of the *Dialogues,* see Kemp Smith's "Introduction" to the *Dialogues,* 87–96.

of the pernicious effects of popular religion, and the importance of separating religion from morality and civic life. Indeed, Part 12 of the *Dialogues* depicts the type of conversation that he himself might have had with one of his friends among the liberal theists.[28] On this view, Hume's strategy in the final section of the *Dialogues* is to uncover and establish common ground, by conceding as much convincing force as possible to the deist argument, and nodding to traditional theism, even though he eventually reaffirms his endorsement of philosophical skepticism. This is similar to the strategy we have encountered in his essays, where he seeks to reconcile opposing views by establishing common ground in various controversies over morals and politics, as in his essays on the four philosophical temperaments (E Ep.138–45; E St.146–54; E Pl.155–58; E Sc.159–80), and on the main political debates in England beginning with the Civil War (E OC.465–87; E PO.488–92; E CP.493–501; E PS.502–11).

This reading is supported by the final comparison of deism and skepticism in the *Dialogues*. Here Philo concludes, on a conciliatory note, that the only people who merit the favor of the Deity are "philosophical theists" such as Cleanthes, since they alone have "suitable notions of his divine perfections." On the other hand, "philosophical sceptics" are the only ones entitled to his "*compassion* and *indulgence*," since these skeptics, from a "natural diffidence of their own capacity," would rather suspend judgment on "such sublime and such extraordinary subjects." Here Hume is apparently flattering the philosophical theists among his readers, while seeking to secure their good will toward the philosophical skeptic, whose outlook Philo is subtly endorsing in his concluding remarks (DNR 12.226–27).[29]

RELIGION AND HUMAN NATURE

The second general question which Hume formulates concerning religion is "its origin in human nature" (NHR Int.21). This is a question that he addresses in the *Natural History of Religion* and in his discussions of the history of Christianity.

The *Natural History of Religion* was written more or less concurrently with the first draft of the *Dialogues* and published in the *Four Dissertations* of 1757.[30]

---

28. On Hume's relations with the moderate clergy in Edinburgh, see Mossner, *Life of David Hume*, 243–45, 274–78, 320–25, and 336–55, and Sher, *Church and University*. A similar view of Part 12 is suggested in Penelhum, *Themes in Hume*, 242–43. See also Stewart, "Hume's Manuscripts," 299–300.

29. Livingston has argued that Hume is in fact endorsing "philosophical theism" through the character of Philo in the *Dialogues*, and in his other apparent affirmations of deism. However, on Livingston's view, Hume considers this view to be justified as a "presupposition of science," which is similar to Kant's later view of purposiveness as a principle prescribed to experience by reflective judgment.

30. For a facsimile of this edition, see Hume, *Four Dissertations and Essays on Suicide and the Immortality of the Soul*, page sequence 1, 1–117.

In this work Hume develops a naturalistic, or what we might now call a social-scientific, account of the origin of religion, by arguing that religion arises from various dispositions within the human mind.[31] He initially observes that religious belief, or belief in some "invisible, intelligent power," appears among human beings in all ages and nations. However, we find little agreement between different cultures in their religious ideas or sentiments, and in some cultures we even occasionally find individuals who reject religious belief. Accordingly, religious sentiments, unlike the ordinary passions, are not "an original instinct or primary impression of nature," but are instead secondary to, or dependent upon, other original passions of the human mind. Religious sentiments may thus be "perverted by various accidents and causes," or even "altogether prevented" (NHR Int.21; cf. 15.75). In other words, the disposition to religion is not universally given in the human species, but when it appears, it arises from "the essential and universal properties of human nature." We may therefore seek the causes of religious beliefs, sentiments, and practices in the basic principles of the human mind (NHR 14.73).[32]

In the *Natural History of Religion* Hume ostensibly endorses the argument from design, though generally echoing Philo's minimal deism rather than the providential deism of Cleanthes (NHR Int.21, 1.24, 2.26, 6.41–42, 15.74). That is, he does not attribute either moral qualities or providential intentions to the creator, although he criticizes the attribution of licentiousness or malevolence to the gods in various religious traditions as impious (NHR 13.65–69). Indeed, he refers approvingly to the view that denies "a *particular* providence" and instead affirms that the "Sovereign mind or first principle of all things" created all of nature, but does not interrupt "the settled order of events by particular volitions" (NHR 6.42; cf. E SU.581–86).

Hume argues that polytheism, which he also calls "idolatry," was "the first and most ancient religion of mankind." The evidence for this claim is provided by ancient documents, by contemporary cross-cultural studies of religion, and also by the improbability that a prehistoric monotheism would be supplanted by polytheism (NHR 1.23–25). In order to discover the origins of religion in human nature, we must therefore begin by considering the origins of polytheism.

As moderns, we might expect that a "contemplation of the works of nature" would lead human beings directly to monotheism. However, Hume argues that the concern of human beings with the "various and contrary events" of our

31. For a discussion of the *Natural History of Religion* and its initial reception, see Mossner, *Life of David Hume*, 319–35. On Hume's approach to religion in this text, and its place in the development of the comparative study of religion, see Malherbe, "Hume's *Natural History of Religion*," 255–74, and Berry, "Rude Religion," 315–34.

32. On Hume's *Natural History of Religion*, see especially Yandell, *Hume's "Inexplicable Mystery,"* and Malherbe, "Hume's *Natural History of Religion*," 255–74. See also Siebert, *Moral Animus*, 62–135; Herdt, *Religion and Faction*, 171–81; and Livingston, *Philosophical Melancholy and Delirium*, 53–79.

lives, including the effects of natural events and human actions on our happiness, is more likely to give us the idea of "a constant combat of opposite powers," or even a "change of intention in the same power." We thus find a tendency for human beings in primitive nations to assign invisible agents to different spheres of natural and human activity, and to invoke or praise whichever agent has authority over their activities and concerns at any given moment. Religious beliefs and sentiments thus arise from the "incessant hopes and fears," or the ordinary passions, of human life (NHR 2.26–27).

Hume argues generally that a concern for our own future happiness and a dread of misery and death move all human beings to seek the hidden causes of any events that influence our lives. This is reflected even in the activities of modern experimental philosophers, in their attempts to show us that these causes are "nothing but the particular fabric and structure of the minute parts of their own bodies and of external objects" which exert their influence by "a regular and constant machinery." However, the "ignorant multitude" does not recognize this operation of mechanical causes in nature. Instead, the human mind has a propensity to form "ideas of those powers, on which we have so entire a dependance," and to generate a "system" of invisible, intelligent agents (NHR 3.29).

Hume argues that this propensity arises from the "universal tendency" of human beings to regard all things as "beings like themselves," and "to transfer to every object, those qualities, with which they are familiarly acquainted, and of which they are intimately conscious." This tendency also appears in childhood fancies, in poetry, in our casual enjoyment of nature, and even in some systems of philosophy (NHR 3.29; cf. T 1.4.3.11 [SBN 224–25]). Similarly, the "ignorant vulgar" regard the unknown causes of events in their lives as "nothing but a species of human creatures," often with "all human passions and appetites, together with corporeal limbs and organs," and multiplied to account for "that variety of events, which happen over the whole face of nature," until "every place is stored with a crowd of local deities." We have thus assigned divine powers variously to celestial bodies, inanimate objects, animals, plants, artifacts, activities, attributes, and even human heroes, all of which have been regarded as deities in different ages and cultures (NHR 3.29–31; cf. 5.38–41). He also notes that the imagination and passions are moved to religion more frequently as a result of fear, disaster, and melancholy, than by prosperity and joy, a view which is reaffirmed by Philo in the *Dialogues* (NHR 3.31–32, 13.65–66; DNR 10.193, 12.225–26). Polytheism has accordingly prevailed as the system of religion among "uninstructed mankind" (NHR 2.26; cf. 5.40, 8.47). Hume's account of the imaginative generation of deities by the human mind is already anticipated in his earlier philosophical writings, and in his essay "On Chivalry and Modern Honour" (T 1.4.7.13 [SBN 271–72]; cf. EHU 1.11 [SBN 11]; CMH 57).

Next, Hume argues that monotheism originally arises from within poly-theism. However, monotheism does not initially follow from any inquiry into the cause of the universe, but from the desire of a community to address their petitions and worship to one god, whom they regard as "the prince or supreme magistrate of the rest," or at least as their own "particular patron." The peti-tioners of this single god seek to flatter their deity by "swelling up the titles of his divinity," or by attributing exaggerated qualities to their god. These qualities correspond to the perfections that are attributed to the creator by philosophical theists, allegedly on the basis of reason, but are suggested to these more primitive worshipers by "the adulation and fears of the most vulgar super-stition." Hume traces the development of monotheism from polytheism espe-cially among the ancient Greeks and ancient Hebrews, and even attributes the elevation of Mary and other saints in Catholic Christianity to the same propensities of the human mind (NHR 6.43; cf. 6.42–45, 7.47, 13.66; CMH 57; EHU 2.6 [SBN 19]).

Indeed, human beings have "a natural tendency to rise from idolatry to theism, and to sink again from theism into idolatry," in a constant "flux and reflux." This cyclical movement arises from the two tendencies in human beings: first, to anthropomorphize and deify the imagined causes of various events in human life, and then, to elevate one of these causes as a protector and patron. However, once the vulgar have moved from polytheism to mono-theism, they find it difficult to maintain a stable conception of the supreme deity. Accordingly, they tend to posit "inferior mediators or subordinate agents" who, by "partaking more of human nature," are interposed between human beings and the supreme deity. Indeed, this tendency is recognized and opposed by strict monotheists, such as Jews and Muslims, who prohibit artis-tic representations of any human figure in order to prevent its deification (NHR 8.46–48).

In comparing the popular versions of polytheism and monotheism "with regard to reason or absurdity," Hume finds the systems of pagan mythology less absurd than they might seem at first. That is, the same "powers or principles" that generated the world could have produced "a species of intelligent crea-tures" that are more ethereal and powerful than visible beings, though resem-bling human beings in their passions and motives. On Hume's view, the main objection to polytheism, as well as against miracles, is that the various poly-theistic systems are not "ascertained by any just reason or authority," that they conflict with each other, and that they partake "more of traditional stories and superstitious practices than of philosophical argument and controversy" (NHR 11.53; cf. E PG.62). Any given system of polytheism also tends to be internally inconsistent, although usually by accident rather than principle (NHR 5.39, 2.58–59).

On the other hand, monotheism is "so conformable to sound reason" that it even tends to incorporate philosophy into its theology. However, this assimilation is complicated by the usual conjunction of popular monotheism with a sacred text or some other authority (NHR 11.53–54). Indeed, Hume further distinguishes between "traditional" and "scriptural" types of religion, and apparently correlates these respectively with polytheism and monotheism. Of these, a traditional or "mythological" religion is diffuse, and allows for variations, contradictions, and even frivolity in its expressions. By contrast, a scriptural, or a "systematical, scholastic" religion, is restricted to a "standard and canon" and to "determinate articles of faith" (NHR 12.61, 12.65; cf. E PG.62; EHU 11.3 [SBN 133]; EPM App.4.21 [SBN 322]). Hume refers to the different types of polytheism and the scripturally based versions of monotheism as "popular religions" (NHR 5.39, 11.53, 12.65, 15.75), and to traditional theology, including Scholastic theology, as "popular theology" (NHR 11.54). All of these popular traditions may be therefore be contrasted to deism, or what he calls "genuine Theism" or "philosophical" theism (NHR Int.21; D 12.226).

While there may be theologians in a monotheistic scriptural tradition who are interested in philosophy, these tend to endorse the distinctive doctrines of their tradition, leaving philosophy "very unequally yoked with her new associate." In these cases, instead of assisting and refining theology, philosophy is "at every turn perverted to serve the purposes of superstition." Indeed, popular theology in its appropriation of philosophy has "a kind of appetite for absurdity and contradiction," arising from the desire among religious leaders to promote awe, amazement, and the subjugation of reason, by obliging their followers to believe in "unintelligible sophisms." By contrast, the heretics denounced by mainstream Christian theologians have generally preferred consistent reasoning to paradoxes; and Hume expects the same anathemas to be directed against philosophers who apply the principles of logic and consistent reasoning to matters of doctrine (NHR 11.53–54).

In considering various absurd beliefs in polytheism and monotheism, Hume notes that we are "so accustomed" to many of the latter, such as the Catholic doctrine of the real presence, that we never think of criticizing them (NHR 12.55–59; cf. 7.45–46). However, he himself criticizes the "impious" concepts of the divine nature in various polytheistic and monotheistic traditions, especially the depictions of any deity as malicious or malevolent, although these qualities are often obscured by "epithets of praise" in the minds of devotees, especially in a monotheistic system (NHR 13.65–67; cf. DNR 12.219, 12.225–26). He even applies this criticism indirectly to Christianity, by quoting a satirical summary of its salvation history from the eccentric Chevalier Ramsay, who apparently intended to attack the supposed misrepresentations of the morality of the Christian God by contemporary freethinkers (NHR 13.68–69n1).

In sum, Hume traces the origin of religious beliefs, sentiments, and practices to the general human propensities to seek the causes of favorable or unfavorable events in our lives; to imagine invisible beings or project human qualities onto objects, especially in the absence of any scientific explanation; and finally, to regarded these beings as susceptible to our praise and petitions. This process of deification is applied to various phenomena in different cultures and historical periods, reflecting the general importance of various objects, dispositions, and activities for human life (cf. NHR 6.41, 7.45–46). Polytheists also tend to develop a monotheistic devotion toward a single god in their pantheon, and monotheists tend to develop a polytheistic elaboration of their doctrine.

Thus far I have considered Hume's "natural history" of religion, or his account, according to the general principles of moral explanation, of the origins of religion in human nature. This analysis is intended to apply to all religions, and in the *Natural History of Religion* he refers to a number of historical examples, but does not attempt to trace the unique history of any religion.

The religion that receives the most sustained attention in Hume's writings is of course Christianity. Hume never devoted a specific work to the history of Christianity. However, he discusses the early history of Christian theology and its relation to philosophy in the *Natural History of Religion* and the *Dialogues;* European church history in the *History of England;* and the seventeenth-century religious conflicts in England in his essays and the *History of England.*[33]

In Hume's view, the most important characteristic of Christianity, at least for its subsequent effects in European history, is its approach to combining theology with philosophy. In "Of Parties in General" he describes the propensity of modern political factions to develop absolutely opposing political principles, and compares this to the tendency of religious sects to establish conflicting doctrines. In both cases this tendency may be traced in part to the universal dispositions of the human mind, which is "wonderfully fortified by an unanimity of sentiments," and "shocked and disturbed by any contrariety." However, this tendency to formulate absolute oppositions has also been promoted by a set of "accidental" or unique causes in the history of Christianity. Since the early church arose in a society where it was rejected by the state and the cultural elite, its positions of power were appropriated exclusively by priests, who absorbed a "spirit of persecution" which continued to pervade Christianity even after it had become the established religion. This spirit of persecution then persisted as "the poison of human society," producing "the greatest misery and devastation" in the subsequent history of Christianity by its tendency to generate divisions, which are "factions of *principle*" for believers, but also "factions of *interest*" for the clergy. In addition, Christianity arose in a culture pervaded by philosophy;

33. On Hume's account of the history of Christianity, see Siebert, *Moral Animus,* 69–95; Bernard, "Hume and the Madness of Religion," 224–38; and Herdt, *Religion and Faction,* 188–218.

its teachers were thus obliged to develop "a system of speculative opinions," and to explain and defend their faith "with all the subtilty of argument and science." This promoted a "keenness in dispute," which persisted as the new religion was "split into new divisions and heresies," and further served the interests of priests by "begetting a mutual hatred and antipathy among their deluded followers" (E PG.60–63).[34] That is, Christianity tends to generate factions through its dual predilections toward philosophy and persecution (NHR 11.53–54; EHU 11.3 [SBN 133]).[35]

A similar view of the relation between Christianity and philosophy is presented in the *Dialogues*. First, Cleanthes observes that ever since "the union of philosophy with the popular religion, upon the first establishment of Christianity," its leaders have tended to denounce reason and even to endorse skepticism. By contrast, Locke seems to have been "the first Christian, who ventured openly to assert, that *faith* was nothing but a species of *reason*" (DNR 1.138–39). Philo notes that there seem to be "strong symptoms of priestcraft in the whole progress of this affair." However, he argues that theologians only promoted skeptical arguments in the "ignorant ages" of church history, in order to challenge any belief "that human reason was equal to everything." On the other hand, modern theologians have adopted the language of the "STOICS, PLATONISTS, and PERIPATETICS" by appealing to reason. It thus seems that "whichever system best suits the purpose of these reverend gentlemen, in giving them an ascendant over mankind" is likely to become "their favourite principle, and established tenet" (DNR 1.139–40).[36]

Hume's most detailed discussion of the history of Christianity appears in the *History of England*. After the reception of the first Stuart volume, Hume recognized that his treatment of the history of Christianity had become, and was likely to remain, the most controversial aspect of his work. Indeed, he drafted a new preface, which he never published but preserved in manuscript.[37] Here he admits to having described "the Mischiefs which arise from the Abuses of Religion" more often than "the salutary Consequences which result from true & genuine Piety." However, since "the proper Office of Religion is to reform

34. On Hume's discussion of the role of philosophy in the history of Christianity, see Livingston, *Philosophical Melancholy and Delirium*, 102–18.

35. Herdt has presented a study of Hume's account of the causes and effects of factions in both religion and politics, in *Religion and Faction*.

36. Goldie provides an intriguing study of the concept of "priestcraft" as a predecessor to the concept of "ideology" in "Ideology," 266–91.

37. This preface is reproduced by Mossner in *Life of David Hume*, 306–7, and noted by Gaskin in "Hume on Religion," 341n2. Mossner also examines contemporary criticisms of Hume's *History of England* in this context, 301–18. Interestingly enough, Hume was apparently more concerned to defend his treatment of political topics than of religion in the *History*. While he attempts to conciliate his religious critics, he "scorns to suggest any Apology" for his approach to political subjects, where he indeed thinks that he is "intitled to Approbation." See Mossner, *Life of David Hume*, 307.

Men's Lives, to purify their Hearts, to inforce all moral Duties, & to secure Obedience to the Laws & civil Magistrate," and since these operations are "secret & silent," they "seldom come under the Cognizance of History" (cf. DNR 12.220). On the other hand, the "adulterate Species" of religion that "inflames Faction, animates Sedition, & prompts Rebellion" is an influential force in the public events of history, and should therefore be considered with all these effects, even if as a consequence "no religious Sect is mentioned in this Work without being expos'd sometimes to some Note of Blame and Disapprobation."

In the first volume of the *History of England* Hume describes the Druidical religion of the Celtic Britons as one of the cruelest systems of superstition in the historical record. The Druid priests fascinated and terrified their subjects by their teachings and practices, including secret rituals, human sacrifices, and threats of eternal punishment. These activities gave them greater influence over their followers than we find in any other known system of "idolatrous worship" (H 1.1.5–6). By contrast, the religion of the Germans, including the Saxon settlers in England, was a more typically diffuse polytheism, with all the usual "air of the wildest extravagance." Woden, their god of war, "by a natural consequence, became their supreme deity, and the chief object of their religious worship" (H 1.1.26–27). Hume also describes the conversion of the various Saxon kingdoms to Christianity, and the influence of the new religion in their social and political life (H 1.1.27–54). However, he reminds us that the Christian faith as received by the Saxons through the "channels of Rome" was a "corrupt species of Christianity." This popular Catholic Christianity included "a great mixture of credulity and superstition," in its preoccupation with saints, relics, miracles, monastic observances, penances, tithes, and reverence for clerical hierarchy, at the expense of the "active virtues" of civic life (H 1.1.51). In addition, the "frivolous controversies in theology" between the Celtic and Roman churches in Britain, especially over the calculation of the date of Easter and the shape of the monastic tonsure, aroused "such animosity" between them that their priests "refused all communion together, and each regarded his opponent as no better than a Pagan" (H 1.1.53–54).

The rest of the *History of England* is pervaded by a continuing discussion of Christianity and its influence in English political and cultural life. In the medieval volumes Hume refers to the history and influence of Christianity both in the main narrative, as in the chapters on Thomas à Becket (H 1.8.306–38) and Joan of Arc (H 2.20.397–410), and in the appendices, in which he considers for example the treatment of Jews in medieval England, and the rise of the Dominican and Franciscan orders (H 2.12.68–72).[38] In his Tudor history he introduces a "digression" on the causes and the social, cultural, and political

38. On Hume's account of Thomas à Becket and Joan of Arc, see also Siebert, *Moral Animus,* 121–29, and Bernard, "Hume and the Madness of Religion," 231–34.

context of the Reformation on the Continent, and its contribution to the ongoing division of the European church (H 3.29.134–42). This is followed by an account of the Reformation in England and Scotland (H 3.31–32.210–90). As we have seen, he traces the role of religion in the conflict between the kings and Parliament in the early Stuart period (cf. H 5.45.10–13; H 5.51.211–14; H 5.52.222–28; H 5.53.249–62), and the nature of Puritan rule and the proliferation of religious sects in the Puritan Republic (H 6.60.3–5; H 6.62.140–46). Finally, he describes various religious developments under Charles II, including the restoration of the episcopacy, the beginnings of toleration, and the emergence of a "spirit of irreligion" in some circles as a reaction against the excesses of Puritanism (H 6.63.164–66; H 6.71.539; cf. E SE.78–79).

Hume provides a further account of the popular tendencies within Christianity since the Reformation in "Of Superstition and Enthusiasm."[39] He describes superstition and enthusiasm, or fanaticism, as "corruptions of true religion," and as "two species of false religion," which are contrary in their tendencies but equally pernicious in their effects. In the first case, the human mind is subject to "unaccountable terrors and apprehensions" arising from external events, ill health, or a melancholy disposition. A person with an apprehensive temperament may also fear "infinite unknown evils" from imaginary agents, who can only be placated by observances that include "any practice, however absurd or frivolous, which either folly or knavery recommends to a blind and terrified credulity." Melancholy, weakness, fear, and ignorance are thus "the true sources of SUPERSTITION." However, the human mind is also subject to "an unaccountable elevation and presumption" arising from success, health, and a confident disposition. In an especially confident person we may even find that "the imagination swells with great, but confused conceptions," and rises to the supposed "invisible regions or world of spirits," in raptures that are attributed "to the immediate inspiration of that Divine Being, who is the object of devotion." Such individuals may regard themselves as the favorites of the deity, and as entitled to reject both reason and morality to follow their own whims, which they regard as expressions of the divine will. Pride, hope, and a lively imagination, along with ignorance, are thus "the true sources of ENTHUSIASM" (E SE.73–74; cf. DNR 10.195, 12.220–23).

These two types of religion also have different effects on government and society. First, superstition tends to promote the development of a priesthood, since the superstitious person is too humble to address the deity directly. By contrast, enthusiasts tend to condemn any outward observances, and to reject the authority of an ecclesiastical hierarchy: tendencies that became progressively more apparent among the English Presbyterians, Congregationalists, and

---

39. For a valuable discussion of "enthusiasm" and its critics in seventeenth-century England, see Beiser, *Sovereignty of Reason,* 148–219.

Quakers in the seventeenth century. Second, enthusiasm is "more furious and violent" than superstition at first, but then becomes "more gentle and moderate." The initial vehemence of enthusiasm, as seen for example among the German Anabaptists, English Levellers, and Scottish Covenanters, arises from the excitement of presumption, novelty, and the sympathetic cohesion of a group, especially in opposition to other groups, and often leads to "the most cruel disorders in human society." However, this fury tends to exhaust itself; and in fact, the members of a fanatical sect often sink afterward into a "remissness and coolness in sacred matters," since their devotion is not supported by any authorities or observances. Indeed, a decline of enthusiasm has tended historically to promote the reappearance of superstition, or, in modern Britain, of deism and free thought (E SE.76–78; cf. H 6.71.539). Third, superstition is opposed to civil liberty, since it supports the authority of priests and the established order, while enthusiasm tends to promote civil liberty, since it rejects ecclesiastical authority and encourages instead a "spirit of liberty" in the individual. For example, during the Civil War the various enthusiastic sects were united by their desire for a republic. Their eighteenth-century successors still tended to support the Whigs, even though the Whig leaders were no longer enthusiasts, but deists or latitudinarians, and were "friends to toleration, and indifferent to any particular sect of *christians*." On the other hand, Catholics and Tories in the mid-eighteenth century both tended to support the privileges of the Crown, although Catholics were also drawn to the Whig party by its principle of toleration. This conflict between superstition and enthusiasm also appears in the competition between the Jesuits and Jansenists in Catholic France since the seventeenth century. Here the Jesuits were supporters of the monarchy and tyrants to the people, while the Jansenists preserve "the small sparks of the love of liberty, which are to be found in the FRENCH nation" (E SE.78–79).

Hume's comparative analysis of superstition and enthusiasm in this essay is based on a combination of "experience" and "reason," by which he evidently means historical evidence and moral causal explanation (E SE.76). In the first edition of his first Stuart volume he applied this analysis at greater length to the conflict between the Catholic Church and Protestant movements during the Reformation. He withdrew these passages after being widely criticized for applying the terms "superstition" and "enthusiasm" to the mainstream Catholic and Protestant sides of the Reformation controversies (cf. H 1.Var.xiv–xviii). However, he apparently prepared a response to this criticism in an unpublished preface to the second Stuart volume, in which he also praises, by contrast, the moderation of both the Anglican Church and the dissident Protestant sects in eighteenth-century Britain.[40]

40. Mossner, *Life of David Hume,* 307.

Finally, we may consider Hume's discussion of the psychological, social, and political effects of religion. He generally offers a more favorable view of polytheism than monotheism in these areas, although he also traces several beneficial effects arising respectively from superstition and enthusiasm in Christianity. However, he tends to regard both types of Christian devotion as harmful, in contrast to a dedication to philosophy, or even to ordinary human reason and the classical virtues. This is especially evident in his description of zealous leaders in either type of Christian sect—especially among the clergy, who also have a professional stake in defending the doctrines and the practices of their particular sect.

First, we may consider the psychological effects of the different types of religion with regard to humility or courage. Since monotheism represents the deity as "infinitely superior to mankind," Hume argues that it tends to produce "the lowest submission and abasement" in its followers, and to promote the "monkish virtues of mortification, penance, humility, and passive suffering." By contrast, polytheism tends to encourage an emulation of the gods, promoting "activity, spirit, courage, magnanimity, love of liberty, and all the virtues which aggrandize a people" (NHR 10.51–52). However, in the monotheism of the medieval church he notes that the "attachment to superstition" was unreserved but not extreme and, like "ancient pagan idolatry," consisted in "exterior practices and observances" more than in any principles of conduct. As a result, medieval Christianity was able to abate "by exterior rites, ceremonies, and abasements," the fears it aroused among its adherents, and also to encourage civil order. On the other hand, enthusiasm furthers an energetic and courageous individualism, but may also promote self-righteousness, vindictiveness, arrogance, and a disposition toward autocracy (H 1.Var.xiv–xvii).

Turning to sincerity and hypocrisy, Hume argues that "the conviction of the religionists, in all ages, is more affected than real," and seldom approaches even the degree of "solid belief and persuasion, which governs us in the common affairs of life." However, since people "dare not avow, even to their own hearts," their doubts concerning religion, they "disguise to themselves their real infidelity, by the strongest asseverations and most positive bigotry." We indeed find many surprising juxtapositions of credulity and infidelity in ancient religious texts, although this tendency is less apparent in modern forms of monotheism, where the insistence upon orthodox belief leads to stronger doubts, and to a more consistent hypocrisy (NHR 12.60–65; cf. 15.75).

Hume also addresses the topic of hypocrisy in a footnote to "Of National Characters," in which he considers, as a "trite, but not altogether a false maxim," the observation that "priests of all religions are the same" (E NC.199). Here he argues that individual clerics are often obliged by their profession to feign a greater religious devotion than naturally belongs to their disposition, and are thus driven toward hypocrisy. On the other hand, those with a strong natural disposition toward piety often regard the intensity of their devotion as compensating for a variety of "vices and enormities" in their private lives. Members of the clergy also tend to be ambitious, deceitful, disputatious, and vindictive. Hume argues that these dispositions in the clerical character tend to arise from "fixed moral causes," mainly their professional commitment to defending paradoxical doctrines that are allegedly derived from a supernatural authority, and to living by principles that are often opposed to the promptings of our natural and moral sentiments. Hume concludes that while some individuals among the clergy may possess "the noble virtues of humanity, meekness, and moderation," these virtues arise from "nature or reflection," rather than their profession (E NC.199–201n3; cf. DNR 12.222–23). In the *Natural History of Religion* he concludes that priests tend to depict the deity as capricious and terrifying, so that we will "abandon our natural reason" and yield to their "ghostly guidance and direction." In this way, the natural weaknesses and follies which give rise to religion are aggravated by the "artifices of men" (NHR 14.73).

Hume gives particular attention throughout his writings to the influence of religion on morality. In the second *Enquiry* he rejects any account of the "monkish virtues" as moral virtues, since they not only "serve to no manner of purpose," but also prevent us from pursuing what is useful or agreeable to the self or to others by cultivating the genuine virtues. Instead, the monkish virtues tend to "stupify the understanding and harden the heart, obscure the fancy and sour the temper" (EPM 9.3 [SBN 270]). In the first *Enquiry* the Epicurean argues that experience and the ordinary human passions provide a foundation for morality that is more secure than any religious motives (EHU 11.19–22 [SBN 139–42]).

In the concluding chapter of the *Natural History of Religion* Hume considers at greater length the "bad influence" of any type of popular religion over morals. He begins by observing that, however sublime the doctrine of a religion might be, its followers will usually seek the favor of their deity, "not by virtue and good morals," but by intemperate zeal, frivolous observances, rapturous ecstasies, or a belief in "mysterious and absurd opinions." Indeed, Hume predicts that human beings would probably rely on such practices even if they were instructed to regard the cultivation of morality as the only service that would be pleasing to the deity. This tendency is especially puzzling, since, on his view, virtuous conduct is generally easier and more agreeable than most religious observances. In order to explain this anomaly, he offers the hypothesis that, since the ordinary practice of virtue does not give the superstitious person a feeling of performing an action exclusively for the sake of the deity, it does not serve to "allay those terrors, with which he is haunted." The superstitious person is instead drawn to practices that are frivolous, disagreeable, or difficult, but which apparently arise from purely religious motives and express a convincing devotion. Indeed, the "greatest crimes" have often been combined with a great deal of "superstitious piety and devotion." The most successful defense against superstition is "a manly, steady virtue," which enables us to endure the accidents of life in a "calm sunshine of the mind," and dissipates the "spectres of false divinity" (NHR 14.70–73). Similarly, Cleanthes and Philo agree that the natural principles of the human mind are the best source for morality. However, Cleanthes also affirms the moral value of providential deism, in its promise of a future reward or punishment. By contrast, Philo argues that the motives for moral action arising from our natural human inclinations are stronger and more reliable than any religious motives, and that our moral inclinations tend to be obscured or warped by the influence of religion (DNR 12.219–23).[41]

Finally, Hume also considers the effects of different types of religion in the social and political order. In the *Natural History of Religion* he compares polytheism and monotheism in their relative tendencies toward toleration or persecution. First, polytheism is "so social" that it is prepared not merely to tolerate, but even to assimilate new deities, and to render their "rites, ceremonies, or traditions, compatible with each other." By contrast, the single deity in a monotheistic religion "seems naturally to require the unity of faith and ceremonies." This tendency toward a unified doctrine and ritual gives to "designing men" within a monotheistic tradition an excuse for depicting their opponents as enemies of God, thereby promoting "sacred zeal and rancour," as found among Christians, Jews, Muslims, and Zoroastrians. Indeed, Hume argues that the principles of toleration only arose in modern England and Holland through "the steady resolution of the civil magistrate, in opposition to the continued efforts of priests and bigots." He even argues that monotheistic intolerance, as a "corruption of theism," has been more "pernicious to society" than any of the cruelties of polytheism (NHR 9.48–51). This view is also reflected in his account of the tendency toward persecution and factionalism in the history of Christianity (E PG.60–63; cf. E SE.73–79; H 1.Var.xiv–xviii; H 6.60.3–5). On the basis of such evidence, Philo argues that religion has been a source of factions, civil war, persecution, subversion, oppression, and slavery throughout history. Cleanthes can only answer that the "proper office" of religion is to reinforce our natural motives toward "morality and justice," and that, whenever it acts "as a separate principle over men, it has departed from its proper sphere, and has become only a cover to faction and ambition" (DNR 12.220).[42]

41. On Hume's criticism of theologically-based ethical systems, and his attempt to develop a secular morality, see especially Norton, *David Hume*, 94–151; Gaskin, *Hume's Philosophy of Religion*, 194–203; Yandell, *Hume's "Inexplicable Mystery,"* 25–39; and Herdt, *Religion and Faction*.

42. For further reflections concerning Hume's discussions of the different types of religion and their influence in society, from both a historical and a social-scientific perspective, see Siebert, *Moral Animus*, 62–135.

Hume concludes his account of the origins, history, and effects of religion by stating that if we consider the principles of religion in the different ages and nations of human history, we are more likely to regard these as "sick men's dreams," or even the playful whimsies of "monkies in human shape," than as the conclusions of rational beings (NHR 15.75). Instead he recommends philosophy, along with the cultivation of ordinary reason and virtue, as the best counterbalance to the dispositions in human nature that tend to promote religion, and the best defense against any type of religion (T 1.4.7.12 [SBN 271]; EHU 11.19–23 [SBN 139–42]; E SE.75; E Su.577–79; DNR 12.221–28). He accordingly ends the *Natural History of Religion* by describing religion as "a riddle, an ænigma, an inexplicable mystery," toward which the best response would be "doubt, uncertainty, suspence of judgment." However, we may find it difficult to sustain this suspense of judgment, especially given the "frailty of human reason" and the "irresistible contagion of opinion." In this case, he advises us to compare "one species of superstition to another" and, once we have observed their quarreling, to "happily make our escape into the calm, though obscure, regions of philosophy" (NHR 15.74–76; cf. EHU 10.24 [SBN 121–22]).

SKEPTICISM, DEISM, AND FIDEISM

In the preceding sections I have traced Hume's criticism of the arguments for revealed religion and natural theology; his causal explanation of the origin of religion in human nature; his account of the history and varieties of Christianity as products of general human dispositions in particular circumstances; and his view of the corrupting effects of various types of religion in human morals and in social and political life. Thus far, the textual evidence seems to support the charges of his contemporaries that Hume was an atheist.

However, and surprisingly, Hume also appears to offer several endorsements of religious faith. Many of these, as I have already indicated, seem to be expressions of caution, irony, a conciliatory strategy, or even an intention to develop only one controversial line of argument at a time. On the other hand, even when we have dismissed many of Hume's apparent endorsements of religion on these grounds, we are still left with several surprising statements concerning the apparent justification and value of religion, in one of its forms or another, which have continued to provoke discussion among later authors.

The first puzzle is Hume's apparent endorsement, through Philo, of a minimal version of deism which is nonprovidential, does not claim to be based on very decisive evidence, neither requires nor justifies any distinctive types of action, and has no implications for morality. Hume describes this minimal deism in two late additions to Part 12 of the *Dialogues*. First, according to

Philo, even the atheist agrees that there is "a certain degree of analogy among all the operations of nature," among which he impishly includes "the rotting of a turnip, the generation of an animal, and the structure of human thought." The atheist may thus agree that whatever principle has given rise to the order of the universe must also bear "some remote inconceivable analogy to the other operations of nature," and among these "to the œconomy of human mind and thought" (DNR 12.218). Philo also indicates that "the whole of natural theology" can be reduced to the proposition "that the cause or causes of order in the universe probably bear some remote analogy to human intelligence."[43] Thus stated, he would expect the "most inquisitive, contemplative, and religious man" to give this proposition a "plain, philosophical assent." However, this conclusion has no further implications for our understanding of any supposed first cause of the universe, or for determining the principles of human action (DNR 12.227).

Philo's concluding statements have recently been regarded as evidence that Hume himself endorses a minimal deism.[44] However, I have already given reasons for regarding Philo's apparent confession of minimal deism as a strategy designed by Hume to conciliate any theists among his readers, especially his friends among the moderate Presbyterian clergy; and for maintaining that Philo ultimately endorses a moderate skepticism toward the design argument. This interpretation is reinforced by Philo's view that the argument for minimal deism is likely to convince the most "inquisitive, contemplative, and religious man." In other words, Philo indicates that this argument is likely to be convincing to a thoughtful person who already has an inclination toward religion; but he does not explicitly state that he expects it to be convincing to an irreligious thinker. If I am right in my view of Philo's skepticism toward the design argument, and also in regarding Philo's general endorsement of moderate skepticism as a restatement of Hume's philosophy, then there are good grounds for regarding Philo's skepticism toward the design argument as an expression of Hume's own position in the *Dialogues*.

On the other hand, it is also possible to regard Philo's apparent endorsement of the design argument, not as a minimal deism, which endorses a probable

43. Philo's reference here to the "cause or causes" of order in the universe might indicate that he is regarding a "minimal polytheism" as equal in plausibility to minimal deism. Hume does not otherwise endorse polytheism here or elsewhere, although he does prefer certain aspects of polytheistic religion to monotheism. I am indebted to David Norton for calling my attention to the polytheistic implications of Philo's statement.

44. For an interpretation of Hume's view as an "attenuated deism," see Gaskin, "Hume's Attenuated Deism," 160–73, and *Hume's Philosophy of Religion,* 209–31. Logan argues that Hume regards minimal deism as a "natural belief," in *Religion Without Talking.* On the other hand, Reich describes Hume as a "religious naturalist," by which he means one who adopts a religious attitude toward philosophical naturalism: see *Hume's Religious Naturalism.* Finally, Livingston regards Hume as a "philosophical theist," who considers theism to be justified as a presupposition of science: see Livingston, *Hume's Philosophy of Common Life,* 172–86 and 331–32, and *Philosophical Melancholy and Delirium,* 61–79.

inference from the observable order in the natural world to the existence of a divine creator, but as a "minimal theism," which arises more directly from the association of ideas and prompting of the imagination. This view is indeed suggested by Hume in his 1751 letter to Elliot, where he notes that we are inclined to accept the design argument through a "Propensity of the Mind," although this propensity is not as "strong & universal as that to believe in our Senses & Experience." He then invites Elliot, though perhaps disingenuously, to help prove that this propensity is "somewhat different from our Inclination to find our own Figures in the Clouds, our Face in the Moon, our Passions & Sentiments even in inanimate Matter" (L 1.155). Hume also suggests this view in the *Natural History of Religion*, where he argues that there is "an universal tendency among mankind to conceive all beings like themselves," and to attribute human qualities to all other objects (NHR 3.29). In other words, Hume appears to be stating here that there is a propensity in the human imagination to personify objects, and to suppose the existence of invisible beings with human qualities, which operates even when we try to form an idea of the origin of the universe. This propensity, which is often compelling and may even be universal in human nature, produces what we may call a "minimal theism" in all of us, at one time or another. However, this propensity of the imagination does not provide evidence that is compelling enough to secure belief, at least in someone who recognizes the nature and origins of this impulse. Consequently, this impulse does not provide convincing evidence for the existence of any deity or deities, or the basis for any principles of moral conduct or religious practice. In this regard, minimal theism agrees with minimal deism in having no further speculative, moral, or religious implications. The only difference between them is that minimal deism is a causal inference, albeit with a low degree of probability, while minimal theism is a direct impulse of the imagination. It is perhaps this minimal theism, rather than minimal deism, which Philo is endorsing in his apparent concessions to the design argument, such as his statement that the "cause or causes" of order in nature exhibit "some remote analogy to human intelligence" (D 12.227; cf. 218). This is an inference from analogy, but the question remains whether it is more properly described as a conclusion of philosophical probable reasoning, or as a more direct association by the imagination.

Interestingly enough, Hume's statements of a minimal deism or minimal theism, as the manifestations of the apparent human tendency to attribute order to the universe, to suppose that this order has a cause, and to personify this cause, are a notable antecedent to Kant's account, a decade later, of the transcendental character of teleological judgments. On Kant's view, our judgments concerning natural beauty, the functions of biological organisms, and progress in human history all reflect a fundamental tendency of the human mind to attribute purposive structures to nature. This, in Kant's view, is to be explained as a basic function of our cognitive faculties, specifically the faculty of judgment, which projects purposiveness onto the phenomena of nature in order to facilitate our explanation and enjoyment of the order we find in it. In other words, the propensity to consider nature as a product of design, which Hume regards as a result of causal reasoning or the imagination, is regarded by Kant as an integral principle of human cognition, although Kant also maintains that we cannot derive any speculative, religious, or moral conclusions directly from this principle.[45]

Two types of evidence indicate that Hume privately refused to call himself a deist, and that he even rejected the title of "atheist," leaving scope for the view that he was a covert theist. The first type of evidence is provided by his letters, in which he frequently expresses annoyance at being charged with deism and atheism.[46] The second type of evidence is that of contemporary anecdotes. In one case, he reportedly responded to the overtures of a freethinking socialite in the following terms: "Madam, I am no Deist. I do na style myself so, neither do I desire to be known by that Appellation." According to Diderot, Hume also stated rather provocatively, while dining with a group of freethinking French *philosophes,* "that he did not believe in atheists, that he had never seen any."[47] On the other hand, Hume does not show any signs, in these private contexts, of professing a religious faith. On the contrary, Boswell reports Hume as stating that "he never had entertained any belief in Religion since he began to read Locke and Clarke."[48] In the absence of any countervailing evidence, and light of his published writings on religion, I would argue that Hume's rejection of the appellations "deist" and "atheist" are best regarded as attempts to avoid social inconveniences, or to avoid dogmatic assertions that he, as a moderate skeptic, might have regarded as unwarranted, rather than as professions of a positive theism. Indeed, his remarks in some conversational contexts, as in the anecdote from Diderot, may even be intended as teasing challenges to his audience. Accordingly, I find the case for attributing a minimal deism or minimal theism to Hume on the basis of these sources less than convincing.

Hume occasionally appears to endorse religion as a positive moral influence. For example, in the unpublished preface to the second Stuart volume of the *History of England,* he states that the "proper Office of Religion" is to support

45. See Kant, *Critique of Judgment,* 20–26; in *Kants gesammelte Schriften,* 5:181–86. On Kant's reception of and response to Hume's philosophy of religion, see Gawlick and Kreimendahl, *Hume in der Deutschen Aufklärung,* 174–98, and Kuehn, "Kant's Critique of Hume's Theory of Faith," 239–55. Livingston has described the "philosophical theism" he attributes to Hume as the view that theism is justified as a presupposition of scientific inquiry: a view which would be similar to Kant's theory of reflective judgment. See *Hume's Philosophy of Common Life,* 172–86 and 331–32, and *Philosophical Melancholy and Delirium,* 61–79.

46. For a survey of these letters, see Gaskin, *Hume's Philosophy of Religion,* 244n4.

47. Mossner, *Life of David Hume,* 395 and 483.

48. Ibid., 51 and 597.

morality.[49] In the first *Enquiry* he leaves open the question of the value of religion for popular morality (EHU 11.28 [SBN 147]). However, these statements are counterbalanced by his more consistent view of the harmful effects of religion on morality, especially in the second *Enquiry* and Part 12 of the *Dialogues* (EPM 9.3; EPM D.52–57 [SBN 270, 341–43]; D 12.220–26). Hume's criticism of religion for its effects on morality is also reflected in his letters and conversation. In his 1751 letter to Elliot he writes that "the worst speculative Sceptic ever I knew, was a much better Man than the best superstitious Bigot & Devotee" (L 1.154). Similarly, Hume is reported by Boswell as stating in a conversation, during his last illness, that "the Morality of every Religion was bad," and that "when he heard a man was religious, he concluded he was a rascal, though he had known some instances of very good men being religious."[50]

Finally, at two crucial points in his writings, Hume seems to affirm a Christian apologetic tradition called "fideism," which endorses a subjective justification for faith, not only apart from any considerations grounded in reason, but also in conjunction with philosophical skepticism. In the first of these cases, in the conclusion to "Of Miracles," he criticizes those "dangerous friends or disguised enemies to the *Christian Religion*" who endeavor to defend it by arguments, without recognizing that "our most holy religion is founded on *Faith*, not on reason." On the contrary, he insists that Christianity was not only "at first attended with miracles, but even at this day cannot be believed by any reasonable person without one." Consequently, "whoever is moved by *Faith* to assent to it, is conscious of a continued miracle in his own person, which subverts all the principles of his understanding, and gives him a determination to believe what is most contrary to custom and experience" (EHU 10.41 [SBN 130–31]). Second, Philo maintains at the end of the *Dialogues* that someone who has been "seasoned with a just sense of the imperfections of natural reason, will fly to revealed truth with the greatest avidity." He therefore concludes that "to be a philosophical sceptic is, in a man of letters, the first and most essential step towards being a sound, believing Christian" (DNR 12.227–28).

Hume's endorsements of fideism are generally regarded as ironic, especially the concluding statement from "Of Miracles," where he glides deftly between respect and ridicule in his description of Christian faith. As we have seen, he did not profess fideism more seriously elsewhere, either in his published writings or in any known private context.

However, Hume's ironic expressions of fideism occupy an important place in the history of Christian fideism. First, Hume is deliberately echoing the tradition of fideism in early modern theology, which had emerged with the

49. Ibid., 306.
50. Ibid., 597.

rediscovery of the ancient skeptics, and was developed by Pierre-Daniel Huet and other theologians, especially in response to the debates within the French Catholic Church between Aristotelian and Cartesian theologians (DNR 1.138).[51] On the other hand, Hume's ironic affirmations of fideism, in conjunction with his skepticism, were important sources for the German tradition of fideism, including the exuberant fideism of Johann Georg Hamann and the more temperate pietism of Friedrich Jacobi, who would in turn be important influences on Kierkegaard.[52]

Hume's approach to the origin of religion in human nature, and its effects on morality and in social and political life, is also reflected in another line of development in modern Continental philosophy, though one which is less easily traced to his direct influence. This trajectory begins with Kant's account of religious traditions as the symbolic expressions and social embodiments of the moral requirements of reason, although they are also subject, as social institutions, to various types of distortion. Indeed, Kant argues that there is a tension, within any church or religious institution, between a purely moral or rational faith and the ritualism and dogmatism of an ecclesiastical faith. In this regard, he is offering a more thorough development of Hume's surmise that even if a popular religion were exclusively devoted to inculcating morality, it would eventually lapse into superstition (NHR 14.70–71).[53] Kant's critique of religion, as taken up and developed by the German idealists, would eventually lead to various theories of religion as a psychologically and socially generated distortion of the natural impulses and values of the human species, in the works of Feuerbach, Marx, Nietzsche, and Freud. Hume's criticism of the arguments for natural and revealed religion, his social-scientific approach to the explanation of religion, and his criticism of the social effects of religion would also be taken up and pursued by empiricists and positivists in the Anglo-American tradition.

What, if anything, can be salvaged from Hume's sweeping cognitive and moral attack on religion? Perhaps, as Hume seems to indicate, and as many today would agree on his grounds, the human species would be better off without religion, although any organized attempt to eradicate any or all of the existing religions from human life would probably provoke conflicts at least as destructive of human happiness and social order as the conflicts between religions. Perhaps, as Kant seems to suggest, critical defenders of religion should attempt to develop a purely ethical religion from within existing religious communities, although this would probably seem artificial and manipulative,

51. See Popkin, *History of Scepticism,* and Kors, *Atheism in France.*
52. For Hume's influence on German fideism, see Berlin, "Hume and the Sources of German Anti-Rationalism," 93–116, and Beiser, *Fate of Reason,* 3–4, 12, 16–17, 24, and 89–91.
53. Kant, *Religion Within the Boundaries of Mere Reason,* 105–91 (parts 3 and 4), in *Kants gesammelte Schriften,* 4: 93–202.

even to those who are sympathetic to this project. It might also be tempting, following Hamann, to cultivate a religious faith apart from any cognitive considerations; but this would also admit the dangerous intellectual, psychological, moral, and social effects of a religion that does not claim rational justification. Or perhaps, to take one example, Christianity in the modern or postmodern world should accept Hume's view of its traditional origins and history and develop an understanding of itself as one among the many religious communities that have developed from a variety of historical traditions. This would invite the Church, considered as a whole, to recognize that many of its teachings are not founded upon evidence which would be convincing apart from faith; to offer its moral teachings without claiming any right of command or social control; and to confess and renounce the history of conflict and persecution arising from its persistent claims to epistemological and moral privilege.[54]

Is it possible, and would it be desirable, not only on secular grounds, but also on grounds internal to Christianity or any other existing religious traditions, to reappraise the traditional faith and practices of these religious communities in the modern world, in light of an honest engagement with Hume's criticism of the claims and effects of religion? This is at least one way of stating the question that confronts members of religious communities of our own day, in light of Hume's compelling and still timely epistemological, psychological, and moral critique of religion.

54. Siebert presents a similar view of the post-Humean prospects for religion in *Moral Animus,* 134–35. Herdt provides a thoughtful response to Hume's criticism of religion in general, and Christianity in particular, in *Religion and Faction,* 206–18. For an assessment of Hume from within the traditions of Anglo-American philosophy and postmodern theology, see Phillips and Tessin, *Religion and Hume's Legacy.*

13

History

Hume's writings testify abundantly to his deep, wide-ranging, and lifelong interest in history. His earliest surviving composition is the first part of an essay comparing the medieval conception of chivalry with modern notions of honor and gallantry (CMH 56–60; cf. E RP.130–34; H I.App.2.486–87).[1] His memoranda include a large number of notes on political, economic, and religious history, both ancient and modern (EM 499–518).[2] He offers a number of reflections concerning the nature of historical knowledge and the methods of historical investigation in the *Treatise* and the *Enquiries.* Several of his essays examine the principles involved in interpreting historical documents and events, and others are concerned with specific historical topics. Hume also considers the history of philosophy, although less explicitly, in his philosophical works and essays; and the history of religion in his essays and in the *Natural History of Religion.*[3] Finally, Hume is the author of a substantial historical work, the six-volume *History of England,* which was not only the

1. See Mossner, "David Hume's 'An Historical Essay on Chivalry and Modern Honour,'" 54–60, and Stewart, "Hume's Manuscripts," 267–76.
2. See Mossner, "Hume's Early Memoranda, 1729–1740," 492–518, and Stewart, "Hume's Manuscripts," 276–88.
3. Livingston reconstructs Hume's view of history of philosophy in *Philosophical Melancholy and Delirium,* 53–172.

most popular of his works during his life, but remained the best known of his writings through much of the nineteenth century.[4]

By the early twentieth century, with the renewal of interest in his philosophy, many commentators came to regard Hume's historical writings as a departure from his philosophical interests, even speculating that he had renounced philosophy for history in discouragement, after pursuing his philosophical reasonings to their skeptical conclusions. Many of his critics have subsequently charged that his approach to history was subverted by the allegedly skeptical and ahistorical character of his philosophy, which supposedly undermined his understanding of history and his approach to historical explanation and narration.[5]

However, this evaluation of Hume's historical work in relation to his philosophy has been challenged by many recent developments in the study of his thought, including the reconsideration of his philosophy that I have considered in this study, along with a renewed attention to his historical writings.[6] These developments have produced a growing literature on Hume's historical thought by both historians and philosophers and a reassessment of the relation between his philosophical and historical writings.[7] In fact, many of these studies have included Hume—along with Vico, Hegel, Marx, and Collingwood—among the modern philosophers who have sought to examine the significance of historical existence for human consciousness, and the implications of modern historical consciousness for the concerns of philosophy.[8]

4. Hume's *History of England* was continuously in print from the first complete edition in 1762 through the nineteenth century. It was then allowed to lapse until the welcome publication of a new edition in 1983 by William Todd under the auspices of Liberty Press. For the reception and bibliographic history of the *History of England*, see Jessop, *Bibliography*, 27–33; Norton and Popkin, *David Hume: Philosophical Historian*, 413–17; Mossner, *Life of David Hume*, 301–18; Todd, "Foreword," xi–xxiii; Phillipson, *Hume*, 3–4 and 137–41; Wootton, "David Hume, 'the historian,'" 281–82; and Ikeda, *David Hume*, 1–181.

5. Examples of these criticisms, extending from the nineteenth century until recently, include Stephen, *History of English Thought*, 1: 57 and 2: 184–85; Hunt, "Hume and Modern Historians," 316–35; Black, *Art of History*, 77–116; Collingwood, *Idea of History*, 76–85; Trevor-Roper, "David Hume as a Historian," 89–100; Berry, *Hume, Hegel and Human Nature*, 57–124 and 207; Dray, "David Hume on History," 735–44; and Pompa, *Human Nature and Historical Knowledge*, 13–66.

6. This new attention to Hume's work as a historian has followed in part from the publication of an anthology of his historical writings, *David Hume: Philosophical Historian*, by Norton and Popkin in 1965; an edition of the first Stuart volume by Duncan Forbes in 1970; an abridged edition of the *History of England* by Rodney Kilcup in 1975; and the complete edition of the *History of England* by William Todd in 1983.

7. See Sabine, "Hume's Contribution," 17–38; Mossner, "An Apology for David Hume," 657–90; Popkin, "Skepticism and the Study of History," ix–xxxi; Norton, "History and Philosophy in Hume's Thought," xxxii–l; Forbes, "Introduction," 7–54; Stockton, "David Hume Among the Historiographers," 14–24; Wootton, "David Hume, 'the historian,'" 281–312; Wexler, *David Hume and the History of England*; Livingston, *Hume's Philosophy of Common Life*, and *Philosophical Melancholy and Delirium*; Phillipson, *Hume*; Siebert, *Moral Animus*; Danford, *Problem of Reason*; and Wertz, *Between Hume's Philosophy and History*.

8. See Livingston, *Hume's Philosophy of Common Life*, ix, 2, and 251–52, and *Philosophical Melancholy and Delirium*, 12–13 and 383–407; Phillipson, *Hume*, 4; and Wertz, *Between Hume's Philosophy and History*, xiii and 115–17. See also Williams, *Cultivated Reason*, 1–20.

HISTORICAL METHOD

Hume does not provide us with a specific work concerning the philosophy or methodology of history. However, he examines various aspects of historical knowledge, historical method, and the principles of historical composition over the course of his writings.[9]

In the *Treatise* and the first *Enquiry,* Hume introduces historical inquiry as a type of causal reasoning in which we judge the probability that an event has occurred in the past by reasoning from evidence that we encounter in the present. This evidence may be conveyed, in whole or in part, through oral reports, extending back to a supposed witness of the event. However, in these cases the historical facts are often "disguised by every successive narration," as a result of feeble memories, exaggeration, or even carelessness, until the report contains little or no resemblance to the original event (NHR 1.25, 5.39–40; cf. EHU 10.15–35 [SBN 116–27]). We accordingly tend to regard textual evidence as a more reliable source for historical knowledge. For example, we believe "that CÆSAR was kill'd in the senate-house on the *ides of March*" because this information has been "establish'd on the unanimous testimony of historians" and transmitted through "certain characters and letters" presented "either to our memory or senses," which we regard as signifying thoughts "either in the minds of such as were immediately present at that action," or "deriv'd from the testimony of others, and that again from another testimony," until we reach "those who were eye-witnesses and spectators of the event" (T 1.3.4.2 [SBN 83]; cf. EHU 5.7 [SBN 45–46]).

However, Hume also considers the possible objection, suggested by his own account of belief, that the number of connections involved in transmitting a report from the witness, though a series of "printers and copists," to the reader, tends to diminish the vivacity of our idea of the event, and thus our estimation of its probability. As a result, we might conclude that "there is no history or tradition, but what must in the end lose all its force and evidence." In response to this concern, he argues that the similarity in our ideas of each successive activity of copying a text tends to enhance the vivacity of these ideas, so that "the mind runs easily along them," and preserves the evidential force of the testimony (T 1.3.13.4–6 [SBN 144–46]).[10]

Hume accordingly includes historical knowledge within the "system of

---

9. For a valuable study of the principles of historical explanation, which summarizes many of the recent debates in analytic philosophy over this topic, see Roberts, *The Logic of Historical Explanation.* For a discussion of Hume in relation to contemporary analytic approaches to the philosophy of history, see Wertz, *Between Hume's Philosophy and History,* 43–58.

10. For a discussion of the antecedents of this argument, and a criticism of Hume's treatment of the problem, see Coady, *Testimony,* 199–223.

reality" constituted by custom and causal reasoning, as these extend the sphere of human knowledge beyond the immediate reach of our senses and memory:

> I form an idea of *Rome,* which I neither see nor remember; but which is connected with such impressions as I remember to have receiv'd from the conversation and books of travellers and historians. This idea of *Rome* I place in a certain situation on the idea of an object, which I call the globe. I join to it the conception of a particular government, and religion, and manners. I look backward and consider its first foundation; its several revolutions, successes, and misfortunes.

Historical beliefs thus consist in ideas, which are distinguished from ideas arising from the imagination "by their force and settled order, arising from custom and the relation of cause and effect" (T 1.3.9.4 [SBN 108]; cf. A 10 [SBN 650]). That is, we conceive of the idea of a historical event as a belief, unlike the idea of a fictional event, which appears to us as a product of our creative fancy. As we have seen, Hume initially describes this distinction as arising from the different degrees of "vivacity" of our ideas, but later restates this as a difference in their "feeling," or in the "manner" in which we conceive our ideas (T 1.3.7.6–8, 1.3.8.15–16 [SBN 97–98, 105–6, 628–29]).

Our belief in a historical event arises from our disposition to regard human testimony as a type of evidence, or an event within a causal sequence. Hume argues that this disposition arises from "our *experience* of the governing principles of human nature," which alone can give us "any assurance of the veracity of men" (T 1.3.9.12 [SBN 113]; cf. EHU 8.18, 10.5–8 [SBN 90, 111–13]). However, we find from experience that our evidence for human veracity is by no means consistent, and that we often have more confidence in human testimony than is reasonably justified by this evidence. Hume describes this disposition toward "CREDULITY," or a "too easy faith in the testimony of others," as one of the most "universal and conspicuous" weaknesses in human nature. Indeed, human beings have "a remarkable propensity to believe whatever is reported, even concerning apparitions, enchantments, and prodigies, however contrary to daily experience and observation," a tendency which may be further stimulated by our love of novelty (T 1.3.9.12 [SBN 113]; cf. 1.3.10.4 [SBN 120]; EHU 10.16–19 [SBN 117–19]). This "too easy faith" in human testimony is also reinforced by sympathy, or our general tendency to adopt the sentiments and opinions of those around us (cf. T 2.1.11.9, 2.3.6.8–10, 3.3.2.2 [SBN 320–21, 427, 592]).

Fortunately, we may counteract our tendencies toward credulity by applying the philosophical principles of probable reasoning to the reports of both witnesses and historians, since these reports are instances of human action that may be explained as products of the beliefs and desires of the agent.[11] First, when we see "certain characters or figures describ'd upon paper," we infer that their author intended to affirm such facts as "the death of *Cæsar,* the success of *Augustus,* the cruelty of *Nero."* Next, by comparing this text to other instances of testimony in our experience, we may conclude "that those facts were once really existent, and that so many men, without any interest, wou'd never conspire to deceive us," since they would have subjected themselves "to the derision of all of their contemporaries" by misrepresenting facts that were so "recent and universally known" (T 2.3.1.15 [SBN 404–5]). However, we also discover by experience that human beings can distort or fabricate information, sometimes as a result of mistaken beliefs, but also through motives which are directed toward some purpose other than accurate reporting. We may accordingly judge the probable influence of such circumstances and motives on any given instance of human testimony. Hume examines the principles involved in the evaluation of human testimony in his essay "Of Miracles" in the first *Enquiry,* and in his writings concerning the poems of Ossian, which we will consider at the end of this section.[12]

As we have seen, many readers have criticized Hume for insisting on the uniformity of human nature, especially in the first *Enquiry,* where he observes that there is "a great uniformity among the actions of men, in all nations and ages, and that human nature remains still the same, in its principles and operations." However, he also argues in this context that one of the main uses of history is to discover the "constant and universal principles of human nature, by showing men in all varieties of circumstances and situations" (EHU 8.7 [SBN 83]). Several recent studies have therefore argued that Hume is locating this uniformity in the "regular springs of human action and behaviour," or in the universal passions whose outward expressions we can trace in the variety of human actions in different ages and cultures. He then indicates that we may account for the evident historical and cultural variety among the objects of the human passions, and among the actions arising from these passions, by arguing that these are influenced by a particular set of beliefs and customs within a given historical context. That is, we should attempt to understand human actions in other nations or ages by considering the "motives, temper and situation" of any given agents in relation to their cultural and historical context (T 2.3.1.15 [SBN 404]). Indeed, he specifically encourages us to examine the

---

11. Hume's application of philosophical probable reasoning to the evaluation of testimony has been overlooked by those who regard his skepticism as entailing that historical judgments are a matter of arbitrary subjective opinion. See Norton, "History and Philosophy in Hume's Thought," xxxix–l, and Main, "Hume's Criterion," 62–74.

12. Coady provides a valuable discussion of Hume's analysis in *Testimony,* 79–176. However, he criticizes Hume, in my view unjustly, for not recognizing the extent to which we rely on testimony, or that we must presuppose the veracity of others in general to understand their use of language.

influence of different cultures on human actions, since whenever we discover any variations in human behavior in different ages and nations, "we learn thence the great force of custom and education, which mould the human mind from its infancy, and form it into a fixed and established character" (EHU 8.11 [SBN 86]). We are thus advised to study the historical context of any given action in order to discover the motive of the agent, or the beliefs and desires that probably determined the action. Hume further recommends and applies this principle in his essays, especially "Of Some Remarkable Customs" and "Of the Standard of Taste," and in "A Dialogue" at the end of the second *Enquiry* (E RC.366–76; E ST.239–40; EPM D.1–57 [SBN 324–43]).

Hume also argues that we may identify patterns in the behavior of various social groups, and even develop "general observations" concerning the causes of historical developments (EHU 8.11 [SBN 86]). He thus distinguishes the study of history, which is concerned with particular facts, from the study of politics, which examines "general facts," or the "qualities, causes, and effects of a whole species of objects" (EHU 12.31 [SBN 165]). However, while he distinguishes between history and the generalizing social sciences as methods of inquiry, he also draws upon history to provide the data for his social-scientific studies and applies the generalizations arising from his social-scientific studies to the explanation of historical developments. As we have seen, in "Of the Rise and Progress of the Arts and Sciences" he argues that "what depends upon a few persons is, in a great measure, to be ascribed to chance, or secret and unknown causes," whereas "what arises from a great number, may often be accounted for by determinate and known causes." For example, "the domestic and the gradual revolutions of a state" are generally easier to trace than "the foreign and the violent," which are usually caused by single persons and are "more influenced by whim, folly, or caprice, than by general passions and interests." It is also easier to explain the rise of commerce than developments in learning and the arts (E RP.112–13). Indeed, many of his essays are specifically concerned with the patterns that we find in political, economic, and cultural history through comparative study. For example, he argues from his own comparative studies of history that republican governments are more oppressive than monarchies toward their colonies; that religious enthusiasm arises from confident individualism; and that the arts and sciences tend to arise in nations with free governments, although they can then be transplanted to nations with other forms of government (E PR.18–21; E SE.76; E RP.115–26).[13]

In several of his essays Hume formulates the idea of a cultural "whole" as a principle of explanation in history and the social sciences. His initial examples

13. For a recent comparative study of the methods of history and the social sciences, see Burke, *History and Social Theory*.

appear in his references to the "spirit" or "genius" of a nation in a particular era of its history. In "Of the Rise and Progress of the Arts and Sciences" he argues that while developments in the arts and sciences might seem to arise from the actions of a few individuals, these innovations also reflect a "spirit and genius" that is already "diffused throughout the people among whom they arise" (E RP.114; cf. H 1.9.375; NHR 12.63–64n7). Similarly, in "Of Refinement in the Arts" he traces the relations among a variety of cultural developments in a given time and place:

> The same age, which produces great philosophers and politicians, renowned generals and poets, usually abounds with skilful weavers, and ship-carpenters. We cannot reasonably expect, that a piece of woollen cloth will be wrought to perfection in a nation, which is ignorant of astronomy, or where ethics are neglected. The spirit of the age affects all the arts; and the minds of men, being once roused from their lethargy, and put into a fermentation, turn themselves on all sides, and carry improvements into every art and science. (E RA.270–71)[14]

This tendency for a spirit of activity to permeate all levels of a given society presumably arises from sympathy, in conjunction with the various motives for productive or creative activity that Hume describes, including our desires for novelty, for material gain, and for a reputation that will attract the love and admiration of others and gratify our own pride.

Hume develops a similar principle in "Of National Characters." In this essay he condemns crude judgments concerning national characters, but then observes that different nations appear to have different customs and manners, which we can attempt to understand. He then argues that the cultural characteristics of a nation arise, not from physical causes, as Montesquieu had suggested, but from "moral causes," or from the influence of history on its social, political, and economic conditions, and on the beliefs and motives of particular individuals. The customs and manners of a social group may accordingly be understood by studying their cultural context, which is in turn a product of history (E NC.197–99; cf. E RC.366–76).

Hume's references to the "genius" of an age, and his reflections concerning the "character" of a nation, anticipate the subsequent development of the concept of the "spirit of an age," or a "culture," as a concept of the organic interrelation of the different activities pursued by the members of a given society during a particular period in its history. This notion is more typically associated with romantic than Enlightenment thought, and would eventually become a

14. See Schmidt, "Shelley's 'Spirit of the Age' Antedated in Hume," 297–98.

methodological principle prescribing that the various activities of a population should be studied as an organic whole. However, we may note that Hume's concept of the spirit or genius of an age, or a national character, is determined by and subordinated to the results of empirical historical investigation. He never takes a speculative view of the "spirit of an age," or of a "national character," as an autonomous force that could exercise any independent influence in history.[15]

In "Of the Standard of Taste" Hume considers the interpretation of a document as an activity that is directed toward discovering the intention of the author, and also the historical situation of the author and the audience. He argues that if a document is to be appreciated and evaluated for its literary merits, and indeed if it is to be understood at all, it must be regarded as addressed by an author to an audience for a particular purpose. Using oratory as his example, he indicates that in order to understand and evaluate a historical text, we must attempt to discover the "genius, interests, opinions, passions, and prejudices" the author is attributing to the audience, sometimes explicitly, but often implicitly. We may then imagine ourselves as members of the audience, in order to evaluate the text for its effectiveness in fulfilling the author's purpose. We must also recognize and take into account any relevant manners and opinions that are foreign to us, but are shared by the author and audience (E ST.239–40; cf. 246–47).

In several of his letters Hume distinguishes between historical facts and the interpretation of these facts by the historian. He writes to Millar in 1762 that Jeremiah Dyson, the Clerk of the House of Commons, had been able to discover only one factual mistake in the Stuart volumes of the *History of England,* although Dyson otherwise "differed from me in my Reasonings & Views of the Constitution" (L 1.354–55). In a letter to the Whig historian Catherine Macaulay in 1764, he again affirms this distinction, and then calls attention to the influence of underlying political assumptions in the interpretation of history: "I flatter myself that we differ less in facts, than in our interpretation and construction of them. Perhaps also I have the misfortune to differ from you in some original principles, which it will not be easy to adjust between us" (NL 81). For example, unlike Macaulay, Hume maintains that any type of government, from an absolute monarchy to a democratic republic, and including the English monarchy under the early Stuarts, is "equally legal, if established by custom and authority." He also maintains that the partisans of liberty in the seventeenth century were motivated by "cant, hypocrisy, and bigotry" more than by a genuine concern for civil liberty (NL 81). In a letter to John Douglas

---

15. For Hume's approach to social and historical wholes, see Sabine, "Hume's Contribution," 17–38; Mossner, "An Apology for David Hume," 666 and 678; Livingston, *Hume's Philosophy of Common Life,* 225–26; and Wootton, "David Hume, 'the historian,'" 295. For a further discussion of the idea of "social wholes," see Jay, *Marxism and Totality,* 32–60, and Burke, *History and Social Theory,* especially 28–33 and 118–26.

in 1770, he doubts that there are any important facts still to be uncovered in modern English history. Accordingly, the task of the historian is to provide an "explication," or explanatory account, of known historical events, rather than to discover any new events in history. On the other hand, we might still hope to discover many details which would "serve to the Embellishment of History" (L 2.229).[16]

Hume's most complete account of historical explanation and interpretation, and of the creative process involved in arranging a historical narrative, is developed in Section 3, "Of the Association of Ideas," in the first *Enquiry*.[17] Here he finds that "in all compositions of genius," both factual and fanciful, the writer must have some "plan or object." We may accordingly trace an intention and design in every literary production, including essays, letters, epic poetry, and history. The design of a literary work arises from the association of ideas in the imagination of the writer and is expressed through a series of connections established by the writer between the ideas in the composition. In cases of narrative compositions, which are Hume's main concern in this passage, this organization may reflect relations of resemblance, as in Ovid's *Metamorphosis,* or contiguity, as in a chronicle of successive events in some specific location. However, the usual connections between the events in a narrative composition, whether fictional or historical, are relations of cause and effect (EHU 3.5–7).

In a historical narrative, the author "chooses for his subject a certain portion of that great chain of events, which compose the history of mankind." He then seeks to identify and explain "each link in this chain," although he is often limited by his "unavoidable ignorance," and must supply "by conjecture what is wanting in knowledge." More specifically, a historian "traces the series of actions according to their natural order," attempts to discover "their secret springs and principles," and finally seeks to delineate "their most remote consequences." In other words, the historian seeks to describe a sequence of actions, to explain these as products of human motives within a particular context, and to describe the effects of these actions on a subsequent series of events (EHU 3.9).

These types of causal connections are also the principles of organization for fictional narratives, which are concerned with the motives of imaginary characters, their actions, and the consequences of these actions within their imagined setting. Indeed, Hume notes that these types of causal connections are often more clearly and precisely indicated in fiction than in "history, biography, or any other species of narration, which confine themselves to strict truth and reality" (EHU 3.10). He concludes that history and poetry are distinguished by the different "degrees of connexion" between the related events, so that it might be

16. See also Wootton, "David Hume, 'the historian,'" 284–85.
17. See Livingston, *Hume's Philosophy of Common Life,* 131–36, and Wertz, *Between Hume's Philosophy and History,* 44–66.

386 · David Hume: Reason in History

difficult or even impossible to establish any absolute boundaries between them (EHU 3.15). Elsewhere, however, he finds that we regard history as a matter of truth and belief because of the "feeling" of its ideas, or their greater vivacity as compared to our ideas of fictional events, in spite of the often greater detail and intimacy of a fictional narrative (T 1.3.7.7, 1.3.10.9, 1.3.10.10–12, App.1–9 [SBN 97–98, 123, 630–32, 623–27]; E SH.564).

Several recent works on Hume's approach to history have called attention to his evident distinction between the perspective of historical agents, who act from a specific set of beliefs and intentions, and the perspective of the historian: a distinction which would later be given a more familiar formulation by Hegel.[18] Of course, a historian often seeks to understand and explain the beliefs and intentions of individual agents. However, the historian is also interested in tracing the effects of these actions in a larger series of events, which is only possible for someone who can view the larger series of events from a later vantage point. This reconstruction of a process of development, in contrast to the sympathetic reconstruction of the beliefs and intentions of an individual agent, often involves considering the competing purposes of various historical agents, the limitations in agents' understandings of their situations, the unintended consequences of their actions, and the fortuitous conjunction of different actions and events. In the *Enquiry* Hume thus assigns to the historian the dual tasks of explaining the "secret springs and principles" of human actions, and of delineating "their most remote consequences" (EHU 3.9; cf. E SH.366; E PS.507). He pursues both types of explanation in explaining the development of the limited monarchy or "mix'd government" of modern Britain. In the *History of England,* he indicates that this system of government emerged gradually through a haphazard series of personal and institutional policies, conflicts, and settlements, with different and competing intentions on the part of the agents. This process would indeed produce "the most entire system of liberty, that ever was known amongst mankind," but none of the agents intended or could have foreseen this result (H 6.71.531; cf. 2.23.525).[19] In his essays comparing the Whig and Tory views of seventeenth-century English history, he again distinguishes the views held by the participants from the views that might be held by later generations. A historian might agree with the Whigs that the success of the present system of government has established the legitimacy of the parliamentary resistance to the Stuart monarchs. However, the royalist arguments

18. Interestingly enough, Hegel seems to have derived this twofold approach to history, and his concept of the "cunning of Reason," partly from his own reading of Hume's *History of England.* See Hegel, "Fragments of Historical Studies," 127–28, and *Lectures on the Philosophy of World History,* 89; along with Waszek, "Hume, Hegel, and History," 379–92. See also Forbes, *Hume's Philosophical Politics,* 264–65; Livingston, *Hume's Philosophy of Common Life,* 104; Phillipson, *Hume,* 81–82; and Wootton, "David Hume, 'the historian,'" 296.

19. See Forbes, *Hume's Philosophical Politics,* 260–96, and Livingston, *Hume's Philosophy of Common Life,* 210–305.

may be justly regarded, in accordance with the Tory view, as having appeared "more solid, more safe, and more legal" at the time, since the outcome "could not reasonably be foreseen at the time when the contest began" (E CP.500, 495; cf. E PS.507).

Indeed, Hume regards the problem of tracing the development of the British constitution, as distinct from the intentions of the agents involved in this development, as his central concern in addressing current debates over the events of British history and their relation to the present system of government. This is especially evident in the final pages of the *History of England,* in which he summarizes the "privilege and prerogative" and "latent claims" of both Parliament and the Crown in the constitutional struggle of the seventeenth century. He concludes that both sides acted from historically justified beliefs concerning the legitimacy of their claims. By contrast, the propagandists of the dominant Whig party, who claim to be defenders of liberty without showing "sufficient liberty of thought in this particular," have promoted "many gross falsehoods" in their depictions of these events, especially by vilifying the first two Stuart monarchs, while praising all republicans and Puritans indiscriminately. Hume indicates that he is seeking to counteract this view with the "moderate opinions" of his own *History,* which are more likely to approach "truth and certainty" (H 6.71.530–34).

Hume's recognition of the importance of the retrospective view that is adopted by the historian is given an especially vivid expression in his own approach to the composition of the *History of England.* After completing his account of recent English history in the Stuart volumes, he worked his way backward in stages through English history, by writing the Tudor volumes and finally the two medieval volumes. In this way, he was presumably able to consider each stage in the development of the English constitution in light of the following one. However, within each pair of volumes he generally adopts the usual order of narration, though with retrospective digressions as needed (cf. T 2.3.7.7 [SBN 430]).[20]

Hume presents his most extensive account of critical historical reasoning in "Of Miracles" and in his discussions of the poems of Ossian.

In "Of Miracles" Hume presents not only a critique of traditional religion and of modern theology, but also a discussion of the principles of historical method involved in the evaluation of testimony. Indeed, he expects to provide a definitive refutation of the accounts of "miracles and prodigies" in any historical writings, whether religious or secular (EHU 10.2 [SBN 110]).[21]

---

20. On Hume's view of the direction of historical narration, see Wertz, *Between Hume's Philosophy and History,* 57–58.

21. On Hume's view of historical method in "Of Miracles," see Stewart, "Hume's Historical View of Miracles," 171–200.

388 · David Hume: Reason in History

First, Hume summarizes his account of philosophical probable reasoning, or reasoning from evidence, as this is developed in the *Treatise*. He now advises us to proportion our belief to the evidence, as this is discovered by "diligent observation," whenever we judge the probability of an event (EHU 10.3 [SBN 110–11]). Among the various types of evidence, he next observes that "there is no species of reasoning more common, more useful, and even necessary to human life, than that which is derived from the testimony of men, and the reports of eye-witnesses and spectators." However, as in all types of causal reasoning, we accept testimony as evidence, not by discovering any *a priori* connection between testimony and reality, but because "we are accustomed to find a conformity between them." On the other hand, since human testimony is often opposed by conflicting evidence, it varies in its evidential force through the entire range of probable assurance, from the certainty of a proof through the different levels of probability. The evidence provided by testimony may in these cases be opposed from "contrary testimony; from the character or number of the witnesses; from the manner of their delivering their testimony; or from the union of all these circumstances" (EHU 10.5–8 [SBN 111–13]). The evidence given by testimony may also be challenged by our own judgment of the probability of the reported event, given our previous experience of related events, and our knowledge of the laws of nature arising from this experience.

In the first part of "Of Miracles," Hume considers the limiting case of human testimony to a surprising event: the case in which the alleged fact is apparently miraculous, and the independent evidence for the veracity of the testimony amounts to a proof. In such a case, however, he argues that we already have a complete proof, from the definition of a miracle, against the occurrence of a miraculous event. That is, since any miracle is by definition "a violation of the laws of nature," and since "a firm and unalterable experience has established these laws," it is impossible for us to regard any individual event as a miracle without subverting our reliance upon experience and our belief in the universality of the laws of nature. We accordingly already have "a uniform experience against every miraculous event, otherwise the event would not merit that appellation." Finally, as a "general maxim" for evaluating the testimony to a miracle, Hume concludes that "no testimony is sufficient to establish a miracle," unless "its falsehood would be more miraculous, than the fact, which it endeavours to establish." He therefore advises to balance the probability of error, even if the testimony seems to amount to a full proof, against the probable occurrence of the miracle, and since it seems that we are weighing "one miracle against the other," to "reject the greater miracle." This will always be the testimony, since an error in human testimony, unlike a miracle, does not violate the laws of nature (EHU 10.12–13; cf. 25–28 [SBN 114–16; cf. 122–25]). In other words, no matter how numerous the witnesses are, or how uniform and extensive their testimony might be, an error or deception in the report is always more likely than a miraculous occurrence.[22]

On the other hand, in Part 2 Hume attempts to show us "that we have been a great deal too liberal in our concession, and that there never was a miraculous event established on so full an evidence" (EHU 10.14 [SBN 116]). He then develops a series of empirical arguments by which we may call into question every miracle report in the annals of history. First, no miracle has ever been attested to by a sufficient number of witnesses, of such confirmed integrity, learning, and sense as to rule out any possibility of error and deceit. Second, human beings tend to accept the accounts of miracles merely because of the agreeable sensations of "*surprize* and *wonder*" stimulated by such reports, especially when these sentiments are reinforced by the "spirit of religion," which promotes credulity in both reporters and audiences (EHU 10.16–17 [SBN 117]). Third, miracle reports tend to arise initially in "ignorant and barbarous nations," and are inherited from their ancestors by civilized nations only because of the "inviolable sanction and authority, which always attend received opinions" (EHU 10.20 [SBN 119]). Fourth, every known instance of testimony to a miracle, even if it has never been shown to be fraudulent, is always opposed by an "infinite number of witnesses." This statement, especially with its manifest hyperbole, might seem to be considerably less compelling than the others as an empirical generalization. However, Hume indicates that the opposition he is describing here is not a conflict between the witnesses who saw an alleged event at a particular place and time, and witnesses who were there but did not. Instead, he is describing the opposition between systems of religious belief, since the use of a specific set of miracle stories by each tradition to confirm its legitimacy, and its rejection of the miracle stories of all other traditions, may be regarded as opposing testimony (EHU 10.24 [SBN 121–22]). Finally, he notes that we should be suspicious of any testimony that favors the inclination of a supposed witness, by elevating "his country, his family, or himself," especially if it is accompanied by religious ambitions or delusions (EHU 10.29 [SBN 125]).

Accordingly, in this part of his essay, Hume indicates not only that reported miracles are improbable but also that such testimony can be explained as a product of human beliefs, desires, and circumstances. We may therefore critically evaluate any instance of human testimony by considering whether it arises from a quality of human nature that tends to produce either true or false testimony, and by considering any independent evidence for the occurrence of the event.

In his writings on the Ossian poems, Hume applies the principles for evaluating human testimony to detecting a forgery. The so-called poems of

---

22. Several authors have questioned whether Hume is able, on this analysis, to allow for the justification of any belief in very surprising reports. For a discussion of this question, see Coady, *Testimony*, 179–98.

Ossian were written and published by James Macpherson in the early 1760s. Macpherson claimed that they were ancient poems by the Scottish bard Ossian, which had survived as an oral tradition among the Highlanders, and were also preserved in a newly discovered manuscript. As a Scottish man of letters, Hume at first welcomed the publication of these poems with enthusiasm, but soon, with others, began to doubt their authenticity. Indeed, he entered indirectly into what became a larger European debate over the poems through his friendship with Hugh Blair, a Presbyterian clergyman who had undertaken to defend Macpherson's supposed discovery.[23] In a letter of 1763, Hume advises Blair, not only to examine the manuscripts, but also to seek evidence that the poems were indeed current in the oral tradition of the Highlanders, as Macpherson had claimed. Hume then offers Blair a series of practical suggestions for pursuing his investigations:

> Your connexions among your brethren of the clergy, may here be of great use to you. You may easily learn the names of all ministers of that country, who understand the language of it. You may write to them, expressing the doubts that have arisen, and desiring them to send for such of the bards as remain, and make them rehearse their ancient poems. Let the clergymen have the translation in their hands, and let them write back to you, and inform you, that they heard such a one (naming him) living in such a place, rehearse the original of such a passage, from such a page to such a page of the English translation, which appeared exact and faithful. (L 1.400)

With this evidence, Blair would be able to publish a convincing defense of the poems as authentic survivals of an ancient Highland tradition. However, Hume advises Blair that "nothing less will so much as command the attention of the public" (L 1.400).

Hume's own later conclusions regarding the Macpherson poems are expressed in an essay entitled "Of the Poems of Ossian," which he apparently wrote around 1775 but never published, probably out of respect for Blair. In this essay, Hume presents a series of arguments against the authenticity of the Ossian poems, in which we find a number of implicit reflections concerning the principles of historical investigation. Several of Hume's criticisms are indeed concerned with Macpherson's methods, and also his reliability, as the supposed discoverer of these poems. For example, he notes that Macpherson has offered no specific information concerning his sources, and that the evidence of his

---

23. For an account of Hume's role in this controversy, see Mossner, *Life of David Hume*, 414–20; Sher, *Church and University*, 242–61; and Raynor, "Ossian and Hume," 147–63.

career and character give us sufficient reason to consider him capable of such a "ludicrous imposition on the public" (PO 390–91, 398). Hume also declares it to be unlikely that these supposedly ancient poems could have remained unknown until the present day, or that they could have been faithfully transmitted by an oral tradition for fifteen centuries among a people who were not only unlettered, but also poor, turbulent, and unsettled. Indeed, he notes that other Celtic peoples, whose circumstances were more favorable for preserving their ancient poetry, could not claim a comparable achievement (PO 391–92).

The rest of Hume's arguments are concerned with the internal evidence of the poems and their inconsistencies with other works of ancient Celtic or Germanic literature, or with the known facts of early Scottish history. First, the Ossian poems are remarkably accurate in their account of ancient Scottish history, even though history is usually distorted in an oral tradition. Next, the poems are inconsistent with the ancient poetic traditions of other Celtic peoples. Indeed, Hume argues that the style is regular and insipid compared to other ancient poems, and that the manners represented in the poems are closer to later ideals of chivalry than to the manners depicted in other ancient poems, especially in their delicacy and respect toward women. On the other hand, they completely lack any of the marvelous and supernatural events that usually appear in ancient literature. Hume regards these two anomalies as especially suspicious, since "manners are the only circumstances which a rude people cannot falsify; because they have no notion of any manners beside their own," while "it is easy for them to let loose their imagination, and violate the course of nature, in every other particular" (PO 392–94).[24] The Ossian poems are also devoid of any references to religion, which would be surprising if they were authentic, but can instead be easily explained as resulting from Macpherson's ignorance of the "Druidical religion." The "state of the arts" in ancient Scotland as described in the poems is also inconsistent with the historical record. For example, the poet refers anachronistically to stone houses, windows, navies, armies, windmills, water-mills, metallurgy, and even to harps, which Hume judged to be historically an Irish rather than a Scottish instrument (PO 394–96).

In response to the alleged endorsement of the poems by present Highlanders, Hume argues that it is easy to account for their evident readiness, when asked by outsiders about the Ossian poems, to claim these as an authentic tradition. Indeed, they may have been "sincere in the delusion," since they may have recognized some of the names, incidents, and sentiments mentioned by Macpherson in his poems, and were "willing to believe, and still more willing to persuade others, that the whole was genuine" (PO 400).

---

24. By contrast, Hume notes that Wilkie was able to depict in his *Epigoniad,* at least to some degree, the roughness and ferocity of the Homeric Greeks (LW 434).

In sum, Hume maintains, on the basis of his study of ancient history and poetry, that the internal evidence of the poems does not support their authenticity, and on the basis of his general study of human passions and motives, that they can be better explained as a modern forgery.[25]

Finally, in several of his writings Hume considers our motives for studying history. The most general reason for our interest in history, as indicated in the *Treatise*, is "curiosity, or the love of truth," which animates not only the researches of scholars but also the interest that many if not all human beings take in "the actions and circumstances of their neighbors." Indeed, we are especially likely to take an interest in the history of a nation after we have visited there and met some of its inhabitants (T 2.3.10.11–12 [SBN 453–54]). Hume also argues that the recognition of a great distance, including a distance in time, tends to enliven the passions, and produces a feeling of awe or reverence toward any objects that we regard as having come from that distance. This feeling of awe toward the past might also stimulate our interest in studying history (T 2.3.7.1–2.3.8.13 [SBN 427–38]; cf. H 5.45.18–19).[26] Hume also regards historical study as a corrective against partisan appeals to past events in order to justify current policies, and, more generally, against a complacent view of modern institutions. That is, he also regards historical inquiry as a basis for criticizing various aspects of contemporary political discourse (T 3.2.10.15–19 [SBN 562–67]; E CP.494, 497–98; H 2.23.524–25; H 4.App.3.354–56; H 6.71.530–34).[27]

Hume also considers the purpose and value of studying history, although in a lighter tone, in his essay "Of the Study of History." This is one of several essays that he came to regard as "frivolous" and out of place in his collection, although they were well received by the public, as he indicates in a 1752 letter to Adam Smith (L 1.168). Indeed, he withdrew it from the editions of his collected works after 1760. This essay, which is especially addressed to female readers, has a rather labored coyness, but also a serious content and intention, both in its consideration of the study of history, and in promoting reading as a means of self-cultivation for women. In this essay Hume recommends history to his female readers as an alternative both to novels and to abstruse philosophy, since the study of history tends to amuse the fancy, improve the understanding, and strengthen virtue.[28] First, the study of history amuses the fancy, not only

25. Hume's discussion of the Ossian poems has been described as one of the earliest discussions of the methods for studying folklore. See Grobman, "Collecting Balladry," 16–31, and Jones, *Hume's Sentiments*, 72–74.

26. See Livingston, *Hume's Philosophy of Common Life*, 120–49.

27. Hume's discussion of the reasons for studying history may be compared to Nietzsche's account of the "monumental," "antiquarian," and "critical" approaches to history, in "On the Uses and Disadvantages of History for Life," 67–77. For a further comparison of Hume and Nietzsche in their use of history, see Hoy, "Genealogical Method," 20–33.

28. For a provocative discussion of Hume's approach to issues of gender in his historical writings, see Temple, "Manly Composition," 263–82. See also Phillipson, *Hume*, 26–34, and Rendall, "Clio, Mars and Minerva," 134–51.

by offering as much intrigue and scandal as a novel, but also by transporting us "into the remotest ages of the world" where we may observe "human society, in its infancy," and trace the development of the arts and sciences, of government and civility, and the rise and fall of empires. The resulting spectacle is more magnificent, varied, and interesting than many of the objects of the senses or imagination. Next, history improves the understanding by extending "our experience to all past ages, and to the most distant nations; making them contribute as much to our improvement in wisdom, as if they had actually lain under our observation." More specifically, history introduces us to other domains of inquiry and provides us with material for most of the other sciences. As a result, someone who has studied history may be said "to have lived from the beginning of the world, and to have been making continual additions to his stock of knowledge in every century." The study of history also introduces us to a wider range of human affairs, and a wider variety of passions, motives, and characters, than we find in our own immediate circles, helping the reader to better understand herself and other human beings. Finally, the study of history tends to promote virtue. In looking for sources of moral inspiration, we find that poets tend to favor vice, at least implicitly, while philosophers tend to obscure morality through their speculations, and men of affairs tend to judge according to their interests. By contrast, historians are usually "true friends of virtue, and have always represented it in its proper colours." This is because historians are "sufficiently interested in the characters and events, to have a lively sentiment of blame or praise; and, at the same time, have no particular interest or concern to pervert their judgment" (E SH.565–68).[29]

THE *HISTORY OF ENGLAND*

Hume's main historical work, the *History of England, from the Invasion of Julius Caesar to The Revolution in 1688,* was also his most popular text for more than a century after its initial publication.[30] We might be tempted to attribute the subsequent decline in its reputation to the advances in historical scholarship during the nineteenth and twentieth centuries. However, many of the criticisms directed against Hume's historical writings between the late nineteenth and the middle of the twentieth century also reflect the renewed popularity of

29. For more on Hume's view of the moral perspective of the historian, see Siebert, *Moral Animus,* 17–61 and 69–169, and Wertz, *Between Hume's Philosophy and History,* 67–87.

30. The first two volumes, covering the seventeenth century, were published in 1754 and 1757, and titled *The History of Great Britain.* The four subsequent volumes, the consolidated edition of 1762, and all subsequent editions during his lifetime were published as *The History of England.* See Jessop, *Bibliography,* 28–30, and Ikeda, *David Hume,* 1–181.

the Whig interpretation of English history during this period. This Whig revival also coincided with the rising interest in the Hume's philosophy and its skeptical implications, and with several persistent misreadings and misunderstandings of his historical writings.

Since the middle of the twentieth century, Hume's methods and achievement as a historian have received a more favorable assessment. I have already considered Hume's approach to the development of the English constitution in the *History of England,* and its affinity with recent approaches to English political and constitutional history, in Chapter 9. In this section I examine his methods as a historian in the *History of England.* However, I also consider his larger project in that work. This project is a study of the progress of civilization in England, as a part of his general study of the nature and causes of cultural progress, and of the obstacles to this progress, which is further developed in his essays and letters.

We may begin by considering Hume's sources and his use of these sources in the *History of England.* Hume has often been criticized for his alleged laziness or carelessness as a historian. This criticism is based at least in part on contemporary anecdotal evidence: "Why, mon, David read a vast deal before he set about a piece of his book; but his usual seat was the sofa, and he often wrote with his legs up; and it would have been unco fashious to have moved across the room when any little doubt occurred."[31] Indeed, Hume himself remarks rather misleadingly in a letter of 1754 to the Abbé Le Blanc that he had followed the "concise manner of the antient Historians" in the first volume of the *History,* instead of the "prolix, tedious Style of some modern Compilers," and explains "I have inserted no original Papers, and enter'd into no Detail of minute, uninteresting Facts." However, he maintains that even without such details, the "philosophical Spirit" may find "ample Materials to work upon" (L 1.193).

However, while he did not seek out manuscript sources, Hume relied extensively upon published sources, such as memoirs and government documents. On the other hand, he did not immediately adopt the practice of referring to these sources systematically in his text. Indeed, in a letter to Horace Walpole in 1758 he acknowledges his negligence in failing to include these references in the initial Stuart volumes, since "such an exactness would have cost no trouble." While he had been following the style of ancient and Renaissance historians, he now recognizes the value of the modern practice of citation, which "having been once introduc'd, ought to be follow'd by every writer." He was "very careful to obviate this objection" by including citations in the succeeding volumes. Finally, as he indicates to Elliot in 1763, he took the opportunity, while preparing the first complete edition in 1762, to add "the Quotations &

31. Quoted in [Palgrave], "Hume and His Influence Upon History," 554.

Authorities for the Reigns of James I & Charles I." In so doing he had even "happily discover'd some more Mistakes" and corrected them (L 1.284–85; NL 69–70). The ease with which Hume was able to incorporate the missing citations into the new edition indicates that he had attended carefully to his sources from the beginning of the project.[32]

Other passages in Hume's letters also reflect his concern for the use of sources, though generally for published rather than manuscript sources. In 1759 he asked Millar, his London publisher, to send him several sources in medieval history that were not available in Edinburgh (L 1.321–24). Writing again to Millar in 1762, he responds to the rumor that he had not consulted the relevant documents for the Stuart volumes of the *History* by stating "there is not a Quotation that I did not see with mine own Eyes, except two or three at most, which I took from Tyrrel or Brady because I had not the Books refer'd to" (L 1.355). Hume also engages in debates with other historians over the interpretation of historical documents, such as those concerning the warrant for Lord Loudon's execution, in a 1755 letter to Millar (L 1.218), and the activities and character of Mary Queen of Scots in a 1760 letter to Alexander Dick (NL 58–64).[33] Finally, in the 1763 letter to Elliot he regrets his lapses into a Whig interpretation of the causes of the Civil War in the first edition of the Stuart volumes, in not considering adequately the justification for many of the apparently arbitrary actions by James I and Charles I. He also corrected these in the 1762 edition (NL 70). Hume's letters accordingly testify to his diligence in seeking the appropriate published sources, and in considering the issues involved in their interpretation.[34]

Several critics of Hume's approach to history have objected that he reduces historical agents to ideal types, instead of considering the actions and characters of human agents in the context of their time and place.[35] This criticism arises at least partly from the assumption that, by affirming the uniformity of human nature, he is justifying the explanation of all human actions on the basis

32. These source citations are included as footnotes in Todd's edition of the *History of England*. For a partial list of Hume's sources, see Norton and Popkin, *David Hume: Philosophical Historian*, 418–24. For further discussions of his sources and models, see Wexler, *David Hume and the History of England*, 97–107; Phillipson, *Hume*, 78–80; and Wootton, "David Hume, 'the historian,'" 282–85.

33. See also Hume, "The Eighteenth-Century Marian Controversy and an Unpublished Letter by David Hume," ed. Bongie, 236–52.

34. For a discussion of Hume's historical scholarship, see Mossner, "An Apology for David Hume," 682–86. Wootton also examines the influence of French philosophers and historians on Hume's approach to history: see "David Hume, 'the historian,'" 285–95.

35. See Black, *Art of History*, 86–87 and 94–103; Collingwood, *Idea of History*, 76–78 and 81–85; Berry, *Hume, Hegel and Human Nature*, 19–20 and 57–65; and Pompa, *Human Nature and Historical Knowledge*, 13–66. For criticisms of this view, see Forbes, *Hume's Philosophical Politics*, 102–21 and 260–307; Wertz, "Hume, History, and Human Nature," 481–96, and *Between Hume's Philosophy and History*, 19–34; and Livingston, *Hume's Philosophy of Common Life*, 214–25.

of eighteenth-century beliefs and principles of conduct, which I have already examined in Chapter 7. However, this criticism also overlooks the evidence of the *History* itself, where Hume applies his approach to the interpretation of human action to historical individuals, by considering their actions as consequences of their motives, characters, and circumstances. This is evident, not only in his account of various individual actions in the main narrative of the *History,* but also in his character sketches with which he concludes his account of the reigns of each of the major English monarchs. Hume's application of these principles in the *History of England* may be illustrated by considering his depiction of three figures, taken from the three main divisions of his work: Joan of Arc, Queen Elizabeth, and Charles I.

Hume's portrayal of Joan of Arc is an especially compelling example, since he rejects the religiously inspired legendary aspects of her life, on the grounds that he had already adduced in "Of Miracles." However, he also acknowledges the remarkable character of her career, even apart from the legend. He then attempts to explain her actions as arising from her motives, character, and historical circumstances, beginning with her background and early life: "In the village of Domremi near Vaucouleurs, on the borders of Lorraine, there lived a country girl of twenty-seven years of age, called Joan d'Arc, who was servant in a small inn, and who in that station had been accustomed to tend the horses of the guests, to ride them without a saddle to the watering-place, and to perform other offices, which, in well-frequented inns, commonly fall to the share of the men servants" (H 2.20.397). During these years she had led "an irreproachable life, and had not hitherto been remarked for any singularity." However, Hume then considers the influence on popular opinion of the unusual political situation then prevailing in France:

> It is easy to imagine, that the present situation of France was an interesting object even to persons of the lowest rank, and would become the frequent subject of conversation: A young prince, expelled his throne by the sedition of native subjects, and by the arms of strangers, could not fail to move the compassion of all his people, whose hearts were uncorrupted by faction; and the peculiar character of Charles, so strongly inclined to friendship and the tender passions, naturally rendered him the hero of that sex, whose generous minds know no bounds in their affections. (H 2.20.397)

The situation of Charles VII, and the siege of Orleans, had caught the imagination of the whole people; and Joan was "inflamed by the general sentiment," and "seized with a wild desire of bringing relief to her sovereign in his present distresses." This desire was combined in her imagination with images from her religious education: "Her unexperienced mind, working day and night on this favourite object, mistook the impulses of passion for heavenly inspirations; and she fancied, that she saw visions, and heard voices, exhorting her to re-establish the throne of France, and to expel the foreign invaders" (H 2.20.397–98). Her "uncommon intrepidity of temper" made her overlook all dangers, and "thinking herself destined by Heaven to this office, she threw aside all that bashfulness and timidity" which we would expect to find in one of "her sex, her years, and her low station," leaving her home to take up arms in the service of the king (H 2.20.398).

In describing her subsequent career, Hume offers the methodological observation that it is "the business of history to distinguish between the *miraculous* and the *marvellous,*" and to reject any appeals to the miraculous in "merely profane and human" narratives, while assenting to what is marvelous only "when obliged by unquestionable testimony, as in the present case." However, even in such a case the historian should still accept "as little of it as is consistent with the known facts and circumstances" (H 2.20.398). He accordingly dismisses many aspects of the reported career of Joan of Arc as legendary, on the grounds of extreme improbability, conflicting evidence, and their more probable explanation as fabrications for various human purposes. That is, many stories were "spread abroad, in order to captivate the vulgar" and "inflame the fond fancy of the people with prepossessions in her favor" (H 2.20.399). He considers it to be highly probable that Joan was active in combat, but not that she took over the command by "directing the troops, conducting the military operations, and swaying the deliberations in all councils of war." These are likely to have been stories circulated by the French court, since it is improbable that she could have, "on a sudden, become expert in a profession, which requires more genius and capacity, than any other active scene of life." Indeed, it is praise enough of her talent that she could "distinguish the persons on whose judgment she might rely," adopt their hints and suggestions, convey them as her own, and sometimes curb her "visionary and enthusiastic spirit" in order to act with "prudence and discretion" (H 2.20.403–4). The story of Joan is perhaps the most remarkable one within the scope of the *History of England,* even when stripped of its miraculous overlay. However, Hume maintains that her actions can be explained as arising from universal passions, in the context of her distinctive background, character, and historical circumstances (cf. EHU 8.8 [SBN 84]).[36]

Hume also describes Queen Elizabeth's political talent as a product of her character and circumstances. Both she and the English public endured great suffering under her Catholic half-sister, Mary Tudor, often called "Bloody Mary,"

36. Black quotes selectively from Hume's account of Joan of Arc to support his claim that Hume presents her as an ideal type; see his *Art of History,* 100–101. The account presented here is also suggested by Sabine: see "Hume's Contribution," 33n1.

who had prolonged the religious persecutions of the English Reformation. Her new subjects when she became queen were therefore eager to overlook their earlier theological divisions and "expressed a general and unfeigned joy that the scepter had passed into the hand of Elizabeth" (H 4.38.3). Her popularity was increased by public compassion for the treatment she had suffered under her sister, which had already made her "to an uncommon degree, the favourite of the nation." At the same time, she had developed "great prudence in her conduct" during the reign of Mary; and with a "prudence and magnanimity truly laudable," she readily forgot upon her accession all the offenses that had been committed against her, and "received with affability even those who had acted with the greatest malevolence against her" (H 4.38.3–4). She also followed a prudent course in her religious policy. Although her own education and interest led her to favor the reforming movement, "she resolved to proceed by gradual and secure steps, and not to imitate the example of Mary, in encouraging the bigots of her party to make immediately a violent invasion on the established religion" (H 4.38.7). Thus, if we make allowances for the "prevailing prejudices of the times," her religious policy "could scarcely be accused of severity or imprudence," since she undertook "no inquisition into men's bosoms" and did not impose an oath of supremacy on anyone except those in government service (H 4.40.176–77). She even accepted some Calvinist reforms in the English church, although she herself preferred a Catholic style of public worship. The prudence and diplomacy arising from her character and experience were also reflected in the "innocent artifices" by which she gained the affection of her subjects: "Open in her address, gracious and affable in all public appearances, she rejoiced in the concourse of her subjects, entered into all their pleasures and amusements, and without departing from her dignity, which she knew well how to preserve, she acquired a popularity beyond what any of her predecessors or successors ever could attain" (H 4.38.8–9). Consequently her authority, "though corroborated by the strictest bands of law and religion, appeared to be derived entirely from the choice and inclination of the people" (H 4.38.9). Hume indeed suggests that Elizabeth's popular success led later politicians and historians to develop a mistaken view of her motives and character:

> The party among us, who have distinguished themselves by their adhering to liberty and a popular government, have long indulged their prejudices against the succeeding race of princes, by bestowing unbounded panegyrics on the virtue and wisdom of Elizabeth. They have even been so extremely ignorant of the transactions of this reign, as to extol her for a quality, which, of all others, she was the least possessed of; a tender regard for the constitution, and a concern for the liberties and privileges of her people. (H 4.App.3.354)

On the contrary, she supported the principles of royal prerogative and "un-limited authority" that she had inherited from her predecessors, while her subjects "entirely acquiesced in her arbitrary administration" because of her popular appeal and her talent for government (H 4.App.3.354; H 4.44.352). In other words, her powers were theoretically unlimited, but were exercised with such moderation and restraint as to be relatively inoffensive to the population (cf. H 5.45.19).

Hume's emphasis upon the relation between circumstances, character, and action is also reflected in his account of Charles I. Like his predecessors, Charles I believed that the English political tradition supported the principle of abso-lute monarchy: "Those lofty ideas of monarchical power, which were very com-monly adopted during that age, and to which the ambiguous nature of the English constitution gave so plausible an appearance, were firmly rivetted in Charles; and however moderate his temper, the natural and unavoidable pre-possessions of self-love, joined to the late uniform precedents in favour of prerog-ative, had made him regard his political tenets as certain and uncontroverted" (H V.50.161). However, this theory was "a very different idea of the constitution, from that which *began*, in general, to prevail among his subjects" (H 5.52.236).

In describing the conflict between Charles I and Parliament, leading to the Civil War and to the execution of the king, Hume maintains that Charles I acted honestly and honorably, in the justifiable belief that the constitutional tradition supported a wide claim of royal prerogative. However, his opponents regarded his actions as an unwarranted and tyrannical attack on the rights of Parliament, and they also justified their view by appealing to the English polit-ical tradition. Hume concludes that Charles I "deserves the epithet of a good, rather than of a great man," and that he was "more fitted to rule in a regular established government, than either to give way to the encroachments of a pop-ular assembly, or finally to subdue their pretensions."

> Had he been born an absolute prince, his humanity and good sense had rendered his reign happy and his memory precious: Had the lim-itations on prerogative been, in his time, quite fixed and certain, his integrity had made him regard, as sacred, the boundaries of the con-stitution. Unhappily, his fate threw him into a period, when the prece-dents of many former reigns favoured strongly of arbitrary power, and the genius of the people ran violently towards liberty. And if his political prudence was not sufficient to extricate him from so perilous a situation, he may be excused; since, even after the event, when it is commonly easy to correct all errors, one is at a loss to determine what conduct, in his circumstances, could have maintained the authority of the crown, and preserved the peace of the nation. (H 5.59.542–43)

In contrast to the prevailing Whig view of his own day, Hume maintains that Charles I should be remembered with honor for his integrity, even though, with the knowledge of later developments, his actions can be considered as a negative contribution to a course of events through which a new and better system of government would emerge. From this perspective Charles I may be regarded a "misguided" prince who overlooked the conflicting precedents within the English constitutional tradition and defied the new spirit of liberty emerging among the people (E PGB.68).[37]

In these examples from the *History,* which could easily be multiplied, Hume is seeking to account for the actions of historical individuals as effects of their passions and beliefs, characters, and circumstances. In so doing he is applying the principle, regarded by Sabine as a discovery of the nineteenth century, that history is "peopled by actual human beings, with human desires and purposes," and that the historian's task includes re-creating the men and women of the past, entering into their feelings and desires, and explaining their actions to posterity.[38]

In addition to his central political narrative, Hume also refers in his *History of England* to developments belonging to what we would now identify as social, economic, and cultural history. Although these themes are apparent in his main narrative, Hume also presents a continuous and relatively systematic account of these developments in a series of supplemental essays, which he variously calls "Appendices" and "miscellaneous transactions," and sometimes includes without any separate designation, after his account of the major periods and reigns in English history.

Hume's treatment of social and cultural history has been regarded, both in own his life and subsequently, as an imitation of Voltaire's historical writings, especially the *Siècle de Louis XIV* of 1751, which is often considered the first work in the "history of manners."[39] In a 1755 letter to Le Blanc, Hume professes to be flattered by the comparison, but maintains that his own history was "plan'd, & in a great measure compos'd" before Voltaire's work was published (L 1.226). Indeed, Hume's interest in social and cultural history is already apparent in his early composition, "On Chivalry and Modern Honour" (CMH 56–60), and in his essays from the 1740s and 1750s, especially "Of Civil Liberty" (E CL.87–96), "Of the Rise and Progress of the Arts and Sciences" (E RP.111–37), and "Of Refinement in the Arts" (E RA.268–80).

In the appendix to the reign of James I, which was the first appendix to be

37. A similar discussion of Hume's account of Charles I is presented in Farr, "Humean Explanations," 69–73.

38. Sabine, "Hume's Contribution," 34.

39. For discussions of this comparison between Hume and Voltaire, see Sabine, "Hume's Contribution," 37–38; Mossner, "An Apology for David Hume," 676–79; Stockton, "David Hume Among the Historiographers," 14–16; and Wertz, *Between Hume's Philosophy and History,* 96 and 111.

written, Hume introduces his readers to the study of social, cultural, economic, and intellectual history and calls attention to their importance for the general study of history: "It may not be improper, at this period, to make a pause; and to take a survey of the state of the kingdom, with regard to government, manners, finances, arms, trade, learning. Where a just notion is not formed of these particulars, history can be little instructive, and often will not be intelligible" (H 5.App.4.124). In the second Stuart volume he adds that "the chief use of history is, that it affords materials for disquisitions of this nature; and it seems the duty of an historian to point out the proper inferences and conclusions" (H 6.62.140). Finally, at the end of the second medieval volume he observes that "the rise, progress, perfection, and decline of art and science, are curious objects of contemplation," and are indeed "intimately connected with a narration of civil transactions," so that "the events of no particular period can be fully accounted for, but by considering the degrees of advancement, which men have reached in those particulars" (H 2.23.519).

The appendices include a history of various general developments in government, law, economics, and military affairs in England, and also in English literature, science, and philosophy, sometimes within the larger European context. Hume also considers the "manners" of the given age, mainly by describing interesting features of the social and cultural life of the period.

In the appendix titled "Anglo-Saxon Government and Manners," which is the first in the complete version of the *History of England,* Hume examines the character and development of the various political and legal institutions of the Anglo-Saxon Germanic kingdoms in England, and also considers the social and economic organization of the Anglo-Saxon kingdoms. He even presents a brief discussion of Anglo-Saxon "manners" or culture, where he observes that they were generally "a rude, uncultivated people, ignorant of letters, unskilled in the mechanical arts, untamed to submission under law and government," and "addicted to intemperance, riot and disorder." Their best talent was their military courage, which was, however, "not supported by discipline or conduct" (H 1.App.I.185).

In considering the early Anglo-Norman period, he examines the further development of English government and society under the Norman feudal system and living conditions in the city of London, along with the development of heraldry, Troubadour poetry, and (recalling his earlier essay) chivalry, including its later influence on the "writings, conversation, and behaviour of men," and its modern cultural legacy (H 1.11.487; cf. 1.9.371–76; H 1.10.404–6; H 1.11.455–88; CMH 56–60). At the end of the second medieval volume, which concludes with the death of Richard III in 1485, he considers learning and the arts during the Middle Ages, especially in relation to the Church and to the development of civil society (H 2.23.518–25).

Turning to the early Tudor period, Hume describes the development of printing, along with the Italian Renaissance, the origins of the Reformation, the study of Greek at Oxford, and the writings of Thomas More (H 3.26.81–82; H 3.33.331–32). In his appendix to the reign of Elizabeth he considers the expansion of industry and commerce in England, and its tendency to promote refinement and hospitality among the nobility, along with an increasing prosperity among the "middle rank of men." He also considers the rising sense of liberty, the decline of serfdom, the first law for poor relief, and developments in learning and literature (H 4.App.3.354–86).

Hume describes a variety of social developments under James I, including the increasing attraction of city life, the decline of small landowners, and the rise of the gentry; along with such "manners" or customs as dueling, and new opportunities for social interaction between men and women. He also presents a history of European literature, including a survey of English authors from Shakespeare to Donne, and examines the origins of natural science and "true philosophy" with Bacon and Galileo (H 5.App.4.124–55). Among the "manners and arts" during the Civil War and the Puritan Commonwealth he considers the conduct of the royalist and Puritan parties, the Quaker movement, the Puritan "blue laws," and the effects of the Civil War and Puritanism on learning and literature (H 6.62.141–54). Finally, in discussing the "manners, arts and sciences" of England from 1660 to 1688, he describes the "licentiousness and debauchery" of the Restoration court, the new "spirit of irreligion" that emerged as a reaction to the hypocrisy and fanaticism of the Puritan era, and the advancing culture of civility and politeness inspired by the royal court. He also traces the establishment of the Royal Society, along with various developments in the natural sciences, culminating in the work of Isaac Newton. He concludes the *History of England* with a description of literature and the arts during the Restoration (H 6.71.530–45).[40]

As we have seen, the central theme of Hume's political narrative in the *History of England* is the development of the English constitution, from the institutions of Anglo-Saxon government to the constitutional settlement of 1689. However, this political narrative is itself subordinate to his larger interest in the rise of modern European civilization, through the interrelated series of political, social, economic, and cultural developments traced in the appendices.[41] He also pursues this theme in his essays, in which he examines the

40. On Hume's contribution to social and cultural history, see Mossner, "An Apology for David Hume," 674–80, and Stockton, "David Hume Among the Historiographers," 17. Wexler discounts the value of these appendices, and regards this material as only incidental to his history of the English constitution: see *David Hume and the History of England*, xi.

41. For a discussion of Hume's history of civilization, see Danford, *Problem of Reason*, 109–64. See also Mossner, "An Apology for David Hume," 657–90; Forbes, *Hume's Philosophical Politics*, 296–307; Livingston, *Hume's Philosophy of Common Life*, 234–46, and *Philosophical Melancholy and Delirium*, 173–216; Phillipson,

interrelations between the development of civil liberty and constitutional government, the rise of commerce and industry, the expansion of prosperity and consumer markets, the emergence of a stable international order, the growth of a middle class, the advancement of learning, the refinement of taste, and improvements in civility, sociability, and humanity since the end of the middle ages.

In three essays, "Of Civil Liberty," "Of the Rise and Progress of the Arts and Sciences," and "Of Refinement in the Arts," Hume draws upon ancient and modern sources, and applies the principles of "moral" or social-scientific explanation, to examine the relation between civil liberty, industry, commerce, the arts and sciences, and the virtues of sociability, civility, and humanity. Here he argues that all of these tend to promote and reinforce one another, so that a commercially productive and prosperous age will tend to enjoy refined arts, advanced science and technology, civic liberty, and political, social, and domestic virtues. However, perhaps because of different projects in these three essays, or because of conflicting trends in the historical evidence, Hume does not argue consistently that any of these is the cause of any other.[42]

In "Of Civil Liberty" and "Of the Rise and Progress of the Arts and Sciences" Hume considers the influence of the various types of government on developments in the arts and sciences, such as "eloquence" or a graceful prose style, the fine arts, scholarship, the natural sciences, and skilled craftsmanship. He distinguishes four types of government: a "despotic" or arbitrary monarchy, a modern "civilized" monarchy such as the absolute monarchy of France, a "free" or republican government, and the "mixed" government or limited monarchy of Britain.[43] Of these, a government that has instituted the principles of "civil liberty," through a system of participatory government and universal law, as opposed to the arbitrary power of any individual, tends to promote the development of the arts and sciences. That is, a participatory government encourages ambition and emulation, while the rule of law provides the security required for the pursuit of knowledge. The arts and sciences thus tend to arise in a nation that is governed by the rule of law, rather than under a despotic government. However, based on the historical evidence, Hume argues that the arts and sciences

Hume, 17–34, 137–41; Siebert, *Moral Animus*, 148–69; and Kolin, *Ethical Foundations*, 71–120; as well as the essays included in Capaldi and Livingstone, *Liberty in Hume's History of England*.

42. Cohen argues that Hume's account of the progress of civilization includes a theory of moral progress. However, unlike many of his contemporaries, Hume regarded moral progress, or the expansion of our sympathy and the improvement of our ability to judge the agreeable or useful tendencies of qualities, as a product of other advances in social and cultural life, rather than as the source of this progress. See Cohen, "Notion of Moral Progress," 109–27.

43. Hume's account of the British constitutional monarchy as a "mixed" government that combines elements of both the republican and monarchical systems is developed at greater length in his essays. See especially "Of the Liberty of the Press" (E LP.9–13), "Of the Independency of Parliament" (E IP.42–46), and "Whether the British Government inclines more to Absolute Monarchy, or to a Republic" (E BG.47–53).

may then be transplanted and flourish under other types of government, even a tyranny. Next, he compares the influence of the two types of "civilized" governments, or governments that are subject to the rule of law: a republic and a constitutional monarchy. Of these, he finds that a republic favors the sciences, which are recognized as useful by society as a whole, whereas a civilized monarchy encourages the development of civility and the fine arts, which are agreeable to the court and aristocracy (E CL.89–93; E RP.115–19, 124–27). For similar reasons, commerce tends to prosper under a free government, but may also flourish under a civilized monarchy if it enforces laws to secure property and regulate the conditions of trade. However, commerce is less honored under a monarchy than hereditary social rank, and tends to receive less attention as a focus of energy and ambition (E CL.93–94).

In "Of Refinement in the Arts" Hume reverses the causal order of this influence. First, he argues that industry and technology tend to promote learning and the fine arts, and that industry is reciprocally promoted by "the knowledge inseparable from ages of art and refinement." Next, he finds that "the more these refined arts advance, the more sociable men become." Accordingly, an increase in "knowledge and the liberal arts" may be expressed in the development of new social institutions, and by improvements in civility, delicacy, sociability, and humanity. Finally, these improvements in commerce, industry, the arts, the sciences, and civility tends to improve the quality of government, and even to promote the development of a free government.[44] In other words, he argues that "laws, order, police, discipline" cannot be developed "to any degree of perfection, before human reason has refined itself by exercise," for example by applying itself to "commerce and manufacture" (E RA.271–74, 277).[45]

Hume rejects the view of other modern authors, such as Rousseau, that "luxury," or the cultivation of the arts, acquisition of material goods, and pursuit of pleasure, tends to undermine both the virtue and vitality of a culture. Instead, he maintains that a refined enjoyment of material goods is blamable only if pursued at the expense of some virtue, such as a prudent regard for our future welfare, a proper care for our family and friends, and an appropriate generosity toward the poor. Indeed, restrictions on the manufacture and trade of luxury items tend to produce sloth and idleness, which undermine the well-being of the individual and society, while the production and exchange of material goods benefits the entire population, and also the state as an institution (E RA.269, 275–76, 279–280; cf. E Co.253–67). In "Of the Middle Station of Life" he argues that the middle class is the most favorably situated for cultivating

44. On Hume's view of the influence of commerce in promoting various social changes that contribute to the advance of civilization, see Manzer, "The Promise of Peace?" 369–82.

45. For a discussion of Hume's ambivalence concerning the order of social, economic, political, and cultural causes in the development of civilization, see Wootton, "David Hume, 'the historian,'" 292–93.

virtue, wisdom, sociability, and natural talent. He therefore maintains that a large middle class tends to promote the progress of civilization (E MS.545–51).[46]

In Hume's view, the good life for human beings thus includes physical security, material prosperity, interesting and satisfying activity, opportunities to pursue knowledge and enjoy the arts, and the sociable pleasures of civility, friendship, and domesticity. A good society is one in which these are available to the whole population: including both men and women, and members of the working classes as well as the gentry and aristocracy, though with differences relative to their different stations in life. Finally, the best political order is one in which the possibility for achieving these is granted to the entire population through equitable laws under a stable and effective government. In his view, these goals were being gradually secured in Britain and in Europe through what we call "progress," or the advance of civilization (E OG.39–40; E BG.51; E RP.111–37).[47]

In the first volume of the *History of England,* Hume contrasts the barbaric cultures of Celtic and Anglo-Saxon England to these modern developments:

> The adventures of barbarous nations, even if they were recorded, could afford little or no entertainment to men born in a more cultivated age. The convulsions of a civilized state usually compose the most instructive and most interesting part of its history; but the sudden, violent, and unprepared revolutions, incident to Barbarians, are so much guided by caprice, and terminate so often in cruelty that they disgust us by the uniformity of their appearance; and it is rather fortunate for letters that they are buried in silence and oblivion. (H 1.1.4–5)

This early medieval period coincided with the decline of the Roman Empire and the legacy of classical antiquity in Europe. Among the few promising cultural achievements attributed by Hume to the Middle Ages are the monastic preservation of ancient texts and the recovery of Justinian's system of Roman law, the *Pandects,* around 1130, which initiated an improvement of law and government throughout Europe, thereby making possible the eventual revival of the other arts and sciences (H 2.23.518, 520–22). After tracing the history of England through a series of "many barbarous ages," he notes at the end of the second medieval volume that by 1485 we have finally "reached the dawn of civility and sciences," with the prospect "both of greater certainty in our

46. For a discussion of Hume's view of the "middle Station of Life," see Forbes, *Hume's Philosophical Politics,* 176–80 and 296–97.

47. Here I am attributing to Hume a relatively optimistic view of human nature, and of progress, although he does not regard a constant progress as guaranteed by human nature. For a more pessimistic reading of Hume's view, see Popkin, "Condorcet and Hume and Turgot," 84–89.

historical narrations, and of being able to present to the reader a spectacle more worthy of his attention" (H 2.23.518).

Next, during the fifteenth century Hume observes that "a general revolution was made in human affairs throughout this part of the world," with improvements in "commerce, arts, science, government, police, and cultivation." He especially calls attention to the effect of the discovery of the Americas in expanding commerce and prosperity throughout Europe, and to the effects of this expanded trade in promoting the development of a middle class and undermining the ancient European nobility. The fifteenth century therefore marks the beginning of modern civilization, which is the most useful and agreeable era for historical study (H 3.26.81–82). On the other hand, the Tudor period from Henry VII to Mary saw a number of impediments to progress, such as a series of ineffective or counterproductive government attempts to regulate the conditions of labor and commerce, the lagging of English manufactures behind those of other European nations, and a series of religious conflicts (H 3.26.74–82; H 3.33.323–32; H 3.37.462–64). Elizabeth presided over a number of more enduring achievements, such as the expansion of English travel and commerce, the spread of learning, and improvements in the mechanical and liberal arts (H 5.45.18). Hume specifically mentions the appearance during this time of new luxuries, such as coaches, pocket watches, and silk stockings (H 4.App.3.354–86). Finally, the emergence of a more "cultivated understanding" among "men of birth and education" by the seventeenth century, including a new interest in Greek and Roman civilization and the history of English government, promoted a "universal fermentation" and an "insensible revolution" in the "minds of men." This led to a new interest in the participatory institutions of government, which was eventually expressed in the assertion of parliamentary privileges against the Crown, leading to the Civil War and to the new constitutional settlement (H 5.45.18–19).

Hume's account of the rise and progress of civilization in England and Europe is not, however, presented as a theory of the continual progress of civilization. On the contrary, he is especially concerned to direct our attention toward any developments in history that have tended to impede, threaten, or reverse the progress of civilization. In "On Chivalry and Modern Honour," and in his later writings, he traces the decline of the Roman Empire to the disorders produced by its system of government and its military structure, along with its extensive conquests (CMH 56–60; E CL.89–90; E RA.275–76; H 1.1.11–13; H 2.23.518–19). In describing the Civil War and the Puritan Interregnum, he considers the destructive effects of factions and fanaticism on manners, sociability, learning, and the arts in England (H 6.62.140–54). He also criticizes the manners of the Restoration court for their licentiousness, frivolity, and detrimental impact on literature and the arts (H 6.71.530–45).

Hume's interest in the developments that tend to threaten the achievements and advance of civilization also appears in his reflections in his essays and letters concerning recent history and current affairs in Europe and England. Indeed, many of Hume's writings may be regarded as attempts to oppose what he regarded as contemporary threats to the precarious achievements of modern civilization. In the *Political Discourses* of 1752 he describes Great Britain, since the constitutional settlement of 1689, as enjoying an unprecedented flourishing of liberty, peace, internal order, agriculture, industry, trade, culture, philosophy, political tranquillity, and religious moderation. Immediately after this, however, he describes the possible sources of civic disorder and cultural decline in Britain, especially the Stuart loyalist movement and the national debt (E PS.508–9). As we have seen, many of his economic essays are concerned with recommending policies to the British government to promote national prosperity, while many of his political essays are attempts to moderate the factionalism of British politics. Finally, in his letters after 1760 he frequently expresses his fear, as in a letter of 1766 to Walpole, that the English public, which still dominated the population of Great Britain, was falling into "barbarism, ignorance, and superstition." He saw this especially in the popular political movements surrounding Pitt and Wilkes, and the demagogic and chauvinistic tendencies in English public opinion (L 2.111). He indeed refers to these developments in a 1768 letter to Turgot, as evidence against any theory of continual progress: "I know you are one of those, who entertain the agreeable and laudable, if not too sanguine hope, that human Society is capable of perpetual Progress towards Perfection, that the Encrease of Knowledge will still prove favourable to good Government, and that since the Discovery of Printing we need no longer Dread the usual Returns of Barbarism and Ignorance. Pray, do not the late Events in this Country appear a little contrary to your System?" (L 2.180). Hume includes the Wilkes and Liberty movement among these "late Events," and also refers to foreign wars as a continuing source of evil in the international order (L 2.180–81).

Accordingly, in writing the last volume of his *History of England*, Hume encourages his readers to study history so that "we may thence learn to cherish with the greater anxiety that science and civility, which has so close a connexion with virtue and humanity, and which, as it is a sovereign antidote against superstition, is also the most effectual remedy against vice and disorders of every kind" (H 2.23.518–19; cf. 525).

As seen in his letter to Turgot, Hume does not defend a theory of continuous historical progress, or indeed any other speculative theory of history, such as a theory of historical cycles or perpetual decline.[48] He clearly considers the

---

48. On Hume's critique of "prophetic" and "providential" approaches to history, both religious and secular, see Popkin, "Philosophical Versus Prophetic Historian," 83–95, and Livingston, *Hume's Philosophy of*

civilization of modern England and Europe to be an advance over earlier civilizations, arising from the general dispositions in human nature toward activity, enterprise, and sociability (E RA.270–72; E Co.260–67). However, he also indicates that the progress of civilization may be subverted by other characteristics of human beings, including insecurity, idleness, discouragement, shortsightedness, insularity, selfishness, factionalism, and stupidity, and indeed even by accident. That is, the progress of civilization can be reversed at any time by individual traits and actions, which may also arise collectively from unfavorable social, political, economic, and cultural circumstances (E CL.94–96: DNR 6.172–74).[49] In Hume's view, the task of the practical moralist is to promote the cultivation of those character traits in individuals which will enable them to contribute to the improvement of government, commerce, industry, learning, the arts, the sciences, benevolence, and sociability, or in other words, to the general advance of civilization.

The most serious deficiency in Hume's writings on history and culture, to readers of our own day, is his apparent indifference to the actions and characters of human beings in cultures and historical periods remote from modern Europe. As is indicated by the preceding discussion, Hume reserves his admiration for those periods in history which have attained what he regards as a high level of achievement in civility, learning, and the arts—classical antiquity, Europe during the Renaissance, and modern Britain. He is less interested in, and is even contemptuous toward, other nations both in history and in the contemporary world—including the ancient Hebrews, the peoples of early medieval Europe, and the native cultures of Africa and the Americas. And, of course, he is critical of religious superstition and fanaticism in every era and culture. On the other hand, several recent studies have pointed out that Hume's failures in sympathy and understanding are also failures to apply consistently his own recommended principles for the interpretation of human action. As we have seen in Chapter 7, Hume argues in his philosophical writings that even the strangest and most surprising human actions can be understood as products of the beliefs and desires of a given agent, as these are influenced by his or her character and circumstances, including his or her cultural setting (T 2.3.1.3–18 [SBN 399–407]; EHU 8.6–35 [SBN 83–103]; EPM D.1–57 [SBN 324–43]). However, Hume apparently fails to apply these principles to actions he finds especially remote or puzzling. For example, Livingston has indicated that Hume departs from his

---

Common Life, 285–305. On the exchange between Hume and Turgot, and their contrasting views on progress, see Popkin, "Condorcet and Hume and Turgot," 76–89.

49. Hume's view of the fragility of civilization is emphasized by Livingston, in *Hume's Philosophy of Common Life* and *Philosophical Melancholy and Delirium,* 217–313. See also Phillipson, *Hume,* 17; Danford, *Problem of Reason,* 135; Popkin, "Condorcet and Hume and Turgot," 76–89; and Haakonssen, "Introduction," xvii–xxv.

principles in regarding the barbarian inhabitants of Britain as prompted by "caprice" rather than by comprehensible motives (H 1.1.3).[50] Similarly, Herdt has shown that Hume tends to reduce the religious motives of monotheistic believers to purely nonreligious and self-serving passions, without attempting to achieve a sympathetic understanding of any autonomous, or generous, religious motives.[51]

The most stark and notorious example of Hume's failure in sympathetic understanding is his discussion of the different races in a footnote to his essay "Of National Characters":

> I am apt to suspect the negroes, and in general all the other species of men (for there are four or five different kinds) to be naturally inferior to the whites. There never was a civilized nation of any other complexion than white, nor even any individual eminent either in action or speculation.... Such a uniform and constant difference could not happen, in so many countries and ages, if nature had not made an original distinction betwixt these breeds of men. Not to mention our colonies, there are NEGROE slaves dispersed all over EUROPE, of which none ever discovered any symptoms of ingenuity; tho' low people, without education, will start up amongst us, and distinguish themselves in every profession. (E Var.629–30; cf. NC.208n10)[52]

In this footnote Hume is attributing the supposed differences between the races in their abilities and achievements, insofar as he has inferred such differences from reports or observation, to an "original" or biological difference that is given with their physiological differences. In doing so, however, he makes no serious effort to consider any cultures or civilizations outside Europe. He also overlooks the effects of social dislocation, racism, and slavery on the Africans who were transported to Europe or America, although he describes the debilitating effects of poverty and slavery on human beings in other contexts. Indeed, he denounces slavery, including both ancient slavery and the modern enslavement of Africans in the New World, as an institution that allows individuals and groups to "trample upon human nature" (E PA.383; cf. E NC.198). In other words, Hume does not present his account of the supposed differences between

50. See Livingston, *Hume's Philosophy of Common Life,* 235–46.

51. See Herdt, *Religion and Faction,* 213–18. A similar criticism of Hume's treatment of religious faith in history, and a detailed critique of his depictions of Alfred the Great and Charles I in this regard, is presented by Palgrave in "Hume and His Influence Upon History," 576–90.

52. "Of National Characters" was first published in 1748. The footnote on race, in the version cited here, was added to it in the 1753–54 edition of Hume's collected essays. Hume revised this footnote for what was to be the posthumous 1777 edition: the 1777 version presents the discussion more exclusively as a contrast between the European and African races.

the races as a justification for slavery, although his essay was used by others for this purpose.[53]

Richard Popkin has called attention to a striking criticism of Hume's discussion of race by James Beattie, the Presbyterian clergyman who was among the most prominent contemporary critics of Hume's philosophy. Beattie's criticism is presented in his *Essay on the Nature and Immutability of Truth,* first published in 1770, in which he offers a general challenge to the skeptical tendencies in Hume's philosophy. Hume did not consider Beattie's interpretation of and challenge to his philosophy to be worthy of much attention, as he indicates to Strahan in 1775 (L 2.301). This dismissal of Beattie was reinforced by Kant, in his famous response to Hume's Scottish critics in the *Prolegomena.*[54]

However, in the *Essay on Truth* Beattie also offers a perceptive and compelling series of answers to Hume's treatment of racial and cultural differences. First, he argues that the European arts and sciences are products of a long and partly accidental process of historical development, not of any special talents in the European race. Second, most Europeans are not sufficiently acquainted with any individual Africans, or with African history, to reach any general judgments concerning their abilities and achievements. Third, the people of Peru and Mexico developed impressive civilizations, and the native peoples of Africa and America have "many ingenious manufactures and arts among them." In addition, Beattie notes that many of the African slaves in Europe have shown "symptoms of ingenuity, notwithstanding their unhappy circumstances," and he observes that racism, slavery, and a lack of education tend to discourage human beings from developing their talents. He also points out that supposing that a slave belongs to "an inferior species" because he has not distinguished himself by any achievements is "just as rational" as supposing any ordinary European to be of an inferior species "because he has not raised himself to the condition of royalty." Finally, Beattie criticizes the tendency among many contemporary writers to denounce as "barbarous" every "practice and sentiment" that does not accord with "the usages of modern Europe," and concludes with his own criticism of slavery.[55]

Beattie's affirmation of a common human nature, and common human abilities across the different races, arises partly from the doctrine of the unity and equality of humankind in the Judeo-Christian tradition. However, he also argues that human actions should be understood in their social, cultural, and

53. For various assessments of the nature and extent of Hume's racism, see Popkin, "Hume's Racism," 251–66, and "Hume's Racism Reconsidered," 64–75; Immerwahr, "Hume's Revised Racism," 481–86; and Palter, "Hume and Prejudice," 3–23.

54. Kant, *Prolegomena,* 8–9, in *Kants gesammelte Schriften,* 4: 258–59.

55. Beattie, *Essay on the Nature and Immutability of Truth,* 479–84. See also Popkin, "Hume's Racism," 251–66, and "Hume's Racism Reconsidered," 64–75; Immerwahr, "Hume's Revised Racism," 481–86; and Palter, "Hume and Prejudice," 3–23.

historical context, thereby reflecting the more distinctively eighteenth-century Scottish interest in the study of history and culture. Indeed, in this regard Beattie is applying the principles that Hume had prescribed for the interpretation of human action, more consistently than Hume does himself, to the native peoples of Africa and America. Beattie even seems to advance a step beyond Hume, by indicating that we should seek to appreciate the distinctive cultures and unique achievements of other peoples and nations.

There are some indications in his writings that Hume was prepared to reconsider his assessment of non-European people and cultures on the basis of a new consideration of the evidence, although he did not do so very extensively. For example, in the revised version of his footnote to "Of National Characters," Hume limits his assertion that "there never was a civilized nation of any other complexion than white" to a claim, now regarding only Africans, that "there scarcely ever was a civilized nation of that complexion" (E Var.629; E NC.208). Immerwahr has suggested that in this revision Hume may be taking into account the cultures of Peru and Mexico, which had been adduced by Beattie as examples of non-European civilizations, while Palter has suggested that by changing "never" to "scarcely ever" Hume might also be acknowledging some evidence of civilization in sub-Saharan Africa.[56] On the other hand, Popkin has summarized the evidence that was probably available to Hume for the achievements of educated and talented individuals of African descent in Europe and America, including above all Francis Williams, a Cambridge-educated mathematician from Jamaica who also wrote poetry in both English and Latin. Hume specifically mentions Williams in this footnote, though not by name, as having probably won fame for slender achievements, though his remark indicates that he knew little about Williams (E Var.630; NC.208n10). Popkin has aptly described Hume as "a lousy empirical scientist" in this regard, in spite of his general empricism.[57]

A more sustained example of Hume's apparent willingness to reconsider his assessment of a remote culture, in this case early medieval European culture, has been pointed out by Livingston, in discussing Hume's review of the second volume of Robert Henry's *History of Great Britain*.[58] As we have seen, in his *History of England* Hume takes a dismissive view of "barbarian" Anglo-Saxon culture, although he praises a few individual rulers, such as Ethelbert and Alfred the Great (H 1.1.3, 32; H 1.2.78–79). However, he welcomed Henry's more thorough and sympathetic portrayal of the history and culture of this period in the second volume, published in 1773, of Henry's *History of Great Britain*. In his review of this volume, Hume finds that it is "wonderful" to discover "what

56. Immerwahr, "Hume's Revised Racism," 483–84; Palter, "Hume and Prejudice," 5.
57. See Popkin, "Hume's Racism Reconsidered," 64–75.
58. Livingston, *Hume's Philosophy of Common Life,* 246.

an instructive, and even entertaining book" Henry was able to compose from "such unpromising materials," and that "when we see those barbarous ages delineated by so able a pen, we admire the *oddness* of their manners, customs, and opinions, and are transported, as it were, into a new world" (RH 378). Here he concedes that a remote culture, when described with eloquence, can interest us by its very strangeness, and provide a "new world" to engage our understanding and imagination. Hume also indicates that, judging by Henry's account, the Anglo-Saxons and other "barbarous" nations of England can be credited with greater achievements than he had found his own study of the period. He gives particular attention to the scholarly interests of Aldhelm and Alcuin, Anglo-Saxon achievements in poetry and music, and the efforts by Alfred the Great to promote trade and exploration. In this review Hume accordingly shows that he is prepared to revise his view of a distant culture in light of further information. He even suggests that our historical curiosity can extend beyond the familiar world of modern civilization to include an interest in a remote and strange culture, a conclusion that indeed reinforces his discussion of curiosity as including a desire for novelty (T 2.3.8.12, 2.3.10.10–12 [SBN 432–37, 452–54]; cf. E SH.565–68).

We may conclude that the inadequacy in Hume's discussion of early medieval history, and in his view of the native peoples and cultures of Africa and America, reflects his failure to apply his own methodological principles consistently. This failure in turn reflects his limited knowledge of the historical and contemporary varieties of human culture, the limitations in his sympathy, and even the limited scope of his curiosity. Apparently, Hume's admiration and concern for the achievements of eighteenth-century European culture prevented him from understanding the motives of individuals in very different cultures, from appreciating their abilities and achievements, and from recognizing the injuries done to non-European peoples and cultures by European hegemony.

On the other hand, an appropriation of Hume in our own day, while not discounting these deficiencies, might argue that Hume is not tracing the progress of civilization in order to glorify the peoples of Britain or Europe. Instead, he is attempting to identify those social and political conditions that tend to foster the development of peace, liberty, civility, and material and cultural prosperity for an entire population, as they may be traced in the history of Europe. In doing so, he is also seeking to promote the development of these conditions, both nationally and internationally, as the context for the general flourishing of human life. Finally, he is also calling attention to various possible threats to these conditions, especially in his own nation. However, he admittedly does not consider our own problem, more recently recognized, of how an emerging global civilization can or should include nations beyond the geographical, cultural, and historical boundaries of Europe in the project of developing a common economic and cultural system, a common moral community, and national and international political structures that establish and promote human liberty.

On this view, Hume's project, in characterizing progress, identifying its sources in human history, and addressing the challenges to progress in his own place and time, is continuous with the problem of progress that confronts us in the contemporary world. This is the problem of how to promote the progress of world civilization, understood not as a homogeneous culture, but as a system that is able to secure and to advance worldwide the material welfare and prosperity of individuals, the civil liberty afforded by modern constitutional government, the flourishing of the arts and sciences, and the increase of benevolence and sociability. If we share his sense of mission and wish to promote his goal, as I have described it here, we must do so under the new and different conditions produced by an industrial—or even a postindustrial—social, economic, political, and technological order, whose subsequent effects upon the liberal commercial civilization of his day Hume did not and could not have foreseen.[59] Even more recently, we have come to recognize that this project must include a historically informed respect for the non-European cultural traditions that have been drawn into this unfolding global civilization, and must also address the challenges involved in incorporating a variety of cultural traditions into this civilization. Accordingly, in reflecting upon the challenges confronting us in attempting to promote a flourishing life for human beings in all nations, we may conclude that Hume's project in attempting to analyze, explain, and promote the progress of civilization, and his weaknesses and limitations in pursuing this project, still remain our own.

59. Here I disagree with Danford's apparent assumption that Hume's "liberal commercial society" is substantially the same as the economic order of the world today: an economic order that is, in Danford's view, wrongly attacked from many directions as "alienating and inhumane, corrupt and vicious." See Danford, *Problem of Reason,* 114, cf. 137. On the contrary, Hume's concept of a commercial society is "radically" pre-industrial, as Livingston notes in *Philosophical Melancholy and Delirium,* 6.

Conclusion

Historians of philosophy are often divided into two types: those who seek to understand earlier systems of thought mainly in relation to their original context, and those who are mainly interested in historical texts as presenting the antecedents of contemporary problems. This has tended to invite charges of antiquarian irrelevance against the former, and of anachronism against the latter.

However, historical and contemporary philosophical interests have also been combined in another way in recent years, as historians of philosophy increasingly seek to uncover unexplored insights and neglected alternatives in many historical texts, and to present these as contributions to current philosophical discussions.[1] This approach is further encouraged by the discovery that our received views of many historical figures in philosophy have been influenced by a subsequent interpretive tradition, which can often be criticized, on the basis of a new examination of the texts, for obscuring or distorting the views of the author. This engagement with historical texts, through what we might

1. This approach to the history of philosophy, as disclosing unexpected alternatives and resources for contemporary discussions, can be found in Taylor, "Philosophy and its History," 17–30, and in other essays in Rorty, Schneewind, and Skinner, *Philosophy in History*. As I was completing the manuscript for this book, I was pleased to find a very similar account of these three approaches to the history of philosophy, in very similar terms, by Zammito in *Kant, Herder, and the Birth of Anthropology*, 13.

call an "archaeological" approach, opens the history of philosophy as a field for new and exciting discoveries, even in relation to contemporary questions.[2]

In this study I have presented a reassessment of Hume according to this method. First, I have shown that Hume develops a constructive account of human cognition, in which he considers the role of various dispositions of the mind in the constitution of experience, and in formulating the principles of critical judgment in different areas of human concern. Next, I have examined his view of the limitations of cognition, and of its subordination to the passions in the activities of life. Third, I have shown that Hume's account of the nature and limitations of cognition is intended to provide the basis for a systematic account of the principles of inquiry in the natural and human sciences, and for his own studies in different areas of the human sciences. Fourth, I have shown that Hume calls attention throughout his works to the influence of social and historical existence on human cognition, passion, and volition. Finally, I have shown that he regards our judgments in the sciences, morals, aesthetics, politics, and religion as products of our participation in a community and a historical tradition, and as subject to criticism on the basis of standards that are articulated historically through reflection upon this experience. In sum, I have shown that Hume's philosophy, his study of history, and his contributions to the development of the other academic disciplines are part of a single integrated project: a constructive study of human cognition in its historical context; or, in other words, a study of reason in history.

HUME ON THE HISTORICITY OF HUMAN NATURE

In concluding this study, it will be helpful to review the main features of Hume's philosophy, or his "science of man," in order to identify those aspects of human consciousness he regards as influenced by historical existence. This historical dimension of human consciousness includes not only the temporality of experience but also the influence of a cultural tradition, which is conveyed to the individual through a process of socialization in a particular historical setting.

First, Hume argues that we develop abstract ideas, including our concepts of species and of qualities, by discovering resemblances among our impressions, as directly given and as recalled by the imagination, and then by sorting these into types, in response to the needs and purposes of life. We then associate these

---

2. I have borrowed this expression from Foucault, *Archaeology of Knowledge*, although I would assimilate traditional intellectual history more closely to this project than he might have countenanced. I will mention several recent examples of this approach in my remarks here, including Brook, *Kant and the Mind*; Pippin on Hegel in *Modernism as a Philosophical Problem*, and *Idealism as Modernism*; and Friedman, *Reconsidering Logical Positivism*.

resembling images with a name or a general term, in order to facilitate our recall of any individual images in the resembling set (T 1.1.7.1–18 [SBN 17–25]).[3] Initially, Hume seems to present the formulation of abstract ideas as an individual process, although he suggests that human beings are likely to form similar concepts of objects and qualities that are especially obvious and important to all of us (cf. T 1.1.4.1 [SBN 10–11]; EHU 3.1 [SBN 23]). However, he also implicitly indicates that social and historical traditions influence concept formation through our use of names or general terms to designate our abstract ideas. As he shows elsewhere, words usually arise as conventions in a particular community (T 1.1.7.7–16, 3.2.2.10 [SBN 20–24, 490]; EPM App.3.7 [SBN 306]). We accordingly acquire most of the words that we use to designate our abstract ideas by learning an existing language. In addition, we also develop many abstract ideas by learning the general terms of a particular linguistic community. That is, the use of words as public symbols not only enables us to communicate with each other regarding a given concept but also allows us to formulate and convey concepts of those objects, activities, institutions, and inventions that are distinctive to a specific community or cultural tradition. This is indicated by Hume in his references to the word "church," or the word "liberty" in its political sense, whose concepts can be fully explained only by referring to institutions arising within a specific historical tradition (T 1.1.7.14, 1.4.6.13 [SBN 23, 258]; E PA.383; E CP.493–501; E PS.505).[4]

Hume also indicates that the rules for philosophical probable reasoning, or standards of justification for empirical knowledge, are products of experience, and also of a historical process of reflection upon experience.[5] He maintains that the principles of scientific reasoning cannot be justified absolutely, either *a priori* by reason, or *a posteriori* by experience. However, he argues that they are relatively justified for practical purposes by experience, as long as we are compelled by habit to presuppose the continuing uniformity of the laws of nature. Indeed, he maintains that we should regard these rules as universally applicable, on the grounds of utility and effectiveness, in both the natural and human sciences. He also indicates that these rules have emerged in the history of modern science, through the work of such figures as Copernicus, Bacon, Galileo, Boyle, and Newton, who developed the experimental method by articulating

---

3. On the historical structure of concept formation in Hume's theory, see Livingston, "Hume's Historical Theory of Meaning," 213–38, and *Hume's Philosophy of Common Life,* 60–149.

4. Contrary to Pompa's assertion, Hume can account for the "social concepts" belonging to the "world of institutional understanding" by considering the role of convention in the development of a term, and by considering the history of any particular term. See Pompa, *Human Nature and Historical Knowledge,* 62–65. On Hume's discussion of the history of the concept of political liberty in England, see Miller, "Hume on Liberty," 53–103, and Livingston, "Hume's Historical Conception of Liberty," 105–53.

5. For discussions of the historical dimension of the various standards of justification in Hume's thought, see Letwin, "New Task," 152–54, and Livingston, *Hume's Philosophy of Common Life,* 150–209.

the implicit principles of ordinary causal reasoning and extended these to the systematic study of objects and events in nature. Other philosophers had sought more recently to apply these principles in the study of human life. Among these founders of the "science of man" Hume includes Locke, Shaftesbury, Mandeville, Hutcheson, and Butler (T Int.7n1 [SBN xviin1]). In both the natural and human sciences, the rules for scientific reasoning are applied to information that is accumulated through a series of experiences, not only in the personal history of each individual scientist, but also in a community of researchers, whose testimony is compared, tested, and transmitted to subsequent generations. Indeed, while many scientific achievements seem to arise from the effort and talents of single individuals, Hume indicates that a research community contributes to formulating the problems addressed by individuals at given times and places, and helps to confirm their discoveries (T Int.7–10, 1.4.1.2 [SBN xvi–xix, 180–81]; H 5.App.4.153–54; H 6.71.541–42; DNR 2.150–51). He also notes that scientific activity tends to be stimulated by certain political and cultural conditions (E RP.115–26; E RA.269–71; E MS.545–51). Thus, in Hume's view, the principles of scientific reasoning have in fact been articulated cooperatively by scientists and philosophers through a process of historical development, and are applied to data provided by the accumulated experiences of individuals in history (cf. EHU 9.5n20 [SBN 107n1]; E SH.566–67).[6]

Next, in his theory of the passions, Hume attributes a set of basic passions to all human beings. As an individual subject, I identify these passions in my own case through introspection, and then attribute these passions to others by observing the resemblances between their behavior and my own outward expressions of a given passion. Our mutual recognition of these similarities in our outward behavior enables us to attribute the same passions to each other, and to develop conventional names for the different passions. However, Hume indicates that while human beings evidently experience the same general passions, any individual assessment of a particular object as good or evil, or as a probable source of pleasure or displeasure, will vary not only according to the temperaments of individuals but also with their cultural context. In order to understand the motives of individuals, as expressed in their actions and discourse, we must rely upon probable reasoning. Our experience of motives, or of the beliefs and desires that determine the actions of human agents, consists in our introspective awareness of our own beliefs and passions, and our awareness, through observation or testimony, of the behavior of other human agents. At first we are likely to attribute beliefs and desires similar to our own to other human agents. However, we may also attribute different beliefs and desires to

---

6. On the historical character of individual experience, and the cognitive value of social experience as conveyed through history, see Wertz, *Between Hume's Philosophy and History,* xiii–xv, 35–42, and 115–17.

an individual, once we have learned to recognize the distinctive experiences and temperament of that individual. Finally, to account for the beliefs and desires of individuals from other times or places, we learn through experience that we must also seek out information concerning the historical and cultural context of their actions. This includes the beliefs, institutions, and customary practices of their culture and its evaluation of various objects, events, and qualities. This information, concerning first the character, and then the circumstances of an agent, enables us to improve the accuracy of our probable judgments concerning the motives that are likely to have prompted the agent to undertake a given action.

On the basis of this analysis, Hume indicates that our disciplined inquiries in the different fields included in the moral or human sciences require us to attain a sympathetic understanding of the beliefs and passions of others, which may also require a study of their social, cultural, and historical context. This twofold approach, which involves understanding the internal motives of individuals in relation to their external context, is reflected in his own contributions to the human sciences, in which he incorporates this approach into both the generalizing method of the social scientist and the contextualizing method of the historian. We find examples of this approach, as applied in both his historical and his social-scientific inquiries, in his writings on economics, demographics, political parties, religion, history, and the customs of different ages and nations. Indeed, as we have seen, he indicates that the study of these aspects of human life through the moral sciences have developed only recently, in response to the intellectual advances of the preceding century and the concerns of contemporary life (T Int.7–10, 1.3.15.11 [SBN xvi–xix, 175]; cf. E CL.88–89).

Finally, Hume indicates that the principles of aesthetics, morality, and political culture are developed collectively by individuals within a community, as we gradually coordinate our sentiments and judgments in order to establish a common set of rules, models, values, practices, and institutions. The results of this process are the moral, aesthetic, and political traditions of a given community. However, Hume maintains that these traditions also include implicit standards of critical judgment that can be discerned by the philosopher.

First, Hume argues that the moral rules and the catalog of virtues within a given moral tradition are generated in order to promote those qualities of character that are generally regarded as useful or agreeable in that historical context. The principles of utility and agreeability are thus the implicit standards of morality, by which we may assess the principles of any specific moral tradition. Any particular moral precepts, such as the monkish virtues, might turn out, by these standards, to be aberrations that were incorporated into a given moral system for other reasons, such as their tendency to advance the interests of certain religious or political leaders. The task of the moral philosopher is to call attention to these aberrations and to promote those qualities of character that are genuinely useful and agreeable to the community as a whole.

In the case of aesthetics, Hume argues that the standard of taste within a given aesthetic tradition is articulated by those individuals, called critics, who are recognized by others as having a special talent for appreciating the merits or demerits of a work of art. This talent, which arises from a delicate taste and from experience in appreciating works in a given genre, is measured by their judgments concerning works that have generally been recognized as classics in that genre by preceding critics and the cultivated public in their cultural tradition. On the other hand, Hume indicates that critics can also discover the merits of a previously unappreciated work and guide the public in appreciating these merits, by an improved delicacy of taste, or by an improved understanding of the historical setting in which the work was created. In this way, a critic may also criticize the rules of art and canon of classics within an existing aesthetic tradition.

Lastly, Hume argues that a political tradition is developed through the history of a given community, to secure the welfare and promote the happiness of its inhabitants by codifying the principles of justice and establishing the means for their enforcement. This tradition is expressed in the political and legal institutions of a given nation, which, however they are established, gain their authority subsequently by the tacit acquiescence of the public. However, the political system of a given society may also be deficient in its tendency to promote the general welfare and happiness of its population. For this reason, a given political system is subject to change through the initiative of its rulers or legislators; the pressures of a political movement; the recommendations of a political scientist or practical moralist; or even, in extreme cases, through a popular uprising. However, he clearly prefers a process of reform, where reform is needed, through discernment, negotiation, and legislation. Finally, he indicates that a process of reform should seek to secure public support by appealing to any precedents that are available in the existing tradition.

Hume therefore indicates that our normative principles, or standards of critical judgment in different areas of thought and action, including the natural sciences, the human sciences, ethics, aesthetics, and politics, are products of philosophical reflection upon our historical experience, as individuals and as participants in a cultural tradition. By contrast, he rejects any claim that these standards are self-evident principles of criticism that can be derived directly from an autonomous faculty of reason, apart from any individual or historical experience.

Hume therefore offers us a diffuse but coherent account of the historical dimension of human consciousness, or the influence of tradition on human cognition, emotion, and volition, along with an examination of the principles of historical and social-scientific study according to which we may explain the effects of tradition. He also seeks to articulate the normative principles that are implicit in the intellectual and cultural traditions of his own time and place, and arguably of our own, as standards for our scientific, moral, aesthetic, and political judgments. These standards may accordingly be used to criticize various other aspects of the existing traditions in these areas of life.[7] He thus presents an account of reason in history, by examining both the historically relative aspects of human cognition and the standards of objectivity that we articulate, as principles of criticism, through reflection upon our historical experience as individuals and as members of a community.[8]

In their recent comparisons of Hume and Hegel, both Christopher Berry and Leon Pompa have attributed to Hume a static account of human nature in general, and also one of rationality, social life, and social institutions. In contrast, both designate as "Hegelian" the distinctively "modern" view that social existence determines human consciousness, including human reflection concerning the standards of rationality. In this study I have shown that Hume also provides an account of the influence of a particular historical and cultural tradition on human consciousness, including our particular concepts and beliefs, the objects of our passions, and our standards of evaluation. He also examines the process by which the standards of critical judgment in different areas of life and thought are developed by human beings within a particular historical society.[9] I would thus maintain that Hume, like Hegel, examines the development and activity of reason in history, not as a separate spiritual or metaphysical principle, as is suggested in some readings of Hegel, but through an empirical account of the use and justification of reason by human beings in history.[10]

HUME, MODERN PHILOSOPHY, AND THE ENLIGHTENMENT AS MODERNITY

Finally, I would like to consider the implications of the preceding interpretation of Hume for understanding his relation, first to several lines of development in

7. For discussions of "tradition" as a social-scientific and historical concept, see Shils, *Tradition;* and Stanford, *Introduction to the Philosophy of History,* 42–48 and 183–205.

8. Hume's approach to the historical dimension of human consciousness is emphasized in the works by Forbes, Capaldi, Jones, Livingston, Whelan, Wilson, and Baier that I have cited in the course of this study. See also Ross, *Human Nature and Utility;* Heruday, *Hume's Theory of Human Assent;* Letwin, "New Task," 134–58; Moore, "Social Background," 23–41; Davie, "Central Problem of Scottish Philosophy," 43–62; and Roth, "Hume's Theory of Human Nature and Community," 331–51.

9. See Berry, *Hume, Hegel and Human Nature* and "Hume on Rationality," 234–47, and Pompa, *Human Nature and Historical Knowledge.*

10. For a useful introduction to Hegel, and to issues in the interpretation of his thought, in relation to the themes that I have examined here, see Beiser, "Hegel's Historicism," 270–300.

German philosophy since the eighteenth century, and then to several recent discussions within the Anglo-American analytic philosophical tradition. I also locate these comparisons in a larger context, by considering the implications of this study for the broader interdisciplinary discussion of the Enlightenment and the tradition of modernity.

First, we may consider Hume's relation to the subsequent German philosophical tradition. Here Hume is especially acknowledged for his role in awakening Kant from his dogmatic slumber and prompting him to address the skeptical challenge by developing his critical philosophy.[11] In this study, however, I have shown that, in addition to his critique of rationalism, Hume develops a constructive theory of human cognition, in which he examines the role of various faculties of the human mind in organizing our subjective impressions into the objects of internal and external experience, a view that is closer to Kant's transcendental idealism than is commonly recognized. Indeed, an increasing number of studies have called attention to the continuities between Hume and Kant and have provided a more focused account of the differences between them, as alternative approaches to the same issues.[12]

According to the view that I have presented here, Hume also indicates that many of our concepts and standards of justification are products of a process of historical development and are transmitted to us through our participation in a given culture. Kant treats this aspect of human cognition only peripherally.[13] However, the historical and cultural aspect of human cognition was emphasized by two of Kant's associates, J. G. Hamann and J. G. Herder, who were also among the earliest critics of his critical philosophy. Of these two, Hamann had already been inspired by Hume's discussions of skepticism, faith, and the imagination in developing his eccentric version of fideism. Indeed, Hamann may have introduced Kant to several passages from Hume's writings that were as yet unavailable in published German translations.[14] For his part, Herder was influenced by the historical writings of Hume and other authors of the Scottish Enlightenment in his approach to history and culture.[15] As I have noted, several

11. Kant, *Prolegomena*, 10, in *Kants gesammelte Schriften*, 4: 260. The precise means and character of this influence has become the subject of considerable scrutiny in recent years: see Wolff, "Kant's Debt," 117–23; Gawlick and Kreimendahl, *Hume in der Deutschen Aufklärung*, 174–98; and Kuehn, "Kant's Conception of 'Hume's Problem,'" 175–93, and *Kant*, 472–73n32.

12. See, for example, Brook, *Kant and the Mind*, 191–95; Falkenstein, "Hume's Answer to Kant," 331–60; and Jacquette, *David Hume's Critique of Infinity*, 181–89.

13. Kant's closest approach to this topic appears in the Transcendental Doctrine of Method in the *Critique of Pure Reason*, 627–704 (A 707–855 / B 735–83); and *Anthropology from a Pragmatic Point of View*.

14. On Hamann's relation to Hume, see Merlan, "From Hume to Hamann," 11–18; Beiser, *Fate of Reason*, 24; Gawlick and Kreimendahl, *Hume in der Deutschen Aufklärung*, 174–98; and Kuehn, *Kant*, 118–26 and 194–201.

15. See Pascal, "Herder and the Scottish Historical School," 23–42, and Zammito, *Kant, Herder, and the Birth of Anthropology*.

recent studies have compared Hume's project to the most ambitious, and influential, synthesis of history and philosophy in the nineteenth century: Hegel's study of the development of human consciousness within a given cultural context; his examination of the history of concepts, practices, standards of judgment, institutions, and philosophical systems; and his approach to forming a critical justification of the cognitive principles, social practices, and institutional structures of modern culture, even while regarding these as products of historical development.[16]

We may also compare Hume with two figures in the later nineteenth-century German tradition who were interested in the relation between history and philosophy: Nietzsche and Dilthey. On the one hand, Hume anticipates many aspects of Nietzsche's thought, such as his criticism of the substance tradition in Western metaphysics, his criticism of Christianity and the moral tradition arising from Christianity, and his use of a historical-genetic method for explaining our concepts, beliefs, and standards of judgment.[17] However, unlike Nietzsche, Hume attempts to offer a straightforward and constructive account of the principles of reasoning and evaluation, including the principles of historical investigation. In this regard he anticipates more nearly the concerns and project of Dilthey, who sought to articulate a method of historical inquiry directed toward understanding the conscious states of individuals, in relation to their historical and cultural setting, as the central method of the human sciences.[18]

Finally, Hume anticipates not only Husserl's phenomenological method, as has often been noted, but also Heidegger's approach to philosophy by means of the "analytic of *Dasein*," or the study of the self-conscious subject as initially finding itself in a world of practical activities and emotional engagements, and as directed by a historical tradition in its interpretation of this world.[19]

Hume may thus be regarded, not only as a direct influence and recurring source of inspiration for German philosophy since the eighteenth century, but also as a harbinger of many of the themes and concerns regarded as characteristic of that tradition.

Next, we may consider Hume's influence in the Anglo-American analytic tradition, and the significance of the present interpretation of Hume for recent developments within this tradition.

16. See Livingston, *Hume's Philosophy of Common Life,* 36; Rorty, "From Passions to Sentiments," 169; and Williams, *Cultivated Reason,* 26. For discussions of Hegel's historical examination and justification of the standards of rationality in modern culture, see Pippin, *Modernism as a Philosophical Problem* and *Idealism as Modernism.*

17. Hoy, "Genealogical Method," 20–38; Beam, "Hume and Nietzsche," 299–324; and Williams, *Cultivated Reason.*

18. See Dilthey, *Introduction to the Human Sciences.*

19. See Mall, *Hume's Concept of Man* and *Experience and Reason;* Murphy, *Hume and Husserl;* and Farr, "Hume, Hermeneutics, and History," 285–310.

The analytic tradition has its most immediate origins in logical positivism, which emerged as a coordinated movement among a network of philosophers, especially in Vienna and Britain, during the 1920s. The leading representatives of this movement identified Hume as one of their historical antecedents, based upon his empiricism, his apparent criticism of metaphysics, his contributions to the philosophy of science, his allegedly emotivist ethical theory, and his attacks on religion.[20] Logical positivism is often regarded as an attempt to explain and justify scientific knowledge, as derived from the immediate data of sensation and the principles of formal logic, without any metaphysical presuppositions, and without reference to any historical context.[21] This project has accordingly been regarded as the latest expression of an allegedly fundamental tendency in the Western philosophical tradition to regard knowledge as the direct reflection of reality in the mind of a passive and ahistorical observer.[22]

In response to the extremes of logical positivism on the one hand, and the apparently relativistic tendencies among its critics on the other, many analytic philosophers have recently sought to develop a more precise account of the social and historical aspects of human cognition. This is reflected in studies concerning a wide variety of topics, including the relation of concepts to particular cultures; the historical development of methods and concepts of the natural sciences; the role of testimony in human cognition; and the nature of conventions and social facts.[23]

On my view, one of the projects still confronting the contemporary analytic philosophical tradition is to develop a systematic account and justification of the principles of cognition in the different areas of human thought, while also considering their social and historical dimension, in response to both positivism and relativism. To be sure, this proposal is daunting in itself, and might also seem disconcertingly Hegelian. However, such a project could be modeled on Hume's systematic examination of the elements and processes of cognition, the methods of the natural and human sciences, and the standards of judgment in

20. See especially Hahn, Neurath, and Carnap, "Scientific Conception of the World," 304, and Ayer, *Language, Truth and Logic,* 31 and 54–55.

21. For a statement and critical discussion of this view of logical positivism, see Friedman, *Reconsidering Logical Positivism,* especially 1–14 and 198–233.

22. See especially Rorty, *Philosophy and the Mirror of Nature.* Rorty's discussions of many figures in the history of philosophy are controversial. In a separate essay, he overlooks precisely those aspects of Hume's project which anticipate his own historicizing and edifying concerns: see "Should Hume be Answered or Bypassed?" 341–52. Interestingly, Hume himself uses the metaphor of a mirror to describe the relation of human minds to each other, rather than the relation of the human mind to reality (T 2.2.5.21 [SBN 365]).

23. See, for example, Schmitt, *Socializing Epistemology;* Hollis and Lukes, *Rationality and Relativism;* Coady, *Testimony;* and Searle, *Construction of Social Reality.* On the implications of recent studies in the history of the natural sciences for recognizing the historicity of their methods and concepts, and for formulating an appropriate conception of objectivity, see Laudan, *Progress and its Problems* and *Beyond Positivism and Relativism;* Shapere, *Reason and the Search for Knowledge;* and Smith, *Realism and the Progress of Science.*

morals, aesthetics, and political life. We would of course also expect to expand upon and improve his discussion, based on our intervening historical experience and further developments in philosophy and other areas of inquiry. However, like Hume's achievement, this project would be an important contribution, from the side of philosophy, to current methodological discussions in the other academic disciplines.

Finally, this reassessment of Hume also contributes to recent discussions, across the academic disciplines, of the Enlightenment and its legacy. The term "Enlightenment" has been used, since the eighteenth century itself, to identify a more or less coherent movement in eighteenth-century thought; although the precise identification of its principles has been a matter of controversy, both then and subsequently. Some of the doctrines that are generally regarded as characteristic of the Enlightenment include a confidence in reason, and especially in the methods and achievements of the natural sciences; a policy of secularization; a conviction that there is a universal human nature that can be explained according to rational principles; a belief in, and commitment to, promoting the continuing progress of humanity; and the defense of intellectual freedom and critical inquiry.[24]

However, since at least the middle of the twentieth century, the intellectual, cultural, and political tradition of the Enlightenment, or the tradition of "modernity," has also been regarded as fundamentally flawed, and has indeed been criticized for giving rise to many of the evils in the subsequent two centuries and in our contemporary world.[25] These criticisms of the Enlightenment and modernism arose from a series of developments in twentieth-century culture, including a recognition of the historical development of modern science; a recognition of the many harmful effects of technological progress; a suspicion toward claims of epistemic privilege for any given conceptual scheme or scientific theory; a renewed appreciation of the destructive potential of the human passions in both individual and social life; a sustained attempt to recognize and understand the diversity of historical and contemporary cultures; and a radical expansion of the Enlightenment program for social and political reform.

Interestingly enough, these challenges to the Enlightenment also indirectly call attention to the persistence of the Enlightenment project among its critics.

24. This is the view presented by Gay in *The Enlightenment: An Interpretation.* For a recent examination of the traditional concept of the Enlightenment and its history, see Outram, *The Enlightenment,* 1–8. Pippin provides an account of the concept of modernity and its relation to the Enlightenment in *Modernism as a Philosophical Problem,* 1–45. For a set of readings on the self-understanding of the German Enlightenment, see Schmidt, *What Is Enlightenment?*

25. See Pippin, *Modernism as a Philosophical Problem;* Gray, *Enlightenment's Wake,* 114–84; Outram, *The Enlightenment,* 8–13; and the twentieth-century essays in Schmidt, *What Is Enlightenment?* For a different version of this criticism, see MacIntyre, *After Virtue* and *Whose Justice? Which Rationality?*

Indeed, many critics of modernity in our own day still pursue its commitment to reason and progress, for example by indicating the inconsistencies and inadequacies in the attitudes of leading Enlightenment figures toward various marginalized groups, such as the working classes, women, and non-Europeans.[26] Any efforts to understand and to improve the contemporary world in this regard are still expressions of Enlightenment principles, and are also still confronted by its problems and challenges.

On the other hand, and perhaps in sympathy with the critics of modernity, a number of recent studies have challenged the interpretation of the Enlightenment as a homogeneous cultural and intellectual movement, or as the only significant intellectual movement of the eighteenth century. Instead, these studies have called attention to other currents of thought during this period, some of which actually anticipate the various criticisms of the Enlightenment project in our own day.

One example of this dynamic has emerged in discussions and criticisms of the supposed Enlightenment belief in a universal human nature. Many modern authors have criticized Hume, Voltaire, and other eighteenth-century figures for allegedly regarding the beliefs and practices of modern Europeans as the standards for explaining, and for judging, human beings all times and places.[27] This supposed universalism has been contrasted, especially by Isaiah Berlin, to the views of other eighteenth-century authors, such as Vico, Hamann, and Herder, who allegedly challenged the Enlightenment by seeking to understand human individuals and cultures in their own unique particularity. These figures, in what is sometimes called the Counter-Enlightenment, are then said to have anticipated and contributed to the romantic and historicist movements of the nineteenth century.[28]

In this study we have seen that Hume's view is considerably more complex than the universalism usually attributed to Enlightenment thinkers. That is, in order to understand human actions, he argues that we must trace these actions to motives arising from various dispositions in human nature, in the context of a particular set of historical circumstances.[29] A number of other studies have challenged the simple contrast between a supposed Enlightenment universalism and a historicizing current emerging only with the Counter-Enlightenment. For example, Vyverberg has examined various views of the influence of history and culture on human beings among the French philosophes, while Reill has

26. This is a central theme in Outram's The Enlightenment. For a valuable discussion of the theoretical achievements, and practical inadequacies, of the attempts by the French philosophes to explain other cultures and historical periods, see Vyverberg, Human Nature.

27. See Collingwood, Idea of History, 76–85, and Gray, Enlightenment's Wake, viii.

28. See Berlin's works on Vico, Hamann, and Herder, collected in Three Critics of the Enlightenment.

29. See Chapter 7 of this book.

traced a number of historicizing currents in the German Enlightenment.[30] On the other hand, Herder and Vico both appeal to various universal characteristics of human nature in order to explain the unique characteristics of human beings in particular cultures and historical periods.[31]

This consideration of one issue in eighteenth-century thought, the universality of human nature, encourages us to avoid easy generalizations concerning the Enlightenment and its critics. Instead, it invites us to examine in detail the views of individual authors on any particular question, such as what is universal to human nature or what is particular to individuals in a specific historical and cultural context. Such studies may, in turn, help us clarify the principles and the underlying assumptions in our own attempts at historical and cross-cultural understanding.

In the same way, a reconsideration of Hume's thought as a whole might contribute to our attempts to understand our own principles of scientific, moral, aesthetic, and political judgment, not only as products of a particular process of historical development, but also as principles that we may continue to examine, criticize, justify, and apply in our own historical and cultural circumstances. In this regard Hume may be regarded as one of several figures in the eighteenth century who sought to articulate, explain, and justify the principles of human understanding in their historical context, in works that both express and challenge what would later be regarded as many of the characteristic doctrines of the Enlightenment. Hume is therefore an important resource and model for our efforts to address the intellectual and moral challenges of the contemporary world from our own location within the tradition of modernity.

30. Vyverberg, *Human Nature;* Reill, *German Enlightenment and the Rise of Historicism.*
31. See, for example, Vico, *New Science,* 60–68 (bk. 1, sec. 2, §§119–64), and Herder, *Outlines,* 71–106 and 163–256 (bks. 4 and 7–9).

Aaron, R. I. *The Theory of Universals.* Oxford: Clarendon Press, 1952.

Acton, H. B. "Prejudice." *Revue Internationale de Philosophie* 6 (1952): 323–36.

Adair, Douglass. "'That Politics May Be Reduced to a Science': David Hume, James Madison, and the Tenth *Federalist.*" In *Hume: A Re-Evaluation,* edited by Donald W. Livingston and James T. King, 404–17. New York: Fordham University Press, 1976.

Agassi, Joseph. "A Note on Smith's Term 'Naturalism.'" *Hume Studies* 12 (1986): 92–96.

Aiken, Henry David. "The Originality of Hume's Theory of Obligation." *Philosophy and Phenomenological Research* 42 (1982): 374–83.

Ainslie, Donald C. "The Problem of the National Self in Hume's Theory of Justice." *Hume Studies* 21 (1995): 289–313.

Allan, David. *Virtue, Learning, and the Scottish Enlightenment: Ideas of Scholarship in Early Modern History.* Edinburgh: Edinburgh University Press, 1993.

Allison, Henry E. *Kant's Transcendental Idealism.* New Haven: Yale University Press, 1983.

Altmann, R. W. "Hume on Sympathy." *Southern Journal of Philosophy* 18 (1980): 123–36.

Anderson, Robert Fendel. *Hume's First Principles.* Lincoln: University of Nebraska Press, 1966.

Annand, M. R. "An Examination of Hume's Theory of Relations." *The Monist* 40 (1930): 581–97.

Árdal, Páll S. "Another Look at Hume's Account of Moral Evaluation." *Journal of the History of Philosophy* 15 (1977): 405–21.

———. "Convention and Value." In *David Hume: Bicentenary Papers,* edited by G. P. Morice, 51–68. Edinburgh: Edinburgh University Press, 1977.

———. "Hume and Reid on Promise, Intention and Obligation." In *Philosophers of the Scottish Enlightenment,* edited by V. Hope, 47–69. Edinburgh: Edinburgh University Press, 1984.

———. "Language and Significance in Hume's *Treatise.*" *Canadian Journal of Philosophy* 16 (1986): 779–83.

———. *Passion and Value in Hume's Treatise.* 2d ed. Edinburgh: Edinburgh University Press, 1989.

———. "Some Implications of the Virtue of Reasonableness in Hume's *Treatise.*" In *Hume: A Re-Evaluation,* edited by Donald W. Livingston and James T. King, 91–106. New York: Fordham University Press, 1976.

Arkin, Marcus. "The Economic Writings of David Hume—A Reassessment." In *Essays in Economic Thought: Aristotle to Marshall,* edited by Joseph J. Spengler and William R. Allen, 141–60. Chicago: Rand McNally, 1960.

Arnauld, Antoine, and Pierre Nicole. *Logic, or the Art of Thinking.* Translated by Jill Vance Buroker. Cambridge: Cambridge University Press, 1996.

Ashley, Lawrence, and Michael Stack. "Hume's Theory of the Self and Its Identity." *Dialogue* 13 (1974): 239–54.

Atkins, J. W. H. *English Literary Criticism: 17th and 18th Centuries.* London: Methuen, 1951.

Atkinson, R. F. "Hume on Mathematics." *Philosophical Quarterly* 10 (1960): 127–37.

————. "Hume on the Standard of Morals." In *David Hume: Many-Sided Genius,* edited by Kenneth R. Merrill and Robert W. Shahan, 25–44. Norman: University of Oklahoma Press, 1976.

Ayer, A. J. *Hume: A Very Short Introduction.* Oxford: Oxford University Press, 1980.

————. *Language, Truth and Logic.* 2d ed. London: Gollancz, 1946. Reprint, New York: Dover, 1952.

Baier, Annette C.. "Artificial Virtues and the Equally Sensible Non-Knaves: A Response to Gauthier." *Hume Studies* 18 (1992): 429–39.

————. "Good Men's Women: Hume on Chastity and Trust." *Hume Studies* 5 (1979): 1–19.

————. "Hume on Heaps and Bundles." *American Philosophical Quarterly* 16 (1979): 285–95.

————. "Hume's Account of Social Artifice—Its Origins and Originality." *Ethics* 98 (1988): 757–78.

————. "Hume's Analysis of Pride." *Journal of Philosophy* 75 (1978): 27–40.

————. *Moral Prejudices: Essays on Ethics.* Cambridge: Harvard University Press, 1994.

————. *Postures of the Mind: Essays on Mind and Morals.* Minneapolis: University of Minnesota Press, 1985.

————. *A Progress of Sentiments: Reflections on Hume's Treatise.* Cambridge: Harvard University Press, 1991.

Barfoot, Michael. "Hume and the Culture of Science in the Early Eighteenth Century." In *Studies in the Philosophy of the Scottish Enlightenment,* edited by M. A. Stewart, 151–90. Oxford: Clarendon Press, 1990.

Bayle, Pierre. *Historical and Critical Dictionary: Selections.* Translated by Richard H. Popkin, with the assistance of Craig Brush. Indianapolis: Bobbs-Merrill, 1965. Reprint, Indianapolis: Hackett, 1991.

Beam, Craig. "Hume and Nietzsche: Naturalists, Ethicists, Anti-Christians." *Hume Studies* 22 (1996): 299–324.

Beattie, James. *An Essay on the Nature and Immutability of Truth in Opposition to Sophistry and Scepticism.* Edinburgh: Kincaid & Bell, 1770. Reprint, New York: Garland, 1983.

Beauchamp, Tom L. "Introduction" to *An Enquiry Concerning Human Understanding: A Critical Edition* by David Hume, edited by Thomas L. Beauchamp, xi–civ. Oxford: Clarendon Press, 2000.

————. "Introduction" to *An Enquiry Concerning the Principles of Morals: A Critical Edition* by David Hume, edited by Thomas L. Beauchamp, xi–lxxx. Oxford: Clarendon Press, 1998.

Beauchamp, Tom L., and Alexander Rosenberg. *Hume and the Problem of Causation.* Oxford: Oxford University Press, 1981.

Beck, Lewis White. *Essays on Kant and Hume.* New Haven: Yale University Press, 1978.

Beckwith, Francis J. *David Hume's Argument Against Miracles: A Critical Analysis.* Lanham: University Press of America, 1989.

Bedford, Errol. "Emotions." *Proceedings of the Aristotelian Society* 57 (1957): 281–304.

Beiser, Frederick C. *The Fate of Reason: German Philosophy from Kant to Fichte.* Cambridge: Harvard University Press, 1987.

————. "Hegel's Historicism." In *The Cambridge Companion to Hegel,* edited by Frederick C. Beiser, 270–300. Cambridge: Cambridge University Press, 1993.

————. *The Sovereignty of Reason: The Defense of Rationality in the Early English Enlightenment.* Princeton: Princeton University Press, 1996.

Beitzinger, Alfons. "The Place of Hume in the History of Jurisprudence." *American Journal of Jurisprudence* 20 (1975): 20–37.

Belshaw, Christopher. "Hume and Demonstrative Knowledge." *Hume Studies* 15 (1989): 141–62.

Bennett, Jonathan. *Locke, Berkeley, Hume: Central Themes.* Oxford: Clarendon Press, 1971.

Berkeley, George. *The Works of George Berkeley, Bishop of Cloyne.* 9 vols. Edited by A. A. Luce and
 T. E. Jessop. London: Thomas Nelson & Sons, 1948–57. Reprint, Nendeln: Kraus, 1979.
Berlin, Isaiah. "Hume and the Sources of German Anti-Rationalism." In *David Hume: Bicentenary
 Papers,* edited by G. P. Morice, 93–116. Edinburgh: Edinburgh University Press, 1977.
———. *Three Critics of the Enlightenment: Vico, Hamann, Herder.* Edited by Henry Hardy. Prince-
 ton: Princeton University Press, 2000.
Bernard, Christopher. "Hume and the Madness of Religion." In *Hume and Hume's Connexions,*
 edited by M. A. Stewart and John P. Wright, 224–38. University Park: Pennsylvania State
 University Press, 1995.
Berry, Christopher J. "Hume on Rationality in History and Social Life." *History and Theory* 21
 (1982): 234–47.
———. *Hume, Hegel and Human Nature.* The Hague: Martinus Nijhoff, 1982.
———. "Rude Religion: The Psychology of Polytheism in the Scottish Enlightenment." In *The
 Scottish Enlightenment: Essays in Reinterpretation,* edited by Paul Wood, 315–34. Rochester:
 University of Rochester Press, 2000.
———. *Social Theory of the Scottish Enlightenment.* Edinburgh: Edinburgh University Press, 1997.
Biro, John. "Hume's New Science of the Mind." In *The Cambridge Companion to Hume,* edited by
 David Fate Norton, 33–63. Cambridge: Cambridge University Press, 1993.
Black, J. B. *The Art of History.* London: Methuen,1926.
Blake, Ralph M., Curt J. Ducasse, and Edward H. Madden. *Theories of Scientific Method: The
 Renaissance Through the Nineteenth Century.* Seattle: University of Washington Press, 1960.
Boatright, John R. "Hume's Account of Moral Sentiment." *Revue Internationale de Philosophie* 30
 (1976): 79–90.
Bongie, Laurence L. *David Hume, Prophet of the Counter-Revolution.* Oxford: Clarendon Press, 1965.
———. "The Eighteenth-Century Marian Controversy and an Unpublished Letter by David
 Hume." *Studies In Scottish Literature* 1 (1964): 236-52.
Boolos, George. "Saving Frege from Contradiction." *Proceedings of the Aristotelian Society* 87
 (1986–87): 137–51.
Bossert, Philip J. "Hume and Husserl on Time and Time-Consciousness." *Journal of the British
 Society for Phenomenology* 7 (1976): 44–52.
Botwinick, Aryeh. *Ethics, Politics and Epistemology: A Study in the Unity of Hume's Thought.* Lanham:
 University Press of America, 1980.
Box, M. A. *The Suasive Art of David Hume.* Princeton: Princeton University Press, 1990.
Bradshaw, D. E. "Berkeley and Hume on Abstraction and Generalization." *History of Philosophy
 Quarterly* 5 (1988): 11–22.
Brand, Walter. *Hume's Theory of Moral Judgment: A Study in the Unity of A Treatise of Human Nature.*
 Dordrecht: Kluwer, 1992.
Bricke, John. *Hume's Philosophy of Mind.* Edinburgh: Edinburgh University Press, 1980.
———. *Mind and Morality: An Examination of Hume's Moral Psychology.* Oxford: Clarendon Press,
 1996.
Broiles, R. David. *The Moral Philosophy of David Hume.* 2d ed. The Hague: Martinus Nijhoff,
 1964, 1969.
Brook, Andrew. *Kant and the Mind.* Cambridge: Cambridge University Press, 1994.
Brown, Charlotte. "From Spectator to Agent: Hume's Theory of Obligation." *Hume Studies* 20
 (1994): 19–35.
Brown, Stuart G. "Observations on Hume's Theory of Taste." *English Studies* 20 (1938): 193–98.
Brunet, Olivier. *Philosophie et Esthétique chez David Hume.* Paris: Librairie A.-G. Nizet, 1965.
Brunius, Teddy. *David Hume on Criticism.* Stockholm: Almquist & Wiksell, 1952.
Bryson, Gladys. *Man and Society: The Scottish Inquiry of the Eighteenth Century.* Princeton: Prince-
 ton University Press, 1945.

Buchdahl, Gerd. *Metaphysics and the Philosophy of Science. The Classical Origins: Descartes to Kant.* Cambridge: MIT Press, 1969.

Burke, Edmund. *Reflections on the Revolution in France.* Edited by J. C. D. Clark. Stanford: Stanford University Press, 2001.

Burke, Peter. *History and Social Theory.* Ithaca: Cornell University Press, 1992.

Burns, R. M. *The Great Debate on Miracles from Joseph Glanvill to David Hume.* Lewisburg: Bucknell University Press, 1981.

Burns, Steven. "The Humean Female." *Dialogue* 15 (1976): 415–24.

Butler, Joseph. *The Analogy of Religion, Natural and Revealed, to the Constitution and Course of Nature.* Edited by Samuel Halifax. New York: Robert Carter & Bros., 1780.

Butler, Ronald J. "*Distinctiones Rationis,* or the Cheshire Cat which left its smile behind it." *Proceedings of the Aristotelian Society* 76 (1976): 165–76.

———. "Hume's Impressions." In *Impressions of Empiricism,* edited by Godfrey Vesey, 122–36. New York: St. Martin's Press, 1976.

———. "T and Sympathy." *Proceedings of the Aristotelian Society,* supplementary vol. 49 (1975): 1–20.

Butterfield, Herbert. *The Whig Interpretation of History.* London: Bell & Sons, 1931.

Butts, Robert E. "Husserl's Critique of Hume's Notion of *Distinctions of Reason.*" *Philosophy and Phenomenological Research* 20 (1959): 213–21.

Capaldi, Nicholas. *David Hume: The Newtonian Philosopher.* Boston: Twayne, 1975.

———. "Hume as Social Scientist." *Review of Metaphysics* 32 (1978): 99–123.

———. *Hume's Place in Moral Philosophy.* New York: Peter Lang, 1989.

———. "Hume's Rejection of 'Ought' as a Moral Category." *Journal of Philosophy* 63 (1966): 126–37.

———. "Hume's Theory of the Passions." In *Hume: A Re-Evaluation,* edited by Donald W. Livingston and James T. King, 172–90. New York: Fordham University Press, 1976.

Capaldi, Nicholas, and Donald W. Livingston, eds. *Liberty in Hume's History of England.* Dordrecht: Kluwer, 1990.

Carabelli, Giancarlo. *On Hume and Eighteenth-Century Aesthetics: The Philosopher on a Swing.* Translated by Joan Krakover Hall. New York: Peter Lang, 1995.

Carroll, Noel. "Hume's Standard of Taste." *Journal of Aesthetics and Art Criticism* 43 (1984): 181–94.

Cassirer, Ernst. *The Philosophy of the Enlightenment.* Translated by Fritz C. A. Koelln and James P. Pettegrove. Princeton: Princeton University Press, 1951, 1979.

Chappell, V. C., ed. *Hume.* Garden City, N.Y.: Doubleday, Anchor Books, 1966.

Cherry, Christopher. "Nature, Artifice and Moral Approbation." *Proceedings of the Aristotelian Society* 76 (1976): 265–82.

Christensen, Jerome. *Practicing Enlightenment: Hume and the Formation of a Literary Career.* Madison: University of Wisconsin Press, 1987.

Church, Ralph W. *Hume's Theory of the Understanding.* London: George Allen & Unwin, 1935.

Clarke, Samuel. *The Works of Samuel Clarke.* 4 vols. London, 1738. Reprint, New York: Garland, 1978.

Coady, C. A. J. *Testimony: A Philosophical Study.* Oxford: Clarendon Press, 1992.

Cohen, Alix. "The Notion of Moral Progress in Hume's Philosophy: Does Hume Have a Theory of Moral Progress?" *Hume Studies* 26 (2000): 109–27.

Cohen, Benjamin. "Contrariety and Causality in Hume." *Hume Studies* 4 (1978): 29–39.

Cohen, Ralph. "Hume's Experimental Method and the Theory of Taste." *English Literary History* 25 (1958): 270–89.

———. "The Rationale of Hume's Literary Inquiries." In *David Hume: Many-Sided Genius,* edited by Kenneth R. Merrill and Robert W. Shahan, 97–115. Norman: University of Oklahoma Press, 1976.

———. "The Transformation of Passion: A Study in Hume's Theories of Tragedy." *Philological Quarterly* 41 (1962): 450–64.

Coleman, Dorothy P. "Hume's Dialectic." *Hume Studies* 10 (1984): 139–55.

———. "Is Mathematics for Hume Synthetic *A Priori?*" *Southwestern Journal of Philosophy* 10 (1979): 113–26.

Collier, Mark. "Filling the Gaps: Hume and Connectionism on the Continued Existence of Unperceived Objects." *Hume Studies* 25 (1999): 155–70.

Collingwood, R. G. *The Idea of History.* Oxford: Clarendon Press, 1946.

Conniff, James. "Hume's Political Methodology: A Reconsideration of 'That Politics May Be Reduced to a Science.'" *Review of Politics* 38 (1976): 88–108.

Connon, R. W. "The Naturalism of Hume Revisited." In *McGill Hume Studies,* edited by David Fate Norton, Nicholas Capaldi, and Wade L. Robison, 121–45. San Diego: Austin Hill Press, 1979.

Costa, Michael J. "Hume and Causal Inference." *Hume Studies* 12 (1986): 141–59.

———. "Hume and Causal Realism." *Australasian Journal of Philosophy* 67 (1989): 172–90.

———. "Hume on the Very Idea of a Relation." *Hume Studies* 24 (1998): 71–94.

———. "Hume, Strict Identity, and Time's Vacuum." *Hume Studies* 16 (1990): 1–16.

Cottle, Charles E. "Justice as Artificial Virtue in Hume's *Treatise.*" *Journal of the History of Ideas* 40 (1979): 457–66.

Cummins, Phillip D. "Hume as Dualist and Anti-Dualist." *Hume Studies* 21 (1995): 47–55.

———. "Hume on the Idea of Existence." *Hume Studies* 17 (1991): 61–82.

———. "Hume on Qualities." *Hume Studies* 22 (1996): 49–88.

———. "Hume's Diffident Skepticism." *Hume Studies* 25 (1999): 43–65.

Danford, John W. *David Hume and the Problem of Reason: Recovering the Human Sciences.* New Haven: Yale University Press, 1990.

———. "Hume's *History* and the Parameters of Economic Development." In *Liberty in Hume's History of England,* edited by Nicholas Capaldi and Donald W. Livingston, 155–94. Dordrecht: Kluwer, 1990.

Darwall, Stephen. "Hume and the Invention of Utilitarianism." In *Hume and Hume's Connexions,* edited by M. A. Stewart and John P. Wright, 58–82. University Park: Pennsylvania State University Press, 1995.

———. "Motive and Obligation in Hume's Ethics." *Nous* 27 (1993): 415–48.

Daston, Lorraine. *Classical Probability in the Enlightenment.* Princeton: Princeton University Press, 1988.

Dauer, Francis W. "Hume's Scepticism with Regard to Reason: A Reconsideration." *Hume Studies* 22 (1996): 211–29.

Davidson, Donald. "Actions, Reasons, and Causes." *Journal of Philosophy* 60 (1963): 685–700.

———. "Hume's Cognitive Theory of Pride." *Journal of Philosophy* 73 (1976): 744–57.

Davie, George. "Berkeley, Hume, and the Central Problem of Scottish Philosophy." In *McGill Hume Studies,* edited by David Fate Norton, Nicholas Capaldi, and Wade L. Robison, 43–62. San Diego: Austin Hill Press, 1979.

Davie, William. "Hume on Monkish Virtue." *Hume Studies* 25 (1999): 139–53.

Dawid, Philip, and Donald Gillies. "A Bayesian Analysis of Hume's Argument Concerning Miracles." *Philosophical Quarterly* 39 (1989): 57–65.

Dean, Dennis R. *James Hutton and the History of Geology.* Ithaca: Cornell University Press, 1992.

Deleuze, Gilles. *Empiricism and Subjectivity: An Essay on Hume's Theory of Human Nature.* New York: Columbia University Press, 1991.

Descartes, René. *Principles of Philosophy.* In *The Philosophical Writings of Descartes,* 1:177–291. Translated by John Cottingham, Rickert Stoothoff, and Dugald Murdoch. Cambridge: Cambridge University Press, 1985.

Devine, T. M., and J. R. Young, eds. *Eighteenth Century Scotland: New Perspectives*. East Linton, Scotland: Tuckwell Press, 1999.

DeWitt, Richard. "Hume's Probability Argument of I, iv, 1." *Hume Studies* 11 (1985): 125–36.

Dicker, Georges. *Hume's Epistemology and Metaphysics: An Introduction*. London: Routledge, 1998.

Dietl, Paul J. "Hume on the Passions." *Philosophy and Phenomenological Research* 28 (1968): 554–66.

Dilthey, Wilhelm. *Introduction to the Human Sciences*. Vol. 1 of the *Selected Works*. Translated by Rudolf A Makkreel and Frithjof Rodi. Princeton: Princeton University Press, 1989.

Dray, W. H. "David Hume on History." *Queen's Quarterly* 90 (1983): 735–45.

Dunn, Richard S. *The Age of Religious Wars, 1559–1715*. 2d ed. New York: Norton, 1979.

Echelbarger, Charles. "Hume on Deduction." *Philosophy Research Archives* 13 (1987–88): 351–65.

Einstein, Albert. *Autobiographical Notes*. Translated by Paul Arthur Schilpp. La Salle, Ill.: Open Court, 1979.

Emerson, Roger L. "Science and Moral Philosophy in the Scottish Enlightenment." In *Studies in the Philosophy of the Scottish Enlightenment*, edited by M. A. Stewart, 11–36. Oxford: Clarendon Press, 1990.

Falk, W. D. "Hume on Practical Reason." *Philosophical Studies* 27 (1975): 1–18.

Falkenstein, Lorne. "Hume on Manners of Disposition and the Ideas of Space and Time." *Archiv für Geschichte der Philosophie* 79 (1997): 179–201.

————. "Hume's Answer to Kant." *Noûs* 32 (1998): 331–60.

————. "Naturalism, Normativity, and Scepticism in Hume's Account of Belief." *Hume Studies* 23 (1997): 29–72.

Farr, James. "Hume, Hermeneutics, and History: A 'Sympathetic' Account." *History and Theory* 17 (1978): 285–310.

————. "Humean Explanations in the Moral Sciences." *Inquiry* 25 (1982): 57–80.

Ferreira, M. Jamie. *Scepticism and Reasonable Doubt: The British Naturalist Tradition in Wilkins, Hume, Reid and Newman*. Oxford: Clarendon Press, 1986.

Fieser, James, ed. *Early Responses to Hume*. 6 vols. Bristol: Thoemmes, 1999– .

Flage, Daniel E. *David Hume's Theory of Mind*. London: Routledge, 1990.

————. "Hume's Relative Ideas." *Hume Studies* 7 (1981): 55–73.

————. "Relative Ideas Re-Viewed." In *The New Hume Debate*, edited by Rupert Read and Kenneth A Richman, 138–55. London: Routledge, 2000.

————. "Remembering the Past." *Hume Studies* 15 (1989): 236–46.

Flew, Antony. *David Hume: Philosopher of Moral Science*. Oxford: Basil Blackwell, 1986.

————. "Did Hume Distinguish Pure from Applied Geometry?" *Ratio* 8 (1966): 96–100.

————. "Hume on Space and Geometry: One Reservation." *Hume Studies* 8 (1982): 62–65.

————. *Hume's Philosophy of Belief: A Study of His First Inquiry*. London: Routledge and Kegan Paul, 1961.

————. "On the Interpretation of Hume." In *Hume*, edited by V. C. Chappell, 278–86. Garden City, N.Y.: Doubleday, Anchor Books, 1966.

————. "Was Berkeley a Precursor of Wittgenstein?" In *Hume and the Enlightenment: Essays Presented to Ernest Campbell Mossner*, edited by William B. Todd, 153–63. Edinburgh: Edinburgh University Press; Austin: Humanities Research Center, 1974.

Fogelin, Robert J. *Hume's Skepticism in the Treatise of Human Nature*. London: Routledge & Kegan Paul, 1985.

Foot, Philippa R. "Hume on Moral Judgement." In *David Hume: A Symposium*, edited by D. F. Pears, 67–76. London: Macmillan, 1963.

Forbes, Duncan. *Hume's Philosophical Politics*. Cambridge: Cambridge University Press, 1975.

————. "Introduction" to *The History of Great Britain: The Reigns of James I and Charles I* by David Hume, edited by Duncan Forbes, 7–54. Harmondsworth: Penguin, 1970.

Force, James E. "Hume's Interest in Newton and Science." *Hume Studies* 13 (1987): 166–216.

Fosl, Peter S. "Doubt and Divinity: Cicero's Influence on Hume's Religious Skepticism." *Hume Studies* 20 (1994): 103–20.

Foucault, Michel. *The Archaeology of Knowledge*. Translated by A. M. Sheridan Smith. New York: Pantheon, 1972.

Franklin, James. "Achievements and Fallacies in Hume's Account of Infinite Divisibility." *Hume Studies* 20 (1994): 85–101.

———. *The Science of Conjecture: Evidence and Probability Before Pascal*. Baltimore: Johns Hopkins University Press, 2001.

Frasca-Spada, Marina. *Space and the Self in Hume's Treatise*. Cambridge: Cambridge University Press, 1998.

Frege, Gottlob. *The Foundations of Arithmetic*. 2d ed. Translated by J. L. Austin. New York: Harper, 1953.

Friedman, Michael. *Reconsidering Logical Positivism*. Cambridge: Cambridge University Press, 1999.

Fry, Michael. "A Commercial Empire: Scotland and British Expansion in the Eighteenth Century." In *Eighteenth Century Scotland: New Perspectives,* edited by T. M. Devine and J. R. Young, 53–69. East Linton, Scotland: Tuckwell Press, 1999.

Gardiner, P. L. "Hume's Theory of the Passions." In *David Hume: A Symposium,* edited by D. F. Pears, 31–42. London: Macmillan, 1963.

Garrett, Don. *Cognition and Commitment in Hume's Philosophy*. New York: Oxford University Press, 1997.

Gaskin, J. C. A. "Hume on Religion." In *The Cambridge Companion to Hume,* edited by David Fate Norton, 313–44. Cambridge: Cambridge University Press, 1993.

———. "Hume's Attenuated Deism." *Archiv für Geschichte der Philosophie* 65 (1983): 160–73.

———. *Hume's Philosophy of Religion*. 2d ed. Atlantic Highlands, N.J.: Humanities Press International, 1988.

———. "Introduction" to *Principal Writings on Religion, Including Dialogues Concerning Natural Religion and the Natural History of Religion* by David Hume, edited by J. C. A. Gaskin, ix–xxvi. Oxford: Oxford University Press, 1993.

Gauthier, David. "Artificial Virtues and the Sensible Knave." *Hume Studies* 18 (1992): 401–27.

Gawlick, Günter, and Lothar Kreimendahl. *Hume in der Deutschen Aufklärung: Umrisse einer Rezeptionsgeschichte*. Stuttgart-Bad Cannstatt: Frommann-Holzboog, 1987.

Gay, Peter. *The Enlightenment: An Interpretation*. 2 vols. New York: Knopf, 1966.

Gill, Michael. "Hume's Progressive View of Human Nature." *Hume Studies* 26 (2000): 87–108.

Glossop, Ronald J. "Hume, Stevenson, and Hare on Moral Language." In *Hume: A Re-Evaluation,* edited by Donald W. Livingston and James T. King, 362–85. New York: Fordham University Press, 1976.

———. "In Defence of David Hume." *Australasian Journal of Philosophy* 55 (1977): 59–63.

———. "Is Hume a 'Classical Utilitarian'?" *Hume Studies* 2 (1976): 1–16.

———. "The Nature of Hume's Ethics." *Philosophy and Phenomenological Research* 27 (1967): 527–36.

Glouberman, M. "Hume on Modes." *Hume Studies* 3 (1977): 32–50.

Goldie, Mark. "Ideology." In *Political Innovation and Conceptual Change,* edited by Terence Ball, James Farr, and Russell L. Hanson, 266–91. Cambridge: Cambridge University Press, 1989.

Gossman, Lionel, ed. "Two Unpublished Essays on Mathematics in the Hume Papers." *Journal of the History of Ideas* 21 (1960): 442–49.

Gotterbarn, Donald. "How Can Hume Know Philosophical Relations?" *Journal of Critical Analysis* 4 (1973): 133–41.

———. "Kant, Hume and Analyticity." *Kant-Studien* 65 (1974): 274–83.

Gower, Barry. "David Hume and the Probability of Miracles." *Hume Studies* 16 (1990): 17–31.
———. "Hume on Probability." *British Journal for the Philosophy of Science* 42 (1991): 1–19.
Gray, John. *Enlightenment's Wake: Politics and Culture at the Close of the Modern Age.* London: Routledge, 1995.
Green, Leslie. "Authority and Convention." *Philosophical Quarterly* 35 (1985): 329–46.
Green, Thomas Hill. *Hume and Locke.* Edited by Ramon M. Lemos. New York: Thomas Y. Crowell, 1968. Reprinted from *The Philosophical Works of David Hume,* edited by T. H. Green and T. H. Grose, 1: 1–299 and 2: 1–71. London: Longmans, 1874.
Greig, J. Y. T. *David Hume.* New York: Oxford University Press, 1931.
Grobman, Neil R. "David Hume and the Earliest Scientific Methodology for Collecting Balladry." *Western Folklore* 34 (1975): 16–31.
Guthrie, Stewart Elliot. *Faces in the Clouds: A New Theory of Religion.* New York: Oxford University Press, 1993.
Haakonssen, Knud. "Hume's Obligations." *Hume Studies* 4 (1978): 7–17.
———. "Introduction" to *David Hume: Political Essays,* edited by Knud Haakonssen, xi–xxx. Cambridge: Cambridge University Press, 1994.
———. *Natural Law and Moral Philosophy: From Grotius to the Scottish Enlightenment.* Cambridge: Cambridge University Press, 1996.
———. "The Structure of Hume's Political Theory." In *The Cambridge Companion to Hume,* edited by David Fate Norton, 182–221. Cambridge: Cambridge University Press, 1993.
Haber, Francis C. "Fossils and the Idea of a Process of Time in Natural History." In *Forerunners of Darwin: 1745–1859,* edited by Bentley Glass, Owsei Temkin, and William L. Straus Jr., 222–61. Baltimore: Johns Hopkins University Press, 1959
Hacking, Ian. *The Emergence of Probability.* Cambridge: Cambridge University Press, 1975.
———. "Hume's Species of Probability." *Philosophical Studies* 33 (1978): 21–37.
———. *Why Does Language Matter to Philosophy?* Cambridge: Cambridge University Press, 1975.
Hahn, Hans, Otto Neurath, and Rudolf Carnap. "The Scientific Conception of the World: The Vienna Circle." In Otto Neurath, *Empiricism and Sociology,* edited by Marie Neurath and Robert S. Cohen, 299–318. Dordrecht: Reidel, 1973.
Halberstadt, William H. "A Problem in Hume's Aesthetics." *Journal of Aesthetics and Art Criticism* 30 (1971): 209–14.
Halévy, Elie. *The Growth of Philosophic Radicalism.* Translated by Mary Morris. London: Faber & Gwyer, 1928.
Hall, Roland. *Fifty Years of Hume Scholarship: A Bibliographical Guide.* Edinburgh: Edinburgh University Press, 1978.
Hampton, Jean. *Political Philosophy.* Boulder, Colo.: Westview Press, 1997.
Harrison, Jonathan. *Hume's Moral Epistemology.* Oxford: Clarendon Press, 1976.
Hausman, Alan. "Hume's Theory of Relations." *Nous* 1 (1967): 255–82.
———. "Some Counsel on Humean Relations." *Hume Studies* 1 (1975): 48–65.
Hausman, David B. "Can Hume's Use of a Simple/Complex Distinction Be Made Consistent?" *Hume Studies* 14 (1988): 424–28.
Hawkins, R. J. "Simplicity, Resemblance and Contrariety in Hume's *Treatise.*" *Philosophical Quarterly* 26 (1976): 24–38.
Hayek, F. A. "The Legal and Political Philosophy of David Hume." In *Hume,* edited by V. C. Chappell, 335–60. Garden City, N.Y.: Doubleday, Anchor Books, 1966.
Hearn, Thomas K., Jr. "General Rules and Moral Sentiments in Hume's *Treatise.*" *Review of Metaphysics* 30 (1976): 57–72.
———. "'General Rules' in Hume's *Treatise.*" *Journal of the History of Philosophy* 8 (1970): 405–22.
———. "Norman Kemp Smith on 'Natural Belief.'" *Southern Journal of Philosophy* 7 (1969): 3–7.

Heath, P. L. "Concept." In *The Encyclopedia of Philosophy*, edited by Paul Edwards, 2: 177–80. New York: Macmillan, 1967.

Hegel, Georg Wilhelm Friedrich. "G. W. F. Hegel: Fragments of Historical Studies," edited by H. S. Harris. *Clio* 7 (1977): 113–34.

———. *Hegel's Philosophy of Mind*. Translated by William Wallace, foreword by J. N. Findlay. Oxford: Clarendon Press, 1971.

———. *Lectures on the Philosophy of World History. Introduction: Reason in History*. Translated by H. B. Nisbet. Cambridge: Cambridge University Press, 1975.

Heidegger, Martin. *Being and Time*. Translated by John Macquarrie and Edward Robinson. New York: Harper & Row, 1962.

Hendel, Charles William, Jr.. *Studies in the Philosophy of David Hume*. Rev. ed. Indianapolis: Bobbs-Merrill, 1963.

Henderson, Robert S. "David Hume on Personal Identity and the Indirect Passions." *Hume Studies* 16 (1990): 33–44.

Henze, Donald F. "The Linguistic Aspect of Hume's Method." *Journal of the History of Ideas* 30 (1969): 116–26.

Herder, Johann Gottfried. *Ideen zur Philosophie der Geschichte der Menschheit*. Vol. 4 of *Herders Werke: in Fünf Bänden*. Edited by Regine Otto. Vol 4. Berlin: Aufbau, 1982.

———. *Outlines of a Philosophy of the History of Man*. Translated by T. Churchill. London, 1800. Reprint, New York: Bergmar, 1966.

———. *On World History: An Anthology*. Edited by Hans Adler and Ernest A. Menze. Translated by Ernest A. Menze with Michael Palma. Armonk, N.Y.: M. E. Sharpe, 1997.

Herdt, Jennifer A. *Religion and Faction in Hume's Moral Philosophy*. Cambridge: Cambridge University Press, 1997.

Herman, Arthur. *How the Scots Invented the Modern World*. New York: Three Rivers Press, 2001.

Heruday, Joseph C. *Hume's Theory of Human Assent*. Rome: Catholic Book Agency, 1950.

Hill, Eric. "Hume and the Delightful Tragedy Problem." *Philosophy* 57 (1982): 319–26.

Hipple, Walter John, Jr. *The Beautiful, the Sublime, and the Picturesque in Eighteenth-Century British Aesthetic Theory*. Carbondale: Southern Illinois University Press, 1957.

———. "The Logic of Hume's Essay 'Of Tragedy.'" *Philosophical Quarterly* 6 (1956): 43–52.

Hiskes, Richard P. "Has Hume a Theory of Social Justice?" *Hume Studies* 3 (1977): 72–93.

Hollis, Martin, and Steven Lukes, eds. *Rationality and Relativism*. Cambridge: MIT Press, 1982.

Hont, Istvan, and Michael Ignatieff, eds. *Wealth and Virtue: The Shaping of Political Economy in the Scottish Enlightenment*. Cambridge: Cambridge University Press, 1983.

Hoy, David C. "Nietzsche, Hume, and the Genealogical Method." In *Nietzsche as Affirmative Thinker*, edited by Yirmiyahu Yovel, 20–38. Dordrecht: Martinus Nijhoff, 1986.

Hudson, Stephen D. "Humean Pleasures Reconsidered." *Canadian Journal of Philosophy* 5 (1975): 545–62.

Hudson, W. D. "Hume on *Is* and *Ought*." In *Hume*, edited by V. C. Chappell, 295–307. Garden City, N.Y.: Doubleday, Anchor Books, 1966.

———, ed. *The Is-Ought Question*. London: Macmillan, 1969.

Hume, David. "An Early Fragment on Evil," edited by M. A. Stewart. In *Hume and Hume's Connexions*, edited by M. A. Stewart and John P. Wright, 160–70. University Park: Pennsylvania State University Press, 1995.

———. "David Hume's 'An Historical Essay on Chivalry and Modern Honour,'" edited by Ernest Campbell Mossner. *Modern Philology* 45 (1947): 54–60.

———. *Four Dissertations and Essays on Suicide and the Immortality of the Soul*. Preface by James Fieser, introductions by John Immerwahr and John Valdimir Price. South Bend, Ind.: St. Augustine's Press, 2000. Facsimiles of the 1757 edition of the *Four Dissertations* and the

1783 edition of the *Essays on Suicide and the Immortality of the Soul.* Reprint of the separate volumes, Bristol: Thoemmes Press, 1992, 1995.

———. *The History of England: From the Invasion of Julius Caesar to The Revolution in 1688.* Abridged by Rodney W. Kilcup. Chicago: University of Chicago Press, 1975.

———. *The History of Great Britain: The Reigns of James I and Charles I.* Edited by Duncan Forbes. Harmondsworth: Penguin, 1970.

———. *The Philosophical Works of David Hume.* 4 vols. Edited by T. H. Green and T. H. Grose. London: Longmans, 1874–75.

Hundert, E. J. "The Achievement Motive in Hume's Political Economy." *Journal of the History of Ideas* 35 (1974): 139–43.

Hunt, William. "Historians I: Hume and Modern Historians." In *The Cambridge History of English Literature,* vol. 10, *The Age of Johnson,* edited by A. W. Ward and A. R. Waller, 316–35. New York: G. P. Putnam's Sons, 1913.

Hunter, Geoffrey. "Concepts and Meaning." In *Hume and the Enlightenment: Essays Presented to Ernest Campbell Mossner,* edited by William B. Todd, 136–52. Edinburgh: Edinburgh University Press; Austin: Humanities Research Center, 1974.

———. "Hume on Is and Ought." In *The Is-Ought Question,* edited by W. D. Hudson, 59–63. London: Macmillan, 1969.

———. "A Reply to Professor Flew." In *The Is-Ought Question,* edited by W. D. Hudson, 70–72. London: Macmillan, 1969.

Hurlbutt, Robert H, III. *Hume, Newton, and the Design Argument.* Rev. ed. Lincoln: University of Nebraska Press, 1985.

Husserl, Edmund. *Formal and Transcendental Logic.* Translated by Dorion Cairns. The Hague: Martinus Nijhoff, 1969.

Ikeda, Sadao. *David Hume and the Eighteenth-Century British Thought: An Annotated Catalogue.* 2 vols. Tokyo: Chuo University Library, 1986, 1988.

Imlay, Robert A. "Hume on Intuitive and Demonstrative Inference." *Hume Studies* 1 (1975): 31–47.

———. "Hume's 'Of Scepticism with regard to reason': A Study in Contrasting Themes." *Hume Studies* 7 (1981): 121–36.

Immerwahr, John. "The Anatomist and the Painter: The Continuity of Hume's *Treatise* and *Essays.*" *Hume Studies* 17 (1991): 1–14.

———. "Hume on Tranquillizing the Passions." *Hume Studies* 18 (1992): 293–314.

———. "Hume's Essays on Happiness." *Hume Studies* 15 (1989): 307–24.

———. "Hume's Revised Racism." *Journal of the History of Ideas* 53 (1992): 481–86.

Jacobson, Anne Jaap, ed. *Feminist Interpretations of David Hume.* University Park: Pennsylvania State University Press, 2000.

Jacquette, Dale. *David Hume's Critique of Infinity.* Leiden: E. J. Brill, 2001.

Jarrett, Derek. *Britain: 1688–1815.* New York: St. Martin's Press, 1965.

Jay, Martin. *Marxism and Totality: The Adventures of a Concept from Lukács to Habermas.* Berkeley and Los Angeles: University of California Press, 1984.

Jeffner, Anders. *Butler and Hume on Religion: A Comprehensive Analysis.* Stockholm: Diakonistyrelsens, 1966.

Jensen, Henning. "Hume on Moral Agreement." *Mind* 86 (1977): 497–513.

Jessop, T. E. *A Bibliography of David Hume and of Scottish Philosophy from Francis Hutcheson to Lord Balfour.* London: A. Brown & Sons, 1938.

Johnson, Clarence Shole. "Hume's Theory of Moral Responsibility: Some Unresolved Matters." *Dialogue* 31 (1992): 3–18.

Johnson, David. *Hume, Holism, and Miracles.* Ithaca: Cornell University Press, 1999.

Johnson, E. A. J. *Predecessors of Adam Smith: The Growth of British Economic Thought.* New York: Prentice-Hall, 1937.

Johnson, Oliver A. "'Lively' Memory and 'Past' Memory." *Hume Studies* 13 (1987), 343–59.
———. *The Mind of David Hume: A Companion to Book I of "A Treatise of Human Nature."* Urbana: University of Illinois Press, 1995.
———. "Time and the Idea of Time." *Hume Studies* 15 (1989): 205–19.
Jones, Peter. "Another Look at Hume's Views of Aesthetic and Moral Judgments." *Philosophical Quarterly* 20 (1970): 53–59.
———. "'Art' and 'Moderation' in Hume's *Essays.*" In *McGill Hume Studies,* edited by David Fate Norton, Nicholas Capaldi, and Wade L. Robison, 161–80. San Diego: Austin Hill Press, 1979.
———. "Cause, Reason, and Objectivity in Hume's Aesthetics." In *Hume: A Re-Evaluation,* edited by Donald W. Livingston and James T. King, 323–42. New York: Fordham University Press, 1976.
———. "Hume's Aesthetics Reassessed." *Philosophical Quarterly* 26 (1976): 48–62.
———. "Hume's Literary and Aesthetic Theory." In *The Cambridge Companion to Hume,* edited by David Fate Norton, 255–80. Cambridge: Cambridge University Press, 1993.
———. *Hume's Sentiments: Their Ciceronian and French Context.* Edinburgh: Edinburgh University Press, 1982.
Kallich, Martin. *The Association of Ideas and Critical Theory in Eighteenth-Century England.* The Hague: Mouton, 1970.
Kant, Immanuel. *Anthropology from a Pragmatic Point of View.* Translated by Mary J. Gregor. The Hague: Martinus Nijhoff, 1974.
———. *Critique of Judgment.* Translated by Werner S. Pluhar. Indianapolis: Hackett, 1987.
———. *Critique of Pure Reason.* Translated by Paul Guyer and Allen W. Wood. Cambridge: Cambridge University Press, 1998.
———. *Kants gesammelte Schriften.* 29 vols. Published by the Royal Prussian (subsequently German) Academy of Sciences. Berlin: Georg Reimer, subsequently Walter de Gruyter; 1900– .
———. *Prolegomena to Any Future Metaphysics.* Translated by Gary Hatfield. Cambridge: Cambridge University Press, 1997.
———. *Religion Within the Boundaries of Mere Reason, and Other Writings.* Edited by Allen Wood and George di Giovanni. Cambridge: Cambridge University Press, 1998.
Kemp Smith, Norman. "Introduction" to the *Dialogues Concerning Natural Religion* by David Hume, edited by Norman Kemp Smith, 1–123. Indianapolis: Bobbs-Merrill, 1947.
———. *The Philosophy of David Hume: A Critical Study of Its Origins and Central Doctrines.* London: Macmillan, 1941.
Kenny, Anthony. *Action, Emotion and Will.* New York: Humanities Press, 1963.
Kenyon, J. P. *Stuart England.* 2d ed. Harmondsworth: Penguin Books, 1985.
King, James T. "Hume on Artificial Lives with a Rejoinder to A. C. MacIntyre." *Hume Studies* 14 (1988): 53–92.
———. "The Place of the Language of Morals in Hume's Second *Enquiry.*" In *Hume: A Re-Evaluation,* edited by Donald W. Livingston and James T. King, 343–61. New York: Fordham University Press, 1976.
Kivy, Peter. "Hume's Standard of Taste: Breaking the Circle." *British Journal of Aesthetics* 7 (1967): 57–66.
Kolin, Andrew. *The Ethical Foundations of Hume's Theory of Politics.* New York: Peter Lang, 1992.
Kors, Alan Charles. *Atheism in France: 1650–1729.* Vol. 1, *The Orthodox Sources of Disbelief.* Princeton: Princeton University Press, 1990.
———. "The French Context of Hume's Philosophical Theology." *Hume Studies* 21 (1995): 221–36.
Korsmeyer, Carolyn W. "Hume and the Foundations of Taste." *Journal of Aesthetics and Art Criticism* 35 (1976): 201–15.

Kuehn, Manfred. *Kant: A Biography.* Cambridge: Cambridge University Press, 2001.

————. "Kant's Conception of 'Hume's Problem.'" *Journal of the History of Philosophy* 21 (1983): 175–93.

————. "Kant's Critique of Hume's Theory of Faith." In *Hume and Hume's Connexions,* edited by M. A. Stewart and John P. Wright, 239–55. University Park: Pennsylvania State University Press, 1995.

————. *Scottish Common Sense in Germany, 1768–1800: A Contribution to the History of Critical Philosophy.* Montreal: McGill-Queen's University Press, 1987.

Kuhns, Richard. "Hume's Republic and the Universe of Newton." In *Eighteenth Century Studies Presented to Arthur M. Wilson,* edited by Peter Gay, 73–95. New York: Russell & Russell, 1975.

Kuypers, Mary Shaw. *Studies in the Eighteenth Century Background of Hume's Empiricism.* Minneapolis: University of Minnesota Press, 1930. Reprint, New York: Russell & Russell, 1966.

Kydd, Rachael M. *Reason and Conduct in Hume's Treatise.* London: Oxford University Press, 1946.

Laing, B. M. *David Hume.* New York: Russell & Russell, 1932.

Laird, John. *Hume's Philosophy of Human Nature.* London: Methuen, 1932.

Laudan, Larry. *Beyond Positivism and Relativism: Theory, Method, and Evidence.* Boulder, Colo.: Westview Press, 1996.

————. *Progress and Its Problems: Toward a Theory of Scientific Growth.* Berkeley and Los Angeles: University of California Press, 1977.

Laursen, John Christian, and Greg Coolidge. "David Hume and Public Debt: Crying Wolf?" *Hume Studies* 20 (1994): 143–49.

Leibniz, Gottfried Wilhelm. *Die Philosophischen Schriften von Gottfried Wilhelm Leibniz.* 7 vols. Edited by C. I. Gerhardt. Berlin, 1875–90; Hildesheim: Georg Olms, 1960–61.

————. *Theodicy: Essays on the Goodness of God, the Freedom of Man, and the Origin of Evil.* Translated by E. M. Haggard, edited by Austin Farrer. New Haven: Yale University Press, 1952.

Lenz, John W. "Hume's Defense of Causal Inference." In *Hume,* edited by V. C. Chappell, 169–86. Garden City, N.Y.: Doubleday, Anchor Books, 1966.

Letwin, Shirley Robin. "Hume: Inventor of a New Task for Philosophy." *Political Theory* 3 (1975): 134–58.

————. *The Pursuit of Certainty.* Cambridge: Cambridge University Press, 1965.

Levey, Ann. "Under Constraint: Chastity and Modesty in Hume." *Hume Studies* 23 (1997): 213–26.

Levine, Michael Philip. *Hume and the Problem of Miracles: A Solution.* Dordrecht: Kluwer, 1989.

Lewis, David. *Convention: A Philosophical Study.* Cambridge: Harvard University Press, 1969.

Livingston, Donald W. "Hume's Historical Conception of Liberty." In *Liberty in Hume's History of England,* edited by Nicholas Capaldi and Donald W. Livingston, 105–53. Dordrecht: Kluwer, 1990.

————. *Hume's Philosophy of Common Life.* Chicago: University of Chicago Press, 1984.

————. *Philosophical Melancholy and Delirium: Hume's Pathology of Philosophy.* Chicago: University of Chicago Press, 1998.

————. "A Sellarsian Hume?" *Journal of the History of Philosophy* 29 (1991): 281–90.

Livingston, Donald W., and James T. King, eds. *Hume: A Re-Evaluation.* New York: Fordham University Press, 1976.

Locke, John. *An Essay Concerning Human Understanding.* Edited by Peter H. Nidditch. Oxford: Clarendon Press, 1975.

Loeb, Louis E. "Causation, Extrinsic Relations, and Hume's Second Thoughts About Personal Identity." *Hume Studies* 18 (1992): 219–31.

————. "Hume's Moral Sentiments and the Structure of the *Treatise.*" *Journal of the History of Philosophy* 15 (1977): 395–403.

Logan, Beryl. *A Religion Without Talking: Religious Belief and Natural Belief in Hume's Philosophy of Religion.* New York: Peter Lang, 1993.

Long, Douglas G. "'Utility' and the 'Utility Principle': Hume, Smith, Bentham, Mill." *Utilitas* 2 (1990): 12–39.

Lyon, Robert. "Notes on Hume's Philosophy of Political Economy." *Journal of the History of Ideas* 31 (1970): 457–61.

MacIntyre, Alasdair C. *After Virtue: A Study in Moral Theory.* 2d ed. Notre Dame: University of Notre Dame Press, 1984.

———. "Hume on 'Is' and 'Ought.'" In *Hume,* edited by V. C. Chappell, 240–64. Garden City, N.Y.: Doubleday, Anchor Books, 1966.

———. *Whose Justice? Which Rationality?* Notre Dame: University of Notre Dame Press, 1988.

Mackie, J. L. *The Cement of the Universe: A Study of Causation.* Oxford: Clarendon Press, 1974.

———. *Hume's Moral Theory.* London: Routledge & Kegan Paul, 1980.

Macleod, Alistair. "Rule-Utilitarianism and Hume's Theory of Justice." *Hume Studies* 7 (1981): 74–84.

MacNabb, D. G. C. *David Hume: His Theory of Knowledge and Morality.* 2d ed. Hamden, Conn.: Archon Books, 1966.

Magri, Tito. "Natural Obligation and Normative Motivation in Hume's *Treatise.*" *Hume Studies* 22 (1996): 231–53.

Main, Edward. "Hume's Criterion for Historical Evidence (Or Lack Thereof)." *Kinesis* 7 (1977): 62–74.

Malherbe, Michel. "Hume and the Art of Dialogue." In *Hume and Hume's Connexions,* edited by M. A. Stewart and John P. Wright, 201–23. University Park: Pennsylvania State University Press, 1995.

———. "Hume's *Natural History of Religion.*" *Hume Studies* 21 (1995): 255–74.

Mall, Ram Adhar. *Experience and Reason: The Phenomenology of Husserl and its Relation to Hume's Philosophy.* The Hague: Martinus Nijhoff, 1973.

———. *Hume's Concept of Man: An Essay in Philosophical Anthropology.* Bombay: Allied Publishers, 1967.

Manzer, Robert A. "The Promise of Peace? Hume and Smith on the Effects of Commerce on War and Peace." *Hume Studies* 22 (1996): 369–82.

Marcil-Lacoste, Louise. "The Consistency of Hume's Position Concerning Women." *Dialogue* 15 (1976): 425–40.

Marshall, Geoffrey. "David Hume and Political Scepticism." *Philosophical Quarterly* 4 (1954): 247–57.

Martin, Marie A. "Hume on Human Excellence." *Hume Studies* 18 (1992): 383–99.

———. "Hutcheson and Hume on Explaining the Nature of Morality: Why It Is Mistaken to Suppose Hume Ever Raised the 'Is-Ought' Question." *History of Philosophy Quarterly* 8 (1991): 277–89.

Maund, Constance. *Hume's Theory of Knowledge: A Critical Examination.* London: Macmillan,1937.

McGee, Robert W. "The Economic Thought of David Hume." *Hume Studies* 15 (1989): 184–204.

McIntyre, Jane L. "Character: A Humean Account." *History of Philosophy Quarterly* 7 (1990): 193–206.

———. "Hume: Second Newton of the Moral Sciences." *Hume Studies* 20 (1994): 3–18.

———. "Hume's Passions: Direct and Indirect." *Hume Studies* 26 (2000): 77–86.

———. "Is Hume's Self Consistent?" In *McGill Hume Studies,* edited by David Fate Norton, Nicholas Capaldi, and Wade L. Robison, 79–88. San Diego: Austin Hill Press, 1979.

———. "Personal Identity and the Passions." *Journal of the History of Philosophy* 27 (1989): 545–57.

McRae, Robert. "Perceptions, Objects, and the Nature of Mind." *Hume Studies,* tenth anniversary issue, supplement (1985): 150–67.

Mercer, Philip. *Sympathy and Ethics: A Study of the Relationship between Sympathy and Morality, with Special Reference to Hume's Treatise.* Oxford: Clarendon Press, 1972.

Merlan, Philip. "From Hume to Hamann." *Personalist* 32 (1951): 11–18.

Merrill, Kenneth R., and Robert W. Shahan, eds. *David Hume: Many-Sided Genius.* Norman: University of Oklahoma Press, 1976.

Middleton, Conyers. *A Free Inquiry into the Miraculous Powers, Which are Supposed to Have subsisted in the Christian Church. . . .* London, 1749. Reprint, New York: Garland, 1976.

Miller, David. *Philosophy and Ideology in Hume's Political Thought.* Oxford: Clarendon Press, 1981.

Miller, Eugene F. "Foreword" to *Essays, Moral, Political, and Literary* by David Hume, edited by Eugene F. Miller, xi–xviii. Indianapolis: Liberty Fund, 1985; revised edition 1987.

———. "Hume on Liberty in the Successive English Constitutions." In *Liberty in Hume's History of England,* edited by Nicholas Capaldi and Donald W. Livingston, 53–103. Dordrecht: Kluwer, 1990.

Monteiro, J. P. "Hume, Induction and Natural Selection." In *McGill Hume Studies,* edited by David Fate Norton, Nicholas Capaldi, and Wade L. Robison, 291–308. San Diego: Austin Hill Press, 1979.

Moonan, Lawrence. "Hume on Is and Ought." *Journal of the History of Philosophy* 13 (1975): 83–98.

Moore, G. E. "Hume's Philosophy." In *Readings in Philosophical Analysis,* edited by Herbert Feigl and Wilfrid Sellars, 351–63. New York: Appleton-Century-Crofts, 1949.

Moore, James. "The Social Background of Hume's Science of Human Nature." In *McGill Hume Studies,* edited by David Fate Norton, Nicholas Capaldi, and Wade L. Robison, 23–41. San Diego: Austin Hill Press, 1979.

Morice, G. P., ed. *David Hume: Bicentenary Papers.* Edinburgh: Edinburgh University Press, 1977.

Morris, William Edward. "Hume's Scepticism About Reason." *Hume Studies* 15 (1989): 39–60.

Morrisroe, Michael, Jr. "Linguistic Analysis as Rhetorical Pattern in David Hume." In *Hume and the Enlightenment: Essays Presented to Ernest Campbell Mossner,* edited by William B. Todd, 72–82. Edinburgh: Edinburgh University Press; Austin: Humanities Research Center, 1974.

Mossner, Ernest Campbell. "An Apology for David Hume, Historian." *Publications of the Modern Language Association* 56 (1941): 657–90.

———. "Deism." In *The Encyclopedia of Philosophy,* edited by Paul Edwards, 2: 326–36. New York: Macmillan, 1967.

———. "The Enigma of Hume." *Mind* 45 (1936): 334–49.

———. "Hume as Literary Patron: A Suppressed Review of Robert Henry's *History of Great Britain,* 1773." *Modern Philology* 39 (1942): 361–82.

———. *The Life of David Hume.* 2d ed. Oxford: Clarendon Press, 1980.

———, ed. "David Hume's 'An Historical Essay on Chivalry and Modern Honour.'" *Modern Philology* 45 (1947): 54–60.

———, ed. "Hume's Early Memoranda, 1729–1740: The Complete Text." *Journal of the History of Ideas* 9 (1948): 492–518.

Mounce, H. O. *Hume's Naturalism.* London: Routledge, 1999.

Murphy, Richard T. *Hume and Husserl: Towards Radical Subjectivism.* The Hague: Martinus Nijhoff, 1980.

Nelson, John O. "The Burial and Resurrection of Hume's Essay 'Of Miracles.'" *Hume Studies* 12 (1986): 57–76.

Neu, Jerome. *Emotion, Thought and Therapy: A Study of Hume and Spinoza and the Relationship of Philosophical Theories of the Emotions to Psychological Theories of Therapy.* Berkeley and Los Angeles: University of California Press, 1977.

Newman, Rosemary. "'Hume on Space and Geometry': A Rejoinder to Flew's 'One Reservation.'" *Hume Studies* 8 (1982): 66–69.

———. "Hume on Space and Geometry." *Hume Studies* 7 (1981): 1–31.

Newton, Isaac. *Sir Isaac Newton's Mathematical Principles of Natural Philosophy, and His System of the World.* 2 vols. Translated by Andrew Motte. Edited by Florian Cajori. Berkeley and Los Angeles: University of California Press, 1962.

Nietzsche, Friedrich. "On the Uses and Disadvantages of History for Life." In *Untimely Meditations,* 57–123. Translated by R. J. Hollingdale. Edited by Daniel Breazeale. Cambridge: Cambridge University Press, 1997.

Norton, David Fate. *David Hume: Common-Sense Moralist, Sceptical Metaphysician.* Princeton: Princeton University Press, 1982.

———. "Editor's Introduction" to David Hume, *A Treatise of Human Nature,* edited by David Fate Norton and Mary J. Norton, I9–I99. Oxford Philosophical Texts. Oxford: Oxford University Press, 2000.

———. "History and Philosophy in Hume's Thought." In *David Hume: Philosophical Historian,* edited by David Fate Norton and Richard H. Popkin, xxxii–l. Indianapolis: Bobbs-Merrill, 1965.

———. "How a Sceptic May Live Scepticism." In *Faith, Scepticism, and Personal Identity,* edited by J. J. MacIntosh and H. A. Meynell, 119–39. Calgary: University of Calgary Press, 1994.

———. "Hume, Human Nature, and the Foundations of Morality." In *The Cambridge Companion to Hume,* edited by David Fate Norton, 148–81. Cambridge: Cambridge University Press, 1993.

———. "Hume's Common Sense Morality." *Canadian Journal of Philosophy* 5 (1975): 523–43.

———. "Hume's Moral Ontology." *Hume Studies,* tenth anniversary issue, supplement (1985): 189–214.

———, ed. *The Cambridge Companion to Hume.* Cambridge: Cambridge University Press, 1993.

Norton, David Fate, and Mary J. Norton. "Substantive Differences Between Two Texts of Hume's *Treatise.*" *Hume Studies* 26 (2000): 245–77

Norton, David Fate, and Richard H. Popkin, eds. *David Hume: Philosophical Historian.* Indianapolis: Bobbs-Merrill, 1965.

Norton, David Fate, Nicholas Capaldi, and Wade L. Robison, eds. *McGill Hume Studies.* San Diego: Austin Hill Press, 1979.

Noxon, James. "Hume's Opinion of Critics." *Journal of Aesthetics and Art Criticism* 20 (1961): 157–62.

———. *Hume's Philosophical Development: A Study of His Methods.* Oxford: Clarendon Press, 1973.

———. "Remembering and Imagining the Past." In *Hume: A Re-Evaluation,* edited by Donald W. Livingston and James T. King, 270–95. New York: Fordham University Press, 1976.

———. "Senses of Identity in Hume's *Treatise.*" *Dialogue* 8 (1969): 367–84.

Oakeshott, Michael. *Rationalism in Politics and Other Essays.* New York: Basic Books, 1962.

Outram, Dorinda. *The Enlightenment.* Cambridge: Cambridge University Press, 1995.

Owen, David. "Hume 'Versus' Price on Miracles and Prior Probabilities: Testimony and the Bayesian Calculation." *Philosophical Quarterly* 37 (1987): 187–202.

———. *Hume's Reason.* Oxford: Oxford University Press, 1999.

Palter, Robert. "Hume and Prejudice." *Hume Studies* 21 (1995): 3–23.

[Palgrave, Francis.] "Hume and His Influence Upon History." *Quarterly Review* 73 (1844): 536–92.

Pap, Arthur. *Semantics and Necessary Truth.* New Haven: Yale University Press, 1958.

Parusnikova, Zuzana. "Against the Spirit of Foundations: Postmodernism and David Hume." *Hume Studies* 19 (1993): 1–17.

Pascal, Roy. "Herder and the Scottish Historical School." *Publications of the English Goethe Society,* n.s., 14 (1939): 23–42.

Passmore, John. *Hume's Intentions.* 3d ed. London: Duckworth, 1980.

Paton, Margaret. "Hume on Tragedy." *British Journal of Aesthetics* 13 (1973): 121–32.

Pears, David F. "Hume on Personal Identity." In *David Hume: A Symposium,* edited by D. F. Pears, 43–54. London: Macmillan, 1963.

———. *Hume's System: An Examination of the First Book of His Treatise.* Oxford: Oxford University Press, 1990.

———, ed. *David Hume: A Symposium.* London: Macmillan, 1963.

Penelhum, Terence. *David Hume: An Introduction to His Philosophical System.* West Lafayette: Purdue University Press, 1992.

———. "Hume on Personal Identity." In *Hume,* edited by V. C. Chappell, 213–39. Garden City, N.Y.: Doubleday, Anchor Books, 1966.

———. "Hume's Moral Psychology." In *The Cambridge Companion to Hume,* edited by David Fate Norton, 117–47. Cambridge: Cambridge University Press, 1993.

———. "The Self of Book I and the Selves of Book II." *Hume Studies* 18 (1992): 281–92.

———. *Themes in Hume: The Self, the Will, Religion.* Oxford: Clarendon Press, 2000.

Philips, John. *Cyder.* In *The Poems of John Philips,* edited by M. G. Lloyd Thomas, 43–87. Oxford: Basil Blackwell, 1927.

Phillips, D. Z., and Timothy Tessin, eds. *Religion and Hume's Legacy.* New York: St. Martin's Press, 1999.

Phillipson, Nicholas. *Hume.* London: Weidenfeld & Nicholson, 1989.

———. "The Scottish Enlightenment." In *The Enlightenment in National Context,* edited by Roy Porter and Mikulás Teich, 19–40. Cambridge: Cambridge University Press, 1981.

Pike, Nelson. "Hume on the Argument from Design." In *Dialogues Concerning Natural Religion by David Hume,* edited by Nelson Pike, 128–238. Indianapolis: Bobbs-Merrill, 1970.

Pippin, Robert B. *Idealism as Modernism: Hegelian Variations.* Cambridge: Cambridge University Press, 1997.

———. *Modernism as a Philosophical Problem: On the Dissatisfactions of European High Culture.* Cambridge, Mass.: Basil Blackwell, 1991.

Pitcher, George. "Emotion." *Mind* 74 (1965): 326–46.

Pitson, Antony E. "Hume on Promises and Their Obligation." *Hume Studies* 14 (1988): 176–90.

Plamenatz, John. *The English Utilitarians.* Oxford: Basil Blackwell, 1949.

Pocock, J. G. A. *The Ancient Constitution and the Feudal Law.* Cambridge: Cambridge University Press, 1957.

———. "Hume and the American Revolution: The Dying Thoughts of a North Briton." In *McGill Hume Studies,* edited by David Fate Norton, Nicholas Capaldi, and Wade L. Robison, 325–43. San Diego: Austin Hill Press, 1979.

Pompa, Leon. *Human Nature and Historical Knowledge: Hume, Hegel and Vico.* Cambridge: Cambridge University Press, 1990.

Ponko, Ted A. "Artificial Virtue, Self-Interest, and Acquired Social Concern." *Hume Studies* 9 (1983): 46–58.

Popkin, Richard H. "Condorcet and Hume and Turgot." In *The Third Force in Seventeenth-Century Thought,* 76–89. Leiden: E. J. Brill, 1992.

———. "David Hume: His Pyrrhonism and His Critique of Pyrrhonism." In *Hume,* edited by V. C. Chappell, 53–98. Garden City, N.Y.: Doubleday, Anchor Books, 1966.

———. *The High Road to Pyrrhonism.* Edited by Richard A. Watson and James E. Force. San Diego: Austin Hill Press, 1980.

———. *The History of Scepticism from Erasmus to Descartes.* Rev. ed. New York: Humanities Press, 1964.

———. "Hume: Philosophical Versus Prophetic Historian." In *David Hume: Many-Sided Genius,* edited by Kenneth R. Merrill and Robert W. Shahan, 83–95. Norman: University of Oklahoma Press, 1976.

———. "Hume's Racism." In *The High Road to Pyrrhonism,* edited by Richard A. Watson and James E. Force, 251–66. San Diego: Austin Hill Press, 1980.

———. "Hume's Racism Reconsidered." In *The Third Force in Seventeenth-Century Thought,* 64–75. Leiden: E. J. Brill, 1992.

———. "Skepticism and the Study of History." In *David Hume: Philosophical Historian,* edited by David Fate Norton and Richard H. Popkin, ix–xxxi. Indianapolis: Bobbs-Merrill, 1965.

Popper, Karl R. *Objective Knowledge: An Evolutionary Approach.* Oxford: Clarendon Press, 1972.

———. *The Logic of Scientific Discovery.* London: Hutchinson, 1959.

Postema, Gerald J. "Hume's Reply to the Sensible Knave." *History of Philosophy Quarterly* 5 (1988): 23–40.

Price, H. H. *Hume's Theory of the External World.* Oxford: Clarendon Press, 1940.

———. *Thinking and Experience.* 2d ed. London: Hutchinson, 1969.

Price, John Valdimir. *David Hume: Updated Edition.* Boston: Twayne, 1991.

———. *The Ironic Hume.* Austin: University of Texas Press, 1965.

Purviance, Susan M. "The Moral Self and the Indirect Passions." *Hume Studies* 23 (1997): 195–212.

Radcliffe, Elizabeth S. "Hume on Motivating Sentiments, the General Point of View, and the Inculcation of 'Morality.'" *Hume Studies* 20 (1994): 37–58.

———. "Hume on the Generation of Motives: Why Beliefs Alone Never Motivate." *Hume Studies* 25 (1999): 101–22.

Raynor, David. "Ossian and Hume." In *Ossian Revisited,* edited by Howard Gaskill, 147–63. Edinburgh: Edinburgh University Press, 1991.

Raynor, Owen. "Hume's Scepticism Regarding 'Probable Reasoning' in the *Treatise.*" *Southern Journal of Philosophy* 2 (1964): 103–6.

Read, Rupert, and Kenneth A. Richman, eds. *The New Hume Debate.* London: Routledge, 2000.

Reich, Lou. *Hume's Religious Naturalism.* Lanham: University Press of America, 1998.

Reid, Thomas. *The Works of Thomas Reid.* 2 vols. 6th ed. Edited by William Hamilton. Edinburgh: Maclachlan and Stewart, 1863.

Reill, Peter Hanns. *The German Enlightenment and the Rise of Historicism.* Berkeley and Los Angeles: University of California Press, 1975.

Reinach, Adolf. "Kant's Interpretation of Hume's Problem." In *David Hume: Many-Sided Genius,* edited by Kenneth R. Merrill and Robert W. Shahan, 161–88. Norman: University of Oklahoma Press, 1976.

Rendall, Jane. "Clio, Mars and Minerva: The Scottish Enlightenment and the Writing of Women's History." In *Eighteenth Century Scotland: New Perspectives,* edited by T. M. Devine and J. R. Young, 134–51. East Linton, Scotland: Tuckwell Press, 1999.

Reventlow, Henning Graf. *The Authority of the Bible and the Rise of the Modern World.* Translated by John Bowden. Philadelphia: Fortress Press, 1985.

Richards, Thomas J. "Hume's Two Definitions of 'Cause.'" In *Hume,* edited by V. C. Chappell, 148–61. Garden City, N.Y.: Doubleday, Anchor Books, 1966.

Roberts, Clayton. *The Logic of Historical Explanation.* University Park: Pennsylvania State University Press, 1996.

Robinson, J. A. "Hume's Two Definitions of 'Cause.'" In *Hume,* edited by V. C. Chappell, 129–47. Garden City, N.Y.: Doubleday, Anchor Books, 1966.

Robison, Wade L. "Hume on Personal Identity." *Journal of the History of Philosophy* 12 (1974): 181–93.

———. "Hume's Causal Scepticism." In *David Hume: Bicentenary Papers,* edited by G. P. Morice, 156–66. Edinburgh: Edinburgh University Press, 1977.

———. "In Defense of Hume's *Appendix.*" In *McGill Hume Studies,* edited by David Fate Norton, Nicholas Capaldi, and Wade L. Robison, 89–99. San Diego: Austin Hill Press, 1979.

Roll, Eric. *A History of Economic Thought.* 4th ed. London: Faber & Faber, 1973.

Rorty, Amélie Oskenberg. "From Passions to Sentiments: The Structure of Hume's *Treatise.*" *History of Philosophy Quarterly* 10 (1993): 165–79.

———. "'Pride Produces the Idea of Self': Hume on Moral Agency." *Australasian Journal of Philosophy* 68 (1990): 255–69.

Rorty, Richard. *Philosophy and the Mirror of Nature.* Princeton: Princeton University Press, 1979.

———. "Should Hume Be Answered or Bypassed?" In *Human Nature and Natural Knowledge,* edited by A. Donogan, A. N. Perovich, and M. V. Wedin, 341–52. Dordrecht: D. Reidl, 1986.

Rorty, Richard, J. B. Schneewind, and Quentin Skinner, eds. *Philosophy in History: Essays on the Historiography of Philosophy.* Cambridge: Cambridge University Press, 1984.

Rosenberg, Alexander. "Hume and the Philosophy of Science." In *The Cambridge Companion to Hume,* edited by David Fate Norton, 64–89. Cambridge: Cambridge University Press, 1993.

Ross, William Gordon. *Human Nature and Utility in Hume's Social Philosophy.* Doctoral dissertation: Columbia University, 1942.

Rostow, W. W. *Theories of Economic Growth from David Hume to the Present.* New York: Oxford University Press, 1990.

Roth, Robert J. "Hume's Theory of Human Nature and Community." *New Scholasticism* 57 (1983): 331–51.

Rotwein, Eugene. "Introduction" to *Writings on Economics* by David Hume, edited by Eugene Rotwein, ix–cxi. Edinburgh: Thomas Nelson & Sons, 1955.

Russell, Bertrand. *A History of Western Philosophy.* New York: Simon & Schuster, 1946.

———. *The Problems of Philosophy.* 1912. Reprint, London: Oxford University Press, 1979.

Russell, Paul. *Freedom and Moral Sentiment: Hume's Way of Naturalizing Responsibility.* New York: Oxford University Press, 1995.

———. "Hume's *Treatise* and the Clarke-Collins Controversy." *Hume Studies* 21 (1995): 95–115.

Russow, Lilly-Marlene. "Simple Ideas and Resemblance." *Philosophical Quarterly* 30 (1980): 342–50.

Sabine, George H. "Hume's Contribution to the Historical Method." *Philosophical Review* 15 (1906): 17–38.

Salmon, C. V. *The Central Problem of David Hume's Philosophy: An Essay Towards a Phenomenological Interpretation of the First Book of the Treatise of Human Nature.* Halle: Max Niemeyer, 1929.

Sapadin, Eugene. "A Note on Newton, Boyle, and Hume's 'Experimental Method.'" *Hume Studies* 23 (1997): 337–44.

Saville, Richard. "Scottish Modernisation Prior to the Industrial Revolution: 1688–1763." In *Eighteenth Century Scotland: New Perspectives,* edited by T. M. Devine and J. R. Young, 6–23. East Linton, Scotland: Tuckwell Press, 1999.

Sawyier, Fay Horton. "A Mark of the Growing Mind Is the Veneration of Objects." *Hume Studies* 18 (1992): 315–29.

Sayre-McCord, Geoffrey. "On Why Hume's 'General Point of View' Isn't Ideal—and Shouldn't Be." *Social Philosophy and Policy* 11 (1994): 202–28.

Schmidt, Claudia M. "Shelley's 'Spirit of the Age' Antedated in Hume." *Notes and Queries* 236 (1991): 297–98.

Schmidt, James, ed. *What Is Enlightenment? Eighteenth-Century Answers and Twentieth-Century Questions.* Berkeley and Los Angeles: University of California Press, 1996.

Schmitt, Frederick F., ed. *Socializing Epistemology: The Social Dimensions of Knowledge.* Lanham: Rowman and Littlefield, 1994.

Schumpeter, Joseph A. *History of Economic Analysis.* New York: Oxford University Press, 1954.

Searle, John R. *The Construction of Social Reality.* New York: Free Press, 1995.

Sedivy, Sonia. "Hume, Images, and Abstraction." *Hume Studies* 21 (1995): 117–33.

Selby-Bigge, L. A. "Editor's Introduction" to the *Enquiries Concerning Human Understanding and Concerning the Principles of Morals* by David Hume, edited by L. A. Selby-Bigge, vii–xxxi. 3d ed. Revised by P. H. Nidditch. Oxford: Clarendon Press, 1975.

Shapere, Dudley. *Reason and the Search for Knowledge: Investigations in the Philosophy of Science.* Dordrecht: Reidel, 1984.

Shapiro, Barbara J. *Probability and Certainty in Seventeenth-Century England: A Study of the Relationships Between Natural Science, Religion, History, Law and Literature.* Princeton: Princeton University Press, 1983.

Shaw, Daniel. "Hume's Theory of Motivation." *Hume Studies* 15 (1989): 163–83.

———. "Hume's Theory of Motivation—Part II." *Hume Studies* 18 (1992): 19–39.

———. "Reason and Feeling in Hume's Action Theory and Moral Philosophy." *Hume Studies* 18 (1992): 349–67.

Sher, Richard B. *Church and University in the Scottish Enlightenment: The Moderate Literati of Edinburgh.* Edinburgh: Edinburgh University Press, 1985.

Shils, Edward. *Tradition.* Chicago: University of Chicago Press, 1981.

Siebert, Donald T. *The Moral Animus of David Hume.* Cranbury: University of Delaware Press, 1990.

Skinner, Andrew S. "David Hume: Principles of Political Economy." In *The Cambridge Companion to Hume,* edited by David Fate Norton, 222–54. Cambridge: Cambridge University Press, 1993.

Smith, Peter. *Realism and the Progress of Science.* Cambridge: Cambridge University Press, 1981.

Snare, Francis. *Morals, Motivation and Convention: Hume's Influential Doctrines.* Cambridge: Cambridge University Press, 1991.

Sobel, Jordan Howard. "On the Evidence of Testimony for Miracles: A Bayesian Interpretation of David Hume's Analysis." *Philosophical Quarterly* 37 (1987): 166–86.

Sokolowski, Robert. "Fiction and Illusion in David Hume's Philosophy." *Modern Schoolman* 45 (1968): 189–225.

Somerville, James. *The Enigmatic Parting Shot: What was Hume's "Compleat Answer to Dr Reid and to That Bigotted Silly Fellow, Beattie"?* Aldershot: Avebury, 1995.

Soule, Edward. "Hume on Economic Policy and Human Nature." *Hume Studies* 26 (2000): 143–57.

Stalley, R. F. "The Will in Hume's *Treatise.*" *Journal of the History of Philosophy* 24 (1986): 41–53.

Stanford, Michael. *An Introduction to the Philosophy of History.* Oxford: Basil Blackwell, 1998.

Steinberg, Eric. "Hume on Liberty, Necessity and Verbal Disputes." *Hume Studies* 13 (1987): 113–37.

Steiner, Mark. "Kant's Misrepresentations of Hume's Philosophy of Mathematics in the *Prolegomena.*" *Hume Studies* 13 (1987): 400–410.

Stephen, Leslie. *History of English Thought in the Eighteenth Century.* 2 vols. 3d ed. New York: Harcourt, Brace & World, 1962.

Stevenson, Charles L. *Ethics and Language.* New Haven: Yale University Press, 1944.

Stevenson, Gordon Park. "Humean Self-Consciousness Explained." *Hume Studies* 24 (1998): 95–129.

Stewart, Carole. "The Moral Point of View." *Philosophy* 51 (1976): 177–87.

Stewart, John B. *The Moral and Political Philosophy of David Hume.* New York: Columbia University Press, 1963.

———. *Opinion and Reform in Hume's Political Philosophy.* Princeton: Princeton University Press, 1992.

Stewart, M. A. "The Dating of Hume's Manuscripts." In *The Scottish Enlightenment: Essays in Reinterpretation,* edited by Paul Wood, 267–314. Rochester: University of Rochester Press, 2000.

———. "Hume's Historical View of Miracles." In *Hume and Hume's Connexions,* edited by M. A. Stewart and John P. Wright, 171–200. University Park: Pennsylvania State University Press, 1995.

———, ed. "An Early Fragment on Evil." In *Hume and Hume's Connexions,* edited by M. A. Stewart and John P. Wright, 160–70. University Park: Pennsylvania State University Press, 1995.

Stewart, M. A., and John P. Wright, eds. *Hume and Hume's Connexions.* University Park: Pennsylvania State University Press, 1995.

Stockton, Constant Noble. "David Hume Among the Historiographers." *Studies in History and Society* 3 (1971): 14–24.

———. "Economics and the Mechanism of Historical Progress in Hume's *History.*" In *Hume: A Re-Evaluation,* edited by Donald W. Livingston and James T. King, 296–320. New York: Fordham University Press, 1976.

———. "Hume—Historian of the English Constitution." *Eighteenth Century Studies* 4 (1971): 277–93.

Stove, D. C. *Probability and Hume's Inductive Scepticism.* Oxford: Clarendon Press, 1973.

Strawson, Galen. *The Secret Connexion: Causation, Realism and David Hume.* Oxford: Clarendon Press, 1989.

Strawson, P. F. *Introduction to Logical Theory.* London: Methuen, 1952.

Streminger, Gerhard. *David Hume: Sein Leben und sein Werk.* Paderborn: Ferdinand Schöningh, 1994.

Stroud, Barry. "'Gilding or Staining' the World with 'Sentiments' and 'Phantasms.'" *Hume Studies* 19 (1993): 253–72.

———. *Hume.* London: Routledge & Kegan Paul, 1977.

Sutherland, Stewart R. "Hume and the Concept of Pleasure." In *David Hume: Bicentenary Papers,* edited by G. P. Morice, 218–24. Edinburgh: Edinburgh University Press, 1977.

———. "Hume on Morality and the Emotions." *Philosophical Quarterly* 26 (1976): 14–23.

Swain, Corliss Gayda. "Being Sure of One's Self: Hume on Personal Identity." *Hume Studies* 17 (1991): 107–19.

Swingewood, Alan. "Origins of Sociology: The Case of the Scottish Enlightenment." *British Journal of Sociology* 21 (1970): 164–80.

Talmor, Sascha. "A Forgotten Classic: Hume's 'Of the Standard of Taste.'" *Durham University Journal* 75 (1982): 15–18.

Taylor, Charles. "Philosophy and its History." In *Philosophy in History: Essays on the Historiography of Philosophy,* edited by Richard Rorty, J. B. Schneewind, and Quentin Skinner, 17–30. Cambridge: Cambridge University Press, 1984.

Taylor, Gabriele. "Hume's Views of Moral Judgments." *Philosophical Quarterly* 21 (1971): 64–68.

Taylor, Jacqueline. "Justice and the Foundations of Social Morality in Hume's *Treatise.*" *Hume Studies* 24 (1998): 5–30.

Temple, Kathryn. "'Manly Composition': Hume and the *History of England.*" In *Feminist Interpretations of David Hume,* edited by Anne Jaap Jacobson, 263–82. University Park: Pennsylvania State University Press, 2000.

Tienson, John. "Hume on Universals and General Terms." *Nous* 18 (1984): 311–30.

Todd, William B. "Foreword" to *The History of England from the Invasion of Julius Caesar to The Revolution in 1688* by David Hume, edited by William B. Todd, 1:xi–xxiii. Indianapolis: Liberty Press, 1983.

———, ed. *Hume and the Enlightenment: Essays Presented to Ernest Campbell Mossner.* Edinburgh: Edinburgh University Press; Austin: Humanities Research Center, 1974.

Townsend, Dabney. *Hume's Aesthetic Theory: Taste and Sentiment.* London: Routledge, 2001.

Traiger, Saul. "Impressions, Ideas, and Fictions." *Hume Studies* 13 (1987): 381–99.

Trevor-Roper, Hugh. "David Hume as a Historian." In *David Hume: A Symposium,* edited by D. F. Pears, 89–100. London: Macmillan, 1963.

Trudeau, Richard J. *The Non-Euclidean Revolution.* Boston: Birkhäuser, 1987.

Tweyman, Stanley. "Hume on Separating the Inseparable." In *Hume and the Enlightenment: Essays Presented to Ernest Campbell Mossner,* edited by William B. Todd, 30–42. Edinburgh: Edinburgh University Press; Austin: Humanities Research Center, 1974.

———. "Hume's Dialogues on Evil." *Hume Studies* 13 (1987): 74–85.

———. *Reason and Conduct in Hume and His Predecessors.* The Hague: Martinus Nijhoff, 1974.

———. *Scepticism and Belief in Hume's Dialogues Concerning Natural Religion.* Dordrecht: Martinus Nijhoff, 1986.

———. "Some Reflections on Hume on Existence." *Hume Studies* 18 (1992): 137–49.

Ushenko, Andrew. "Hume's Theory of General Ideas." *Review of Metaphysics* 9 (1955): 236–51.

Van Leeuwen, Henry G. *The Problem of Certainty in English Thought, 1630–1690.* The Hague: Martinus Nijhoff, 1963.

Van Steenburgh, E. W. "Hume's Geometric 'Objects.'" *Hume Studies* 6 (1980): 61–68.

———. "Hume's Ontology." *Journal of Critical Analysis* 4 (1973): 164–72.

Vanterpool, Rudolph V. "Hume's Account of General Rules." *Southern Journal of Philosophy* 12 (1974): 481–92.

Velk, Tom, and A. R. Riggs. "David Hume's Practical Economics." *Hume Studies* 11 (1985): 154–65.

Venning, Corey. "Hume on Property, Commerce, and Empire in the Good Society: The Role of Historical Necessity." *Journal of the History of Ideas* 37 (1976): 79–92.

Vesey, Godfrey. *Personal Identity: A Philosophical Analysis.* Ithaca: Cornell University Press, 1974.

Vico, Giambattista. *The New Science of Giambattista Vico.* Translated by Thomas Goddard Bergin and Max Harold Fisch. 1948. Rev. ed. Ithaca: Cornell University Press, 1968.

Vitek, William. *Promising.* Philadelphia: Temple University Press, 1993.

Vyverberg, Henry. *Human Nature, Cultural Diversity, and the French Enlightenment.* New York: Oxford University Press, 1989.

Wadia, P. S. "Philo Confounded." In *McGill Hume Studies,* edited by David Fate Norton, Nicholas Capaldi, and Wade L. Robison, 279–90. San Diego: Austin Hill Press, 1979.

Wallis, Wilson D. "David Hume's Contribution to Social Science." In *Philosophical Essays in Honor of Edgar Arthur Singer, Jr.,* edited by F. P. Clarke and M. C. Nahm, 358–71. Philadelphia: University of Pennsylvania Press, 1942.

Walton, Craig. "Hume and Jefferson on the Uses of History." In *Hume: A Re-Evaluation,* edited by Donald W. Livingston and James T. King, 389–403. New York: Fordham University Press, 1976.

Warner, Stuart D., and Donald W. Livingston. "Introduction" to *Political Writings* by David Hume, edited by Stuart D. Warner and Donald W. Livingston, vii–xxvi. Indianapolis: Hackett, 1994.

Waszek, Norbert. "Hume, Hegel, and History." *Clio* 14 (1985): 379–92.

———. *The Scottish Enlightenment and Hegel's Account of Civil Society.* Dordrecht: Kluwer, 1988.

Waxman, Wayne. "Hume's Quandary Concerning Personal Identity." *Hume Studies* 18 (1992): 233–53.

————. *Hume's Theory of Consciousness.* Cambridge: Cambridge University Press, 1994.

Weiand, Jeffrey. "Hume's Two Standards of Taste." *Philosophical Quarterly* 34 (1984): 129–42.

Werner, John M. "David Hume and America." *Journal of the History of Ideas* 33 (1972): 439–56.

Wertz, Spencer K. *Between Hume's Philosophy and History: Historical Theory and Practice.* Lanham: University Press of America, 2000.

————. "Hume, History, and Human Nature." *Journal of the History of Ideas* 36 (1975): 481–96.

Westerman, Pauline C. "Hume and the Natural Lawyers: A Change of Landscape." In *Hume and Hume's Connexions,* edited by M. A. Stewart and John P. Wright, 83–104. University Park: Pennsylvania State University Press, 1995.

Wexler, Victor G. *David Hume and the History of England.* Philadelphia: American Philosophical Society, 1979.

Whelan, Frederick G. *Order and Artifice in Hume's Political Philosophy.* Princeton: Princeton University Press, 1985.

White, Thomas I. "Some Remarks on Hume's Conversion Theory in 'Of Tragedy.'" *Philological Quarterly* 55 (1976): 287–91.

Wilbanks, Jan. *Hume's Theory of Imagination.* The Hague: Martinus Nijhoff, 1968.

Williams, Christopher. *A Cultivated Reason: An Essay on Hume and Humeanism.* University Park: Pennsylvania State University Press, 1999.

Williams, Michael. "Hume's Criterion of Significance." *Canadian Journal of Philosophy* 15 (1985): 273–304.

Williams, William H. "Is Hume's Shade of Blue a Red Herring?" *Synthese* 92 (1992): 83–99.

Wilson, Fred. "Association, Ideas, and Images in Hume." In *Minds, Ideas, and Objects: Essays on the Theory of Representation in Modern Philosophy,* edited by Phillip D. Cummins and Günter Zöller, 255–74. Atascadero, Calif.: Ridgeview Publishing, 1992.

————. "Hume and Derrida on Language and Meaning." *Hume Studies* 12 (1986): 99–121.

————. "Hume on the Abstract Idea of Existence: Comments on Cummins' 'Hume on the Idea of Existence.'" *Hume Studies* 17 (1991): 167–201.

————. "Hume's Critical Realism: A Reply to Livingston," *Journal of the History of Philosophy* 29 (1991): 291–96.

————. *Hume's Defence of Causal Inference.* Toronto: University of Toronto Press, 1997.

————. "Is Hume a Sceptic with Regard to the Senses?" *Journal of the History of Philosophy* 27 (1989): 49–73.

————. "The Logic of Probabilities in Hume's Argument Against Miracles." *Hume Studies* 15 (1989): 255–75.

————. "Was Hume a Subjectivist?" *Philosophy Research Archives* 14 (1988–89): 247–82.

Winkler, Kenneth P. "The New Hume." In *The New Hume Debate,* edited by Rupert Read and Kenneth A. Richman, 52–87. London: Routledge, 2000.

Wolff, Robert Paul. "Hume's Theory of Mental Activity." In *Hume,* edited by V. C. Chappell, 99–128. Garden City, N.Y.: Doubleday, Anchor Books, 1966.

————. "Kant's Debt to Hume via Beattie." *Journal of the History of Ideas* 21 (1960): 117–23.

Wolin, Sheldon S. "Hume and Conservatism." In *Hume: A Re-Evaluation,* edited by Donald W. Livingston and James T. King, 239–56. New York: Fordham University Press, 1976.

Wood, P. B. "Hume, Reid and the Science of the Mind." In *Hume and Hume's Connexions,* edited by M. A. Stewart and John P. Wright, 119–39. University Park: Pennsylvania State University Press, 1995.

Wood, Paul, ed. *The Scottish Enlightenment: Essays in Reinterpretation.* Rochester: University of Rochester Press, 2000.

Wootton, David. "David Hume, 'the historian.'" In *The Cambridge Companion to Hume,* edited by David Fate Norton, 281–312. Cambridge: Cambridge University Press, 1993.

———. "Hume's 'Of Miracles': Probability and Irreligion." In *Studies in the Philosophy of the Scottish Enlightenment,* edited by M. A. Stewart, 191–229. Oxford: Clarendon Press, 1990.

Wright, John P. *The Sceptical Realism of David Hume.* Minneapolis: University of Minnesota Press, 1983.

Yalden-Thomson, D. C. "Hume's View of 'Is-ought.'" *Philosophy* 53 (1978): 89–93.

———. "Recent Work on Hume." *American Philosophical Quarterly* 20 (1983): 1–22.

Yandell, Keith E. *Hume's "Inexplicable Mystery": His Views on Religion.* Philadelphia: Temple University Press, 1990.

Zabeeh, Farhang. *Hume: Precursor of Modern Empiricism.* 2d ed. The Hague: Martinus Nijhoff, 1973.

Zammito, John H. *Kant, Herder, and the Birth of Anthropology.* Chicago: University of Chicago Press, 2002.

Zartman, James F. "Hume and 'The Meaning of a Word.'" *Philosophy and Phenomenological Research* 36 (1975): 255–60.

probable or causal reasoning, philosophical, 6–7,
69, 79–96, 146, 344–45, 353–54, 388,
417–18. *See also* rules for judging causes and
effects
as affirmed by moderate skepticism, 153–60
as applied in natural sciences, 96–103, 359
as applied to human testimony, 104–6, 182,
344–47, 379–81, 397
as applied to judgments of identity, 135
as applied to religion, 323–47, 349–55, 360,
362, 370–72
as applied to the interpretation of human action,
88–90, 106, 192, 198, 202–9, 363, 418–19
probable or causal reasoning, unphilosophical,
78–91, 93–95, 146, 181–82
professions, as correlated with character traits,
201–2, 367–68
progress
moral progress, 255–56, 288, 333, 403–5
of civilization, 255–56, 394, 401–6, 408, 410,
412–13, 425–27
of taste in aesthetics, 329–30, 336–37
uncertainty of progress, 256, 406–8, 412–13
promises and promising, 236, 241–42, 244,
265–67
proofs, causal, 44, 82–83, 90, 344
property
property and property rights, 47, 236–41, 244,
262–64, 300, 302–10, 312–13, 420
possessions as secondary object of indirect
passions, 170, 175–76, 186, 237
proportion (aesthetic quality), 317–18
proportion in quantity or number, as a
philosophical relation, 30, 44, 52–56, 66,
112
propositions. *See* judgments
Protestant succession, 267–68, 280, 291
Protestants and Protestantism, 279, 365–66
providence of God, 341, 347, 349–51, 358,
369–70
punishment, 238, 250, 263–64, 369
in the afterlife, 341, 349–50, 369
Puritan Commonwealth, 267, 282, 342, 365, 402,
406
puritans and puritanism, 279, 282, 365, 387, 402.
See also England, history of
Pyrrho and Pyrrhonism, 154–56, 159. *See also
under* skepticism, types of

qualities of character. *See* dispositions of character
qualities
as sources of causal efficacy in objects, 86–88,
91, 96–100, 349–50

degrees of. *See* degrees of quality
ideas of, 16–17, 35–37. *See also* distinctions of
reason
primary and secondary, 15, 116–17, 139, 141,
146–49, 227, 317
role in ideas of relations, modes and substances,
35–38, 40–42, 144–45

race and racism, 217, 409–11
radicalism and radical tradition (politics), 282,
295–97, 342
Ramsay, Andrew Michael (Chevalier Ramsay), 361
rational, use of the word, 80, 95–96
realism
causal, 99–100
naïve, 117–18
reason in history, use of the phrase, 6, 11, 416, 421
reason, 94–95, 138, 367, 370, 420
as term for cognition, 2, 6
as term for motive, 199, 203, 210–12
considered as a ground for religious belief,
339–57
influence over volition and action, 195, 217,
220–22, 226, 230, 416
not a motive for action, 218–22, 225–26, 230–
31, 416
not source for moral distinctions, 225–29
not source of idea of external existence, 115–16,
121, 148–49
reasonable and unreasonable, Hume's use of the
words
as pertaining to cognition, 84, 95–96, 196,
202–3, 267, 301
as pertaining to passions and volition, 220, 222,
225–26
reasoning
as a type of conception, 38
causal. *See* probable or causal reasoning
deductive. *See* logic, deductive
demonstrative. *See* demonstration and
demonstrative reasoning
division into two types, 30, 43, 94–95, 218, 226
Hume's use of the word, 30, 52, 70, 94–95,
141, 149, 218
purposes of, 191–93, 218–19
similarity to calm passions, 218–22
rebellion, right of, 267–69, 420
reform, political, 288, 290–92, 295–97, 420,
425–27
Reformation
in Europe, 279, 341n4, 343, 364–66, 402
in England, 397–98
Reid, Thomas, 1, 3, 26n21, 102, 228

in modern civilization, 246–47, 249–50, 253, 256–57, 403–8, 412–13
  military, 249–51, 256, 401
  monkish, 251, 253, 367–68, 419–20
virtues, natural, 234–36, 244–53
  as useful and agreeable, 245–53, 255–56, 368–70, 404, 419–20
  common point of view toward, 235, 247–49, 254–55
  cultural relativity of, 249–53, 404
  degrees of obligation in, 248–49
  sentiments of approval toward, 245–48, 252–53
vision, 58–60, 109, 147, 247–48
volition. *See* will
Voltaire, François-Marie Arouet, 400, 426
voluntary action. *See also* liberty and necessity
  and morality, 195, 209, 231–32, 250–51
  idea of, 198, 207–10, 250–51
  subjective feeling of, 196–97, 203–4, 208–9
vulgar
  Hume's use of the word, 113n10
  vulgar idea of external existence, 113, 116–22

wages, 304, 306–7, 311–13
Walpole, Robert, 181, 291

war and warfare, 262, 264, 274, 293, 311, 397, 407
Weber, Max, 212
Whig party
  history and principles of, 265–68, 279–84, 286, 290, 294–95, 386–87
  religious views in, 342, 366
  response to Hume's writings, 294
Whig interpretation of English history, 283–84, 289, 294, 384, 393–95, 399–400
Wilkes, John, 284–89, 293, 295, 407
Wilkie, William, 319, 326, 391n24
will (volition), 128, 161, 163, 182, 195. *See also* liberty and necessity; voluntary action
  as impression of reflection, 196–97, 204, 212, 218
William and Mary (king and queen of England), 267, 283
Williams, Francis, 411
Wilson, Fred, 6, 23
wit, 170, 245–46, 321, 323, 334
Wolff, Robert Paul, 23
Wollaston, William, 225
women, 242–44, 252, 392–93, 402
words. *See* language